A GAME OF INCHES

The Game on the Field

A GAME
OF INCHES

The Stories Behind the Innovations
That Shaped Baseball

THE GAME ON THE FIELD

Peter Morris

Ivan R. Dee
CHICAGO

www.ivanrdee.com

Library of Congress Cataloging-in-Publication Data:
Morris, Peter, 1962–
    A game of inches : the game on the field : the stories behind the innovations that shaped baseball / Peter Morris.
        v. cm.
    Includes bibliographical references and index.
    Contents: v. 1. The game on the field.
    ISBN-13: 978-1-56663-677-3 (cloth : alk. paper)
    ISBN-10: 1-56663-677-9 (cloth : alk. paper)
        1. Baseball—United States. 2. Baseball—United States—History.
I. Title.
GV863.A1M65 2006
796.35709—dc22
                                        2005031597

To my father, Dr. Raymond Morris, with love and gratitude

Contents

CHAPTER 2: BATTING

(i) Variations on a Theme: Refinements to Approaches, Swings, and Stances

(ii) Less Is More: The Bunt and Other Novel Approaches to Hitting

(iii) And When All Else Fails: Trying to Be a Successful Hitter Without Hitting

CHAPTER 4: FIELDING

CHAPTER 5: BASERUNNING

(i) Stolen Bases

(ii) Bats

(iii) Gloves

(iv) Protective Equipment

(v) Miscellaneous Equipment

CHAPTER 10: UNIFORMS

CHAPTER 11: SKULLDUGGERY

(i) Garden Variety Trickery

(ii) Gardening Variety Trickery

CHAPTER 12: TIMEOUTS

Preface: Who Cares Who Was First?

"Of course, all those deliveries must have new names today or they would not be considered new. It's the same principle as at a French restaurant, where you get the same dish every day, but with a new name. According to a certain line of baseball logic, Smith is not Smith if he wears a different suit of clothes from that he had on when he was known as Smith. Vanity is a great thing in this world of baseball. One generation does not want you to tell it of the mighty deeds, or of the merits of that which preceeded [sic]. The present generation insists upon being regarded as the pioneer in the inventive or strategical features of the game."—Ted Sullivan, quoted in A. H. Spink, *The National Game* (1911), 152

"The oldest inhabitants are still claiming credit for unearthing all new wrinkles in baseball."—*Washington Post*, September 15, 1904

"Our game has at last reached a point whence we may look back only. Ahead we cannot well go, except in perfecting ourselves in the science of the game as already established. And yet, perhaps we are saying, as the Danish king said to the waves, 'Thus far shalt thou go, and no farther.' But they did not see fit to obey the monarch, and kept rising higher and higher, until at last they touched his feet. So may it be now. Some pen may be saying, 'Base ball has gone far enough; farther it cannot go; the rules now comprehend every position of our game and any more improvements will be useless.' Perhaps it has; yet who can tell? Does any one think that . . . the veteran Knickerbockers had an idea of what was to result from their early and primitive attempts at playing ball? Were there not many, who, after reading the rules adopted by the first National Association were satisfied that the game was as complete as need be, nothing more being necessary? Is it not so in nearly everything? Every improvement is looked upon as the last."—A. H. Brasher, *The Ball Player's Chronicle*, June 6, 1867

"[Babe] Pinelli says he worked that hidden-ball trick once too often. He tried to pull it on Ivy Olson in Brooklyn one day. 'Ivy stood there on the base and looked at me with great scorn,' Babe recalled. 'Then he sneered: "Say, you busher, don't you know I INVENTED that play.""—J. G. Taylor Spink, *Sporting News*, August 20, 1942

BASEBALL has a sense of tradition that is powerful enough to be described as a burden. Yet paradoxically, its collective memory is often short and nostalgia too frequently passed off as history. It is always fashionable for older fans to denounce the limited historical perspective of younger ones, but many who do so also have a knowledge base that spans only their own lifetime.

As the above epigraphs show, this is not a new phenomenon. There is nothing like a claim of invention or originality to stir up a passionate debate with often wildly conflicting views. This may seem confusing or dispiriting, but I think it is actually just the opposite. The history of a sport that has been so large a part of American culture for 150 years cannot rely simply on the memory of anyone now alive and thus must be passed along to survive. This in turn means that no generation has an exclusive claim on historical perspective; it is something that we collectively participate in and agree upon.

Nowhere is this more evident than in the subject of this book. In his later years, 1930s player Frenchy Bordagaray recounted an encounter with Reggie Jackson. Bordagaray called Jackson "that stinker" for being billed as the first twentieth-century player to wear a mustache, a distinction he claimed for himself. When the two men met, Bordagaray made Jackson go down on his knees as penance (Tony Salin, *Baseball's Forgotten Heroes*, 183).

That's a nice story, but Bordagaray had no more right to the distinction than Jackson. In fact, both men did exactly the same thing by reviving a dormant tradition—mustaches were common in nineteenth-century baseball and were carried into the twentieth century by players like John Titus, Jake Beckley, and Allen Benson (see **26.1.1** "Beards and Mustaches").* So an alternate reading of this story is that, rather than representing the righting of a wrong, it demonstrates Ted Sullivan's contention that each "generation does not want you to tell it of the mighty deeds, or of the merits of that which preceded" (quoted in A. H. Spink, *The National Game*, 152).

---

*These references in the text are to other sections of this work. Some of them, including this one, appear in the companion volume, *A Game of Inches: The Game Behind the Scenes*, now in preparation.

Many who set out to read about early baseball history find the Knickerbockers rather alien figures and give up. Perhaps this book will prove to be a sneaky way of making history seem relevant to fans both young and old. Young people notoriously ask, "Why does this matter?" and "How do I use this in real life?" These can be prickly questions, but they are legitimate ones. If one generation can't explain why an event matters, it won't continue to interest succeeding ones. Baseball is a shared cultural legacy, but it needs to be fully understood to be fully shared.

The inability to explain many of baseball's customs is one of the reasons why the game seems stodgy to many of today's young people. Baseball's rules and customs have changed little in the last thirty years, and even a suggestion of innovation can elicit a reactionary, even apocalyptic backlash. It is as though each generation is asserting anew: "Our game has at last reached a point from which we may only look back. Ahead we cannot go, except in perfecting ourselves in the science of the game as already established." Yet baseball's history is filled with dramatic changes based upon competing visions of what the game should become. Gaining an appreciation of the factors that produced today's game helps us understand such instinctive defensiveness toward change.

One important point to note as we examine baseball firsts is how many revolve around the issue of competitiveness. Baseball's earliest players viewed baseball primarily as a recreation rather than as a competition, and although this changed quickly, many of the game's rules and customs were much slower to change. This led to cycles in which an innovative player or manager found a strategy not covered by the rules but not deemed entirely sporting. New rules were introduced to eliminate or govern the new tactic; more new strategies were brought forward as a result of the new rule; new techniques emerged to counteract them, and so on until a compromise was reached.

For early clubs like the Knickerbockers, how the game was played was the primary consideration. Who won was less important. We now take the pursuit of victory for granted, yet that is a relative difference rather than an absolute one. We all want our favorite team to win, yet for most of us it is even more important to be able to use baseball as an instructional experience for a young person.

As a result, while many of the "firsts" in this book are resisted because they seem unlikely to produce victories, even more innovations have drawn criticism because they didn't correspond to how someone believes baseball *ought to be played*. In such cases the subtext of the complaint was: "Here is what I believe baseball should be about and how I have depicted baseball to my child, and this is an innovation that doesn't belong." Such assertions have led to passionate debates that are filled with insight into exactly what it is about baseball that matters so much to so many people.

For example, a reporter in 1886 wrote these scathing words: "For this babyish performance [Arthur Irwin] was roundly hissed by the spectators, and concluded to abandon it. Base ball is essentially a manly spirit, and its patrons object to such infantile tricks" (*Detroit Free Press*, May 9, 1886). The tactic that drew the reporter's wrath was nothing other than the bunt, which many of today's fans regard as the epitome of how baseball should be played. But nineteenth-century aficionados had a very different perspective.

Throughout the 1890s there were efforts to eliminate the bunt because it was viewed as an unmanly act. In 1905 a sportswriter claimed that its effect had been "to kill base running, diminish individual effort, and curtail the use of better though more risky plays" (*Sporting Life*, July 8, 1905). That same year Ted Sullivan wrote that baserunning was becoming a lost art because of the prevalence of the bunt (*Sporting Life*, March 25, 1905). There is thus unappreciated irony in the now commonplace lament that the bunt has become a lost art.

Many of the other items mentioned in this book had to overcome such brickbats, including gloves, masks, and even the intentional walk. Off-field innovations such as baseball's transmission via telegraph, radio, and television have been on the receiving end of similar criticisms. But just as some firsts were gloomily viewed as signs of doom, others were hailed as signs that baseball was progressing toward perfection. Readers will be surprised by which ones were viewed in which way. The reasoning behind these conclusions runs the gamut from profound to absurd, but all are impassioned. Reading them should deepen our understanding of why baseball matters to so many of us.

A memorable short story by Raymond Carver bore the intriguing title "What We Talk About When We Talk About Love." The tale is a penetrating study of the ways our values are illuminated both by what we say and by what we leave unsaid. I hope that readers, in the course of this book, will similarly come to a deeper appreciation of what we talk about when we talk about baseball's traditions. And perhaps readers will also come to see the game's rules, customs, and traditions in a new light—not as immutable laws established long ago but as the results of a century and a half of lively negotiations about how best to make baseball embody such ideals as fair play, manliness, equality of opportunity, and what it means to be an American.

Many entries detail occurrences that fans see every day on the ball field but may never have understood why they are part of the game. Other entries describe something that is no longer part of the game, and these may seem much less relevant. I believe that in many instances we gain even more understanding about baseball today from its forgotten details.

P. M.

Haslett, Michigan
January 2006

Acknowledgments

A WORK as ambitious as this one relies on the diligent work of many earlier researchers, and the bibliography reflects many of those debts. In addition I am deeply grateful to the many researchers, almost all of them members of the Society for American Baseball Research (SABR), who have graciously permitted me to cite their unpublished research and/or have read preliminary entries and offered perceptive critiques. These include Bruce Allardice, Bill Anderson, David Anderson, David Arcidiacono, Jean Hastings Ardell, Priscilla Astifan, Bob Bailey, David Ball, Evelyn Begley, Charlie Bevis, Cliff Blau, David Block, Darryl Brock, Bill Carle, Frank Ceresi, Dick Clark, Jack Daugherty, Harry Davis, Bill Deane, Paul Dickson, Jane Finnan Dorward, Stefan Fatsis, Scott Flatow, John Freyer, Cappy Gagnon, Glenn Guzzo, Ron Haas, Reed Howard, Paul Hunkele, John Husman, Bill Kirwin, Jim Lannen, R. J. Lesch, Larry Lester, John Lewis, Richard Malatzky, Skip McAfee, David McCarthy, Bob McConnell, David McDonald, Wayne McElreavy, Eric Miklich, Sammy Miller, Art Neff, Rod Nelson, David Nemec, Gene Newman, Marc Okkonen, Pete Palmer, Greg Rhodes, Kevin Saldana, Jay Sanford, John Schwartz, Joe Simenic, Steve Steinberg, Bob Schaefer, Tom Shieber, David W. Smith, Alan Smitley, Dean Thilgen, Richard Thompson, John Thorn, Bob Timmermann, Frank Vaccaro, David Vincent, and Mike Welsh.

Ivan Dee has shown enormous faith in this project and contributed meticulous editing. I am very appreciative of the many friends, family members, and co-workers who have offered moral support—or at least refrained from laughing at the idea of a work of such specificity and length. A special thanks to all of the members of the Michigan State volleyball community, both past and present, for their friendship and support. Go Green!

Naturally, the errors and shortcomings that remain are solely my responsibility.

A GAME OF INCHES

The Game on the Field

Introduction: What Makes an Innovation Dangerous?

"But the exact year was not given, so it is impossible to say that [Charles] Bennett's contribution was a 'first,' a very dangerous word to employ in writing baseball history."—Lee Allen, *Sporting News*, April 6, 1968

"Many plays . . . have been 'discovered' about once a decade, and then neglected, if not forgotten, until some other genius brought them into action. In the pioneer days of the game, it seemed that if a player invented or evolved a play, the others, instead of seizing upon it to use, gave him a kind of patent-right to it."—John J. Evers and Hugh S. Fullerton, *Touching Second* (1910), 198

"I'm not the first 400-pound player. I'm just the first to admit it."—NFL player Aaron Gibson, quoted in *Sports Illustrated*, July 29, 2002

A BOOK of baseball firsts could of course be endlessly long. A *Sporting News* publication entitled *Baseball: A Doubleheader Collection of Facts, Feats and Firsts* includes such items as Don Drysdale throwing the first pitch in the first indoor All-Star Game, and Jamie Quirk and Dan Quisenberry forming the first battery where the surnames of both players began with a Q. While it undoubtedly tells us something significant about baseball that anyone would keep track of such firsts, it is not the object of this book to capture such minutiae. For the purposes of this book, firsts are defined more narrowly.

Toward that end, I have by and large defined a first as having only one condition. In other words, I'm interested in the origins of the batting crouch, but not in determining the first left-handed batter to crouch. I have made a few exceptions when the category seemed important or interesting enough but have tried to stick to that rule as much as possible. I have also considered statistical accomplishments to be "mosts" rather than "firsts," and omitted them: Babe Ruth was the first player to hit fifty home runs in a major league regular season, but for my purposes, that is a "most." Baseball already has many record books, and this book is not intended to poach on their territory.

As a rule I have avoided firsts that were primarily chance events that could not be intentionally replicated (for example, the first stray dog to run onto a field, the first time a batted ball rolled into a tin can or hit a bird, etc.) in favor of events that became—or at least had the potential to become—a significant part of baseball. I also generally ignore new names for the same old thing, except as a part of their history. Admittedly these can all be somewhat arbitrary distinctions, and I freely admit that I have included some borderline cases simply because there are good stories involved.

Finally, there are no separate entries for the first time that something happened in the twentieth century. I regard with dismay the willingness of many baseball historians to class the nineteenth century as a different sort of animal. The notion that something called "modern baseball" originated in 1900 or 1901 is as untrue as the idea that baseball began in Farmer Phinney's pasture in 1839. There are times when, for the purposes of a record book, important rule changes may make it necessary to treat records in a particular category this way, but there can be no purpose to doing so in a book of firsts, nor indeed in any book of history.

Perhaps there is no baseball subject on which as much nonsense is written as firsts. There has been a tendency to attribute every innovation of the nineteenth century to a few famous players, such as the White Stockings of Cap Anson and Mike "King" Kelly, or the Orioles of John McGraw and Hughey Jennings. And there are countless accounts of firsts that do not pass the most rudimentary scrutiny.

Accordingly, I have tried as far as possible to present documented evidence for all firsts that appear in this book with specific dates and places and, wherever possible, excerpts of contemporary newspaper coverage. I have used exact quotations as much as possible because they tell us so much about how an innovation came about and how it was received. It may appear that I have been inordinately preoccupied with providing contemporary documentation for firsts, but that is made necessary by the distressingly large number of apocryphal stories that are passed off as history.

Of course, a newspaper account does not necessarily mean that something happened exactly as reported. But it is certainly very important evidence that warrants treating an event differently than one for which there is no contemporary testimony. Readers are strongly encouraged to regard all such accounts as evidence rather than as definitive proof, and to render their own judgments as to the credibility of any report.

I have tried to help in this process by providing any evidence that leads me to take a particular account more or less seriously. I try to weigh all evidence in reaching this conclusion, but a few factors are always paramount: (1) whether the writer is a firsthand witness of the events; (2) any other claims made by the writer that either weaken or strengthen that writer's credibility; and (3) whether the account appeared soon enough after the events and in a sufficiently prominent publication that any errors could be pointed out by other witnesses.

In sifting through contradictory claims, I have given much more weight to ones that seem to bear up to such scrutiny but have tried at least to mention any that cannot be definitively discredited. I have not hesitated to point out trends or draw conclusions when I believed the facts clearly warrant them, but I have been equally willing to withhold judgment when the matter is less clear-cut so that readers can decide for themselves. I have tried to make the distinction between my interpretations and the testimony of witnesses as clear as possible, and thus I have generally resisted the urge to put firsthand evidence in my own words. "The document speaks for itself" is a tenet of the legal profession that I have kept in mind. Readers will find that many of these documents speak powerfully.

Many claimed firsts are challenged in this book. This does not necessarily diminish the accomplishments of those who are displaced. Jackie Robinson was not the first African American to play major league baseball, and neither was Fleet Walker, but this surely does not in any way lessen the importance of either man. In many cases the first practitioner of a tactic may not have perfected or really appreciated it, and my intention is not to make value judgments but merely to document as far as possible.

Some erroneously claimed firsts are attempts to deprive the rightful originator, but most simply reflect lack of awareness. Many of the innovations I describe were essayed several times before they caught on, and a later claimant would have no way of knowing of the earlier efforts. If a first immediately caught on, I generally have given an account only of its origination. But if, as often happens, the new creation took a while to become a significant part of baseball, I try to trace its history until it attained permanence.

One point that I have become very aware of while researching this book is that most firsts did not occur because of a "Eureka!" moment. They occurred when they did because conditions had changed—rules, ethics, finances, etc.—and a strategy became practical, not because earlier generations had lacked imagination. For example, in the early 1870s first basemen stayed relatively close to the base and pinch hitters were not used. To a twenty-first-century observer this may seem primitive, and readers may find themselves wishing to be able to go back in time and set the ballplayers right.

As this book will show, such time travelers would usually be met by reasonable objections. Pinch hitters did not exist for two simple reasons: the rules prohibited them, and clubs could not afford to carry extra players (see **6.2.5**). The positioning of first basemen in these years was a recent and logical response to the rules and conditions, as discussed in greater depth under "Guarding the Lines" (**4.2.3**). Whether this positioning is optimal can be debated, but it should at least be apparent that the placement was not due to a lack of imagination.

Even with the restrictions I laid down, the task of determining any first remains a daunting one. No matter how thoroughly a researcher scours the microfilm, there is always the possibility that an earlier occurrence lurks. Moreover, the danger of committing firsts to paper is increased by the reality that innovators have not always been anxious to claim credit for their breakthroughs. There have been two especially good reasons for this reticence.

The first factor is baseball's traditional role as a test of manliness, embodied by the saying, "There's no crying in baseball." Predictably, the acceptance of many forms of protective equipment was slowed by such concerns. But readers may be surprised by some of the other innovations that have been condemned as unmanly.

For example, sportswriter John B. Sheridan in 1924 denounced an element newly introduced to baseball as: "Spoon-feeding baseball players. Giving them setups. Making things soft for them. Coddling them. Softening them morally. . . . Permitting them to become soft of muscle and weak of will, discontented loafers or semi-loafers" (*Sporting News*, August 7, 1924). The object of Sheridan's venom was platooning. Baseball firsts may truly be said to be a dangerous subject not only for the historian but also for the inventor!

The second factor is that someone who believed they had happened upon a competitive advantage wasn't necessarily eager to share it. Johnny Evers and Hugh Fullerton observed, "In the pioneer days of the game, it seemed that if a player invented or evolved a play, the others, instead of seizing upon it to use, gave him a kind of patent-right to it" (John J. Evers and Hugh S. Fullerton, *Touching Second*, 198).

This was particularly true of early pitchers, who justifiably were wary that if they acknowledged having come up with a clever new idea, the game's rule makers would be swift to ban it. One of the many versions of the origins of the curveball (see **3.2.3**) had "Candy" Cummings unveiling the pitch in an 1867 game and then asking mischievously afterward, "Does it curve?" (*Washington Post*, September 8, 1907). Cummings himself acknowledged having been "jealous of his discovery" and he was not alone (*Sporting News*, December 29, 1921). When asked by St. Louis's George Bradley to show him how to throw the curveball, Louisville's Jim Devlin "refused to explain it to him" (*St. Louis Globe-Democrat*, December 13, 1875).

Nor was this proprietary outlook entirely restricted to the early days of baseball. Pitcher Russ Ford gave a fascinating description of his reasoning process after realizing that his 1909 discovery of a new pitch known as the emery ball (see **3.2.13**) could change the game. Upon consideration, he decided that he had a "pig in a poke" and that it would be of no benefit to him or anyone else if he allowed it to escape (Russell Ford [as told to Don E. Basenfelder], "Russell Ford Tells Inside Story of the 'Emery' Ball After Guarding His Secret for Quarter of a Century," *Sporting News*, April 25, 1935, 5). His discretion turned out to be warranted, as in 1915 the emery ball became the first specific pitch ever banned from baseball.

The length and content of the entries in this book vary considerably as I have sought to fit the format to the facts, rather than the other way around. But in general I have tried to answer a few basic questions: When did the tactic originate? Why didn't it emerge earlier? Was the significance of the innovation immediately appreciated or did it take someone later to fully appreciate it? Did the innovation come as a result of a rule change? Was it immediately accepted as a good thing, or were objections raised? If there were objections, what was the nature of the objections and what do they reveal about how the people playing baseball at that period viewed the game? When did it become a permanent part of baseball?

As a result, I hope this study of firsts will accomplish two basic aims. The first is to serve as testimony to the inventiveness, ingenuity, and resourcefulness that ballplayers and managers have always brought to the national pastime. The second is a reminder that the way baseball is played today is not necessarily the way it has to be played. Rather it is the legacy of an enormous number of people who used both words and actions to create the framework for the way baseball is still played.

Baseball was a popular game with a loose and incoherent structure until the mid-1840s, when a New York club called the Knickerbockers imposed a "frame" upon it by writing down standardized rules. This new frame allowed a boy's game to be reinvented as a man's activity.

Beginning in the mid-1850s the newly elevated game was again repackaged and reframed as the "national game." Distinctions between baseball and cricket were emphasized to characterize baseball as quintessentially American. The game associated itself with the traditional institution of social clubs and thereby appeared unthreatening to social order. Early newspaper coverage also helped by stressing the healthful aspects of the game and downplaying its competitive aspects.

By the mid-1860s the journalist Henry Chadwick had emerged as the game's preeminent creator of baseball's traditional outlines. Chadwick covered baseball for some fifty years, right up to his death in 1908, and yet in many ways he seemed like an old man from the outset. He was a rigid fellow whose austere countenance and flowing beard caused him to be referred to as "Father Chadwick." This impression was reinforced by his fussy prose style and his ceaseless repetition of the same basic themes.

Not surprisingly, Chadwick frequently opposed change. Yet he was far from a reactionary. Indeed, he often embraced radical changes to baseball, such as his long-running campaign to change the game to encompass ten players and ten innings. Such inconsistencies are initially baffling, but they make sense when we recognize Chadwick as a builder of a basic framework for baseball, much of which endures to this day.

In Chadwick's view, a particular strategy, club, player, or result was not of much importance in and of itself. These items gained his approval only if they helped demonstrate one of the planks of his conception of baseball's underpinnings. The most prominent of these themes included: baseball is a healthful game; baseball is a test of manliness; fair play is more important than winning; umpires should be treated with courtesy and respect; baseball is a scientific game, in that success is based upon practice, discipline, and what Chadwick called "headwork," rather than raw talent; low-scoring games are better than high-scoring ones; teamwork wins baseball games; games are won by steady contributors rather than flashy ones; individual statistics should be measured and analyzed because they reveal who those steady contributors are; batters should aim for open spaces rather than swinging for the fences; specialization is good up to a point, but only after the basic skills of hitting and fielding have been mastered.

These themes will all seem familiar, but they are that way in large part because of Chadwick's incessant repetition of them. They have taken on still greater significance as they have been passed down by generations of fathers to their sons, making them our just-so stories. And their whole is greater than the sum of their parts because collectively they form a framework that supports one of the game's most enduring themes—that baseball can be viewed as a test of character.

Not all the planks that Chadwick used to build this framework remain intact, but a surprising number of them do. Fathers who teach their sons baseball still often give them simple moral lessons disguised as playing tips. And when one of these basic tenets is attacked, the offender is greeted with resistance that seems wildly disproportionate. Thus the designated-hitter rule still generates passionate opposition because it challenges the principles that every player needs to master all the skills of baseball and that people should complete what they start. Even when one of the elements of Chadwick's framework seems to become obsolete—as with the emphasis on home runs in today's game—we feel a seemingly irrational guilt about it.

When resistance to a new idea is surprisingly strong, it is a sure sign that it has challenged a fundamental element that we use to construct a meaning for baseball. Thus what is most dangerous about introducing an innovation is that it may threaten something that is perceived to be essential to baseball.

When Malcolm McLean wrote in 1913 that it was a historical fact that "every innovation in base ball has been bitterly fought until finally adopted," he was exaggerating—but not all that much (*Collier's*, reprinted in *Sporting News*, October 23, 1913). Labor-saving devices such as tarpaulins and batting cages, which threaten no underlying principles, have generally been accepted without a fuss. But a surprisingly large number of innovations have been deemed to tread on the toes of some tradition.

In sorting though the wildly conflicting claims regarding firsts and the diverse responses to them, a few basic features have recurred so frequently that it may be helpful to introduce them briefly:

(1) *Clinging to the Center*. As Robin Lakoff has noted, modern politics is often a linguistic war in which each side tries to gain the center by depicting its own position as "moderate" and "mainstream" and its opponent as "extremist" (Robin Tolmach Lakoff, *The Language War*, 66–67). Baseball firsts have been the subject of similar linguistic wars. While the terms have changed slightly over time, the fight has usually been to associate one's side generally with tests of character and specifically with magic words like "manliness," "science," "American," and "teamwork." For example, in 1887 walks (see **17.10**) were counted as base hits. At season's end, the *New York Times* observed, "It is true that patience and good judgment on [the batter's] part may help to earn a base under such circumstances, but it is mainly due to the pitcher's error, and the phrase 'phantom hits' shows the popular estimation of such additions to batting records" (*New York Times*, October 9, 1887). The demise of this scoring practice was virtually ensured by its opponents' success in popularizing such a negative term.

(2) *Glory or Guilt by Association*. Similarly, a first is greatly helped when introduced by players who are successful and generally admired. In the early 1880s, pitcher J Lee Richmond, a Brown University graduate who threw the first perfect game in major league history, began keeping a book on the strengths and weaknesses of opposing batters. The tactic received generally favorable press. In the following decade the same tactic was used by an eccentric pitcher known as "Crazy" Schmit and became the subject of ridicule (see **3.3.4**). During the late nineteenth and early twentieth centuries, sportswriters placed a special emphasis on depicting baseball as a thinking man's game, with the result that any tactic introduced by a collegian was likely to be accorded a favorable reception.

(3) *The Good (or Bad) Old Days*. As shown in the epigraphs to the Preface, disputes about firsts are often part of an underlying hostility between

generations. The process is usually along these lines: something unfamiliar is used and described as a first. There seems to be an implication that baseball is improving, and old-timers react by saying that they used the same play/tactic/approach to illustrate that baseball isn't what it once was. The debate escalates and often obscures the question of who was actually first.

(4) *Competitive Balance.* While the initial reception of a first is often determined by the terms and players with which it is associated, its long-term success also depends upon competitive balance. Most obviously, any significant new element will give some advantage to specific clubs and players. Which clubs and players benefit, and by how much, will have an important effect on its long-term survival, as will be illustrated in the next three principles.

(5) *Everyone's Contribution Matters.* Whenever the role of one kind of player becomes too great, strong pressure will be brought to bear to increase the involvement of others. This has been most apparent when pitchers' strikeouts are on the rise. The legalization of overhand pitching in the mid-1880s led to several pitchers striking out more than five hundred batters in a season. The game's rule makers tried a series of new approaches in succeeding years to remedy such imbalances, but generally satisfied no one. Ned Hanlon complained in 1888 about rules changes favoring the pitcher: "There is one thing I do know, and that is, there will not be so much interest taken in or as much excitement in the games this year as last. There will be little or no betting at all. This year is going to be a pitchers' contest, and the rest of the players will stand there on the field like wooden men. The pitchers will also have the batsmen at their mercy, and you will find that the managers, or rather the club officials, will be the greatest sufferers in the end" (*Grand Rapids* [Mich.] *Daily Democrat*, March 24, 1888). A series of important rules changes were then implemented to favor batters, as baseball desperately sought "the restoration of the proper equilibrium between the two great principles of the game—attack and defense" (*Sporting Life*, November 12, 1892). Yet by 1905 the *New York Times* was complaining, "The pitcher is now too important and the other players too unimportant" (quoted in Roger Kahn, *The Head Game*, 134). Adjustments were again made to the conditions and rules to reemphasize hitters and fielders. The cycle has continued to this day, with tinkering every time it has seemed that the contributions of one group of players are receiving short shrift.

(6) *Speed Versus Power.* The Knickerbockers brought power to what had primarily been a game of speed by adopting a harder ball and encouraging grown men to participate. The change to a deader ball in 1870 put a renewed emphasis on speed and led to the introduction of the bunt. In the years since then, the pendulum has swung back and forth. There appears to

be a fundamental belief that both speed and power should be part of baseball, because this in turn makes the game accessible to men of different sizes and ages. It is equally clear that it is difficult to make both part of the game at the same time, since speed favors small, young men while power favors larger and older men. As a result, one or the other skill tends to dominate and a balance has proven difficult to attain. Attempts to shift the emphasis of the game have been greeted with stiff resistance because they throw men out of work.

(7) *Risk on Both Sides.* The principle of competitive balance is especially applicable to individual plays. Plays in which risk is entirely on one side will offend the sense of fair play and create pressure to abolish them. For example, in early baseball, batters often stood at the plate without swinging with runners on base. Eventually a passed ball would occur, and the runner would advance without risk. The unsporting nature of this tactic led to one of baseball's most fundamental rules: called balls and strikes. Similarly, foul strikes were added because of the tedious practice of "blocking a ball off" by "holding the bat slightly behind the home plate, in no case in front of the center of the plate, and allowing the pitched ball to glance off, with no intention of hitting at all" (Doc Bushong, letter to *National Base Ball Gazette*, reprinted in *Cleveland Leader and Herald*, April 24, 1887). A current example of this is the reaction when a pitcher fakes to second or third to drive a runner back but does not make a throw (see **5.3.7**). At least a few fans will always call for a balk, and they are wrong, for the rules allow such fakes at bases other than first. But such fans are articulating a deeper antipathy to any play in which an advantage is gained without any risk.

(8) *Majority Rules.* If one club—especially the current champion—is particularly well suited to take advantage of a particular innovation, the others may disregard other factors and vote it down out of self-interest. At the rules meeting after the 1878 season, a bloc of National League clubs led by Cincinnati apparently conspired to make things difficult for specific players. One new rule was "a direct slap" at Boston's Harry Wright (the only nonplaying manager) by barring nonplayers from the bench; another modified the pitching box to the disadvantage of Boston's Tommy Bond; a third banned Providence pitcher Johnny Ward's tactic of turning his back to the hitter. The intent of hindering individual players was so apparent that "some joker" introduced a motion that pitchers be prohibited from wearing glasses, in reference to Cincinnati's bespectacled pitcher Will White (*New York Clipper*, December 14, 1878). Henry Chadwick justifiably groused about clubs that voted for rule changes based on the "selfish principle" of "How will this, that or the other new rule or revised section affect the play of our pitcher or our catcher?" (*New York Clipper*, November 29, 1879; also December 14 and 28, 1878). The guilty clubs responded by

becoming subtler about enacting such rules, but it would be naive to think that self-interest has ever ceased to be a consideration. In 1939 the American League tried to slow down the Yankees' juggernaut by introducing a bizarre rule that prevented the defending league champion from making trades without obtaining waivers (see **13.3.7**). This principle also applies to pitchers, who were outnumbered eight to one on most early clubs, which resulted in a barrage of rule changes directed at them that will be discussed in Chapter 3. Johnny Evers and Hugh S. Fullerton commented in 1910 that "the batters, being the majority on each team," were able to "override the pitchers" on many crucial points (John J. Evers and Hugh S. Fullerton, *Touching Second*, 117). This tendency gradually diminished over the years as the number of pitchers on a roster has approached and occasionally surpassed the number of hitters.

(*9*) *Jocko's Law*. Hall of Fame umpire Jocko Conlan once succinctly observed, "I've never claimed to be a psychic. Fair or foul. Safe or out. Ball or strike. All of that is plenty tough enough" (quoted in Roger Kahn, *The Head Game*, 217). Rule makers have not always taken this into account in their initial formulation of new rules, often expecting umpires to judge the motives of players. Such rules have quickly proven to be unenforceable. As a result, many rules have been fine-tuned by a two-stage process. The first spells out the general principle that is desired, but does so in such broad strokes that the rule cannot be effectively enforced. A revision generally follows a year or two later that allows umpires to make decisions based upon their eyesight rather than their intuition.

(*10*) *Eureka!* Stories of firsts are often told as "Eureka!" moments in which a new idea—previously overlooked—suddenly occurred to the storyteller. In fact it is rare for a first to originate in this way. In particular, complex maneuvers such as the wheel play or the various cutoff plays are developed through a give-and-take between offense and defense and cannot be invented in one step.

Similarly the word "invent" always needs to be scrutinized carefully. Sometimes these statements are simply false (e.g., "Abner Doubleday invented baseball"). Far more often they oversimplify by taking a complex development and reducing it to a statement like "Branch Rickey invented the farm system" or "Candy Cummings invented the curveball." Claims such as these are often more dangerous than out-and-out fictions because they contain a grain of truth that makes them more difficult to refute. This tendency stems from the natural impulse "to make a long story short," but in doing so a critical part of that story is omitted.

(*11*) *Good Stories Often Outlive Good History*. If we want to learn the truth, we need to be especially suspicious of memorable stories about a new invention. The picturesque image of Candy Cummings discovering the curveball while throwing clamshells, for example, has become part of the lore of the curveball precisely because it is such an appealing tale. But in order to gain a more nuanced understanding of baseball history, it is often necessary to reject such simple and colorful tales in favor of more complex and homelier ones. As we shall see (**3.2.3**), the clamshell version has survived primarily because it was what Malcolm Gladwell has termed the "stickiest" version—the rendering of events best suited to stick in people's memories (Malcolm Gladwell, *The Tipping Point,* 25). The premise of this work is to present the version of events most consistent with the evidence at hand, whether or not that makes a good story.

(12) It's New to Me. As we shall see, a great many claims of firsts are not really firsts but merely someone saying that something was new to him. Sometimes such claims merely reflect the ignorance of the speaker. If such a contention is extremely ill-informed or comes long after the fact, I have felt free to ignore it. But I have done so only when it is clear that the item in question was firmly established before the date being claimed.

If a claim of a first is made within a reasonable time span or by a credible source, I have made sure to mention it. Even if it is clearly not a genuine first, such a claim usually shows that the item in question was not yet fully accepted or known. On other occasions such claims demonstrate that a once-standard practice had fallen into disuse.

(13) Victors Write History. There has been a strong tendency to credit all firsts to a few champion teams and players, and more generally to the National League rather than its less successful nineteenth-century rivals. In large part this reflects the fact that influential clubs like the Red Stockings of Cincinnati and charismatic people such as Mike "King" Kelly and Ted Sullivan were able to use their popularity to ensure that someone else's idea caught on. Nonetheless it is important to remember that innovations are not the exclusive province of the victors.

The saga of baseball firsts offers the peculiar corollary that *survivors* often write history. Quite a few players have waited until their contemporaries have died before claiming to have themselves played an important role in a first. In particular, the late 1930s and 1940s saw the *Sporting News* publish interviews with a number of elderly players whose hazy recollections have often been uncritically accepted as firsts. While these players are not to be blamed, their claims must be scrutinized with great care.

(14) Exceptions Prove Rules. The saying "exceptions prove rules" is sometimes met with the retort, "No, exceptions *disprove* rules." In fact, exceptions can prove rules. This is particularly true when history is being viewed through the prism of daily newspapers, as is often the case in this

book. The fundamental principle of journalism is that "man bites dog" is news while "dog bites man" is not. This is because news is fundamentally about exceptions. To take a simple example, a 1905 note stated that "Umpire Tom Connolly is wearing shin pads" (*Sporting Life*, June 17, 1905). This does not mean it was the norm in 1905 for umpires to wear shin pads. In fact it strongly implies just the opposite, for there would be no reason to remark on this if umpires were already commonly wearing shin pads. This principle that exceptions prove rules is essential to bear in mind when using newspapers to determine when and how particular items were introduced to baseball.

(*15*) *Outs Were Not Routine.* In today's game it is pretty safe to assume that an out will be recorded whenever a ground ball is hit at an infielder or a ball is hit in the air in the direction of any fielder. Once in a long while something surprising happens, but not very often. That simply wasn't the case in the 1860s, when the rules and customs of baseball were being established. Everything favored hitters: fielders didn't wear gloves or sunglasses; playing grounds were uneven and often included obstacles; and balls were lively and rubbery. The easiest way to record an out was to capture a ball on the first hop, but the eccentricities of the playing field rendered even "bound catches" uncertain. Once the bound rule was eliminated following the 1864 season (see **1.21**), it became even more the case that there was no such thing as a routine out.

It is hard to overstate the effect that this had on the way the game was played. As we shall see, many of baseball's fundamental precepts developed during this era, and in some cases they persisted long after the conditions of the game had changed.

(*16*) *The Enemies of Change.* Before new inventions or innovations were accepted into baseball, especially in early baseball, they had to pass two litmus tests: Is this manly? Can we afford this? Both are such deep-rooted issues that any time an invention seems to come about later than might be expected, it is worth examining whether one of these factors was involved. For example, trainers (see **21.10**) were resisted until a *Sporting News* correspondent observed that the cost of having two star players disabled for a month would exceed the annual salary of a trainer who might have prevented those injuries. Clearly it would have been just as much of a competitive advantage to employ a trainer before this time, yet it didn't become part of baseball until player salaries had reached the point where this innovation made economic sense.

(*17*) *I Can Hold My Breath Longer Than You.* Once an enterprising player, manager, or owner decided that an innovation passed both of those tests and showed that it could be successfully used to win games, the pressure would shift to those who had not adopted it.

An instinct against rapid change is especially true in the fiercely competitive environment of professional sport. In consequence, once a new concept is finally accepted in baseball, there is often a race to exploit a strategy that had previously been viewed as unmanly or unaffordable. For example, gloves were still viewed as unmanly by many until the late 1880s. But within a few years of catching on, infielders were taking catcher's mitts out to their positions (see **9.3.3** "Snaring Nets").

(18) There's No Place for Condescension. The rules and conditions of baseball in the nineteenth century were constantly changing. The players, out of necessity, were highly adaptable, constantly revisiting and revising their techniques, tactics, and strategies. By contrast, the twentieth century saw great stability, which enabled the development of a basic consensus on the fundamentals of play and a "book" of strategies. Unfortunately, far too many baseball historians have failed to grasp this reality and have leaped to the conclusion that nineteenth-century players were unimaginative because they did not evolve the tactics now in use.

I hope readers will come away from this work with an appreciation that such condescension is almost always inappropriate. One of the basic premises of this work has been that, whenever early ballplayers did something differently from how it is now done, the first place to look for an explanation is in the rules and conditions of their era. We shall see time and again that just as many nineteenth-century tactics would not work today, so too many of today's strategies would have been ill-suited to early baseball or would have been too costly for a sport that was still struggling to survive.

In old age, turn-of-the-century ballplayer Bobby Lowe discussed the 3-6-3 double play and said, "I believe [Fred] Tenney was the originator, but I know any such observation will be subject to controversy" (*Sporting News*, July 16, 1942). Bobby Lowe was a wise man. I started out thinking it strange that no one had studied this topic before, but I soon came to understand why. Not only was I rehashing old controversies, I was starting new ones. Worse, my research was never done; just when I thought I had traced something back as far as possible, an earlier claimant emerged.

I have done my best to find and document the earliest instance of all the categories that follow, but it goes without saying that this is not always possible, hence this is a work in progress. Nearly a century ago a sportswriter noted that "no 'new play' ever materialized but there were several claimants for the honor accruing from it" (H. G. Merrill, *Sporting News*, December 22, 1906). Even that early, the complexity was enough to deter any writer from attempting systematically to sort these matters out. The passage of a hundred years makes the task infinitely harder and often makes me feel that I have rushed in where angels fear to tread.

Notes on Nineteenth-century Baseball

Several elements of early baseball will come up repeatedly and confuse twenty-first-century readers, so it is important to address them before we proceed.

Until the 1880s the word "base ball" was almost exclusively written as two words. After that the word began sometimes to be hyphenated and other times to be written as one word. By the early twentieth century it had become most common to write it as one word. This change is sometimes described as puzzling or mysterious; in fact it is a common pattern for compound nouns.

The American Association was a major league formed in 1882 as a rival to the National League. The two leagues reached a truce after one year (see **18.2.3** "National Agreement") but continued to operate as separate leagues for nine years, after which they merged. This American Association has no relationship to the minor league of the same name.

The National Association was baseball's first major league, formed in 1871 and after five years succeeded by the National League. A committee created by major league baseball in 1969 decided that the National Association should not be regarded as a major league because of various irregularities. I believe this to have been an extraordinarily wrongheaded decision that somehow considers minor irregularities to be more important criteria than the fact that the National Association (unlike the early National League) included all the best players of the era. The two points that need to be stressed here are: (1) I describe the National Association as a major league throughout the text, and (2) references to the "National Association" are to this league and not to two entities with confusingly similar names. The National Association of Base Ball Players (NABBP) determined the rules of baseball from 1857 to 1870. To avoid confusion, I will refer to the NABBP by this acronym or by its full name. In addition, the International Association (see the next paragraph) became known as the National Association in 1879. That league was fading out by that point and will not be referred to in this text.

The International Association was a rival founded in 1877 to compete with the National League. It bears no relationship to the International League, a minor league formed in 1885 and still in existence.

Until the 1870s, club names almost always took the following form: the Atlantic Base Ball Club of Brooklyn. Because of the length, the name was often abbreviated to the Atlantic Club of Brooklyn, or the Atlantics of Brooklyn. The modern formulation of "the Brooklyn Atlantics" only began to become common in the 1880s, so I have retained the correct version of these names in referring to earlier clubs.

As this discussion suggests, the distinction between major and minor leagues was not clear-cut in the nineteenth century. Indeed, well into the twentieth century, there continued to be players who preferred to play in what are considered minor leagues rather than major leagues. For the purposes of this book, I have described the National League, American League, American Association, Players' League, Union Association, and National Association as the nineteenth-century major leagues.

Another confusing topic is the names by which players were known. To avoid confusion I wanted to use the same name for a player throughout the book, but which name to choose? The various baseball encyclopedias have been forced to choose a single "use name" for players and have generally chosen the most colorful nickname. This has created the erroneous impression that nicknames were more plentiful in those days than they actually were, and that a single name clung to a player throughout his career. I have done my best to use the version most common during the player's career, and thus have referred to "Old Hoss" Radbourn as Charley, and to "King" Kelly as Mike. Adrian "Cap" Anson was a particularly difficult case; "Cap" wasn't predominant during his career, but neither was any other name. In fact, Anson was such a larger-than-life character that he was usually just referred to as Anson. Since that wouldn't do for this book, I reluctantly opted for Cap.

Finally, I have tried hard to document the source of every quotation used in this book. It has not always been possible. Even when I do cite a source, it needs to be emphasized that this is not necessarily the original source. Nineteenth-century newspapers, especially sporting ones, frequently stole one another's material without attribution. The *Chicago Tribune* harrumphed in 1877, "There is an evening paper in Cincinnati which prints accounts of Chicago games under the heading 'Special Dispatch,' when it is beyond question that said scores were nailed out of the *Enquirer* printed the morning before" (*Chicago Tribune*, May 13, 1877). In 1885 the Cleveland correspondent to the *Sporting Life* complained: "The gentleman who is in charge of [the sporting] department of the [Cleveland] *Leader* evidently has a pair of long scissors, with which he completely cuts up the *Sporting Life* and Cincinnati papers, but fails to credit the source for the news stolen. Nothing original in the sporting line emanates from the *Leader*" (*Sporting Life*, May 13, 1885). This state of affairs naturally makes it impossible to be certain that a note originated in the source cited. When a source was acknowledged in the original, a date was never provided, so I cite such articles in this manner: *Cincinnati Enquirer*; reprinted in *Chicago Tribune*, January 1, 1880. If I feel certain that the item first appeared elsewhere but no acknowledgment appeared (or if the source is listed as "Exchange," which meant an early wire service), I note: reprinted in *Chicago Tribune*, January 1, 1880.

A related problem is that bylines were rare in nineteenth-century periodicals, making it necessary to refer vaguely to a correspondent or reporter. In the case of Henry Chadwick, who served as the exclusive baseball correspondent for many periodicals, I have sometimes taken the liberty of attributing an unsigned piece to him. I have done so only when the article was long enough to exhibit both Chadwick's characteristic style and his point of view; in most cases, passages were verbatim from his other works. If I have any doubt about the authorship of a piece, I left it unattributed.

A Note on Ghostwritten Books

It was common for the books of ballplayers of the late nineteenth and early twentieth centuries to be ghostwritten by sportswriters who received no credit. How much of the content originated from the anonymous author and how much from the ballplayer varied considerably, and the precise ratio for any book is unknowable at this point. Obviously some books and newspaper columns were almost entirely the work of ghostwriters, but these were not the ones that are substantive enough to quote in a book like this. Accordingly, in quoting from works that may have been or are generally accepted to have been ghostwritten, I have credited the ballplayer. While this designation may not be entirely accurate, I feel confident that most of the respective ballplayers played major roles in the books that bear their names.

Christy Mathewson's *Pitching in a Pinch*, for example, was ghostwritten by sportswriter John Wheeler, yet I feel certain that Mathewson, a Bucknell graduate, at the very least approved its content. Ty Cobb used Stoney McLinn as a ghostwriter, but it is inconceivable that the strong-willed and highly intelligent Cobb would have allowed someone else's words to appear as his own. Indeed, a 1939 account said that when McLinn told Cobb that he would be ghostwriting his book, Cobb responded: "No, sir, we don't do it that way. Ty Cobb's name won't be over a story he did not write. You sit down to that typewriter and I'll tell you what to write." Cobb then dictated the copy to McLinn and read it and corrected it (*Sporting News*, January 5, 1939).

I have made similar assumptions about the books of John Montgomery Ward (a Columbia Law School graduate), A. G. Spalding, and Adrian "Cap" Anson. John J. Evers and sportswriter Hugh S. Fullerton are jointly credited as authors of *Touching Second*, so that is how I have designated quotations from that work. I feel much less certain about *Babe Ruth's Own Book of Baseball*, but it is such a perceptive work that I have quoted from it on a number of occasions.

Chapter 1

THE THINGS WE TAKE FOR GRANTED

BASEBALL abounds with the kinds of questions that inquisitive young children love to ask and that their parents dread trying to answer: Why does the home team bat last? Why are the bases run counterclockwise? Why can't a player come back into a game as in other sports?

It is not entirely a cop-out to say, "Because that's the rule." In some cases, the closest we can come to the origins of these underlying rules and customs is that someone (we're not sure who) decided it should be that way (we're not sure why). But this chapter will, at the very least, try to illuminate the historical developments that helped make possible many of the things we take for granted when we watch a baseball game.

1.1 Clubs. Baseball teams are still often referred to as clubs, but the current meaning bears little relationship to the original one. Early baseball matches were contested by clubs, and when the term "team" first appeared in the mid-1860s it was an indication that the way the game was being played had changed for good.

The change in terminology is significant because clubs were such an integral element of nineteenth-century life. A club was a restricted group of people from similar backgrounds and was primarily social in nature. As Americans moved from the farms to the cities and began to lead less active lives, clubs began to experiment with sporting diversions to give their members much-needed exercise.

The Olympic Ball Club of Philadelphia was founded on July 4, 1833, playing what is now generally described as "town ball." The club survived long enough to celebrate its golden anniversary, though by 1860 it had switched to baseball. Rochester, New York, also had a club devoted to bat and ball games in the 1830s (Stephen Fox, *Big Leagues*, 168–172).

But the club that is generally credited with being the first baseball club is the Knickerbocker Base Ball Club of New York City, because this club introduced so many of the elements of today's game. Formally organized on September 23, 1845, the Knickerbockers quickly adopted detailed rules for playing baseball and modified them over the next decade. Many of the rules they developed—two sides, nine players a side, base runners not being retired by being hit by a thrown ball—form the basis of today's game.

Just as important, the Knickerbockers wrote down their rules and arranged for them to be distributed. (The Olympic Ball Club had had a written constitution as early as 1837, which still survives and is reprinted in Dean Sullivan's *Early Innings*, pages 5–8. But the rules were all administrative in nature, so there is no reason to think that other clubs would have requested copies.) As will be explained in the next two entries, the Knickerbockers' rules were a vital step that made it possible for the game to spread.

1.2   Rules. Of course baseball has always had rules, right? Only in a limited sense. In the first half of the nineteenth century, bat and ball games were almost exclusively children's activities. Similar to hopscotch or tag or marbles, a game might be played on a particular day and in a particular place according to specific conventions, but the same rules wouldn't necessarily apply the next day or in the next county. Baseball in those days was truly "just a game."

The Knickerbockers adopted their first rules on September 23, 1845, which represented a significant step toward a more organized and formal game. Their rules were as follows:

1. Members must strictly observe the time agreed upon for exercise, and be punctual in their attendance.

2. When assembled for exercise, the President, or in his absence, the Vice-President, shall appoint an Umpire, who shall keep the game in a book provided for that purpose, and note all violations of the By-Laws and Rules during the time of exercise.

3. The presiding officer shall designate two members as Captains, who shall retire and make the match to be played, observing at the same time that the players opposite to each other should be as nearly equal as possible, the choice of sides to be then tossed for, and the first in hand to be decided in like manner.

4. The bases shall be from "home" to second base, forty-two paces; from first to third bases, forty-two paces, equidistant.

5. No stump match shall be played on a regular day of exercise.

6. If there should not be a sufficient number of members of the Club present at the time agreed upon to commence exercise, gentlemen not members may be chosen in to make up the match, which shall not be broken up to take in members that may afterwards appear; but in all cases, members shall have the preference, when present, at the making of a match.

7. If members appear after the game is commenced, they may be chosen if mutually agreed upon.

8. The game to consist of twenty-one counts, or aces; but at the conclusion an equal number of hands must be played.

9. The ball must be pitched, not thrown, for the bat.

10. A ball knocked out of the field, or outside the range of the first or third base, is foul.

11. Three balls being struck at and missed and the last one caught, is a hand out; if not caught is considered fair, and the striker bound to run.

12. If a ball be struck, or tipped, and caught, either flying or on the first bound, it is a hand out.

13. A player running the bases shall be out, if the ball is in the hands of an adversary on the base, or the runner is touched with it before he makes his base; it being understood, however, that in no instance is a ball to be thrown at him.

14. A player running who shall prevent an adversary from catching or getting the ball before making his base, is a hand out.

15. Three hands out, all out.

16. Players must take their strike in regular turn.

17. All disputes and differences relative to the game, to be decided by the Umpire, from which there is no appeal.

18. No ace or base can be made on a foul strike.

19. A runner cannot be put out in making one base, when a balk is made by the pitcher.

20. But one base allowed when a ball bounds out of the field when struck.

In mentioning the Knickerbockers, historians often stress the rules that are still part of today's game, such as Rule 15's establishment of three outs per inning and Rule 13's prohibition on throwing the ball at a base runner. Some sources even print only Rule 4 and the last thirteen rules, since these are the playing rules (see, for example, George L. Moreland, *Balldom*, 6).

While understandable, this emphasis is unfortunate because it creates a distorted portrait of the club. The Knickerbockers viewed these playing rules as very provisional and changed many of them in the ensuing years. The club's organizational rules were just as important—both to them and to the history of baseball—because they suggested a seriousness of purpose and a permanence that was essential in reinventing a child's game as an acceptable activity for adults.

1.3   Mass-circulated Rules. The Knickerbockers' rules appeared on December 6, 1856, in a publication called *Porter's Spirit of the Times*. This was an important step for a country that was still making the transition from oral communication to print. It enabled baseball to spread rapidly and also helped the game to make a valuable ally in the burgeoning American newspaper industry. Tom Melville has concluded that "baseball was the first game Americans learned principally from print," noting that town ball was "handed down from generation to generation orally" but that baseball was learned by reading "printed regulations" (Tom Melville, *Early Baseball and the Rise of the National League*, 18).

This process was directly responsible for the 1857 founding of the Franklin Base Ball Club of Detroit, which was likely the first club west of New York to use the Knickerbocker Rules. The December 13, 1856, issue of the *New York Clipper* included a copy of the rules. In an 1884 interview, founding club member Henry Starkey explained, "There was an old fiddler here in the city named Page. . . . He used to take the *New York Clipper*, and one day he showed me a copy in which there was quite a lengthy description of the new game of base ball. . . . There was quite a number of us who felt an interest in the game, and we came to the conclusion that the new way must be an improvement over the old. Anyway, we decided to try it, so I wrote to the *Clipper* for a copy of the new rules, and paid $1 for it. After we got the rules we organized a club—the first in Detroit" (*Detroit Free Press*, April 4, 1884).

1.4   Matches. Early clubs made a sharp distinction between informal games and matches, which were formal contests between two clubs. It was long believed that the first official match played under the Knickerbockers' rules took place on June 19, 1846, when the Knickerbockers were beaten at their own game by an informal group known as the New York Club, 23-1. But research by Melvin Adelman and Edward L. Widmer has established that two games had been played between the New York Ball Club and nine Brooklyn players the previous fall, on October 21 and 24, 1845 (Melvin L. Adelman, "The First Baseball Game, the First Newspaper References to Baseball, and the New York Club: A Note on the Early History of Baseball," *Journal of Sport History*, vol. 7, no. 3 [Winter 1980], 132–135). There is no proof that these games were played by the Knickerbockers' rules, but Frederick Ivor-Campbell concluded that "it is reasonable to suppose the games were played wholly under the rules that had been codified and formally adopted by the Knickerbockers just a month earlier" (Frederick Ivor-Campbell, "When Was the First Match Game Played by the Knickerbocker Rules?" *Nineteenth*

Century Notes 93:4 [Fall 1993], 1). Contemporary newspaper accounts of both matches are reprinted in Dean Sullivan's *Early Innings*. Matches remained very rare for the next decade but then grew exponentially between 1855 and 1857.

1.5 Uniforms. On April 24, 1849, the Knickerbockers adopted a uniform of blue woolen pantaloons, a white flannel shirt, and a straw hat. Jimmy Wood said these choices were prompted by a previous game in which the players had found "that trousers impeded their movements and that the wearing of linen shirts was a handicap" (James Wood, as told to Frank G. Menke, "Baseball in By-Gone Days," syndicated column, *Indiana* [Pa.] *Evening Gazette*, August 14, 1916).

1.6 Nine Innings. The Knickerbockers' rules called for the game to be played until "21 counts, or aces" had been scored by one side. Playing until one side scored a predetermined number of runs continued to be the custom for the next decade. Nine innings was adopted as the length of the game on March 7, 1857, by the rules committee formed at the meeting that led to the creation of the game's first organizing body, the National Association of Base Ball Players. While the exact reasons for the choice of nine innings remain murky, researcher John Thorn believes there was general agreement that the number of players and innings should correspond. Thus the adoption of the nine-player game meant that nine would also become the number of innings.

1.7 Running Counterclockwise. In many of the forerunners of baseball, the bases were run clockwise. The reasons for the change are not known, but it's interesting to speculate on the consequences. Imagine how different baseball would be in a parallel universe in which the bases were run clockwise. With the extra edge in getting to first base, would all the greatest hitters in baseball history be right-handers? Would the left-handed pitcher, accordingly, be a rare bird? Would all the great defensive catchers, middle infielders, and third basemen be left-handers? Would great players like Ozzie Smith and Luis Aparicio even have played in the major leagues?

Incidentally, softball incorporated a peculiar rule in 1908 by which the leadoff hitter could choose to run the bases clockwise *or* counterclockwise. The other base runners were then obliged to follow the leadoff hitter's cue (Lois Browne, *Girls of Summer*, 15).

1.8 Overrunning Bases. The rules of early baseball did not allow base runners to overrun bases, including first base, which had a number of important consequences. For example, the *Brooklyn Eagle* noted in 1865, "It is a noticeable fact this season thus far, that so many of the players overrun their bases and slip away from them. It has been found, upon investigation, to arise from the fact of their playing without spikes. Complaint is also made that shoes with spikes in, cannot be obtained. Every ball player should wear shoes with good spikes, that he can break up at short notice, and stop short, without slipping down" (*Brooklyn Eagle*, June 19, 1865).

Allowing runners to overrun bases was a hot topic for a number of years. Some observers contended that runners should be allowed to overrun any base while others argued for the status quo. Finally, before the 1871 season, a compromise was reached and runners were allowed to overrun first base only.

According to Jimmy Wood, the impetus for the rule change came from a surprising source. Baseball on ice (see **19.6**) was popular in the 1860s, but players on the base paths "found it impossible to stop at bases after skating out a hit. Many of them were injured by skating into bases, their skates tripping them and sending them to the icy surface. To prevent further accidents the captains decided to permit players to overskate the bags without penalty of being touched out if they turned to the right on their way back to base. When summer baseball was resumed it was decided that the rule made for skater-players should be extended to the regular diamond" (James Wood, as told to Frank G. Menke, "Baseball in By-Gone Days," part 2, syndicated column, *Marion* [Ohio] *Star*, August 15, 1916). Although this explanation sounds farfetched, Wood was a star player of the era and was not known for fanciful tales, so his account must at least be considered.

The decision to let runners overrun first but not the other bases was one of those compromises that seem to have satisfied neither side. Supporters of allowing overrunning at all the bases were particularly outspoken, with Henry Chadwick declaring with his customary assurance: "This rule is confined to the first base, but it should have been applied to all, and no doubt the Amateur Convention will amend it to that effect" (*New York Clipper*, March 4, 1871). But that never happened.

In 1888 it was reported that the owners were tired of losing players to sliding injuries and were considering legalizing the overrunning of all bases (*Brooklyn Eagle*, November 9, 1888). The Lester Plan of 1892 called for runners to be allowed to run past second or third base, which gave Henry Chadwick the opportunity to reiterate his support (*Sporting Life*, November 12, 1892; *Brooklyn Eagle*, November 14, 1892). In 1894, John B. Foster of the *Cleveland Leader* advocated allowing runners to overrun second and third base in order to reduce the amount of spiking (quoted in the *Brooklyn Eagle*, November 7, 1894).

Others, however, preferred things as they were. One scribe complained that such a rule change would "kill some very exciting incidents. What is more interesting than to watch a runner and a fielder both jabbing at the base like a couple of bantams slugging a third party?" (*Brooklyn Eagle*, September 8, 1894). Whether this argument persuaded anyone or not is unclear, but for whatever reason the campaign to legalize the overrunning of second and third base never picked up enough steam to accomplish its aim.

As a result, what appears to have been a compromise when adopted in 1870 has been retained ever since. It has had far-reaching consequences, contributing to such developments as slides, the use of spikes, and the baseball player's own distinctive injury, the charley horse.

1.9   Pitchers Trying to Retire Batters. In many of the bat and ball games that were popular in the first half of the nineteenth century, the action was initiated by a "feeder" who tossed the ball to the batter without any thought of making it difficult to hit. Under the Knickerbockers' rules, the pitcher was initially still expected to simply toss hittable balls to the batter, but this soon changed. The identity of the first pitcher to seek a greater role is unknown, and indeed unknowable, but it can be safely said that the innovation occurred no later than the first great spurt of competitive play between 1855 and 1857. An 1856 account remarked that Knickerbockers pitcher Richard F. Stevens "sends the ball with exceeding velocity, and he who strikes it fairly must be a fine batsman. It is questionable, however, whether his style of pitching is most successful, many believing a slow ball curving near the bat, to be the most effective" (*Porter's Spirit of the Times*, December 6, 1856; quoted by William Rankin, *Sporting News*, May 25, 1901). It is worth noting in passing that Stevens was a member of the family that owned the Elysian Fields on which the Knickerbockers played, which may have made batters reluctant to complain about this tactic! As will be noted in the introduction to Chapter 3 on pitching, rule makers tried everything they could think of to reduce the role of the pitcher, but without success.

1.10   Balls and Strikes. As a result of the pitcher's limited role in very early baseball, batsmen accumulated no balls while strikes were recorded only on a swing and a miss. The premise was that each batter got to strike the ball once and that the pitch was the prelude to the fundamental conflict: the batter's effort to make his way home before the fielders could put him out.

This changed forever when pitchers began to enlarge their role. As noted in the previous entry, pitchers were using speedy pitching and spinning their pitches as early as 1856. Other pitchers hit upon the simpler and maddeningly effective approach of deliberately throwing wide pitches to tempt batters to swing at pitches that were difficult to hit squarely. Not only was no skill required for this tactic, but there was also no penalty in the game's rules.

Batters retaliated by playing what was known as the "waiting game" and not swinging at all. This earned them rebukes from journals like the *New*

York Clipper, which wrote in 1861, "Squires was active on the field, but in batting he has a habit of waiting at the bat which is tedious and useless" (*New York Clipper*, August 24, 1861). Two years later the *Clipper* added, "The Nassaus did not adopt the 'waiting game' style of play in this match as they did in the Excelsior game. We would suggest to them to repudiate it altogether, leaving such style of play to those clubs who prefer 'playing the points,' as it is called, instead of doing 'the fair and square thing' with their opponents" (*New York Clipper*, October 31, 1863).

But these were appeals to the gentlemanly spirit, and that spirit was giving way to competitive fervor. While the rules had allowed umpires to call strikes since 1858, few did so, and players were increasingly taking the view that any tactic they could get away with was acceptable.

The result was gridlock. Bob Ferguson recalled in an 1884 interview that "a pitcher had the prerogative of sending as many balls as he wanted to across the plate until the batsman made up his mind to strike at one. In an ordinary game, forty, fifty and sixty balls were considered nothing for a pitcher before the batsman got suited" (*St. Louis Post-Dispatch*, July 10, 1884). Ferguson wasn't exaggerating.

Writing in 1893, Henry Chadwick described the first game of the Atlantics of Brooklyn in 1855: "It will be seen that it took the players over 2 hours to play three innings [2:45], so great was the number of balls the pitcher had to deliver to the bat before the batsman was suited" (*Sporting Life*, October 28, 1893). Baseball historian William J. Ryczek reported that the third game of an 1860 series between the Atlantics and Excelsiors saw Jim Creighton deliver 331 pitches and Mattie O'Brien throw 334 pitches in three innings. Ryczek also cited a tightly contested game on August 3, 1863, in which Atlantics pitcher Al Smith threw 68 pitches to Billy McKeever of the Mutuals in a single at bat (William J. Ryczek, *When Johnny Came Sliding Home*, 45).

This presented a grave dilemma for the game's rule makers. The pitcher was not supposed to have such a large role, so almost everyone agreed that something must be done to effect "the transfer of the interest of a match from the pitchers to the basemen and outfielders" (*New York Clipper*, May 7, 1864). Yet any course of action would disrupt the fundamental balance of the game—exactly what they were trying to prevent. So they attempted to address the problem with a series of tweaks.

In 1864 the concept of called balls and called strikes was added to the rulebook along with a warning system by which the count began only when the umpire decided that either the pitcher or the batter was deliberately stalling. As Henry Chadwick explained, "The correct thing for the umpire to do is this: When the striker takes his position, ask him where he wants a ball, and see that the pitcher is made aware of the point to which he must

deliver the ball; then, if the first ball pitched is out of the legitimate reach
. . . call out 'Ball to the bat,' or some similar warning; and after this is done
and two unfair balls are delivered, you can legitimately call 'one ball' on the
second one so delivered, and 'two' and 'three balls' on the very next unfair
balls sent in. The same rule should be observed in regard to strikes—first a
warning, and then a repeated refusal to strike at fair balls" (*The Ball Player's
Chronicle*, July 4, 1867; quoted in William J. Ryczek, *When Johnny Came Sliding Home*, 46).

As a *Sporting News* article explained many years later, "This rule was construed so that very many real 'balls' as they would be called now, could be
delivered to the 'striker' before he was allowed to 'walk.'" Accordingly, "not
until the third ball was pitched could a real 'ball' be called. If a 'strike' inter-
vencd, another 'ball' would go unchallenged until the charge of 'repeatedly'
could be brought by another wide one, and so on until the 'striker' had three
called" (*Sporting News*, based on information provided by George L. Moreland, November 4, 1909). The umpire thus had a great deal of discretion
and, if he believed that the pitcher was trying to pitch fairly, the pitcher
could "send a score or more unfair balls over the base before the umpire
picked out the three bad ones" (John H. Gruber, "Bases on Balls," *Sporting
News*, January 20, 1916).

This was an imaginative approach, similar to a parent threatening a child
with punishment while at the same time explaining that it can be averted if
the child just goes back to playing appropriately. Unfortunately this carrot-
and-stick approach led only to more creative efforts to grab the carrot while
avoiding the stick.

The rule change had been intended to restore baseball to a battle between batters and fielders by reducing the pitcher's resources. Instead it had
the unintended consequence of elevating a new figure to prominence—the
umpire. For it was the umpire who was now charged with determining the
players' intentions, and many umpires were reluctant to fulfill this responsibility. Henry Chadwick wrote of an 1867 game: "both nines had played in
somewhat too much of the waiting game style at the bat, ball after ball being sent in by both pitchers, but especially by [Charley] Walker, within the
legitimate reach of the bat, but because they were either 'too far out,' 'too
close in,' 'too low' or 'too high,' in fact, not just within an inch or two of the
spot indicated, the batsman would refuse to strike, the Umpire allowing
them full liberty to thus delay the game and make it tedious" (*The Ball
Player's Chronicle*, June 20, 1867).

Making the umpire responsible for making such subjective determina-
tions put him in an untenable position. A typical example took place in a July
20, 1868, match in which the Detroit Base Ball Club hosted the Buckeye
Club of Cincinnati. When the umpire did not appear, that role was filled by

Bob Anderson, a highly respectable citizen who around 1859 had helped found the Detroit Base Ball Club. Steeped in the gentlemanly tradition, Anderson occasionally called balls but never strikes. The visiting players took advantage of this by standing at the plate for up to fifteen minutes before swinging at a pitch. As a result, darkness fell with only seven innings having been played. Most of the crowd had departed long before then.

A match in Rochester, New York, on August 9, 1869, saw the umpire similarly allow a tedious number of pitches to pass without issuing a warning. One spectator became so exasperated that he finally read the rules aloud to the umpire (*Rochester Evening Express*, August 10, 1869; cited in Priscilla Astifan, "Baseball in the Nineteenth Century, Part 3: The Dawn of Acknowledged Professionalism and Its Impact on Rochester Baseball," *Rochester History* LXIII, no. 1 [Winter 2001], 8).

William J. Ryczek reported that an umpire once called star player George Wright out on a called strike. The crowd complained vociferously about the ruling because Wright did not have a reputation for stalling. Having to take such factors into account put the umpire in an impossible position (William J. Ryczek, *When Johnny Came Sliding Home*, 46).

It thus became clear that the warning system had failed to accomplish its purpose, and there was a gradual acceptance that the increase in the pitcher's role was permanent. An 1872 account noted: "Harry Wright went to bat and waited, as is his custom, until the umpire, Mr. Hannan, reminded him of his duty by calling a strike" (*Cleveland Plain Dealer*, August 20, 1872). Harry Wright's use of a tactic was important in legitimizing it, since Wright had played with the Knickerbockers on the Elysian Fields and was universally regarded as an exemplar of fair play.

The approach of waiting out the pitcher soon gained another influential supporter in Henry Chadwick, who commented in 1876, "a batsman, when he finds balls sent in so wide of the base as not to yield one fair ball in six should wait for good balls; for it is no discredit to him to take his base on called balls under such circumstances" (*New York Clipper*, November 11, 1876).

The rules were modified several times between 1867 and 1875 in hopes of finding a more satisfactory system. In 1875 the rule was again changed so that "the umpire must call one ball on each third unfair ball delivered. . . . When three balls have been called, the striker shall take his first base." As the *Sporting News* later explained, "This somewhat disguised nine-ball rule held until 1879, when the rule plainly states what it really meant—'when nine balls have been called, the striker shall take first base'" (*Sporting News*, based on information provided by George L. Moreland, November 4, 1909).

Beginning in 1879, each pitch had to be declared a ball or a strike except for a two-strike warning pitch. Since 1881 the umpire has been obliged to call every pitch one way or the other.

The number of balls and strikes allowed changed frequently over the next decade as rule makers sought the ideal balance between hitters and pitchers. Further confusing matters was a peculiar rule that the batter could be thrown out after a base on balls if he walked to first base instead of running (John H. Gruber, "Base on Balls," *Sporting News*, January 20, 1916). (This explains why they were not known as walks until later!)

In 1889, three strikes and four balls were finally settled upon as the parameters for an at bat. And it was not until the early twentieth century that fouls began to count as strikes, a rule change that will be discussed under "Deliberate Fouls" (**2.3.2**).

1.11   Strike Zones. The concept of a strike zone began to develop once called strikes were established in the late 1850s, but it took a roundabout course. As Paul Hunkele has pointed out to me, in the early days of called strikes there was no real "strike zone," since an umpire could call a strike only if a pitcher hit a precise location.

In 1868, Henry Chadwick offered this explanation: "When the batsman takes his position at the home base, the umpire asks him where he wants a ball, and the batsman responds by saying 'knee high,' or 'waist high,' or by naming the character of the ball he wants, and the pitcher is required by the rules to deliver the batsman a ball within legitimate reach of his bat and as near the place indicated as he can" (Henry Chadwick, *The American Game of Base Ball*, 15).

A peculiar element of this rule was that batters apparently could not change their requested pitch location during the game. Henry Chadwick observed: "Many players, when men are on the bases, call for 'low balls,' although they may be in the habit of striking at high balls. This the rules do not admit of, and whenever the umpire sees this trick resorted to, he should consider every ball as a ball 'fairly for the striker,' if it is within his fair reach" (*The National Chronicle*, July 3, 1869; see also Henry Chadwick, *The American Game of Base Ball*, 75). Indeed in 1867 Chadwick even implied that a batter could not change his request from game to game (Henry Chadwick, *Haney's Base Ball Book of Reference for 1867*, 41).

A. G. Spalding later recalled: "The pitcher was required not only to deliver the ball over the home base, but at the height called for by the batsman. This, of course, gave the batsman considerable latitude in judging the balls to suit him, and was a handicap on the pitcher. I remember asking the batsman: 'What was the matter with that ball?' referring to a ball over the base and within fair reach of bat, and his reply would be either 'It was not high enough' or 'It was too low.' It was some years before this old rule was changed" (*Sporting News*, May 23, 1896). As this suggests, even after balls and called strikes were introduced, the batter played at least as great a role as the umpire in determining the strike zone.

Moreover, umpires had different interpretations as to how close the pitch had to be to the designated location. As noted in the previous entry, some umpires considered a pitch as having to hit "within an inch or two" of an exact spot. Umpires were criticized if they expected too much precision from the pitcher, but overly lenient umpires were also subject to criticism (*New York Clipper*, June 18, 1864).

Some umpires sought the advice of the two clubs as to how strict they should be. The two sides wouldn't necessarily agree; even if they did, it essentially meant a different strike zone for each match. As a result, it was announced before the 1865 season that "the practice of taking the opinion of the two nines or their captains as to the degree of latitude to be observed in making allowance for unfair balls is to be entirely done away with" (*New York Clipper*, March 25, 1865).

Another vexing question was what an umpire was supposed to do if the batter chose to swing at a pitch outside the area he had designated. Henry Chadwick described a play that occurred on June 1, 1867, in a match between a club from Lowell and the Harvard nine in which a batter called for a knee-high ball but then struck at a shoulder-high ball. Even though the ball was put in play, the umpire had called a "ball" while it was still in flight and accordingly ruled that the play was of "no account" (Henry Chadwick, *The American Game of Base Ball*, 88–89).

With no meaningful strike zone, the calling of balls was just as problematic. Early in the 1864 season the *Brooklyn Eagle* reported that the "new rules were strictly enforced throughout . . . balls being called on [the pitcher] when he pitched the ball either over the head of the batsman or on the ground before reaching the home base" (*Brooklyn Eagle*, May 2, 1864). But even that enormous range did not suit everyone, and at season's end it was acknowledged that "No two umpires last year agreed upon what constitutes a fair ball . . . some almost ignored that part of the rule which required umpires to call balls on a pitcher" (*New York Clipper*, December 17, 1864).

The confusion was finally cleared up in 1871 when the rule makers restricted the batter to calling only for a "high" or "low" pitch. This created two different strike zones—between the waist and shoulder for a batter who requested "high," and between the knee and the waist for one who chose low balls. Since the pitcher could aim for anywhere within the area the batter had selected, the basic concept of a strike zone had been established.

Henry Chadwick explained in 1874 that the strike zone varied in both height and width depending upon the batter's size: "The umpire, whenever the striker takes his position at the home base, should satisfy himself as best he can as to what constitutes the fair reach of the batsman. No regular rule will apply, as a ball which would be within the legitimate reach of a tall, long armed man would be out of the reach of a short armed man, and vice versa.

. . . The circle of the striker's legitimate reach being ascertained, the umpire will then find no difficulty in deciding the question of whether the pitcher sends in balls within the striker's reach or not" (Henry Chadwick, *1874 Chadwick's American Base Ball Manual*, 77–78).

In 1885, Harry Wright suggested doing away with the requests for high and low pitches and just having a single strike zone that stretched from the shoulder to the knee (*St. Louis Post-Dispatch*, June 27, 1885). His idea was implemented after the 1886 season, which meant that for the first time each batter had to defend a standard strike zone. The exact parameters have changed only slightly since, but there have been bigger changes in how umpires interpret the strike zone. One could, as a result, view today's strike zone as having reverted to that of a batter between 1871 and 1886 who requested a low pitch.

1.12   Umpires. The umpire has been part of baseball since the game's earliest days, but the responsibilities of the position have undergone a dramatic transformation. The Olympic Ball Club of Philadelphia, a club that played a version of baseball now known as town ball, recognized the need for an umpire as early as the 1830s. The Olympics' constitution, published in 1838, specified that one of the duties of the team recorder was to act as "umpire between the captains on Club days, in the event of a disputed point of the game, and from his decision there shall be no appeal, except to the club at its next stated meeting" (reprinted in Dean A. Sullivan, ed., *Early Innings*, 6).

The Knickerbockers' rules outlined a similar role for the umpire. William R. Wheaton officiated during a game of October 6, 1845, that appears in the club's scorebooks.

Researchers Edward L. Widmer and Melvin L. Adelman discovered a box score for an October 23, 1845, game between the New York Ball Club and the Brooklyn Club that stated, "Messrs. Johnson, Wheaton and Von Nostrand were the umpires" (*New York Herald*, October 25, 1845; reprinted in Melvin L. Adelman, "The First Baseball Game, the First Newspaper References to Baseball, and the New York Club: A Note on the Early History of Baseball," *Journal of Sport History*, 7, no. 3 [Winter 1980], 134). In their more celebrated match on June 23, 1846, the umpire issued a six-cent fine to one of the players for swearing.

In all these examples, however, the responsibilities of the umpire were to enforce decorum and club rules. Befitting this role, the umpire of this period was usually a prominent member of the community. Jimmy Wood later recollected: ". . . In the early part of my baseball career—from 1859 to 1869— an umpire was highly honored. After each game the players would give three cheers for each other and then, as a grand finale, they would bellow forth with three more—and sometimes nine—for the umpire.

"Arbitrators in the early days were chosen from among the crowd. In most cases, at least up to 1865, the umpire often was one of the most distinguished men in the city. The clubs vied with each other in trying to secure the most prominent personages.

"The old time umpires were accorded the utmost courtesy by the players. They were given easy chairs, placed near the home plate, provided with fans on hot days and their absolute comfort was uppermost in the minds of the players. After each of our games in the early '60's, sandwiches, beer, cakes and other refreshments were served by the home team. The umpire always received the choicest bits of food and the largest glass of beer—in case he cared for such beverage. If he didn't, he needed but to express his desires in the thirst-quenching line before the game started—and he got it" (James Wood, as told to Frank G. Menke, "Baseball in By-Gone Days," part 2, syndicated column, *Marion* [Ohio] *Star*, August 15, 1916).

Clarence Deming offered this similar description: "The umpire's place was usually a point even with home plate and about twenty feet away. There an armchair was set for him and, on sunny days, he was entitled to an umbrella, either self-provided or a special one of vast circumference, fastened to the chair and with it constituting one of the fixtures of the game. He had freedom of movement, but the prerogative was rarely used. In his pocket was a copy of 'Beadle's Dime Baseball Book,' then the hornbook of the game, and often in requisition. In his airy perch, shielded by his mighty canopy, the umpire of those days made an imposing figure, bearing his honors with Oriental dignity, though hardly with Oriental ease" (Clarence Deming, "Old Days in Baseball," *Outing*, June 1902, 357–358).

By the late 1860s a dramatic change in the umpire's role was under way. Before long, instead of being provided with easy chairs and canopies, umpires found themselves on the figurative hot seat. Rather than receiving such comforts as the largest glass of beer, these poor men all too often had to dodge glasses of beer that were hurled at them (see **8.2.3**). One major component of that transformation was the umpire's assumption of additional responsibilities, a development already touched upon under "Balls and Strikes" (**1.10**). The umpire's new duties will be described more fully in the next entry.

1.13 Judgment Calls. Today's fans assume without question that the umpire's role is to make decisions and to make them immediately. An umpire nowadays is likely to be criticized for a belated call even if the decision is correct. The situation could scarcely be more different from the early days of baseball when, as Clarence Deming observed, the umpire's decisions were always expected to be *ex post facto* (Clarence Deming, "Old Days in Baseball," *Outing*, June 1902, 358). Yet even in today's game a curious remnant of baseball's early days persists in the fact that players must initiate an appeal in certain circumstances.

In the 1850s, matches were officiated by two umpires, representing the two clubs, and an impartial referee. Their roles are nicely illustrated in this 1857 account: "At the desk are the umpires, watching the game, and noting its progress. The referee, solitary and alone, is seated between the batsman and the marquee, taking an impartial survey of the proceedings, and ready to mete out justice to all when appealed to" (*New York Clipper*, September 19, 1857).

This proved a cumbersome system, as this later description shows: ". . . There were a referee and two 'umpires,' so called. The referee was really the only judge. The 'umpires' were simply special advocates of their respective nines. Upon appeal being made, one umpire would invariably shout 'Not out!' while the other would call 'Out!' The question would have to go the referee, the same as if there had been no umpire" (*New York Clipper*, June 21, 1884).

The threesome was thus replaced in 1858 by a single umpire, but it continued to be his function to make few rulings except "when appealed to." A dissatisfied party would call out "judgment" or "how's that?" to invoke the umpire's intervention. But if his opinion was not solicited, he remained silent unless there was a specific need for a ruling. For example, umpires called out fouls so that runners knew to return to their base, but they remained silent on fair balls. (This is still true today, though the reason now is that the words "fair" and "foul" sound similar enough that it is feared that a fielder might mishear a call of "fair" and not play the ball.)

During the Civil War, umpires were still reticent about passing judgment. Henry Chadwick had to explain in 1864, "We were pleased to see [umpire John Grum] refuse to be guided by the statement of the player on the second base in the case of his touching a man. In the excitement of a play of this kind, one party is just as certain he touched his adversary as the latter is certain he did not, although neither the one or the other may be right, and for this reason, if none other, the umpire should be guided by his own impression of the play" (*Brooklyn Eagle*, July 27, 1864).

By the end of the war, the decision-making function was established as the umpire's unpleasant duty. Even then, it applied only to specific plays, as is shown by this 1864 account: "In the instance where Wood and Miller were put out at first base, Wood made a mistake in thinking the ball foul; it was not only fair, but the Umpire was right in not saying anything until appealed to, it being his duty only to call foul balls and not fair ones" (*New York Clipper*, September 3, 1864).

After the war, competitiveness became rampant, and incessant calls for judgment transferred more and more decisions to the umpire. Henry

Chadwick complained in 1867, "The constant cry of 'judgment on that,' 'how's that,' & c., in reference to unfair balls by the pitcher, or refusal to strike at fair balls by the batsman, has become almost a nuisance . . . there should be but one spokesman in a nine, and he should be the captain; and no captain, knowing his duties or having any judgment, will make appeals on points of play which it is the duty of the umpire to decide without any appeal whatever, such as calling baulks, balls and strikes" (*The Ball Player's Chronicle*, July 11, 1867).

The natural result was described by Chadwick in an 1868 game account: "Frequent appeals to umpire for judgment, when nothing necessitated it, became the order of the day, 'How's that,' from the players were quickly caught up by the crowd, and from this the umpire, because he had not four pair of eyes in his head, was insulted and abused by both nines. . . . Who, after this exhibition, wishes to act as umpire?" (*Brooklyn Eagle*, August 15, 1868).

This development could give an advantage to a contentious club that was playing against one that followed more gentlemanly customs. A Detroit reporter complained after an 1866 match: "McNally, the Chicago pitcher, did not pitch his balls but bowled instead. That the Detroit boys did not ask judgment and obtain the ruling out of this pitching, can only be explained on the supposition mentioned that they thought themselves able to beat their opponents against all odds" (*Detroit Advertiser and Tribune*, July 3, 1866).

On the other hand, it could also backfire against a disputatious player or club. Henry Chadwick's account of an 1868 game between the Athletics of Philadelphia and the Atlantics of Brooklyn stated: "in trying to reach second, however, [Dick Pearce of the Atlantics] was captured by [Al] Reach [of the Athletics]. . . . Dick did not think he was out, but as Reach appealed, and the Col. well knew that 'Al.' is too square a man to appeal except he thinks he has put his man out, the Col. promptly decided him out."

The game was umpired by Colonel Thomas Fitzgerald, who had formerly been president of the Athletic club. Instead of condemning his decision as being partisan, Chadwick editorialized, "The tricky men, who are constantly appealing even when they know the player is not out, too frequently over-reach themselves, as Umpires, when appealed to by men of this tricky style of play, pay no regard to their movements, and the result is that men are sometimes given in who are really out" (*New England Base Ballist*, September 10, 1868).

There is a subtle but important change in Chadwick's logic. Instead of advocating that clubs restrict appeals because it is the right thing to do, he is now suggesting that should they do so to avoid hurting their club. A similar shift from moral to pragmatic reasoning was demonstrated in 1871 when he chastised Dick McBride for having "overdone one thing, and that is in appealing to the umpire. . . . It may lead to a favorable decision in one or two instances, but only at the cost of adverse ruling in a majority of appeals made, as umpires are bound to revenge themselves in nine cases out of ten for the annoyances the pitcher thereby subjects them to" (*New York Clipper*, February 4, 1871).

By the early 1870s the sense of having the umpire rule on every play was becoming evident. Of course this didn't satisfy everyone either. The *Chicago Tribune* noted in 1870: "[Charley] Hodes tried to steal second, but was decided out—one of the closest and most unsatisfactory decisions of the game, which the boys took to unkindly, as the second baseman of the [Brooklyn] Atlantics was so well satisfied that Hodes got his base that he did not call for a decision" (*Chicago Tribune*, July 6, 1870).

The idea of an umpire who rules only when appealed to is not merely a quaint part of baseball's ancient past. The practice continued with respect to the legality of pitching deliveries for many years afterward. For example, an 1887 account noted: "[Detroit captain Ned] Hanlon called for judgment on [pitcher John Clarkson's delivery] and [umpire Ed] Hengle ruled that it was a balk" (*Chicago Tribune*, reprinted in the *Detroit Free Press*, May 14, 1887).

Remnants of this practice still exist in today's game. In 1928 sportswriter Frank H. Young noted, "There are three rule infringements which may happen in a game and which, even if he sees them, the umpire will not pass on unless asked to by an opposing team. They are: (1) A batsman hitting out of turn; (2) a base runner failing to touch a base on a long hit, and (3) a player leaving a base too soon after the catch of a sacrifice fly."

Young asked several umpires for an explanation and was told, "it's up to the opposing team to ask for our ruling. We can't be expected to play their game for them." He found this reasoning unsatisfying and wrote that he could "not see where it helps the game any to make flesh of one ruling and fowl of another. The umpires are placed on the field to see that games are played according to the rules and no good explanation has ever been made as to why some rules have to be asked for and others are given as fast as the plays are made" (Frank H. Young, "Umpires Work at 'Trick' Plays Despite Rules of Game," *Washington Post*, June 10, 1928).

Young was quite correct. There is no logical reason for these few remnants of the gentlemanly era to persist while all other areas are governed by a more legalistic approach. And yet all three continue to this day, and yet another partial example has been added—the checked swing, on which either the catcher or the plate umpire may initiate the appeal.

Occasionally this quaint custom has significant consequences. A particularly dramatic instance occurred in the fifth game of the 1911 World Series when Larry Doyle of the Giants missed the plate as he came home with the winning run in the tenth inning. Home plate umpire Bill Klem noticed the oversight and was prepared to call Doyle out, but the Athletics did not appeal so the Giants won the game. Fortunately for the Athletics, they rebounded the next day to capture the series.

This state of having vital information but being unable to convey it puts umpires in an awkward position. Umpire Billy Evans conveyed this nicely in describing a 1914 minor league game in which the base runner had missed home plate but not been tagged. After the runner had returned to the dugout, "the catcher asked the umpire what ruling he made on the play. The umpire diplomatically replied that a runner was always safe when not touched with the ball." The significance of this cryptic response gradually dawned on the catcher, and he "asked the umpire what he should do, and the umpire replied that he was there to decide plays, not to make them" (syndicated column, *Boston Globe*, January 23, 1915).

This temptation proved too great for one early umpire. In an 1878 game, Syracuse player Michael Mansell hit a home run, but the Auburn club appealed that he had missed second base. The umpire, a Mr. Woodlin, "said, 'Safe on *second*,' placing a suggestive emphasis on the last word. The hint was accepted and the ball was thrown to [Auburn third baseman George] Fair, when the umpire called Mansell out" (*New York Clipper*, May 18, 1878). A heated argument ensued, and the game was eventually forfeited.

1.14 Nine Players. The Knickerbockers' initial rules said nothing about the number of players. There was good reason for this; the club frequently had to scrounge to find enough players for any sort of organized game. Daniel Adams later recalled, "I had to employ all my rhetoric to induce attendance." In spite of his efforts, he reported limited success: "I frequently went to Hoboken to find only two or three members present, and we were often obliged to take our exercise in the form of 'old cat,' 'one' or 'two' as the case might be" (*Sporting News*, February 29, 1896). John Thorn notes that between 1845 and 1849 the Knickerbockers played matches with eight, ten, and eleven players a side, before nine gradually became the norm during the 1850s. In 1857 the rules for the first time mandated the use of nine players. Beginning in 1874, Henry Chadwick unsuccessfully campaigned to have a tenth player—a right shortstop—added to the game (see **19.12**).

1.15 Shortstops. The positions of pitcher, catcher, and basemen were already established by the time the Knickerbockers wrote their rules, with the remaining players—however many—acting as fielders. Accordingly, the only position to have developed since then is the shortstop, which began to evolve around 1849.

In an 1896 interview, Daniel Adams, one of the leading members of the Knickerbockers, claimed that "I used to play shortstop and I believe I was the first one to occupy that place, as it had formerly been left uncovered."

Adams made the move because a more resilient ball had begun to be used that could be hit and thrown farther (*Sporting News*, February 29, 1896). This caused the outfielders to play deeper and made relay throws necessary, which was Adams's primary function.

The player-turned-sportswriter Tim Murnane, who was apparently referring to the 1850s, offered this explanation: "As near as one can learn the position of short-stop was the last one to be added to the make-up of a baseball nine. In the early days the game was played on large open fields, and the out-fielders had some long runs to get a ball hit by them. Sometimes they were obliged to go to the extreme end of the field. Men played but few games and their arms were not in condition to make long throws, and the basemen hugged their bases much closer than at the present time. The short-stop acted as a utility man and would go out in the field to take the ball from the out-fielders and send it to the home plate or to the in-field" (*Cincinnati Enquirer*, April 1, 1888).

As these two accounts suggest, the position appears to have been in a state of flux in the 1850s, with significant variations between clubs. According to Clarence Deming, the shortstop sometimes also acted as a sort of rover: "The short-stop for many years shifted ground to a point between first and second bases if a left-handed striker was at bat" (Clarence Deming, "Old Days in Baseball," *Outing*, June 1902, 358). Meanwhile other clubs seem to have been slow to adapt, with one reporter offering this description of the division of labor in 1859: "At each of the bases is stationed one man to watch the runner, and the fielders, who are outside throw the ball to him in order that he may touch the runner with it before he reaches the bag" (*New York Herald*, October 16, 1859).

Since all these functions were to some extent afterthoughts, shortstop was not a very glamorous position during these years. That started to change in 1856 when Dickey Pearce joined the Atlantics of Brooklyn. Pearce was probably put at shortstop because he was short and chubby, but he helped to transform the position into a key defensive one. Tim Murnane explained, "Dickey Pearce . . . was the first man to play the position as it is played now. . . . George Wright was the first man to play the position deep and close to second base, so as to give the baseman an opportunity to move away from his position, and in 1869 Wright and Charley Sweasy were the first players to work the two positions as they are worked to-day" (*Cincinnati Enquirer*, April 1, 1888). The later development of the position is discussed in **4.2.6**.

1.16   Ninety Feet. The Knickerbockers' fourth rule used paces to set the distances between the bases, and there is dispute as to how to convert these. Some experts believe the initial distance was about ninety feet while others think it may have been shorter.

John Thorn, for example, believes that until the mid-1850s the bases were only about seventy-five feet apart. Still others, such as Fred Ivor-Campbell, have suggested that paces were used to produce "scalable" dimensions: adults could use something close to ninety feet while children would use a shorter distance. Support for either of these views may be derived from the *1864 American Boy's Book of Sports and Games*, which reprinted the official rules and observed "that boys should reduce the distances there set down about one-sixth" (*1864 American Boy's Book of Sports and Games*, 83).

The length was finally clarified in 1857 when the rules were codified. In an 1896 interview, Daniel Adams, one of the leading members of the Knickerbockers, explained that he prepared a set of rules for that convention: "The distance between bases I fixed at thirty yards—the only previous determination being 'the bases shall be from home to second base 42 paces equidistant'—which was rather vague" (*Sporting News*, February 29, 1896).

1.17   Sixty Feet, Six Inches. By 1854 the Knickerbockers had established the pitcher's distance at fifteen paces. This was clarified to mean forty-five feet in 1857, with the distance being marked by an iron plate. In 1881 the pitcher was moved back another five feet to fifty feet. By the end of the decade the advent of overhand pitching had created an abundance of strikeouts and led to consideration of another change. There was serious discussion of moving the pitcher back another five feet, but no action was taken (*Boston Globe*, September 17, 1888).

In the early 1890s, moving the pitcher back became a key plank of the Lester Plan, a series of changes proposed by *Philadelphia Record* sportswriter W. R. Lester. Lester's ideas gained a key ally in *Sporting Life* editor Francis Richter, who argued that another five feet between the pitcher and batter would result in "the restoration of the proper equilibrium between the two great principles of the game—attack and defense. With the pitcher reduced to the ranks, nine men instead of two will play the game" (*Sporting Life*, November 12, 1892).

As a result, the current distance of sixty feet, six inches was adopted by the National League on March 7, 1893, in a 9-3 vote. This change from fifty feet to sixty feet, six inches is sometimes depicted as having moved the pitcher ten and a half feet farther from the plate, and the mysterious six inches is sometimes attributed to a surveyor's error. Neither is the case.

It was actually the intention of the rule makers to move the pitcher back about five feet. But the five-and-a-half-foot pitcher's box had been the limit for the pitcher's front foot, while the new rubber effectively determined the location of the pitcher's rear foot. The result was that the five-foot change was added to the five-and-a-half-foot box in the wording of the new rule, which created the magic number of sixty feet, six inches. For several technical reasons, Tom Shieber contended that the move was actually only four feet, three and a half inches farther from the plate (Tom Shieber, "The Evolution of the Baseball Diamond," in *Total Baseball IV*, 118).

After two years, A. J. Flanner of the *St. Louis Post-Dispatch* concluded that the main objective of the change had been accomplished: "The monotonous strike out game has been legislated into a reminiscence" (quoted in the *Brooklyn Eagle*, November 7, 1894).

1.18   Diamonds. The baseball infield isn't really a diamond at all, since a diamond has two acute and two obtuse angles. The reasons for the inaccurate name have not been definitively established, but it dates back to long before the Knickerbockers. David Block reported that the diamond configuration of the infield had emerged as early as 1834, and the term "diamond" was being used by 1835 (David Block, *Baseball Before We Knew It*, 197–198). At that time it would have been silly to call the resulting shape a square, since the use of "convenient trees, posts and pumps" for bases meant that in most instances "the distance [was] not alike between any two" (*New England Base Ballist*, August 6, 1868). As with so many items of baseball, the name "diamond" was retained long after changes to the game rendered it inaccurate.

1.19   Other Dimensions. The most conspicuous changes to the configurations of the baseball diamond after 1857 were the ones noted in the preceding two entries. But there were also a great number of less noticeable changes, which are enumerated in Tom Shieber's outstanding article "The Evolution of the Baseball Diamond." (The article originally appeared in *The National Pastime* but was reprinted in editions of *Total Baseball*.)

1.20   Foul Ground. The concept of foul territory is one of baseball's distinguishing characteristics. David Block pointed out that most previous bat and ball games had no foul territory at all and that in the two exceptions, trapball and rounders, a foul counted as an out (David Block, *Baseball Before We Knew It*, 84–85). While it is unknown why the Knickerbockers made the novel decision to count a foul as no play, my theory is that the troubles the club had in finding suitable grounds in the rapidly developing New York City area played an important role. The early rules treated a ball as fair or foul based on where it first struck. The reasons for this rule being changed are discussed under the entries for "Fair-Fouls" (**2.2.2**) and "Deliberate Fouls" (**2.3.2**).

1.21   Out on Fly. In early baseball, a batter was out if a fielder caught his hit on the first bounce. By the late 1850s the Knickerbockers and at least one other club, the Excelsiors of Brooklyn, had begun experimenting with allowing only fly catches. They were pleased with the results, and the

Knickerbockers led a campaign to permit an out only for catching a ball on the fly. The issue was heatedly debated for the next few years and was brought up at the annual convention of the National Association of Base Ball Players no fewer than six times. As Warren Goldstein described, advocates of the change used the potent technique of characterizing the bound rule as a childish custom that was unworthy of men. On December 14, 1864, they finally carried their point, and fielders were required to catch fair balls on the fly, though fouls could still be caught on the first bounce until the 1880s (*New York Clipper*, December 24, 1864; Warren Goldstein, *Playing for Keeps*, 48–53).

1.22   Tagging. Early versions of baseball allowed fielders to retire base runners by throwing the ball at them and hitting them before they could reach a base. This tactic was variously known as "soaking," "patching," and "plugging." The Knickerbockers explicitly prohibited this practice in their thirteenth rule, and replaced it with tagging and force-outs. Historian David Block observed that "Without a doubt, this rule is the Knickerbockers' single greatest contribution to the game of baseball. . . . It was sparklingly original, given that a central feature of every previous description of baseball and related games mandated throwing the ball at base runners to put them out" (David Block, *Baseball Before We Knew It*, 87).

While hindsight now enables us to perceive the Knickerbockers as visionaries for doing away with soaking, many of their contemporaries did not consider this a change for the better. As one observer recalled in 1873: "thirty years ago the now national game of base ball was unknown, except in its old original form, as played by the school boys, when to put a man out all you had to do was to throw the ball at him while he was running from base to base. This was half the fun of the game at that time" (*Brooklyn Eagle*, July 16, 1873).

Many others thought that baseball without soaking was no fun at all. The pioneer Jerome Trowbridge gave this description of how baseball came to Kalamazoo: "John [McCord] used to play the old game of patch ball with us when he was here, but he went down to Poughkeepsie to school and when he came back to Kalamazoo he told us of the other game and prevailed upon us to try it. We tried it and were thoroughly disgusted with the whole thing and wanted to go back to the old game, but John kept at us telling us that this would soon be the only game that would be played and he was right. We kept at it but there were a great many things that we could not get used to. We still wanted to patch a man and some way we could not get used to this new way of putting a man out" (*Kalamazoo Gazette*, February 11, 1906).

A transplanted Brooklynite named Merritt Griswold encountered similar resistance when he tried to convince a town ball club in St. Louis to adopt the Knickerbockers' brand of baseball: ". . . After considerable urging and coaxing on my part they passed a resolution at one of their meetings that they would try the national rules for one morning if I would . . . teach them, which I consented to do if they would agree to stick to it for the full hour without 'kicking,' for as I told them they would not like it until after playing it for a sufficient length of time to be familiar with some of its fine points, all of which they agreed to and kept their words like good fellows as they were, but in ten minutes I could see most of them were disgusted, yet they would not go back on their word and stuck to it for their hour's play. At the breaking up of the game to go home they asked me if I would coach them one more morning as they began to 'kindy like it'" (quoted in A. H. Spink, *The National Game*, 406).

Soaking was retained in the Massachusetts version of baseball, which was popular in New England until the early 1860s, but when it died out so did the custom. As difficult as this change was for some to accept, the elimination of soaking was crucial to baseball being reinvented as an activity for men. As long as the rule was in effect, the game had to be played with a soft ball and bore the stigma of being a child's activity. The removal of this feature enabled baseball to be viewed in a fresh light.

The Knickerbockers did not immediately develop the current system of force-outs at first and tags at other bases unless all the bases behind are occupied. According to their initial rules, a player could be put out at any base, including home, by holding the ball on the base to which he was running, even if the base preceding him was unoccupied. This would have drastically reduced the amount of running and chasing in the game, and it must have seemed very anticlimactic for a base runner's mad dash for a base to end with a fielder stepping on that base. The Knickerbockers must have concluded that things had gone too far in that direction, and by 1848 tags were required at every base except first. Conventions about when a force-out applied developed gradually in the succeeding years, and by 1864 today's compromise was in place.

It has not gone entirely unchallenged. In 1914 concern about the number of violent collisions on the base paths had prompted calls to eliminate tagging from the game. By then, tagging was firmly entrenched, causing a *Washington Post* reporter to observe: "The plan is not feasible, and it would rob baseball of many of its most picturesque features. Tagging, or 'putting the ball on a runner,' is really one of the fine points of baseball, and to eliminate it would virtually kill base stealing, which is an art in itself" (*Washington Post*, July 26, 1914).

1.23 Touching Bases. Early base runners were required only to "make" their base—in yet another reflection of an environment in which competitiveness was considered ungentlemanly. This custom was also shaped by a more practical reality: bases were often posts or hard objects, and landing upon them was at best unpleasant and at worst could cause serious injury. Indicative of changes to both baseball's conditions and attitudes, a rule change after the 1863 season required runners to specifically "touch" their base. Base runners apparently were not keen on this change, as Henry Chadwick wrote in 1867 that it was pretty much a dead letter to get runners to actually tag a base (*The Ball Player's Chronicle*, July 25, 1867). But the next few years saw baseball increasingly governed by the letter rather than the spirit of the law, with the result that base runners who adhered to the old custom were both literally and figuratively put out.

1.24 Batting Orders. The Knickerbockers' sixteenth rule dictated that players bat "in regular turn," but early batsmen did not always take their turns in the strict rotation that is now customary.

Once an inning begins, it has always been required for batters to come to the plate in the designated order. But the early rules were vague about which batter should lead off the next inning if the preceding inning had ended on an out made by a base runner.

According to Henry Chadwick, the generally accepted custom of the era differed from the current practice. He explained in 1876 that if a base runner made the third out of an inning, the next inning would be led off by the batter who followed that base runner in the lineup. Chadwick was adamant that "This has been the rule of play since the National Association of 1857 first adopted a regular code" (*New York Clipper*, January 1, 1876).

After the 1878 season the rule was changed so that a new inning was led off by the batter following the last one to complete his at bat. Henry Chadwick commented that this would eliminate a lot of confusion: "Under the old rule, [the fourth] batsman might force [the] third man out at second base, and in the next inning take his strike over again. . . . Under the new rules each batsman will have the same number of times at bat in a match so far as the rules can possibly control the matter" (*New York Clipper*, December 28, 1878).

Even this revamped version led to confusion under some circumstances. In an exhibition game between Troy and the Metropolitans on April 19, 1881, "two men were out on the Metropolitan side, [Jerry] Dorgan was at bat and [Ed] Kennedy was on third base. After a strike had been called, Dorgan hit a foul ball along the line towards third base, which was passed in quickly enough to [pitcher Tim] Keefe to throw out Kennedy, returning on the foul hit, thus ending the inning. In the next inning Dorgan claimed his turn at the bat on the basis of the league rule that said term begins when he takes his position at the bat, and continues until he is put out or becomes a base-runner. Captain [Bob] Ferguson, however, claimed that the fact of his foul hit having put the third hand out was equivalent to a turn at the bat, and [Lew] Say was given his place as first striker" (*Boston Globe*, May 1, 1881).

1.25 "Walkoff" Hits. Once it was established that a game was to last nine innings, the requirement was taken literally. If the club batting last was ahead after eight and a half innings, it wouldn't have occurred to early players not to complete the game. After all, a baseball match was a ceremony rather than a competition, and for the losers to walk off the field would be the ultimate act of poor sportsmanship.

This custom of completing the game persisted throughout the increasingly competitive 1870s while many other gentlemanly traditions died out. Nor was it simply a case of going through the motions in the bottom of the ninth; in many cases a side that had already won piled up many additional runs against demoralized opponents.

In the deciding match of a tournament in Blissfield, Michigan, held on August 22 and 23, 1879, the Nine Spots of Sturgis led the Adrian Club 5-4 in the bottom of the ninth. But a two-run single won the game and the tournament for Adrian. The Nine Spots glumly walked off the field and the umpire ruled the game a 9-0 forfeit. The newspapers criticized the club for the breach of etiquette (*Adrian* [Mich.] *Weekly Press*, August 29, 1879). More important, their action in walking off the field helped to pave the way for the "walkoff" hit.

This and similar incidents made it obvious that a custom once designed to promote good sportsmanship was instead creating ill will. The rule was finally changed that offseason, so that "if the side at bat in the ninth innings secures the winning run, the game is to be called without putting out three men as heretofore" (*Stevens Point* [Wisc.] *Journal*, December 13, 1879).

The first sudden-death victory in major league history took place on opening day of the National League's 1880 season and, with the visiting team still generally batting last (see **1.31**), the road team was victorious. In Cincinnati, Chicago rallied with two runs in the bottom of the ninth inning to defeat their hosts 4-3. The *Chicago Tribune* triumphantly reported that "It was nobody's victory till the last moment" (*Chicago Tribune*, May 2, 1880). The dramatic circumstances surrounding the National League's first "walkoff" home run are described in the entry "Rotations" (**6.3.13**).

1.26 New Balls. In early baseball it was customary to use a single ball in a match unless it was lost or entirely demolished. This reflected the simple reality that early baseballs were difficult to obtain and costly to replace.

For example, at one of the first matches ever played in San Francisco, a field had been found and teams arranged before it was realized that no suitable ball was available. A committee was formed, and the problem was solved only when one of its members "came across a German immigrant who was the possessor of a pair of rubber overshoes. These he bought, after much dickering, for $10, and with the yarn unraveled from a woolen stocking and a piece of a rubber overshoe the first ball ever used in this city was made" (ex–Fire Marshal Durkee, quoted in the *San Francisco Examiner*, November 19, 1888).

A similar response was elicited in Rochester, New York, when the secretary of the Flour City Club "ordered the first white horsehide ball, just one" from the Atlantic Club of Brooklyn. He later recalled the reverence with which it was treated: "What a host of the boys came to see it and to have a kindly handling" (quoted in Priscilla Astifan, "Baseball in the Nineteenth Century," *Rochester History* LII, no. 3 [Summer 1990], 10–11).

John Gruber noted that the ball's status as a precious commodity was reflected in the syntax of baseball's early rules: "Until 1876, the word 'ball' was never used in the plural number. One ball was expected to be sufficient. In that year, for the first time, a second ball was provided for. The rule said: 'Should the ball be lost during the game, the umpire shall, at the expiration of five minutes, call for a new ball,' and in 1877, 'the player looking for it shall call "lost ball," so that the umpire can note the time and wait five minutes.' The five-minute rule held until 1886, when it was abolished" (*Sporting News*, November 11, 1915).

The practice of looking for the ball for only five minutes was an improvement over the previous custom of having no limit on such searches. This could lead to long delays, especially when the club that was losing thought that darkness might avert a loss (*New York Clipper*, December 11, 1875). Al Pratt later recalled: "We used but one ball then, too, and when some strong batter would lose it, the whole gang, including the spectators, would set out to find it. Occasionally some scamp would run away with it, and then there would be all kinds of trouble" (quoted in *Sporting News*, March 23, 1895).

Only when baseball became more financially stable did this begin to change. Gruber adds, "In the olden days, when the ball was cut or ripped, needle and thread were brought into requisition there and then and the break mended. If the ball became out of shape, it was squeezed into some semblance of its natural form" (*Sporting News*, November 11, 1915). In 1876 the National League allowed the umpire to replace a damaged ball at the end of a complete inning, if requested to do so by either captain. In 1884 the umpire was given the authority to immediately replace an unfit baseball.

This did not mean that misshapen balls were being replaced with brand-new ones. Clubs were still highly cost-conscious about baseballs and would roll out a slightly less used one as a replacement. As late as the 1880s, managers like Harry Wright were keeping logs of the condition of every ball owned by their team.

Sporting Life reported in 1885, "In Chicago the umpire starts into the game with a couple of extra balls in his pocket and when a foul tip sends the sheepskin over the fence he merely rolls one of the 'extras' to the pitcher and goes right on with the game" (*Sporting Life*, July 15, 1885). But clubs were still not abandoning balls to spectators and passersby. The novelty introduced in Chicago was merely that club employees, rather than the players themselves, were responsible for retrieving foul balls. It was not until well into the twentieth century that clubs began willingly to relinquish game balls, a development that is discussed under "Keeping Balls in Stands" (see **16.2.7**).

The Chicago model appears to have worked well, and in 1887 the rules formally required the home club to provide two balls for each game. At the end of that campaign the *New York Times* hailed the success of "the rule requiring the use of 2 balls, to avoid awaiting return of a foul ball batted out of the grounds" (*New York Times*, October 9, 1887).

The presence of multiple balls offered clubs an opportunity for subterfuge that often proved irresistible. Sometimes this entailed clearly illegal efforts to replace the game ball with a dead or lively one, as discussed under "Double-ball Rackets" (see **11.1.12**). But other clubs found more subtle ways to use the presence of an extra ball to their advantage.

Late in the 1884 season, a row took place during a game in St. Louis: "[Henry] Boyle, of the St. Louis, knocked a foul ball over the inner fence separating the field seats from the playing grounds. Captain [Phil] Baker, of the Nationals, called for a new ball under the rule allowing a new ball when the old one was knocked over the fence—the rule having been made to save time. [St. Louis] Captain [Fred] Dunlap ran and got the ball, and asked that the game go on, claiming that the rule about the new ball applied only to the outer fence." The visitors, hoping to benefit from a livelier ball, refused to continue play with the old ball and eventually the game was forfeited to St. Louis (*Cincinnati Enquirer*, October 12, 1884).

Tim Murnane later recalled an 1888 game in which Boston hosted Washington with a steady rain falling. Both game balls became sodden, so Boston manager John Morrill craftily ordered the groundskeeper to pretend to lose foul balls when Boston was at bat so that new, livelier balls would have to be introduced. Instead, every time a foul was hit, a ball would immediately be thrown back on the field. Morrill accused the groundskeeper of insubordination but found that he was not at fault. Washington manager Ted Sullivan had anticipated the ploy and "had borrowed all of their old practice balls, gone into the grandstand and as fast as the balls disappeared sent an old one back in its place" (*Sporting News*, November 21, 1907).

Nor were these the only types of shenanigans that took place as a result of having only two baseballs. Another tactic is described in this 1891 account: "After Terre Haute had piled up eight runs and the visitors only one, Manager [Rasty] Wright made a hard kick because there was no new ball in play. One had been fouled over the fence and was not in play. The other one had been lost or hidden. Wright demanded that the game should be forfeited to him, and after a wrangle of about forty minutes, a new ball was brought out from town. All this 'rag chewing' did not change the result of the game" (*Grand Rapids* [Mich.] *Democrat*, May 21, 1891).

In 1896 the rules compelled the home club to have at least twelve balls available for each game. An 1893 article suggested one possible reason for the sudden extravagance: "It is one of the unwritten rules that the professional clubs, whose prowess is the source of such enthusiastic delight to Young America, get their balls for nothing, the advertisement they give to a brand by using it being considered an equivalent. This is an important item, inasmuch as half a dozen baseballs are often lost in a single game" ("How Base Balls Are Made," *Manufacturer and Builder*, April 1893).

Yet if this claim were true, the giveaways may not have continued for long, since clubs remained very unwilling to part with baseballs. A 1912 article made this rather perplexing claim: "The manufacturers are understood to donate the balls for the privilege of using the National and American League's endorsement; the balls are furnished the leagues by the makers, but the individual clubs pay the regular price for them to the league headquarters" (*Sporting News*, November 28, 1912).

The nineteenth century closed with owners remaining adamant about using no more baseballs than absolutely necessary. An 1897 *Sporting News* editorial criticized the regular "delay in providing a new ball when one of the two in play is 'batted out of sight of the umpire'" (*Sporting News*, January 9, 1897). Only in the twentieth century did it became customary to replace a baseball that had been damaged. A 1906 article referred to "the rule of furnishing new balls to umpires, instead of throwing out discolored ones from the bench" (*Sporting Life*, March 31, 1906).

In the teens and twenties, as baseball authorities tried to eliminate the emery ball and other trick pitches, balls began to be removed from play at the first sign of damage. Umpire Billy Evans claimed that during the 1915 season "hardly a game passed by in any league without some manager making accusations against the opposing pitcher. In addition, there was the 'mud ball,' the 'fingernail ball,' the 'talcum ball' and a host of others too numerous to mention." As a result, "the moment a pitcher got his fast ball to sailing, the batter would insist on an examination, a rough spot would usually be found," and the ball would be removed from play (*Atlanta Constitution*, January 16, 1916). As a result, between 1909 and 1916 the number of balls used per season in the major leagues nearly quadrupled (Vince Staten, *Why Is the Foul Pole Fair?*, 163).

Pitcher Eddie Cicotte observed in 1918 that the paranoia remained rampant: "Ban Johnson must have a whole truck full of balls that were thrown out of various games and forwarded to him for inspection. I understand that a number of these balls were analyzed by a chemist to determine if any foreign substance were rubbed on the surface. This analysis, so I am informed, showed that the ball had been treated with tobacco juice" (Eddie Cicotte, "The Secrets of Successful Pitching," *Baseball Magazine*, July 1918, 268).

As will be discussed in a later section, this new attitude toward replacing baseballs was largely responsible for ushering in the home run era. In 1931, with many feeling that home runs had become too commonplace, Lena Blackburne suggested keeping every ball in play until it became lost.

Professional baseball had become too lucrative an industry ever to go back, but the use of a single ball persisted at other levels of play. Early Wynn grew up in depression-era Alabama and recalled playing other towns with a single ball: "So if someone hit the ball into the bushes, it meant the game was over, unless we found it. We always found it. You had the whole population of two towns looking for that one baseball" (quoted in Roger Kahn, *Memories of Summer*, 209).

Nowadays the phrase "taking his ball and going home" is primarily a metaphor, yet it is one that powerfully evokes an era when such events could bring a ballgame to a premature end.

1.27 Catchers Signaling to Pitchers. A child learning the game of baseball is likely to wonder why the catcher signals the pitch to the pitcher rather than the other way around. It is a good question that once caused considerable discussion.

As late as 1896 an observer claimed that "all a catcher cares to know is whether his pitcher is about to throw a curve or a straight ball" (*Sporting News*, March 7, 1896). It might reasonably be supposed that signals were not used before the curveball came to prominence in the 1870s, but this is not entirely the case. The innovative Dickey Pearce, while filling in as a catcher, was already signaling locations to the pitcher in the mid-1860s. While catching Tommy Pratt, Pearce "kept his eye on the striker, and let Pratt know just where to deliver the ball" (*National Chronicle*, May 15, 1869).

In the pre-curve era, however, it appears to have been more common for the pitcher to give the signals, when signals were given at all. Henry Chadwick noted in 1871 that pitcher George Zettlein "will send the ball just where the catcher wants him to; and in this respect, perhaps, he is too compliant, for while the catcher should be allowed to have some influence over the pitcher in directing his fire, the pitcher ought to be master of his own actions" (*New York Clipper*, February 11, 1871).

By 1874, Chadwick was counseling, ". . . If the pitcher is familiar with a certain habit of the batsman before him of hitting at a favourite ball, he should give the catcher a sign informing him that he is going to send in a slower or swifter ball or a higher or lower one than ordinarily is pitched" (Henry Chadwick, *1874 Chadwick's American Base Ball Manual*, 14–15).

Arthur "Candy" Cummings, who retired in 1878, later reported: ". . . We used to have signals, but our catchers did not take care of them as they do now. I did all this myself, and they were so simple, too, that no opposing batsman got on to them for that reason" (*Sporting News*, February 20, 1897).

John Ward wrote in 1888: "Every battery, by which is meant a pitcher and catcher, must have a perfectly understood private code of signals, so that they may make known their intentions and wishes to another without at the same time apprising the opposing players. . . . Until within a few years this sign was always given by the pitcher, but now it is almost the universal practice for the catcher to give it to the pitcher, and if the latter doesn't want to pitch the ball asked for he changes the sign by a shake of the head" (John Ward, *Base-Ball: How to Become a Player*, 53).

Despite Ward's apparent certainty, the issue is not as clear-cut as he suggested. In 1871 the *New York Clipper* noted that it was common for the catcher to do "the 'headwork' in strategic play by directing—through private signals—the pitcher how to deliver particular balls" (*New York Clipper*, October 28, 1871). In 1883, *Sporting Life* reported disapprovingly, "In these days it has become almost a fashion for old catchers to give the pitcher signs to pitch. Such is not the catcher's office" (*Sporting Life*, December 12, 1883).

Accordingly it appears that there was no uniformity as to which member of the battery gave the signals until the 1880s, when the catcher took control. That same decade saw the emergence of "sign stealing" (see **6.5.2**), and it seems safe to assume that the primary reason for the change was that the catcher is out of the batter's range of vision and is also in better position to keep his signals hidden from the coaches and the bench.

Even after it became the norm for the catcher to give the signals, there were exceptions. An 1886 article offered only a conditional endorsement, suggesting that allowing the catcher to give the signs "is a better plan when the catcher is a cool and experienced man" (*Boston Globe*, June 26, 1886). Star pitcher Charley Radbourn continued to do "all the signaling himself, and only [use] a sign for his outcurves" (*Williamsport Sunday Grit*, May 24, 1891). And researcher Frank Vaccaro directed my attention to an article that same year which observed that Chicago pitcher Bill Hutchison called his own pitches but "shakes head 'yes' or 'no' pretending the catcher is calling them" (*Milwaukee Daily Journal*, April 25, 1891).

Christy Mathewson noted that during the 1911 World Series he gave the signs to catcher "Chief" Meyers in order to thwart the Athletics' sign stealers (Christy Mathewson, *Pitching in a Pinch*, 151). Cy Young and Lou Criger went one step further, simply dispensing with signs if they suspected sign stealing (Reed Browning, *Cy Young*, 159).

At least one pitcher felt that catchers took advantage of the prerogative to call pitches by requesting only pitches that were easy to catch. Al Krumm complained in 1889: "At Dayton catchers would catch nothing but a straight ball and out-curve, and when a pitcher shook his head and delivered anything else, they jumped aside and let it pass as a wild pitch" (*Dayton Journal*, August 14, 1889).

1.28   Specialization. Early baseball clubs selected their nine best players and then assigned them to positions without much agonizing. If that combination did not seem to work, a different one was tried. As Henry Chadwick noted in 1867, "Some ten years ago, and even later, it was a rare sight to witness a ball match, played anywhere, or by any parties, which was not marked by changes in the positions of the players in nearly every innings" (*The Ball Player's Chronicle*, June 13, 1867).

The idea that each position required specialized skills developed very quickly. Championed by Chadwick, this notion soon became an important part of the game's ideological underpinnings. Chadwick, typically, lost no opportunity to remind readers of the principle. In 1865 he pointed out that "the Stars had not once played their nine together—their practice-game being played according to the old-fogy style of making up even sides on practice-days rather than of playing each member of their nine on their regular positions, and all on one side, so as to make them familiar with each other's play" (*New York Clipper*, June 10, 1865).

In an 1867 article he contended that "The change in regard to keeping players in their regular positions was a natural sequence of an improved knowledge of the points of the game" (*The Ball Player's Chronicle*, June 13, 1867). A few weeks later he offered this illustration of his point: "it is injudicious to take an outfielder, accustomed to running catches and long throws, and place him in the in-field, where his business is to stop hot ground balls and to make short and accurate throws" (*The Ball Player's Chronicle*, July 4, 1867).

Other writers picked up on the theme. An 1866 victory was described as "a striking illustration of the advantages arising from playing a nine in their regular positions always and as a whole" (*New York Tribune*, June 11, 1866). An 1874 defeat led the local paper to "suggest to the Modoc club that they practice oftener, and that each man be assigned the position he is best capable of playing, and retain and play in that place in every game" (*Adrian* [Mich.] *Daily Press*, April 27, 1874).

How this general principle manifested itself in specific requirements for the various positions is discussed in Chapter 4 on fielding.

1.29   Competitiveness. Competitiveness became a part of baseball very early, but the willingness to acknowledge this fact came much more gradually.

Whatever may have been in the hearts of baseball players of the 1860s, maxims about chivalry were on their tongues. Indeed, in the 1860s many clubs seemed to protest too much that they didn't really want to win.

A perfect example occurred after two Michigan clubs met on Independence Day, 1863. The Monitor Club of Niles lost to the Daybreak Club of Jackson and was dissatisfied with the outcome. Nonetheless, in voicing this sentiment the club was anxious not to be perceived as caring about the result: "we do not claim [the game], nor do we care for it, but we have made these statements for the purpose of showing that if we were beaten, we were not beaten by the Day Breaks [sic] as a club but by a single member of the club and that member the Umpire." The Daybreaks responded in similar fashion: "we cared very little at that time to win the game . . . [and] regret exceedingly that anything occurred to mar the pleasure of the game" (*Niles Republican*, July 25, 1863).

Clubs were chastised if they gave the impression of caring about "vulgar" considerations like winning and losing. Henry Chadwick wrote in 1862 that "There is far too much of this great desire to win matches prevalent for the best interest of the game" (*Brooklyn Eagle*, July 28, 1862). Chadwick frequently denounced clubs that obeyed the letter rather than the spirit of the rules for what he termed "playing the points." One club's song counseled, "And should any club by their cunning and trick / Dishonor the game that it plays / Let them take my advice and go to 'Old Knick' [the Knickerbocker Club] / And there learn to better their ways" (quoted in James DiClerico and Barry Pavelec, *The Jersey Game*, 27).

By the end of the decade, times were changing. Reflecting the changing times, the 1870s saw baseball's rule makers begin the long slow process of converting the game's governing principles into a set of rules that covered every contingency. They had plenty of help in this endeavor, because every loophole they left was quickly exploited.

An 1885 writer noted: "In the 'good old days' it was considered dishonorable for a player to claim he had put a player out when he knew he hadn't. Now every player is expected to make the claim of bluff, as they call it, and if they can work the umpire so much the better. This is certainly a most reprehensible practice, as it has more to do with putting an audience onto an umpire than any other thing. It is a common thing to see a player make a bluff at putting out a man and throw down the ball, and the whole side start in as a matter of course. . . . It is a common occurrence for the captains and members of the different teams to claim men are out or not, as their interests may dictate, and when they fail to get the decision they want they make remarks or motions indicative of disgust, as much as to say 'we are being robbed of the game'" (*Sporting Life*, June 3, 1885).

Acceptance of this new ethos was not universal. The *Washington Post* reported in 1887, "[Jim] Fogarty, the tricky right fielder of the Quaker City club, endeavored to hide a ball about his clothes, but the boys on the bleaching boards caught on to the trick and called [Umpire John] Wilson's attention to it, and Fogarty was made to give it up. Spectators pay to see clean, fair playing, and such tricks should be discountenanced by every honest player, whether it is done to advance the interest of his side or not" (*Washington Post*, May 7, 1887). This account might not seem especially noteworthy except for the detail that this game was played in Philadelphia!

In 1886, John I. Rogers, co-owner of the Philadelphia club, accused Chicago of embodying the maxim "Anything to Win" by using "questionable tactics and dishonest points of play, which the rules seem powerless to prevent." Rogers cited these examples: "Disconcerting the opposing pitcher, catcher, or fielder by loud yells or irrelevant remarks under pretense of coaching. Knocking or bunting foul balls with the object of wearing out or demoralizing a pitcher. Colliding with or spiking an opponent. Falling upon or tripping an opposing baserunner. When the baserunner is on third for the coacher to run in along the foul line so that the opposing pitcher or catcher may confuse him with the baserunner. When a baserunner is on second, while the umpire is looking at an 'out on first,' for the former to steal from short field to home plate without crossing third. Constant kicking, bulldozing, and appeals to the umpire on points not at all doubtful with the hope that the subsequent and really close decisions will compensatorily be in their favor. Objecting to the substitution of a new player for one manifestly injured in the game, as in the subject of this inquiry, and the hundreds of other unmanly, unchivalrous, and unsportsmanlike acts and deeds which have so often disgusted the losers of fair play and honorable rivalry in athletic contests" (*Chicago Tribune*, September 22, 1886).

A generation earlier, the mere mention of terms like "unchivalrous" and "unsportsmanlike" would have been enough to ensure an apologetic reply. Instead the response of the *Chicago Tribune* showed how much the times had changed: "talk about 'chivalry' is nonsense. The best ball-players are those who, keeping within the rules of the game, resort to all manner of devices to bring them success. Rattling the pitcher by bunting a number of foul balls or in any other way under the rules is proper. It is a point of the game, and the Captain of the nine and his men are not earning their salaries if they fail to do it. There is no chivalry about it. Everything a club can legally get . . . is so much to its credit" (*Chicago Tribune*, September 23, 1886).

This new attitude created a generation of players for whom the letter of the law was all that mattered. The 1890s spawned players like John McGraw, who freely admitted, "I had trained myself . . . to think up little and big things that might be anticipated by the rule changers. . . . With us, only the written rule counted . . . and if you could come up with something not covered by the rules, you were ahead of the slower-thinking opposition by at least a full season" (quoted in David Voigt, *The League That Failed*, 63).

Such sentiments were very upsetting to old-timers like Henry Chadwick. The venerable sportswriter wrote in 1887, "'hustling,' in base ball parlance— as far as my experience in watching the movements of 'hustling' managers goes—is to gain your ends in working up a team without regard to the character of the means to be employed. 'He's a hustler' means, generally, that the club manager in question is unscrupulous in his methods, tricky in his ways, and only kept within the bounds of honesty in his business by the controlling power of the law. I'd have none such in my club if I was a club president" (*Brooklyn Eagle*, February 6, 1887).

He elaborated on the theme in 1895: "I have noticed of late among correspondents of the sporting papers a tendency on the part of base ball scribes to advocate brutal and unfair methods in professional base ball under the guise of having teams play their game in what is called the 'hustling' and aggressive style of play so much in vogue among the League teams in 1894. The interpretation of the words 'manliness in sports' is in striking opposition to the true definition of the sentence. Too many scribes—one in particular— appear to regard 'aggressiveness' and hustling as especially applicable to manly play in the field, whereas both are terms appropriate to the very reverse object. It is worth while to define these two terms as applied to base ball.

"Webster defines 'hustling' as 'shaking together, pushing and crowding.' The base ball definition of the word as illustrated in the professional arena, is simply to endeavor to win a game either by fair means or foul. 'Hustling' is, according to the base ball definition of the word, to yell like a mad bull on the coaching lines; to prevent a batsman or a fielder or base runner from making his point of play by irritating or balking him; by wilfully colliding with him, or tripping him up by striking him on his arm to prevent his throwing accurately, by yelling at him when about to catch a ball; in fact by any one of the means of prevention of playing his point known under the generic term of 'dirty ball playing.'

"The other favorite term with the scribes in question as well as magnates and team managers is that of having their team made 'aggressive.' Now Webster defines this word as 'the first act of hostility; also of injury and of calling to war,' and the 'aggressor' he defines as he who first begun a quarrel or an assault. Here have the correct definition of the terms 'aggressive' and 'hustling.' It is simply quarrelling and assaulting, so forcibly illustrated in the hustling game of foot ball of the period.

"There is a 'spirit of rivalry' in base ball circles which, while it is a spirit of earnest, energetic effort, full of life, vigor and legitimate excitement, is at the same time manly, chivalric and honorable. But there is also 'a spirit of rivalry' which revels in ill nature and even brutality, together with low cunning. The one characterizes the true, manly and honorable ball player; the other is characteristic of the 'hoodlumism' of the professional ball fields and belongs in the 'aggressive' 'hustling' method advocated by certain scribes and managers" (*Sporting News*, March 23, 1895).

Chadwick was fighting not merely a losing battle but one that had already been lost. The more he denounced "the 'aggressive hustling' method of play" as "nothing but rowdy ball playing," the more obvious it became that no one was listening (*Sporting Life*, June 9, 1894). Terms like "aggressive" and "hustling" may have been restricted to those meanings to men of Chadwick's generation, but a new generation was adopting them as a badge of honor.

This brash announcement appeared in *Sporting Life* in 1895: "Jimmy Gilman wishes to go on record as prophesying that his Houston team will win the pennant in the Texas League. Jim has surrounded himself with an outfit of hustlers" (*Sporting Life*, March 30, 1895). The *Boston Globe* noted in 1896 that "Baltimore always appreciates the services of faithful, hustling players like McGraw" (*Boston Globe*, July 2, 1896).

By the early twentieth century the term's new connotations were so established that the *Cleveland News* wrote in 1909, "Hustlers are admired the world over. Men who never will admit defeat, but will keep on fighting to the end always make their marks in the world" (*Cleveland News*, reprinted in *Sporting News*, July 1, 1909). Just as the nineteenth century had seen the connotations of terms such as "prejudice" and "discrimination" transformed from positive to negative, so too formerly derogatory terms such as "aggressive" and "hustling" had been reinvented as the property of overachievers.

By the twentieth century, the rulebook had been tightened to virtually eliminate loopholes. As a result, the few remnants of the days when competitiveness had been frowned upon began to seem increasingly anachronistic. Jim Brosnan commented on the injunction against "deception" in the balk rule: "Deceive is a most ponderous choice of words. What in hell do they think a pitcher is doing when he throws a curve ball? If deceit is, in truth, a flagrant violation of baseball morality, then the next logical step is to ban breaking balls, and let the hitter call his pitch" (Jim Brosnan, *The Long Season*, 86).

1.30 Low Scoring. Most knowledgeable baseball fans today have a sense that a low-scoring game is baseball at its finest. For many of us, this is not really our preference. Yet just as we may read best-sellers while thinking that we ought to be reading classics, there is an indefinable sense of guilty pleasure in watching an 11-9 game. Like so many elements of baseball, this guilt is a legacy of the early days of baseball and, in particular, the influence of pioneer sportswriter Henry Chadwick.

Baseball in the 1850s and 1860s was a very high-scoring game. The combination of rubbery baseballs, restrictions on pitchers, and poor field conditions made it very difficult for gloveless fielders to record outs. As a result, a base hit came to be viewed as nothing special while a putout was a sign of great skill. Reporters picked up on this and heaped praise on great fielders and on clubs that played low-scoring games. As early as 1860 it was becoming a byword that "in baseball low figures represent good play" (*Troy Daily Whig*, account of July 3, 1860, match; quoted in Richard A. Puff, ed., *Troy's Baseball Heritage*, 6).

This tendency was so pronounced that it began to exert a powerful influence on how the game was played. Until 1869 most baseballs contained two and a half ounces of rubber, but the next two seasons saw a dramatic reduction in that amount. By the middle of the 1870 season, adoption of a dead ball was a foregone conclusion: "From the many accidents which have lately happened in consequence of using a 'lively' ball, one in which there is a large quantity of rubber, it has been pretty generally determined by the leading clubs of the country to employ what is known as the 'dead' ball in future" (*Chicago Post*, reprinted in the *Detroit Advertiser and Tribune*, August 1, 1870). The dead ball was formally adopted at the convention of the National Association of Base Ball Players on November 30, 1870, with balls being limited to no more than one ounce of rubber.

Scores naturally plunged as a result, and the trend was accelerated by liberalized pitching rules, improved playing fields, and, eventually, fielder's equipment. By the mid-1870s, shutouts had become commonplace and the 46-38 scores of the 1860s had vanished forever.

What is most surprising about this development is the response from sportswriters, with Chadwick at the forefront. Instead of attributing this trend to changed conditions, they extolled lower scores as proof that baseball had become a "scientific" game. A typical 1878 report exclaimed that "Base ball has been reduced to an exact science, and we read of fifteen innings with only one tally" (*Fremont* [Mich.] *Indicator*, May 15, 1878). In contrast, an 1874 game with a 28-14 score was dismissed out of hand as having a "score too large to call it a good game" (*Adrian* [Mich.] *Press*, June 11, 1874).

In addition to trying to convince readers that lower-scoring games were aesthetically superior, sportswriters of the 1870s and 1880s sought to portray such games as more exciting. Part of this view was that low-scoring games tended to be close, but it went well beyond that. For example, a twelve-inning 1-0 game caused a reporter to gush, "Altogether the closest and most exciting game ever played in the city. . . . From the time the game commenced until the close of the long contest the interest was at fever heat" (*Grand Rapids* [Mich.] *Times*, June 17, 1883). Yet after a ten-inning 10-9 thriller, the players were dourly admonished to "bear in mind that such games are calculated to shake the confidence their backers and the public have had in them, and will have a tendency to lessen their receipts at the turnstile" (*Detroit Free Press*, June 15, 1881).

It is harder to determine whether fans actually found low-scoring games more exciting or whether this notion was a creation of the press. There is some evidence of the latter. The *Williamsport Sunday Grit*, for example, observed in 1891 that in spite of Henry Chadwick's advocacy of 1-0 games, "The public's idea of an exciting game is one where the pitchers are not effective and the game see saws first one way and then another" (*Williamsport Sunday Grit*, April 12, 1891).

Either way, the press's insistent preference for low-scoring games had an enormous effect on the perception of baseball. Scores have fluctuated in the years since, but there has remained a sense that low-scoring baseball is purer and that a high-scoring game is, at best, a guilty pleasure.

1.31 Home Team Last. It was not until 1950 that the home team was required by rule to bat last. By then, what had once been viewed as a significant strategic decision had become so routine that hardly anyone noticed.

Robin Carver wrote in 1834 that in "base, or goal ball," play began when "chance decides which shall have the first innings" (Robin Carver, *The Boy's and Girl's Book of Sports*, 37). This custom was maintained by the Knickerbockers, whose third rule dictated a coin toss for first ups. This practice continued for many years, though exactly what was tossed is less clear. A 1921 *Sporting News* article about Candy Cummings noted, "In [Candy] Cummings' days ball clubs at the start of the game tossed up for their raps" by playing "'hand over hand' on the bat" (*Sporting News*, December 29, 1921). But the contemporary accounts that are specific invariably refer to a coin toss. For example, a player in Albany, New York, wrote after an 1864 game, "Upon threwing [sic] up the cent for chose [sic] of innings, Hodgkins called head, and it came down head. We took last inning" (Scott S. Taylor, "Pure Passion for the Game: Albany Amateur Baseball Box Scores from 1864," *Manuscripts* LIV, no. 1 [Winter 2002], describing a collection of letters about baseball in Albany written in 1864 recently donated to the Georgetown University Library).

The decision of the Albany club seems to have reflected the consensus of the time, as Henry Chadwick wrote in 1867, "The Lowells won the toss and went to bat. Here [in New York], our players generally take the field when they win the choice, in order to have the last chance at bat" (*The Ball Player's Chronicle*, June 6, 1867). Note how similar this reasoning is to today's philosophy. The issue drew little attention in the 1860s, however, suggesting that it was not considered particularly important.

The change to less elastic balls in the early 1870s appears to have changed thinking. Captains increasingly began to choose to bat first in order to have the first crack at the new ball. The *Sporting News* article about Candy Cummings noted that "Both teams wanted to be on the offensive right off the reel." When Cummings was victorious, as he usually was, "his club took the first clouts and proceeded in a lusty endeavor to whale in enough runs to discourage the opposition at the outset and incidentally put the ball in such a delapidated [sic] condition that it could not be batted far when the opposing team arrived at bat" (*Sporting News*, December 29, 1921).

A 1914 article noted: ". . . Many years ago, it was equally the rule for the home team to bat first, and the argument on which the managers maintained the system was the supposed advantage of 'getting the first crack at the new ball!' When the game was played with only one ball, and was held up till that ball came back after every journey, a hard-hitting club could, very often, get a flock of runs by starting right in at the jump, taking first bat and collecting hits before the other team had any chance. By the time that ball was turned over to the other club it was black and hard to hit— hence an actual and indisputable advantage for the team first at bat" (*Detroit News*, September 1, 1914).

Reflecting this apparent consensus, an 1877 rule change dictated that the home team bat first. After one season the pregame toss was restored, and most sources suggest that it continued to be the norm for the winners to choose to bat first. Perplexingly, however, Henry Chadwick wrote in 1879: "In the Boston-Syracuse games at Boston, Mass., the home team has almost won the toss, and, instead of sending their opponents to the bat, as is usual, they have taken the bat first themselves, and in such cases invariably started off with too strong a lead to overcome" (*New York Clipper*, August 30, 1879).

On June 5, 1885, the American Association adopted a new rule making it the home captain's choice, and the National League followed suit in 1887 (David Nemec, *The Beer and Whisky League*, 101). In the mid-1880s most captains elected to bat first, with the *Detroit Free Press* offering this explanation in 1886: "Why does the captain who has won [the coin toss] send his team to bat? Simply this, gentle reader: The ball is new and white and the ball-tosser loves a shining mark to bang at with a bat. Again the new ball is so smooth and slippery, the pitcher cannot grasp it firmly, and is unable to impart to the sphere the delusive drops, or the deadly in-shoot, with as much effect as when the ball has become black from the pounding it has received, and from incidental excursions into the mud. Thus it is that Captain [Ned] Hanlon and all other field captains when they win the toss, elect to go to bat" (*Detroit Free Press*, May 17, 1886).

By 1887, however, the question was again being reexamined: "Some managers believe that it is an advantage to go to bat first in a game, because the opposing pitcher has not yet settled down and the batsmen are fresh and eager. Other managers, however, consider it a special advantage to go to bat last, as in event of a close game the pitcher knows that his side has an extra opportunity to overcome any lead of their opponents, and is therefore not as apt to become uneasy and nervous as if his opponents had another inning to play" (*St. Louis Post-Dispatch*, June 25, 1887).

A later article gave this account of the reasons: ". . . When the statute was introduced providing a fresh white ball whenever the original ball vanished, this advantage was destroyed. . . . And yet, though the situation was thus altered, it took seven or eight years to wake up the managers and make them realize that they didn't get anything by taking first bats any more. Now, you couldn't get them to budge from the present custom. [Cap] Anson was the last manager who occasionally changed round. If the Old Man saw a young, green and nervous pitcher getting ready—especially on a cold day—he'd take first bats, and his sluggers would make life a burden for the kid before he got his bearings. Many and many a time Anson's men rolled up 6 or 7 runs on kid pitchers in the first inning—and if the other manager replaced his novice with a veteran, the vet probably had a chilled arm, went in unprepared to pitch, and got his beatings likewise" (*Detroit News*, September 1, 1914).

By 1891 batting last had become the norm, though there were still exceptions. A game account that year observed: "Captain [Johnny] Ward varied his point of going in last at the bat on this occasion for a special reason. In the first place it was a batsman's day in having the wind with him; secondly, it was a good point to play to try and take the wind out of the sails of the enemy by a brilliant onslaught on their works at the outset, and it worked beautifully in yesterday's game" (*Brooklyn Eagle*, June 13, 1891).

A rule change the following year gave managers an added incentive to bat last, as the *Brooklyn Eagle* explained: "There is an important advantage accruing to the position of being last at the bat which the new rule governing the ending of a game after four and a half innings have been played has very plainly developed, and the Philadelphia team was the first to benefit by it. The rule in question provides that, if four and a half innings are played, the side that has not been at bat wins if it was in the lead at the close of the first part of the inning. Suppose that in Monday's game, with the score of 3 to 2 in favor of Cleveland at the end of the fourth inning, Brooklyn had drawn a blank in their fifth inning, and at the close of the first part of the fifth inning a storm of rain had set in and stopped play for the day, Cleveland would have won the incompleted four and a half inning game legally by 3 to 2, owing to their being last at bat. This advantage causes Harry Wright to send his team last to the bat every time they play on home grounds. Captain [John] Ward, apparently, loses sight of this new rule" (*Brooklyn Eagle*, June 8, 1892).

Eventually it became customary for the home captain to choose last ups. A rare but noteworthy exception took place when Frank Chance chose to bat first in a July 16 game against the Giants during the legendary 1908 pennant race; the strategy did not work, however, as Chicago lost the game.

The introduction of the cork-centered ball and the increased use of new baseballs eliminated the one perceived benefit to batting first. By 1914 "all clubs go to the field first when on the home grounds; the custom has become firmly rooted, and no manager ever thinks of changing" (*Detroit News*, September 1, 1914). Nevertheless it was not until 1950, with a general recodification of the rules, that what had become the universal practice of the home team batting last was written into the rules.

1.32   Substitutions. In early baseball the nine players in a club's lineup were usually the only ones who participated in the game. Clubs generally brought no more than ten men to a game, and the substitute was not allowed to enter the game unless one of the starters became ill or injured. This was typical of nineteenth-century team sports; even early hockey did not allow substitutes (Michael McKinley, *Putting a Roof on Winter*, 7).

For many years the opposing team's captain actually had to approve injury substitutions, which could lead to conflict. In an 1867 match between the Mutuals and Irvingtons, a brawl broke out in the stands and Hugh Campbell of the Irvingtons was injured in trying to break it up. The Mutuals at first refused to allow a substitute, but the captain finally relented when the Irvingtons said they would have to play with only eight players. Henry Chadwick wrote that the Mutuals were correct that the substitution did not have to be accepted since it did not occur during the game. But he commended them for their sportsmanship (*The Ball Player's Chronicle*, July 4, 1867).

The lone exception to the prohibition on substitutions was the courtesy runner (see **6.2.6**). But it was other members of the starting lineup who were used in this role, rather than reserve players. The concept of replacing a player during a game for poor performance or for tactical reasons was simply not part of early baseball. Players were expected to finish what they started—a mind-set that continued to be part of baseball for many years and, to some extent, still is.

The rules were modified in the 1870s to allow a substitution in the early innings. The purpose of this rule was not to enable strategic substitutions but instead had a more practical intention. If a game was scheduled to begin and a starter had not made his appearance, that player's club was likely to try to stall until he arrived. Early-innings substitutions were designed to allow a backup to begin the game and be replaced by the regular when he appeared.

In 1881 the old rule that replacements were allowed only in the case of injury or illness was restored. In an increasingly competitive era, the provision that the opposing captain had to approve these substitutions led to a great deal of wrangling. During an 1886 game, Chicago captain Adrian

Anson refused to allow an injured Philadelphia player to be replaced, caus-ing Philadelphia co-owner John I. Rogers to denounce Chicago for its "questionable tactics and dishonest points of play, which the rules seem powerless to prevent" (*Chicago Tribune*, September 22, 1886).

Since strategic substitutions were illegal, clubs usually had only nine or ten players on hand. If there was an extra, he often manned the turnstile or had other duties, with the result that many early diamonds featured only one bench (see **14.4.6**). The *Cincinnati Enquirer* suggested in 1878, "The tenth man should be held ready in uniform to take the place of a disabled player at a moment's notice. Then there would be no unpleasant delay" (*Cincinnati Enquirer*, May 3, 1878). An 1887 rule mandated that substitute players be in uniform, but few clubs seem to have heeded this advice.

Substitutions for healthy players were finally made legal in 1889, but only one elective substitution could be made per game, and the player had to be specified on the scorecard. The number of substitutes was increased to two in 1890, but they still had to be designated beforehand. Unlimited sub-stitutions were finally legalized in 1891.

This development brought a new degree of complexity to the manager's role, as is discussed in part two of Chapter 6. It also had a pervasive but sub-tler influence on many other elements of baseball, such as making it feasible for umpires to eject players from games (see **8.3.2**) and leading to a change in the numbering system used by scorekeepers (see **26.3.6**).

In a 1958 column, Red Smith reported that Lew Fonseca had proposed that players be allowed to return to the game after being substituted for, as happens in most other sports (Red Smith, August 7, 1958, reprinted in *Red Smith on Baseball*). In some ways this notion represented the logical culmi-nation of the direction in which baseball had been heading since its earli-est days.

Nonetheless baseball has been reluctant to go too far down the path of specialization, as demonstrated by the strong feelings that are still gener-ated by the designated hitter. The continued influence of the belief that one should finish what one started is also reflected in the frequent com-plaints about "seven-inning pitchers" and the demise of the complete game. Yet this principle is at odds with another important one: the belief that baseball should include and value the participation of as many people as possible. The inevitable clash between these two underlying principles is, I believe, the reason for the passion engendered by debates about the designated hitter.

1.33 Overhand Pitching. In early baseball the pitcher was restricted to a fully underhand, straight-arm motion. The term "pitching" was thus very apt, because the motion was akin to pitching a horseshoe. But very early on, pitchers began to bend their arm or break their wrist in order to create greater speed or spin.

A series of rules were enacted in the 1860s and 1870s to try to restrict pitchers, but they quickly found ways around them. In 1872 pitchers were allowed to release the ball from the hip, but the liberalized rule only encouraged many of them to try to get away with still higher release points. When the National League legislated in 1878 that pitchers had to release the ball from below the waist, pitchers began wearing their belts deceptively high (A. G. Spalding, *America's National Game*, 484; James Wood, as told to Frank G. Menke, "Baseball in By-Gone Days," part 2, syndicated column, *Marion* [Ohio] *Star*, August 15, 1916). Each new rule change just led to more bickering and more hardships for umpires. The pitcher's motion eventually bore so little resemblance to the original intent that the *New Orleans Times* quipped in 1877, "[Ed "The Only"] Nolan, it may be remarked, is called the pitcher of the Indianapolis club; but why pitcher does not appear upon the surface, for the reason that his delivery of the ball is an underhand throw" (*New Orleans Times*, March 15, 1877; reprinted in *New York Clipper*, March 24, 1877).

Finally, in 1884, "the league gave up trying to fight the pitchers who wanted to deliver the ball with a swift overhand motion, and the pitching rules were so amended that the pitcher could throw or pitch the ball as suited his fancy. It was found useless trying to contend against the advances of the pitcher, and, in order to even matters as much as possible, the number of balls entitling a batter to first base was reduced" (*Detroit Free Press*, March 31, 1895). The American Association followed suit on June 7, 1885, in a rare mid-season rule change. Pitchers' deliveries are discussed at much greater length in Chapter 3, part one.

Chapter 2

BATTING

THE ART of hitting has been aptly described as the paradox of swinging a round bat at a round ball and trying to hit it squarely. Lengthy treatises are now written on the proper biomechanical and psychological approaches to hitting. In the early days of baseball, however, hitting didn't seem all that difficult, and with good reason. Pitchers were restricted to underhand tosses to batters, who could request high or low pitches. Fielders wore no gloves and played on wildly uneven surfaces with nothing to shield their eyes from the glare of the afternoon sun. With everything in their favor, batters understandably saw little reason to do anything other than whale away and try to hit the ball out of sight.

Robert Smith captured the spirit when he claimed: "The Knickerbockers had taken it for granted that any red-blooded man would want to take a healthy cut at the ball to see how far he could drive it" (Robert Smith, *Baseball*, 42).

Things began to change when new pitching techniques, new equipment, and better playing fields began to alter the balance of power. The 74-56 scores of the 1860s gave way to 4-2 results in the 1870s. As a result, frustrated hitters began to develop new techniques and tactics and even to define success differently.

These innovations have been divided into four categories: (i) evolutionary attempts that modified the approach but didn't directly challenge the premise that success was a ball well struck; (ii) the revolutionary approach of trying to achieve success without hitting the ball squarely, as represented by the bunt and its offspring; (iii) the openly subversive efforts that could enable the batter to declare success without hitting the ball at all; (iv) the possibly even more subversive notion that preparation done before the game even started could help the batter in the split-second during which he swung.

(i) Variations on a Theme: Refinements to Approaches, Swings, and Stances

2.1.1   Place Hitting. As long as there has been baseball, hitters have recognized the benefit of a well-placed hit. But a far more contentious issue, then as now, is how much it is within a batter's power to place a ball. Baseball, after all, is not like golf or T-ball, where the ball just sits there waiting to be hit. When thrown by a skillful pitcher, it is a feat to make contact with the ball at all, let alone to determine where it will go. Moreover it is generally necessary to cut down on a swing to gain even a measure of control over the baseball's destination. Thus the perception of place hitting has fluctuated throughout baseball history based on whether conditions favored offense or defense.

The lively ball, uneven fields, and gloveless fielders of the early 1860s all favored the hitters and meant that a solidly hit ball was far from a routine out even if it headed straight toward a fielder. Batters of the period consequently concluded that they would be doing fielders a favor if they cut down on their swings in an attempt to place the ball.

The lone advantage that fielders did have was the bound rule, by which a batter was retired if his hit was caught on the first bounce. But this too discouraged place hitting, since a batter who seemed to have found a hole between fielders was liable to see one of them run in and scoop it up on the hop for an out.

After the 1864 season the bound rule was eliminated, offering a little more incentive for place hitting. Henry Chadwick immediately picked up on this and began one of the most doggedly persistent of his many long crusades by observing that "one of the 'beauties' of the 'fly' game" was that hitters "who can send a ball about where they please, need not be put out often by fly catches from fair balls. If the field [i.e., the outfielders] be stationed far out, then by batting ball just beyond [the infield], the bases are certainly secured" (*Brooklyn Eagle*, May 6, 1865).

At the end of the decade, with the introduction of the first dead balls, hitters received another incentive to try to place balls. One of the first players to emphasize place hitting was the five-foot-three Dickey Pearce, whom veteran baseball writer William Rankin later described as "the first to place the ball in any part of the field he desired" (*Sporting News*, March 3, 1910). The *Boston Chronicle* observed in 1869, "Pearce in an important match comes to bat, views the position of the field and finds an open spot or weak point on the field and aims to send the ball there" (quoted in Duane Smith, "Dickey Pearce: Baseball's First Great Shortstop," *National Pastime* 10 [1990], 38–42). In 1870 the *Chicago Tribune* praised Pearce for having "demonstrated the difference between wild hits to the field and scientific batting" (*Chicago*

Tribune, July 6, 1870). The *Tribune* pointed out the benefits of this tactic the next day: "The Mutuals [of New York] patiently waited, and, after they got the ball in the desired place, scientifically batted it to where there was nobody. The White Stockings batted more with a desire to knock the ball a great, rather than a safe, distance" (*Chicago Tribune*, July 7, 1870).

Thus encouraged, batters began to experiment with techniques that would make place hitting easier. Henry Chadwick continued to advocate this approach, leading John Thorn and Pete Palmer to suggest that he viewed it as baseball's equivalent to the cricket concept of "good form" (John Thorn and Pete Palmer, *The Hidden Game of Baseball*, 16). Chadwick repeatedly extolled the merits of "facing for position," his fancy term for a batter using the positioning of his feet to influence the direction in which the ball went (e.g., *Spalding's Official Base Ball Guide, 1902*, 90: "facing for position, that is, standing in such a manner as to ensure the bat's meeting the ball so as to have it go to the right, the centre or the left, just as you stand to ensure such a hit").

Chadwick brought all his rhetorical force to bear on the question. He wrote approvingly, "[Ross] Barnes is not one of the class of chance hitters who, when they go to the bat, simply go in to hit the ball as hard as they can, without the slightest idea as to where it is going; but he studies up the position, and makes his hits according to circumstances. . . . In fact, as 'a scientific batsman'—one who goes in to place a ball advantageously—we never saw his superior" (*New York Clipper*, May 3, 1879). In contrast, he sneered that "going in to hit a ball blindly, as it were, not knowing where it is going, is child's play at the bat" (*Brooklyn Eagle*, April 24, 1876).

In 1890, Chadwick noted that the previous season had seen "increased attention paid to *place hitting* by the more intelligent class of batsmen. Under the rule of the swift pitching which has been in vogue for several years past, there was a general idea prevalent among batsmen that it was next to an impossibility to *place* a ball from the bat in the face of the swift pitching batsmen had to encounter; but this rutty idea has been got rid of by headwork batsmen, and last year saw many very successful attempts made to place balls against the fire of a swift delivery" (*Spalding's Official Base Ball Guide, 1890*, 59).

Thus for Chadwick, place hitters were "scientific" and "intelligent" while hitters who took other approaches were compared to children who relied upon "chance" and clung to "rutty ideas." It seems safe to say that Chadwick was writing less about the mechanics of hitting—something at which he had almost no experience—than about what he had to believe in order to conceptualize baseball as a test of character. Such ideologically charged language had its effect, but it still didn't make it easy for batters actually to hit the ball where they were aiming.

A bat with one flattened side was made legal in 1880 by the body governing amateur play, in the hope it would "give the power to batsmen to 'place' balls better than is possible from the use of round bats" (Henry Chadwick, *New York Clipper*, January 10, 1880). As is discussed under "Shapes" (see **9.2.4**), it was rarely used but was nonetheless legalized by the National League after the 1884 season. Instead of leading to more place hitting, the innovation had the unexpected result of helping to bring back the bunt (see **2.2.1**), and it was banned after the 1893 season when many were calling for the bunt to be abolished altogether.

One 1880s batter who seems to have had success with place hitting was Charley Ganzel. The *Detroit Free Press* reported that Ganzel's "style of batting differs materially from that of other members of the team and in fact from any ball player on the diamond. He does the work with the forearm. Gently swinging his bat perpendicularly, he watches the ball like a hawk. When he sees one that suits him, quick as a flash he meets it squarely with a firm but gentle rap and it darts out on a line over the heads of the infield, but usually plows the ground before the outfield can reach it. It is seldom he hits for more than a base, but almost always puts the ball out of everybody's reach. He comes nearer to 'placing' the ball, if such a thing is possible, than any player in the country, his favorite spot being between left and center. With men on bases it is a most satisfactory thing to see him come to the plate because it is almost a certainty he will hit the ball" (*Detroit Free Press*, April 28, 1887).

Other batters also discovered success by cutting down on their swings. Chris Von der Ahe wrote that "The nickname 'Tip' was given to [Tip O'Neill] because he merely seemed to 'tip' the ball when batting. He stood at the plate straight as an arrow, a giant in physique, and it seemed that he would just push out his bat and the ball would shoot like lightning. He seldom drew back and made a 'swipe' at the ball" (*St. Louis Post-Dispatch*, April 17, 1904).

Before long the dominant philosophy of batters was to "hit 'em where they ain't," a phrase that became associated with Wee Willie Keeler. This philosophy became so dominant that many made it sound as though it was the only possible approach to hitting. Bill Carrick said in 1901, "About the only man that I know who can swing hard to good effect is [Buck] Freeman. Lajoie sometimes uses the body swing, but his general action is all in the forearm" (quoted in *Washington Post*, July 1, 1901). Christy Mathewson wrote in 1912: "In the history of baseball there have not been more than fifteen or twenty free swingers altogether, and they are the real natural hitters of the game, the men with eyes nice enough and accurate enough to take a long wallop at the ball." He cited Honus Wagner as an example, noting that the great Pittsburgh shortstop "takes a long bat, stands well back from the plate, and steps into the ball, poling it" (Christy Mathewson, *Pitching in a Pinch*, 7).

It may thus be argued that place hitting was the method of hitting best suited to the 1890s and the first decade of the twentieth century. According to this view, it was the introduction of the cork-center ball (see **9.1.6**) in 1909 that swung the pendulum away from place hitting.

There is also, however, the possibility that place hitting was at least in part an illusion supported by rhetoric like Chadwick's. Johnny Evers and Hugh Fullerton, though advocates of place hitting, remarked that many believed it to be "more or less of a myth" (John J. Evers and Hugh S. Fullerton, *Touching Second*, 160). Proponents of the view that place hitting was a myth contended that the shorter swings only ensured more solid contact, not precise placement.

For example, in 1875 a *Hartford Courant* sportswriter denounced place hitting as an "absurd notion." He contended: "More games than a few have been lost by players who have forced themselves to believe that a ball should only be hit at scientifically, and with a view of sending it to some particular point in the field. There probably is not a player in the profession who would not admit that he has driven a ball in a contrary direction to that intended more times than he has where he set his mind upon sending it . . . scientific batting is an absurdity. The only thing to do is to hit the ball, and its course after is as much a matter of luck as science" (*Hartford Courant*, reprinted in the *Chicago Tribune*, October 10, 1875).

In addition, an 1883 article in a publication called *American Sports* described a heated debate between Cap Anson and Larry Corcoran about place hitting. Anson claimed that he could hit the ball wherever he wanted to; Corcoran offered to bet him that he couldn't. Anson declined the bet but indicated that he would prove his ability to place his hits in that afternoon's game. Instead Anson went hitless in six at bats, and only half the balls he hit went in the intended direction, prompting the author to crow: "Admitting that Anson can probably come nearer to controlling the direction of a batted ball than any other batsman in the league can do, it will be seen that he cannot do it more than half of the time, and even then cannot regulate the hits as between high balls, grounders or fouls. Like every other batsman who faces curve-throwing, Anson will accomplish more for his side and will improve his individual batting record by limiting his efforts to hitting the ball hard and strong" (*American Sports*; quoted in *Chicago Tribune*, September 9, 1883). Longtime *Chicago Tribune* sports editor T. Z. Cowles vividly recalled this incident many years later, though his colorful version added some impossible details (*Chicago Tribune*, May 26, 1918).

Skeptics about place hitting can gain further support from the highly ambiguous nature of the phrase "Hit 'em where they ain't." Nap Lajoie was

quoted in 1904 as saying: "I am heartily in accord with that wise youth—
I think it was Schmidt, the old pitcher—who, when asked the best way to
bat, replied, 'Hit 'em where they ain't'" (*Washington Post*, July 24, 1904,
reprinted from a source identified only as the *Evening Journal*). Lajoie's sin-
cerity must be doubted since he was noted as a free swinger. Moreover,
"Schmidt the old pitcher" was none other than "Crazy" Schmit, a pitcher
who was notorious for his crackpot theories (see **3.3.5, 14.3.2**).

Lajoie accordingly seems to be implying that place hitting is an illusion.
Is he also suggesting that the phrase "hit 'em where they ain't" was an inside
joke by which hitters told reporters what they wanted to hear? Was this a
case like the Emperor's New Clothes, in which sportswriters, especially
Chadwick, breathlessly informed their readers of the merits of place hitting
while the hitters quietly guffawed?

Willie Keeler similarly seems to have regarded his signature phrase as a
bit of a joke. When a fan wrote and asked if he had written a hitting instructional, Keeler quipped, "I've already written that treatise and it reads
like this: 'Keep your eyes clear and hit 'em where they ain't'" (*Brooklyn Eagle*, August 7, 1901; quoted in Al Kermisch, "From a Researcher's Note-
book," *Baseball Research Journal* 28 [1999], 141).

This possibility is lent additional credence by the unidentified reporter
who wrote in 1889: "If some of the wild-eyed scribes who have been spoiling good paper with idiotic slush about place batting would get in front of
the cyclone pitchers of to-day, they would change their opinion materially.
It would take about three hard pitched balls to convince them that the players are unable to hit the ball, much less to place it. 'Place' hitting in the days
of straight-arm pitching and slow-coach deliveries was a possibility. Now
there is no such feature in base ball" (*Perry* [Iowa] *Chief*, September 6, 1889).

Even more emphatic was Ginger Beaumont who, after leading the National League in batting average in 1903, proclaimed, "There are no place
hitters." He maintained, "When a player tells you that he can put a ball
where he pleases, he is insinuating that you are weak-minded and woefully
gullible. Don't take any stock in such twaddle. When it comes to delivering
the goods I have noticed that they are generally short of stock" (quoted in
Oshkosh Northwestern, July 16, 1904).

The most compelling evidence for this viewpoint comes from none other
than Ty Cobb, who condemned "the futility of trying to place hits instead of
merely concentrating the mind and muscles on hitting the ball on the nose"
(Ty Cobb, *Memoirs of Twenty Years in Baseball*, 79). Cobb instead advised young
hitters: "never try to place a hit. In the first place, you can't do it, and it is not
a good idea, anyway. Very few batters ever successfully acquired the art. I never
try to place hit. I have tried simply to meet the ball solidly and let the hits find
holes for themselves" (Ty Cobb, *Memoirs of Twenty Years in Baseball*, 78).

Cobb called Willie Keeler "the best of the so-called place hitters." He explained that Keeler was really a poke or slap hitter rather than a place hitter: "Keeler combined several things to make this possible. He gripped his bat far down toward the middle and poked at the ball, rather than hit at it. His swing was short and naturally more accurate than the longer swings of the average batter. He was able to wait until the ball was almost upon him before poking at it. Many of Keeler's hits were pokey little flies, just past the infield" (Paul Purman, "Place Hitting," syndicated column, *Sheboygan* [Wisc.] *Press*, July 9, 1918).

In either case, it was only with the success of Babe Ruth that swinging hard without regard to placement gained general acceptance. According to Ty Cobb, Ruth was allowed to develop his batting style because he was a pitcher. Cobb explained that "A pitcher is not expected to hit. Therefore, he can follow his own system without managerial interference. Ruth made the most of this opportunity. As a pitcher he took a tremendous cut at the ball. At first he was awkward. . . . Gradually he gained confidence, experience and knowledge of pitchers" (quoted in F. C. Lane, *Batting*, 71).

2.1.2 Swings. Henry Chadwick wrote in 1860, "Players have different modes, and adopt different styles of batting; some take the bat with the left hand on the handle, and slide the right from the large end toward the handle; others grasp it nearly one-third of the distance from the small end, so that both hands appear near the middle of the bat; others again take hold with both hands well down on the handle, and swing the bat with a natural and free stroke, while great force is given to the hit; all give good reasons for their several styles" (*Beadle's Dime Base-Ball Player*, 19).

An 1864 book added, "Some give a blow like a woodman, grasping the handle with the left hand, and sliding the right toward it; some take the bat near the middle, with both hands; others seize that handle with both hands, and give a swinging hit" (*1864 American Boy's Book of Sports and Games*, 19).

Gradually a single basic approach gained approval. In 1867, Henry Chadwick criticized a Columbus club whose "players, in batting, held their bats in front of them before they struck, a style of play which necessitates a double swing with the bat, backward and forward, thereby rendering the aim difficult. The proper way is to half shoulder the bat, bringing it down to meet the ball, especially for swift pitching" (*The Ball Player's Chronicle*, July 4, 1867). A few years later he observed that "The batsman is only in proper 'form' for a good hit when he stands squarely on his feet . . . with the point of the bat resting over his shoulder" (*New York Clipper*, April 12, 1873).

While this element of hitting has remained virtually unchanged, form follows intended function, and other elements of the swing have been modified in accordance with changes in the approach to hitting.

2.1.3   Follow-throughs. It is not clear that early batters followed through on their swings, but it seems very likely. In the 1870s the follow-through fell victim to new approaches to hitting. An 1875 article noted: "As batters, the Bostons are making a big record this season. Harry has trained them to hit to right field, where pretty much all their hitting is now done" (Randolph, the New York correspondent for the *Chicago Tribune*, reprinted in *St. Louis Globe-Democrat*, June 1, 1875).

Boston would compile the most dominant record in major league history that season. How much this hitting approach had to do with their success is debatable, but winners are often imitated uncritically. Before long, the follow-through seems to have passed entirely out of baseball.

In 1906 sportswriter George M. Graham wrote as though the follow-through was unheard of in baseball: "Possibly batters could improve their hitting by learning to 'follow through,' as the golfer and billiardist do, but if batters stopped to follow through their batting swing the chances are they would be thrown out on what would be otherwise base hits" (*Sporting Life*, January 6, 1906). Another article implied the same thing a decade later when it referred to "Chick Evans, the well-known golfing star, who thinks he can improve the batting of the players by teaching them the 'follow through' that is necessary in swinging golf clubs" (*Sporting Life*, January 13, 1917).

It was not until Babe Ruth initiated the home run revolution that it became common for batters to follow through on their swings. F. C. Lane referred in 1925 to "the Babe Ruth follow through motion," suggesting that the swing was inextricably linked to the Bambino (F. C. Lane, *Batting*, 29). Lane cited Walter Johnson's description of Ruth's swing: "He grasps the bat with an iron grip and when he meets the ball he follows it through with his full strength and weight" (F. C. Lane, *Batting*, 66).

Ruth attributed his success with this new technique to the banning of trick pitches. He explained that when he reached the major leagues "a fellow had to choke his bat, take a short swing and be prepared for anything, or else be 'whiffed'" (Babe Ruth, *Babe Ruth's Own Book of Baseball*, 152).

Even the Babe's success did not convince everyone. Bill Jacobson told Lane, "Perhaps with a heavier bat and a follow through motion, I could hit the ball harder, but I wouldn't hit anywhere near so often" (F. C. Lane, *Batting*, 28). Ruth himself noted that Lou Gehrig had a much shorter follow-through (Babe Ruth, *Babe Ruth's Own Book of Baseball*, 153–155).

2.1.4   Choking Up. The tactic of choking up on the bat was used very early on, as Henry Chadwick noted in 1872: "The batsman is only in proper form for a good hit when he stands squarely on his feet, with the bat grasped firmly about 6 or 8 inches from the end of the handle, and with the point of the bat partly resting over his shoulder. He should never hold it horizontally, and especially should he avoid pointing it toward the pitcher" (*Brooklyn Eagle*, April 20, 1872; almost the exact same words appear in the *New York Clipper*, April 12, 1873).

But choke hitting became particularly closely associated with five-foot-four Willie Keeler and his catchphrase "Hit 'em where they ain't." John B. Sheridan recalled later, "The 'choke' craze first began about 1894, when [John] McGraw, [Willie] Keeler, [Hughey] Jennings and [Joe] Kelley choked up a bit and did wonderful things. Keeler was the only real 'choke' hitter of the lot. The others did shorten up a bit, but none so far as Keeler" (*Sporting News*, April 21, 1922). The *Washington Post* referred in 1904 to the "Willie Keeler method of holding the stick a foot from the end and simply bumping the ball" (*Washington Post*, September 25, 1904). The 1905 comments of Skel Roach, reprinted under "Keeping the Ball Down" (3.3.3), describe how "an army of others" adopted Keeler's approach and how dramatically this style of hitting influenced other aspects of the game.

Choke hitting remained the dominant approach until around 1910, when the introduction of the cork-centered baseball began to change things. Even afterward, the conventional wisdom seems to have remained that a skilled hitter should choke up in certain situations. Honus Wagner noted: "Often I swing from the handle, but a good deal of the time I choke up. [Napoleon] Lajoie always did the same thing." Ty Cobb added: "My idea of a real batter is a man who can choke up on the bat when he feels like it or slug from the handle when it is necessary" (quoted in F. C. Lane, *Batting*, 44). It is noteworthy that, as is discussed in the next entry, both Cobb and Wagner were known for splitting their hands on the bat.

2.1.5   Split Hands. As noted in the entry on "Swings," the technique of dividing the hands on the bat was in use as early as 1860. It appears to have remained in use throughout the nineteenth century by batters who were seeking bat control. The *St. Louis Post-Dispatch* explained in 1888, "Nearly all the heavy batters, except Mike Kelly, grasp the bat close to the end with both hands and swing it around from their shoulder. The sacrifice hitters and the ones who seem to rarely strike out hold one hand close to the end of the bat and the other several inches further up on the stick" (*St. Louis Post-Dispatch*, September 6, 1888).

While the split-hands grip had become less common in the twentieth century, that did not stop two of the greatest hitters of all time from adopting it: Ty Cobb and Honus Wagner. Cobb gave this explanation: "I learned [as a teenager] that the way to hit a ball sharply was to meet it in front of the plate just as it broke. That is how I developed the habit of holding the bat with my hands apart, well up on the handle. I have always batted that way.

Hans Wagner batted the same way. He tells me that style came to him just as it did to me."

Cobb appreciated the irony of two of the game's greatest hitters using an approach that was deemed unorthodox: "Two or three years ago one of the bat manufacturers got out a little book on how to bat. Pictures were given of all the different styles. It was pointed out that Cobb and Wagner both used the style of keeping their hands apart on the bat handle. A note said, however, that this style wasn't recommended. Wagner and I both had a laugh about that. At the time we were both leading our leagues—in a style not recommended" (Ty Cobb, *Memoirs of Twenty Years in Baseball*, 16).

Grantland Rice attributed the demise of this batting technique to the home run era. He observed in 1923, ". . . In the old days Keeler held his hands well apart; there were six inches separating Lajoie's hands, and fully that much separating Ty Cobb's. But now [Rogers] Hornsby, [George] Sisler, [Babe] Ruth and most of the leading swatsmen of the era keep their hands in close contact upon the bat, where they can feel the weight of the heavier end of the big mace. And in this fashion there is also more leverage for the long and lusty blow" (Grantland Rice, "The Sportlight," syndicated column, April 17, 1923).

2.1.6   **Open Stances.** Batting stances are too idiosyncratic to be easily categorized, making it extremely difficult to determine firsts. But it can be said that the extreme open stance of recent players like Tony Batista is not new.

Early rules mandated that the batter stand with at least one foot in line with home plate (see **14.3.5**). As a result, researcher Paul Hunkele reported that an illustration in an 1867 guide edited by Henry Chadwick showed a batsman taking his position with his forward foot turned out with his toe pointing toward the pitcher and his rear foot perpendicular to the batsman's line. The result was a sort of a "T" stance, "as a backwoodsman does when using his axe in cutting down a tree" (Henry Chadwick, *Haney's Base Ball Book of Reference for 1867*, 112, 115).

This illustration continued to appear in Chadwick's guides until 1874 when, as noted under "Batters' Boxes" (**14.3.5**), the batter's box was introduced. At that point Chadwick's recommendation changed dramatically, though the change may have had more to do with a new emphasis on hitting to right field than on the batter's increased freedom. The 1876 *DeWitt's Guide* includes an illustration of "The Correct Position in Batting," in which the batter employs a radically closed stance "so as to face for a right field hit" (Henry Chadwick, *1876 DeWitt's Base Ball Umpire Guide*, 10).

Even after the introduction of the batter's box, many hitters continued with an open stance. Dasher Troy, an infielder of the 1880s, later explained that facing the pitcher was considered the best approach during his playing days. He provided this description of Cap Anson's stance: "he grasped the bludgeon firmly, faced the pitcher, with his feet squarely on the ground, and as the ball whirled from the pitcher's hand he stepped forward to meet it" (F. C. Lane, *Batting*, 32–33). Sportswriters George M. Graham and Hugh S. Fullerton both confirmed that Anson "faced the pitcher squarely" throughout his lengthy career, which extended from 1871 to 1897 (*Sporting Life*, January 6, 1906; *Chicago Tribune*, April 29, 1906).

An 1888 article that included detailed descriptions of the batting stances of a dozen star batters made clear that facing the pitcher was still the preferred approach, though far from the only one. It noted that Scott Stratton, a left-handed hitter, "is said by some to have the best position for hitting the ball of any player in the Association. He gets exactly in the center of the batter's box, on the left hand side, and places the toes of the left foot close against the front line of the box, the right foot being back several inches. When he strikes he steps squarely forward and swings his entire body toward the pitchers" ("How to Hit a Ball," *New York Sun*, reprinted in *Birmingham* [Ala.] *Evening News*, October 2, 1888).

By the twentieth century this once-dominant approach had become less common. George M. Graham wrote in 1906, "[Napoleon] Lajoie is what might be described as a three-quarters face hitter. His whole body is turned toward the pitcher. . . . Lajoie is turned toward the pitcher more than most batsmen, but his position in that regard is not as pronounced as was Anson's" (*Sporting Life*, January 6, 1906). In 1925, F. C. Lane reported that Heinie Groh was "the only batter of recent days who won any prominence by following this once approved old style method of facing the pitcher" (F. C. Lane, *Batting*, 33).

2.1.7   Leg Kicks. This device is probably most closely associated with slugger Mel Ott and with Japanese home run king Sadaharu Oh. More recent practitioners, such as Harold Baines and Ruben Sierra, have also generally been sluggers who used it to generate power. But the leg kick dates back to the nineteenth century and seems to have been designed simply as a timing device to help the batter make contact.

An 1884 article noted that when the amateur Empire club of Detroit played the professional Red Stockings of Boston in 1872, future major leaguer Dan O'Leary of the Empires "had the habit of making his right leg go through the swinging motion of the pitcher's arm as the ball was delivered" (*Saginaw Evening Express*, April 24, 1884). An 1891 *Brooklyn Eagle* article remarked that "[Boxer Dick] Connor has a peculiar style of lifting his right leg something after the manner of Jack Nelson, the base ball player, who lifted one of his limbs whenever he got ready to hit a curve" (*Brooklyn Eagle*, December 17, 1891).

Others were even more idiosyncratic. F. C. Lane gave this description of Jack Bentley's approach: "As the pitcher released the ball, Bentley would step back, raise himself slowly on one foot, much the same as a shot putter would do, and lunge forward. When he met the ball he was literally standing on one leg" (F. C. Lane, *Batting*, 36). Hugh S. Fullerton wrote in 1906, ". . . The oddest of all batters was Doggy Miller. He was short and stout with plump little legs. He stood perfectly still at bat until just as the pitcher was winding up to deliver the ball, then he suddenly stuck his left leg out straight in front of it, gave a funny little ballet girl kick, and threw himself forward to meet the ball. His performance caused so much laughter that Doggy tried earnestly to stop kicking—but he couldn't hit unless he did" (*Chicago Tribune*, April 29, 1906).

2.1.8 Foot in the Bucket. The "foot in the bucket" stance was the signature trait of Al Simmons. While he didn't invent it, he did a much more extraordinary thing by bringing it a legitimacy as a batting stance that would have previously been unthinkable.

Before Simmons, the foot-in-the-bucket stance was inextricably associated with cowardice. Its name was a less than subtle suggestion that the batter was so afraid of being hit by the ball that he was preparing to exit the batter's box. Christy Mathewson in 1912 cited a typical catcher talking to an intimidated young batter: "Yer almost had your foot in the water-pail over by the bench that time" (Christy Mathewson, *Pitching in a Pinch*, 42).

When Al Simmons first joined Connie Mack's Athletics in 1924, a coach reportedly said, "That boy Simmons never will make a hitter. He pulls away from the plate. He has one foot in the water bucket." But Connie Mack replied, "I don't care if he has both feet in the bucket as long as he keeps on hitting the ball" (*Washington Post*, December 2, 1928).

Simmons confirmed that "Connie never once suggested that I change my style. He always claimed that I was a natural hitter, and that he might ruin me if he tried to move my feet. He probably would have. It is the only way I have ever hit" (quoted in Ed Rumill, "Al Simmons a Natural Hitter," *Christian Science Monitor*, March 13, 1939).

Babe Ruth believed that Simmons was able to overcome the inherent disadvantage of his stance by "using an exceptionally long bat—the longest in the league I think. . . . The result is that he can reach the outside corner for a curve if he has to, and at the same time he's far enough away that the inside stuff doesn't bother him" (Babe Ruth, *Babe Ruth's Own Book of Baseball*, 167).

Early in his career, Simmons was rarely referred to without his unorthodox stance being mentioned, and this scrutiny seems to have irritated him. Sportswriter Frank Young reported: "An interesting discussion was had in the Nats' dressing room before the fracas regarding the batting of Al Simmons, flashy Athletic flyhawk. The general opinion was that continued reference to the player as 'Foot in the Bucket Al' was getting on his nerves, and that he is changing his stance. As a result, the 'experts' claim that this season he neither is hitting as often nor as hard as he did last" (Frank H. Young, *Washington Post*, June 29, 1926).

By this time, however, Simmons was so closely associated with the foot-in-the-bucket stance that nothing could rid him of the label. Sportswriter Edward J. Neil claimed that Simmons made some adjustments in 1931: "Now he steps forward more than he steps away, but his reputation still clings to him" (Edward J. Neil, *Washington Post*, September 23, 1931).

Ultimately the attention turned to admiration. In 1947, Specs Toporcer said that Simmons "always had his foot in the 'bucket,' which is decidedly unorthodox, yet he was one of the greatest hitters the game ever produced. You can frown at his style up at the plate, but you can't laugh off his record. Geniuses have the privileges of being different" (quoted in *Christian Science Monitor*, March 6, 1947).

2.1.9 Batting Left-handed. *Sporting Life* recorded in 1885, "Johnny Ward says he will continue batting left-handed. He does not make a large number of base hits, but he stands a better chance of beating a slow grounder or a fumbled ball to first base. He says that a left-handed man has an advantage of ten feet or more over a right-handed man in reaching first base. There's meat in this" (*Sporting Life*, September 2, 1885). Of course Ward was not the first man to notice such an obvious fact, and there were natural right-handers in the 1870s who batted left-handed.

But a couple of important factors prevented this from becoming a common strategy before the 1880s. First, until the mid-1870s the shorter distance to first base was the only advantage to batting left-handed. This advantage was apparent to anyone, but it was not perceived as being large enough to relinquish the benefit of batting with one's natural hand. Then around 1876, "pitchers first introduced the wide-out curve. [Terry] Larkin had the first one ever seen [in Chicago] and it was thought to be a wonder. In fact, the papers and people generally refused to believe that it was possible to curve a ball. A great many writers insisted that there was some trick about it. [Jimmy] Hallinan was the only batter that could hit him, and he because he was left-handed" (*Chicago Tribune*, April 1, 1894).

The perception that left-handed batters gained a second important advantage thus emerged around 1876, but there was still a lag before a significant number of natural right-handers began to bat left-handed. This makes sense because batting with the nondominant hand is easiest to pick up when young. Thus there had to be a perception of a sizable advantage to batting left-handed for a couple of years before there could be a generation that fully capitalized on this new state of affairs.

One of the first was Hall of Famer Roger Connor, who signed with New Bedford in 1878, only to be "released because he could not bat. Roger batted right-handed in those days. He went home and turned around and practiced batting left-handed, and blossomed out as one of the greatest hitters of the age" (*Sporting News*, January 9, 1897). After the 1879 campaign, Henry Chadwick noted that one of that season's important developments was the "introduction of batting quartets of left-handed hard hitters" (*New York Clipper*, December 20, 1879). The 1880s saw substantial numbers of natural right-handers batting left-handed for the first time, though it soon became clear that this was not a cure-all.

2.1.10   Switch-hitter. Today's switch-hitters do so primarily because of the advantage of never having to flail at curveballs that are breaking away from them. But the first known switch-hitter, Bob Ferguson, began doing so before the curveball was a large part of baseball.

As William J. Ryczek explained, "[Bob] Ferguson was a switch hitter, but batted right- or left-handed according to disposition or situation, not based upon whether the opposing pitcher threw right- or left-handed" (William J. Ryczek, *When Johnny Came Sliding Home*, 212). At a crucial moment in the game on June 14, 1870, that ended the Red Stockings' winning streak, Ferguson "took the bat, and with commendable nerve batted left hand, to get the ball out of [Cincinnati shortstop] George Wright's hands" (*Brooklyn Eagle*, June 15, 1870). In a National Association game on August 12, 1875, Ferguson came up with two outs in the ninth, a runner on third, and his Hartford team trailing 1-0. After fouling off several pitches left-handed, he turned around to bat right-handed and drove in the tying run "by the safest kind of a hit over the third-baseman's head" (*New York Clipper*, August 21, 1875).

Left-handed pitchers (see **3.3.6**) were scarce in early baseball, while the curveball (see **3.2.3**) did not become a major force in most pitchers' arsenals until the late 1870s. Almost as soon the left-handed curveball pitcher emerged, left-handed batters seized upon switch-hitting as a way to strike back. The *Chicago Tribune* reported in 1878, "[Bob] Ferguson and [Larry] Reis bat about as well one way as the other" (*Chicago Tribune*, March 31, 1878). The *Cleveland Plain Dealer* observed the following year, "[John] O'Rourke tried to hit [southpaw Bobby] Mitchell's pitching right handed and struck out. Then he tried it left handed and struck out twice" (*Cleveland Plain Dealer*, July 21, 1879).

That setback wasn't enough to end the strategy, and it became even more relevant in response to the success of southpaw J Lee Richmond. In a game on May 26, 1880, three left-handed Chicago batters—Abner Dalrymple, George Gore, and Larry Corcoran—batted right-handed against Richmond. In an 1883 game, "[Sam] Trott and [George] Weidman both took a turn at right-handed batting yesterday on account of Richmond's left-handed delivery. The results were very favorable" (*Detroit Post and Tribune*, May 24, 1883).

2.1.11 Changing Batter's Boxes. The *San Francisco Examiner* reported in 1887, "The Metropolitans have introduced a new and clever play in order to get first base on called balls. After a batter has had four balls called on the pitcher and has less than three strikes against himself he changes position to the opposite side of the plate, and the chances are strongly in favor of the next ball being called. Thus far it has worked like a charm" (*San Francisco Examiner*, July 25, 1887). This tactic remains legal, but a few inventive players tried to take it further.

A piece in *Sporting Life* in 1897 noted that the wording of the rule mandated only that the batsman must be in his box when he hits the ball. Accordingly, in a game in Pittsburgh, Bill Lange of Chicago jumped from the right-handed batter's box to the left-handed batter's box just as the pitcher was about to throw, and whacked a double. "Cap" Anson argued successfully that Lange was in the batter's box, and the hit stood (*Sporting Life*, December 11, 1897).

For whatever reason, rule makers did not get around to explicitly banning this tactic until 1907, when it was decreed that "the batsman is out if he steps from one batsman's box to the other after the pitcher has taken his position" (John H. Gruber, "Out for Interference," *Sporting News*, February 24, 1916). Even this didn't stop Honus Wagner from stepping from one batter's box to the other to distract Cincinnati pitcher Harry Gaspar in a game on April 23, 1909. Umpire Bill Klem was aware of the rule but allowed Wagner to do this because he felt that Gaspar was trying to intentionally walk Wagner. But Cincinnati successfully appealed the game, and it was replayed on September 10 (with Pittsburgh winning again) (*Sporting Life*, June 12, 1909; John H. Gruber, "Out for Interference," *Sporting News*, February 24, 1916).

2.1.12 High-low. As discussed under "Strike Zones" (1.11), the rule that batters could call for either high or low pitches was eliminated after the 1886 season. This change affected batters in a number of ways.

Shortly after the rule was implemented, the *New York Sun* suggested that it would alter the approach of some batters: "The Detroits, in their practice at Macon, learned a fact about batting under the new rules. They say that if a player holds his bat in the usual position to strike at a low ball he cannot raise it in time to hit a high ball, but if he holds the bat in the position to hit a high ball, it is easy enough to come down on a low one" (*New York Sun*, April 17, 1887).

Connie Mack claimed in 1924 that many hitters could not make the adjustment, including himself: "as I had already tipped off the big league pitchers to my weakness by asking for a high ball every time I went to the bat, when the season of 1887 opened I never got a look at a high ball, but was fed low ones from that time on" (Connie Mack, "Memories of When the Game Was Young," *Sporting Life* [monthly], June 1924).

Historian David Nemec noted that at least one player found a clever strategy to prevent a similar fate. Bob Caruthers was a high-ball hitter, but during the 1886 season "he had craftily concealed his weakness for low pitches to an extent by occasionally calling for low ones, especially against hurlers he knew he couldn't hit anyway. As a result, pitchers did not catch on to Caruthers' game immediately" (David Nemec, *The Beer and Whisky League*, 123).

2.1.13   Peeking. Not surprisingly, trying to catch a glimpse at the catcher's positioning is an ancient tactic. Connie Mack observed in 1904, "Many batters watch the catcher closely to see what position he settles himself in before the ball is delivered" (Connie Mack, "How to Play Ball," multi-part series, *Washington Post*, March 20, 1904). Others went further, forcing one sportswriter to counsel that the catcher "must guard against the batsman peeking back to catch his code. That is why the backstop stoops in calling for balls . . . by crouching he shuts out all possible vision of the batsman" (*Washington Post*, July 18, 1909).

(ii) Less Is More: The Bunt and Other Novel Approaches to Hitting

2.2.1   Bunts. Today the bunt is regarded as the epitome of good fundamental baseball. Any time a player is unable to execute a bunt successfully, fans and broadcasters tut-tut and mutter about the "lost art of bunting." This is ironic, considering the history of the bunt.

Bunts were an important part of other bat-and-ball games. Irving A. Leitner gave this description of town ball as played in Philadelphia in 1833: "If the striker used two hands, the bat was broad and flat, closely resembling a cricket bat. If he used one hand, the bat was shaped like a miniature baseball bat and was called a 'delill.' A good player was able to use either type. However, when 'delilling,' the striker, instead of swinging at the ball, would simply allow the ball to be deflected off his bat, directing it to whatever area of the playing field he chose by holding the delill at a given angle" (Irving Leitner, *Baseball: Diamond in the Rough*, 32).

David Block has pointed out that as late as 1856 supporters of the Massachusetts version of baseball "considered the art of tipping a ball over the catcher's head to be one of a batsman's greatest skills" (*Porter's Spirit of the Times*, December 27, 1856; quoted in David Block, *Baseball Before We Knew It*, 85). Similarly, in cricket it was and still is considered good technique for a batsman to simply deflect a ball that might strike his wicket. By contrast, one of the distinctive features of early baseball was that it was taken for granted that batsmen would try to hit the ball as hard and as far as possible. This mind-set would result in significant controversy when the tactics of other bat-and-ball games were used in baseball.

Researcher Tom Shieber found what appears to be the earliest instance of a bunt in baseball in an account of a match game played between the Atlantic and Putnam Base Ball Clubs on June 29, 1860. The following description appeared in the *New York Clipper*: "A circumstance occurred in the 2d innings which we deem worthy of notice: Brown was at the bat, and [John G.] Price pitched him a low ball, which, in bringing his bat down, Brown hit with the bat in a similar manner to that in which a cricketer blocks a straight ball; judgment was asked, and as the Umpire deemed it an accident, it was decided 'no hit,' but we think it should have been considered fair, for the reason, that had a player been on the first base at the time, he could easily have made his second base before the pitcher could have fielded it, and the decision may lead to similar accidents on other occasions when such play would have a more important bearing on the game. If, in the act of striking, the ball be hit forward of home base, however light the touch, it ought to be considered a fair ball, otherwise accidents similar to the above will be of frequent occurrence" (*New York Clipper*, July 14, 1860).

In spite of the umpire's ruling that this bunt was "no hit," the tactic soon reemerged. Its development was spurred by the fact that the rules of the day considered any ball fair if it initially struck in fair territory. This made possible the "fair-foul," a ball struck with sufficient English to bounce once in fair territory and then go well into foul territory. Not only was this extremely difficult to defend against, but there was also little penalty for attempting such a hit since foul balls did not count as strikes (though a foul ball caught on the first bounce was an out). The bunt complemented the fair-foul, either as an accidental consequence of an attempted "fair-foul" or as an intentional means of keeping the fielders from overcommitting to prevent the fair-foul.

There remains some uncertainty as to whether the bunt or the fair-foul came first, but it seems clear that the two are closely linked. Robert H. Schaefer gives a thorough summary of the issue in his article "The Lost Art of Fair-Foul Hitting" (*National Pastime* 20 [2000], 3–9), which in turn relies heavily on sportswriter William M. Rankin's research on the topic in the 1890s.

The two names that surfaced over and over were Dickey Pearce and Tom Barlow, both Brooklyn natives and teammates on the Atlantics of Brooklyn. Pearce was unanimously credited with inventing the fair-foul, but the testimony regarding bunts was divided. Rankin found three players—Billy Barnie, Henry Dollard, and Herbert Worth—who credited Barlow with inventing the bunt. Worth was particularly adamant, stating: "Tommy Barlow was the inventor of the bunt hit, and was famous throughout the country for his skill. He had a short bat, not over two feet long, which when he hit the ball (if it could be called a hit) he imparted a wrist motion which gave the ball, when it came in contact with the bat, a sort of reversed twist and the ball after striking the ground would almost seem to remain where it struck and then dart off at an angle out of reach of the third baseman or the pitcher should they endeavor to field him out at first" (*Sporting News*, January 1, 1898).

Nonetheless Rankin concluded that Dickey Pearce was responsible for both the first bunt and the first fair-foul hit. George Hall, a teammate of Barlow and Pearce, recalled both men bunting but was convinced that Pearce was first. Another teammate of both players, Jack Chapman, confirmed: "It was early in the sixties that he introduced the fair foul hits and a few years later he adopted the bunt. I remember the late Tommy Barlow and how clever he used to make a bunt hit. Barlow always carried a little bat, about two feet long, and made a great reputation for himself in bunting the ball, but that was in 1871, when he was a member of the Star nine. Pearce, however, had made the bunt hit several years prior to that season. It was from Pearce that Barlow got the idea, although the latter had it down to such a science that he could not be beaten in making a bunt hit." In addition, Rankin found descriptions in the *New York Clipper* of bunts by Pearce in games played on August 17, 1868, and September 10, 1868, before Barlow's professional career had begun (*Sporting News*, January 1, 1898).

Bob Ferguson, another teammate of both players, initially credited Barlow with inventing the bunt but demurred when told that Pearce also claimed the distinction (*Sporting News*, January 13, 1894). These accounts suggest that the bunt was initially used by Dickey Pearce, but as a rare, and possibly accidental, variant to the more lethal fair-foul. Hall was especially explicit that "the bunt sprang from the fair foul hits." Thus when Rankin first researched the subject he concluded that the bunt "is unequivocally the offspring of the 'fair-foul hit'" (*Sporting News*, January 1, 1898). This view was also supported by Henry Chadwick, who claimed that it was his suggestion that spurred Dickey Pearce to invent the fair-foul in 1864, and that the bunt evolved from it (*Sporting Life*, January 27, 1894).

But Rankin later wrote that the order was reversed—that Dickey Pearce "invented the bunt in the early '60's, and some years later in trying to draw a bunt away from the third baseman he discovered the fair-foul hit, which was impossible to field, except from foul ground" (*Sporting News*, March 3, 1910; also, *Sporting News*, July 1, 1905, and A. H. Spink, *The National Game*, 58: "[Pearce] invented the bunt, and some years later when trying to draw a bunt away from the third baseman, he discovered the fair-foul hit"). Was Rankin confused, or had he found additional information that caused him to change his mind? There is no way to be certain, but the former possibility seems more likely.

Even if Pearce preceded him in using the bunt, Tommy Barlow added a distinctive twist with his miniature bat. In so doing he caused considerable controversy over whether this was how baseball should really be played. The *Boston Globe* wrote, "Barlow acknowledged his weakness at the bat by attempting the black game, but [A. G.] Spalding got him out twice, and the attempt, which is rather a weak one for a professional club, was a failure" (*Boston Globe*, September 9, 1873).

Others were more indulgent. The *New York Clipper* gave this account: "After the first two strikers had been retired, [Tommy] Barlow, amid much laughter and applause, 'blocked' a ball in front of the home plate and reached first base before the ball did" (*New York Clipper*, June 15, 1872). The *Brooklyn Eagle* offered this description of a game in which Barlow made six of "what Nick Young calls 'baby hits' . . . by the little judgment shown by Radcliffe [John Radcliff] in his position at third base. All Barlow had to do to secure his base safely with Radcliffe playing his position as he did, was to allow the ball to fall dead from the bat to the left of the base, and so as to touch the ground fair. This he did, and as Radcliffe had to run up and field the ball from third base, the result was Barlow reached first base ahead of the ball. This style of hitting annoys a field exceedingly, besides which it corners a pitcher. As for sneering at it and calling it baby hitting, that is absurd. The object of the batsman is to reach first base, and if by any style of hitting he can send the ball fairly to the field, and in such a way that it cannot be caught on the fly or fielded to first base in time to put him out, he earns his base by skilful, scientific batting. The real baby hits are those which give easy chances for fly catches" (*Brooklyn Eagle*, July 23, 1873).

Whether it was because of the scorn he received or just that it wasn't very effective, Barlow and his little bat had few if any imitators. Henry Chadwick accordingly referred to the bunt as Tommy Barlow's "patent hit." Even the tactic's use by a widely respected player like George Wright was received with condescension; an 1877 account noted that Wright had "made a 'baby-bunting' hit near home plate" (*Louisville Courier-Journal*, July 12, 1877). The effectiveness of the bunt was further diminished that year by the banning of the fair-foul and the introduction of the catcher's mask, which enabled catchers to play closer to the plate. When Barlow's career ended prematurely, it seemed that the bunt would also be abandoned.

Jim O'Rourke later explained, "There were two other wonderful hitters that I saw when a mere boy. They were Dicky Pierce [sic], shortstop, and Tommy Barlowe [sic], catcher of the Brooklyn Mutuals [sic], back in 1870. I have seen these men with little short bats, which I believe were later ruled out of the game, make the wonderful bunt hit which we have taken to calling a modern institution. Pierce and Barlowe were famous over the country for their little bats and their bunt hits; but as soon as the short bats were ruled out Pierce and Barlowe, not realizing that a bunt could be made with a long bat, gave up the bunt hits and became ordinary players" ("Forty Two Years of Base Ball: Wonderful Life Story of Jim O'Rourke," *Kalamazoo Evening Telegraph*, March 3, 1910).

After a decade of disuse, the bunt made a dramatic comeback in 1886, spurred on by the legalization of flattened bats (see **9.2.4**). In 1905 a *New York World* reporter credited Arlie Latham and Johnny Ward with inventing the bunt in 1888 (*New York World*, June 15, 1905; cited and disparaged by William Rankin, *Sporting News*, July 1, 1905). While this attribution is certainly mistaken, it gives an indication of how completely the bunt disappeared between the mid-1870s and 1886.

Not everyone was pleased by the bunt's return, and questions were again raised about the manliness of its practitioners. The *Detroit Free Press* was particularly dismissive: "[Arthur Irwin] is evidently too weak physically to swing a bat and he therefore holds out the willow and 'bunts' the ball. For this babyish performance he was roundly hissed by the spectators, and concluded to abandon it. Base ball is essentially a manly spirit, and its patrons object to such infantile tricks" (*Detroit Free Press*, May 9, 1886).

But the reemergence of the bunt gained momentum from the recognition that the tactic had benefits besides the possibility of a base hit. The primary one was the advancement of base runners. As players and managers realized that bunts were reliable means of moving runners along even when the batter failed to reach safely, they came into much greater favor. *Sporting News* later credited Arlie Latham and the Browns with having popularized the sacrifice bunt (*Sporting News*, October 30, 1897).

This association of the bunt with a successful team and a colorful player certainly added to its appeal. The *New York Sun* reported, "[Arlie] Latham has a great way of butting the ball out in front of the plate, and depending upon his running to get to first. He generally does it" (*New York Sun*, May 23, 1886; "butting" was a common variant of "bunting"). A few weeks later it added, "Several of the Metropolitan players are practising Latham's mode of 'bunting' the ball" (*New York Sun*, June 6, 1886).

Another benefit was that, as discussed in the next entry, the fake bunt emerged as an excellent complement to the bunt, just as the fair-foul had been in the previous decade.

Finally, as discussed under "Deliberate Fouls" (2.3.2), the bunt proved to be an effective way to wear opposing pitchers down by deliberately spoiling their best pitches. Near the end of the 1886 season, John I. Rogers, secretary and co-owner of the Philadelphia club, accused Chicago of embodying the maxim "Anything to Win" by using "questionable tactics and dishonest points of play, which the rules seem powerless to prevent." One of the examples he cited was "Knocking or bunting foul balls with the object of wearing out or demoralizing a pitcher" (*Chicago Tribune*, September 22, 1886).

Chicago won the National League pennant in 1886 while St. Louis captured the American Association flag. With both clubs being prominently associated with the bunt, the play was restored to popularity.

That did not, however, mean that everyone liked it. There continued to be calls to ban the bunt for several years afterward. Opponents continued to refer to the bunt as the "baby hit," thereby invoking ridicule, the most powerful tool available. Indeed the term "bunt" itself appears to have derived from the lullaby "Bye, Baby Bunting" in an attempt by its detractors to associate it with childishness (Peter Morris, "Baseball Term 'Bunt' Was Originally Called 'Baby Hit'; Popular 19c. Lullaby 'Bye, Baby Bunting' May Have Produced 'Baby Bunting Hit,' Shortened to 'Bunt,'" *Comments on Etymology*, vol. 34, no. 1 [October 2004], 2–4).

Calls to ban the bunt grew louder in the 1890s, and rule makers addressed the issue in 1893 by banning the flat bat and in 1894 by counting a foul bunt as a strike. This compromise approach seemed to satisfy most critics. J. H. Anderson of the *Baltimore Herald* wrote, "With proper restrictions the bunt is a very scientific play and should be kept in the game" (quoted in the *Brooklyn Eagle*, November 7, 1894).

It takes a long time to change a mind-set, however, and critics of the bunt did not disappear altogether. Frank Selee called for a ban in 1904 (*Sporting Life*, January 9, 1904). In 1909, President William Howard Taft mentioned his dislike of the bunt to reporters. When told that the bunt was considered a key element of scientific baseball, Taft was unimpressed and declared, "I like to see them hit it out for all that is in them" (*New York Times*, May 31, 1909).

2.2.2 Fair-fouls. All the evidence points to Dickey Pearce having invented the fair-foul in the 1860s. In addition to the statements gathered by William Rankin and Robert Schaefer that were cited in the preceding entry, an account of an 1875 game noted, "Bad Dicky hit one of those fair-foul for which he is famous and made first" (*St. Louis Post-Dispatch*, April 20, 1875). An 1888 article added, "It was Dicky Pearce who conceived the idea of touching the top of the ball with his bat and making the famous fair-foul hits, which were practiced by others with such telling effect" (*Sporting News*, March 10, 1888).

The tactic continued to develop in the 1870s, with Ross Barnes becoming the most expert practitioner of the technique. Whereas Pearce's fair-fouls appear to have been closer to bunts, Barnes generally used a full swing. Jim O'Rourke recalled that Barnes's method was "hitting the ball so it would smash on the ground near the plate just inside of the third base line, and would then mow the grass over the line, away out into the field" ("Forty Two Years of Base Ball: Wonderful Life Story of Jim O'Rourke," *Kalamazoo Evening Telegraph*, March 3, 1910).

As the fair-foul became more lethal, it grew increasingly controversial. At the 1873 annual convention in Baltimore, an unsuccessful proposal was made to designate balls as foul if they hit the ground before the pitcher's area. The advocates of adding a tenth player in 1874 also pointed to the difficulty of defending against the fair-foul (see **19.12**).

Several other attempts were made to restrict the fair-foul, but they met with limited success (Tom Shieber, "The Evolution of the Baseball Diamond," *Total Baseball IV*, 116; Robert H. Schaefer, "The Lost Art of Fair-Foul Hitting," *National Pastime* 20 [2000], 5). Spectators perceived the play as unsporting and often became openly hostile, such as at an 1875 game in Chicago where "The derisive cheers, cat calls, hisses and groans that greeted Dicky Pierce's [sic] first attempt at one of his patent tips were repeated throughout the entire game" (*St. Louis Republican*, July 5, 1875). (Obviously there was more of a consensus about Pearce inventing the fair-foul than about the spelling of his name.)

Most sportswriters continued to express admiration for the fair-foul because it demanded a high degree of skill. Henry Chadwick defended it for "requiring the most skillful handling of the bat, and a quick eye and a steady nerve, besides" (*New York Clipper*, April 12, 1873; while Chadwick liked the fair-foul, he acknowledged the difficulties it caused umpires and advanced several ideas for remedying the problem). This again shows Chadwick's determination to view baseball as a test of character, but it misses the point of the criticism.

What ultimately provided the impetus to abolish the fair-foul was the fact that it was very difficult for umpires to determine whether a ball that was hit into the ground first hit fair or foul. Accordingly, the rule makers redefined the concepts of fair and foul in 1877 and, in the process, eliminated the fair-foul. The *Chicago Tribune* pointed out that the legislation that abolished the fair-foul had simultaneously created a new breed of hits: "By the rule of this year a ball which strikes foul ground first, and then bounds into fair ground before passing first or third bases, is a fair ball. Inasmuch as it struck foul ground first, it must be called a 'foul-fair,' following the custom of last year" (*Chicago Tribune*, April 29, 1877).

The definition of a fair ball created to eliminate the fair-foul remains the basis of the current interpretation, though in 1931 rule makers made one important amendment. In light of the difficulties that Babe Ruth's monster shots were causing umpires, they decided that a ball hit over the outfield fence would be considered fair if it was between the foul poles when it left the playing field.

2.2.3 Fake Bunts. One of the reasons for Arlie Latham's success in reviving the bunt in 1886 was his use of the fake bunt as an effective complement. Obviously this tactic had not been available to earlier practitioners like Barlow who had used a miniature bat. Jim Galvin described Latham's technique as "making believe you are about to bunt the ball, and when the infielders have come up close to field such a ball, then just tap a swift-pitched ball with his bat—a wrist-play hit—and it will go safely out of the reach of any infielder and short of those in the outfield" (_Louisville Courier-Journal_, reprinted in _New York Sun_, October 3, 1886). Tommy McCarthy has been credited with helping to popularize the fake bunt (James D. Smith and Robert L. Tiemann, "Thomas Francis Michael McCarthy," in Frederick Ivor-Campbell, Robert L. Tiemann and Mark Rucker, eds., _Baseball's First Stars_, 102).

2.2.4 Bunting Backward. Jake Beckley apparently turned his bat around to bunt and used the handle side. Half a century later, Casey Stengel recalled Beckley's technique and tried to teach it to some of his Yankee players. He reported: "they say it's the silliest thing they ever saw, which it probably is but Beckley done it" (quoted in David Fleitz, "Jacob Peter Beckley," Tom Simon, ed., _Deadball Stars of the National League_, 232).

2.2.5 Baltimore Chop. Early in the 1896 season a sportswriter for the _Baltimore News_ remarked: "The Baltimore Club has already originated several distinctive plays which have made it famous and which have been copied with more or less success by others. Foremost among these are the 'hit and run' tactics. Now a new style of hitting will be recorded in the base ball history of '96 and credited to the Orioles. It is 'chopping' the ball, and a chopped ball generally goes for a hit. It requires great skill in placing to work this trick successfully, and it is done in this fashion: A middle-height ball is picked out and is attacked with a terrific swing on the upper side. The ball is made to strike the ground from five to ten feet away from the batsman, and, striking the ground with force bounds high over the head of the third or first baseman. In nearly every game lately has this little teaser been successfully employed, and yesterday two such hits were made" (unidentified

1896 clipping, Jordan Deutsch, Richard M. Cohen, Roland T. Johnson, and David S. Neft, eds., *The Scrapbook History of Baseball*). The Orioles' success with this approach was augmented greatly by the skill of groundskeeper Thomas J. Murphy, who made sure that the ground in front of home plate was as hard as possible.

While the joint efforts of the players and their groundskeeper created a play that was novel enough to be named in honor of the Baltimore club, it was not entirely new. At least in part, the Baltimore chop was an updated and modified version of the fair-foul as executed by masters like Ross Barnes. Robert Schaefer explained that batters deliberately hit the ball off the cast-iron home plate until an 1875 rule change that placed home plate in foul territory (Robert H. Schaefer, "The Lost Art of Fair-Foul Hitting," *National Pastime* 20 [2000], 5).

Other related hitting tactics, such as the hit-and-run and the squeeze play, will be discussed under "Baserunning" (Chapter 5, part four).

(iii) And When All Else Fails: Trying to Be a Successful Hitter Without Hitting

2.3.1   Waiting Out the Pitcher. As noted under "Balls and Strikes" (1.10), the waiting game was a familiar element of baseball by the early 1860s. But in those years it was a widely reviled strategy, and many viewed it as scarcely better than cheating. Henry Chadwick wrote dismissively in 1860, ". . . It is preferable to play the game manfully and without resorting to any such trickery—for it is little else—as this, which not only tires the spectator, but detracts from the merit of the game itself" (*Beadle's Dime Base-Ball Player*, 16).

This perception changed dramatically in the 1870s. In 1876, Chadwick wrote, "Some batsmen, who have not the moral courage to play their own game without regard to the comments of the crowd, are very apt to be intimidated into a reckless style of hitting, for fear of being considered 'a waiter at the bat.'" He thus maintained that "it is no discredit to him to take his base on called balls under such circumstances" (*New York Clipper*, November 11, 1876).

This represents an extraordinary reversal in the perception of a base on balls—from a sign of moral cowardice to the epitome of courage. Once this new mind-set had taken hold, batters felt empowered to originate a whole set of new approaches to getting on base.

2.3.2   Deliberate Fouls. Baseball batting tactics reached a new level of evolution or devolution, depending on your perspective, when batters began to unashamedly seek ways to reach base without hitting the ball. These strategems had begun to emerge by the 1870s and have since polarized the baseball community.

On the face of it, the tactic of deliberate foul balls does not seem that different from the waiting game of the 1860s (see **1.10**). But the "waiting game" merely provided the batter with an advantage in his battle with the pitcher, and in many cases was a response to deliberate wild pitching.

The deliberate foul was an entirely different matter, since it seemed to allow the batter to avoid the conflict altogether and be rewarded for doing so. This new reality—that a batter could use the fact that fouls did not count as strikes to reach base without even giving the fielders a chance to make a play—flew in the face of the accepted wisdom that taking "bases on called balls [is] something no good batsman likes to do" (*Brooklyn Eagle*, May 9, 1871).

By the late 1860s some batters were taking advantage of the catcher being back of the plate by craftily stepping back into foul territory to swing at pitches. By doing so, they took advantage of the rule of the day, which specified that a ball was fair or foul based on where it first struck the ground or a fielder. Thus if the batter took a swing at a ball and dubbed it, it simply counted as a foul ball. It was also easier for batters to wait until the last minute and spoil a good pitch (Tom Shieber, "The Evolution of the Baseball Diamond," in *Total Baseball IV*, 115).

The dissatisfaction created by these tactics had a dramatic effect on the rulebook. There were calls throughout the 1870s to eliminate the foul bound rule, by which batters were out if a foul was caught on the first bounce. But defenders of the rule contended that it was necessary to discourage foul-ball hitting, and the antiquated rule was not permanently repealed until the early 1880s.

The controversy also helped to spawn a couple of important rule changes. First, the rule makers endeavored to force the batter to be in line with the plate when he swung. In doing so, they created early versions of the batter's box (see **14.3.5**), but they failed to accomplish their desired goal. As a result, in 1877 they introduced the current definition of foul territory in which a ball is fair or foul depending on its status when it passes first or third base or is touched by a fielder.

This latter change seems to have reduced the use of the intentional foul for a few years, but the tactic made a comeback in the 1880s. Johnny Evers and Hugh S. Fullerton later recalled, "Many of the old timers were skilful in 'pulling' the ball foul in order to wear down pitchers, and by hitting late in fouling off" (John J. Evers and Hugh S. Fullerton, *Touching Second*, 161). As long as such hitters used a full swing, there was little resentment of this ploy since it required skill and entailed risk on both sides.

That perception began to change when such hitters as Mike "King" Kelly found different ways to accomplish the same end. As early as 1880, Kelly was reported to have fouled eleven balls out of play in one game (*New York Clipper*, May 29, 1880). The return of the bunt in 1886 (see **2.2.1**) gave him a more effective way of doing so, as is shown by this account: "Kelly maneuvered to get first on balls. When a fair ball was pitched he held up his bat and tipped it, making it foul. [Pitcher Charles] Getzein pitched seven or eight balls right over the plate, and Kelly made fouls of them. This trick of Kelly's is on a par with his cutting home from second when the umpire is not looking. Some means should be found of making him play an honorable game of ball, as he seems to depend chiefly on trickery. He finally got his base" (*Detroit Free Press*, May 10, 1886).

Kelly accomplished this by "poking out his bat," a tactic that "caused laughter from the spectators at first, but by and by it became as fatiguing to them as to the pitcher" (John H. Gruber, "Strikes," *Sporting News*, January 13, 1916). Others indulged in the still more tedious practice that Doc Bushong described as "blocking a ball off" by "holding the bat slightly behind the home plate, in no case in front of the center of the plate, and allowing the pitched ball to glance off, with no intention of hitting at all" (letter to *National Base Ball Gazette*, reprinted in *Cleveland Leader and Herald*, April 24, 1887).

The need for a solution became readily apparent during the postseason series between the champions of the two leagues. St. Louis' Arlie Latham "started in the first inning with Kelly's trick of bunting fouls. When after knocking ten of these, he struck out, the crowd howled its approval. When the Chicagos went to bat and Kelly's turn came he bunted 4 or 5 fouls and then, when the crowd had begun laughing heartily, he hit the ball hard enough to get his base, and the laugh turned to cheers" (*Chicago Tribune*, October 19, 1886).

In an attempt to again create risk on both sides, a new rule was introduced after the 1886 season that authorized the umpire to call a strike on "any obvious attempt to make a foul hit." This was a big improvement, but it still left plenty of grey area, which Arlie Latham was one of the first to exploit. Early the next season, the *St. Louis Post-Dispatch* reported, "Latham has been attracting no little attention by a habit he has fallen into of late; namely, at peculiar stages of the game when he comes to the bat he hits foul after foul, some of which go over the fence, the grand-stand and out into the street. On one occasion he was warned by the umpire" (*St. Louis Post-Dispatch*, August 13, 1887).

The new rule thus cut down on the most blatant attempts to foul pitches off, but with umpires having to determine that the act was deliberate, borderline cases were not usually called. After the 1893 season the rule was reworded with the intent that "the unskilled will be charged with a strike for 'fouling off' whether through intention or inexpertness" (*Sporting News*, December 23, 1893).

National League President Nick Young instructed umpires to call a strike on any foul bunt, defining "a bunt hit as being made when the bat is pushed or held forward so as to allow the ball to rebound from the bat without its being struck at" (*Sporting Life*, April 21, 1894). This was clear enough, and subsequent tinkering made it possible for umpires to assess a strike on a fouled-off bunt attempt without eliciting much of a protest.

But this hardly eliminated the deliberate foul. Standout hitter Jesse Burkett pointed out immediately that "by stepping either forward or back in the box the ball can be sent foul, so as to worry the pitcher and the fielders just as much as if there were no new rules" (quoted in *Sporting Life*, April 14, 1894).

Moreover the tactic gained favor as it became apparent that it had additional benefits when a teammate was on base. Horace Fogel explained: "Fouling off balls enabled [a batter] to protect his base runners in stealing, when it was pretty certain they would be thrown out, because of a poor start they had made" (Horace S. Fogel, "Foul Strike Rule Spoils Team Work," syndicated column, *Nevada* [Reno] *State Journal*, February 14, 1909).

An 1897 account noted that Dibby Flynn of Indianapolis "is an adept at driving fouls near left field, and will worry the life out of any pitcher. . . . It is not chance with Flynn, but intent, pure and simple. [Detroit pitcher Thomas R.] Thomas played against him in the Western Association and says that he can bat foul balls all day long against any kind of pitching. If he tries it on here the attention of the umpire will be called to it, as foul balls of this sort are strikes under the rule. Flynn is clever in hitting them, but he does not carry it out well, as he fails to move after hitting the ball, when he would naturally run were he trying to hit it out" (*Detroit Free Press*, May 2, 1897).

But in fact calling the attention of umpires to such tactics was becoming futile. While the "skill of batters in that direction increased through steady practice," umpires found it harder and harder to gauge batters' intentions (John J. Evers and Hugh S. Fullerton, *Touching Second*, 161). Worse, they found that they were only courting controversy by trying to read the minds of batters who fouled off a pitch with a full swing. As a result, as Francis Richter later recalled, "the question of 'intention' raised such incessant argument that umpires permitted the rule to fall into desuetude" (Francis C. Richter, *Richter's History and Records of Base Ball*, 357).

Johnny Evers and Hugh S. Fullerton indicated that this problem was dealt with swiftly: "The rule makers promptly legislated against foul balls" (John J. Evers and Hugh S. Fullerton, *Touching Second*, 161). Actually, the response was anything but prompt. It was not until 1901, when the warning for an intentional foul had essentially become a dead letter, that the rule makers finally took drastic action (*Sporting Life*, August 17, 1901). The National League legislated that year that any foul with less than two strikes would be a strike, and the American League followed suit two years later.

The new rule proved very unpopular in many circles, and opposition mounted in the years to come as offensive production dropped sharply. Nonetheless the foul strike was retained because the alternative was just as unpalatable. Umpire Hank O'Day regarded the rule change as "one of the best things that ever happened" because it "stopped the tireless process of the batter always trying to get his base on balls. People like to see batters hit. They don't want too much waiting out" (quoted in F. C. Lane, *Batting*, 123).

O'Day claimed in 1901 that the foul strike rule was made necessary by a dramatic increase in the prevalence of deliberate fouls: "When players first made a practice of trying to foul off balls there were only 2 or 3 that could do it. The next year there were about a dozen and this year would have seen still more who were adept at the trick, as players were in the habit of practicing such things in the morning" (*Sporting News*, May 4, 1901).

While O'Day did not name names, others were less reticent, and they almost invariably identified Roy Thomas and John McGraw as the originators. According to the baseball scribe John B. Sheridan: "Batters of the '90s, led by John J. McGraw, made a specialty of fouling off good balls. When fellows like McGraw or Roy Thomas, then with Philadelphia, went to bat the pitchers could expect to have anywhere from 10 to 20 good strikes deliberately fouled off. McGraw would run up half way to the pitcher, swing hard, but late, check his swing and cut fouls along the left line for an indefinite period. Roy Thomas was more skillful than McGraw in this line of work. Thomas had the practice of turning good strikes into mere fouls so perfected that he could take his usual cut at the ball and, getting a piece of it, foul it straight over the catcher's shoulders" (*Sporting News*, February 5, 1925). Connie Mack, reminiscing in 1924, cited Thomas, McGraw, and Hughey Jennings as batters who were adept at using this tactic to draw walks (Connie Mack, "Memories of When the Game Was Young," *Sporting Life* [monthly], June 1924). One Cincinnati pitcher became so annoyed by Thomas's persistence during a game in August 1900 that he sucker-punched him (Jerrold Casway, *Ed Delahanty and the Emerald Age of Baseball*, 189).

Other sources have filled in the names of the less notorious practitioners who began to imitate Thomas and McGraw. Sportswriter John B. Foster recited a longer list: "The [foul ball] rule was made to stop the dilatory work of McGraw, Thomas, Jennings, [Joe] Kelley, [Cupid] Childs, [Jesse] Burkett, [Win] Mercer, [Fielder] Jones, there are half a score more, who could stand at the plate and knock fouls by the hour" (*Sporting Life*, April 6, 1901). Johnny Evers and Hugh S. Fullerton listed "McGraw, Keeler, Roy Thomas,

[Jimmy] Slagle and others" as batters who "could prolong the games indefinitely and tire out any pitcher" (John J. Evers and Hugh S. Fullerton, *Touching Second*, 161).

Of course the rule that fouls counted as strikes did not entirely end the practice. Batters continued to foul off pitches that they could not hit effectively, as they still do today. And some teams made a deliberate effort to force an opposing pitcher to throw a lot of pitches so that they could get to him late in the game. John J. Evers and Hugh S. Fullerton wrote in 1910: "Frequently a manager, feeling certain the game will be close, orders his men to wait. . . . Each batter then, instead of hitting, tries to make the pitcher throw as many balls as possible. If a batter can get three balls, foul off three, and then strike out, he may have accomplished far more toward the final result than he would have done had he made a base hit off the first ball pitched . . . every additional ball pitched wearies the pitcher" (John J. Evers and Hugh S. Fullerton, *Touching Second*, 165). They credited Chicago with using this approach to beat Detroit in the second game of the 1908 World Series (John J. Evers and Hugh S. Fullerton, *Touching Second*, 266–267).

The effectiveness of the tactic was diminished, however, by the increased likelihood that an unsuccessful attempt to foul the ball off could bring an end to the at bat. As with the 1894 legislation that introduced the automatic strike on a foul bunt, there was now risk on both sides, and that proved a satisfactory compromise. While the years following the creation of the foul strike saw offense decline dramatically and prompted frequent calls to repeal the rule change, the rule was retained.

During the so-called deadball era, batters found an entirely different advantage that could be derived from the deliberate foul. Until the twentieth century, umpires rarely put a new ball in play until the old one was unplayable. This changed during the first two decades of the new century, but it was still common until about 1915 for a misshapen or soiled ball to be in play. Accordingly, a later article in *Sporting News* explained that 1910s slugger Gavvy Cravath would deliberately foul an old ball out of play in order to get the opportunity to hit a new one (*Sporting News*, March 20, 1941).

Needless to say, Cravath was not the only player to recognize this benefit. Roger Peckinpaugh later recalled that, when he first came up in 1910, "if you were behind two or three runs and an old ball was in there, a leadoff man's duty was to get up there and try to foul the ball into the stands so they would have a new ball to hit against" (Eugene Murdock, *Baseball Between the Wars*, 19).

Yet even in the twentieth century the mind-set that taking "bases on called balls [is] something no good batsman likes to do" continues to exert influence, as is shown by the differing perspectives of the sabermetric community and traditional baseball analysts about the value of bases on balls.

2.3.3   Crouches. The next logical step after batters began to deliberately strive to gain bases on balls was for them to start trying to help their chances by means of batting crouches. Charley Farrell was one of the first, if not the actual originator. A *Chicago Tribune* reporter observed in 1889, "Charley Farrell gets many a base on balls by a clever trick that fools most umpires, and he worked it today on [umpire John] McQuaid as he has done before. In bracing himself to hit the ball he drops his shoulder a foot or possibly fifteen inches, and a ball which would be perfectly fair with the batsman standing erect is called 'ball'" (*Chicago Tribune*, reprinted in *Cleveland Plain Dealer*, May 26, 1889).

This *Tribune* sportswriter clearly felt that McQuaid should not have modified the strike zone for a batter who crouched. It would be nice to know how other umpires interpreted this situation, but unfortunately this is the type of question that is difficult to resolve at this late date. What we can say is that many batters of the era perceived the crouch as a means of drawing bases on balls, which strongly suggests that at least some umpires were reducing the strike zone of these batters. In 1903, *Sporting Life* noted, "The 'Elberfeld crouch' is the latest thing in Metropolitan base ball. The kid's position in trying to work the pitcher for a base on balls is what earned him the new name" (*Sporting Life*, August 8, 1903).

The crouch also came to be perceived by some batters as an effective means of hitting the ball. As noted by Skel Roach in "Keeping the Ball Down" (3.3.3), Willie Keeler made use of a crouch to chop and cut the ball. Another influential practitioner of a pronounced crouch was George Stone, whose peculiar stance prompted Billy Evans to observe, "[George Stone] uses a very heavy bat and assumes a crouching position at the plate, so much so that a spectator not knowing Stone would believe he was humpbacked. Stone stands close to the plate and in reality half of his body is extending over it when he crouches" (*Sporting News*, February 27, 1908). When Stone led the American League in batting average in 1906, he naturally attracted imitators. Washington's Bob Ganley observed in 1907 that his rookie teammate Clyde Milan "has the George Stone crouch at the bat" (quoted in *Washington Post*, August 29, 1907).

Of course the ultimate example of this tactic was Eddie Gaedel, the three-foot-seven midget hired by Bill Veeck. Gaedel pinch-hit for the St. Louis Browns in the second game of a doubleheader on August 19, 1951. He crouched so as to have virtually no strike zone and drew a four-pitch walk. Since Gaedel had an official contract that had been submitted to the league, he was allowed to appear in that one game. But American League president Will Harridge refused to approve Gaedel's contract, ending his career.

A James Thurber short story, "You Could Look It Up," features a midget who is used in a similar fashion, but Veeck claimed that the story had not been the source of his inspiration. Researcher Joe Overfield, however, discovered that Gaedel was not the first midget to appear in a professional game. In an inconsequential late-season 1905 Eastern League game at Baltimore, Buffalo manager George Stallings sent midget Jerry Sullivan up to pinch-hit. The first pitch was far too high, but the second was in Sullivan's tiny strike zone and he singled over the third baseman's head. Sullivan ended up scoring and ended his professional career with a 1.000 batting average (Joe Overfield, "You Could Look It Up," *National Pastime* 10 [1990], 69–71).

2.3.4   Getting Deliberately Hit by Pitches. The rule entitling a hit batsman to take first base was introduced in the American Association in 1884 and the National League in 1887. It would accordingly seem reasonable to assume that hitters didn't deliberately allow themselves to be hit by pitches until after this rule was adopted, but that was not the case. In early baseball the ball was not dead upon hitting the batter, so with a teammate on base, batters could allow a pitch to deflect off them to enable the base runner to advance.

The rule makers attempted to address this in 1872 by instructing umpires to call a batter out if he "willfully" stood "in the way of the ball when pitched to the catcher so that it may touch them and glide off." Unfortunately, like so many rules that required the umpire to determine intent, this was doomed only to start arguments. As a result, two years later a new rule made the ball dead when it hit the batter (John H. Gruber, "Out for Interference," *Sporting News*, February 24, 1916).

This approach solved one problem but created another. Pitchers no longer faced any penalty for trying to intimidate batters by pitching at them. Moreover this change came during the years that pitchers' release points were moving steadily upward, allowing pitchers to generate frightening speed. When brushback pitching (see **3.3.2**) became a major part of the game, the rule entitling a hit batsman to take first base became necessary.

There is of course no way to definitively identify the first man who intentionally allowed himself to be hit by a pitch in order to reach base. We can establish that it did not take long after the American Association's rules first allowed a base to a hit batsman, and that Curt Welch was one of the leaders. In 1907, "Someone accused Hughie Jennings of being one of the first men to conceive the idea of getting hit by the pitch in order to get his base. 'I never did such a thing,' said Hughie, trying awfully hard to appear indignant. 'That gag was working before my time. Quirt Welch [sic], I guess, was the first man to ever reduce it to a science. That old St. Louis outfielder had them all beaten at that game'" (*Detroit News*, March 18, 1907). Indeed, *Sporting News* reported in 1886, "Welch, who led off for the Browns, pretended to be hit by a pitched ball, and started to first. [Umpire Jim] Clinton did not see it in that light, and called him back" (*Sporting News*, May 16, 1886).

The next month Fred Dunlap was asked if the National League should allow batters their base if hit by a pitch. He replied, "I will not favor that rule. I think, if we had such a rule as that in the League the players would be colliding with the ball early and often, and that a continuous wrangle would follow" (*Sporting News*, June 28, 1886).

His prediction proved accurate. John B. Foster wrote in 1901, "There were batters in the National League last year who played regularly to be hit by the pitcher . . . so many of the pitchers have become perfect in the use of a slow ball that the batters have taken advantage of the fact, and have been schooling themselves in methods to get their base without going to the trouble to hit the ball. Hughey Jennings had lots of fun flirting that big glove of his [presumably a batting or protective glove] into the ball, and many and many a time he was made a present to first when he was no more entitled to it than the Kohinoor [a very valuable diamond]" (*Sporting Life*, April 6, 1901).

And John J. Evers and Hugh S. Fullerton observed in 1910, "The practice of getting to first base by allowing the pitched ball to hit them, is more general with batters than usually is supposed. It is not indulged in as extensively as in former years when 'Red' Galvin used to allow the ball to carrom off his head in order to reach first, but it still is used extensively, despite rules forbidding umpires to allow batters to take first when purposely hit. There is scarcely an important game between contenders for pennant honors, in which a dozen batters do not strive to make the ball hit them" (John J. Evers and Hugh S. Fullerton, *Touching Second*, 165–166).

F. C. Lane, writing in 1925, described this tactic as being used "occasionally." He recalled that Fred Snodgrass was accused of getting on base in this way several times during World Series games (F. C. Lane, *Batting*, 142).

This tactic has of course remained a part of baseball and has become less painful to batters in recent years due to the increasing use of bulky padding.

2.3.5 Deliberate Strikeouts. On at least a couple of occasions, a batter has been heady enough to anticipate that a two-strike wild pitch presented a novel opportunity to reach base. A *Sporting News* correspondent reported in 1894: "One of the smartest schemes that has been worked on a base ball diamond was that of [Abner] Powell's in a Southern League game last week. After two strikes, [Harrison] Pepper pitched a wild ball which went behind Powell's back and he swung his bat as though he expected to drive a home run. He was past first when [August "Duke"] Jantzen got the ball, and beat the throw to second" (*Sporting News*, June 16, 1894).

Sportswriter Paul H. Bruske gave this description of a play that took place in the second game of a doubleheader between Detroit and Cleveland on June 29, 1905: "[Bill] Donovan was pitching, and Detroit was two runs ahead in the last half of the ninth. [Cleveland batter Bill] Bradley missed two of Bill's benders, and then the twirler let the ball off his wrong finger. It came up ten feet wide of the plate, like a cannot [sic] shot. Bradley's mind worked lightning fast. He whipped his bat around like a flash for the third strike and started for first, all in one motion. The ball was clear out of [catcher Lew] Drill's reach, and Bradley got second on the play" (*Sporting Life*, July 8, 1905).

In 1868, Henry Chadwick instructed umpires that should a batsman "willfully strike at balls for the purpose of striking out, then such strikes are not to be called" (Henry Chadwick, *The American Game of Base Ball*, 52). An addition to the 1872 rules, Rule 3, Sections 5 and 6, seemed to prohibit it. Of course, this is a judgment call, so it would have been possible for a cunning batter to get away with this ploy no matter what the rules might say. There no longer appears to be any rule to prevent this tactic.

(iv) Preparation

2.4.1 Muscle Building. Until very recently, weight training was considered counterproductive for baseball players, because it was believed that the added bulk was offset by lost flexibility. For example, Bob Shaw told a *Sporting News* reporter in 1960 that he worked with five-pound weights to strengthen his wrist and forearm. But he maintained that heavy weight lifting would be injurious to a baseball player: "Some of this weight lifting is done by people just to build up muscles. In the case of ballplayers, that would be harmful because you might get muscle bound. The entire object of the exercising I'm doing is for strengthening and flexibility. I want to build up my stamina, endurance and power in the throwing arm. However, I'm not seeking bulging muscles. An athlete like a ball player wants to retain fast reflexes and speed" (Edgar Munzel, "Daily Workouts Put Shaw in Pink for Comeback Pitch," *Sporting News*, November 16, 1960).

Of course there have always been exceptions. In 1960, Wally Shannon described his weight-lifting regime to Jack Herman of *Sporting News*, and indicated that he was not alone: "Ralph Kiner lifted weights. So did Hank Greenberg. Jackie Jensen still does and, if I'm not mistaken, Ted Williams did too" (*Sporting News*, January 13, 1960). Williams was endorsing a line of barbells for Sears by 1969, which couldn't have hurt their popularity among aspiring players (*Mansfield* [Ohio] *News*, December 17, 1969).

In the early 1960s, Tony Conigliaro ignored the conventional wisdom and had a grueling weight-lifting regimen. Conigliaro, however, believed that his right arm was what generated his batting power, and focused almost exclusively on that arm. Teammate Rico Petrocelli recalled: "The definition

in his arm was just incredible; his right arm. His left arm was sort of atro-
phied" (quoted in David Cataneo, *Tony C.*, 40).

The Cincinnati Reds of the mid-1970s are usually credited with being
the first club to make extensive use of weight-training machines. As usual,
the success of the Big Red Machine led to imitators. Red Smith reported
near the end of the 1979 season that Carl Yastrzemski had decided to purchase Nautilus equipment because it had helped teammate Fred Lynn (Red
Smith, September 14, 1979, reprinted in *Red Smith on Baseball*). Robin
Yount's MVP season in 1982, after an offseason of weight training, convinced many others and led John Lowenstein to grumble, "They tell you all
your life never to lift weights, then you find out it's just what you should have
been doing all along" (quoted by Tom Boswell, *Washington Post*, September
5, 1982; reprinted in Paul Dickson, ed., *Baseball's Greatest Quotations*, 257).
Positive results by many of the imitators have made the practice generally
accepted, though it is sometimes blamed for a greater frequency of muscle
pulls and other specific injuries.

The fact that weight lifting is primarily a recent phenomenon does not
of course mean that early baseball players did not have serious workout reg-
imens that were designed to develop their muscles. According to Jimmy
Wood, young pitcher Jim Creighton approached Joe Leggett of the Excelsiors of Brooklyn for advice after the 1859 season. Leggett suggested that he
spend the winter throwing an iron ball that was the same size as a regular
baseball. By the spring, Creighton's "speed was blinding," and he established
himself as the game's first dominant pitcher (James Wood, as told to Frank
G. Menke, "Baseball in By-Gone Days," part 2, syndicated column, *Marion*
[Ohio] *Daily Star*, August 15, 1916).

A reporter observed before the 1872 season, "I called in at the Gymnasium, on Elliott street, this forenoon, and found the Red Stocking boys in
full preparatory career, pending the opening of the base ball season on next
Thursday. As I entered, Calvin McVey was throwing [A. G.] Spalding over
his head; George Wright was hanging by his little fingers on a trapeze bar,
away up close by the ceiling; Charley Gould was holding Schaefer [Harry
Schafer] by the ankles, at arms' length, and about four feet off the floor—the
two looking as rigid as if they had been hewed out of granite; Harry Wright
was swinging a couple of logs about his head with wonderful ease and per-
severence [sic]; [Andy] Leonard and [Fraley] Rogers were climbing what
looked like greased poles, but which had no tempting leg of mutton on top
to excite their aspirations; [John J.] Ryan, the new man . . . was getting off
his lazy muscle through the use of all sorts of pulling and haulings of weights
and swinging of dumbbells, each weighing thirty pounds, and [Ross] Barnes
was diverting himself on the horizontal bar in a way most cruelly suggestive
of hard work. All the boys were as full of health as they could look or be, and

if they are not the champions of 1872 it will not be for lack of determination" (Boston correspondent, *Cleveland Leader*, April 5, 1872).

Tim Murnane later recalled: "The spring practice of the Boston team in the early history of the club consisted of several weeks' training in the old Association gym on Elliot street, commencing March 15 and winding up when the grounds became fit to work on." He reported that a Professor Roberts supervised the workouts (Tim Murnane, *Boston Globe*, February 19, 1900, also April 19, 1896).

The effectiveness of such a regimen in developing muscles was demonstrated when the Red Stockings visited Detroit to play the Empires, an amateur club that held the championship of Michigan. The local paper was struck by the contrast: "the Empire nine is made up of vigorous and rather athletic young men, all of whom are just attaining mature life. The members of the Boston are athletes, brawny men, trained by long practice to immense muscular power and endurance" (*Detroit Advertiser and Tribune*, August 22, 1872). Another commented that the Empires appeared "ludicrous by comparison" with their muscular opponents (*Detroit Daily Post*, August 22, 1872).

But the emphasis was on flexibility, and muscle building continued to be discouraged. Henry Chadwick was especially adamant on the subject, writing in 1880: "What is necessary for a baseball player in gymnastic exercise is to take only that exercise which makes him agile and quick of movement, and which trains the eye to judge the ball, the arms and chest to wield the bat, or the legs to run the bases. Lifting heavy weights, or excercise [sic] which is calculated to develop strength for such purposes is useless. Swinging clubs is carried to excess; jumping is unnecessary; work on the parallel bars, the trapeze, etc., is needless" (*New York Clipper*, December 25, 1880).

Baseball clubs thus stressed general fitness, as this 1883 account suggested: "The Chicago nine are at work practicing general athletics under the orders of Captain Anson, who acts as trainer, overseeing the work of each of his men. He puts them through a course of running, jumping, weight-lifting, walking and general work. He has not put a ball in their hands yet, saying he has not yet reached the proper point for that" (*Chicago Inter-Ocean*, reprinted in *Cleveland Leader*, April 13, 1883).

New York captain John M. Ward told the *New York Sun* in 1887, "Gymnasium apparatus and gymnastic exercise are going out of favor among ball players for several reasons, and very few of them now attempt to keep in condition through the winter. When you hear of a player going into a gymnasium that usually means he goes in there, tries some feat and lames himself, and then drops in two or three times a week to look on. It is not a good thing for a player to fool with the apparatus. He does not want to develop big bunches of muscle. What he needs is agility, suppleness, quickness of eye, hand and foot. If he goes into a gymnasium he exercises muscles that he does not use in the field, and he either developes [sic] them at the expense of his useful muscles, or he puts too much strain upon them . . . [and] injures himself" (*New York Sun*, March 20, 1887).

Walter C. Dohm noted in 1893 that college players were beginning to focus more on muscle building: "while the snow still lies deep on the ground, the collegian who hopes to get a place on the nine commences putting his muscles in shape in the gymnasium. He pulls chest weights, handles dumb-bells and swings light Indian clubs" (Walter C. Dohm, "College Baseball," *Los Angeles Times*, May 21, 1893).

One professional who followed their example was Buck Freeman, who hit twenty-five home runs in 1899 and credited the development of the muscles of the back and arm. He explained, "I am a crank on exercise. The gymnasium is the best sanitarium on earth. . . . The parallel bars, wrist, and weight machine, and the punch bag are the apparatuses used by me in my winter exercises." But even Freeman stressed that muscle alone did not make a good hitter (*Washington Post*, October 15, 1899).

The general disapproval of muscle building was appropriate to baseball as it was played in the late nineteenth and early twentieth centuries. It is harder to explain why it persisted for so much of the twentieth century in the face of a growing emphasis on power. One likely reason for this lag is the belief that bulky athletes are more prone to pulled muscles.

2.4.2 Swing Practice. Deacon White borrowed from boxing when he devised a regimen for maintaining his swing over the winter. An 1887 article noted that he had been showing it to teammate Charlie Bennett: "It consists of a canvas bag of sawdust suspended from a rafter by a single piece of rope. To keep his arms from becoming too soft during the winter months Deacon White exercises quietly by taking a bat and striking the bag in the same manner that he would strike at a ball. It is not intended to give the eye any practice, but it keeps the arms in good shape without giving them too violent exercise" (*Boston Globe*, February 20, 1887).

Walter C. Dohm noted in 1893 that it had been a common preseason drill for any collegian who hoped to make his school's baseball nine to train "his eye for the elusive curve ball by banging away for twenty minutes a day with his bat at a big knot at the end of a rope" (Walter C. Dohm, "College Baseball," *Los Angeles Times*, May 21, 1893).

2.4.3 Batting Practice. From time immemorial, batters engaged in some form of pregame practice. In the early days, however, it consisted largely of "fungo hitting," and its development into a more formal process was slow and uneven.

The largest obstacles seem to have been practical ones. Baseballs represented a major expense for early baseball clubs, and they could ill afford to lose or deface them for the sake of a little practice. Nor did it make much sense to them to spend their time retrieving baseballs. As a result, the gentler and more controlled practice of fungo hitting was generally used.

The invention of batting practice is sometimes credited to either George or Harry Wright, but there is little evidence to support that assertion. Harry Wright was noted for instilling discipline in his players, and they no doubt went about their pregame practice in a more orderly fashion than other clubs of the era. But Wright also kept a tight rein on expenses, and it seems unlikely that he would have been willing to sacrifice many balls to pregame hitting.

One man who may have played a significant role was Henry Chadwick, who, in his dogged way, regularly inveighed against fungo hitting. Chadwick lost no opportunity to denounce "the absurd fungo practice, which only gives the outfielders practice and is death to good batting" (*Brooklyn Eagle*, April 1, 1889).

For whatever reason, by the 1880s batters' pregame rituals had begun to take on greater order and purpose. *Sporting Life* recorded in 1885: "There are well-developed indications that [Bill] Traffley has improved his batting over last season's record. Judicious practice, and not too much 'batting up' before the commencement of a game, may do much to assist him in this regard. It is believed by many practical base ball men that 'batting up' develops a tendency in some players to hit under the ball, which they are unable to overcome when at the plate" (*Sporting Life*, April 8, 1885).

The new approach to batting practice was also reflected in batters using the warm-ups to address specific weaknesses. An 1886 account noted, "The left-handed hitters of the Detroit team—and seven of them bat this way—practice batting a 'south paw' pitcher every morning. His name is Howard Lawrence, and the managers hope that he may develop into a valuable man in time" (*Boston Globe*, May 21, 1886).

Henry Chadwick noted approvingly in 1889 that Louisville captain "Dude" Esterbrook was rotating hitters during pregame practice: "his rule is to have the players take their regular positions on the field and one of the batteries officiate in the points. The other pitchers and catchers will take their turn at the bat" (*Brooklyn Eagle*, April 1, 1889).

By the 1890s, new inventions were promoting more productive batting practices. Batting cages originated in college baseball in the 1880s (see 14.4.10), and by 1894 their benefits had become evident to major league clubs. Tim Murnane explained: "Members of the Boston baseball team are badly in need of a little batting practice. All the work they have been able to get in the way of batting is during the games. When they return to the South end grounds next Thursday the mornings will be devoted to practice, and manager [Frank] Selee will suggest to the owners of the club the putting up of nets such as they use at the big colleges for batting practice" (*Boston Globe*, May 7, 1894).

Two years later a singular invention (see **14.4.11**) was unveiled: "Professor [Charles H.] Hinton of Princeton has, it is said, invented a machine that will pitch balls automatically, and that will curve them also. The apparatus will deliver a ball every twenty seconds, but the time between balls can be changed. The speed of the balls can be regulated as well as the curves. The balls always go directly over the plate. It is said that the Princeton tigers will use this for batting practice next year" (*Boston Globe*, April 16, 1896).

Still, it does not seem to have been until the twentieth century that batting practices became highly structured. Benton Stark, for example, claimed that batting practice was still a casual affair in 1904 (Benton Stark, *The Year They Called Off the World Series*, 102). The *Detroit News* informed its readers in 1907, "[Hugh] Jennings gets each man to bat about forty times in the course of a day's practice. This shows the system. As soon as the ball has been lined out by one, another steps to the plate. It's like standing in line at a barber shop. 'You're next,' cries Jennings, and each man tries to put one over the fence, while Hughie tells the pitcher how to serve the unhittable ones" (*Detroit News*, March 18, 1907).

2.4.4 Swinging Multiple Bats in the On-deck Circle. Swinging multiple bats was already a common practice by 1904, when Nap Lajoie said, "I have been asked why batters just before they go to the plate swing two bats. It is to make the bat you use feel lighter" (quoted in *Washington Post*, July 24, 1904). Ty Cobb claimed to have improved on the idea: "Another idea that I worked out was the carrying of three bats to the plate so that when two were thrown away the remaining one would feel light. I had seen a batter swing two bats in practice, so I tried three" (Ty Cobb, *Memoirs of Twenty Years in Baseball*, 8).

With such star players using this form of preparation, it was inevitable that it would be copied. A 1915 article reported, "You will often see a player advancing to the plate swinging two or three bats as he walks. Practically all the good batters in both the National and American Leagues are in the habit of going through this performance before they face the pitcher. Watch men like Ty Cobb, Tris Speaker and Hans Wagner, who are famous for their batting ability, and you will conclude that they consider it part of their day's work" ("Superstition in Baseball," *Washington Post*, September 19, 1915; credited to the *New York Times*, but I could not find the original).

It gradually became standard to recommend this tactic to youngsters, as Billy Evans did in 1922: "As you walk to the plate swing two or three bats until you step into the box. That tends to make the regular bat feel much lighter after you discard the others" (Billy Evans, "How to Play Baseball," syndicated column, *Lima* [Ohio] *News*, May 26, 1922).

2.4.5 Batting Tees. The batting tee was developed by a coach and former player named Bert Dunne and was unveiled by Dunne's 1945 book *Play Ball Son!* Joe Cronin, in the introduction to the 1951 edition of Dunne's book *Play Ball!*, wrote, "In the summer of 1946 [Dunne] came East with the Tee which he had finally perfected as a device for teaching hitting." Red Sox teammates Cronin and Ted Williams both saw value in the device, and Williams appeared in a movie that helped popularize the batting tee.

2.4.6 Steroids. The first ballplayer to admit to having taken illegal steroids was the late Ken Caminiti, in a *Sports Illustrated* article published in June 2002. Caminiti acknowledged that steroids helped him win the National League MVP award in 1996. Of course Caminiti wasn't the first major leaguer to take illegal steroids, and other players, most notably Mark McGwire, have acknowledged taking products such as androstenedione, which were not prohibited by baseball at the time.

Chapter 3

PITCHING

OF ALL of the things that it is necessary to understand about early pitching, perhaps the most important is this: almost everyone except the pitchers themselves viewed them as intruders in a game that was supposed to pit fielders against hitters. This perception endured long after pitchers had carved out a larger role for themselves.

Whenever rule changes were contemplated, the opinions of the eight hitters on a club counted for more than the lone pitcher. As a result, while the history of hitting is a tale of techniques, the history of early pitching is a saga of legislative attempts to restore baseball to the way it had once been but would never be again—when the pitcher's role was to give the batter something to hit. As Bozeman Bulger observed in 1912, "Practically every important change in the rules has been aimed at the pitcher. The bat, the ball, the distance between the bases and the fundamental rules of the game have stood for half a century, while the pitching has gone through a steady grind of evolution" (Bozeman Bulger, "Pitching, Past and Present: The Evolution of the Twirler's Art," *Baseball Magazine*, February 1912, no. 4, 71–73).

It appears that the intention of the Knickerbockers was for pitchers to be the least important players on the field, their role being simply to lob fat pitches to the batter. As their name implied, they were required to "pitch" the ball in the manner of a horseshoer. Instead pitchers almost immediately began to hew out a larger role in the game, and rule makers tried in vain to reclaim the lost ground and restore baseball to a game of hitting and fielding.

Again and again, baseball legislators wrestled with the issue neatly summarized by the *Brooklyn Eagle* in 1885: "The question now is, therefore, how can the rules be made so as to not interfere with strategic play in the delivery of the ball, and yet be such as to give greater freedom of play to the batsman, with a view to doing away with the style of play known as 'the pitcher's game,' in which the brunt of the work of the attack in a contest falls upon the pitcher and catcher, while the majority of the fielders stand idly by as mere lookers on" (*Brooklyn Eagle*, November 8, 1885). Again and again, they failed to hit upon a workable solution.

The art of pitching can be divided into two stages: the delivery (what the pitcher does while he still holds the ball) and the pitch itself (the trajectory taken by the ball after it is released). Of course the two are directly and intimately related, yet there is a fundamental distinction. Baseball's rule makers have generally concluded that there is no feasible way to pass legislation based directly on what a ball does after its release—how quickly it travels, how sharply it breaks, etc. But until the mid-1880s they showed no qualms about trying to prevent specific pitches by restricting what the pitcher could do while the ball was in his possession.

The Knickerbockers initially thought it was enough to assert that the ball should be "pitched" rather than "thrown." They saw no need to put any other restrictions on the pitcher. But by the mid-1850s pitchers had begun to make incursions upon those rules in ways that forced the creation of additional rules. This would become a vicious cycle, with each new rule leading to inventive ways of flouting at least the spirit of the rule. The details of this struggle are discussed below.

(i) Deliveries

James A. Williams was a top amateur pitcher in Columbus, Ohio, in the late 1860s when pitching still resembled the act of tossing a horseshoe. By 1884, he was manager of the St. Louis Brown Stockings of the American Association and had seen rule makers struggle for nearly two decades to prevent pitching from becoming overhand throwing. He offered his unique perspective on why it was time to wave the white flag and let pitchers do as they chose.

Williams explained: "The history of the past clearly proves that the pitcher has not been restrained by the rules. That he has always encroached upon them. That for the past two seasons, at least, he has delivered the ball as he pleased." With pitchers in both leagues showing rampant disregard for the rules, the American Association had instructed umpires to strictly enforce the written rules. In contrast, the National League, "recognizing the fact that no rules could be framed that would hold the pitchers in check, as was evidenced by the history of the past years and also believing that no style of pitching or throwing could be invented that would be more effective than the present that would not be used by the pitchers, wisely, in my opinion, discarded all restrictions and thus did away with a rule that has always been a dead letter on the book." Williams believed that the National League's course was the right one because "there is no one point in the game so sure to create a wrangle as for the umpire to attempt to interfere with the pitcher's delivery."

He continued, "So much has been said in the papers in the cities where American Association clubs are located about the great mistake made by the League in doing away entirely with all restrictions in regard to the delivery of the ball by the pitcher, thus allowing him to throw overhand, underhand, round-arm, or even jerk the ball, that it may be of some interest to look at the question minutely, to see if the change is such a great and radical one, and also what effect it is likely to have upon the game.

"Those of your readers who are familiar with the history of the game of base-ball will readily remember the old rule that required the pitcher to keep both feet on the ground when delivering the ball and it was delivered with the arm swinging perpendicular and the hand passing below the knee. That is what is known as a square pitch, and there are many old timers who would like to see it brought into vogue again. Those were the days of lively balls and large scores. With this style of delivery, very little latitude was given the pitcher. The only way of outwitting the batsman was by a change of pace. A few pitchers—notably [Dick] McBride of the Athletics, [Asa] Brainard of the Cincinnatis, and [George] Zettlein of the Atlantics—were able to pitch with considerable speed by an imperceptible whip-like motion of the arm. [A. G.] Spalding of Chicago was perhaps the best exponent of this school of pitching, he having so well disguised the change of pace that he was very effective.

"Then came the underhand throw, and with it a change in the rule allowing an outward movement of the arm but still requiring the hand to pass below the hip. This was gradually encroached upon until the curve was introduced, about 1876, when there was hardly a pitcher who pitched strictly under the rules. Arthur Cummings and Bob Matthews [sic] had pitched a small lateral curve as early as 1868, but it was done by a regular pitch and not by a throw, as later. Later, the rule was still further amended, allowing the hand to pass as high as the waist. But, as before, the pitchers paid but little or no heed to it, and almost every pitcher in the profession got his hand above the prescribed line, the fact being that no curve pitcher can pitch a drop ball, which is one of the most effective of all balls pitched, without getting his hand above his waist. So open and flagrantly was the rule violated that in 1883 the rule was changed so as to allow the hand to pass as high as the shoulder. This concession seemed to make no difference to the pitchers, who pursued the even tenor of their way and delivered the ball in the most effective manner they could; if that required the hand at times to pass as high or higher than the head, that is where they put it. The writer does not

remember of seeing but three pitchers in the American Association last season, and he saw all of them, who did not deliver some ball in an illegal manner with the hand passing above the shoulder. The three exceptions were
[Will] White and [Jim] McCormick of Cincinnati and [George] Bradley of
the Athletics" (*St. Louis Post-Dispatch*, January 2, 1884).

Others echoed Williams's conclusion that the time had come to admit
the futility of trying to legislate against specific delivery techniques. Indeed,
many considered the question to be already academic. Early in the 1884
campaign, a Boston sportswriter remarked that the National League's new
rule "has not made any noticeable change in deliveries, as had been expected,
this well showing that the rule was a recognized dead letter in 1883" (*New
York Clipper*, May 17, 1884).

By the end of the first month of the 1885 season, both leagues had abandoned for good the effort to place restrictions on how a ball was released, effectively legalizing overhand pitching. Restrictions continued to be placed
on the pitcher's location when he released the ball, his application of substances foreign and organic to it, and his making motions that deceived a
base runner. But never again would the pitcher be told that he could not
pitch the ball as he saw fit.

How baseball came to that juncture is a fascinating story that begins
with a jerk. The Knickerbockers' ninth rule had stated, "The ball must be
pitched, not thrown, for the bat." By 1854 the pitcher was required to release the ball from behind a line fifteen paces from the batter and, since
there were varying interpretations of the length of a pace, it was clarified
in 1857 that this meant forty-five feet. This would be the last time for
many years that a restriction on pitching would be introduced without creating turmoil.

The trouble began when the game's legislative body, the National Association of Base Ball Players (NABBP), tried to be more specific about how the
pitcher should throw. The rules of 1860 included only one small modification to those of the Knickerbockers: "The ball must be pitched, not jerked
nor thrown to the bat." Since the addition of the word "jerked" is the only
substantive change, it is clearly significant. But while this term had had a
clearly understood meaning when used in cricket, its borrowing by baseball
only caused confusion.

The NABBP's rules committee attempted to clarify the intended meaning,
but without much success. In 1864 the *Brooklyn Eagle* commented on the latest interpretation: "In reference to the jerking of the ball, no movement can
be called a jerk in which the arm used does not touch the side of the body
while the body is in an upright position. But when a pitcher stoops on one
side in order to deliver the ball, thereby getting all the motive power of a jerk
without actually touching the body, then the Umpire is empowered to call a

baulk for jerking the ball. According to this interpretation, nearly every swift pitcher now in our clubs jerks the ball every time he delivers it" (*Brooklyn Eagle*, March 28, 1864).

In contrast, *The Ball Player's Chronicle* gave this explanation in 1867: "A 'pitched' ball is one that reaches the batsman without touching the ground. If it touches the ground it becomes a 'bowled' ball. A 'jerked' ball is a ball delivered swiftly from the hand by the arm first touching the side of the pitcher; if the arm does not touch his side the ball is not 'jerked'" (*The Ball Player's Chronicle*, July 18, 1867). (While neither piece is bylined, Henry Chadwick wrote for the *Eagle* and was the editor of *The Ball Player's Chronicle*, so he could well have been responsible for both pieces.)

The inevitable result of these differing interpretations was that every time a pitcher experienced some success, questions were raised as to "whether his pitching was a 'jerk,' 'an underhand throw,' or a 'fair square pitch,'" as Chadwick noted in 1860 (*Brooklyn Eagle*, August 6, 1860). All too often, different authorities had different answers.

Pitchers naturally began to work on deliveries of borderline legality, and the NABBP made a renewed effort to define exactly what the pitcher could and could not do. The first step was to dictate that both of the pitcher's feet must be on the ground at the time the ball was released. (In 1865 it was clarified that a step was permissible before the release.) This rule proved very tricky to enforce since the feet were allowed to leave the ground as soon as the ball was released.

At the same time an even thornier problem had begun to surface. "Pitching" the ball was universally understood to mean a straight-arm motion and a release from an underhand position. Unfortunately, enforcing these requirements was no easy task for umpires. Determining whether a pitcher's hand was low enough at the instant of release was an onerous judgment call. Getting pitchers to adhere to the straight-arm requirement proved still more difficult.

A few pitchers were effective by going to the other extreme. Henry Chadwick reported in 1860, "whenever [Jim] Creighton pitched his balls, he delivered them from within a few inches of the ground, and they rose up above the batsman's hip, and when thus delivered, the result of hitting at the ball is either to miss it or to send it high in the air" (*Brooklyn Eagle*, August 6, 1860). Jim "Deacon" White got around the requirement that a pitcher "stand flat-footed in the box and swing his arm perpendicular without bending his wrist" and achieved greater speed by "[getting] my shoulder behind my heave, and my knuckles almost touched the ground" (Martin Quigley, *The Crooked Pitch*, 44–45). The techniques of Creighton and White seemed to comply with the rules, but this didn't stop both from being accused of illegal pitching.

An even more important new rule in 1863 limited the pitcher from running starts by dictating that he begin and end his delivery from within the confines of two parallel chalked lines. This was the first rudimentary version of what eventually became known as the "pitcher's box" (see 14.3.7). Over the next thirty years, the dimensions and/or location of the box were altered seven times. The one constant was that the pitcher was boxed in while performing—unless he had the misfortune to be knocked out of the box.

Umpires had trouble keeping the pitcher within the exact constraints of the box, but at least the pitchers couldn't stray too far outside of it. In contrast, the other pitching rules created by the NABBP were proving unenforceable and were only creating disputes. As pitchers routinely ignored them, these rules became dead letters and were eventually removed.

In 1868 the NABBP scrapped the rule that the pitcher's feet had to be on the ground when the ball was released. The Red Stockings' pitchers took advantage by "[advancing] the leg, at the same time they brought the arm forward, and thus gave to the ball the impetus of the whole body and leg" (*Daily Alta California*, September 26, 1869; quoted in Stephen Guschov, *The Red Stockings of Cincinnati*, 85).

By the 1870s, arguments of the legality of specific pitching techniques were rampant, and games often ended with one club marching off the field in a huff. Rule makers had little choice but to liberalize the pitching rules. Before the 1872 season, the bent-arm delivery was explicitly permitted, and the release point elevated to the hip, meaning that "the only style of delivery in pitching in base ball that is illegal now is the overhand throw and the round arm delivery as in bowling in cricket" (*Brooklyn Eagle*, August 13, 1872). Legalizing the bent elbow and pitching from hip height made it much easier to throw curves.

Albert Goodwill Spalding, probably the most effective pitcher under the old restrictions, gave a couple of intriguing accounts of the reasons for the change. In 1879 he cited competitive balance: "it was found a matter of difficulty to secure good pitchers for all the clubs. In order to remedy the evil the bars which had been built by legislation around the pitcher's position were let down, and the first thing the public knew throwing had come into fashion. At the time I thought it would lead to bad results, but Harry Wright said there was no help for it; there were not first-class pitchers enough in the country" (*Detroit Post and Tribune*, May 31, 1879). He later elaborated that the effect of that scarcity "was to put the question up to the umpire, and if he ruled against the pitcher there was a disappointed crowd, no game, or an utterly uninteresting exhibition." Consequently there was "a growing tendency on the part of umpires to be lax in the enforcement of the rule . . . rather than stop the game and disappoint the crowd" (A. G. Spalding, *America's National Game*, 482–483).

Umpires were no more vigilant about enforcing the new rule, but there was a very important practical consideration that kept release points from going much higher. The *Brooklyn Eagle* noted in 1872 that even "if overhand throwing were allowed, it could never be indulged in to the extent of the full power of the thrower to deliver the ball, simply because no man could stop a ball from an overhand throw—like [John] Hatfield we'll say—thrown with all the speed he could deliver it, consequently such throwing would be useless" (*Brooklyn Eagle*, August 13, 1872).

That restraint was removed when catchers began to wear equipment, and pitchers immediately began to push the limits. An attempt was made in 1878 to make things easier for the umpire by specifying that the pitcher's hand be below his waistline when he released the ball. Predictably, pitchers "elevated their trousers to a point where the 'waist line' was on a level with their chests" (James Wood, as told to Frank G. Menke, "Baseball in By-Gone Days," part 2, syndicated column, *Marion* [Ohio] *Star*, August 15, 1916). Efforts by umpires to enforce shoulder-height delivery were met with similar resistance: "Repeatedly, when the umpire issued a warning note to the pitcher, the latter would answer back: 'Where's your tape measure?'" (John B. Foster, "The Evolution of Pitching" (part 4), *Sporting News*, January 7, 1932). This relentless process led to the sense of resignation articulated by James Williams and made the elimination of virtually all restrictions on pitching techniques inevitable. In 1883 pitchers were allowed to throw from shoulder height, and by 1885 straight overhand pitching was legal in both major leagues.

Thus by the 1880s, experienced observers such as Williams realized that restricting the pitcher's motions was futile. But more than a decade of ceding ground to pitchers had drained the game of much of its offense, making some action essential. Accordingly, rule makers sought to restore some balance by using the only tools that had not sparked controversy: modifying the pitcher's distance from home plate and the size of his box.

In 1881 they moved the front line of the pitcher's box back five feet, to fifty feet from the plate. But the ground thus gained by batters was again lost when first shoulder-height deliveries and then overhand pitching were legalized.

To offset these concessions, a volley of rule changes was made in 1887. The size of the box was reduced, the pitcher was restricted to one step during his delivery, and the pitcher had to begin his delivery with a foot on the back line of the box. Between them, the latter two rules created what was essentially the first pitching rubber, though it was merely a chalk line. (As is discussed under "Pitching Rubbers" [14.3.8], slabs had been part of the pitching area earlier, but they were in areas where the pitcher was not supposed to step.)

These changes were effective at reducing strikeouts because they denied the pitcher the source from which "he derives the power to give the lasting impetus to the ball in delivery" (*Sporting News*, January 29, 1887). Nonetheless, offense remained lethargic and batters pressed for additional relief. In 1893 the box was finally scrapped for good and replaced with a rubber, located sixty feet, six inches from the plate. (See **1.17** for an explanation of why this actually represented a move of less than five feet for the pitcher.)

The second move proved to be sufficient, as offensive production soared in 1894 and 1895. In the years since 1893 there have been occasional calls to revisit the restrictions placed on the pitcher. But the compromise finally hit upon in 1893, after thirty years of trial and error, has proved an enduring one.

3.1.1 **Windups.** As a result of the frequent changes in the rules governing deliveries, pitchers' windups developed in fits and starts. John B. Foster noted that, before 1863, "The pitcher could take a short preliminary run with the ball, which some of them did" (John B. Foster, "The Evolution of Pitching," part 4, *Sporting News*, January 7, 1932). For example, in a game on October 11, 1862, the pitcher for the Stars of New Brunswick "seized the ball and swinging his hand behind him as if in an effort to dislocate his shoulder, put his head between his legs—almost—and running furiously, discharged the ball some yards away from home base." This pitcher understandably had difficulty with his control, as he had to repeat it "an indefinite number of times" before the Princeton batter got a pitch that "suited him" (James M. DiClerico and Barry J. Pavelec, *The Jersey Game*, 173).

As discussed in the introduction to this chapter, such contortions led to three important rule changes being adopted in the following year: pitchers were required to keep their feet on the ground when releasing the pitch, the prototype of the pitcher's box was introduced, and balls began to be called when they missed their target. As intended, these new restrictions brought a temporary end to elaborate deliveries. It also ended a number of pitching careers prematurely, as many pitchers could not adapt (John H. Gruber, "The Pitcher," *Sporting News*, December 23, 1915).

R. M. Larner claimed that as a result of these new rules, "The pitcher was required to plant both feet firmly in two holes in the pitcher's box, two feet apart. In that rather uncomfortable attitude the 'slab artist' of ye olden times was obliged to deliver the ball to a batsman by a fair, square pitch. No throwing, or side-stepping, or gymnastic contortions to intimidate the batsman were permitted" (R. M. Larner, "Old-Time Baseball in the White Lot," *Washington Post*, June 26, 1904).

The 1870s saw a few pitchers attempt to conceal the ball from the batter, a development that is discussed in the next entry. By and large, however, deliveries remained fairly simple. In the 1880s, as the pitcher's release point was elevated, elaborate motions made their return. The most celebrated delivery was that of a Yale pitcher named Daniel Jones, whose gyrations earned him the nickname "Jumping Jack" Jones.

Jones was not especially effective in the major leagues, but his technique attracted imitators. It was said that the delivery of Washington pitcher John Hamill "takes the cake; he turns his back to the umpire with a get-thee-behind-me-Satan sort of an air, dances a double shuffle on the four corners of the box, and for want of something else to do, pitches" (*Toledo Commercial Telegram*, reprinted in *Sporting Life*, July 23, 1884). A description of Frank Hengstebeck, who pitched in the major leagues under the name Frank Beck, noted that he "shuts himself up like a jack knife and pitches" (*Port Huron Daily Times*, September 20, 1882).

Another scribe later claimed that at this time "the twirler was allowed to take a deliberate run of several feet or even yards before delivering the ball to the bat. Some of the big men, Jim Whitney of Boston, for instance, got the method down so fine that they managed to work up speed which not only puzzled the batsman to a ridiculous degree, but also frightened many of them out of their wits. A pitcher weighing 200 pounds had a tremendous advantage for the reason that he was enabled to put just so much more momentum into his delivery" (*Ottumwa* [Iowa] *Courier*, March 16, 1903). His "hop, step and jump" not only frightened batters but also proved too much for his catchers: "Whitney, with his long legs and preliminary movements, was able to soak the ball to his catcher with frightful power. He used up both Mike Hines and Mertie Hackett, his backstops, that year, but he puzzled the best batters in the National League" (*Washington Post*, February 11, 1906).

To remedy this situation, the National League dictated before the 1885 season that the pitcher would have to keep both feet on the ground during his preliminary movements. According to Tim Keefe, however, the rule "was brought in only as an experiment and a protest from any one club against it was to be deemed sufficient to bring back the old 'hop and skip' style" (*San Francisco Examiner*, November 18, 1888).

That was exactly what happened on June 7, and Keefe believed it was self-interest that led to the return of "contortionist's movements": "During the season of 1885 the New York club was playing in Boston when everything looked favorable for the Giants winning the championship. But here they struck a snag. . . . Mr. [James] Billings, one of the Boston club Directors, came to the rescue. He held a consultation with the Providence club, and after considerable pleading they joined hands with him and objected to the new rule. It was immediately changed, previous to the New York club going on the grounds that day. . . . The retrogression to the hop, skip and jump pitching again placed a premium on brute strength. All it demanded to be an effective pitcher was plenty of speed and strength and a series of gymnastics to terrify the batter" (*San Francisco Examiner*, November 18, 1888).

Tony Mullane took advantage of the liberalized rules to unveil a "jumping-jack style. He pauses, then throws both arms aloft, and, taking a short run, delivers the ball hot as a cannon shot to the batter" (*Boston Globe*, June 30, 1886). But as pitchers found new ways to increase the speed of their pitches, it became clear that the equipment of catchers (see **9.3.2**) had not kept up with their new deliveries. A pitcher named Dan Bickham evolved a style that generated great speed but found that such "pace is useless, as no one could stand the punishment involved in facing such a delivery behind the bat" (*Cleveland Leader and Herald*, April 25, 1886). Bickham's major league career lasted only one game, and experiences like his led to significant adjustments.

In 1887 rule makers mandated that a pitcher hold the ball in front of him and then take only one step during his motion. Instead of eliminating preliminary movements, this placed a greater emphasis upon arm pumps, which several pitchers were already employing. Pitchers "began to study deliveries more, and with the swing of the arms over the head coupled with a sort of hitch and kick movement with the feet, they were able to get almost as much speed as formerly" (*Ottumwa* [Iowa] *Courier*, March 16, 1903).

Even before the rule change, pitchers began to adjust to the fact that the benefits of great speed were often offset by the toll it took on catchers. Thus some enterprising souls worked on deliveries that sacrificed pace for deceptiveness. Detroit southpaw Lady Baldwin was described as being "as gentle as a lamb when in the box. He pitches steadily and without any delay or waiting. Usually he throws his arm in a circle about his head, then raises one leg, and a moment later comes down hard with both feet on the ground, when the ball leaves his left hand like a flash" (*Boston Globe*, June 30, 1886).

Another pitcher who had a stint with Detroit, the left-hander Dupee Shaw, was known for a still stranger set of motions: "There have been long fought and dangerous disputes about the exact number of motions through which Shaw puts himself before delivering the ball. One man claimed thirty-two, holding that he had counted them. An attempt to give all of them would be foolish. A few will be enough. When Shaw first lays his hands on the sphere he looks at it. Then he rolls it around a few times. Then he sticks out one leg; pulls it back and shoves the other behind him. Now he makes three or four rapid steps in the box. When he does all this he holds the ball in his left hand. After he has swapped it to the right he wipes his left on his breeches, changes the ball to his left again and pumps the air with both arms. Then he gets down to work and digs up the ground with his right foot. Then you think he is going to pitch. But he isn't. He starts in and reverses the programme and does it over again three or four times, and just as the audience sits back in the seats with a sigh, the ball flies out like a streak. Nobody

knows how it left his hand, but it did" (*St. Louis Post-Dispatch*, June 19, 1886).
A later account observed: "Dupee Shaw, left-handed, was one of the first
pitchers to use the 'wind-up' motion of the arm before delivering the ball,
and his antics caused much merriment and good-natured joshing wherever
he appeared" (*Washington Post*, February 11, 1906).

The peculiar motions of Washington pitcher Bob Barr inspired one
writer to comment that Barr "steps into the box parrot-toed, and, as he un-
winds himself to deliver the ball, he looks not unlike the dissolving view in
'The Black Crook.' From the many preparatory motions he goes through,
one might suppose that he was trying to mesmerize the batters" (*Philadelphia
North American*, reprinted in the *Boston Globe*, June 12, 1886).

Other onlookers noticed that the pitchers who replaced leg movements
with arm movements bore a resemblance to clock-winders. The *New York
Sun* remarked in 1889: "[Bert] Cunningham, Baltimore's clever little pitcher,
still does the 'wind-the-clock act' while delivering the ball when none of the
bases are occupied" (*New York Sun*, April 30, 1889). The *Detroit Free Press*
noted in 1902: "Al Orth is not very popular with the Washington fans. His
slow motion in delivering the ball has caused it all. He takes plenty of time
to wind himself up" (*Detroit Free Press*, May 2, 1902). Thus was born the
word "windup."

The 1887 rule changes significantly reduced the variety of deliveries and
led to much speculation about which pitchers would be able to remain successful. Larry Corcoran predicted that only Phenomenal Smith and Harry
Pyle would suffer greatly, claiming that several other jumpers did so only out
of habit (*Detroit Free Press*, February 5, 1887). It turned out that pitchers who
had relied upon the banned deliveries had mixed success at adapting. Tom
Shieber noted that Guy Hecker, who had used a running start, was never the
same. Ed Morris, who used a skipping motion, struggled in 1887, then rebounded in 1888 for one last big season (Tom Shieber, "The Evolution of
the Baseball Diamond," in *Total Baseball IV*, 117). Tony Mullane, however,
never missed a beat, recording his fifth straight thirty-win season.

After the 1887 changes, a few pitchers still essayed elaborate motions.
Baseball writer E. K. Rife offered this description of St. Louis' Cy Duryea
in 1891: "He poses on one foot, and executing a grand *pas de seul*, like a
$4-a-month man opening a keg of nails, casts his mild blue eye toward [St.
Louis first baseman Charles] Comiskey with a sort of 'Willie-do-you-miss-
me' look, and sends the ball hustling through the air" (*Williamsport Sunday
Grit*, August 9, 1891).

During his first two seasons of 1890 and 1891, Cy Young employed an
elaborate pitching motion that sportswriters expended considerable ink in
trying to describe. One observed that "he winds up his arm, then his body,
then his legs, bows profoundly to his great outfield, straightens up again,

then lets her go. It is difficult to tell whether the ball comes from his hands or his feet" (*Boston Globe*, quoted in *Cleveland Plain Dealer*, June 5, 1891; quoted in Reed Browning, *Cy Young*, 151). Other scribes settled for fanciful analogies, comparing Young's delivery to "a man climbing a stake-and-rider fence" and "a corkscrew with an ecru handle" (*Sporting News*, October 10, 1891; *Cleveland Plain Dealer*, May 9, 1891; both quoted in Reed Browning, *Cy Young*, 151).

Ted Breitenstein was reported in 1892 to have a delivery that "beats [Scott] Stratton's all to pieces for contortion business. He shakes the ball behind the back of his neck a couple of times, brings it around in front of him with a double shuffle, draws back his head and body, pirouettes like Carmencita and then lets the ball go across the plate with a speed that is truly wonderful. When men are on the bases he leaves out the funny business, which lessens his speed considerably" (*Brooklyn Eagle*, May 27, 1892).

In 1898, *Sporting News* reported: "Another 'Jumping Jack' is liable to be seen on the diamond again this year. Jerry Nops, of the Baltimores, is said to be developing a new style of pitching which for weird and eccentric movements is said to far exceed anything ever attempted by the famous Jones, and is most startling in its effect. Nops faces the batter, when with a jump, he lands himself in the box facing second base. Pausing a moment his next move is an awe-inspiring jerk of the ball as he twists around, and another kangaroo jump completes the movement. The effectiveness of the delivery depends upon how badly the paralyzed batter is frightened" (*Sporting News*, May 7, 1898).

But such innovators were members of a dying breed. Reed Browning speculated that Cy Young may have scrapped his elaborate windup when he recognized that Kid Nichols was just as successful as Young with no windup at all (Reed Browning, *Cy Young*, 151–152).

Whatever the reason, the twentieth century saw a tendency toward orthodoxy in delivery techniques. The selection process begins with scouts, who generally presume that a successful pitcher with an awkward delivery will be unable to sustain his performance. Hugh Jennings recalled that the Tigers once turned down an opportunity to acquire a promising young pitcher because a scout was adamant that his sidearm delivery would never succeed in the major leagues: "If he's going to get anywhere in the major leagues with the stuff he's got, he must pitch overhand, and I don't think this fellow will ever learn to pitch overhand. He's one of those that you can't change the style of." The pitcher in question was Grover Cleveland Alexander (Hugh Jennings, *Rounding First*, Chapter 75).

Despite such blunders, scouts have grown increasingly picky in evaluating pitchers' deliveries. Sportswriter David Rawnsley observed: "Scouts are often quick to classify pitchers according to perceived flaws in their mechanics (i.e., arm action and delivery). One pitcher is a 'stabber,' another one 'wraps,' a third pitcher 'pole vaults' over a stiff front leg, a fourth might be a 'slinger.'. . .'Slingers,' for instance, are considered bigger injury risks because they are opening the front of their shoulder early and exposing both their rotator cuff and the inside of their elbow to more pressure" (*Baseball America*, August 9–22, 1999).

The few pitchers with unorthodox deliveries who make it into professional ball are further winnowed down by pitching coaches. Roger Kahn noted that "Most contemporary pitching coaches preach against elaborate windups. They reason that the more motion, the greater the chance for something to go out of whack." He quoted pitching coach Dick Bosman's maxim: "The simpler the mechanics of a delivery, the easier it is for most pitchers to master it" (Roger Kahn, *The Head Game*, 167).

3.1.2 Deception. Few pitchers wore gloves before the 1890s, which of course made it difficult to conceal the ball. Moreover rules in the 1880s often specified that the pitcher face the batter and present the ball. Nonetheless pitchers were trying to hinder the batter from picking up the ball long before Luis Tiant came along.

Speaking of Luis Tiant, by the late 1870s, a few pitchers were experimenting with deliveries in which they turned their backs to the batter. In an 1876 game, Cincinnati pitcher Dory Dean "brought out a new delivery, which consisted in facing second base with the ball in hand, and then turning quickly, letting it come in the general direction of the stand, without any idea of where it really was going to land" (*Chicago Tribune*, July 28, 1876). The *Chicago Tribune* characterized this as a "foolish boy's trick," and the White Stockings might have questioned its legality if they hadn't been too busy running around the bases in a 17-3 win.

Dory Dean compiled a 4-26 record that year and never again appeared in the major leagues, but he did leave a legacy. By 1878, Harvard pitcher Harold Ernst was using a similar delivery and he taught it to Johnny Ward of Providence (*New York Clipper*, December 14, 1878, January 25, 1879). Ward's "fore and aft style of delivery" during the 1878 campaign proved very "puzzling" to National League hitters (*Milwaukee Sentinel*, September 13, 1878).

This led to the introduction of a new rule on December 4, 1878, barring pitchers from completely turning their back on the batter during their delivery. Henry Chadwick noted that there had been "but one pitcher of the League who pitched in that way" and therefore "it certainly looked like an instance of special legislation" against a specific player (*New York Clipper*, December 28, 1878). Ward, however, expressed less concern, telling a reporter that it was "not necessary for him to turn his back to the batsman in pitching in order to be effective. It was only a dodge of his—learned from Ernst of the Harvards—to prevent the batsman from judging the ball. He can pitch with more accuracy by facing him" (*New York Clipper*, January 25, 1879).

Indeed Ward unveiled a new wrinkle the next spring: "In facing the striker he completely hides his delivery by seizing the ball in his right hand, carrying it to the small of his back, then by the aid of his left arm carries over to the right in front of his body, he fixes the ball in preparation for a curve-pitch" (*New York Clipper*, April 26, 1879).

The technique of turning the back to the batter seems to have largely disappeared during the 1880s as pitchers adapted to a series of rules changes. One exception was John Clarkson, yet the sportswriter who described his motion clearly did not think that he benefited from it, writing that he "stands with his face to the second baseman and suddenly whirls around and sends the ball to the plate with a rapidity of motion that should be startling to the batter. Of course, on the man that knows Clarkson's style it hasn't the least effect, but Clarkson thinks it has, and that's just as good" (*St. Louis Post-Dispatch*, June 19, 1886).

The ensuing years saw this technique occasionally reemerge. Cy Young turned his back to the hitter while winding up (Robert L. Tiemann, "Denton True Young," in Frederick Ivor-Campbell, Robert L. Tiemann and Mark Rucker, eds., *Baseball's First Stars*, 180; Reed Browning, *Cy Young*, 151). *Sporting Life* reported in 1908, "Jake Stahl says there are only three pitchers who have the out-of-sight delivery, [Fred] Glade, [Addie] Joss and [Jack] Chesbro. 'Glade,' says Stahl, 'faces the second baseman and then wheels around. That sort of a delivery makes any batter pull a little, and that's the reason Glade is so effective'" (*Sporting Life*, April 18, 1908).

This was not the only means by which nineteenth-century pitchers sought to disrupt batters' vision. John J. Evers and Hugh S. Fullerton explained in 1910, "Shadowing the ball, which was an art in former days, is almost lost. A few pitchers try it, but without the skill of Bert Cunningham, Mattie Kilroy, Willie McGill and many of the old school. [Clark] Griffith was the last pitcher to use it steadily. Shadowing consists of the pitcher side-stepping and placing his body on the line of the batter's vision, so that the ball has no background except the pitcher's body and the batter cannot see it plainly until the ball almost is upon him" (John J. Evers and Hugh S. Fullerton, *Touching Second*, 116).

3.1.3 Crossfire. Until 1872, pitchers were required to use an underhand motion. But this was difficult for umpires to enforce, and pitchers like Boston's Tommy Bond "kept inching up on the rules until he was throwing from a point several inches above his waist" (Bozeman Bulger, "Pitching, Past and Present: The Evolution of the Twirler's Art," *Baseball Magazine*, February 1912, no. 4, 71–73).

In 1872 the crossfire or sidearm delivery was legalized and many pitchers used it to great effect, with Bond being one of the most successful. Having won this concession, pitchers continued to try to get away with higher and higher release points. Eventually overhand pitching was legalized in the early 1880s, and the crossfire became an endangered species.

When Boston signed sidearm pitcher Willie Mains in 1896, the reaction to his pitching style gives a perfect indication of how rare it had become. The *Boston Globe* remarked in 1896: "Willie [Mains] was wilder than a stray cat, but was full of interest for the crowd, who enjoyed seeing him cutting semicolons with his left toe just before letting go a fast 'cross-fire.' Captain [Hugh] Duffy has impressed the Maine sapling with the importance of throwing a ball from the direction of third base, while Foot No. 1 is attached to the pitcher's rubber plate." Another article the same day observed that Mains "has a peculiar style. As he starts to pitch he steps into the extreme corner of the box towards third base and delivers the ball cat-a-cornered across the plate. On account of this angle, the batsmen seemed to be easily deceived" (*Boston Globe*, April 21, 1896).

The crossfire made a significant comeback in the next few years and through the first decade of the twentieth century. A primary reason for its success was the deceptiveness inherent in the delivery. Ty Cobb noted that one of the factors in Eddie Plank's success was that his "cross-fire was one of the most deceptive deliveries that I have ever seen" (Ty Cobb, *Memoirs of Twenty Years in Baseball*, 112). Other pitchers whom Cobb credited with inspiring the delivery's revival were Billy Donovan, Addie Joss, and Fred Glade (Ty Cobb, *Memoirs of Twenty Years in Baseball*, 119). Note that in the preceding entry, Joss and Glade were singled out by Jake Stahl for their ability to keep the ball out of the batter's sight during their deliveries.

By 1910, however, Johnny Evers and Hugh Fullerton were reporting that "the deadly cross fire used with wonderful effect fifteen years ago, almost has been abandoned" (John J. Evers and Hugh S. Fullerton, *Touching Second*, 115). Throughout the remainder of the twentieth century the sidearm delivery remained uncommon. While the term "crossfire" has fallen out of use, there always seem to be a few pitchers who are successful enough with the delivery itself to keep it from becoming extinct. Moreover a significant number of pitchers who usually throw overhand find it effective to vary things occasionally by dropping down to a sidearm delivery.

3.1.4 **Submarine.** Pitchers were restricted to underhand deliveries until 1872. Once higher release points were legal, most pitchers felt they had to use them in order to continue to pitch in the major leagues. This perception was reinforced by the simultaneous development of the curveball, which broke much more sharply when thrown with the extra speed enabled by a higher release point.

By the 1890s, however, a few pitchers began to rediscover how hard the underhand delivery could be for batters to pick up. In the process they learned that while an underhand curve might not break as dramatically as an overhand one, its unfamiliar trajectory could render it just as baffling. In 1896, *Sporting News* reported, "[Al] Orth, of the Philadelphias, is copying the underhanded movement of Billy Rhynes [Rhines]. This motion, though an old swing, is new to the majority of major league batsmen, and therein lies its effectiveness."

As with the sidearm delivery, the submarine motion enjoyed a vogue of popularity in the early twentieth century, with such pitchers as Bill Phillips, Deacon Phillippe, Jack Warhop, Joe McGinnity, and Carl Mays experiencing success with it. By the 1930s it had receded again, with the notable exception of Elden Auker.

This trend would suggest that the underhand style was most effective when batters were unaccustomed to seeing it, which may account for why its reemergence in the 1970s was largely restricted to relievers. Since then there have always been a few effective submariners manning major league bullpens. Some of the more renowned practitioners have included Ted Abernathy, Kent Tekulve, Dan Quisenberry, Mark Eichhorn, Chad Bradford, and Byung-Hyun Kim. There has been no corresponding success among starters.

3.1.5 Leg Kicks. The development of the leg kick came relatively late because of delivery restrictions and the ease of stealing against it. An 1886 description of Charley Sweeney's motion explained that he used a leg kick but modified it according to the situation: "When men are on bases Sweeney rolls the sphere continuously between both hands, meanwhile watching the bags carefully. Suddenly his right leg comes up, and, as it comes down, the ball speeds away" (*St. Louis Post-Dispatch*, June 19, 1886). Clark Griffith claimed to have scuffed the ball during his delivery, which implies both a high leg kick and impressive balance. Chief Bender was one of the first pitchers who became well known for a high leg kick.

(ii) Pitches

The development of the pitcher's basic weapons—the pitches—is a fascinating saga of ingenuity, resourcefulness, happenstance, and even intrigue. That might not appear to be the case at first pass. Eddie Lopat once described the introduction of new pitches as "sometimes a pitcher falls into something. George Blaeholder fell into the slider. Elmer Stricklett fell into the spitter. Tom Seaton or somebody else fell into the knuckler. Candy Cummings, back there in Civil War times, fell into the curve ball." Lopat, however, added an all-important qualifier: "But all of these men must have had basic assets of more than ordinary value before they tried to hit the moon" (quoted in *Sporting News*, April 6, 1960). In addition, as we shall see in this chapter, new pitches have arisen in clusters when the success of one pitch has inspired others to try new grips and techniques.

The two most fundamental pitches, the fastball and the change of pace, were in place in the 1860s. These were the only two pitches that could be fully mastered while adhering to the delivery restrictions of the day. Both have remained a basic part of the pitcher's repertoire ever since, even while those repertoires have expanded to include many fancier pitches. Both continue to present the batter with the same fundamental challenge—the fastball overpowers him while the change of pace disrupts his timing.

Most of the additions to the two fundamental pitches have taken place during two revolutionary flurries of inventiveness, which occurred a generation apart. The first was the curveball family of pitches, most notably the sinker and the curve, which began in the mid-1870s when liberalized delivery rules made the curveball practical. The second was the spitball family of pitches, including the forkball, the palm ball, the knuckleball, the emery ball, and the screwball. This second revolution was initiated less predictably shortly after the turn of the century.

It may be argued, especially by those who know a great deal more about pitching than I do, that the pitches included in these families are not similar enough to warrant this classification. But my designation of them is not based primarily on mechanical likeness. Rather, my contention is that the curveball and the spitball created climates in which pitchers felt that it was worth putting in the considerable time necessary to master a new pitch.

The second of these revolutions had finished running its course by about 1915. Since then the number of new pitches has been quite limited, which is not to say insignificant. The primary additions to the pitcher's repertoire since then have been hybrids—the slider, the circle change, the split-fingered fastball, and the cutter—and novelty pitches, such as the eephus and the extremely short-lived kimono pitch (see **3.2.17**).

3.2.1 Fastball. The fastball must have already been a familiar part of baseball by 1854, when rule makers first specified the distance that the pitcher must stand from the batter. As baseball's first pitch, it was also the first pitch to prompt talk of banning. It would of course have been impossible to legislate the maximum speed at which a ball could travel, but consideration was given to delivery restrictions that would accomplish this aim. A piece in the

New York Clipper in 1864 counseled: "Umpires must remember, in deciding on this movement of the feet, that no one can lift his foot in delivering a ball until the ball leaves his hand, the lifting of the hind foot being the result of this delivery, as it is from the pressure of the foot on the ground that he derives the power to impel the ball with speed." The same article later noted: "A strict adherence to these new rules must perforce result in there being less speed in pitching, the making of accuracy in aim the great desideratum in effective play, and the transfer of the interest of a match from the pitchers to the basemen and outerfielders" (*New York Clipper*, May 7, 1864). As discussed throughout the section on "Deliveries" (3.1), that strict adherence did not occur, and bases on balls became the primary curb on fast pitching.

3.2.2 Change of Pace. The change of pace, then known as the slow ball, is the only other pitch to have been extensively used before 1870. Its most celebrated early practitioners were Alphonse "Phonney" Martin of the Eckfords of Brooklyn and Harry Wright, who would pitch in relief when opposing batters were teeing off on a fastball pitcher. *Sporting News* noted in 1891, "Martin was celebrated for his slow drop ball up to 1872, depending on his field for outs. Harry Wright was effective with the same ball until the players got more proficient in the use of the bat" (*Sporting News*, December 19, 1891).

A. H. Spink added that Martin was known as "Old Slow Ball," and that his "slow ball came to the plate at such a snail-like pace that it nearly drove the batsman crazy and when he got ready to hit it good and hard it seemed to carrom away from him. Martin pitched the ball with a twist of the fingers and the wrist, manipulating the sphere about as you would a billiard ball when you wanted to put the English on it. His delivery set the spectators as well as the opposing batsmen nearly wild. It was so long and drawn out that it tired the spectators and so slow that it maddened the batsman so that he tried to kill it. Instead of doing that he usually drove the ball high and generally to the left field where Al Gedney, the Eckfords' speediest and best outfielder, generally took good care of it" (A. H. Spink, *The National Game*, 57, 139).

Some have questioned whether Martin or Wright was really throwing a change of pace, since neither had an effective fastball. John Thorn and John Holway suggested that A. G. Spalding was the first to utilize a pitch with the same motion as a fastball but at slower speed (John Thorn and John Holway, *The Pitcher*, 152). A *Sporting Life* correspondent concurred: "Spalding got his first idea of slow pitching from [Harvard catcher] Archie Bush, and is credited with being the first to combine the two styles of slow and swift delivery, or 'change of pace,' without varying the motion of the arm and body" (*Sporting Life*, September 10, 1883). Hugh Fullerton called Charlie Radbourn "the pioneer of the 'slow ball' and the inventor of the change of pace" (*Chicago Tribune*, August 12, 1906).

It seems clear, however, from Henry Chadwick's contemporaneous descriptions that the pitch was being used in the 1860s just as it is today. Chadwick explained in 1867 that Phonney "Martin is not a slow pitcher, his delivery is medium paced, and, what is more, varies in pace as much as any pitcher's delivery we know of, and therein lies much of his success against all but the most experienced batsmen" (*The Ball Player's Chronicle*, June 13, 1867). Two years later he suggested that Rynie Wolters should "try to acquire Harry Wright's strong point of changing his pace in delivery without any change of motion—one of the most effective points there is in pitching" (*National Chronicle*, February 13, 1869). Elsewhere he described Wright as "a great coaxer, the ball coming at one time so slow that the striker will hit too quick, either missing or making a weak blow; or little above medium pace causing them to strike too slow, with the same result" (*National Chronicle*, June 5, 1869).

Chadwick also observed that "J. Williams, the Capital pitcher, would occasionally drop a ball short, but the change from swift to slow was too apparent to be effective. This style to work well must be done on the sly, the change of pace not being perceptible" (*The Ball Player's Chronicle*, July 18, 1867). That same James Williams was the manager of the St. Louis Brown Stockings seventeen years later when he reviewed the history of pitching. Williams observed then that until the 1870s "very little latitude was given the pitcher. The only way of outwitting the batsman was by a change of pace" (*St. Louis Post-Dispatch*, January 2, 1884).

Chadwick summed up in 1871: "Nothing so bothers the general class of batsmen as a sudden change of pace in pitching, but to be effective in deceiving the batsman, it must be disguised. For instance, when taking his position at the bat to face a swift pitcher he sees the balls pass him at great speed and at once settles himself to strike quickly at the ball. Just as he is prepared to do this the ball is 'dropped short,' that is, it is sent in at a pace a third less swift than before—not tossed in, however—and the batsman, not expecting it, strikes too quickly" (*New York Clipper*, February 4, 1871).

3.2.3 **Curves.** Few if any origins have been as heatedly disputed as those of the curveball. Sometime during the 1870s, Fred Goldsmith gave a demonstration of the curveball at the Capitoline Grounds in Brooklyn. By the time Goldsmith died in 1939, however, Arthur "Candy" Cummings was generally considered to have invented the curveball. The *Detroit News* announced Goldsmith's death with the headline "Goldsmith Dies Insisting He Invented Curve Ball," and this was almost literally true. Goldsmith still had in his possession a newspaper clipping about his demonstration, in which Henry Chadwick wrote, "This feat was successfully accomplished six or eight times and that which had up to this point been considered an optical illusion and against all rules of philosophy was now an established fact." (The event was said to have taken place on August 16, 1870, but there is no contemporary account of it, and Goldsmith's age suggests that it was actually several years later.)

Writer Bob Carroll asked rhetorically, "Who cares? All right, let's say Candy [Cummings] DID invent the curveball; it makes a nice footnote. . . . Some other guys invented the sacrifice, the hit-and-run, the stolen base, and on and on. How come none of those people—and most of them are known—have not been elected to the Hall of Fame? Is the curveball really of such overriding importance in the history of baseball that its inventor alone gets a plaque at Cooperstown?" (Bob Carroll, *Baseball Between the Lies*, 27). Well, yes.

The first known effort to determine the inventor of the curveball was made by the *Philadelphia Press* in 1883, and there were already "a good many claimants." That list has only grown since then, and the entrants range from the sublime to the ridiculous. Let's consider the more serious claims in reverse chronological order.

Yale pitcher Charles Hammond Avery reportedly used the curveball to pitch a celebrated shutout of Harvard in 1874 and another one against Princeton on May 29, 1875. As a result, the *Philadelphia Press* article observed, "College men, with the exception of those from Harvard, always insist that Avery brought [the curve] to light at Yale, while the Harvard men, who naturally would refuse to see a curve of two feet in a Yale pitcher's delivery, incline to the opinion that [Joseph McElroy] Mann of Princeton was first on the diamond with it. Harvard's men have grounds for their belief, from the fact that the Harvard team first had practical sight of the curve at Princeton in 1874; but, as it did not have the effect of winning the game from them there, they regarded it more as a curiosity than anything of importance in the game. The fact was that Mann was so much excited about his new delivery that he did not know when to quit, and after the Harvard men had noticed that the ball always turned about a foot outward after leaving the pitcher's hand they made their calculations and hammered at it accordingly. Mann had only one curve, and he did not even vary it by straight balls, so it failed of success against the straight pitching and fine headwork of [Harold] Ernst and [James] Tyng. Avery, at Yale, came out with his curve the same year, and the next year, by his effective pitching, helped his team to the championship" (*Philadelphia Press*, reprinted in the *Grand Rapids* [Mich.] *Morning Democrat*, September 2, 1883).

In 1900, Mann wrote to the *New York Times* to give his version of events after twenty-six years during which "I have never written a line to establish my claim to the honor of its introduction." He acknowledged that nobody really invented the curveball: "As long as baseball has been played and baseballs have had seams with which to catch the air curve balls have been thrown, and the curve was especially noticeable in the case of a left-handed thrower, whose curve was in the opposite direction from that of a right-handed thrower."

Mann went on to make the odd claim that even though "curve balls have always been thrown . . . no one thought of using them in the pitching department till 1874" when he conceived of the idea. His inspiration was Cummings, who "came to Princeton, and before the game and between innings he would stand on the home plate and pitch (he did not throw underhand) the ball down to second base, starting it at an angle of about forty-five degrees. I was greatly interested and wondered how he got the ball to curve as it did. It was said by his catcher that sometimes he pitched a ball that curved, but I failed to notice any curve that day."

Mann was further intrigued when the Philadelphia club came to Princeton and, during practice, the left fielder "would throw the ball with force sufficient to carry it all the way to right field, but after going part of the way the ball would suddenly shoot down and fall far short of right field." Mann thought the matter over, practiced a number of approaches, and finally found one that worked. He spent the winter refining his technique while also arriving at an understanding of the aerodynamics of the pitch (which he explained in considerable detail).

Mann concluded, "In the Spring I had the pleasure of seeing many surprised batters, who did not seem to be able to comprehend the situation. Unfortunately I was quite young at the time and did not know how to conceal the manner in which I produced the curve, and it was only a short time before it spread all over the country, which accounts for the confusion as to who introduced it. I was on the Princeton nine in 1873, 1874, 1875, and 1876 and batted against all the then famous pitchers, and I do not recall a single one who could curve a ball prior to 1874, when I, as I said above, accidentally stumbled upon it and then worked it out. . . . I think I have said enough to establish the fact that I was the one who initiated the movement and revolutionized the pitching department of baseball."

Mann believed that Avery didn't use the pitch until 1875, and his teammate W. J. Henderson vouched for this version of events. But a Yale alumnus asserted in the same issue that "Avery certainly pitched with a curve in 1874" (*New York Times*, June 10, 1900).

It is beyond question that Mann and Avery played an important role in popularizing the curveball. The comments of Harvard's James Tyng, reprinted later in this entry, attest to the fact that the pitch was new to many observers. But it is hard to make a serious case that either Mann or Avery "initiated the movement." Despite his obvious intelligence, Joseph Mann seems not to have realized how inconceivable it was that Cummings had been practicing throwing a curve but that neither he nor anyone before Mann had thought of using it for pitching. Mann's claims are further weakened by his later declaration that his inspiration to develop the curve came when he faced Cummings and Cummings threw a pitch that caused catcher Doug Allison to say, "'That ball went zig-zag.' He meant, of course, that the curve was too great for him to judge" (J. C. Kofoed, "Early History of Curve Pitching," *Baseball Magazine*, August 1915, 56).

Moreover, as the *Press* pointed out, before either Mann or Avery came along, "curve pitching was practiced in professional games and, though its nature was not much understood, everybody seemed to know that a peculiar kind of ball could be delivered, and that Matthews [Bobby Mathews], the present 'curver' for the Athletics, was the man who was doing it" (*Philadelphia Press*, reprinted in the *Grand Rapids* [Mich.] *Morning Democrat*, September 2, 1883).

Bobby Mathews occupies a unique role in this saga. While everyone agreed that Mathews was one of the earliest pitchers to master the curveball, he himself disavowed any credit for inventing the pitch: "Matthews himself says that Cummings was curving the ball before he knew anything about it, and he gives further credit to Cummings by adding that he got his first lessons in the art by watching the Mutual pitcher's delivery. Cummings' delivery was known to every man in the profession as very peculiar, and Matthews, whose straight work was beginning to give way before it, made up his mind to take advantage of a position near the bat to learn the secret. He watched Cummings' hands carefully, noting how he held the ball and how he let it go, and after a few weeks' careful practice in the same way could see the curve in his own delivery. Then he began to use it in matches, striking men out in a way that no one but Cummings had ever done before, and in a short time he was known as one of the most effective pitchers in the field" (*Philadelphia Press*, reprinted in the *Grand Rapids* [Mich.] *Morning Democrat*, September 2, 1883).

Fred Goldsmith's case rested almost entirely upon his claim of having given the first exhibition of the curveball. But I have found no support for Goldsmith among his contemporaries, and what really militates against him is his year of birth—1856. To give precedence to Goldsmith, all earlier claimants must be refuted. That would be difficult to do if Goldsmith's demonstration actually occurred in 1870 and impossible if, as seems much more likely, it actually happened in the mid-1870s.

Candy Cummings, in contrast, did have support from his peers. In addition to Mathews's previously mentioned statements, Joe Start told *Sporting Life* in 1895 that he had no doubt that Cummings invented the curveball.

Start explained that he and Cummings grew up on the same lots and that Cummings was working on the pitch between 1866 and 1870 (*Sporting Life*, November 16, 1895). A. G. Spalding also endorsed Cummings as the first pitcher to throw a curve (*Fort Wayne News*, May 6, 1895; A. G. Spalding, *America's National Game*, 484).

Tim Murnane considered it an open-and-shut case: "There may be some doubt as to who discovered the North Pole, but none whatsoever as to the boy who discovered and first brought into practical use the curving of a base ball. . . . 'Did Shakespeare write Hamlet?' 'Did Edison invent the kinetiscope [sic]?' They surely did. Well, just as certain did Arthur Cummings not only discover but was the first to make use of curved pitching" (*Sporting News*, November 4, 1909).

On another occasion, Murnane noted that George Wright also credited Cummings with throwing the first curve. Wright informed Murnane that forty years after the fact he still remembered the first time he saw Cummings's curve "as if it were only yesterday." The ball "came straight for the center of the plate and then took a wide curve." Wright said that the pitch was quite unlike anything he had previously seen from Bobby Mathews (who he claimed didn't have a true curve until 1879) or Phonney Martin (*Fort Wayne News*, March 28, 1911).

Cummings himself gave several different accounts of how he first came to throw the curveball, and while many of the details remained the same, there was a noticeable shift in emphasis over the years. The first two that I'm aware of appeared in the *Boston Globe* on April 6, 1896, and in the *Sporting News* on February 20, 1897. They have such similar passages that it is quite possible the author of the second piece relied in part on the earlier article.

The latter version began with a very intriguing fact: "Mr. Cummings was born in Ware, Mass., on October 17, 1848, and played the old-fashioned game that prevailed in the Bay State before he moved to Brooklyn with his parents." In the earlier article, much of which was a letter from Cummings to Tim Murnane, Cummings confirmed that he played the "old Massachusetts game" before the family's move.

While neither account elaborated on the significance, this is a potentially crucial detail. In the "Massachusetts game" of the 1850s, pitchers threw overhand, which made the curveball much more viable than under the restrictions imposed by the Knickerbockers. The 1860 census shows the Cummings family already in Brooklyn, and there is contradictory evidence as to when they arrived there; but Cummings's exposure to the "Massachusetts game" may have been a key factor in his subsequent interest in the curveball.

Cummings's comments did not discuss this point, but he did make several of the assertions that would later become celebrated: "It was in a game against the collegians that I first used the curve. I got my theory from throwing clam shells in playing with boys. I saw that they curved to the right and left and I conceived the idea of trying to make a base ball do the same thing. After a great deal of constant practice I accomplished the feat. I received no encouragement from base ball experts and was, in fact, laughed at as no one thought it could be done."

He continued to recount how he "went to work secretly" because of the "chaffing" from his friends and "kept on practicing for it was the dream of my boyhood days." Finally he was able to unveil the pitch against the celebrated Harvard catcher Archie Bush and realized with exultance: "I had succeeded at last" ("Curved Balls," *Sporting News*, February 20, 1897).

Cummings also included some important details that would be conspicuously absent from later versions. In his letter to Murnane he pointed out that it was "no easy job for a pitcher to deliver a ball in those days, as he had to keep both feet on the ground and not raise either until after the ball left his hand, and had to keep the arm close to his side and deliver the ball with a perpendicular swing." In the version published the following year, Cummings added, "Some of the pitchers who have claimed to be the inventor of curving the ball, but who did not introduce it in their work until several years afterward, had to deliver the ball on a level with their waist to make it curve at all. Keeping both feet on the ground while delivering the ball was a hard strain, as the wrist and second finger did all the work. I snapped the ball like a whip and this caused me to throw my wrist bone out of place quite often. During one season I was compelled to wear a rubber supporter the whole time. I had great speed, however, even if I was of light frame and apparently not powerful" ("Curved Balls," *Sporting News*, February 20, 1897).

These two accounts suggest an explanation of how Cummings learned to throw the curve that to my mind is more plausible than the version that later emerged. He had probably seen rudimentary curves thrown as a youngster in Massachusetts, but when he moved to Brooklyn and began playing the "New York game," the delivery restrictions made the pitch seem impossible. Yet the example of throwing clamshells made him think that it might be possible, and his arm strength and relentless practice enabled him to realize his ambition.

Unfortunately this version is too complex to make for good storytelling, and in later renderings the crucial factor of the delivery restrictions disappeared. In 1900, Tim Murnane presented a simplified version in which Cummings began trying to master the curve around 1866 but did not succeed until facing Archie Bush two years later. He gave the ball an extra twist, and "When Bush struck at the ball it seemed to go about a foot beyond the end of his stick. I tried again with the same result, and then I realized at last that I had succeeded in mastering the curve, something I had been after for two years" (*Boston Globe*, February 20, 1900). While the basic details are similar, the emphasis has begun to shift to the moment of discovery.

A 1902 book by Seymour Church included this account: "Cummings was one day pitching against a picked nine, and noticed the ball curving. He had no difficulty in striking the batsmen out, and went home that night and tried to study the phenomena [sic]. The next day he invited some gentlemen friends out to see him work. They laughed at him, and when he tried to convince them that he could accomplish what he claimed, he failed, as no doubt, in his anxiety, he sent the ball too fast, and very little curve can be gotten out of a speedily pitched ball. The next day he went out with his catcher, and discovered that the curve came from a certain twist he gave his wrist. He worked hard until he secured full control of the new movement, and then astonished the base ball and scientific world" (Seymour Church, *Base Ball*, 33). In this version, not only have important details begun to disappear but also a gradual process of discovery has begun to give way to a "Eureka" moment.

Cummings also wrote a 1908 article entitled "How I Curved the First Ball," and the account shows that he had begun to emphasize the details that would appeal to an audience too young to remember the delivery restrictions of the 1860s. In it, Cummings recalled that in the summer of 1863 he and some other boys were throwing clamshells when "it came to me that it would be a good joke on the boys if I could make a baseball curve the same way." He experimented with deliveries for a year and a half, receiving "not one single word of encouragement in all that time, while my attempts were a standing joke among my friends." But he persevered and by 1867 was able to use the pitch to great effect (Arthur Cummings, "How I Curved the First Ball," *Baseball Magazine*, September 1908; reprinted in John Thorn and John Holway, *The Pitcher*, 150 and Roger Kahn, *The Head Game*, 18–21).

In 1910, Alfred Spink reported that Cummings had recently said, "I don't think I was the first man to pitch a curved ball. I think that [Alphonse "Phonney"] Martin of the old Eckfords had the curve—not mine but a kind of curve; and I am sure that [George] Zettlein . . . pitched a curved ball, and that [Charley] Pabor . . . pitched a curve when he was playing with the old Unions of Morrisania, New York. . . .

"But none of these pitchers knew that he had a curve, and I suppose it is fair to say that I was the first to find out what a curve was and how it was done.

"[Nat] Hicks was catcher and I was pitcher of the semi-professional Stars of Brooklyn. I noticed that very few batsmen could hit me, and finally I saw that when I pitched the ball it swerved outward before it reached the batsman. Then, when I had thought about this a little, I said to myself: 'That ball does not go in a straight line until it begins to fall; it curves outside of the horizontal line, and that is the reason why batsmen can not hit it.'

"Well, I studied and experimented until at last I found that if I held the ball between my fingers and thumb in a certain way, and gave it a certain twist of the wrist just as I delivered it, then the resultant motion that the ball took produced a curve. I wondered how that could be, and I made up my mind that the rotary motion of the ball created a vacuum on one side, the outside, and the pressure of the air on the other side caused it to swerve. I had found out the secret of the curved ball. I afterwards taught it to Tommy Bond, and he could make a ball curve either way" (A. H. Spink, *The National Game*, 139–140).

In 1919, Cummings was quoted thus: "I hit upon the curve ball quite accidentally. Just as I was about to deliver the ball in the usual way one day I lost my balance. That threw my arm out of line and when the ball left my hand there was a twist of my wrist. Imagine my surprise when the ball went sailing up to the plate on a direct line only to take a sharp outcurve as the batsman swung for it. Naturally, noticing the effect on the ball with such wrist motion I practiced the next morning with my catcher and very shortly I had perfected an outcurve" ("Sport World with James J. Corbett," syndicated column, *Fort Wayne News and Sentinel*, February 18, 1919).

In 1921, Cummings provided the *Sporting News* with another account that included many of the by now familiar details. He explained that throwing clamshells as a boy "gave me the idea and the inspiration" that a baseball might be made to curve in a similar manner. He continued to try, though his friends told him it couldn't be done, and finally got the motion down. Cummings also mentioned the role of the restrictions on deliveries, claiming that the only others who ever mastered the underhand curve were Mathews, Avery, and Mann. But there was an intriguing new element. Cummings now maintained that he pitched his first curveball in 1864 yet was "jealous of his discovery" and did not tell anyone about it so that he could be the only one to benefit from it (*Sporting News*, December 29, 1921).

Cummings died in 1924, but even this did not staunch the flow of accounts of the origins of the curveball. Five years later sportswriter Bozeman Bulger maintained that he had been told yet another version: "Cummings often said that he got the idea from watching a billiard ball spin and curve when the player applied English—hitting the ball on one side, with the tip of the cue" (Bozeman Bulger, "Curveball Cause [sic] Revolution," *Lincoln* [Nebr.] *Evening Journal*, January 22, 1929).

Finally we come to a ghastly history of the curveball written by a man named Harold C. Burr and published in *Sporting News* in 1942. Burr embellished the story with invented dialogue ("Gee whillikins! Wouldn't it be great if I could make a baseball curve like that?") and colorful details ("One of the other boys overheard young Art Cummings at his day-dreaming. He nudged those nearest, beckoned to others to come a-running, and they gathered around Cummings in the glee of ghoulish youth . . .") (*Sporting News*, November 19, 1942). It is sad that such obvious fabrications are passed off as baseball history.

Many different interpretations may be placed on this wide variety of accounts. One is to focus on the inconsistencies and simply disregard all the stories, but this seems extreme. Cummings never comes across as a blowhard, and the role he gives himself is no greater than the one with which he is credited by some of the disinterested firsthand observers. His first account was given about thirty years after the events being described, so we may expect him to be hazy about some of the details, yet he was only in his late forties at the time.

The many subsequent versions include some apparent contradictions, but by and large what changes is the emphasis: a complex sequence of events revolving around pitching restrictions was gradually simplified to a "Eureka!" moment. The reporters who recounted these versions were undoubtedly one factor in their variations. In addition, any oft-told story usually starts to take on some of the characteristics that its audience hopes to hear, and Cummings obviously was asked about the curve many times. In his later years his audience was too young to appreciate the pitching restrictions of the 1860s, so they seized instead upon the now-famous "clamshells" image and the triumphant moment in which he realized he had mastered the pitch. As researcher Joe Overfield asked rhetorically after analyzing yet another account: "Is this history, or is it a case of history being created simply because a story has been repeated so many times?" (Joseph M. Overfield, "William Arthur Cummings," in Frederick Ivor-Campbell, Robert L. Tiemann and Mark Rucker, eds., *Baseball's First Stars*, 43).

In any event, while Cummings unquestionably played a major role in popularizing the curveball, he is far from the earliest candidate for the first pitcher to throw it. Jimmy Wood, who saw all the great early pitchers, nominated Joe Sprague as the first to throw the curveball: "Sprague threw a curve ball—that was back in 1862—which means that Sprague, not Arthur Cummins [sic], of the Brooklyn Stars of 1863–64, or Bobby Mathews, of the Baltimores of 1866–67 was the original curve ball pitcher. . . . We always noticed that some of Sprague's deliveries took a sharp twist, sometimes turning in and sometimes turning away from the batter. All of us used to remark about the peculiar gyrations of the ball that he threw. It was not until some years later, however, when curved balls became an established fact, that we recognized the delivery, then called a curve as the same kind of ball that Sprague had thrown in 1862 and 1863" (James Wood, as told to Frank G. Menke, "Baseball in By-Gone Days," part 3, syndicated column, *Indiana* [Pa.] *Evening Gazette*, August 17, 1916). Another teammate, Waddy Beach, also maintained that Sprague "could and did curve the ball while pitching for the Eckfords in 1863" (quoted by William Rankin in *Sporting News*, May 25, 1901; he cites it as originating in the *New York Clipper* in the summer of 1883 but does not provide an exact date).

Cummings himself, on a couple of different occasions, allowed that Phonney Martin "was throwing something akin to a curve some years before my time" ("Sport World with James J. Corbett," syndicated column, *Fort Wayne News and Sentinel*, February 18, 1919; also A. H. Spink, *The National Game*, 139–140, as noted earlier). A. H. Spink claimed that Martin's slow ball would reach the plate and take "a sudden swerve away and the batter would miss. Martin pitched the ball with a twist of the fingers and wrist, manipulating it much as does a billiard player when he wants to put English on a billiard ball" (A. H. Spink, *The National Game*, 139). William Rankin cited an 1870 reference to "the Martin style of curved line delivery" (*New York Clipper*, April 2, 1870; quoted in *Sporting News*, May 25, 1901). On the other hand, George Wright maintained that Martin "simply had a slow 'teaser,' as we called it, something after the style of a slow ball tossed up by my brother Harry. The ball Martin tossed up was hard to meet fair, as he sent it in with a spin, but it was a slow ball, usually sent very high, that dropped as it reached the plate without the semblance of a curve" (quoted by Tim Murnane, *Fort Wayne News*, March 28, 1911).

There are still earlier intimations of the pitch beginning to develop. An 1863 account described Princeton pitcher Frank Henry as having given his pitches "a heavy twist that was extremely irregular" (J. C. Kofoed, "Early History of Curve Pitching," *Baseball Magazine*, August 1915, 56). Jim Creighton is sometimes said to have pitched a curve, though contemporary descriptions of his pitches sound more like fastballs with considerable movement. Henry Chadwick noted in 1860 that it was advantageous to "impart a bias or twist to the ball" (*Beadle's Dime Base-Ball Player 1860*, 22). One of the participants in the first intercollegiate match, played between Amherst and Williams in 1859, later recalled that Amherst's pitcher, Henry D. Hyde, "had a wonderful knack of making the ball curve in to the catcher" (quoted in Joel Zoss and John Bowman, *Diamonds in the Rough*, 72). Melvin Adelman discovered an 1857 article that noted, "many think that a ball that will curve as it approaches the striker is much more difficult to bat than one that takes a straight course" (*Porter's Spirit of the Times*, March 7, 1857; quoted in Melvin Adelman, *A Sporting Time*, 129).

William Rankin cited this description of a Knickerbockers player named Richard Stevens in 1856: "as pitcher [he] sends the ball with exceeding velocity, and he who strikes it fairly must be a fine batsman. It is questionable, however, whether his style of pitching is most successful, many believing a slow ball curving near the bat, to be the most effective" (*Porter's Spirit of the Times*, December 6, 1856; quoted in *Sporting News*, May 25, 1901). The *Detroit Free Press* reported in 1881, "On the last day of June, 1854, the valiant Knickerbockers were humbled. On that day the feeder of the Gothams resorted to what is now known as the 'Chicago snake ball,' and the Knickerbockers could not get a nick of it" (*Detroit Free Press*, August 27, 1881). David Block discovered an 1845 reference to "one who, in playing 'base,' screws his ball, as the expression is among boys" (*The Knickerbocker*, vol. 26, November 1845, 426–427; quoted in David Block, *Baseball Before We Knew It*, 207–208).

In 1923, Grantland Rice used his syndicated column to revisit the question of who pitched the first curveball and got an unexpected response. A man named William H. Allison wrote, "In July, 1897, I sat at table in a boarding house in London, by the side of a Dartmouth graduate of the class of 1844. He told me one day that when he was in college he discovered that he could throw a ball so that it would curve. As a result, in the crude game which preceded baseball the boys would not allow him to pitch. This man, who for years was president of the Newton Theological Institution and had been my own teacher of systematic theology, was Dr. Allan [sic] Hovey, whose youngest son made a reputation in baseball at both Brown and Harvard and won the tennis championship at Newport in 1895" (Grantland Rice, "The Sportlight," syndicated column, April 13, 1923).

A second letter writer, W. D. Q., Dartmouth, '87, added: "My father was of the class of 1846 at Dartmouth, and he told me of the peculiar ability of Hovey, '44, to throw a ball with a strange curve, 'benders,' they called it then. Everyone was puzzled to know how such a ball was thrown. But it seems to me, looking back upon the feat, that it must have been the original curve. I don't believe anyone can go back of 1844 and it is now perfectly established that Hovey, Dartmouth '44, was curving the ball" (Grantland Rice, "The Sportlight," syndicated column, April 24, 1923).

Finally, a letter from one of Dr. Alvah Hovey's sons read: "I had no idea any one outside of the family had ever heard him speak of it. Not until many years later, when the curve ball had become common, did he recognize just what he had been doing with the ball in the old days. He merely remembered that the ball seemed to jump away from the bat at the critical moment. How he did it he said he never knew.

"It was a fact, however, that his opponents in the informal games then played refused to play if he was put in to pitch. Perhaps that entitles him to another record—that of being the first pitcher too good to be allowed to play. I can picture him saying in his quiet vein of humor: 'I have not noticed Yale refusing to play Harvard because you are on the team'" (Grantland Rice, "The Sportlight," syndicated column, April 28, 1923).

How do we make sense of these wildly divergent claims? It's actually not as difficult as it may appear, for three reasons. First, the curveball occupies a singular place among baseball firsts since it is difficult to identify (unlike, say, a shin guard). Many have assumed that the first to demonstrate a curveball *to them* must have invented it.

Second, once its existence is conceded, a true curveball can be difficult to distinguish from a pitch with a slightly different break. Even today, differences in trajectory, direction of break, and the natural movement produced by a pitcher's arm action combine to make the distinctions between pitches less than crystal clear.

Fans who struggle to tell one breaking ball from another may take some consolation from the words of former Atlanta Braves pitching coach Leo Mazzone: "I don't really like the terms slider or curve all that much. . . . Give me a hundred experts, show them a good sharp breaking pitch. Half will say it was a curve and the other half will say it was a slider. What we want at Atlanta is a quality breaking ball. To us, that isn't a nasty curve or a nasty slider. We call it an Atlanta Braves–quality breaking ball. The opposition can call it whatever the hell they like" (quoted in Roger Kahn, *The Head Game*, 291). The difficulty of distinguishing one breaking pitch from another was even more pronounced in the days when the whole idea of a curve was still a novelty. While it is safe to assume that very early descriptions of pitches with a "twist" or "bias" are not referring to a true curveball, it is significant that the idea of such trajectories was in currency that early.

Third, and most important, the curveball was difficult if not impossible to pitch in games played by the Knickerbockers' rules before restrictions on deliveries began to be relaxed in 1872. Yet the "Massachusetts" version of baseball played in New England in the 1840s and 1850s allowed overhand deliveries, which makes the claims on behalf of Henry Hyde and Alvah Hovey very plausible and potentially puts the origins of "Candy" Cummings's curve in a very different light.

Under the New York rules, only a few pitchers were able to throw curves before the 1870s, and even they probably had to bend the rules to do so. Deacon White later claimed that Candy Cummings "used to curve a ball as early as 1868, but not in regulation games. That was impossible, because the rules then prohibited a wrist throw. Pitchers then were forced to throw underhanded with a stiff arm. If a pitcher bent or twisted his wrist, he was disqualified. Cummings curved a ball across the infield by using a wrist snap during practice, but he couldn't use it in a game—that is, until the rules were changed in 1872" (Gene Kessler, "Deacon White, Oldest Living Player, at 92 Recalls Highlights of Historic Career That Started in 1868," *Sporting News*, June 22, 1939, 19).

As Johnny Evers and Hugh Fullerton explained in 1910: "The first curves pitched were of the variety now known as the 'barrel hoop.' It was a slow curve, pitched underhand, with the hand swung nearly to the level of the knee, fingers downward and hand held almost at right angles with the wrist. As the hand was swung the wrist was jerked sharply and the ball, sliding off the first finger, revolved rapidly and the air pressure on one side of the sphere and the partial vacuum on the other caused by the rotation, forced the ball to move in a slow wide arc. All curves are developments of the 'barrel hoop,' the same principle entering into each" (John J. Evers and Hugh S. Fullerton, *Touching Second*, 103–104).

Note, however, that even the barrel hoop curve was not being pitched with a straight arm. Sportswriter J. C. Kofoed similarly offered a detailed description of the efforts of an early Princeton pitcher named Ed Davis to make the ball swerve but stressed that Davis did so only by breaking the rule that "called for a straight arm delivery" (J. C. Kofoed, "Early History of Curve Pitching," *Baseball Magazine*, August 1915, 56).

This distinction makes it possible to make sense of the baffling number of claimants to having introduced the curveball. As long as the pitch remained tantalizingly just outside the reach of being delivered legally, it was inevitable that a series of pitchers would discover it, experiment with it, find it impossible to pitch legally, and concentrate on other aspects of the art of pitching.

Perhaps the best concise summary of the origins of the curveball is to say that the idea is an old one, predating even the Knickerbocker rules in areas where overhand deliveries were allowed. But the idea was not truly a practical one for the New York version of baseball as long as the rules mandated a straight-arm delivery and a release point below the knee. Henry Chadwick maintained that "the horizontal curve of the ball through the air" was "practically unknown in the days of the old club at Hoboken" (Henry Chadwick, "The Art of Pitching," *Outing*, May 1889, 119).

According to Cummings, the only pitchers who threw a true underhanded curve were himself, Mathews, Mann, and Avery (*Sporting News*, December 29, 1921). Even though the hip-level release was legalized in 1872, Tim Murnane claimed that Cummings and Mathews were still the only pitchers throwing curves in 1873 (*Boston Globe*, January 31, 1915). The situation began to change in 1874, with Chadwick writing at the season's end: "There is a peculiarity of delivery which Creighton had not, and which some of our pitchers now possess, which is worth mentioning, and that is the power to deliver the ball with that puzzling horizontal curve which marks the delivery of Mathews and Cummings" (undated review of 1874 season, Chadwick Scrapbooks).

This delay does not mean that pitchers were not experimenting with the pitch before the rule change of 1872. Deacon White later recalled that pitchers were practicing curves seriously as early as 1870, in anticipation that the delivery rules would be relaxed (Gene Kessler, "Deacon White, Oldest Living Player, at 92 Recalls Highlights of Historic Career That Started in 1868," *Sporting News*, June 22, 1939, 19). Yet the curve is not an easy pitch to master, especially with no one willing to act as tutor, and it took a couple of years for the pitch to spread.

This version of events may be much less appealing than the story about clamshells, but it seems to me to be more satisfactory. The sportswriter and historian William Rankin considered the matter in 1901, after Cummings had first claimed credit and when many of the principles were still alive, and reached a similar conclusion: "It is no unusual thing to hear one or more persons coming to the front and posing as the inventor of some important discovery, especially if the real inventor has been unknown to fame. The curve in pitching seems to belong to this class of invention. Many persons have gained renown on the ball field by their cleverness in pitching curves, drops, etc., and may have added to the effectiveness and general conduciveness of that style of delivery, but that does not entitle any of them to the honor of having discovered the curve" (*Sporting News*, May 25, 1901).

Whether or not anyone deserves credit for inventing the pitch, it is difficult to overstate the extent to which the curveball revolutionized baseball in the years after the breakout year of 1874. Most obviously, it changed pitching so fundamentally that "Other pitchers had to take up the curve or quit playing" (*Philadelphia Press*, reprinted in the *Grand Rapids* [Mich.] *Morning Democrat*, September 2, 1883). The success of a curveball pitcher in a tournament in Atlanta around 1879 "ended the 'tournamena' [sic] and 'straight' pitching in Atlanta. . . . The Cranks began to clamor for 'curved' pitching and never stopped until the Southern League was formed" (*Atlanta Constitution*, February 12, 1893).

Henry Chadwick observed after the 1877 season that club managers "seemed to turn up their nose at any man who 'hadn't got the curve'" (*New York Clipper*, December 8, 1877). A year later he added: "during 1878 a pitcher without the 'curve' was nowhere" (*New York Clipper*, January 11, 1879). With their livelihoods at stake, and the ever-present threat that a ban would be placed on any effective technique, pitchers often became secretive or proprietary. An 1875 account noted: "[George] Bradley, of the St. Louis Base Ball Club, has been after Jim Devlin, of the Louisville Nine, and endeavored to learn his 'curve.' But Devlin has refused to explain it to him" (*St. Louis Globe-Democrat*, December 13, 1875). As noted earlier, late in life Candy Cummings said that he had been "jealous of his discovery," and he reported with evident satisfaction that Jim Galvin inspected Cummings's delivery "closely and confessed that he could not see what was going on" (*Sporting News*, December 29, 1921).

Another example of the ability of the curveball to turn baseball on its head was offered in 1897 by a man named Bennett Wilson. In the 1870s, Wilson had been the pitcher on a club called the Lurlines of Brooklyn that included future major league pitching stars Larry Corcoran, Terry Larkin, and Mickey Welch. Welch was his catcher, but that was to change: "When curve pitching came into vogue, Mr. Wilson says, he and his associates gathered in a big back yard almost every day and used a clothes line horse, which was used by an old widow on which to dry her washing, with which to gain control of the various curves. The horizontal bar across the horse was supposed to represent the height of the batter's knees or waist and the ball was curved around the main sticks. This afforded an effective means of practice and Corcoran and Wilson soon had all the curves at their command" (*Brooklyn Eagle*, April 2, 1897). Before long, Welch was experimenting with the pitch as well, and his days as a catcher were numbered.

The curve also proved to be a litmus test for batters, producing precursors of what Grantland Rice would call the "favorite baseball story . . . about the training camp rookie who wired back to his folks: 'You can expect me any day, now, they're beginning to curve 'em'" (Grantland Rice, "The Sportlight," syndicated column, March 10, 1932).

Harvard's James Tyng later offered a captivating account of how his team responded to Joseph Mann's curveball in 1875: "Out of the first nine men at the bat eight, I think, were unable to hit the ball. We had no idea what was the trouble, except that the bat and ball seemed to have a repulsion for each other which we could not overcome. About the fifth inning one of our men, who had been standing behind the catcher, came back with the announcement that the balls were curving away from the batsman. There was a general exodus on our part to the backstop to watch this unheard of phenomenon. Sure enough, there were the balls coming in for the middle of the plate and curving off beyond the reach of the bat" (*Harper's Weekly*; quoted in Mann's letter to the *New York Times*, June 10, 1900).

There was similar pathos in an 1877 lament from Owosso, Michigan, where the batters found they could not reach the pitches of a curve pitcher from Flint and thought it unfair that they were called out for trying to move to a place where they could reach them (*Owosso Weekly Press*, August 8, 1877).

When a touring club from San Francisco played a game in Detroit in 1876, they got the surprise of their lives. The Aetnas of Detroit club had acquired a curve pitcher named J. A. Sullivan and a catcher named Edward Brown who knew how to hold him: "Brown would stand away back in the grass to the right of the pitcher, and Sullivan would work the out curve, which was the only one he knew, and man after man was mowed down before him" (*Boston Globe*, October 12, 1887). Eighteen of the visiting batters had the same demoralizing experience: "When the ball starts the striker would wager that it was coming just where he wanted it, but just as he nerves up to bat the ball dodges away and just out of the reach of the bat" (*Detroit Free Press*, July 16, 1876).

The frustration of flailing away at a ball that suddenly veered out of reach was especially palpable for right-handed hitters. A writer later reminisced that in 1876 "pitchers first introduced the wide-out curve. [Terry] Larkin had the first one ever seen [in Chicago] and it was thought to be a wonder. In fact, the papers and people generally refused to believe that it was possible to curve a ball. A great many writers insisted that there was some trick about it. [Jimmy] Hallinan was the only batter that could hit him, and he because he was left-handed" (*Chicago Tribune*, April 1, 1894).

The curve changed not only the lives of batters and pitchers, but also the competitive balance of baseball by renewing the hopes of many clubs. The rise of professionalism in the late 1860s and 1870s had presented a great challenge to the game. Clubs felt pressured to choose between hiring nine professionals and becoming noncompetitive, a dilemma that created a wide talent gap and did great damage to baseball. The curveball revolution changed that by showing that it only took a curve pitcher and a reliable catcher to elevate a club's fortunes.

For example, in 1877 a Savannah pitcher named Frank Lincoln was the first Georgian to master the curveball. It soon became obvious that this one pitch more than offset the advantages held by a larger city like Atlanta. Savannah became state champions, but more important was the renewed sense of hope across the state: "The curved pitching, as done by Lincoln, aroused the amateur clubs in Georgia" (*Atlanta Constitution*, February 12, 1893).

For the 1876 season, Chicago had signed A. G. Spalding, the game's premier pitcher. But Spalding did not throw a curve, and the public fascination with the pitch was so great that Spalding later remembered that the club's supporters became "greatly worried back in 1876 because the White Stockings had no 'curve pitcher'" (*Fort Wayne News*, May 6, 1895). The curveball had emerged as the great equalizer.

This new dynamic dashed any remaining hopes that baseball could return to the days when the pitcher was little more than a bystander in a contest between batters and fielders. But that was a small price to pay for reawakening the sense that a small-town club again had a fighting chance. The curveball had, one might say, introduced to baseball the precept that "good pitching beats good hitting."

As the curveball appeared across the country, it was greeted with a mixture of amazement, befuddlement, and disbelief. A player named James Fitzgibbon of the Charter Oak club of Hartford, Connecticut, traveled to Brooklyn in 1867 to play the Excelsiors and found himself unable to hit Candy Cummings's pitching at all (A. H. Spink, *The National Game*, 41). Jacob Morse described the introduction of the curve to Boston around 1874 by a pitcher named George Griffin and observed that it was a life-changing event for at least one batter: "'Jack' Lanning, the veteran . . . made thirteen futile attempts to hit the ball and then congratulated the young man on his success" (*Sporting Life*, March 5, 1898).

Jimmy Clinton had similar memories: "I shall never forget the first curve pitching I ever saw. Tommy Bond did it. It was in a game of the Hartford against St. Louis in '75, and I was umpire. . . . Excitement ran high and all the heelers were on hand, together with an immense crowd. From the first Hartford took a decided lead, and the ill success of the home pets was visited on the umpire, especially as batter after batter of the St. Louis was seen by the audience to jump back from the plate for balls on which I called strikes. The people could not understand it, and hooted and yelled and threatened, and I was beginning to feel rather shaky when I called Pierce [Dickey Pearce] and two or three others of the St. Louis to witness that the balls on which I called strikes cut the plate in two, although they seemed until nearing the plate to be going right for the batter. Pierce confirmed this to the crowd and told them, 'I-hope-I-may-die if it ain't so,' but they wouldn't have it that way. I thanked my lucky stars for a whole hide when the game was over and took the first train for Louisville, without waiting to umpire the other two games for which I had been engaged" (*Sporting Life*, December 3, 1884).

A Kalamazoo paper informed its readers in 1878: "After our boys came back from Ann Arbor they explained the fact of there being such a thing as 'curve pitching,' that being the trick by which the university boys 'foolished' them so badly, and some of our citizens have seemed to doubt it. But WILLIAM L SERGEANT has since got on to the 'curve balls' and has given good practical demonstration of that style of pitching to the entire satisfaction of the incredulous ones. . . . The Sturgis batters would stand up to the home plate grating their teeth and suggestively gazing on the back fence in a manner calculated to impress their many friends and backers that they would make a clean 'three baser,' but to their undisguised astonishment, Sergeant would pitch them one that would make them 'saw the wood'" (*Kalamazoo Daily Telegraph*, May 27, 1878).

John Montgomery Ward was greeted with similar skepticism when he introduced the curveball in Williamsport, Pennsylvania: "Even after observing the uncanny bends and twists that Ward put on the sphere, many refused to believe their eyes. Among them was Ephraim H. Page. Mr. Page scoffed and said it was nothing more than an optical illusion. As proof of this he offered to stand around a corner and let Ward hit him with the ball if such a thing was possible. Ward accepted the defi. Mr. Page took a position out of sight and serenely awaited the result. Ward cut loose with a 'roundhouse' curve that, to the horrified amazement of Ephraim, described a parabola around that corner and plunked him a sickening thud precisely in the tonneau. No further demonstration was needed to convince Mr. Page" (*Williamsport Sunday Grit*, November 7, 1915).

Charley Lamar gave this description of the reception accorded Frank Lincoln when he introduced the curve to Georgia: "In June, 1877 the

'Dixies' met a picked nine at Macon and beat them by a score of 11 to 0. Tom Clayton, of Atlanta, played short for Macon, and did it well, but 'Old Twist 'Em,' as he called Lincoln, had too much 'curve' for the Macon boys, and they met an inglorious defeat." Two months later the Dixies faced a club from Charleston, South Carolina, for the championship of the two states: "The Carolinas were confident of victory. They were fine amateur ball players and their pitcher was very speedy. When assured by the Savannah cranks that they would be unable to hit Lincoln they readily offered to bet any amount that they could 'kill him.' . . . A large amount of money changed hands and the Carolinas and their friends returned to Charleston minus their enthusiasm and their money. They ran the bases and fielded well. But alas! the 'curved' pitching was a 'Jonah.' It was out of the question to master it, and they went down like chaff before the wind, and Lincoln was a hero" (*Atlanta Constitution*, February 12, 1893).

George Cuyler, the father of Hall of Famer "Kiki" Cuyler, was playing for a town team in Kincardine, Ontario, around this time. He later recollected being scheduled to play a match against the club from the county seat but, "upon learning that the county seat nine had imported a curveball pitcher, refused to play as none of the team had ever batted against the then-new curve ball" (R. E. Prescott, *Historical Tales of the Huron Shore Region*, vol. VII, 63).

While Ted Sullivan's tales always need to be taken with at least a grain of salt, there is probably a kernel of truth in a story he told about a game in a small town in Wisconsin around this time. Ted's team was playing a town team in either La Crosse or Prairie-Duchien with Charles Radbourn pitching. Radbourn was throwing curves over the plate, but the home town umpire would not call them strikes. When Radbourn complained, the umpire told him, "I'm agoin' ter give yer snap away! You're a pitchin' with a trick ball! The ball ain't official. Every time it leaves yer hand it ducks in and out so that our boys can't hit it! If yer can't pitch the ball straight or get a new one that ain't a trick ball I'll give the game to our team, b'gosh!" (*Sporting News*, March 19, 1898; A. H. Spink, *The National Game*, 150).

Others sought to use the scientific method to make sense of the mysterious new pitch. In 1876 a student at the Michigan Agricultural College reported: "A considerable discussion is going on among the members of the class in mechanics as to whether it is possible for a pitcher, in playing ball, to give a ball such a combination of forces as to send it for a distance in a straight line and then cause it to make an angle or curve. Those who say it can be done say they have seen it, but do not pretend to explain it, while those opposed think they can prove by the action of forces that it must go in the direction of the resultant, except as it is drawn towards the earth by gravity. If any one . . . can do it, they can get their expenses here paid for and good pay for their time to come and prove it" (*Paw Paw* [Mich.] *True North-erner*, October 13, 1876).

In 1877 the students were taken up on this offer, and team captain William K. Prudden later recalled: ". . . We heard of the 'curve' ball, and made up a purse of $10 to get a player from Detroit to demonstrate it. At the exhibition the Faculty were among the spectators, and we received a demonstration of the curve ball. The $10 was easy to get, as some of the sub-scribers expected a return of their money, the curver having agreed to per-form gratis in case he did not curve the ball" (*M.A.C. Record*, XXI, no. 29, May 2, 1916). The curve pitcher satisfied the skeptics and got his money.

Some of the confusion stemmed from the fact that many more pitchers tried to master the curveball than were successful in doing so. Accounts such as this 1879 one became familiar: "One of the pitchers is a splendid 'curve' pitcher, i.e., . . . his balls generally land nearer the first or third baseman than the striker" (*Manistee* [Mich.] *Advocate*, May 31, 1879).

Most of the successful curveball pitchers seem to have had far less cu-riosity about how the pitch worked: "The reason for the curve is something that professional players have never troubled themselves about, and though Matthews [Bobby Mathews] and [John] Coleman, and, in fact, any of them can tell exactly how a ball will go if it leaves the hand in a certain way, with a certain amount of force, but why or how it does it they decline to explain" (*Philadelphia Press*, reprinted in the *Grand Rapids* [Mich.] *Morning Democrat*, September 2, 1883).

In 1878 righty Tom Bond and left-handed pitcher Bobby Mitchell gave a demonstration of throwing balls that curved around two posts, and ac-cording to Spink this settled the question (A. H. Spink, *The National Game*, 124). Nonetheless claims that the curveball was just an optical illusion con-tinued to surface on a regular basis for the next seventy-five years.

3.2.4 The Curve Family. The awe and astonishment created by the curve-ball led to a flurry of reports of dazzling new variants. Curves were reported to be breaking in every conceivable direction. But the curveball revolution did not produce as many permanent additions to the pitching repertoire as it might have, at least in part because many of these proved to be exagger-ated or entirely fictitious.

The *Philadelphia Press* observed in 1883: "Every pitcher was popularly supposed to have a choice selection of curves which he sent in at pleasure, and his value was usually reckoned on the number of different ones he could use. That idea, by the way, is still prevalent, and there are many people who believe in an 'up' curve and a 'down' curve, an 'in' curve and an 'out' curve, a 'zig zag' and a 'double' curve, and 'shoots' and 'jumps,' and fast and slow balls to match. 'That's all a mistake,' said Matthews [Bobby Mathews], while talking over some of his experiences. 'I never saw but one curve, and never made any more. Of course, a ball will shoot in a little distance, but you can't call it a curve, because you can't hold that kind of a ball so as to make a curve out of it. The only genuine curve is the one that turns out from the batsmen; but after two or three of that kind a straight ball, if it is properly pitched, looks as if it was turning the other way. 'Drop' balls, or balls which apparently shoot or curve downwards, are all deceptive work, and are thrown from the highest start the rules allow. Rising balls are the same thing, started from as near the ground as possible and pitched upward. 'Slowed' balls are started slow with an apparently fast flourish, for if they were ever started fast I don't know what skill could hold them back, and, as to balls which go both in and out, why that is a manifest impossibility. No, sir. Good, straight pitching, thorough command over the ball, a good 'out-curve' and a good 'in-shoot' are what the great pitchers are working with today, and I, for my part, don't believe in anything else.' Matthews has had enough experience to know all about pitching, but there are other players who disagree with him and believe in balls which change their course downwards or upwards" (*Philadelphia Press*, reprinted in the *Grand Rapids* [Mich.] *Morning Democrat*, September 2, 1883).

Mathews and the author of this article were either overreacting or being somewhat disingenuous, since many of the pitches being described are legitimate ones. But this response is understandable in light of the proliferation of implausible claims about curves. The *Washington Post* summed up the mood aptly when it reported, "[Will] White has got a new curve. It is called the patent-combined-tripartite-quadruplex-quiver" (*Washington Post*, March 16, 1884).

Especially persistent were reports of the "'double shoot,' a ball which so defied the laws of gravitation that it would curve twice in its course, first in and then out, or combining a drop and an up curve" (*Washington Post*, September 4, 1904). The *Chicago Tribune* asked sarcastically in 1877, "A careful scrutiny of the Cincinnati papers fails to show anything about [Bobby] Mitchell, the sensation of the week. It is easy to find out that he is young, an amateur, 'a second Nolan,' left-handed, has 'a double curve,' and is 'the coming pitcher,' but who is he?" (*Chicago Tribune*, April 29, 1877).

Others, however, took the pitch more seriously. In the early 1880s, Larry Corcoran was said to be pitching the "Chicago snake ball," which writhed its way to the plate. The *Zanesville Times-Recorder* noted in 1887: "[Frank] Lemons has marvelous speed and [is] the only man except one that has ever pitched on our diamond that could throw the S curve. This difficult ball is produced by firmly grasping the ball and imparting such a twist to it as to cause it to curve to the right until it comes within ten or twelve feet of the batter, when it takes a sudden shoot to the right thus forming a complete

S curve" (*Zanesville Times-Recorder*, February 25, 1887). (The double shoot later found an appropriate home as the core pitch of Frank Merriwell, the hero of a series of baseball tales for juveniles.)

A few sources took advantage of the mushrooming of alleged curves to divvy up credit for invention of the pitch. In 1891, *Sporting News* credited Will White with the first sharp curve and "The Only" Nolan with the first outcurve (*Sporting News*, December 19, 1891). A 1903 attempt to sort the matter out credited Fred Goldsmith with having "discovered the 'in shoot,' that is, he was able to deliver a swift ball with a distinct swerve toward a right-handed batter" (*Grand Rapids* [Mich.] *Herald*, May 17, 1903). Charles Francis Carter, who pitched for Yale from 1876 to 1878, claimed later that others beat him to the curve, but "I was one of the early curve pitchers, developing all the variations of the curve and using the inshoot, which I discovered, incidentally, in a Princeton game, earlier than any one else had it, so far as I know" (letter to Grantland Rice, "The Sportlight," syndicated column, April 3, 1923).

But by and large the number of outrageous claims resulted in a jaundiced eye being cast at all of the variants of the curve. After a few years of experimentation, the search for new curves fell into disrepute and faded out. It did, however, produce a few pitches of note and tentative steps toward some others that would later reemerge.

3.2.5 Sinker. The sinker, then known as the drop ball, was the most successful of the pitches derived from the curveball. Its early development was uneven, but several nineteenth-century pitchers seem to have mastered it. Stray references appear in the 1870s, including a mention in 1870 that Charles Bierman "pitches a slow drop ball which is very effective" (*New York Clipper*, April 2, 1870; quoted by William Rankin in *Sporting News*, May 25, 1901).

The Boston pitcher Charles Buffinton was one of the pioneers in the early 1880s. An unspecified Buffalo paper wrote, "The secret of [Buffinton's] success, the players say, is a peculiar twist that he gives the ball. It comes straight enough to deceive the eye, but shoots downward just before it crosses the plate" (reprinted in *Boston Globe*, July 6, 1884). The *Detroit Free Press* later noted that in 1883, "The fame of Buffington's [sic] drop ball traveled from one end of the country to the other and hundreds of people went miles to see the Bostons play in order that they might see what a 'drop' looked like. It was an innovation in professional pitching" (*Detroit Free Press*, March 31, 1895).

The pitch proved an effective way of negating the batter's advantage of being allowed to call for a high or low pitch. As columnist "Cy" Sherman later explained, Buffinton's delivery "would look like the high ball the batsman called for and its deceptiveness fooled the man at the plate into swinging at it and missing it by a foot or two. Now the batsman who called for a low ball would gaze at the evident high ball sent through by the great Buffinton and settle back with a look of proud disdain, but when the ball took a sudden downward flight and passed the mark at the height called for and a strike call [sic], the look was changed to disgust" ("Cy" Sherman, "Hitting the High Spots on the Sporting Pike," *Lincoln* [Nebr.] *Star*, November 6, 1917).

In 1887 batters were deprived of the ability to call for high or low pitches, but by then the drop ball had caught on around the league, with such pitchers as Al Mays, Ed Seward, Nat Hudson, and Charlie Getzein featuring it. According to an 1888 account discovered by the researcher David Ball, the pitch was the key to the success of Toad Ramsey, who threw "a combination down and in ball. He brings a ball higher than any pitcher in the profession. When it starts out it seems above the batter's head, but, taking a quick shoot, it passes over the plate waist high, having taken a wonderful drop." But none of his imitators seem to have surpassed Buffinton, who still had "one of the best drop balls ever seen and when he can command it is almost invulnerable" (*Cincinnati Commercial-Gazette*, January 19, 1888).

Johnny Evers and Hugh S. Fullerton described Charles Radbourn as featuring a pitch in which "he held the ball exactly as if pitching a fast ball, with the thumb on one side and the first two fingers on the other, and at the moment of releasing it from his hand clinched the finger tips tightly into the seams of the ball and jerked backwards with the hand, the ball not only would revolve rapidly but would travel almost on a straight line—yet slowly. The revolution, which was the reverse of the natural twist, helped the ball to hold its straight course, and it lost speed quickly after exhausting the reverse revolution and fell rapidly towards the ground at a point in front of the batter." Evers and Fullerton credited Radbourn with teaching the pitch to Clark Griffith, and suggested that Christy Mathewson's fadeaway was evolved from this pitch (John J. Evers and Hugh S. Fullerton, *Touching Second*, 107–108). Ted Sullivan also attested to Radbourn throwing a drop ball (A. H. Spink, *The National Game*, 152).

For reasons explained by Skel Roach in the entry for "Keeping the Ball Down" (3.3.3), a combination of factors caused the pitch to fall out of favor in the 1890s and to remain so for two decades. One of the few notable exceptions was Amos Rusie's drop ball, which derived much of its effectiveness from the way it complemented his legendary fastball. Catcher Malachi Kittridge later observed that the greatest asset a pitcher can possess is "the drop ball that does not break from the right-handed batters. I don't mean one of those outdrops, but a ball that comes up to the plate squarely in the center and falls from one to two feet without changing its lateral direction. Amos Rusie had that ball and he threw it with tremendous speed. Rusie pitched that drop thing and mixed it up with a fast one in close, and the batter who could meet it with any regularity never lived. They tell me that Ramsey and other old-timers depended on it extensively" (quoted in A. H. Spink, *The National Game*, 126).

Around 1910 the pitch began to return to prominence and received its current name. *Sporting Life* reported during spring training, "A new curve which promises to gain fame equal to that of the spit ball or Christy Mathewson's noted fadeaway, is announced today from the training camp of the New York Giants. The discoverer of the new ball is [Ed] Keiber, one of [manager John] McGraw's new pitchers. The ball has been christened a 'sinker.' With Keiber's delivery the ball starts high, apparently rises a few feet, and then sinks suddenly to about the height of the batter's knee. It can be curved a trifle, either out or in, and though a slow ball, is said to be very effective. McGraw fanned on it Wednesday" (*Sporting Life*, March 12, 1910).

3.2.6   Upshoot or Raise Ball. The "up-shoot" or "raise ball"—a pitch thrown by submarine-style pitchers—is probably not a true member of the curve family. Yet since it is essentially an inverted sinker, this seems the best place to discuss it.

As already noted, Jim Creighton and Deacon White were both throwing pitches in the 1860s that baffled batters by seeming to curve upward. In addition, Henry Chadwick observed after an 1867 game, "The pitching of Hoy [Patrick Hoey of the Excelsiors of Rochester] in this game was very effective. His delivery is from the ground, and the ball comes to the batsman 'on the raise,' so that they are hard to control" (*The Ball Player's Chronicle*, August 29, 1867).

A. G. Spalding, the premier pitcher of the early 1870s, later said, "Although I couldn't pitch a curve, I managed to get a 'sail' on a slowly pitched ball that kept it in the air and really did make it rise" (*Fort Wayne News*, May 6, 1895). Spalding was said to have learned the "slow raise" ball from Archie Bush of Harvard (*Oshkosh Northwestern*, December 9, 1905).

Several pitchers experimented with the pitch in the wake of the curveball revolution. But no one seems to have mastered it, and changing rules soon deterred experiments with the pitch. With pitchers being allowed to throw sidearm and then overhand, there was less reason to want the ball to rise. The introduction of the mound in the 1890s seemed to be the pitch's death knell. And yet it is strangely appropriate to the upshoot's fragmentary history that it was again the featured pitch of an active pitcher in the early twenty-first century—Byung-Hyun Kim.

3.2.7   Spitball. The spitball is a pitch of enormous historical significance, and its origins are convoluted. Yet the story of its history is singular, if not unique, because no one ever appears to have claimed more credit for its invention than he deserved.

The spitball came to prominence in 1904, and its impact was extraordinary. The *Washington Post* noted, "This year, however, Jack Chesbro has introduced a novelty into pitching, which, while it is not as wonderful as the visionary double shoot, still is very effective in aiding the possessor to puzzle the opposing batters. This innovation is known as 'the spit ball'" (*Washington Post*, September 4, 1904). Chesbro won forty-one games that season, a total not matched since, which naturally attracted attention and imitators.

Their efforts that season were largely unsuccessful, and it was reported toward the end of the year that "The so-called 'spit ball' has become famous this season, and but few have been able to master it" (*Washington Post*, September 23, 1904). But that changed dramatically in 1905, beginning with reports from spring training that "nearly every slabman in both major leagues has been practicing it all winter" and estimates that three-quarters of them now featured the pitch (*Detroit Times*, reprinted in *Sporting News*, April 22, 1905; *Sporting News*, April 29, 1905).

The spitball became such a big story that the 1905 season was soon dubbed "the spit ball year" (Timothy Sharp, *Sporting News*, May 6, 1905). At least with the curveball, batters knew the direction in which it would break. The spitball presented an entirely new problem, as the sportswriter Bozeman Bulger explained: "The spot on the ball that is usually covered by the tips of the fingers is so moistened with saliva that the fingers slip off without causing any friction. The less friction the greater the break. Therefore, when the ball leaves the hand it is directed by the thumb. This gives it a peculiar wabbling motion and it is liable to 'break' either to the right or to the left" (Bozeman Bulger, "Pitching, Past and Present: The Evolution of the Twirler's Art," *Baseball Magazine*, February 1912, no. 4, 71–73).

The pitch became so popular in the American League that the sportswriter Charles Dryden quipped, "The American League consists of Ban Johnson, the 'spit ball' and the Wabash Railroad" (quoted in John J. Evers and Hugh S. Fullerton, *Touching Second*, 114). But its effects were also felt in the National League, where the Pirates' Fred Clarke observed, "the foul-strike rule never caused one-half the havoc that this ball is doing with the batting" (*Sporting Life*, May 14, 1905). The sportswriter Timothy Sharp noted succinctly: "You are not in it these days if you are a pitcher without the spit ball" (Timothy Sharp, *Sporting News*, May 6, 1905).

As hitting was virtually submerged by saliva, numerous theories emerged as to how to counteract the spitball. The simplest method was to ban the unhygienic pitch: "The suggestion of Captain [Tommy] Corcoran of the Cincinnati team that the 'nasty' spit ball be referred to the national board of health doubtless will receive the approbation of the White Sox and Cleveland teams" (*Chicago Tribune*, April 30, 1905). This approach received a boost when Dr. Herman C. H. Herold, president of the Newark Board of Health and a baseball fan, called for the abolition of the pitch on sanitary grounds (*Sporting Life*, June 17, 1905).

Others turned to chemistry for relief: "Every city has a scheme to cripple the 'pesky pitch.' In Chicago mustard is the favorite. [Jack] Chesbro awards the palm to Cleveland for originality in that line. The Naps annointed [sic] the sphere with tincture of capsicum, the effects of which remained with him for several days. The capsicum idea is credited to Bradley, who played first base behind a drug store counter in his early days" (*Sporting Life*, August 5, 1905). Cleveland was one of several teams that put licorice on the ball to dissuade the spitball, but resourceful pitchers countered by using benzene to clean off the licorice (*Sporting Life*, May 20, 1905).

John Anderson, who was a bit of a wag, claimed that he had invented a technique called the "Tungent," which he described as "a method of putting an 'English' on the ball when he hits it that will cause it to deflect from its true course in a similar manner to a billiard ball that has been 'Englished' by a player." Appropriately enough, Anderson's comments were published in the April Fool's Day issue of *Sporting Life*.

So why wasn't the spitball banned? One obvious reason is that a significant percentage of the players believed they had a vested interest in the spitball. The most conspicuous members of this group were the pitchers who used the new pitch. But they also received support from batters who thought their team's chances might be improved by a pitch which, like the curveball a generation earlier, represented a great equalizer. The sportswriter A. H. C. Mitchell argued: "If the spit ball were eliminated I believe the pennant races would not be so close, especially in the American League" (*Spalding's Guide, 1909*; quoted in David W. Anderson, *More Than Merkle*, 124).

There was even a bit of a public relations campaign mounted to aid the spitball. The *Chicago Tribune* reported that "The players have evolved another name for the spit ball, less offensive than the expressive but inelegant title by which it was christened. They call it the 'eel' ball now, because it has all the characteristics of that aquatic article and is harder to handle generally. They don't expect to hit it any oftener under the new name, but believe it will be more acceptable to the public" (*Chicago Tribune*, April 26, 1905). The *Tribune* made a concerted effort to use the term, but it did not catch on.

A more compelling explanation was given by Ned Hanlon when he grudgingly conceded, "The 'spit ball' is one of the scientific evolutions of the game, and as such I suppose it ought to be encouraged" (*Sporting Life*, June 3, 1905). Equating spitting on a baseball with science seems like twisted logic, but it fits nicely with the spirit of the times.

The efforts of Henry Chadwick and others had succeeded in convincing many that a low-scoring game represented a superior brand of baseball (see **1.30**). One of the basic underpinnings of this contention was the designation of low-scoring baseball as "scientific." In an era where science was making the lives of Americans vastly easier, this was a magic word. An association with science was the equivalent of an endorsement from an unassailable source.

Hanlon's choice of the word "evolution" is also significant. Social Darwinism was at its apex at the turn of the century and exerted a widespread influence. Its emphasis on the "survival of the fittest" lent credence to any advantage gained through innovation and cunning. In contrast, banning such advances seemed to go against the natural order.

A few observers sagely anticipated that the effectiveness of the new pitch would diminish once batters became familiar with its peculiar breaks. Timothy Sharp predicted, "There never was a wrinkle in the pitcher's art that was not solved sooner or later, and I look for the batters to size up this spit ball article before the summer is over" (Timothy Sharp, *Sporting News*, May 6, 1905).

Others argued against outlawing the spitball on practical grounds rather than philosophical ones. The sportswriter I. E. Sanborn believed that a ban would be "difficult to accomplish" while his colleague George M. Graham wrote resignedly, "it would be impossible to formulate a rule which would do away with it" (both in *Spalding's Guide, 1909*; quoted in David W. Anderson, *More Than Merkle*, 124).

For whatever reason, the initial attempt to ban the spitball stalled. Only after the pitch had frustrated batters for more than a decade was the effort successfully renewed. The American Association banned the pitch in 1918, and the circuit's umpires claimed to have "rigidly enforced" the prohibition (Billy Evans, syndicated column, *Atlanta Constitution*, January 5, 1919). The first vote to abolish the spitball was made by the National League on December 10, 1919. On February 9, 1920, the Joint Rules Committee announced that the pitch would be phased out, with a few spitballers being grandfathered.

The timing of the ban is intriguing, because all indications are that by then the spitball was no longer feared in the way it had once been. Batters had learned that the pitch would often drop out of the strike zone and had begun to resist the urge to swing at it. Former pitcher Ralph Works contended that only three pitchers still used the pitch effectively and applauded the ban for sending pitchers the message "play to win—but lose rather than use discredited pitching" (*Sporting News*, February 19, 1920).

Veteran sportswriter Hugh Fullerton maintained that "an examination of the records of the spit ball pitchers over the last eight years shows them losers." He reported that the ban was unpopular only among a few veteran pitchers "who have little else in their repertoire," while the "great majority of pitchers who have used freak deliveries now agree that it is a good thing to get rid of all that kind of stuff" (Hugh S. Fullerton, "On the Screen of Sports," *Atlanta Constitution*, March 21, 1920). Roger Peckinpaugh similarly contended that the spitball was banned only as part of an effort to rid the game of all pitches that relied upon defacing the ball (Eugene Murdock, *Baseball Between the Wars*, 19).

This suggests that ideological concerns, rather than competitive ones, prompted the ban. It seems likely that two factors were of particular importance. First, the esteem in which science was held had been eroded by the devastating uses to which scientific advances had been put during World War I. Second, the popularity of Babe Ruth and his towering home runs demonstrated that the public was not as enamored with low-scoring baseball as had been assumed. These shifts apparently were enough to tip the balance and change the perception of the pitch from "scientific" to "tricky."

The way in which the ban on the spitball was implemented was, to put it mildly, extraordinary. Pittsburgh owner Barney Dreyfuss proposed that a one-year reprieve be granted to recognized spitballers, even though Dreyfuss's Pirates had no pitchers who used the pitch. American League clubs were required to submit the names of two pitchers who would continue to use the pitch, while the National League placed no limit. The Braves and Cardinals accordingly submitted three names apiece (*Sporting News*, February 19, 1920).

At the end of one year it was decided to continue to let acknowledged spitballers throw the pitch, and the names of the seventeen designated pitchers were written into the rulebook. As a result, it was not until Burleigh Grimes was released at the end of the 1934 season that the pitch became entirely illegal. It seems likely that this indulgence was a compromise to gain acceptance for the abolition of the pitch. But it certainly underscores the fact that the pitch was no longer viewed as the threat it had once been.

Of course the pitch has continued to be used illicitly, and enforcing the ban has proved very difficult for umpires. The first pitcher ejected for throwing a spitball was the Browns' Nelson Potter on July 20, 1944 (William Mead, *Even the Browns*, 157–159). The second such pitcher to be ejected was John Boozer, of the Phillies, who was tossed on May 1, 1968, for throwing spitballs during his warm-up pitches. The Cubs' Phil Regan was ejected for throwing a spitball or doctored ball on August 18, 1968, and Gaylord Perry of Seattle was ejected from a game on August 23, 1982.

But who was responsible for inventing the spitball? Jack Chesbro was most responsible for popularizing the pitch and received some initial credit for its invention. The *Washington Post* reported during the 1904 season, "It was Mr. J. Dwight Chesbro who invented the puzzling delivery to fool batsmen" (*Washington Post*, August 28, 1904). The *Post* corrected its mistake within a month: "The so-called 'spit ball' has become famous this season, and but few have been able to master it. Chesbro, while not the originator of the odd delivery, is superior to all others handling it" (*Washington Post*, September 23, 1904).

Moreover Chesbro made no claim to having invented the pitch, acknowledging that he had learned it from a pitcher named Elmer Stricklett. Stricklett later explained: "After I had got the ball down fine Jack Chesbro saw me pitching it at Columbus, O., and he took it up" (*Sporting News*, January 1, 1920). Reporter Joe S. Jackson similarly concluded that "while no one tried to rob Stricklett of any credit, Jack Chesbro got most of the glory that went with the introduction of the delivery, speedily getting the spit ball down to such a fine point that he made all other users of the delivery look like imitators" (*Detroit Free Press*, March 22, 1908).

Another early master of the pitch, Ed Walsh, also credited Stricklett with having shown him the pitch one spring training when both were with the White Sox: "You hear all kinds of stories about the birth of the spitball, but I believe that Elmer Stricklett was the first pitcher who used it" (quoted in "Walsh Credits Stricklett with Discovery of Spitball," *Washington Post*, March 15, 1914; reprinted in Barry Popik and Gerald Cohen, "Material on the Origin of the Spitball Pitch," *Comments on Etymology*, May 2003 [32:8], 21–28).

So that moves the credit back to Elmer Stricklett, but Stricklett was equally reluctant to accept the mantle of inventor. In 1920 he told a reporter: "The man who discovered the spitball was Frank Corridon. I saw him throwing it in practice and I immediately set about to master it" (*Sporting News*, January 1, 1920). In 1940 he reiterated, "I never discovered the spitball. In countless magazine articles, radio skits and even in some of the baseball records I've been called the originator of the spitter though I never claimed credit for it. A fellow named Frank Corridon really discovered the spitball" (*San Francisco Call-Bulletin*, July 2, 1940; Peter Tamony Collection).

That same year, Edgar Brands of *Sporting News* was producing a radio quiz show when the question arose. A letter was thereupon written to Elmer Stricklett, and this time he tabbed George Hildebrand as the originator, a designation that Hildebrand confirmed (*Sporting News*, June 8, 1960). Hildebrand's role in the saga is especially curious since he was an outfielder and of course did not use the pitch in games.

The two different names cited by Elmer Stricklett reflect not a contradiction but the pitch's convoluted history. Corridon gave this account: "It was back in 1901 that I fell into the knack of throwing it and it was some 'feel' as nobody ever accused me of possessing any inventive genius. I was playing at that time for that famous old manager, Billy Murray, who was then piloting the Providence Grays of the old Eastern League. . . .

"The day in question was one of those where it had rained just enough to make things disagreeable and to make the handling of the ball very uncertain. I was warming up with the catcher, and after throwing five or six balls, I found it impossible to control their course with any degree of accuracy, as the ball was very wet and soggy. I then began fooling and experimenting with the wet ball more in a manner of fun than anything else. To my surprise one ball took a sudden break just before it reached the catcher and landed against his shins. What he said I guess you can figure out for yourself.

"George Hildebrand, now an umpire in the American League, and who was a member of the Providence team at the time, was idly standing by watching the fun. He was much surprised with the way the ball 'broke' and urged me to try again and this time cut out the foolish antics. . . . I took his advice and the next ball acted in the same way as the previous one, except that it didn't get anywhere near the catcher. After a few attempts to control it I gave it up as a hopeless task.

"The thought still stuck with me, though, that perhaps under better conditions and a closer study of it there might be a chance to master it. On the day that followed I practiced it continually, experimenting in every conceivable manner; first, by trying to get the exact amount of moisture on it, and in the right spot on the ball, and also the proper grip. After months of patience and practice success finally crowned my efforts, and I was satisfied that this style of delivery would in future help a pitcher overcome the many handicaps that were being placed in his path to help the batter" (*Sporting News*, January 1, 1920).

George Hildebrand explained how the pitch made its way to Stricklett: "Back in the early part of 1902, Frank Corridon, a young pitcher who was afterward with the Chicago Cubs, was with the Providence Club. He had a habit of spitting on his slow ball, and in fun one day I imitated him in practice, and then said 'Why don't you shoot 'em in faster?' Then I moistened up the ball again and threw a fast one. I noticed it took a peculiar shoot, and I experimented with it a number of times, and even discussed it with Corridon. He used it and in one game I remember he struck out twelve men in six innings, and then wrenched his arm. I doubt if he even realized that it was of much value even then.

"Toward the end of the 1902 season I jumped organized ball to play with Mike Fisher's Sacramento Club. Stricklett was a member of the club. . . . During the warm-up in Los Angeles one day, I said to Stricklett, 'Let me show you something they can't hit,' and I showed him this ball that I had experimented with in the East. He immediately began to experiment with it. That was the beginning of spit ball pitching. Stricklett got so he could control the ball, making it break in any direction he chose" (*Sporting News*, December 11, 1913).

Mike Fisher was present when Hildebrand demonstrated the pitch, and he picked the story up from that point: "Hildebrand saturated the ball and his pitching hand with a generous supply of saliva. 'Now watch me,' he said.

"The ball approached the plate in a manner entirely different from any Stricklett had ever seen. Thereupon followed a long and earnest conversation between the two, Hildebrand agreeing to teach his partner the mystery of the new shoot.

"Some weeks later a company of big leaguers visited the coast and a series of games was arranged in which Stricklett, with a number of others, was to uphold the honor of the west coast pitchers. The big leaguers expected a lot of fun. The day arrived when it came Elmer's turn to assume box duty and, nothing reluctant, he essayed the task.

"When the game was over the visitors were thoroughly subdued. One hit they secured, and they were lucky to get that. Stricklett was besieged by the foreigners to reveal the secret of his craft. A few years previous he had been one of their company and he was never known to be possessed of the effectiveness he displayed that day.

"'What do you call it?' one of them asked.

"Stricklett smiled and replied in a very superior way, 'That's the 'spit ball'" (Francis J. Mannix, "Hildebrand Gave Stricklett First Lessons with 'Spitball,'" *The* [San Francisco] *Bulletin*, September 24, 1913; reprinted in Barry Popik and Gerald Cohen, "Material on the Origin of the Spitball Pitch," *Comments on Etymology*, May 2003 [32:8], 21–28).

Although the story comes to us piecemeal from three different sources, the inconsistencies are minor. Corridon incorrectly gave the year as 1901, but that is the kind of mistake that can be expected after the passage of nearly twenty years. More important, each man was an eyewitness to the events he described, and none claimed a larger role for himself than is justified by the other accounts.

This basic version of events was corroborated by an article that first appeared in the *Washington Post* in 1913 and then in *Sporting News* in 1916. Curiously, when the article appeared in the *Washington Post*, no source or byline was listed, yet when it was reprinted almost verbatim in *Sporting News* three years later, the San Francisco writer Ed Lanhart was cited as its source. Lanhart was in turn said to have been told the story "by a certain party who ought to know." Since George Hildebrand was the only man present at both of the events being described, Gerald Cohen pointed out that he is very likely the unnamed source.

The article presented the same basic facts as the *Bulletin*'s account but added a few new details. For one thing, the Providence catcher who tried to catch Corridon's spitball was identified as Pat McCauley. In addition, it indicated that Elmer Stricklett was on the verge of being released when he mastered the spitball. The later article also claimed that Jack Chesbro toured California after the 1902 season and learned the pitch then (*Washington Post*, April 27, 1913; "History of Two Freak Deliveries," *Sporting News*, May 25, 1916; reprinted in Barry Popik and Gerald Cohen, "Material on the Origin of the Spitball Pitch," *Comments on Etymology*, May 2003 [32:8], 21–28). The researcher Wayne McElreavy discovered that Stricklett beat Chesbro's barnstorming team 13-1 on December 13, 1902, and believes that is when Chesbro first learned of the pitch.

The *Sporting News* version of the article also noted that two other Sacramento pitchers, Win Cutter and Bull Thomas, experimented unsuccessfully with the spitball. Indeed, Elmer Stricklett was not the only pitcher to master the spitball in 1903 and bring the pitch back east. *Sporting Life*'s Chicago correspondent reported at the end of the 1903 season: "Local base ball players and incoming professionals have one topic of conversation now, and that is the new ball the California pitchers are bringing back with them. Among this lot is Skel Roach, who has it down to a science. It is said that every pitcher, big and little, is working on it, and before long there will be fifty, at least, who will have mastered the mysterious 'drop.' It is called the 'spit-ball,' from the fact that the pitcher moistens his pitching forefinger just before delivering the ball. This act in some way takes from the ball all the twist which ordinarily gives the ball its curve near the plate. The result is that it comes from the pitcher's hand with all the speed motion, comes up fair and fast and then drops dully, all speed gone from it, all the twist washed out" (*Sporting Life*, November 7, 1903).

The correspondent also made clear that the 1905 efforts to use chemistry to combat the pitch were not the first such endeavors: "Out in California, they say, the wise manager whose pitcher had not yet learned the drop tried to put red pepper in the seams of the playing ball, figuring this would stop it. It did while the red pepper lasted" (*Sporting Life*, November 7, 1903).

And so the spitball would seem to have resulted from a tag-team effort by several men in the first few years of the twentieth century. Frank Corridon had used it but not appreciated it; George Hildebrand realized what it was and showed it to Elmer Stricklett; Stricklett mastered it and shared it with many others, including Jack Chesbro and Ed Walsh; Chesbro and Walsh brought the pitch to its highest level of attainment.

The astonishment with which the pitch was met would seem enough to establish that it was new. And yet, no sooner did the pitch attain popularity than an extraordinary number of earlier claimants emerged.

Billy Hallman maintained in 1907 that Stricklett may have perfected the pitch, "but he never discovered it. Long before Stricklett was heard of in base ball [catcher] Frank Bowerman had it. When he was with Baltimore in the old National League days he used to use this same ball to have fun with the boys. One day he called me up to play throw and catch and commenced smearing the ball with spit. He called my attention to the way it fooled a fellow and we had considerable fun over it. Just ask 'Robby,' [Wilbert Robinson] or any of the boys on the old Baltimore team, and they'll tell you that Bowerman had it in a limited way, and they all recognized the 'freak work' of the ball when delivered in that way" (quoted in H. G. Merrill, "Jogged to Bench," *Sporting News*, February 9, 1907).

Pitcher-turned-umpire Billy Hart also endorsed Bowerman: "I notice they claim Chesbro and Stricklett were the first to discover the 'spit ball.' Well, back in 1896, when I was pitching for St. Louis, I met Catcher Bowerman, who was with Baltimore that year. Calling me aside in St. Louis one day, he took the ball and requested me to get back of the catcher and watch his curves. I did so and was surprised to see how the ball acted as it neared the catcher. I asked Bowerman what made the ball act so. He explained that he simply spat on the ball, held onto it with his thumb at the seam and let it go. The odd part of it was that there was no speed to the ball that Bowerman pitched, whereas today they claim that the 'spit ball' can only be delivered with speed. I mastered it after a while, but found that it injured my arm, as it brought into play muscles not generally used. I advise any pitcher with good speed and curves to let the 'spit ball' severely alone. It will ruin an arm of steel in due time" (quoted in the *New York Sun*, February 10, 1908).

Christy Mathewson added, "Bowerman, the old Giant catcher, was throwing the spit ball for two or three years before it was discovered to be a pitching asset. He used to wet his fingers when catching, and as he threw to second base the ball would take all sorts of eccentric breaks which fooled the baseman, and could explain why it did it until Stricklett came through with the spit ball" (Christy Mathewson, *Pitching in a Pinch*, 223).

In 1904, *Sporting Life* unearthed another candidate: "Pitcher George Cuppy, of the Clevelands, had the 'spit ball' seven or eight years ago, and he didn't know it. He had it on the Baltimores all the time and that was why they couldn't hit him" (*Sporting Life*, December 31, 1904).

An 1880 account of James "Pud" Galvin's delivery noted that he "licks the end of his fingers" (*New York Clipper*, January 17, 1880). In 1887 the *Chicago Herald* similarly described Galvin as "a fat, good-natured little fellow who used to go through the business-like performance of expectorating on his fingers before delivering the ball" (*Chicago Herald*, reprinted in the *Detroit Free Press*, May 4, 1887).

Galvin was far from alone in this practice. Sportswriter Walter Barnes wrote in the *Boston Journal* in 1905 that Tim Keefe "wet his thumb before delivering the ball" (*Boston Journal*, reprinted in *Sporting Life*, January 21, 1905). Charley Snyder told an interviewer in 1907, "They tell us of the new ball this or that pitcher has discovered, but they are not new. I caught the spit ball 25 or more years ago, but we did not call it the spit ball then. Tommy Bond used to wet his fingers and produce a peculiar shoot on his ball, yet he was never given much credit for it, nor was he advertised all over the country as a spit-ball pitcher" (*Cleveland Press*, reprinted in *Sporting News*, December 26, 1907). An 1886 description noted that Mickey Welch "expectorates on either hand" during his preliminary motions (*St. Louis Post-Dispatch*, June 19, 1886). Jim McGuire claimed that Charley Buffinton was the first spitballer while the two were teammates in Philadelphia in 1887 (*Washington Post*, December 26, 1907). And Ted Sullivan made this confusing claim about Charley Radbourn: "He had a drop ball that he did not have to spit on, and called it a 'spit ball'" (A. H. Spink, *The National Game*, 152).

The cases for Galvin, Keefe, Bond, Welch, Buffinton, and Radbourn are weakened by the fact that I have found only one attestation for each. On the other hand, none of the claims was made by the men themselves. And while the descriptions of Galvin and Welch are contemporaneous, the others emerged soon after the spitball became prominent.

Bobby Mathews has far and away the best-documented case of any nineteenth-century spitballer. The *Washington Post* reported in 1904, "Umpire Billy Hart says he use [sic] the 'spit ball' when he pitched in the Union Association back in 1884, and that it was one of Bobby Mathews' best 'foolers,' and yet some say that it is new. The oldest inhabitants are still claiming credit for unearthing all new wrinkles in baseball" (*Washington Post*, September 15, 1904). Note, however, that Hart later was quoted as saying he had been introduced to the pitch in 1896 by Frank Bowerman.

Many other sources gave the credit to Mathews. Ted Kennedy, a pitcher of the 1880s, wrote to Cap Anson in 1905: "What they call the 'spit' ball has moss four ft. thick on it [i.e., is not new]. The old thumb drop ball has found a new name. Bobby Mathews, the grandest little man of the box, used it" (letter to Cap Anson dated May 3, 1905, printed in *Chicago Tribune*, May 5, 1905). Anson later echoed Kennedy: "The spitball. Yes, that may be a new wrinkle, and it may not. I remember how Bobby Matthews [sic] used to pitch. He used to keep wetting the ball, and when he was pitching there was always a nice clean spot on the pill about the size of a half a dollar. Now, that spot was the result of Matthews' wetting the ball, and I believe he was a 'spit ball' pitcher" (quoted in *The* [San Francisco] *Bulletin*, March 6, 1913; reprinted in Barry Popik and Gerald Cohen, "Material on the Origin of the Spitball Pitch," *Comments on Etymology*, May 2003 [32:8], 21–28).

Phonney Martin recalled many years later that as early as 1868, Mathews "rubbed the balls with his hand and kept one side perfectly white, then he would moisten it with his fingers and let it go. The ball would not only take a decided curve at times, but at other times would drop and curve in" (Francis C. Richter, *Richter's History and Records of Base Ball*, 270). Pitcher-turned-umpire Hank O'Day added that "Mathews used to cover the palm of his left hand with saliva and rub the ball in it" (quoted in John Thorn and John Holway, *The Pitcher*, 164).

Columnist James J. Corbett wrote in 1919: "Mathews threw a wider and more vicious breaking curve than any other moundsman of his time. And always as a preliminary to throwing such a ball, he would spit on it and then, without rubbing it on his glove, would pitch to the plate. The resultant twister baffled batsmen such as did no other delivery in the days before the National League began" ("Sport World with James J. Corbett," syndicated column, *Fort Wayne News and Sentinel*, February 18, 1919).

Two of the most knowledgeable sportswriters also credited Mathews. Tim Murnane, who was also a former player, wrote: "[Bobby Mathews] became a famous pitcher by what is now known as the spit ball" (*Sporting News*, November 4, 1909). William Rankin similarly concluded, "There is no doubt that [Bobby] Mathews was the originator of the 'spit ball.' He used to rub the ball on the breeches until there was a white spot or one much lighter than the rest of the ball, and then wet his finger. He used to say the grass made the ball slippery, that was why he rubbed it on his breeches, and then he wet his fingers to get a good hold on the ball" (*Sporting News*, February 13, 1908).

A. H. Spink came to a different conclusion: "Some of the players of the present day claim that the ball which Matthews [sic] was pitching then was nothing more nor less than the 'spit' ball now used by many of the best pitchers. But this is hardly possible for the 'spit' ball is fearfully wearing on the pitcher and soon retires him from service" (A. H. Spink, *The National Game*, 140).

Spink is clearly basing his conclusion on an assumption, however, and that assumption is dubious at best. Many of the early spitballers had abbreviated careers, but it is more reasonable to attribute this to the extraordinary workloads they handled. Ed Walsh and Jack Chesbro both exceeded 450 innings in their best season—more than "Iron Man" McGinnity ever worked—and both had arm problems soon thereafter. Later spitballers, when assigned more reasonable workloads, proved much more durable.

It is an unfortunate fact that, by the time the spitball made its extraordinary rise to prominence in 1905, Bobby Mathews had been dead for eight years. (Galvin and Radbourn were also dead by then.) Given that Mathews declined to take credit for the curveball, it would have been fascinating to have the benefit of his comments on the spitball.

While the history of the spitball is thus a very complex one, a few conclusions seem warranted. One reason for the extraordinary number of claims for nineteenth-century spitballers is apparent from this 1893 account: "Most pitchers when they want to moisten the tips of their fingers expectorate freely on the ball, rub it briskly with both hands and then wipe the aforesaid hands along the front of their curtailed pantaloons, leaving the brand of their tin-tag tobacco on the surface of their clothing. Mr. [George] Nicol does not do this. He fastens a dampened handkerchief to the surcingle of his uniform, with which he moistens the ball, thus doing away with the time-honored tobacco-juice bath. This act of true gentility on his part was freely and favorably commented on, and it is said the Colonel's pitchers have been ordered to follow his example" (*San Francisco Examiner*, April 15, 1893).

Baseball historian John B. Foster offered support for this contention: "[Fred] Goldsmith has been quoted as saying that he knew of the spitball and if he is quoted rightly, perhaps he did, because the spitter was known in those early days, although it was not generally used, or called such, and it was not pitched after expectorating on the ball, as became the custom. It was more due to occasional wetting of the fingers of the pitching hand" (John B. Foster, "The Evolution of Pitching," part 3, *Sporting News*, December 24, 1931).

Many contemporaries were aware that this spitting affected a pitcher's control of the ball. In 1886, Pittsburgh manager Horace Phillips blamed a bad outing by pitcher Frank Mountain on the fact that catcher George Miller "is an incessant chewer of tobacco and is ever spitting on his gloves to keep them moist. That makes the ball slippery, and Mountain couldn't grip it firmly at all. However, Miller will chew something else than tobacco henceforth, and that may mend matters" (*Cleveland Leader and Herald*, April 19, 1886).

Indeed, a rule was implemented in 1890 that "Players will not be allowed to spit and rub dirt on the ball this year when a new sphere is thrown upon the diamond" (*Columbus* [Ohio] *Press*, March 16, 1890). It does not appear to have been very strictly enforced. So this raises yet another question: how well the nineteenth-century pitchers who ostensibly used saliva to improve their grip understood and could control its effect upon the pitch's trajectory.

With so many different issues to consider, there are a wide variety of perspectives as to whether the spitball was being thrown in the nineteenth century. Candy Cummings's view was that "when he was pitching they had no spitter but had something like it. He used a similar delivery by gripping the ball on the seams and shooting it over much the same as the spitter does now. He claims, however, that the delivery was dangerous because of the impossibility to control it and as a result it was much like the dreaded 'beaner'" (*Sandusky* [Ohio] *Star-Journal*, May 13, 1921). The *New York Times* rendered this verdict: "Old timers contend that they got peculiar breaks in pitching by wetting the ball, but none specialized in this peculiar delivery up to the time of Stricklett" (*New York Times*, October 31, 1919). Note that both of these viewpoints suggest an awareness of the possibility of producing "peculiar breaks" but question whether it was possible to control the resulting pitch.

Frank Corridon was thus skeptical about claims that any early pitchers had mastered the spitball: "at various times old-time pitchers—twirlers of the 80's and 90's—have declared they used to moisten the ball before delivering it to the batsmen. That may be so, but it is doubtful if they did it with a definite purpose. They may have done so without method or system of distinctive feature. If they used a wet ball, maybe it was not with the knowledge that they were using something they considered better than the dry ball and perhaps they did not use the wet ball twice in the same fashion. Anyway, the peculiar breaks generally attributed to the spitball were not gained by the old-timers, who were not conscious of the possibilities of the ball they claimed to have thrown. They may have used moisture but they did not gain from nor recognize peculiarly definite results therein" (*Sporting News*, January 1, 1920). Connie Mack went further, contending that nineteenth-century pitchers "never heard of the spit ball and don't let anybody try to tell you that they did" (*Sporting Life*, July 18, 1908; quoted in David W. Anderson, *More Than Merkle*, 126).

Still, it is one thing to presume that many nineteenth-century pitchers were inadvertently throwing spitballs and quite another to take it for granted that none of them were aware of what they were doing. It is hard to escape noticing that Keefe, Welch, Galvin, Bond, Radbourn, and Mathews averaged well over three hundred wins apiece. Johnny Evers and Hugh Fullerton later observed that "In the pioneer days of the game, it seemed that if a player invented or evolved a play, the others, instead of seizing upon it to use, gave him a kind of patent-right to it" (John J. Evers and Hugh S. Fullerton, *Touching Second*, 198). The fact that these pitchers performed in an era when effective pitching tactics were often banned would have given them another good reason to be secretive. It seems reasonable to conjecture that at least one of these six greats—especially Mathews—was aware of both the pitch and how to control it, but chose not to publicize the fact.

3.2.8 **"Dry Spitters."** By the time the spitball came along, the search for new curves had ceased to be taken seriously. Indeed, Christy Mathewson claimed that one reporter who filed a story about the spitball received a telegram from his skeptical editor that read: "It's all right to 'fake' about new curves, but when it comes to being vulgar about it, that's going too far. Either drop that spit ball or mail us your resignation" (Christy Mathewson, *Pitching in a Pinch*, 223).

The remarkable success of the spitball changed everyone's perspective and started the cycle all over again. Innumerable new pitches were soon being invented, and the common aim of most of these efforts was to replicate the break of the spitball without using saliva. As a result, these pitches were often collectively referred to as "dry spitters." A few of these were successful enough to contribute to the actual pitches described in the entries that follow, but most never made it off the drawing board.

Mathewson, who disliked the spitball because he couldn't control it, was one of the experimenters (Christy Mathewson, *Pitching in a Pinch*, 222). *Sporting Life* reported in 1908: "A topic of much discussion among the Giants this morning is the 'dry spitter,' a new pitching delivery of which Chris Mathewson claims to be the originator. Matty calls his freak ball the 'spitless spitter,' for he does not moisten the ball, yet it breaks like a spitter. . . . The 'dry spitter' differs radically from the common spitball not only because the ball is not moistened, but because it is a slow instead of a fast ball. Speed and a quick break have been the essential qualities heretofore, of the 'spit ball' delivery, but Matty throws his deceiver without any effort. In yesterday's game the ball floated up to the plate without any force behind it, and just as the batter would take a healthy swing at it the sphere would suddenly waver and drop dead into [catcher Tom] Needham's mitt. It was like a piece of paper fluttering along and encountering a puff of wind from the opposite direction" (*Sporting Life*, April 18, 1908).

Minor league pitcher Evan "Rube" Evans developed a similar pitch four years later: "The ball is delivered in exactly the same manner as the spitball, but he does not moisten it. Instead of using moisture to slip his first two fingers from the ball he lets them drag off. The ball then takes a peculiar wabbling motion and then jumps as it gets to the batter. The ordinary spitter usually breaks into a right-handed batter, but this one takes an outward and upward jump that is very puzzling" (*Sporting Life*, March 9, 1912).

Sportswriter J. W. Foley wrote in 1915, "[Pete] Standridge was secured from Frisco and is a right-hander. He has a delivery called the 'fork ball' in addition to the regular assortment of twisters. This freak ball is held between the middle and index fingers and is what is sometimes called a 'dry spitter'" (syndicated column, *St. Louis Post-Dispatch*, April 2, 1915).

The constant experimentation during spring training amused veterans like Cy Young, who said in 1905: "This talk about the bewildering shoots that are expected to make the batsmen hammer the atmosphere until they are blue in the face is enough to make one smile. When the season opens such twists as the 'spit ball,' 'snake twist,' and the 'grasshopper shoot' will be relegated to the icebox, and it will be a case of play ball" (*Chicago Tribune*, April 16, 1905).

Christy Mathewson was also struck by the number of pitchers working on new curves in spring training. He commented, "Pitchers, old and young, are always trying for new curves in the spring practice, and out of the South, wafted over the wires by the fertile imaginations of the flotilla of correspondents, drift tales each spring of the 'fish' ball and the new 'hook' jump and the 'stop' ball and many more eccentric curves which usually boil down to modifications of the old ones" (Christy Mathewson, *Pitching in a Pinch*, 222).

Pitchers as successful as Young and Mathewson could afford to poke fun at such extravagant claims. Yet the relentless experimentation by those seeking the "dry spitter" did uncover enough gems that Ty Cobb would later write that the result of "the hullabaloo over the spitball" was that "every pitcher in the land was sitting up at night thinking up ways of doing tricky things to the ball. . . . Most of these pitchers, too, were really clever inventors. They got away with the most astonishing tricks, some of which have not been solved or exposed to this day" (Ty Cobb, *Memoirs of Twenty Years in Baseball*, 65). The next entries will describe a few of those success stories.

3.2.9 Forkball. John Thorn and John Holway traced the origins of the forkball back to "Chattanooga in about 1905, when outfielder Mike Lynch, who had had a cup of coffee with the White Sox a few years before, experimented with the pitch and found he could get 'astonishing' breaks. But the style tired his fingers, and he could not control it. Three years later, playing with the Tacoma Tigers, he taught it to pitcher Bert Hall, who experimented with it in secret for about three weeks, learning to control it." Hall unveiled the pitch against an "unsuspecting Seattle club and shut them out on four hits. BERT HALL HAS NEW FANGLED BALL WORSE THAN SPITTER, the local paper headlined. That day the pitch—and the name forkball—were both born" (John Thorn and John Holway, *The Pitcher*, 158).

Rob Neyer discovered that the game in question took place on September 18, 1908. An account the following day observed that Hall "simply put the ball between his first two fingers, drew back his arm and let fly. The result was a lot of wiggles on the ball that had the local help completely mystified, and when they hit the ball at all they were so surprised that they sometimes forgot to run. Hall's assortment yesterday beats all the spit-ball and knuckle ball combinations to death, for he used it overhand, side arm and any old way and kept the ball breaking over the plate" (*Seattle Times*, September 19, 1908; quoted in Bill James and Rob Neyer, *The Neyer/James Guide to Pitchers*, 47).

Hall credited his apprenticeship as a plumber with giving him the wrist strength necessary for the pitch. He explained, "I hold the ball between the first and second fingers, jammed back as far as possible. The ball sort of floats up to the batter with almost no whirling at all, and then, just as the batter is ready to strike, down it shoots to one side or the other, whichever way I let it go from the hand" (quoted in Gerard S. Petrone, *When Baseball Was Young*, 94).

The pitch attracted occasional practitioners in the years that followed, including Pete Standridge, Dave Keefe, and Joe Bush. But it remained cnough of a novelty that when Tiny Bonham had success with the forkball in the 1940s, some sources credited him with inventing the pitch.

As has been discussed at some length by Rob Neyer, the distinction between the forkball and the modern splitter is far from clear-cut (Rob Neyer, "The Forkball Fast and Slow," Bill James and Rob Neyer, *The Neyer/James Guide to Pitchers*, 45–51).

3.2.10 Knuckleball. The knuckleball is one pitch that has had no strong claimants for nineteenth-century origination. The drop curve thrown by 1880s pitcher Toad Ramsey is sometimes said to have been a knuckleball. Ramsey had suffered an injury to his pitching hand that necessitated an unusual grip. But the name of his pitch alone would seem to suggest that it did not have the unpredictable movement that characterizes the knuckleball.

Ed Cicotte and Nap Rucker are usually credited with inventing the pitch in 1905 while teammates with Augusta of the Sally League. Unlike later practitioners, both Cicotte and Rucker used their knuckles in throwing the pitch. Rucker gave this description: "The knuckleball is held tightly by the thumb and little finger and the knuckles of the other fingers are closed, the ball resting against it. When the ball is pitched it is sent spinning on a horizontal axis. The downward thrust of the hand as the ball leaves, causes the ball to make a spin toward the box artist instead of against him. If this ball could be thrown fast enough, pitchers who have used it say, it would curve upward—something, however, impossible. In its efforts to climb, however, it slows up as it reaches the plate and then shoots quickly as the spinning motion dies, to one side or the other" (quoted in John Thorn and John Holway, *The Pitcher*, 156).

Neither pitcher mastered the pitch immediately, but by the 1908 season it had begun to emerge as a potent weapon. The sportswriter Joe S. Jackson wrote during spring training that "the 'knuckle ball,' so called . . . which Cicotte is credited with inventing" was the talk of the camps: "Following the stories of this delivery that went out of Little Rock come tales from the training camp of the Brooklyn club, in which the credit for discovery of the 'knuckle ball' is given to Nap Rucker, the big left-hander whom the Superbas got from Augusta. Rucker is using the delivery in the spring games, and is doing wonders with it. His team mates say that he used the ball in games last fall. However, minor leaguers here in the south who came from the American association discount this by claiming that they saw Cicotte use the ball when he was pitching for the Indianapolis club.

"The knuckler is pitched by pressing the knuckles against the seams, instead of folding the fingers over it. It is a medium-paced delivery. In throwing the spit ball there is very little rotary motion. In the 'knuckle ball' those who have watched it, or who have batted against it, say that there is no rotary motion at all. It goes to the batter like an ordinary slow ball, but has a break like a spitter, shooting down, and apparently breaking either to the right or the left of the plate.

"Cicotte used it in games at Little Rock. He had good control of it, and hitting it was about as difficult as hitting the spit ball when the latter is used by a man like [Jack] Chesbro or [Harry] Howell.

"'The way Cicotte used it,' said Lou Criger, 'it's the best slow ball I ever caught. And it's also the hardest slow ball to handle that was ever sent up to me'" (*Detroit Free Press*, March 22, 1908).

Another candidate for having invented the pitch is Lew Moren, who pitched briefly in the major leagues in 1903 and 1904. When he was returned to the minor leagues in 1905, it is said that he recognized the need for another pitch and came up with the knuckleball. It proved his ticket back to the big leagues, where he was hailed as the "inventor" of the knuckleball (*New York Daily Press*, April 17, 1908; quoted in Craig R. Wright and Tom House, *The Diamond Appraised*, 107).

Early in the 1908 season, Clark Griffith predicted that "The knuckle ball will ultimately replace the spit ball and be even more effective than that famous twist" (*Sporting News*, May 7, 1908). Instead a curious thing happened.

That same spring Ed Summers of Detroit unveiled a variant of the pitch. Paul H. Bruske reported that Summers's "slow ball which he pitches from his finger-tip . . . is his adaptation of the knuckle-ball which Eddie Cicotte used last year in the Western League. Cicotte and Summers worked out the thing together with Indianapolis in the spring of 1906, and each did well with it last season. [Detroit catcher] Freddie Payne, who has caught Summers in most of his work down here, says that Summers' particular pet delivery is certainly unique and thinks it should be baffling. The pitcher throws it overhand, underhand or sidearm and gets a different break on every delivery" (*Sporting Life*, March 28, 1908).

Bruske added that Summers "throws the new contrivance in a manner which would better qualify it for the name of 'finger-tip' or 'finger-nail' ball. He clutches it away from the palm of his hands, his finger nails gripping it at the seams. The ball comes up something like a spitter, though with less speed. It actually 'shimmers' before taking the final dive." Grand Rapids manager Bobby Lowe tried to catch "five or six of the finger-tip balls and failed to catch a single one, being hit on the back of the hand with one and missing one other completely, though it lodged in the pit of his stomach" (*Sporting Life*, March 28, 1908).

Sportswriter W. W. Bingay gave a thorough explanation of the difference between the two methods of throwing the pitch: "Baseball's new delivery requires strong, wiry fingers, and these Summers possesses. His fingers are well shaped but long, remarkably long, and he has a grip like that of a vise.

The finger nails must be kept down or they will turn in delivering the ball. . . . Summer's [sic] finger nail ball and the knuckle ball are entirely different. As used by Cicotte, Moren, Rucker and others who have mastered it, the knuckle ball is held tightly by the thumb and little finger, and the knuckles of the other fingers are closed, the ball resting against it. When the ball is pitched it is sent spinning on a perfectly horizontal axis." He quoted Summers's explanation that Cicotte rested the ball against his knuckles, but "I found by holding the ball with my finger tips and steadying it with my thumb alone I could get a peculiar break to it, and send it to the batters with considerable speed and good control" (*Sporting Life*, May 16, 1908).

Detroit catcher Charles Schmidt believed that the new method of throwing the pitch had an important advantage, noting that Summers "has as much control of it as any ordinary pitcher has of any ball he uses. The knuckle ball you hear about hasn't this virtue. The pitcher hardly knows where it is going when it starts. It is hard to handle and hard to get over the plate. Summers uses this finger nail ball, or reverse curve, or whatever you want to call it, any old time, and can almost always get it over" (*Sporting Life*, May 16, 1908). But the pitch also featured the unpredictability that still confounds batters. Summers perhaps said it best when he observed, "You can't describe the darn thing. The nearest I can come to it is a staggering jag coming home" (*Sporting News*, May 12, 1910).

For whatever reason, Summers had greater immediate success with the pitch than did Cicotte or Rucker. Summers won twenty-four games that year, and his use of the pitch in the World Series drew added attention. Gradually the fingernail ball increased in popularity at the expense of the knuckleball.

Most prominent among those who threw the fingernail ball was Ralph Savidge, who apparently developed the pitch independently at about the same time as Summers, and may have preceded him in using it. A *Sporting Life* correspondent filed this report before the 1908 season: "Ralph Savidge, the promising young pitcher purchased from the 1907 Jacksonville South Atlantic League Club by the Memphis club, believes he has invented a new wrinkle in curves. Savidge has mastered the 'finger nail curve.' He believes it is an improvement of the 'fadeaway,' the 'boomerang,' the 'spitter,' or 'knuckle curve.' . . . The 'finger nail' curve is pitched with thumb nail and as many other nails as possible penetrating the covering. The fingers are kept rigid and the ball is thrown with full force. In practice Savidge has baffled the efforts of the best batters. The ball floats lazily toward the batter. There is no revolution at all, but just before the ball passes the plate it takes a quick dart in one of three directions, as desired by the pitcher, certain movement being used to cause the 'finger nail' curve to dart out or in toward the batter" (*Sporting Life*, May 9, 1908).

The following year Savidge gave this description of the pitch and its origins: "All I know about it is that I hold the ball with the tips of all my fingers and there is a sort of a reverse English on it when it leaves my hand. It floats up to the plate very slowly and does not revolve at all until it gets close to the rubber; then it darts suddenly up or down or to one side. It really is not a 'fingernail' ball, for it never comes in contact with my fingernails. Some one just got the idea that it did and gave it that name. I discovered the 'fingernail' by accident while fooling around trying to learn something new. Like Topsy [a character in *Uncle Tom's Cabin*], the 'fingernail' ball wasn't born: 'it just growed.' I never know which way the ball is going to break when I start it toward the plate. If the wind is blowing against the ball it causes it to break sharply and wickedly, but when there is not a breath of air stirring, the break is not so pronounced. The spitball pitcher generally has a faint idea of the direction the ball will take when it breaks, but I never know what's going to happen after the ball leaves my hand. Sometimes it breaks upward and sometimes it drops and it is just as liable to break to either the right or left" (*Sporting Life*, March 20, 1909).

It is not surprising that the fingernail grip became dominant, since most pitchers found it to be easier to control. What is intriguing and rather perplexing is the fact that the fingernail pitch assumed the name of the knuckleball, even though the pitch does not use the knuckles at all.

In 1912 the *Chicago Tribune* reported: "The knuckle ball is thrown by pitcher [Flame] Delhi by pressing the fingernails against the surface of the ball instead of grasping it in his hand. When it travels to the catcher it doesn't even make one revolution. One can see the seam of the ball throughout the entire distance. With sufficient speed back of it it takes a quick break downward or either in or out, just before reaching the batter" (*Chicago Tribune*, March 6, 1912). Delhi pitched only one major league game yet is still remembered for another distinction. He was the first major leaguer to hail from Arizona, and a regional chapter of the Society for American Baseball Research is named in his honor.

Tom Seaton was also successful with the pitch, but it seemed to be dying out by the end of the decade. Then it got a new lease on life when the spitball was banned. Ed Rommel, a minor league spitballer, was one of those for whom the prohibition on his specialty pitch was a major crisis. But a plumber named Cutter Dreuery offered to show him an even better pitch. Rommel soon reached the majors, where he claimed to have been "the first pitcher to make the knuckleball his standby" (Dan Daniel, "Batters Going Batty from Butterflies," *Sporting News*, June 12, 1946).

By this time the distinction between the fingernail ball and the knuckleball was beginning to disappear. The sportswriter Rodger Pippen wrote indignantly in 1923 that Ed Rommel's knuckleball was a myth. He explained: "Rommel's famous ball is a fingernail ball. His knuckles never touch the cover. . . . Wright of the St. Louis Club is said to employ a real knuckle ball." Pippen blamed the confusion on an ill-informed reporter from a Newark newspaper and noted that Rommel himself "had been under the delusion for five years that he was a knuckle-ball artist" (*Sporting News*, February 1, 1923). As unassailable as Pippen's logic is, by then he was fighting a losing battle. That battle was clearly over by 1953 when Johnny Lindell said, "As a youngster, I had fooled around with what is known as a knuckleball. Actually, mine is a fingertip ball because I hold it with the tips of the three fingers" (*Sporting News*, April 15, 1953).

Bill James and Rob Neyer have noted that when Rommel retired in 1932, the knuckleball again appeared to be on the verge of dying out. At that point there were only two pitchers who relied on the pitch: Jesse Haines and Fred Fitzsimmons (both of whom threw the pitch with their knuckles) (Bill James and Rob Neyer, *The Neyer/James Guide to Pitchers*, 42–43). Nonetheless they were succeeded by a new generation of knuckleballers who threw the pitch with their fingertips, and since then the pitch has almost exclusively been thrown that way.

The resurgence of popularity reached its peak in the mid-1940s when the Washington Senators featured four knuckleball pitchers—Roger Wolff, Emil "Dutch" Leonard, Johnny Niggeling, and Mickey Haefner. Dan Daniel observed in 1946, "Freakish pitching deliveries run in cycles. The current sensation in the major leagues is the knuckleball. There is scarcely a pitcher in the Big Time who is not either using the butterfly, or fooling around with it in his on-the-field off-time. Infielders and outfielders knuckle the ball to each other in warm-ups" (Dan Daniel, "Batters Going Batty from Butterflies," *Sporting News*, June 12, 1946).

Most of these experimenters found it impossible to control the knuckleball and quickly abandoned it. The extraordinary difficulty the pitch poses to catchers has also limited its spread. But the knuckler has remained a lethal weapon for the select few who master it, and such pitchers as Hoyt Wilhelm, Joe and Phil Niekro, Wilbur Wood, Charlie Hough, Tom Candiotti, and Tim Wakefield have parlayed it into long careers.

Since World War II the pitch's usage has been characterized by several elements that distinguish it from other pitches. First, most knuckleballers either throw the pitch almost exclusively or not at all. Bill James has observed that this was not the case before World War II, with many pitchers using it as part of their arsenal (Bill James, *The New Bill James Historical Baseball Abstract*, 864; see also Rob Neyer, "The Dancing Knuckleball," Bill James and Rob Neyer, *The Neyer/James Guide to Pitchers*, 40–44). Attention to this new trend may have been first drawn by Jim Tobin's 1944 no-hitter while "relying almost solely on a knuckleball," according to a *Sporting News* editorial (*Sporting News*, May 4, 1944).

Pitcher Dick Hall reported that Branch Rickey wanted all the pitchers on the Pittsburgh staff in the early 1950s at least to experiment with the knuckler (quoted in Marty Appel, *Yesterday's Heroes*, 124). Rob Neyer estimated that half the major league pitchers of the 1940s and early 1950s used the pitch at least occasionally (Bill James and Rob Neyer, *The Neyer/James Guide to Pitchers*, 438). Since then, however, it has become a pitch that is either featured or not used at all.

Another distinguishing characteristic of the knuckleball's usage since the 1950s is that its practitioners have ended up as starters, though many of them began as relievers. In addition, knuckleballers rarely enjoy major league success before age thirty, but they often last well into their forties.

Since the 1930s it has also become almost automatic for the pitch to be gripped with the fingernails, rather than the knuckles. When a recent pitcher named Jared Fernandez threw the pitch with his knuckles, this was considered such a novelty that his pitch was dubbed the "hard knuckleball" to distinguish it from what was viewed as the real knuckleball.

3.2.11 Knuckle Curve. Like most hybrid pitches, the origins of the knuckle curve are extremely difficult to pin down. Nonetheless it appears clear that the idea of combining a knuckleball grip with a curveball delivery is as old as the knuckleball itself.

For example, the *Lansing Journal* reported in 1907, "Pitcher Morgan of the Philadelphia club has a new curve that he calls a 'knuckle curve'" (*Lansing* [Mich.] *Journal*, June 5, 1907). There was no pitcher named Morgan on either Philadelphia club that season, so the writer almost certainly meant Lew Moren, whose knuckleball was described in the preceding entry. As noted in that same entry, Ralph Savidge called his pitch a "finger nail curve."

The pitch has never been common, but it resurfaces occasionally. Ed Rommel noted that George Earnshaw, a star of the early 1930s, "had a knuckler, but he pitched it with only one finger. It had more curve and spin than the knuckle pitches you see now" (Dan Daniel, "Batters Going Batty from Butterflies," *Sporting News*, June 12, 1946). Bill James and Rob Neyer noted that Dave Stenhouse in the 1960s and Burt Hooton in the 1970s brought the pitch back to some level of prominence (Bill James and Rob Neyer, *The Neyer/James Guide to Pitchers*, 16).

3.2.12 Screwball. Christy Mathewson, with his legendary fadeaway, was the first pitcher to bring widespread attention to the pitch now known as the screwball. Mathewson disavowed having invented it, claiming that he learned it around 1900 from a man named Dave Williams (Bozeman Bulger, "Pitching, Past and Present: The Evolution of the Twirler's Art," *Baseball Magazine*, February 1912, 71–73; Dick Thompson, "Matty and His Fadeaway," *National Pastime* 17 [1997], 93–96).

It is therefore safe to assume that the pitch is of nineteenth-century origin. The evidence also makes it possible to draw some general conclusions about the screwball's history. Like several other pitches, it first emerged during the curveball revolution but either it was not fully mastered by any pitcher, or those who did master it successfully kept it under wraps. Only the spitball revolution spawned renewed experiments that led to general recognition of the screwball's effectiveness.

It is much more difficult to pinpoint who actually invented the pitch, as the claims are many and varied. Some accounts of Fred Goldsmith's curve-throwing exhibition have him throwing a screwball (William E. McMahon, "Fred Ernest Goldsmith," in Frederick Ivor-Campbell, Robert L. Tiemann, and Mark Rucker, eds., *Baseball's First Stars*, 69). A 1903 account claimed that Goldsmith "discovered the 'in shoot,' that is, he was able to deliver a swift ball with a distinct swerve toward a right-handed batter" (*Grand Rapids* [Mich.] *Herald*, May 17, 1903).

Ted Sullivan said that Charles Radbourn "had a perplexing slow ball that was never duplicated on the ball field. The nearest approach to him in this delivery was by John Clarkson and Tim Keefe of Rad's time. To this slow ball he could give a lot of speed. It would come toward you and then change its route all of a sudden. It was the delivery they call today the 'fadeaway'" (quoted in A. H. Spink, *The National Game*, 152).

Mickey Welch later stated: "I had a fadeaway, although I didn't call it that. I didn't call it anything. It was just a slow curveball that broke down and in on a right-handed hitter, and I got a lot of good results with it in the ten years I pitched for the Giants. Not until Matty came along and they began to write about his fadeaway did I realize that I had pitched it for years. Why, I learned it within a couple of years after I started to play ball and I had no copyright on it. There were several other old pitchers who used it" (Frank Graham, *New York Sun*, reprinted in *Sporting News*, March 2, 1933).

Johnny Evers and Hugh S. Fullerton wrote that "before [Christy] Mathewson learned the trick of pitching his 'fader,' there was one who pitched the same ball in even more wonderful style." The pitcher whom they had in mind was Virgil Garvin, who "pitched it with his middle finger lapped over his index finger and when he released the ball his hand was turned almost upside down." But Evers and Fullerton believed that Garvin "did not understand its use or worth" (John J. Evers and Hugh S. Fullerton, *Touching Second*, 108–109).

Faith has been a recurring theme in the pitch's history. Bobby Mathews indicated in 1883 that he did not believe that such a pitch was possible at all. He acknowledged that there was an "inshoot" but not an "incurve," explaining, "Of course, a ball will shoot in a little distance, but you can't call it a curve, because you can't hold that kind of a ball so as to make a curve out of it. The only genuine curve is the one that turns out from the batsmen; but after two or three of that kind a straight ball, if it is properly pitched, looks as if it was turning the other way" (*Philadelphia Press*, reprinted in *Grand Rapids* [Mich.] *Morning Democrat*, September 2, 1883).

It would thus appear that, as with many other pitches but to a still greater degree, the pertinent question is not who invented the fadeaway but who believed in the pitch enough to develop it to its full potential. And that man, unquestionably, was Christy Mathewson.

The pitch receded into the background after Mathewson's retirement, only to make a dramatic comeback with another Giant great, Carl Hubbell. Hubbell called his pitch a screwball; the reasons for the name change are complex. Rob Neyer has made a persuasive case that "screw ball" was the name of a different pitch in the 1920s, which was closer to a sinker (Rob Neyer, "The Screwball: Fading Away," Bill James and Rob Neyer, *The Neyer/James Guide to Pitchers*, 52–55). My own findings support Neyer's contention. According to *Babe Ruth's Own Book of Baseball*, the "screw ball" was developed in response to the banning of the spitball (Babe Ruth, *Babe Ruth's Own Book of Baseball*, 78). A 1921 article confirmed this view, noting that "The day of the spitball and other freak deliveries may be over, but [the Browns'] Dixie Davis displayed an entirely new brand of hurling [today] . . . in the shape of a screw ball that enabled him to stand [George] McBride's hirelings [Washington] on their heads" (John A. Dugan, "Davis Has Equal of Freak Pitching," *Washington Post*, May 21, 1921).

Such questions can never be definitively resolved, but there seem to be more similarities than differences between the fadeaway and the screwball. Al Lopez believed that some of Hubbell's effectiveness with the pitch was the result of a change to the ball in 1933: ". . . In '33 they raised the seams on the ball. This let Hubbell get a better grip to turn the ball over and get a better snap with that long wrist he had. That's when his screwball faded away into a real butterfly and he became a big winner" (quoted in Walter M. Langford, *Legends of Baseball*, 218).

3.2.13   Emery Ball. While the emery ball is part of the doctored-ball family discussed in the next entry, it warrants its own entry due to its historical significance. One major part of the emery ball's legacy is that it became the first pitch ever banned when the American League outlawed it on February 3, 1915. Another singular element of the pitch's history is that it was primarily associated with one pitcher, Russell Ford. And while Ford began using the emery ball around 1910 and was highly successful with it, he kept its secret so well that he was its sole practitioner for most of the period until it was banned.

The secrecy that surrounded the pitch helped keep its origins shrouded in mystery. Fortunately Ford eventually provided his own account of the origins and history of the emery ball. Writing in 1935, he observed, "Many stories have been told and yarns spun by the yard during the years that have passed, relating to the discovery of the emery ball. None of them came from me, because I never talked about that 'delivery'" (Russell Ford as told to Don E. Basenfelder, "Russell Ford Tells Inside Story of the 'Emery' Ball After Guarding His Secret for Quarter of a Century," *Sporting News*, April 25, 1935, 5). In fact, Ford's memory was faulty in this regard, as he had given a similar account to F. C. Lane of *Baseball Magazine* in 1915 (F. C. Lane, "The Emery Ball Strangest of Freak Deliveries," *Baseball Magazine*, July 1915, 58–72).

According to Ford, the story begins in the spring of 1908. Ford and Ed Sweeney had formed a battery with Atlanta the preceding year, but Sweeney had been sold to New York near the end of the season. Nonetheless the two practiced together in Atlanta to prepare for the 1908 campaign.

One of Ford's pitches got away from Sweeney and struck a wooden upright behind the plate. Ford's next pitch, which was supposed to be a fastball, instead broke viciously and sailed sideways by about five feet. When Sweeney retrieved the pitch, Ford examined the baseball and noticed that the surface had been roughened by the impact of hitting the stands.

Suspecting that the rough surface may have caused the peculiar break, Ford threw another pitch with a completely different grip. The ball confirmed his hunch by again taking a mysterious sailing dip. But Ford dismissed the pitch to Sweeney as "a funny one I learned how to throw" and did not use it at all that year.

Russell Ford was drafted by New York at season's end and reported to spring training with the major league club. Because his arm was sore, he was shipped to Jersey City. At that point Ford recalled the funny ball of the previous spring and decided to give it another try. Before a batting practice session, he used a broken pop bottle to roughen the surface of the ball.

Several slow tosses produced nothing out of the ordinary. Then Ford threw the ball harder and the miraculous break returned: "A double curve! Could any baseball pitcher dream of a sweeter thing than that?" Three Jersey City teammates, Earl Gardner, Dan Moeller, and Eddie "Kid" Foster, flailed at the pitch throughout the session without success. When it was finished, the befuddled players told Ford that he was either a one-day "flash" or they were losing their eyesight.

Ford now realized that he was on to something. He faced an important dilemma: "I had come across a new delivery that without doubt would make me the greatest pitcher in big league baseball—if I kept it to myself!

"But should I conceal my secret or impart it to the rest of the baseball world? If I did the latter I would lose it and others would also benefit from it. What should I do? I realized you couldn't sell a pig in a poke and once the pig is out, it was anybody's pig.

"I didn't want to talk it over with anybody, so I carried the problem to my Jersey City boarding house when practice was over. Going to my room, I sat down on the bed and pondered the situation.

"Somewhat selfish, perhaps, I felt that the discovery belonged to me and if anything came of it, I should benefit through its use.

"Then again, if I told other baseball pitchers about it and they started to throw the emery ball, it would soon become outlawed because of the advantage it gave the hurler over a batter. Nothing can survive in baseball which impairs the balance of the game."

Thus, according to Ford, before having ever used what would become his signature pitch in a game, he had made a conscious decision to keep it secret. Realizing that he could not bring broken glass out to the mound with him, he experimented until he found that he could create a similar effect with emery paper, a type of sandpaper. So he cut a piece of emery paper into pieces and sewed a three-quarter-inch square of it into his glove.

Ford took several additional precautions to guard against the discovery of his secret. He pointedly carried his glove back to the dugout with him between innings, defying the custom of leaving gloves on the field. He went through an elaborate pretense of wetting the ball to create the impression that he was throwing a spitball. And he took none of his teammates into his confidence regarding the ruse, not even catcher Larry Spahr.

Once the 1909 Eastern League season began, Ford had the emery ball mastered, and he experienced immediate success with it. He continued to modify his technique for roughening the surface of the ball. First, he moved the emery paper from the outside of his glove to the webbing. Then he moved the emery paper to a ring he wore on his finger. Ford then cut a hole in his glove, allowing him to scuff the ball surreptitiously.

Ford characterized these changes as "seeking to improve ways of pitching the emery ball." It seems a safe assumption, though, that their real intent was to ensure the secrecy of the pitch. No doubt Ford was worried that carrying his glove off the field between innings would attract attention and lead to the discovery of the emery paper.

In July, New York manager George Stallings repurchased Ford's contract, but a spike wound sidelined him for the remainder of the season. The following spring he took the American League by storm, winning his first eight decisions en route to a 26-6 record and a 1.65 earned run average. He followed that up in 1911 with another 22 victories.

Moreover his secret seems to have remained safe, as opposing batters seem to have believed it was a spitball that was baffling them. Ed Sweeney was Ford's personal catcher and was in on the secret, as was his roommate Eddie Foster, but otherwise Ford continued to keep even his teammates in the dark about the pitch.

After two spectacular seasons, Ford's bubble burst in 1912. Sweeney was a holdout that spring, and no other catcher was as accomplished at receiving the emery ball. More important, Ford suffered a series of arm problems and posted losing records in both 1912 and 1913.

Insult was added to injury when the secret of the emery ball finally leaked. Early in the 1913 season Ford realized that Cy Falkenberg of Cleveland was pitching the emery ball. Ford confronted Falkenberg, trying to learn who had revealed the secret of the pitch. Falkenberg offered an unconvincing denial, and Ford warned him not to tell anyone else about the pitch.

Ford now mulled over the question of how his secret had gotten out. Eventually he recalled that one teammate on New York, an infielder, "used to pick up the ball I used, every time an opportunity presented itself, and examine it." According to Ford, after this teammate "ferreted" out the secret, he told Cleveland owner Charles Somers that he could teach the pitch to the journeyman Falkenberg.

Ford deliberately withheld the name of this teammate from the account, and added: "He has never told me to this day [that he revealed the secret] and I have made no effort to find out. There was never any question of a violation of confidence in this matter." Nonetheless Ford offers enough clues that it is easy to deduce the player's identity.

Earl Gardner had been one of the three Jersey City players on whom Ford had first sprung the emery ball in batting practice in 1909. He and Ford were reunited in New York the following season, and Gardner remained a semi-regular at second base until 1912. Midway through that season he lost his job with New York and caught on with Toledo, where one of his new teammates was Falkenberg.

The pitch rejuvenated Falkenberg's previously undistinguished career, and he won twenty-three games in his 1913 return to the majors. He also apparently disregarded Ford's advice and took at least one Cleveland teammate, pitcher George Kahler, into his confidence. (Ford also cited Ed Klepfer as having been taught the pitch by Falkenberg, but Klepfer was not with Cleveland that year.)

Both Cy Falkenberg and Russell Ford jumped to the Federal League in 1914, and both were twenty-game winners that season. But Ford's proverbial pig was now out of the poke. The number of players who knew the secret had grown too large.

Ford noted, "It wasn't two months after the opening of the 1914 American League campaign before everybody in the circuit sought to take his turn on the pitching peak and fling the emery ball." The pitch soon made its way to the National League, and Ford suspected that the responsible party was his former manager George Stallings, now with the Boston Braves.

The secret finally came out in September. In a game on September 14, Eddie Collins of Philadelphia accused New York pitcher Ray Keating of illegally defacing the ball. Umpire Tom Connolly checked Keating's glove and found emery paper. Nine days later Jimmy Lavender of the Cubs was caught scratching the ball against a piece of emery paper that he had taped to his uniform.

The rules could not be changed in mid-season, but American League president Ban Johnson made quick and decisive use of the powers he did have. He announced that any pitcher using sandpaper or emery paper to scuff the baseball would face a thirty-game suspension and a $100 fine.

Once Keating and Lavender were caught, it didn't take long to trace the technique back to Russell Ford. The word was soon out that Ford's "freak or double barreled spitball was nothing more than the emery papered style" (*Sporting News*, October 1, 1914). It turned out that Keating and several other Yankee pitchers had been taught the pitch by Ford's old batterymate, Ed Sweeney.

According to Frank Chance, "Sweeney was in on the secret. But he kept the secret well. He was the only man in the business outside of Ford who had the faintest idea of Russ' secret up to a few weeks ago." Chance said that Sweeney decided to show the pitch to others only when he saw George Kahler using it (*Sporting News*, October 1, 1914). Roger Peckinpaugh confirmed that Sweeney had been the one who had taught the emery ball to the Yankee pitchers (Eugene Murdock, *Baseball Between the Wars*, 18).

That offseason, the pitch was banned and Ford realized that his "bubble had burst." Ford also struggled with arm troubles that year and posted a 5-9 mark. When the Federal League folded at the end of 1915, he wrote to New York owner Colonel Jacob Ruppert that he doubted he could win without the emery ball. Ruppert gave him his release and, as Ford poignantly puts it, "wearily I backtracked the paths of my greatest successes to the baseball minors."

The ban on the pitch also brought an end to Cy Falkenberg's success. After two straight twenty-win seasons, he posted a losing mark in 1915. He was back in the minors in 1916, and resurfaced in the American League just long enough to put up a 2-6 mark which confirmed that his magic had deserted him forever.

Ty Cobb acknowledged that American League batters did not recognize the nature of the pitch, noting that Ford "kept his secret a long time by pretending he was pitching a spitter. He would deliberately show his finger to the batter and then wet it with saliva. This covered up his real trick of using the emery finger-ring to rough the ball" (Ty Cobb, *Memoirs of Twenty Years in Baseball*, 70).

Roger Peckinpaugh suggested that another key to Ford's keeping the pitch a secret was his restraint: "He was satisfied that he could sail the ball just a short distance with a small spot on it the size of a dime. He got away with it for so long because he would go to his mouth every time as if he was throwing a spitter. Everyone thought he was throwing a spitter." Once other pitchers learned the pitch, they "weren't satisfied with a little spot the size of a dime, they wanted a bigger spot. They wound up scuffing half the ball, so it wasn't long until the emery ball was outlawed" (Eugene Murdock, *Baseball Between the Wars*, 18).

Russell Ford's account of the history of the emery pitch included one more intriguing element, though he acknowledged it to be only a "strong hunch" on his part. He suggested that Braves manager George Stallings might have taught the emery ball to pitchers Dick Rudolph, Lefty Tyler, and Bill James during the 1914 season.

Something certainly got into these three pitchers. The Braves had posted thirteen consecutive second-division finishes and were in the National League cellar on July 4, 1914. Then they were transformed into the "Miracle Braves" and stormed to the National League pennant and a World Series sweep of the heavily favored Philadelphia Athletics. The key was the trio of starting pitchers; after posting only one shutout before July 4, they posted eighteen afterward.

The record of the Braves' trio of pitchers in 1915 also seems to support Russell Ford's hunch about the secret of their success. After being virtually unbeatable for much of 1914, Tyler, Rudolph, and James were only five games over .500 in 1915.

Once the emery ball became famous, there were at least a couple of claimants to prior invention. Clark Griffith confessed to having used the emery ball during the 1890s (*Atlanta Constitution*, September 19, 1913). Hugh S. Fullerton wrote that turn-of-the-century pitcher Bert Briggs carried emery powder in his hip pocket and applied it to the ball, making it take "the most extraordinary 'hops,' some of which fooled his catchers" (Hugh S. Fullerton, syndicated column, *Reno Evening Gazette*, April 29, 1915). But it is clear that even if others experimented with the pitch earlier, Russell Ford was the man who perfected it.

3.2.14 Doctored-ball Family. In early baseball a single ball was usually used for the entire game, which meant that a pitcher who doctored the ball might

hinder the opposing batters but would similarly handicap his own team's hitters. This did not, of course, entirely prevent such tactics.

Several clubs attempted the ethically dubious practice of switching balls
between half-innings, as is discussed under "Double-ball Rackets" (**11.1.12**).
Other pitchers reasoned that, if it helped them get batters out, they didn't
much care if it had a similar effect on their team's batsmen. George W.
"Grin" Bradley pitched for Chicago in 1877, but the club did not attempt to
resign him for the following season. Bradley caught on with New Bedford
and eagerly awaited the opportunity to face his old team and exact revenge.

Bradley "took the box containing the ball into the kitchen of the hotel
and steamed it so the label would come off. Then he carried it to a carpenter's shop, wrapped it in the heel of a stocking, put it in a vise and pressed it
until it was as mellow as a ripe pear. Then he put it back in the box, sealed
it up and took it out to the game. The ball was thrown to the umpire, who
broke open the box and tossed it to Bradley. The latter grinned in his own
original, fiendish style and took his place in the box. Brad could make the
soft ball do everything but talk. He sent it in with all kinds of shoots and
curves. In consequence we knocked the Windy City team out by a score of
5 to 1" (*Cincinnati Enquirer*, April 17, 1892; see also Tim Murnane, *Boston
Globe*, May 14, 1888).

There was a very fine line between rubbing up a ball and defacing one,
as is clear from this 1891 description: "On the occasion of a pitcher entering the box in the first inning having a brand new white ball tossed to him,
he thereupon goes through a little performance previous to delivering the
ball, for the same reason probably that a violinist tunes up before playing. To
deliver a new ball to the bat without this bit of preliminary acting would be
considered evidence that the pitcher was not in good trim. Upon receiving
the ball from the umpire, the pitcher first examines it in a critical manner.
Convinced that it is a regulation ball without flaw, he then rolls it around in
his hands with great vigor. Formerly he took up a handful of dirt and rubbed
it all over the ball, in order to render it a less shining mark for the batsman,
but the rules now forbid that. He is, therefore, compelled to do the rubbing
with his hands, and this is done in an energetic manner, as though determined to rub the cover off. Having rubbed the ball until all the dirt on the
palm of his hands is transferred to the corner of the sphere, the pitcher looks
around to see if all his fielders, in and out, big and little, are alive and in good
spirits. Satisfied on this point, he gives the ball one parting rub, and with a
look which expresses great dissatisfaction with its bright exterior, he finally
throws it" (*Sporting Life*, November 7, 1891).

Al Maul, who pitched in the majors from 1884 to 1901, was particularly
vigilant in these efforts. An 1896 account reported that Maul "is said to have
an invention of his own of breaking in a new ball. When the new white spheroid is passed to him he anoints it with a piece of pumice stone concealed in

a handkerchief. This removes the gloss and roughens the smooth surface, thus giving the fingers a firm grip on the ball" (*Brooklyn Eagle*, May 5, 1896).

But Maul was interested in more than just improving his grip. He later explained, "It's impossible to make a ball with a new, shiny cover break right. . . . In my time, we only used two or three balls to a game. If it was fouled off we waited until it was retrieved and put it in play again, and when a new ball was thrown out we were allowed to saturate it with tobacco juice, rub it in the dirt and roughen it up a bit. Then we could put the old stuff on it. Yes, sir, the batters in those days used to see some funny shoots breaking over the corners of the plate" (*Sporting Life* [monthly], December 1922).

Others went further. Arthur Cummings, for example, had a way of pinching the ball that elevated the cover temporarily and gave it an erratic motion. At inning's end he could smooth it back to its original form (*Sporting News*, December 29, 1921). An 1894 account noted, "In Cleveland [Brooklyn] Pitcher [Sadie] McMahon is accused of carrying lamp black in his pocket to use on new balls" (*Brooklyn Eagle*, July 7, 1894). Researcher David Ball directed my attention to an 1891 claim that George Cuppy "is accused of smearing the ball so thickly with licorice, which he carries in his mouth for that purpose, that opposing pitchers cannot control it" (*Sporting Life*, July 11, 1891).

Hugh S. Fullerton later enumerated others: "The first record we have of the tricky use of outside agents to cause a ball to perform strange antics in the air was when Tom Bond, pitching for New Bedford, used glycerine and delivered a form of what is now known as the spit-ball. Al Orth, who, according to many old-time players, was the only man to pitch an 'up curve,' used slippery elm, which he applied to his fingers and, throwing underhand, caused the ball to seem to curve upward. Clark Griffith . . . used to knock the dirt from his spikes by striking the ball against his shoe. Grif would strike the ball sharply against his spikes, cut two abrasions in the hide, grip his fingers into them and pitch his famous slow ball. He learned the trick from Hoss Radbourn. While trying to 'wing' the ball Griffith discovered by accident that on some diamonds the grit from his heel, adhering to the ball, made the sphere act strangely in the air. He was pitching a 'sail ball' as long ago as 1896. Bert Briggs, now dead, used emery powder, which he carried in his hip pocket, and his fast ball took the most extraordinary 'hops,' some of which fooled his catchers" (syndicated column, *Reno Evening Gazette*, April 29, 1915; the source of Fullerton's information on Bond was a 1911 interview with Michael Scanlon tracked down by researcher Steve Steinberg. Scanlon told Fullerton that "Bond used to carry a small bottle of glycerin in his hip pocket, and when he wanted to pitch a spitball, he smeared the ends of his fingers with the glycerin. The ball broke exactly as the spitball of today does, and perhaps in Bond's hands as sharply as [Ed] Walsh's does. Old-timers who hit against him will recall it" [*Detroit News*, August 21, 1911]).

The most famous instance of doctoring a baseball came when William "Blondie" Purcell of Buffalo earned the nickname "Cut-the-ball" (and a ten-dollar fine) by taking his penknife to a baseball in a game on June 6, 1882. Ironically, Purcell's intention was to force the umpire to remove the sodden ball from the game so that his team's pitcher could throw his curveball properly.

In 1897 it was made illegal for a player deliberately to deface the baseball. This was followed in the ensuing years by an increased emphasis on discarding frayed baseballs, as discussed under "New Balls" (1.26). Instead of eliminating ball scuffing, this had the opposite effect.

For one thing, the rule was extremely difficult for umpires to enforce. A perfect example was the effort to stop Clark Griffith's previously noted "habit of hitting the ball against the heel of one of his shoes." A *New York Times* article later recalled that "opposing batsmen were always calling the umpires' attention to this, claiming that Griffith nicked the cover of the ball, which aided him in using a freak delivery. After a while the umpires came to the conclusion that this was just a nervous habit of Griffith's, and he merely knocked the ball against the heel of his shoe and had no intention of cutting the cover" ("Leagues May Ban Weird Deliveries," *New York Times*, October 19, 1919).

In addition, pitchers soon realized that more frequent ball changes meant that they alone would benefit if they doctored the ball. They soon found that with practice such pitches could often be controlled. This led to what Ty Cobb called the "long siege of trick pitching," and even he expressed grudging admiration for the inventiveness behind it (Ty Cobb, *Memoirs of Twenty Years in Baseball*, 119). After it ended, Cobb commented, "While the development of trick ball pitching was not a good thing for baseball, the inventors of those mysterious devices for fooling batters are really entitled to more credit than they ever received" (Ty Cobb, *Memoirs of Twenty Years in Baseball*, 68).

The spitball's rise to prominence in 1904 accelerated this trend, and both Cobb and Johnny Evers explicitly linked the two developments. Ty Cobb offered this description: "Every pitcher in the land was sitting up at night thinking up ways of doing tricky things to the ball. This came right on the heels of the hullabaloo over the spitball. Most of those pitchers, too, were really clever inventors. They got away with the most astonishing tricks, some of which have not been solved or exposed to this day. A rule was adopted to do away with all freak pitching, but it still crops out in spots" (Ty Cobb, *Memoirs of Twenty Years in Baseball*, 65).

The rule makers tried to prohibit pitchers from defacing the ball, but the rules proved easy to get around. Fred Snodgrass later recalled that when an umpire would toss a new ball to the mound, the pitcher "would promptly side step it. It would go around the infield once or twice and come back to the pitcher as black as the ace of spades. All the infielders were chewing to-bacco or licorice, and spitting into their gloves, and they'd give that ball a good going over before it got to the pitcher. Believe me, that dark ball was hard to see coming out of the shadows of the stands" (Lawrence Ritter, *The Glory of Their Times*, 99).

Johnny Evers and Hugh Fullerton wrote in 1910: "Immediate variations of the [spit] ball were developed. Slippery elm, talcum powder, crude oil, vaseline were used to lessen the friction of the fingers while other pitchers, to get more friction on the thumb, used gum, pumice stone, resin or adhe-sive tape" (John J. Evers and Hugh S. Fullerton, *Touching Second*, 113).

Dan Daniel later pinpointed the 1914 and 1915 seasons as the height of the "era of screwy slinging." He noted: "Mud ball, talcum ball, shine ball, phonograph needle ball, raised-seams ball, emery ball, tobacco juice ball—all these daffy inventions made life miserable for the hitters—and the catch-ers, too. Finally, when Joe Tinker came out with a large steel file and rubbed a ball right out in the open, the time had come to put a stop to the extrava-ganza" (Dan Daniel, "Batters Going Batty from Butterflies," *Sporting News*, June 12, 1946).

But these years also proved to be the swan song for such tactics. Connie Mack spent much of a game on September 14, 1914, arguing that New York pitcher Ray Keating was illegally defacing the ball with emery paper. The emery ball was banned the following year, and pitchers who engaged in "screwy slinging" began to come under intense scrutiny. Billy Evans ex-plained that during the 1915 season "hardly a game passed by in any league without some manager making accusations against the opposing pitcher. In addition, there was the 'mud ball,' the 'fingernail ball,' the 'talcum ball' and a host of others too numerous to mention." As a result, "the moment a pitcher got his fast ball to sailing, the batter would insist on an examination, a rough spot would usually be found," and the ball would be removed from play (Billy Evans, syndicated column, *Atlanta Constitution*, January 16, 1916).

As a result, pitchers who wanted to doctor the ball had to become more and more devious. Eddie Cicotte, for example, threw a mysterious pitch that Ty Cobb called a "sailor." The ball "would start like an ordinary pitch and then would sail much in the manner of a flat stone thrown by a small boy" (Ty Cobb, *Memoirs of Twenty Years in Baseball*, 68). The *New York Times* ob-served, "Eddie Cicotte and Hod Eller are supposed to be shine ball experts, but the methods used in doctoring this particular ball never has [sic] been clearly explained" (*New York Times*, October 31, 1919). Cobb was convinced that Cicotte used some illegal tactic to achieve this effect, but even his team-mates were in the dark about his method.

No doubt Cicotte was mindful of what had happened to Russell Ford's emery ball and remained tight-lipped about the pitch, even around teammates. Cobb noted that all that Cicotte "asked was for the ball to be rolled to him on the ground. With a brand new ball that had not touched the dirt he couldn't deliver the sailor" (Ty Cobb, *Memoirs of Twenty Years in Baseball*, 69). Cicotte was banned from baseball in 1920 for his role in the Black Sox scandal, and took the secret of this pitch with him.

The shine ball became a cause celebre during the 1917 season, but the term was a catchall for any pitch that generated a peculiar movement. Sportswriter Paul Purman noted that the shine ball was also referred to as the licorice ball or the talcum powder ball and was "caused by rubbing talcum powder, licorice or any other smooth, slippery substance on the ball." He explained that the pitch "depends upon air pressure for its peculiar defiance of the laws of the moving bodies and of gravitation. The shineball is only effective when the shiny spot is on one of the poles of rotation" (Paul Purman, syndicated column, *Fort Wayne Sentinel*, July 5, 1917).

Near the end of the 1917 season, American League president Ban Johnson responded by ordering the elimination of the shine ball and decreeing that pitchers could henceforth only use dirt or sand to rub the ball (*Sporting Life*, September 8, 1917). Needless to say, this was easier said than enforced.

Umpire Billy Evans wrote that what he termed the loaded ball was popular among pitchers during the 1918 season: "Through the use of paraffine, an oil rubbed into the palm of the glove, or merely through the use of tobacco licorice juice, or plain saliva, the ball was moistened at the seams. Such moistening acted as a base. A pitcher then rubbed the ball into some dirt, which he managed to get on the palm of his glove. In a short while that seam would become thoroughly loaded, making it considerably heavier at a certain spot. Through proper delivery, and the air resistance which the ball encountered, some fancy dips were possible" (Billy Evans, syndicated column, *Atlanta Constitution*, January 5, 1919).

While it was impossible to eliminate entirely the doctored-ball family of pitches, increased replacement of baseballs and relentless scrutiny by umpires did the next best thing. Suspected shine-ball practitioner Dave Danforth "was subjected to a showdown test of his alleged illegal pitches. With Commissioner Kenesaw M. Landis and American League President Ban Johnson in the stands, Umpire Billy Evans was instructed to hand Danforth a new ball every time one was hit foul or even into the outfield. Moreover, Danforth was forbidden to rub the ball" (Bob Wolf, "Controversy Like Screaming at Danforth 40 Years Ago," *Sporting News*, May 1, 1957). Such tactics ensured that moundsmen could no longer rely upon these pitches.

Sporting News correspondent Francis J. Powers wrote in 1921 that pitcher Eric Erickson of Washington was following Al Maul's lead in using the pitcher's prerogative to rub up the ball to further his own ends: "With a grip that would put many a professional wrestler and strong man to shame, the Jamestown (N.Y.) Swede can twist the cover loose from a ball with a couple of turns. And once the tightly sewed horsehide is loosened from the interior it is an easy matter to knead it so the ball will sail and dip as it leaves the pitcher's hands and darts toward the batter" (*Sporting News*, December 8, 1921). He seems to have had some imitators, as the writer of a 1923 article reported on the practice of pitchers loosening the cover of baseballs by grasping it with both hands and twisting in opposite directions (*The Literary Digest*; quoted in Dan Gutman, *It Ain't Cheatin' If You Don't Get Caught*, 52).

Apparently at least some umpires considered this technique legal, perhaps because it used no foreign substance. But it didn't help Erickson much, as he never posted a winning record in his seven-year major league career.

3.2.15 Slider. Despite its relatively recent emergence, the origins of the slider are cloaked in considerable mystery. Sportswriter Joseph Durso aptly observed in 1968, "Nobody knows for sure who invented the slider or whether it was just there all the time waiting to be harnessed" (Joseph Durso, "Slider Is the Pitch That Put Falling Batting Averages on the Skids," *New York Times*, September 22, 1968).

The two names that come up most frequently are George Blaeholder and George Uhle. John Thorn and John Holway observed that Blaeholder is usually credited with discovering the pitch in the late 1920s (John Thorn and John Holway, *The Pitcher*, 154). Others have suggested that Uhle developed the pitch around 1930.

George Uhle himself commented: "I think I was the first one to throw the slider. At least I happened to come up with it while I was in Detroit. And I gave it its name because it just slides across. It's just a fastball you turn loose in a different way. When I first started throwing it the batters thought I was putting some kind of stuff on the ball to make it act that way" (Walter M. Langford, *Legends of Baseball*, 128).

On another occasion, Uhle added: "Harry Heilmann and I were just working [on the sideline with catcher Eddie] Phillips. It just came to me all of a sudden, letting the ball go along my index finger and using my ring finger and pinky to give it just a little bit of a twist. It was a sailing fastball, and that's how come I named it the slider. The real slider is a sailing fastball. Now they call everything a slider, including a nickel curve" (quoted in John Thorn and John Holway, *The Pitcher*, 154).

For many, the pitch was just a reincarnation of an older pitch. Phil Rizzuto suggested that it evolved from the "slip pitch" taught by Paul Richards (Joseph Durso, "Slider Is the Pitch That Put Falling Batting Averages on the Skids," *New York Times*, September 22, 1968; according to Rob Neyer, the slip pitch is very similar to the palm ball [Bill James and Rob Neyer, *The Neyer/James Guide to Pitchers*, 21]). Frank Frisch was particularly vociferous in denouncing the slider as just a nickel curve or a dinky curve. He considered the success of the pitch to be a prime example of that eternal lament of retired ballplayers—that baseball was not as good as it had been in his day (Frank Frisch and J. Roy Stockton, *Frank Frisch: The Fordham Flash*; quoted in Dan Daniel, "Fordham Flash Casts Vote for Old-Timers," *Sporting News*, August 4, 1962, 5).

Bucky Walters claimed that Chief Bender had taught him the pitch and had used it as early as 1910. The only difference was that Bender didn't call it a slider, nor did he have any name for the pitch. Martin Quigley cited Frank Shellenback and Elmer Stricklett as other early pitchers who may have used sliders (Martin Quigley, *The Crooked Pitch*, 102–103). Additional names that have come up include Cy Young, Clark Griffith, and Grover Cleveland Alexander (John Thorn and John Holway, *The Pitcher*, 153–154; Bill James and Rob Neyer, *The Neyer/James Guide to Pitchers*, 7). The nature of the pitch and the passage of time make such claims impossible to resolve.

What is not in dispute is the extraordinary growth in the slider's popularity during the '40s and '50s. Phil Rizzuto claimed that when he debuted in 1941, only Cleveland's Al Milnar threw the slider regularly (Joseph Durso, "Slider Is the Pitch That Put Falling Batting Averages on the Skids," *New York Times*, September 22, 1968). But within a few years the pitch had begun to catch on.

Bill James and Rob Neyer called it "the pitch of the 1950s" (Bill James and Rob Neyer, *The Neyer/James Guide to Pitchers*, 7). By 1960 the slider was so firmly established that sportswriter Dan Daniel could claim that there was "a strong coterie of mound coaches which holds that if you cannot throw a slider, you had better open a shoeshine store" (Dan Daniel, "Lopat Using 'Soft Sell' on Yankee Pitchers," *Sporting News*, April 6, 1960). That master of the turn of phrase, Roger Angell, aptly dubbed it "the pitcher's friend" (Roger Angell, "On the Ball," *Once More Around the Park*, 90).

Stan Musial explained that the slider "changed the game" because its very existence altered a batter's approach. An astute batter, according to Musial, could distinguish a curve from a fastball in plenty of time to take a full swing. The late break of the slider forced batters to remain wary of another option and made it more difficult to attack any pitch (Roger Kahn, *The Head Game*, 157).

Ted Williams observed that, just as important, the pitch proved easy for pitchers to learn and master: "The big thing the slider did was give the pitcher a third pitch right away. With two pitches you might guess right half the time. With three your guessing goes down proportionately. . . . It immediately gives a pitcher a better repertoire" (Ted Williams with John Underwood, *My Turn at Bat*, 234).

Musial concurred, observing in 1961: "When I came to the majors in 1941, only a few pitchers had the slider. Now almost all of them can throw it effectively. It breaks in on the thin handle where there is no wood. I'd say the slider increases the hitter's problem 25 per cent" (quoted in *Sporting News*, November 8, 1961).

Musial's comments raise the interesting possibility that the success of the slider can be at least partially attributed to the tapered bat. It also seems logical that the trend toward fuller swings and follow-throughs (see Chapter 2, section 1, especially **2.1.3** and **2.1.1**) would have made the pitch more effective. This would help explain why old-timers like Frisch considered the slider to be a retread of an old pitch that had not been effective. Musial has also suggested that the slider spurred the trend toward lighter bats (Martin Quigley, *The Crooked Pitch*, 103).

3.2.16   Eephus Pitch. After so many years of hurlers spending their spare time trying to evolve new pitches, Rip Sewell tried a deceptively simple idea in a major league game on June 1, 1943. Sewell simply turned back the clock a century by lobbing a high, slow ball up to the plate and daring batters to hit it. What was so amazing about the pitch, which Sewell initially called his dew-drop ball but which later became known as the blooper or eephus ball, was that it worked—at least until Ted Williams connected with Sewell's novelty pitch for a memorable home run in the 1946 All-Star game.

   Given the simplicity of the pitch, it is not surprising that there were earlier pitchers who appear to have experimented with variations of it. In an 1867 match, a pitcher from the Athletic Club of Dansville, New York, arced his pitches as high as twenty feet in the air with great success (*Rochester Evening Express*, August 3, 1867; reprinted in Priscilla Astifan, "Baseball in the Nineteenth Century, Part Two," *Rochester History* LXII, no. 2, Spring 2000, 17). In an 1869 match against the Stars of Brooklyn, Jack Chapman of the Atlantics of Brooklyn pitched "the last five innings in so peculiar a manner that the Stars could not hit him. The ball was delivered very slowly, and tossed high in the air, descending over the plate and the spot which the striker designated as the place where he wanted a ball. The Stars looked upon this style of pitching as little short of robbery, although they acknowledged it was in accordance with the rules" (*New York Clipper*, January 24, 1880). John Thorn and John Holway cite Harry Wright and Bill Phillips as pitchers who evolved similar techniques (John Thorn and John Holway, *The Pitcher*, 153). The *Steubenville Herald Star* noted many years later that turn-of-the-century pitcher James "Slab" Burns "won considerable fame as a pitcher, and is reported to be the first hurler to pitch the 'balloon' ball which Rip Sewell of the Pittsburgh Pirates has made famous" (*Steubenville Herald Star*, June 22, 1945).

After Sewell revived the unique delivery, pitchers who have experimented with it have included Bill Lee, Steve Hamilton, with his folly floater, and Dave LaRoche, who dubbed his pitch LaLob.

3.2.17   Kimono Ball. Baseball historian Martin Quigley called the kimono ball the "only new pitch introduced to baseball during the latter half of [the twentieth] century." It was the brainchild of Yankee southpaw Tommy Byrne, who invented the pitch during a 1955 postseason exhibition tour of Japan. Quigley gave this description: "From a set position, looking in, he would take his arm back normally and, while striding forward, continue a backward swing and deliver the ball from behind his back. He got so he could control it pretty well. While it did not have much velocity and only a slight rainbow drop, its charm was that it came to batters who were expecting to see it coming toward them from one side, the meanwhile it was still revolving around his back."

While the bizarre pitch was originally intended only to entertain Japanese fans, Byrne showed it to Yankee manager Casey Stengel during spring training and received permission to use it in a preseason game. He did so on March 26, 1956, in a game in Miami against the Brooklyn Dodgers. Batter Pee Wee Reese was too surprised to swing, but umpire Larry Napp called it a "discard" pitch and told Byrne not to throw it again (Martin Quigley, *The Crooked Pitch*, 143–144).

A few days later, Cal Hubbard, umpire-in-chief of the American League, announced that the kimono pitch would not be permitted. He agreed that there was no specific rule against the pitch but said it fell under the provisions against making a mockery of the game (Ed Nichols, "Shore Sports," *Salisbury* [Md.] *Times*, March 29, 1956). Hubbard authorized umpires to fine or eject pitchers for using the pitch, and the ultimate novelty pitch passed out of baseball.

Perhaps the most amazing thing about the pitch is that Byrne, whose control problems were legendary, was somehow able to throw a pitch from behind his back and get it over the plate.

3.2.18   Palm Ball. Early pitchers lumped all changes of pace as slow balls, without making distinctions based on the technique used to throw the pitch. Bill James and Rob Neyer have noted that it is still very difficult to differentiate the palm ball from other pitches that function as changes of pace (Bill James and Rob Neyer, *The Neyer/James Guide to Pitchers*, 17). As a result, it is impossible to determine the originators of pitches like the palm ball and the circle change, and the best we can do is get some sense of when these deliveries began to be viewed as distinct pitches.

Negro Leagues star Chet Brewer claimed that fellow Negro Leaguer Bullet Rogan invented the palm ball (John Holway, *Blackball Stars*; quoted in Bill James and Rob Neyer, *The Neyer/James Guide to Pitchers*, 17). The pitch gained renown in the late 1940s and early 1950s when it was used by such pitchers as Ewell Blackwell and Jim Konstanty, and it has periodically resurfaced with such pitchers as Dave Giusti.

But with almost all organizations teaching the circle change, the pitch remains scarce. For example, when Cleveland prospect Todd Pennington developed a palm ball, farm director John Farrell remarked, "He's the only pitcher in our system that throws one. You don't see it very often because it's a difficult pitch to command" (quoted in *Baseball America*, September 1–14, 2003).

3.2.19 Circle Change. The circle change is really not a new pitch but at most just a new grip for one of the most ancient pitches. Yet it has become such a major part of pitchers' repertoires in recent years that it deserves to be mentioned.

A recurring theme of baseball firsts is that the subtler an innovation is, the harder it will be to identify its origins. The circle change is a classic example of this, since its distinguishing feature is a grip in which the pitcher's index finger and thumb form a circle (Roger Kahn, *The Head Game*, 290–291). As a result, accounts of how it entered baseball are wildly disparate.

Tim McCarver claimed that Johnny Podres threw the pitch, but other sources suggest that Podres used the conventional grip (Tim McCarver with Danny Peary, *Tim McCarver's Baseball for Brain Surgeons and Other Fans*, 54–55; quoted in Bill James and Rob Neyer, *The Neyer/James Guide to Pitchers*, 12). Roger Angell described Warren Spahn teaching a pitch that he called a sinker-screwball, but which was thrown with the grip of the circle change (Roger Angell, "The Arms Talk," *Once More Around the Park*, 292; quoted in Bill James and Rob Neyer, *The Neyer/James Guide to Pitchers*, 12). Still others try to trace the circle change back to Paul Richards's slip pitch.

While at least a few pitchers undoubtedly threw the pitch earlier, it was not until the 1990s that it began to attract much attention.

3.2.20 Splitter. There are two basic schools of thought on the delivery that became known as "the pitch of the '80s." The first contends that the split-fingered fastball is just a new name for the forkball, albeit thrown with greater speed. The second holds that the pitch's speed and precipitous drop are such an unprecedented combination that it must be considered an entirely new pitch.

Whitey Herzog offered support for the latter viewpoint, arguing, "A fork ball is a fork ball. This is a faster pitch." His explanation of the pitch's effectiveness bears some similarities to Stan Musial's comments on the slider.

Herzog noted that batters are forced to commit themselves to swing before the pitch drops out of the strike zone: "The speed doesn't give away anything. It's pretty fast. You can't pick up the rotation, so you don't know what the hell it is" (quoted in Roger Kahn, *The Head Game*, 244).

Roger Craig is generally associated with the pitch, but Roger Kahn suggested that the credit should actually go to a more obscure pitcher named Freddie Martin. Martin pitched for the Cardinals in 1946 but jumped to the ill-fated Mexican League. Toward the end of his career he began to experiment with the grip for the splitter, but he made little use of it.

Martin became a minor league pitching coach, and 1973 found him working for the Chicago Cubs' Quincy team in the Midwest League. One of his charges was Bruce Sutter, a not particularly promising or hard-throwing prospect. Martin showed him the split-fingered grip, and Sutter's exceptionally large hands and long fingers made the pitch extraordinarily effective. According to Sutter, "I threw it, and the first time I did it, it broke down" (quoted in Roger Kahn, *The Head Game*, 247–253).

The results were spectacular. Sutter noted that "Before I learned the splitter, the Cubs were ready to release me from a bottom-level minor league team. . . . Two years after I learned the splitter, I was pitching in the major leagues." After another four years, Sutter captured the National League Cy Young Award.

That kind of success automatically attracts imitators, and Sutter helped the process along by demonstrating his grip to anyone who asked. Sutter noted, "I was the guy who showed Roger Craig how to throw the splitter. I was with the Cubs. Craig was pitching coach for San Diego. Fred Martin was there with me on the major league club that day, and on the sideline there I showed Roger how to throw it. Then Fred spent some time talking to him about it. I'm sure Roger came up with some modifications. But it was Fred Martin and I [who] showed him the pitch" (quoted in Roger Kahn, *The Head Game*, 257).

Roger Craig then brought the pitch to a new level of acclaim. In several high-profile stops as pitching coach, he encouraged his entire staff to throw the splitter. It became known as "the pitch of the '80s."

3.2.21   Cutter. Like the splitter, the cutter is a hybrid, but there is more of a consensus that the cutter is just a fastball thrown with a different grip. Bill James and Rob Neyer discussed the subject at some length and concluded that the terms "cutter" and "cut fastball" are only some twenty years old, but "the pitch itself has been around for a long, long time" (Bill James and Rob Neyer, *The Neyer/James Guide to Pitchers*, 12). Nonetheless, when thrown by a master like Mariano Rivera, the pitch's combination of speed and late movement makes it seem like a new pitch to the unhappy batters who must contend with it.

(iii) Pitching Tactics

3.3.1   Getting Batters to Chase. Of all the tactics in a pitcher's arsenal, none is older or more enduring than trying to get batters to go after bad pitches. Indeed, pitchers were trying to get batters to chase pitches outside the strike zone before there even was a strike zone (see **1.11**).

The approach of the early star Jim Creighton was particularly effective, as this 1862 account shows: "Suppose you want a low ball and you ask him to give you one, you prepare yourself to strike, and in comes the ball just the right height, but out of reach for a good hit. You again prepare yourself, and in comes another, just what you want save that it is too close. This goes on, ball after ball, until he sees you unprepared to strike, and then in comes the very ball you want, and perhaps you make a hasty strike and either miss it or tip out. And if you do neither and keep on waiting . . . being tired and impatient you strike without judgment, and 'foul out' or 'three strikes out' is the invariable result" (*New York Clipper*, August 2, 1862, reprinted in James L. Terry, *Long Before the Dodgers*, 31).

The following year rule makers took action by introducing the concepts of balls and bases on balls. The change had a dramatic effect, as the *New York Clipper* noted: "Last season, McKever's [Billy McKeever's] pitching, like several others, was made effective by his skill in what is called 'dodgy delivery,' that is, the balls he pitched, though apparently for the striker, were not such as he would strike at with any chance of hitting fairly. This style of pitching, and likewise the inaccuracy resulting from efforts to excel in speed, it was that led to the introduction of the new rules in reference to pitching, and hence McKever's style is this season deprived of all its effect" (*New York Clipper*, July 9, 1864).

The introduction of these penalties made this style of pitching more potentially costly, but it did not eliminate it. The large number of balls initially needed for a walk (near ten) left the pitcher with considerable leeway to tempt the batter to expand the strike zone. Hugh Fullerton cited 1880s pitcher Tony Mullane as being particularly effective at testing the patience of batters, noting that Mullane "had the art of wasting a ball down long before the other pitchers thought of it, and, aside from his speed, Tony's greatest success was in making batters hit bad balls" (*Chicago Tribune*, August 12, 1906).

The number of balls required for a walk continued to be reduced until the current total of four was reached in 1889. With less margin for error, the number of waste pitches was again reduced. Pitchers adapted by trying to get ahead of batters so they could afford to tempt them. For example, a 1908 game summary recounted that with two strikes on a batter, "[base runner Harry] Davis figured it out that [pitcher Tom] Hughes would waste a ball, and as it turned out he figured correctly" (*Washington Post*, April 28, 1908). And of course this basic approach continues to this day (see **6.6.4**).

3.3.2 Brushback Pitching. The Knickerbockers' ninth rule specified that the ball be pitched "for the bat." There is no reason to think that they foresaw that pitchers might choose instead to throw "for the batter," but it was less than a generation before brushback pitching began.

In early baseball there was no penalty for hitting a batter. Pitchers were taking advantage of this loophole by the early 1860s, causing one reporter to observe in 1863, ". . . All the heavy work of the game [lay] between the pitchers and catchers, the efforts of the former apparently being devoted to the intimidation of batsmen by pitching at them instead of for them as the rules require. . . . Every striker who faces such pitchers as the two in this match is as much engaged in efforts to avoid the ball pitched at him as he is to select one suitable for him to hit at" (*New York Clipper*, October 17, 1863). According to the researcher Tom Shieber, the introduction of the base on balls that offseason was intended to eliminate not only wild pitching but also this intimidating style of pitching (Tom Shieber, "The Evolution of the Baseball Diamond," in *Total Baseball IV*, 114).

As discussed in the preceding chapter (see **2.3.4**), brushback pitching was also kept within limits in the 1860s by other considerations. The fact that pitchers released the ball from below their waist conferred two important benefits for batters: it kept the pitchers from generating great speed and meant that a pitch that did hit a batsman would be likely to do so in less vulnerable spots. In addition, the ball was not dead if it hit the batsman and bounded away, which made it easy for base runners to advance.

These restraints were gradually removed, and by the mid-1870s the predictable increase in brushback pitching had begun. The ascendance of the curveball (see **3.2.3**) in the late 1870s brought the issue to a head. The curve put a batter in an unenviable position: a pitch that appeared to be headed for him might suddenly break back over the plate, while one that he had started to swing at might suddenly veer toward him.

Moreover the curve was very difficult for most pitchers to control. Ernest Lanigan later maintained that the hit-batsman rule was necessitated by a pitcher named "Wild Bill" Serad who "couldn't make his curves behave" (*Sporting News*, November 28, 1912). With bases on balls requiring close to ten balls, pitchers had plenty of opportunities to experiment. Unfortunately for batters, this meant that pitchers with good control could afford to waste pitches. It is hard to miss the hint implicit in Henry Chadwick's reference to Bobby Mathews's "habit of throwing away the first ball to each striker by tossing it over the batsman's head" (*New York Clipper*, August 14, 1875).

Then as now, knockdown pitches caused accusations to fly. When Boston pitcher Tommy Bond hit two Cleveland batters with pitches in an 1879 game, he was criticized by the *Cleveland Leader*. The *Boston Herald* responded by castigating the *Leader* for having "contemptibly insinuate[d] that it was done on purpose" (the entire exchange was reprinted in the *Chicago Tribune*, May 25, 1879). With no way of knowing what was going on in the heads of pitchers, such disputes were inevitable.

By the end of the decade, pitchers were throwing from shoulder height or higher, making brushback pitching more dangerous and more effective. It was becoming clear that bases on balls were not enough of a deterrent, so a rule was enacted before the 1879 season that empowered umpires to levy a fine of between ten and fifty dollars against pitchers who they believed were deliberately throwing at batters. This was a very sizable amount and certainly got the attention of pitchers.

But there was an obvious problem with the rule, as Henry Chadwick immediately noted: "How is the umpire to judge whether the pitcher intended to hit the batsman or not?" (*New York Clipper*, December 28, 1878). Or, as umpire Jocko Conlan later observed succinctly, "I've never claimed to be a psychic. Fair or foul. Safe or out. Ball or strike. All of that is plenty tough enough" (quoted in Roger Kahn, *The Head Game*, 217). The new rule indeed proved unenforceable, and the situation continued to deteriorate.

A pitcher named John Schappert became notorious for this approach, causing the *New York Clipper* to scold in 1883: "Schappert in his delivery of the ball to the bat has adopted a line of conduct which is hardly worthy a manly player, and one which is in direct violation of the American rules of the game; and that is his intimidation of batsmen by sending the ball to them so as to either hit them or oblige them to look more to avoiding a dangerous blow than to hitting the ball" (*New York Clipper*, August 11, 1883, quoted in James L. Terry, *Long Before the Dodgers*, 129).

Tony Mullane was another pitcher who specialized in intimidation. As early as 1881 it was reported that "Mullane for the Whites [of Cleveland] pitched wildly at times, landing the ball among batsmen's ribs quite too often to please the victims of his uncertain aim" (*Detroit Free Press*, May 1, 1881). It soon became clear that there was nothing wrong with Mullane's aim.

Chris Von der Ahe recalled in 1904 that Mullane "was a great hand at frightening the batters. 'Watch me polish his buttons,' he would frequently say as a good batter faced him. He would throw the ball right at the batter sometimes, particularly if he was a strong batter" (*St. Louis Post-Dispatch*, April 17, 1904). Hugh Fullerton gave this account: "Another point on which the Count [Mullane] insisted was that no player ever should crowd the plate on him. It interfered with his plans of making them hit bad balls. To keep them a proper distance from the plate Tony tried a system which modern pitchers would do well to follow. When a batter got up on the edge of the plate Tony hit him with the ball. After he had wounded half a dozen there was no more crowding the plate" (*Chicago Tribune*, August 12, 1906).

Another star pitcher of the 1880s with a reputation as a brushback pitcher was Tim Keefe. After an inside pitch by Keefe in 1888 injured Boston's Kid Madden, the *New York Sun* wrote, "While Boston people always have recognized the merits of Keefe as a pitcher, nevertheless they have no particular love for him, on account of his peculiar habit, fault, call it what you will, of hitting the batsman. In fact, it used to be said here that half of his skill was due to his intentional delivery of the ball so close to the batter as to intimidate constantly and finally actually frighten him into inability to hit the ball" (*New York Sun*, May 6, 1888).

With more and more pitchers throwing overhand pitches at batters, it became apparent that something stronger than a warning had to be added to the rulebook. The *Brooklyn Eagle* complained in 1883, "Nothing was done to punish the pitcher for trying to intimidate a batsman by throwing the ball at his person—the Schappert style of pitching" (*Brooklyn Eagle*, December 2, 1883).

A new rule was introduced by the American Association in 1884 allowing a hit batsman first base. At least one umpire appears to have felt that the wrong person was being protected and added a novel twist to the new hit-batsman rule during a preseason game. Indianapolis manager Bill Watkins complained that umpire John McQuaid "would not permit a batsman to take a base on being hit by a pitched ball; then again he allowed Columbus men to take bases on balls which struck him (the umpire)" (*Sporting Life*, April 30, 1884). A reply from Columbus manager Gus Schmelz the next week acknowledged that to have been the case but claimed that McQuaid was actually following a directive to that effect.

Once the wrinkles had been ironed out, the rule proved effective. One observer remarked: "The new rule punishing a pitcher for hitting a batman with the ball is working admirably. Under the old rule the pitcher could not be punished except for intentional hitting, and this could not be proved. Now he is punished whether it is intentional or not, and justly so; for if not intentional it is from want of proper command of the ball, and if he has not that the rule will teach him to acquire it. The blow must be a solid one, however, and not one in which the ball simply glances from his person" (*Sporting Life*, April 30, 1884). The National League adopted the rule three years later.

As with many other compromises, the new rule didn't eliminate brushback pitching, but it did the next best thing by ensuring that there was again risk on both sides. In the years that followed, there were hopes that reducing the number of balls required for a walk would bring an end to the brushback pitch. As late as 1901, John B. Foster wrote, "This talk about any pitcher deliberately driving a man away from the plate by trying to knock out his brains might have had some weight in the old days, when the pitcher had six and eight times to try that little performance, but it is not likely that it will be attempted very often under present conditions" (*Sporting Life*, April 6, 1901).

Eventually it became clear that no rule would eliminate this style of pitching. Instead, inside pitching has come to be governed by a generally agreed-upon set of principles. Johnny Evers and Hugh Fullerton wrote in 1910, "Spectators are not aware that one of the greatest and most effective balls pitched is the 'bean ball.' 'Bean' is baseball for 'head' and pitching at the batter's head, not to hit it, but to drive him out of position and perhaps cause him to get panic-stricken and swing at the ball in self-defense is an art" (John J. Evers and Hugh S. Fullerton, *Touching Second*, 91–92).

As this suggests, it was acceptable in the early twentieth century intentionally to pitch near the batter's head as long as he was given a chance to get out of the way. Christy Mathewson, for instance, wrote about the bean-ball at length in 1912 without expressing any ethical reservations. Instead Mathewson presented it as a good way to determine if a batter had a "yellow streak" and was not manly enough to belong in baseball (Christy Mathewson, *Pitching in a Pinch*, 35–36).

As the century wore on, beanballs became increasingly unacceptable. This trend is often attributed to the fatal beaning of Cleveland shortstop Ray Chapman in 1920, and yet this conclusion is difficult to justify. Bill James has noted that hit batsmen declined steadily during the first two decades of the twentieth century, then actually increased briefly after the Chapman tragedy. Totals of hit batsmen again dropped steadily from the mid-1920s until the mid-1940s, then increased dramatically over the next two decades, before beginning to drop in 1968.

The causes for these tendencies are more difficult to determine, because no single reason predominated. Instead a number of factors contributed, including changing interpretations of the strike zone, new approaches by batters, and the introduction of the batting helmet (Bill James, "A History of the Beanball," *The Bill James Baseball Abstract 1985*, 131–140).

Through the ups and downs there developed an unwritten but generally understood code that spells out the circumstances in which it was acceptable for a pitcher to hit a batter. Of course there are always instances where a pitcher goes beyond these constraints or where a batter expresses his displeasure by charging the mound.

Speaking of batters charging the mound, this is primarily a recent trend. But there were isolated incidents in earlier eras. Cap Anson's father Henry claimed to have charged A. G. Spalding when hit by a pitch in the late 1860s

(Adrian Anson, *A Ball Player's Career*, 43). An 1884 account noted, "In one of the recent Muskegon-Grand Rapids games [Charles] Eden, of the latter club, was hit by a ball pitched by [William F.] Nelson. This angered him, and refusing to take an apology, he rushed at Nelson, bat in hand, to punish him for it." In an incredible instance of *deus ex machina*, it began to rain heavily at that very moment, and tempers were calmed (*Sporting Life*, August 13, 1884).

3.3.3 Keeping the Ball Down. While keeping the ball down has long been a standard precept of pitching, that wasn't always the case.

As discussed under "Strike Zones" (**1.11**), until 1871 pitchers had to fulfill batter's requests for specific locations, and until 1887 batters requested low or high pitches. In addition, pitchers were not allowed to throw overhand until 1884. Since a pitch that changes planes causes difficulties for batters, many felt that "what is called a 'raise ball' (a ball delivered from below the waist for a batter calling for a high ball) is the most difficult to hit" (*Saginaw Evening Express*, May 24, 1884).

Once the pitcher was given the choice of where to throw the ball and the freedom to throw overhand, low pitching quickly came into favor. According to the pitcher "Skel" Roach, by the start of the 1890s "the man who threw low balls was the master of the situation, and the low drop curve was in great demand. Men like [Toad] Ramsey and [Charley] Buffinton, masters of low drop balls, were kings and every pitcher had a drop in his repertory. . . . The old-time slugger stood right up to his work, grasping the handle of the stick and swatting with all his might. He could kill a waist ball and could reach up after a high shoot with tremendous effect. A ball coming by his knees or sinking as it reached the plate was his hoodoo, and he would break his bat bending down for them" (*Sporting News*, February 18, 1905).

By the start of the twentieth century, many batters had switched to slap and chop hitting, and this in turn convinced many pitchers that it was wiser to keep the ball up. *Sporting Life* reported in 1903: "Charley Phillippi [Phillippe] gave the gang at headquarters a surprise when he said that he had found out more men were weak on low balls these days than on the high pitch. The veteran gave it as his opinion that this fact was due to the habit of all twirlers for years past in pitching high, so as to force the man to put the ball on the ground or lift it into the air. Phil found out not long since that a swift, waist-high pitch worried some of the best batsmen in the League" (*Sporting Life*, September 26, 1903).

Two years later pitcher Skel Roach observed a perceptive analysis that foreshadowed his later career as a distinguished judge: "A pitcher of the present time must keep the ball up, and must send in high shoots continually. If he puts them down and lets them drop around the batter's knees, he will be getting the release envelope in a hurry."

Roach acknowledged that one reason for this trend was the strain that drop balls put on pitchers' arms, but he cited "the changed condition of the batting" as the primary consideration: "One day Willie Keeler arrived, and after him an army of others who realized that it was time for a new era in batting. Keeler and the other fellows caught the bat halfway up the bat. They cut, chopped and bunted. They found low balls just the thing to be whacked under this new system. At about the same time the pitching distance was increased and the drop ball found its funeral. Not only had it became easy prey for the hitters, but it could not be controlled as formerly and, with the changed distance, was breaking anywhere but the proper place. The pitchers had to begin over again, and devise new means of fooling the hitters. While they were doing so, there was plenty of batting, but it wasn't long until the slabmen had the batters gauged again. They began bringing in the shoots right by the neck, and the crouching batsman, waiting to chop on the low balls were deceived.

"The pitchers, I think, accommodate themselves to changed conditions much faster than the batsmen. It took only a few seasons for the pitchers to master the changed style of batting, but the batters could not work either their brains or minds fast enough to cope with the change in pitching. They didn't even go back to the old style of slugging, but just plugged away as best they could—and got the worst of it. The only low ball that's really effective now is Joe McGinnity's raise, and that works because it is just the reverse of a drop—while it sails low, it comes slowly upward just as it reaches the batter" (*Sporting News*, February 18, 1905). This is very insightful commentary, which shows how a rule change and a new technique can work in tandem to have a ripple effect in many seemingly unrelated areas of the game.

While Roach's dig at slow-witted batters may seem gratuitous, the implication that batters were being foolish by not reverting to slugging tactics is not an unreasonable one. As discussed at some length in the entry on "Place Hitting" (**2.1.1**), and more briefly under "Choking Up" (**2.1.4**), many of the greatest hitters in these years were men like Napoleon Lajoie and Honus Wagner who did indeed revert to the slugging tactics of earlier generations.

Hitters were provided with an additional reason for modifying their tactics by the introduction in 1909 of the livelier cork-center ball (see **9.1.6**). Many remained unwilling to change, but enough did so that pitchers once again began to alter their tactics. Within a couple of years Ty Cobb noticed another dramatic change in pitching tendencies: "pitchers who are keeping the ball low are those who are getting away best. The ball has much to do with this, and furthermore there are more high ball hitters now than there used to be. The batters have mastered the high ball, but most of them are weak on the low ball" (quoted in *Sporting News*, June 29, 1911).

The following year Addie Joss told the *Washington Post*, "There was a time when it was the accepted theory that one of the requisites of the first-class pitchers was ability to keep the ball around the batter's neck" (*Washington Post*, September 5, 1912). Joss credited the prevalence of the hit-and-run play with having forced pitchers to again rethink their approach.

Several factors have contributed to the development of a consensus that keeping the ball down is the most effective style of pitching. The first and most obvious is the livelier ball, which transformed fly balls from likely outs into peril. At the same time larger gloves and smoother fields have made ground balls routine outs and thus more desirable than in early baseball. The hinged or one-handed catcher's mitt of the 1960s was another important factor as it reduced the risk of a wild pitch or passed ball on a low pitch.

In addition, some believe that the lights used in night baseball make it easier for batters to pick up high pitches and have therefore increased the emphasis on keeping the ball down. Bob Feller commented in 1962, ". . . To win under the arcs you must keep the ball low. The high, hard one doesn't rate with the sinker for success under the lamps" (*Sporting News*, August 4, 1962).

3.3.4 Keeping a Book on Hitters. Until the 1887 season, batters could specify that they wanted a high or low pitch. As a result, Connie Mack later claimed that before 1887 "there was no use in [the pitcher] knowing a batter's weakness, because the rules prevented him from pitching to it" (Connie Mack, "Memories of When the Game Was Young," *Sporting Life* [monthly], June 1924).

At least one pitcher disagreed. It was reported in 1880 that Worcester pitcher Lee Richmond, a Brown University alumnus, "has a little book in which he has noted the batting peculiarities of all the League batsmen who played against him last year. This book he has thoroughly studied, and will endeavor to put it to good use the coming season" (*St. Louis Post-Dispatch*, March 27, 1880).

Tracking hitters' weaknesses became more viable when batters were stripped of the right to request pitches. At the same time, however, the tactic once used by an Ivy League graduate lost prestige when it became associated with an eccentric and not very successful turn-of-the-century pitcher known as "Crazy" Schmit. Schmit's insistence on referring to the book between pitches caused considerable amusement.

One 1890 note explained: "Schmitt [sic], one of the pitchers of the Pittsburg League Club, carries a book when pitching, which contains the weaknesses of all the League batters. He consults this as he faces each man. He must have had the weaknesses wrong last Saturday, for the New York Club made something like twenty-four hits off him" (*Sporting News*, May 31,

1890). Another skeptical reporter observed that all Schmit "has to do is to ask the umpire the name of the man at bat and in less than five minutes he finds his man's weak points by a reference to his library, and then he has him at his mercy. Just exactly how this German scientist is going to pan out it is difficult to tell, but the chances are that he will go the way of all the other brilliant men and land deep in the soup" (*Sporting News*, June 7, 1890).

The strategy eventually overcame the stigma of being associated with Schmit, and a 1903 account observed: "Nowadays . . . few pitchers of note go into the box without knowing the weak points of every batsman who may come to the plate. In other words, they know or feel sure that they know just what kind of a pitched ball each batsman cannot hit safely, and as a result they 'feed' each hitter what they believe will retire him" (*Ottumwa* [Iowa] *Courier*, March 16, 1903).

Many pitchers kept this information in their heads, but some literally kept books. White Sox pitcher Doc White, for instance, was reported to be "following in the footsteps of the late Win Mercer, and keeps a 'dope' book on all the men he has to work against. He has a neat little vest pocket book, carefully indexed by clubs, in which he writes the weaknesses and strong points of the batters he faces" (*Sporting Life*, May 2, 1903). White was reportedly so proud of the accuracy of his book that he intended to publish it—but only after he retired (Gerard S. Petrone, *When Baseball Was Young*, 71).

3.3.5 Reading Batters. Some pitchers found they could enhance their success by studying not only batters' tendencies but their stance at the plate. Henry Chadwick explained in 1879, "The moment the pitcher faces the batsman in the first inning of a match he should begin to study his man and endeavor to find out his weak points of play." Chadwick suggested that this could be done by studying "how he holds his bat" and "the speed of his stroke" (*New York Clipper*, March 15, 1879).

Unlike some of Chadwick's ideas, this tactic has continued to be successfully used by pitchers. Clark Griffith explained in 1902: "There is a great deal in understanding a batter's feet. It is by studying them that I am able to tell what kind of a ball the man is expecting, and consequently give him something he doesn't want. Every batter has a different position of the feet when he expects a fast one or a floater, a high or a low ball. They try to fool the pitcher when they are going to bunt, and can, too, in the way they hold the bat, but their feet give it away almost invariably. A batter's feet are better to watch than his head in this respect" (*Sporting Life*, May 31, 1902).

In the 1920s, Urban Shocker remarked that a pitcher "can often tell what is in the batter's mind by the way he shifts his feet, hitches his belt or wiggles his bat" (quoted in F. C. Lane, *Batting*, 33). Warren Spahn suggested that this tactic can be especially effective when facing a batter for the first time: "A man who drops the front shoulder when he cocks the bat is a high-ball hitter. If he drops the back one, he's a low-ball hitter. After he takes one swing you know whether he has good wrists" (quoted in Roger Kahn, *The Head Game*, 176–177).

Stance-reading became such an established part of the pitcher's arsenal that some batters have devised countermeasures. Mike Flanagan cited Chet Lemon as a hitter who would try to mislead pitchers by moving "way up in the box like he was looking for a curve so that you'll throw him a fastball" (quoted in George F. Will, *Men at Work*, 92).

3.3.6   Advantage to Pitching Left-handed. As early as 1867 a *Dayton Journal* reporter wrote that the Buckeyes of Cincinnati "had a conspicuous advantage in a left-handed pitcher, which baffled the Daytons" (*Dayton Journal*, reprinted in *The Ball Player's Chronicle*, June 13, 1867).

When the curveball revolutionized the game in the mid-1870s, there was a general belief that it was easier for a southpaw to throw a curve. John B. Foster explained: "The boys of that day and the fathers, too, for that matter, were certain that the lefthanded pitcher could throw a natural curve better than a righthanded pitcher, or, to put it another way, did throw a natural curve, while the righthander had to acquire the skill to curve a ball" (John B. Foster, "The Evolution of Pitching," part 1, *Sporting News*, November 26, 1931).

In addition, clubs responded to the curve by stacking their lineups with left-handed hitters, which increased the advantage of a left-handed pitcher. The result was an awed reaction when the first great post-curve southpaw, J Lee Richmond, burst on the scene in 1880 with a dominant season that included major league baseball's first perfect game (see **3.4.4, 6.3.9**). In addition, as discussed under "Pickoff Moves" (**5.3.1**), the development of windups during the 1880s provided another advantage to left-handers since base runners can break with less risk when a right-hander begins his windup.

3.3.7   Switch-pitcher. The advent of the curveball gave right-handed pitchers a distinct advantage over right-handed batters, and southpaws the upper hand against left-handed batsmen. Some right-handed batters adjusted to this new state of affairs by learning to hit left-handed or to switch-hit. Pitchers, of course, had no such option open to them. Or did they?

With pitchers not yet wearing gloves, several of them saw no reason not to try using both hands for pitching. On July 18, 1882, in the fourth inning of a game against Baltimore, right-handed pitcher Tony Mullane of Louisville began to pitch with his left hand to left-handed batters. He continued to alternate for the rest of the game but lost 9-8 in the ninth when left-handed batter Charles Householder hit his only home run of the season off one of Mullane's left-handed offerings. (Mullane gave a very confused account of this game in an interview with the *Washington Post* in 1899. Mullane had himself pitching for Baltimore against Louisville and surrendering the home run to Chicken Wolf) (Lee Allen, *The Hot Stove League*, 35).

The disastrous result deterred Mullane from left-handed pitching for many years, though David Nemec reported that "Mullane would sometimes hide his hands behind his back as he began his delivery, keeping a batter guessing until the last instant as to which arm would launch the ball" (David Nemec, *The Beer and Whisky League*, 130). Researcher Cliff Blau has discovered that Mullane again pitched left-handed in a major league game on July 5, 1892. And the following year, on July 14, 1893, Mullane pitched the ninth inning of a game against Chicago left-handed, surrendering three runs.

Larry Corcoran may have experimented with ambidextrous pitching even earlier than Mullane, as the *Chicago Tribune* noted in 1880: "Corcoran has developed into a left-handed pitcher, and it is expected that his double method of delivery will prove extremely puzzling to batsmen" (*Chicago Tribune*, April 4, 1880). Corcoran is known to have pitched with both hands in a major league game only once, against Buffalo on June 16, 1884. In addition, researcher Steve Steinberg discovered a 1915 article that claimed that after Corcoran's right arm went lame in 1885, he attempted a comeback as a left-hander, only to injure that arm too (*New York Times*, March 14, 1915).

Elton "Icebox" Chamberlain was more persistent in his efforts to gain the platoon advantage against major league hitters. On May 9, 1888, with Louisville ahead 18-6 after seven innings, he pitched the final two innings with his left hand. Cliff Blau discovered that Chamberlain repeated the endeavor on October 1, 1891. *The Official Baseball Record* reported that Chamberlain threw right-handed to home but left-handed to first base on pickoffs (*The Official Baseball Record*, September 20, 1886).

A 1936 letter writer to the *New York Times* claimed to have witnessed John Roach pitching with both hands for the Giants in his only major league game on May 14, 1887. The writer correctly recalled that the Giants had lost the game 17-2. But there is no contemporary documentation of Roach using both hands during that game, and no mention of his being ambidextrous has been found during his lengthy minor league career (letter from "D.F.P.," *New York Times*, August 8, 1936). Another player on the 1887 Giants, outfielder and occasional pitcher Mike Tiernan, had been described as "the ambidextrous pitcher" while playing for Trenton two years earlier (*Washington Post*, September 18, 1885).

At least one Hall of Famer also pursued the elusive goal of ambidextrous pitching. An 1883 note observed that "[Charles] Radbourn, of the Providence nine, can pitch either right or left handed" (*Washington Post*, May 6,

1883). Philadelphia experimented with an ambidextrous pitcher named Waring before the 1884 season. Unfortunately, when Waring used both hands alternately in an exhibition game, "the Whites found no difficulty in hitting him either way" (*New York Clipper*, April 12, 1884). J. H. Campbell, who pitched for a number of clubs in the mid-1880s, was also ambidextrous (*St. Louis Post-Dispatch*, February 24, 1886).

According to a *New York Times* article many years later, a minor league pitcher accomplished the ultimate in ambidextrous achievement in 1885. While pitching for Youngstown, Ohio, a pitcher named Owen Keenan pitched both ends of an Independence Day doubleheader against New Castle, winning one game with each arm (*New York Times*, March 14, 1915).

By the 1890s this unique period of experimentation was coming to an end. The lack of success of the switch-pitchers was the most obvious reason. Just as important, a left-handed pitcher was no longer regarded as a panacea; managers again realized that effective stuff and good control were more important than the pitching hand. The fact that pitchers were now wearing gloves may also have contributed to the end of this era.

The twentieth century has seen occasional efforts to bring back the ambidextrous pitcher. Harold Friene, who went to spring training with the Athletics in 1910 and 1911 but never pitched in a major league game, was billed as an ambidextrous pitcher (*Washington Post*, February 27, 1910; A. H. Spink, *The National Game*, 132). Cal McLish was billed as a switch-pitcher when he arrived in the majors in the mid-1940s but used only his right hand when facing major league competition. On July 4, 1952, in a Longhorn League game, right-handed pitcher Rudie Malone pitched left-handed to the left-handed slugger Joe Bauman. Bert Campaneris pitched ambidextrously in a Florida State League game on August 13, 1962.

Most organizations frowned on such experiments, but at one point the Dodgers farm system had three pitchers—Ed Head, Paul Richards, and Clyde Day—who experimented with ambidextrous mound work. Researcher Steve Steinberg found a 1928 account in which Richards, while playing for Muskogee against Topeka, gave a preview of the innovative spirit that would characterize his later work as a major league manager and general manager: "[Richards] went along in fine style as a left handed pitcher, until Wilson, a turn-over hitter came to bat. Wilson went to bat right handed and Richards asked for a left handed glove and wound up right handed. Wilson jumped to the other side of the plate and Richards decided to throw left handed again. Finally he discarded the glove and pitched alternately with his left and right hand. But Wilson was too smart for him and waited him out for a base on balls" (*New York Evening Journal*, July 24, 1928).

The switch-pitcher finally made its return to the major leagues in 1995 after an absence of more than a century. Greg Harris had long experimented with left-handed pitching, though he used his right hand exclusively when facing major league competition. On September 28, 1995, pitching for the Montreal Expos, Harris used both hands to throw a shutout inning against the Cincinnati Reds. He wore a special six-fingered glove that he could use on either hand.

3.3.8   When All Else Fails/Grooving. Researcher Bill Kirwin reported that former Milwaukee catcher Sammy White told him of an unusual ploy that he and Lew Burdette used against Orlando Cepeda in 1961. Kirwin explained that "they both agreed that whatever they tried was unsuccessful. White came up with the idea that they should tell Cepeda what was coming because 'nothing else worked.' Burdette agreed. White crouched behind the plate and told Cepeda what was coming. Cepeda protested to the umpire that this was illegal and was told it was not. From that point on, in that game, White told Cepeda every pitch that he signaled to Burdette and he was retired easily each time." Kirwin later asked Cepeda about the incident, and Cepeda confirmed White's account.

Birdie Tebbetts similarly claimed that the Tigers once let Ted Williams call his own pitches, and he was so unnerved that he went 0-for-5 (Jonathan Fraser Light, *The Cultural Encyclopedia of Baseball*, 566). There are a few other pieces of anecdotal evidence to support that possibility. Ty Cobb, for example, related a story in which Al Bridwell went 0-for-5 on the last day of the season in spite of being allowed to call the pitches. But the details that Cobb provided do not correspond to the known facts (Ty Cobb, *Memoirs of Twenty Years in Baseball*, 86).

This tactic seems so foolish that it seems safe to assume that it would not work if widely used. But considering the old formulation that hitting is timing and pitching is disrupting timing, perhaps with the right hitter the surprise of being told the pitch might disturb that delicate balance. While such sketchy anecdotal evidence doesn't prove anything, it at least suggests that knowing what pitch is coming is less of an advantage than might be expected.

(iv) Measures of Success

While I have generally deemed statistical accomplishments to be outside the scope of this book, I have made an exception for the basic yardsticks used to measure the success of pitchers because these standards have become such a fundamental part of baseball.

3.4.1   Shutouts. On November 8, 1860, Jim Creighton of the Excelsiors of Brooklyn beat the St. George Cricket Club 25-0 at the Elysian Fields. The game was hailed as "the first match on record that has resulted in nine innings being played without each party making runs. The contest with the Flour City Club, wherein they made one run the [sic] Excelsior's 26, was the nearest to it" (*Brooklyn Eagle*, November 10, 1860).

This does appear to have been the first shutout in baseball history. But it was considered a reflection of the unfamiliarity of the cricket players with baseball rather than an accomplishment by Creighton: ". . . The St. George nine were players selected for their ability as fielders, and the pitcher and catcher were experienced ball players; whereas the Excelsiors had two of their muffin players in their nine. The fact is it was a mere practice game for them. Judging from the result we think we could name two or three of our junior clubs that could easily take down the St. George nine at baseball." The catcher for the St. George club was none other than Harry Wright (*Brooklyn Eagle*, November 10, 1860).

Shutouts remained an extremely rare event during the high-scoring 1860s. According to John H. Gruber, "there were exactly five shutouts prior to 1870" (John H. Gruber, "Scoring Rules," *Sporting News*, November 4, 1915).

That changed in 1870. Inspired by the success of the Red Stockings of Cincinnati, a professional nine was organized in Chicago at great expense. The White Stockings initially struggled, especially at the bat, but received little sympathy from other cities or the hometown press. After one lackluster performance the *Chicago Tribune* wrote: "that 'our terrific batters,' 'our scientific hitters,' 'our heavy strikers' should have failed to make more than four runs against any club on earth, was a circumstance of stupendous unaccountability" (*Chicago Tribune*, July 7, 1870).

That was nothing compared to the reaction a few weeks later when the White Stockings were whitewashed 9-0 by Rynie Wolters of the Mutuals of New York. The baseball world erupted with amazement and more than a bit of *schadenfreude*. Because the name "Chicago" derived from an Indian word for "skunk," the word "Chicago" had begun to appear in game accounts in the late 1860s to refer to a score of zero in an inning or game.

But in the aftermath of Wolters's historic accomplishment, the popularity of the term exploded. Within a week, the sports pages were filled with such passages as: "The first two innings gave two 'Chicagos' for the Forest Citys" (*Cleveland Herald*, July 30, 1870). The word continued to be a major part of the baseball lexicon for the remainder of the nineteenth century.

As noteworthy as this game's impact on baseball vernacular was, it had even more significant consequences for baseball play. Harry Wright's Red Stockings had already helped to popularize a deader ball the preceding season (see **9.1.5**). The shutout of the White Stockings went further—by showing that one good pitcher backed by a solid defense could offset an all-star unit gathered at great expense, it made low-scoring baseball trendy! Clubs across the country jumped on the bandwagon, using increasingly dead balls in hopes of reproducing Wolters's result.

Dead balls did indeed produce the desired effect. Shutouts increased dramatically in the next few years, and the trend accelerated with the introduction of the curveball. By the end of the 1870s, shutouts were so common that Harry Wright, who had helped to start the trend, thought it had gone too far.

3.4.2 1-0 Games. The first 1-0 game apparently took place on August 12, 1874, when the White Stockings of Burlington, New Jersey, defeated the Haymakers of Philadelphia. The first major league 1-0 game took place in a National Association game on May 11, 1875, with Chicago beating the Reds of St. Louis. For several years after this, a 1-0 game was regarded as the ultimate baseball accomplishment by many observers, led as usual by Henry Chadwick.

As the balls used became less and less lively, and batters puzzled over curveballs, 1-0 games became relatively common. To differentiate them, a consensus emerged that the longest 1-0 game was the best. By this criterion, the greatest game of the 1870s was a twenty-four-inning game on May 11, 1877, between Harvard and the Manchester, New Hampshire, club. It appears that the most remarkable thing about this game was that the condition of the ball and the field made scoring almost impossible. Nonetheless the game was talked about for many years afterward.

The Harvard game was finally surpassed on August 17, 1882, when Detroit and Providence played an eighteen-inning 1-0 game. It was immediately and for many years afterward hailed as the greatest game ever played.

3.4.3 No-hitters. On May 29, 1875, Joseph McElroy Mann of Princeton threw a no-hitter against Yale. The feat was accorded little attention. A four-sentence account of the game in the *New York Mercury* noted that "Mr. Mann's pitching for the Princeton nine was so effective that the Yales did not make a single base hit." The report gave similar accolades to two Princeton fielders for their defensive play (reprinted in H. Allen Smith and Ira L. Smith, *Low and Inside*, 238).

Joseph Borden pitched the National Association's first no-hitter on July 28, 1875. Borden's feat was also reported in only the most matter-of-fact fashion (William J. Ryczek, *Blackguards and Red Stockings*, 218). When George Bradley pitched the first National League no-hitter the following season, the event was heralded with more enthusiasm, but the accomplishment was portrayed as belonging as much to the fielders as to the pitcher: "Bradley's pitching, and the magnificent backing given it by the fielders, won the day for St. Louis. For the first time in the annals of the League, nine innings were played without a single base hit being placed" (*St. Louis Globe-Democrat*, quoted in David Falkner, *Nine Sides of the Diamond*, 10).

The fact that the response to early no-hitters was so subdued is somewhat puzzling in light of the acclaim being accorded low-scoring games during this period. My conjecture is that, as implied by the account of Bradley's no-hitter, this was a reflection of the continued perception that baseball ought to be a battle between hitters and fielders and a resulting resentment of pitchers for having usurped too great a role. Low-scoring games could be viewed as the product of good defense, but the absence of any hits at all evoked suspicion that the pitcher had exerted too great an influence.

3.4.4 Perfect Games. The first major league perfect game was pitched by left-hander J Lee Richmond of Worcester against Cleveland on June 12, 1880. An apparent clean single was foiled when Worcester right fielder Lon Knight threw the batter out at first base.

The first perfect game known to have been pitched at any level was tossed by James "Pud" Galvin of the Reds of St. Louis against the Cass Club of Detroit on August 17, 1876, in a tournament in Ionia, Michigan. The feat attracted little notice, but the *Ionia Sentinel* did comment: "The game was in some respects one of the most remarkable on record. The Cass boys did not make a base hit or reach first base during the game. Each man of the club batted three times and each was put out three times" (*Ionia Sentinel*, August 25, 1876).

More extraordinary was the fact that it was Galvin's second no-hitter of the day. That morning he had blanked the Mutuals of Jackson, allowing only three runners to reach base on errors. Thus only three fielding misplays prevented Galvin from accomplishing twice in one day a feat that had never before been accomplished. Nor was his opposition weak; the Cass and Mutuals were both strong professional nines, stocked with former and future major leaguers.

A related question is how "perfect" came to characterize a game in which nothing happened. Henry Chadwick again appears to have played a role. In the 1870s, Chadwick began using the term "model game" to describe a low-scoring game with few hits or errors. The term became so closely associated with Chadwick that those seeking to take shots at the sportswriter did so by assailing this concept. The *Chicago Tribune*, for instance, referred derisively to "what is absurdly called a 'model' game—that is, a game equally devoid of base hits and errors" (*Chicago Tribune*, June 20, 1880).

It took some time for the current mind-set to become widespread. It was not until the early twentieth century that the term "perfect game" originated or that much notice was taken of such games. Perhaps this change in outlook reflects the longing of our hectic times for less eventful ones, as was articulated by David Byrne's memorable lyric, "Heaven is a place where nothing ever happens."

Chapter 4

FIELDING

IT MIGHT seem logical to assume that there would be few fielding firsts to record. After all, the fielder's role is not to initiate action but to react to the batter, who is in turn reacting to the pitcher. In addition, the nine fielding positions haven't changed since the 1850s. Neither have the basic ways in which the defensive team can retire their opponents: they can catch a batted ball on the fly, they can touch a base that a runner or batter is forced to run to, they can tag a runner between bases, or they can strike a batter out.

Considering these limitations, the number of new stratagems that have been introduced by fielders is impressive. I've subdivided them into four basic categories: (1) choosing how to fill each position, (2) positioning the nine fielders, (3) combination plays or teamwork, and (4) devising alternate methods of retiring players.

(i) Choosing How to Fill Positions

The most basic element of defensive strategy is deciding which player is best suited for each of the nine positions. As discussed under "Specialization" (1.28), the benefits of specialization were recognized by the 1860s, and clubs tried as much as possible to let a player remain at a single position so that he could master it.

The next question to be resolved was what made a player best suited to a particular position. With any out far from routine in the 1860s, the predominant philosophy was to view the defensive positions hierarchically. Catcher was the most important position, followed by shortstop, and since these players were offered the most chances and the most demanding ones, clubs customarily used their two most agile, sure-handed, and strong-armed players in these roles. The three basemen ranked next in importance, and the next most agile players were assigned to them. The three least defensively skilled regulars generally occupied the outfield.

The ensuing years brought shifts in this hierarchy, as rule changes, the use of gloves, new tactics such as the bunt, and better fields increased the role of positions like shortstop and second base and diminished the importance of the first baseman and catcher. There are still, however, discernable remnants of the original philosophy. The positions at which twenty-first-century managers will sacrifice offense to have a good glove man correspond quite closely to the hierarchy of the 1860s.

The period between the 1860s and the 1890s also brought new ideas about the qualifications for specific positions. The emphasis on a player's basic fielding skills—throwing, catching, and agility—was gradually supplemented by the notion that innate characteristics such as size, dexterity, and left- or right-handedness were assets or liabilities at specific positions. This section will discuss the emergence of those perceptions.

4.1.1 Stretches by First Basemen. The idea that height was an important asset at first base was well established by the 1870s. A typical example was an 1879 profile that noted: "This season [Levi Meyerle] joined the Nationals of Washington as their first-baseman, a position which he is peculiarly adapted to by reason of his height—6 ft. 1 in" (*New York Clipper*, June 21, 1879).

This, however, was primarily because height meant greater reach. The stretches now performed by first basemen are quite another matter. First of all, what constitutes a stretch is a matter of degree.

There are vague claims that Charles Comiskey or Cap Anson may have originated the stretch (Harold Dellinger, "Theodore P. Sullivan," in Robert L. Tiemann and Mark Rucker, eds., *Nineteenth Century Stars*, 120; William P. Akin, "Bare Hands and Kid Gloves: The Best Fielders 1880–1899," *Baseball Research Journal* 10 [1981], 60–65). Undoubtedly these men and many early first basemen reached far out to stab errant throws. As early as 1860, Henry Chadwick was advising first basemen to practice standing "with one foot on the base, and see how far he can reach and take the ball from the fielder; this practice will prepare him for balls that are thrown short of the base" (*Beadle's 1860 Dime Base-Ball Player*, 24). But the more difficult stretches and scoops performed by today's first basemen would be impossible without a large, sophisticated fielding glove. Given the additional complication of uneven grounds, my sense is that a nineteenth-century first baseman would have been expected to vacate the bag on throws that were not within his reach and do his best to stop them.

The stretch seems to have begun to develop in earnest only when first basemen's mitts became larger (see **9.3.3**). William Curran said that the tactic was well established in 1905 and suggested that Fred Tenney may have popularized the technique (William Curran, *Mitts*, 121). Turn-of-the-century first baseman George Carey was known by the suggestive nickname of "Scoops" and was known for his "wonderful pick-ups of balls thrown to him on the bound and his great stops of wide thrown balls" (Henry Chadwick, *Sporting News*, December 21, 1895). And a 1904 article referred to the one-handed stops of badly thrown balls made by Philadelphia's Harry Davis (*Sporting Life*, May 21, 1904).

4.1.2 Left-handers Excluded from Positions. The poor fields and absence of gloves in early baseball meant that quickness, sure-handedness, and accurate throwing arms were the main qualifications looked for in catchers, second basemen, shortstops, and third basemen.

The disadvantage that left-handers had in making throws from these positions did not go unnoticed. But the slight delay in making a throw was considered a relatively minor factor at a time when conditions made no play routine. Thus left-handedness was viewed as a handicap but not a bar to playing these positions. For example, Henry Chadwick observed in 1863, "[Joe] Start was placed at third base, a position any player of the nine can fill better, because he is a left-handed player, and for that reason just the man for the opposite base" (*New York Clipper*, September 12, 1863).

As playing conditions improved there was a corresponding increase in the perception that right-handers were best suited to these positions. By 1868, Chadwick was insisting: "the first base is the only position in the infield, except that of pitcher, a left-handed man should occupy" (Henry Chadwick, *The American Game of Base Ball*, 34). In 1879, with gloves still being used only by catchers and first basemen, Chadwick elaborated: "Another mistake last season in the make-up of base-teams was that of placing left-handed men on any base but the first. A left-handed first-baseman finds the hand he can use with greatest facility ready to pick up balls which come on foul ground to the left of him; while, on the other hand, the third-baseman finds his right hand most available to cover a similar class of balls to his right. At third or second base a left-hand player is unquestionably out of position, as he is also at short-stop, though not to so great an extent" (*New York Clipper*, December 13, 1879).

Once gloves came into wider use in the 1880s, the frequency with which plays were executed increased dramatically. This in turn greatly accentuated the previously small edge held by right-handers. Double plays slowly became more common, which increased the importance of having right-handers in the middle infield. The prevalence of bunts similarly helped to drive out the left-handed third baseman (*Sporting Life*, March 12, 1898). By the 1890s, left-handers had become rare at these positions.

As a result the *Cincinnati Times-Star* observed in 1905 that it was a fairly recent tradition "that an infielder, the first baseman excepted, who would be successful must be a right hand thrower. Since the days when 'Hick' Carpenter, covering third base for the Cincinnati team, was a star at that position [1879–1890], but one man has broken into fast company who played the infield for any length of time and used his left wing wherewith to propel the ball to various parts of the field. That man was Billy Hulen, and with all his cleverness he was unable to hold his place in the big League for the reason that his offside throwing disconcerted the other members of the infield, and incidentally made him a somewhat slower man than was desirable for a first-class team" (*Cincinnati Times-Star*, reprinted in *Sporting Life*, April 22, 1905).

4.1.3 Left-handed Catchers. After the emergence of the curveball (see 3.2.3), it was considered advantageous to pair a left-handed catcher with a left-handed pitcher. The *Detroit Free Press* explained the reasoning: "[Dupee] Shaw's left-handed out-shoots are responsible for [Walter] Walker's sore hand. With a right-handed pitcher, the catcher can do most of the stopping with his left hand, protected by a thickly padded glove. Such a glove cannot be worn upon the right hand as it renders accurate throwing impossible" (*Detroit Free Press*, May 2, 1884).

As the nineteenth century wore on, left-handed catchers became increasingly rare. The last one to enjoy a lengthy career was Jack Clements, who played in the major leagues from 1884 to 1900. The primary reasons seem to have been the greater difficulties left-handers faced in throwing to bases and in fielding bunts.

Interestingly, Bugs Baer argued in 1923 that those reasons no longer applied: "In those days a catcher with a left-hand drive-wheel was handicapped in throwing to second and third. Right-handed batters would easily balk him when he attempted to put the subpoena on a baserunner. He had to step out to right-field when throwing to second and also had to do a sun dance when tossing to third. He could whale away at first base all he wanted without competition. That was the reason left-hand catchers faded out like a blue serge coat in the land of eternal sunshine. There were too many right-handed batters encouraging him to throw wild. . . . Traditions croak hard. One old folk fable is that left-handed catchers are taboo. But with every batter transferring his batting affections to the wrong side of the plate, there doesn't seem to be any reason against left-handed catchers" (*Detroit Free Press*, April 17, 1923).

Nonetheless the left-handed catcher seems to have gone the way of the dodo bird. Even if a youngster today were determined to prove otherwise, he would probably be hard-pressed to find a catcher's mitt for his right hand.

Perhaps even more important, a left-hander with the necessary arm strength would likely be asked instead to pitch.

4.1.4   Left-handed Outfielders. While the custom of not placing left-handers at catcher, second base, shortstop, or third base has become deeply entrenched, a similar practice involving outfielders emerged at about the same time and is now entirely disregarded. In 1905 the *Cincinnati Times-Star* remarked: ". . . There was once a feeling that no left-hand thrower ever should play left field or no man who threw right-handed would make a success playing the long field back of first base, but these traditions have proven fallacies by such clever left-hand throwers as Jimmy Ryan, Jesse Burkett, Topsy Hartsel and others who are or were stars in left field, and by 'Dusty' Miller, Hans Wagner, Jack Barry and others who shone brilliantly in the right garden." The *Times-Star* indicated that it was only recently that this rule of thumb had fallen by the wayside (*Cincinnati Times-Star*, reprinted in *Sporting Life*, April 22, 1905).

4.1.5   First Base for Left-handers. When Henry Chadwick observed in 1863 that a left-handed player was "just the man" for first base, he certainly implied an advantage. He was more explicit a decade later: "The first base can be best occupied by a left-handed player, as the hand most at command with such players faces the balls going close to the line of the base; while a left-handed player is decidedly out of place at either of the other infield positions" (*New York Clipper*, March 7, 1874).

When bunting became prevalent in the 1880s, first basemen assumed more responsibility for making throws. This provided more reason for concluding that first base was the one infield position where not only was left-handedness not a handicap but an actual advantage.

Hal Chase, widely acclaimed as the best defensive first baseman in the first decade of the twentieth century, explained: "I believe a left-handed first baseman is better fitted for the position than a right-hander. He uses the left hand for throwing. This makes a snap throw to second or third much easier. He naturally faces these bags. The right-hander has to turn around, losing valuable time. As to throwing to the plate, there is no advantage at either style. I believe the time will come when a right-handed first baseman will be almost as rare as a left-handed third baseman now is. Fred Tenney was the pioneer southpaw first sacker. He originated the sacrifice killing play. That is, on a bunt to him, he tried for the man that was to be advanced. I did the same thing before I heard of Tenney. It was as natural for me to do it as to play for the plate with bases full and none out. For a right-hander, the play is more difficult. He loses too much time in turning after getting the ball" (quoted in A. H. Spink, *The National Game*, 174).

4.1.6   Catcher Size. Early catchers were often regarded as occupying the most important position on the field. It was no coincidence that in the first known fixed game, in 1865, it was the catcher who was the central figure (see **11.1.1**).

Because catchers of this era stood well behind the batter, the position's two main requirements were a strong arm and the ability to stop wild pitches. The latter requirement meant that a catcher needed either agility or a long reach, which led many observers to conclude that a large man was best behind the plate. In 1868 the *Brooklyn Eagle* noted that the six-foot-two Charlie Mills "has an advantage over all other catchers, in his long reach" (*Brooklyn Eagle*, August 15, 1868). As a rule, however, early clubs put one of their best athletes behind the plate, which more often meant a small, athletic man.

Once catchers began to play directly behind the plate (see **4.2.1**), the focus shifted away from agility and toward size. The lanky Connie Mack, who had been a catcher during his playing days in the 1880s, later explained why height was a major advantage for a catcher. He observed that a longer reach cut down on wild pitches and also gave a pitcher "greater confidence, inasmuch as he is given a bigger mark behind the plate to throw at." He added, "Weight is also an important factor in blocking a base runner. In case of a collision, a heavy catcher will have the greater advantage with desperate base runners" (Connie Mack, "How to Play Ball," multi-part series, *Washington Post*, March 20, 1904). John McGraw noted in 1900, "A catcher ought to be a man of considerable weight to hold the heavy and speeding pitches" (*New York World*, reprinted in *Milwaukee Journal*, April 19, 1900).

In the next few years, blocking the plate (see **4.4.11**) would become an even more prominent part of the catcher's responsibilities. But this requirement was offset by two other developments that set the stage for the small, agile catcher to return to the fore. By this time mitts (see **9.3.2**) were lessening the force that was borne by catchers' hands, and bunts (see **2.2.1**) were coming into prominence. With all these factors to consider, it took some time for the prejudice against small catchers to be overcome, as Red Dooin discovered.

Dooin was born in Cincinnati in 1879 and weighed only 110 pounds when he started college at St. Xavier's (now Xavier University). He went out for the baseball team, but the captain took one look at him and said that he didn't want any "little runts" around. After graduation, Dooin got a trial with St. Paul of the Western League, but Charles Comiskey advised him to stick to his trade of tailoring. He caught on with a low minor league club in 1900 and did well enough that he was drafted, sight unseen, by St. Joseph. When Dooin reported to St. Joseph the following spring, manager Byron McKibbon asked him, "What can I do for you, sonny?" Red replied, "I'm

Dooin, your new player." McKibbon sized him up carefully and then said, "Why, my boy, I want a catcher, not a jockey" (*New York World*, September 21, 1913).

Nonetheless Dooin went on to become a star catcher in the National League and eventually player-manager of the Phillies. When a slightly built young catcher named Bill Killefer was having a hard time breaking into the major leagues, Dooin was naturally willing to consider him. He liked what he saw and groomed Killefer to be his successor.

Bill Killefer came to be regarded as the prototype of a new breed of catcher: "The time has gone by when the ideal catcher was considered a mountain of beef and bone, something that could stand any kind of knocks and, as long as he was successful as a battering ram, mattering not what his other qualities might be. The catcher now is more than a mere backstop, inserted to break the impact of pitched balls against the grand stand planks. Bill Killifer [sic] of the Phillies is an illustration. The St. Louis Browns disposed of him because he was considered too light for catching, but now he is doing the bulk of the work for the Phillies and showing that it does not take beef to make a catcher. The old iron man has given way to the more delicate structure of steel and Killifer is one of that sort, built on graceful lines, but able to give and take with the best of them" (*Sporting News*, August 14, 1913). According to the 1928 *Babe Ruth's Own Book of Baseball*, "The old idea used to be that a catcher had to be a big, strong oversized fellow in order to stand the gaff of holding up a pitcher and blocking runners. That's bunk" (Babe Ruth, *Babe Ruth's Own Book of Baseball*, 131).

In the years since Red Dooin showed that a small man could be successful behind the plate, the bunt has become less common, and there has been a slight trend back toward catchers being larger men. Nonetheless catchers come in a variety of shapes and sizes, and ability is deemed more important than stature. The requirements of the position are thus now not all that different from what they were in the 1860s, with a strong arm and either agility or reach being necessary.

4.1.7 Outfielders' Roles. The current mantra that the fastest outfielder covers center field and the best thrower goes in right field was not accepted in early baseball. The extent to which gloves have changed baseball will be a recurring theme in this book, but it bears repetition. Today's enormous gloves make catching a ball a simple feat and enable managers to concentrate on other factors in assigning fields for their outfielders. But until outfielders began using gloves in the mid-1880s, the first and foremost consideration with any outfielder was his reliability at catching fly balls.

As a result, there were a number of theories about where to place one's outfielders, but no clear consensus. Henry Chadwick wrote in 1860 that the left fielder had the most important duties and the right fielder the least (*Beadle's Dime Base-Ball Player*, 25–26). But by 1877 he observed, "In old ball-playing days, the left-fielder was the king-pin of the outfield, but this idea has long since been exploded. In fact, if there be any one of the three positions which requires more skillful play than another, it is that of right-field, for the right-fielder has the most frequent opportunities to throw out men on the bases" (*New York Clipper*, February 10, 1877).

A *Sporting Life* correspondent wrote in 1884: "If there 'happens to be a weak spot' on the nine—well, it is better not to have a weak spot—but if there should be a weak spot centre field or first base—preferably the former—should bear it. Centre field has less work to perform on the average than left field and less responsible work generally than right field" (*Sporting Life*, April 16, 1884).

As noted in "Left-Handed Outfielders" (4.1.4), in the 1890s an emphasis was placed on using a right-handed thrower in left field and a left-handed thrower in right field. Henry Chadwick suggested that the "peculiar character of the ground" could be the most important factor. He explained that at the Union Grounds in Brooklyn, "the services of the sharpest outfielder are required at right field" because the hills there were so difficult to negotiate (*New York Clipper*, January 12, 1878). Others implied that consideration be given to finding the right man to play the demanding sun field (*Chicago Tribune*, March 12, 1901). These two issues meant that a club might choose to rearrange its outfielders based upon the ballpark.

It does not appear to have been until well into the twentieth century that it became the conventional wisdom for the fielder who covers the most ground to be placed in center field and the strongest thrower in right field. This development is primarily attributable to the advent of the home run era in the 1920s, which forced outfielders to position themselves much deeper.

(ii) Positioning of the Fielders

4.2.1 Catchers Playing Close. As simple a question as when catchers began to be positioned directly behind the plate remains a confusing topic. We do know that very early catchers stood well back of the batter, that they had begun to venture closer by the 1860s, and that it was only near the start of the twentieth century that it became routine for them to be positioned close to the batter. The exact details are more difficult to pin down, but let's consider the evidence.

Early catchers positioned themselves well behind the batter for an obvious reason: self-preservation. This natural instinct was encouraged by the rules, since a foul ball caught on the first bounce counted as an out until the

1880s, which meant that by standing well back a catcher could range far and wide to record such outs. This positioning also gave them more time to react and prevent wild pitches. Strikeouts were rare in early baseball, and the catcher had only to catch the pitch on the first bounce to complete the out.

Catchers had begun to play closer by 1870, but the originator is more difficult to pin down. Doug Allison of the Red Stockings of Cincinnati is occasionally cited, but this is just another example of the tendency to credit this club with every first. Deacon White's name comes up more frequently, as a result of Al Pratt's statement to that effect in 1895 (*Sporting News*, March 23, 1895).

Pratt's testimony has to be taken seriously since he was a prominent player in the 1860s. But the evidence suggests that other catchers were employing this positioning before White. Indeed, a New York paper reported in 1870 that Deacon White's cousin Elmer "played up close to the bat" while catching the pitching of Deacon White himself (*New York Daily Tribune*, August 19, 1870).

The practice can be pushed still earlier, but in doing so we quickly run into the problem that "close" is an imprecise term. Henry Chadwick counseled in 1860, "when a player has made his first base, the Catcher should take a position nearer the striker, in order to take the ball from the pitcher before it bounds" (*Beadle's Dime Base-Ball Player*, 21). But how much nearer?

An 1891 article claimed that early catchers stood twenty to twenty-five feet behind plate, and this seems consistent with other evidence (*Williamsport Sunday Grit*, June 7, 1891). Yet how much closer did the catcher have to move before he would be considered "near"? Two feet? Five feet? Ten feet? Fifteen feet? There is obviously no way to answer this question.

It seems unlikely that any catcher in the days before masks was foolhardy enough to position himself directly behind the plate. None of the sources that give credit to a particular catcher specify exactly what distance they regard as close, though Chadwick wrote in 1874 that "moving up behind the bat" saved the catcher three to four yards on his throws (Henry Chadwick, *Chadwick's Base Ball Manual*, 14). Yet, as we shall see, Chadwick tried in 1872 to prohibit catchers from standing within six feet of the plate, from which it can be inferred that at least a few catchers were coming that near. Thus it seems likely that much of the confusion results from different understandings of what was meant by "close." Pratt's statement—like many of the others we are forced to rely on—most likely means that White played closer to the plate than any previous catcher *that he had seen*.

The vagueness of terms like "close" and "near" and the imprecision of memory itself have led to a baffling array of claims. The issue is further complicated by the fact that positioning was situational, as T. Z. Cowles, sports editor of the *Chicago Tribune* from 1868 to 1875, explained many years later:

"A writer in the *New York Sun* of recent date, in reviewing the baseball of long ago, errs in saying that the catcher always played twenty feet or more behind the home plate, and never came up any closer until the rules were changed. This is a mistake. The star catchers played back until a man was on base, and then they went forward to the plate. Some of them would play back on the third strike, which was out when the ball was caught on the first bound, but always came up close to prevent the stealing of bases" (*Chicago Tribune*, June 2, 1918).

There are at least a couple of contemporary attestations to catchers playing close in the 1860s. In 1868 catcher George Dawson of the Detroit Base Ball Club was described as "standing close to the batter" in order to hold opposing base runners near to their bases (*Detroit Advertiser and Tribune*, September 10, 1868). Four years earlier this intriguing description had appeared in the *Brooklyn Eagle*: "Harris 'struck out' the balls he failed to hit, being held close behind the bat in Joe 'Howards' [sic] peculiar style, a style, by the way, that rather astonished the Hoboken crowd" (*Brooklyn Eagle*, August 18, 1864). But most of the claims were made after the fact, which further clouds the issue of exactly how close to the plate these catchers stood.

A. H. Spink indicated that several catchers were playing close to the batsman during the 1860s, including Bob Ferguson (A. H. Spink, *The National Game*, 10). Spink also described Nat Hicks and Fergy Malone as members "of the old army who caught up close to the bat without glove or mask to protect them" (A. H. Spink, *The National Game*, 92). Jonathan Fraser Light cited an undated account that said of Hicks: "Player after player went down before his unfaltering nerve, and although struck four times during the game—once squarely on the mouth by the ball and once on the chest and twice with the bat—he could not be driven away from his position" (Jonathan Fraser Light, *The Cultural Encyclopedia of Baseball*, 140). Early sportswriter William Rankin, however, denounced "that fake about Nat Hicks being the first man to play close up behind the bat" (*Sporting News*, September 9, 1909).

Rankin instead claimed the distinction for a still earlier catcher for the Atlantics of Brooklyn who bore the imposing name of Folkert Rappelje Boerum. According to Rankin, Boerum began playing close to the batter in the summer of 1859 at the suggestion of Atlantics president William V. Babcock. He added that the tactic "proved so great a success that it was adopted by all the leading clubs in the vicinity of New York" (Francis C. Richter, *Richter's History and Records of Base Ball*, 220).

Early ballplayer William Ridgely Griffith reported that when Joe Leggett of the Excelsiors of Brooklyn visited Baltimore in 1860 he was "the first to ever take fly-tips close behind the bat" (William Ridgely Griffith, *The Early History of Amateur Base Ball in the State of Maryland*;

reprinted in *Maryland Historical Magazine*, vol. 87, no. 2 [Summer 1992], 204). At around this time a Rochester, New York, catcher named John Morey was also said to "get under the bat and catch the hot delivery without even dodging" (quoted in Priscilla Astifan, "Baseball in the Nineteenth Century," *Rochester History* LII, no. 3 [Summer 1990], 15).

Whoever originated catching close to the plate, by the early 1870s it was unquestionably becoming more common. Henry Chadwick did not like this innovation and advocated that catchers be required to remain at least six feet from the plate. He explained: "The necessity for a rule of the kind has been apparent by the play of the last season. In fact, the position taken by some catchers who are apparently reckless of injuries in their strenuous efforts to take sharp fly tips close to the bat, has been such as to really amount to an obstruction to the batsman in striking at the ball" (*New York Clipper*, November 25, 1871).

Some important tactical considerations influenced when and how close a catcher should approach the plate. A Boston ballplayer later reported that when the Excelsiors visited Boston in 1862, Joe Leggett "caught on a bound except when a man was on third base, and then he went up behind the bat." Three years later another Brooklyn catcher, Frank Prescott Norton, "caught up behind the bat when there was a man on any base, and on a bound when the bases were free" (*Boston Journal*, February 22, 1905).

In 1875, with most catchers inching closer, Jim "Deacon" White made the opposite decision: "We no longer see him come up close to the bat after two strikes have been called on a batsman, he preferring to stay back and take the chances on a foul, and, not getting one, throwing the man out at first base" (Randolph, the New York correspondent for the *Chicago Tribune*, reprinted in the *St. Louis Globe-Democrat*, June 1, 1875).

Another problem that resulted from bringing the catcher up close was that he had to adjust to his dangerous proximity to the batter. The point was demonstrated in a September 4, 1877, game by a predictable figure who was playing a surprising position: "An amusing incident in this inning was [catcher Cap] Anson's appealing to the umpire to prevent Burdick [Jack Burdock] from swinging his bat too far back, by which Anson claimed that his play behind the bat was interfered with. It is the catcher the umpire has a right to make stand back, so as not to interfere with the batsman's movements in batting, the catcher having no right to stand so close to the batsman as to cramp his movements in any way" (*New York Clipper*, September 15, 1877).

Other variables such as the conditions of the grounds could also play a crucial role. Many years after the fact, a player named Jim McTague recalled why he began playing close to the plate in 1874 while catching for St. John's College in Minnesota. He explained that the area behind the plate was very sandy, making it almost impossible to catch a ball on the bound (*The Campion*, May 1916; reprinted in *Sporting News*, June 1, 1916).

The invention of the catcher's mask (see **9.4.2**) in 1877 eliminated one of the main reasons for catchers to set up well back of the plate. Catchers moved noticeably closer to the action, but their positioning remained situational. Henry Chadwick noted at the season's end that catchers were now playing up close with runners on base, and he endorsed that choice. He observed that they also generally played close with two strikes, but he questioned this strategy, claiming that it often resulted "in the loss of chances for long foul-bound tips and high foul balls." Chadwick was even more dubious about the benefit of playing close at other times, noting that it was handy for catching "waist and shoulder balls" but that "difficult low side balls" all too often turned into passed balls (*New York Clipper*, December 1, 1877).

The next few years saw catchers receive a couple of additional incentives to move closer to the plate. In 1879 the strikeout rule was changed to require the catcher to catch the ball on the fly to complete the out. The foul bound rule was permanently eliminated by the National League in 1883, and in the American Association in 1885. (The National League initially revoked the foul bound in 1879 but restored the old rule a year later.)

These rule changes pretty much forced receivers to position themselves behind the plate once a strikeout was possible, and some catchers also moved up when a walk appeared imminent. The *Atlanta Constitution* explained in 1885: "An inquirer asks why the catcher goes up to the bat when six balls are called. Because by standing right at the batter the catcher gives the pitcher a guide by which to throw the seventh and decisive balls" (*Atlanta Constitution*, May 16, 1885).

Catchers continued to play back early in the count with no runners on base, but even in that situation they seem to have been moving gradually closer. Researcher Greg Rhodes reviewed the diagrams of the diamond in the annual *Spalding Guide* between 1876 and 1892. He found that "the diagrams change from year to year, but for the most part the players stay in the same positions, with the exception of the catcher. He starts off in 1876 many steps behind home, but by 1892, he is within a couple of steps of home (although not yet in the position we see him today)."

It was several more years before the rules required the catcher to remain directly behind the plate throughout an at bat. Connie Mack later recalled that this was done for practical reasons: "Jim Hart, owner of the Chicago National League Club, was the father of this rule, which was made primarily to prevent the tiresome delays which occurred many times during the progress of a game by reason of having to wait for the catcher to come up and don his mask, and other paraphernalia every time a runner got on base or the batter had two strikes" (Connie Mack, "Memories of When the Game Was Young," *Sporting Life* [monthly], June 1924).

Mack's memory seems to have been a bit off, because he recalled this rule change taking place in 1896 or 1897. In fact it appears to have been introduced in the Western League in 1899 by Charles Comiskey (Jim McTague, writing in *The Campion*, May 1916; reprinted in *Sporting News*, June 1, 1916). The National League made it a requirement in 1901 and the American League one year later. (Since the American League grew out of the Western League, this would suggest that the Western League had dropped the rule at some point.)

The new rule also enabled umpires to move closer to the plate, which Hank O'Day felt made for better officiating. He explained that now an umpire "can tell better when a ball that rolls close along the base line is fair or foul, and on a slow hit he can step out on the diamond and he is in a better position to judge the decision at first base than when he stood back with the catcher" (*Sporting News*, May 4, 1901). This shift also provided the impetus for much of today's umpire's equipment to emerge over the next decade, as will be discussed in part six of Chapter 8.

4.2.2 Catching from a Crouch. Early catchers stood upright, although usually with a bit of a stoop. An 1871 article noted of the Red Stockings' Doug Allison: "In standing close to the bat, too, he takes a ball hot from the pitcher, while perfectly upright. Most catchers take a stooping position" (*New York Clipper*, January 21, 1871).

Their stance did not immediately change once catchers began to position themselves closer to the plate. There were a number of good reasons for this. Since the emphasis on pitchers keeping the ball low was not yet in place, the advantage of being better positioned to catch the pitch was not a major factor. An upright posture made it a little easier to adjust to stop wild pitches or dodge hot fouls. In addition, catchers who crouched had to expend valuable time uncoiling in order to make their throws. Perhaps most important, a crouch is uncomfortable.

With so many disadvantages, the crouch was slow to catch on. Baseball historian William Curran cited Buck Ewing, a star catcher of the 1880s, as the first catcher to crouch (William Curran, *Mitts*, 103). Curran noted that Ewing overcame one of the drawbacks of the crouch by making snap throws from the position. In 1891, Germany Smith credited Cincinnati catcher Jim Keenan, whose career began in 1885, with being the first to squat down and give signals from between both knees. Interestingly, Smith made the claim during a discussion of the 1889 World's Series during which, according to Smith, Brooklyn used signs stolen from Ewing to take a 3-1 lead in games. Ewing then changed his signs and New York came back to win the series (*Cincinnati Commercial-Gazette*, reprinted in *Sporting News*, April 25, 1891).

Nonetheless there seems to have been no reason compelling enough for most nineteenth-century catchers to change their stance, and the twentieth century opened with crouches still unpopular. Connie Mack advised in 1904: ". . . When a catcher takes his position he should assume a stooping posture. The body should be well bent forward from the hips, so as to enable the player to handle the ball at any height. Crouching to the ground should not be considered, as a player who insists on so doing will never become a first-class catcher. An easy position should be assumed as far as possible. Where the catcher crouches he is unable to control the erratic flight of the ball" (Connie Mack, "How to Play Ball," multi-part series, *Washington Post*, March 20, 1904).

The stoop advocated by Mack appears to have been more pronounced than those of earlier years because of the increased emphasis on shielding signals from the prying eyes of the opposing players (see **6.5.2**). An 1896 article explained, "In these days the most effective method used by catchers in giving signs is by placing the fingers of the right hand in the centre of the big mitt worn on the left hand. The catcher stoops until one knee rests upon the ground and then turns the middle of the mitt toward the pitcher" (*Sporting News*, March 7, 1896). Yet within a few years it became clear that precautions were essential, with one of the factors being the permanent return of first-base coaches after an absence of several seasons (see **7.1.4**).

In response, catchers concluded that it was no longer sufficient to "work the signals from within the shadow of the knee and the big mitt so that they are exposed for the gaze of the pitcher alone and can not be seen from the coaching boxes" (*Sporting News*, June 24, 1899). The return of the first-base coach was accompanied by a rapid increase in sign-stealing, and the price for these transgressions would be borne—quite literally—on the backs of catchers.

According to a 1909 article in *Sporting News*, crouching had become a necessity because of the need for catchers to give their signals confidentially (*Sporting News*, April 29, 1909). The *Washington Post* confirmed that same year that catchers "must guard against the batsman peeking back to catch his code. That is why the backstop stoops in calling for balls . . . by crouching he shuts out all possible vision of the batsman" (*Washington Post*, July 18, 1909).

Catchers were forced to crouch still lower a couple of years later when word got out that the Athletics had stolen "the signs of big Ed Sweeney, catcher of the Yankees, by having one of the A's players hide behind the water cooler on his stomach. When the backstop gave his signals, he dropped his fingers to the ground and they were clearly visible from beneath the cooler" (Stan Baumgartner, "Signals," *Baseball Guide and Record Book 1947*, 127).

Thus it seems that sign stealers are primarily responsible for nearly a century of catchers' aching backs and legs, though other factors also contributed. The trend toward lower pitching after 1910 (see **3.3.3**) was undoubtedly one such factor. It is also possible that catchers were trying not to block the umpire's view. The 1960s saw catchers given reason to crouch still lower when the introduction of improved mitt designs made it easier to catch low pitches (see **4.4.1**).

4.2.3 Guarding the Lines. The late 1870s saw a dramatic shift as the infield gradually began to assume its current functions. The key event was the elimination of the fair-foul after the 1876 season. Within weeks of the rule's passage, Henry Chadwick noted perceptively that "the infielders will be able to consolidate their forces so as to secure more ground-balls than they did before" (*New York Clipper*, January 13, 1877).

Many chroniclers of baseball history have appreciated the basic fact that a repositioning of the infield took place at this time. But in doing so they have too often misrepresented or grossly oversimplified the reasons for the change. This regrettable trend began soon after the events themselves.

In 1887, for example, a Detroit sportswriter offered this description of how baseball had been played in 1874: "The basemen played throughout the game with one foot on the base and never thought of trying for a ground ball unless it came straight to them" (*Detroit Free Press*, December 18, 1887). Sportswriter Malcolm McLean went further in 1913, penning this florid account of first-base play in 1876: "Like all first basemen who guarded the position since the game graduated from the 'o'cat' stage, [Cap] Anson kept one foot firmly planted on the sack. This was the custom. If he was so careless as to remove said shoe for an instant he quickly corrected himself. First basemen were hired to act as targets and to slug the ball. It was up to their mates to throw within fairly easy reaching distance. Grounders hit a few feet to the right of them went as singles—that is, if the second baseman couldn't cover that far. First-base tactics were in the cave-dwelling age" (Malcolm McLean, *Collier's*, reprinted in *Sporting News*, October 23, 1913).

Both comments are emblematic of a condescending attitude toward early baseball. While these descriptions of the first baseman's positioning have some basis in fact, these writers are engaging in both exaggeration and oversimplification as well as displaying a degree of ignorance. In fact the positioning of first basemen in relation to their base did not betray a lack of imagination but instead fluctuated in response to the rules and conditions of the day.

Henry Chadwick recommended in 1860 that the first baseman "should play a little below his base and inside the line of the foul ball post, as he will then get to balls that would otherwise pass him" (*Beadle's 1860 Dime Base-Ball Player*, 23). While this player was clearly not standing on the bag, his relative proximity to it reflected the unique demands of play at first base. From very early in the game's history, sure-handedness and height were stressed as requirements, while foot speed, mobility, and a strong, accurate throwing arm were not particularly important. Since every other position on the field *did* reward these skills, players who lacked them naturally gravitated to first base.

This began to change when left-handers began to be excluded from the other infield positions, which meant that more agile and proficient fielders started to be stationed at first base. The most notable was southpaw Joe Start, a forgotten superstar who remained the standard for first basemen from the early 1860s until his retirement in 1886. Sportswriter William Rankin noted in 1910: "It was Joe Start who made first base a fielding position. Up to the early sixties the first baseman stood at the base and caught, or tried to do so, all balls thrown there, but made no attempt to leave the base to get batted balls. In the early '60's Start revolutionized the first base system of play. It was easy for him to go after hits in his direction with a man like Freddy Crane playing second, for the latter would cover first when Joe had played deep for the ball" (*Sporting News*, March 3, 1910).

Chadwick was a great admirer of Start, and by 1867 he was advising, "In taking his position in the field, he should stand about twenty or thirty feet from the base towards the right field . . . he will of course be guided by the style of batting opposed to him" (Henry Chadwick, *Haney's Book of Base Ball Reference for 1867*, 128). The following year he instructed first basemen to stand eight to ten yards from the base and four to five yards inside the foul line except when a runner occupied first base (Henry Chadwick, *The American Game of Base Ball*, 30). Of course not every first baseman had the skill to follow Chadwick's counsel, yet it seems safe to assume that most were positioning themselves at least a few feet from their base. So why were later observers convinced that they never left the base?

The answer is quite simple. The fair-foul hit (see **2.2.2**), which was still unknown in 1867, emerged in the next few years and remained a major part of batters' arsenals until it was banned in 1877. The fair-foul hit meant that first and third basemen were suddenly responsible for covering the ground both to the left and right of their base.

This new factor combined with an existing one to force first and third basemen to regard their respective bases as the midpoint of the territory they were expected to cover. Foul balls that were caught on the first bounce counted as outs until the mid-1880s, meaning that a corner baseman who guarded the lines would have many extra opportunities to record outs.

Fair-fouls and foul bounds applied to both the first and third basemen, but several additional factors led first basemen to remain close to the bag.

The first and most obvious is the large number of outs that are registered at first base. The nonroutine nature of outs in early baseball made it helpful for the first baseman to be stationed on the base to await throws. The bases were not always easily visible from afar, so the first baseman could naturally elicit more accurate throws by providing a stationary target. Being on the base beforehand also made it easier for a first baseman to adjust to wild throws, an important and difficult feat in the days before trapping mitts were introduced.

Place hitting (see **2.1.1**), curveballs (see **3.2.3**), left-handed hitters (see **2.1.9**), and closed batting stances (see **2.1.6**) were also uncommon before the mid-1870s. The result was that relatively few balls were hit between first and second base, providing another good reason for first basemen not to stray far from the base.

In consequence, first basemen again positioned themselves close to their base between the late 1860s and the mid-1870s, but this reflected not thoughtlessness but a very reasonable decision. The responsibility for covering foul territory meant that even agile players such as Joe Start moved closer to the base. Moreover this trend reinforced itself because the tendency to assign the position to slow-footed players reemerged.

The pendulum swung back after a couple of rule changes reinvented foul territory. The fair-foul was eliminated in 1877, and the consequences for the first baseman were immediately appreciated by Henry Chadwick, who observed, "Under the new rule, the first and third baseman will not be required to stand as near to the foul-ball line as hitherto" (*New York Clipper*, January 13, 1877). The "foul bound" was permanently removed from the books in the early 1880s. (The foul bound was eliminated in the National League in 1879 but restored a year later. It was permanently abolished in the National League in 1883 and in 1885 in the American Association.)

The first baseman was thus liberated from much of the responsibility of covering foul balls. Holdovers who had been placed at first base because of their lack of mobility were not quick to reposition themselves, but newcomers to the position began to experiment.

Lee Richmond credited Walter Meader, the first baseman on his college championship team at Brown University, with being a pioneer at playing off the base. He claimed that Meader was responsible for assisting on putouts more frequently than any first baseman he saw in professional baseball (Ronald A. Mayer, *Perfect!*, 12).

Charles Comiskey is often referred to as having been the earliest first baseman to play off the base. There are many descriptions of Comiskey and Ted Sullivan developing this new tactic while with Dubuque in 1879. As with so many events in which Ted Sullivan figured, the accounts are rather hyperbolic in presenting it as a "Eureka!" type of idea that the two men then honed in clandestine fashion at a freight yard.

Malcolm McLean gave a particularly far-fetched account: ". . . The base ball world was shaken to its foundation. A tall, slender boy named Charley Comiskey had started in to revolutionize the system of playing the initial station. From the first day he signed with the St. Louis Browns, he sprinted after grounders which had formerly been considered hits—and got them. Fouls caught on the first bound were called outs in those first years of the big leagues. Few made much of an effort to trap them. Not so with Comiskey. He took such long chances it became dangerous to foul within running distance of him. Great ball players shook their heads gravely. Other first basemen were furious. It was plainly up to them to wise up and hustle. Yet they were slow in realizing something new had been added to the sport. This is a historic fact—every innovation in base ball has been bitterly fought until finally adopted" (Malcolm McLean, *Collier's*, reprinted in *Sporting News*, October 23, 1913).

This description reads much more like myth than history, and, as we have already seen, Comiskey was at most bringing back a trend introduced by Joe Start a decade and a half earlier. Moreover the extent to which Comiskey was ahead of his peers is doubtless exaggerated, especially since Start was still considered the master of the position. Indeed, Comiskey himself later wrote that his contribution was to "[play] my position 10 or 15 feet deeper than the other first baseman." He added that although he played deeper, he did not stray far from the baseline: "I always played the foul lines safe, for a hit along the foul lines is the most dangerous of any" (Charles A. Comiskey, "How to Play the Infield," A. H. Spink, *The National Game*, 394–395).

Other evidence seems to confirm that Comiskey played an important role but that the change was evolutionary rather than revolutionary. For example, the sportswriter Revere Rodgers wrote, "Comiskey played the deepest first base of any professional I ever saw. It was almost akin to a short right field and he drilled it into his pitching staff that they should cover the sack" (*Sporting News*, July 16, 1904).

Consequently the role of the first baseman began to change dramatically in the early 1880s. A *Sporting Life* correspondent observed in 1883, "The old style first baseman was required to play his base—that is, to hug it closely—attend to throwing, and but that. In the modern game the first baseman is required to play half of the right short field ground, to which the superior batting sends many hot, ugly balls, for the reason that it is regarded as safe ground" (*Sporting Life*, December 12, 1883). As this suggests, the new rules concerning foul territory were combining with new hitting approaches to move the first baseman farther from the bag.

4.2.4 Pitchers Covering First. The most obvious consequence of the first baseman moving farther from the base was that pitchers began to routinely cover first base. As might be guessed from the previous entry, this was not entirely a new phenomenon.

Henry Chadwick remarked in 1860, "The Pitcher will frequently have to occupy the bases on occasions when the proper guardian has left it to field the ball" (*Beadle's 1860 Dime Base-Ball Player*, 22). An 1861 account of a game in Hoboken between the Eureka of Newark and the Enterprise of Brooklyn reported: ". . . There were two or three plays made then that were so superior in their character that we cannot help noticing them. One was the putting out of Leland, in the third innings, when [first baseman Harry] Northrop fielded the ball to [pitcher] Linen, who was running to first base to receive it, Linen catching the ball on the run in beautiful style, and touching the base before Leland could reach it" (*New York Clipper*, July 20, 1861). The *Brooklyn Eagle* recorded that in an 1865 game, "[Jack] Chapman was next put out at first, the 'pitcher' covering the base" (*Brooklyn Eagle*, August 31, 1865).

The Red Stockings of Cincinnati also pulled the play at least once. Researcher Darryl Brock reported that the opponents were the Nationals of Washington and that future National League president Nick Young hit a ball to Red Stockings first baseman Charlie Gould. Gould fell down while fielding the ball, so he completed the putout by flipping it to pitcher Asa Brainard. Although the fact that Gould had fallen down suggests that the play was a bit of a fluke, Brainard would not have been in position unless it was customary for him to cover the bag on such plays (*Cincinnati Commercial*, July 4, 1869).

The prominence of the fair-foul in the early 1870s kept first basemen very close to the bag, and pitchers were thus able to conserve their energies. But the changes described in the preceding entry meant that by the early 1880s pitchers were again getting plenty of exercise. *Sporting Life* observed in 1883: "Lately pitchers have added to their play the part of covering first when the baseman has to leave his ground for a safely hit ball" (*Sporting Life*, December 12, 1883).

As captain of St. Louis, Charley Comiskey naturally drilled his pitchers to cover first base when he was drawn away from it. Comiskey found a novel way to impress upon the team's pitchers how important it was "to get over to cover the bag." According to Comiskey, "If I saw the pitcher was loafing on me I fielded the ball and then threw to first whether anyone was there or not. Then the crowd saw who was to blame, and pretty soon the pitchers got in the habit of running over rapidly rather than be roasted" (Charles A. Comiskey, "How to Play the Infield," A. H. Spink, *The National Game*, 394–395; see also Revere Rodgers, *Sporting News*, July 16, 1904, and Malcolm

McLean, *Collier's*, reprinted in *Sporting News*, October 23, 1913). Harry Wright had a different method of ensuring compliance: "One of Harry Wright's new rules is that every time a pitcher fails to cover first base when [Sid] Farrar goes for a ball he is fined $1" (*Sporting Life*, May 13, 1885).

The tactics of Comiskey and Wright suggest that it was far from easy to convince pitchers to add regular sprints to their duties. Deacon Phillippe reported in 1904 that Comiskey's method was still in use: "Several National and American league first basemen follow Comiskey's advice and throw the ball whether the pitcher covers the bag or not, the idea being to 'show him up' if he is lazy or neglectful" (Deacon Phillippe, "Phillippe of Pittsburg Team Discusses Requirements of Successful Pitchers," *Syracuse Post Standard*, March 27, 1904).

In the next few years this technique grew to become a point of emphasis in spring training drills. A 1905 description noted that Washington manager Jake Stahl "believes in the value of pitchers covering first base while the baseman is fielding the ball, and he firmly impressed it upon the minds of all. Stahl proposes to have his boxmen so well drilled in this point of play that he can play a deep field and feel certain that the pitcher will go over to take his throws. Washington pitchers have been prone to remaining in the box when the ball was batted to the first baseman, and often it was impossible for the baseman to get to the bag ahead of the runner, hence a chance was lost owing to the stupidity or indifference of the pitcher" (*Washington Post*, March 16, 1905).

The increased reliance on "inside ball" left other pitchers with little choice about making a habit of covering first.

4.2.5 Second Basemen Leaving the Bag. A number of diagrams, drawings, and early photographs show a second baseman standing on second base as a pitch is delivered. Such evidence has led some to conclude that early second basemen invariably stationed themselves on the base.

In fact this was not the case. While early second basemen played closer to the base than is the case today and occasionally even stood on it, they changed their position according to the situation. Henry Chadwick recommended in 1860 that the second baseman "should play a little back of his base, and to the right or left of it, according to the habitual play of the striker, but generally to the left as most balls pass in that direction" (*Beadle's 1860 Dime Base-Ball Player*, 24).

An 1864 book advised that this player "should play generally to the left and a little back of his base, though he should be guided in it by the customary play of the striker. When the striker reaches the first base, he should return to his base, prepared to receive the ball from the catcher, and be ready to put out the striker by touching him with the ball" (*The American Boy's Book of Sports and Games*, 87). In 1867, Chadwick counseled captains that with a slow or medium-paced pitcher working, "prepare your field for catches by placing your basemen out further, letting the short stop nearly cover second base, and the second baseman play at right short well out, and extending your out-fielders about ten yards or so" (*Haney's Base Ball Book of Reference for 1867*, reprinted in *The Ball Player's Chronicle*, August 22, 1867).

The second baseman was especially likely to move away from the base when there were no runners on base, as is shown by Chadwick's description of an 1867 match between the Atlantics and the Mutuals: "[John] Hatfield, of the Mutuals, . . . led off with a fine hit to [Atlantics second baseman] Charley Smith, who was playing almost at right short, and though Charley found it a hot one to field, he got it to [first baseman Joe] Start in time to send Hatfield back" (Henry Chadwick, *The American Game of Base Ball*, 126).

Another factor in the placement of the second baseman was the skill of the shortstop. An 1869 article noted that second baseman Albert DeGroot Martin and shortstop Albro Akin of the Unions of Morrisania "were extremely active and quick runners, and would support one another effectively, thus allowing Martin to play farther from his base than he could with a less active short" (*National Chronicle*, June 12, 1869).

A similar repositioning occurred when a left-handed batter was at the plate. Henry Chadwick explained in 1871 that the second baseman "is required, also, to cover second base and to play 'right short stop,' but his position in the field must be governed entirely by the character of the batting he is called upon to face. If a hard hitter comes to bat and swift balls are being sent in, he should play well out in the field, between right field and second base, and be on the *qui vive* for long bound balls or high fly balls, which drop between the out-field and the second base line. When the batsman makes his first base the second baseman comes up and gets near the base in readiness to receive the ball from the catcher" (*New York Clipper*, March 11, 1871).

In the ensuing years the second baseman also began to inch farther from the bag against right-handed batters. Henry Chadwick noted before the 1874 season: "Of late seasons it has been the custom to cover the open gap between first and second bases by making the second baseman play at 'right short,' but this has left a safe spot for sharp grounders close to second base, while it has also drawn round the short-stop to second, and the third baseman to short-field to such an extent as to make fair-foul hitting a sure style of play for earned bases" (*New York Clipper*, March 7, 1874).

It is thus simply untrue that early second basemen remained planted in one place. In actuality they took a remarkable number of factors into account and changed their position accordingly.

Unlike the first and third basemen, the second baseman's positioning does not seem to have changed dramatically as a result of the abolition of the fair-foul. Researcher Greg Rhodes reported that the second baseman remained a few steps from the bag in the diagrams that appeared in the annual *Spalding Guide* between 1876 and 1892. But the responsibilities of the position did increase as a result of the "marked increase of right-field hitting" (*New York Clipper*, December 20, 1879).

Sporting Life observed in 1883, "The second baseman of to-day is an entirely different unit in the field work of a team that [sic] was his fellow tradesman of ten years ago. There is a wide difference between the play of a [Tommy] Beals, a [Wes] Fisler and a [Jack] Burdock of 1873 and a [Fred] Dunlap, a [Jack] Farrell and a [Jack] Burdock of 1883. Not only has the territory over which the second baseman of the first class does not permit a grounder to pass grown larger, but the work in throwing and attention to fly balls has increased nearly as much. To the short stop and the second baseman has gradually been assigned the work of attending to all fly balls 'between the fields' as the gap between the infielders and outfielders of a team in play is called" (*Sporting Life*, December 12, 1883).

As will be suggested in the next entry, the current custom of having the second baseman and shortstop roughly equidistant from the base dates from around the beginning of the twentieth century. It is no coincidence that the hit-and-run play became a major offensive weapon at the same time (see 5.4.7).

4.2.6 Shortstops Become Responsible for Base Play. As discussed in the first chapter (see 1.15), the shortstop originated as a fourth outfielder and then during the 1850s gradually evolved into a rover. By the 1860s he was playing much closer to the infield but continued to have much more license to roam about than the basemen. Henry Chadwick wrote in 1867, "In selecting your short-stop, let him be an accurate thrower to begin with, but especially should he be noted for his activity in backing up every player in the in-field as occasion may require. The short-stop should always be on the move and on the lookout, first behind third base, then running home to help the catcher, anon playing second base, and even running out to long field for a high ball" (Henry Chadwick, *Haney's Base Ball Book of Reference for 1867*, reprinted in *The Ball Player's Chronicle*, August 15, 1867).

By 1879 the role had changed enough for Chadwick to observe that "short-stops are now required to cover bases so frequently—second base in particular—that they have come to be almost part and parcel of the basemen-team of a nine" (*New York Clipper*, December 20, 1879). An increased emphasis on hitting to right field would promote this trend in the next few years.

In 1883, *Sporting Life* remarked upon the shortstop's growing responsibilities: ". . . A change has come to the short stop of this day, when his work is contrasted with the short stops of ten years ago. The short stop not only plays the ground half way from third base to second, but he attends to the base play when the players leave them for stops, backs up the infield throwing, has rambling orders for pop flies in the space between fields, and is especially useful in the run-outs that are so frequent in these days of fast and daring base running" (*Sporting Life*, December 12, 1883).

It was several more years before shortstops began truly to share the responsibility for covering second base. Honus Wagner remarked in 1904, "The position of shortstop has come to be practically a duplicate of that of second base, except that one man plays to the right of the bag while the other plays to the left. Ten years ago the short fielder had a position all to himself, and one which gave him a full share of the work done at that time. The large increase in the number of left-hand batters has brought about a change, and the shortstop is as much a second baseman as the player so designated" (*Washington Post*, July 3, 1904).

4.2.7 Third Base Becomes a Hitter's Haven. As discussed in "Guarding the Lines" (see **4.2.3**), a number of factors caused third basemen of the late 1860s and early 1870s to stay close to their bag. The *New York Clipper* observed in 1871: "The third baseman takes a position closer to his base than either of the other basemen. Sometimes, however, he takes the place of the short stop when the latter covers the second base in cases where the second baseman plays at right short for a right-field hitter, a position frequently taken by a first class nine" (*New York Clipper*, March 4, 1871).

Some batsmen of the early 1870s were so adept at the fair-foul that third basemen must have wished they could stand in foul territory. Jim O'Rourke recalled that Ross Barnes "had a trick of hitting the ball so it would smash on the ground near the plate just inside of the third base line, and would then mow the grass over the line, away out into the field, where, of course, the fielders did not stay. No third baseman could get away from his position quickly enough to stop one of Barnes' hits" ("Forty Two Years of Base Ball: Wonderful Life Story of Jim O'Rourke," *Kalamazoo Evening Telegraph*, March 3, 1910).

As also noted in "Guarding the Lines," that began to change when the fair-foul was banned in 1877. At season's end, Henry Chadwick remarked that "the cutting off of the fair-foul hitting lessened some of the difficulties of the third baseman's work" (*New York Clipper*, December 29, 1877). The basic duties of the third baseman have not changed much since. What has changed is the desirability of having a skilled gloveman at third base, which has corresponded closely to whether the bunt (see **2.2.1**) was in or out of favor.

Sporting Life noted in 1883: "In old times the third baseman was perhaps the most important man on the nine, as the position was regarded as the key of the infield. Those were the days when fair-foul hitting and blocking the ball [i.e., bunting] flourished. Nowadays the third baseman has much less to do than formerly, the changes in the rules and in styles of pitching being responsible therefor. In fact, the second baseman, of the infielders, exceeds in importance" (*Sporting Life*, December 12, 1883).

Just when it appeared that third base was no longer an important defensive position, the bunt made its comeback in the late 1880s. But playing far enough in to defend against the bunt put the third baseman in great peril from a hot line drive. It was no coincidence that in these years third base began to be referred to as the "difficult corner," a term that eventually evolved into the "hot corner" (*Sporting Life*, December 30, 1885; *Sporting News*, August 17, 1889).

The frequency of bunting continued to increase in the 1890s. In an 1892 editorial, the *New York Times* suggested that due to the requirement of having to guard against bunts as well as field line drives, it might be appropriate for third basemen to wear masks and other equipment reserved for catchers (*New York Times*, June 23, 1892). By 1904, Connie Mack observed that "third base has always been considered as the most difficult position on the diamond to play" (Connie Mack, "How to Play Ball," multi-part series, *Washington Post*, April 3, 1904).

Even after the power explosion of the 1920s, bunting remained a common part of baseball (albeit one that many recent analysts believe is overused). Not until the 1950s did the emphasis on the bunt begin to wane and third base begin to be viewed as a hitter's position.

4.2.8 Outfield Placement. Some writers believe that outfielders in early baseball stood in the same location for each batter. Some clubs do indeed seem to have been unimaginative in this regard, as the *Boston Globe* wrote in 1889, "The [Harvard] outfield seemed all right, but played their positions as they did twenty-five years ago. They went out and stood in the same spot for every man that came to the bat, without any regard to the way the batsman faced" (*Boston Globe*, April 9, 1889).

That was not generally the case, however. Henry Chadwick instructed captains as early as 1867 that it was worth "extending your out-fielders about ten yards or so" when a slow or medium-paced pitcher was working. He added, "Always have an understanding with your two sets of fielders in regard to private signals, so as to be able to call them in closer, or place them out further, or nearer the foul-ball lines, as occasion may require, without giving notice to your adversaries. . . . Warn your out-fielders also to watch well the batsmen, so as to be ready to move in the direction he faces for batting" (*Haney's Base Ball Book of Reference for 1867*, reprinted in *The Ball Player's Chronicle*, August 22, 1867).

By 1881 outfielders were being advised to "strictly obey the signals from the pitcher for all such changes of position. Time and again this past season we have seen a pitcher's strategy entirely nullified by the stupidity or obstinacy of some one or other of the outfielders to quickly obey the pitcher's signal to play deeper, or closer, or to get round more to the right or to the left, when he has been preparing to outwit a batsman by something besides the mere speed of his delivery" (*New York Clipper*, December 31, 1881).

4.2.9 Right Fielders Playing Very Shallow. Right fielders in the very early days of baseball played so shallow in some circumstances that they became essentially right shortstops. Even when they played at more normal depth, they remained alert for opportunities to throw runners out at first on apparent base hits. A 1915 article observed, "In the bygone days of baseball the speediest outfielders were stationed in right field so that they could come in fast on a bounder hit into right field, scoop it up and throw the batter [sic] at first base. In these days such a trick is a rarity; but twenty and thirty years ago it was common. A right fielder who could not arrange an assist on every three bounders hit out his way was considered too slow to keep" (*Nevada* [Reno] *State Journal*, September 14, 1915).

The piece cited Billy Sunday, Mike Tiernan, Mike Kelly, Jake Evans, Tom McCarthy, and Hugh Nicol as right fielders who were proficient at executing this play. The garrulous George "Orator" Shafer was especially skilled at the tactic. A contemporary report observed, "Without exception he is the best right-fielder in the country today, a position in which he has always played, and which he has down to a very fine point. His record of assist on put-outs at first base beats anything that has ever been heard of" (*Cleveland Leader*, March 23, 1882). In 1925 the sportswriter John B. Sheridan described Shafer as "one of the greatest right fielders that I have ever known in one point, throwing out base runners at first base on apparently safe hits" (*Sporting News*, November 26, 1925).

A. H. Spink claimed that in the 1870s and 1880s this play was "pulled off three or four times in each and every contest" (A. H. Spink, *The National Game*, 270). This is probably a slight exaggeration, but not as much as might be expected, as Shafer had fifty outfield assists in seventy-two games in 1879, a major league record that still stands. A particularly historic instance of this play occurred in an 1880 game when Providence right fielder Lon Knight threw out a batter at first base on what appeared to be a clean single. The play preserved Lee Richmond's 1880 perfect game— the first in major league history.

Gradually a greater emphasis on left-field hitting forced right fielders to play deeper, and this once-common play began to disappear. A notable exception occurred during the second game of a Decoration Day double-header on May 30, 1895, when an overflow crowd forced Cincinnati right fielder "Dusty" Miller to play very shallow. He took advantage by throwing out four Philadelphia batters on apparent singles (Greg Rhodes and John Snyder, *Redleg Journal*, 117).

4.2.10   Infield Depth. We have already seen in the entry for "Catchers Playing Close" (4.2.1) that terms like "close" and "near" are too subjective for exact interpretation. This is even more the case with infield depth, but I will venture a few generalizations.

Early infielders did not play particularly deep, typically no more than a step or two behind the base paths. There were several reasons for this. One was so that they could return to their bases in time to provide a target for other fielders, if necessary. Another was that, with all the obstacles that prevented any out from being routine, it made sense to reduce the length of throws.

Connie Mack noted an additional factor that complicated the positioning of early infielders. He explained that old-time fielders had to take account of a "narrow path running between the bases from which the turf was skinned. If an infielder played in front of this path a hard hit ball was apt to kill him, and if he played back of it the ball often hit the edge of it and bounced over his head to the outfield" (Connie Mack, "Memories of When the Game Was Young," *Sporting Life* [monthly], June 1924).

Clubs certainly did play their infielders deeper or shallower depending on the situation, however. In 1905 the sportswriter H. G. Merrill wrote that "bringing the infield in is an antiquated play" and cited Ted Sullivan as one proponent of this philosophy when he managed the St. Louis Brown Stockings in 1883 (*Sporting News*, April 29, 1905).

Sullivan's protégé, Charlie Comiskey, took over the reins of the Brown Stockings later that season and became noted for playing a deep infield. Johnny Evers and Hugh Fullerton reported that the 1885 and 1886 post-season series between Chicago, champions of the National League, and the American Association pennant winners from St. Louis provided a vivid contrast in defensive philosophies, with the Brown Stockings playing much deeper (John J. Evers and Hugh S. Fullerton, *Touching Second*, 201).

Once infielders began to play deeper, a manager's decision about whether to move the infielders closer in critical situations became more conspicuous and began to attract more attention. Comiskey commented in 1910 that "unless the score is very close and it is near the end of a game, I never pull in my infielders for a possible play at the plate, but rather play for the base runner" (Charles A. Comiskey. "How to Play the Infield," A. H. Spink, *The National Game*, 395).

4.2.11   Moving In During the Pitch. As the preceding entry shows, since deep positioning for infielders was a relatively late development, it is probably impossible to determine the first club to play their infield in or at double-play depth. There is one variant, however, that has developed much more recently. Tim McCarver reported that in the 1990s the Montreal Expos unveiled the tactic of having their middle infielders move in during the pitcher's windup. McCarver noted that this puts pressure on a base runner on third base, since he has already received his instructions from the third-base coach (Tim McCarver with Danny Peary, *Tim McCarver's Baseball for Brain Surgeons and Other Fans*, 322, 324).

4.2.12   Shifts. On July 14, 1946, Lou Boudreau unveiled the famous Williams Shift against Ted Williams, which featured only one defensive player to the left of second base. But clubs had been using shifts against Williams as early as 1941 (Michael Seidel, *Ted Williams*, 103–104). Moreover David Nemec has pointed out that this was not even the first Williams Shift—shifts were used against left-handed pull hitters Ken Williams and Cy Williams in 1922! (David Nemec, *Great Baseball Facts, Feats and Firsts*, 122). Boudreau's version wasn't remotely a first—it just attracted a lot of attention because it was so dramatic.

As this suggests, shifts are a vexed subject. Since there is no clear-cut distinction between shading and a full-fledged shift, there is no way to determine the first shift. It is worth noting, however, that some extreme positioning was in use in the nineteenth century, with Bob Ferguson at the forefront. By 1877 he was adjusting to right-handed pull hitters by placing the second baseman on the left side of the infield (*Louisville Courier-Journal*, May 19, 1877; quoted in David Arcidiacono, *Grace, Grit and Growling*, 61).

An 1879 game account showed that Ferguson was expanding and refining the shift: "The game opened with the Athletics at the bat, and as Cramer—a left-handed striker—took up his position it was noteworthy how finely [captain Bob] Ferguson placed his field for him. [Third baseman] Smith stood at left-short, [shortstop] Ferguson covered second, [second baseman Sam] Crane was deep right-short, and [first baseman George] Latham covered first well back, while [right fielder John] Cassidy was ready for a right-field assistance, [center fielder Lip] Pike at right-centre, and [left fielder Phil] Powers at left-centre. The moment a right-handed batsman took his place, the field was moved round to the regular positions to suit the probable hitting" (*New York Clipper*, May 24, 1879).

Similarly, an 1895 exhibition game saw Chicago position all three outfielders in left field when John Shearon came to the plate. Shearon tried in vain to hit the ball into the gaping hole in right field (*Sporting News*, December 7, 1895).

While shifts are generally used on power hitters, Ed Reulbach claimed that one of the most effective ones was used on turn-of-the-century Philadelphia outfielder Roy Thomas, a singles hitter. Reulbach explained that Thomas "not only hit almost all the time to left field, but he was a short field hitter as well. This tendency handicapped him tremendously. When Thomas was at bat, the left fielder moved close to the foul line and came well in. The center fielder shifted away over toward left and at the same time advanced close up behind short and second. Third baseman moved over nearly to the foul line, and the shortstop followed him to a point at least fifteen feet beyond his natural position. At the same time he fell back and played a rather deep field. With this combination against him, Thomas was like clay in the hands of the pitcher" (F. C. Lane, *Batting*, 50).

(iii) Teamwork

4.3.1 Calling for Fly Balls. Given the danger of collisions, it is not surprising that calling for fly balls developed very early. Researcher Priscilla Astifan discovered an 1860 game account in which the catcher of the touring Excelsiors of Brooklyn was praised "for the manner in which he would telegraph advantages to be gained, or the direction as to which one of the fielders should take a 'fly.' There was no rushing for a ball, but each man of the Excelsiors knew his place and kept it, a point which our ball-players will please make a note of" (*Rochester Evening Express*, July 9, 1860).

Henry Chadwick advised in 1860: "The Catcher, whenever he sees several fielders running to catch a ball, should designate the one he deems most sure of taking it, by name, in which case the others should refrain from the attempt to catch the ball on the fly" (*Beadle's 1860 Dime Base-Ball Player*, 21).

Researcher Darryl Brock discovered that the Red Stockings drew praise for the sophistication of their system during their 1869 tour of California: "The Red Stockings have arranged a set of orders so brief that frequently only the name of the player is called and he hastens to do what is requisite: an instance of their alacrity and perfect understanding was given on Saturday—a sky ball was sent between short-stop and right field, for which either might have gone, but the captain called 'McVey,' and right field [Cal McVey] at once put himself in position to catch it, but the captain also called 'Wright' in the same breath, and short-stop [George Wright] ran and dropped on his knee under McVey's hands, so that if missed by the first it could still be caught before reaching the ground" (*Daily Alta California*, September 27, 1869).

The primary responsibility of calling for fly balls initially fell upon the captain. In 1879 the *Cleveland Plain Dealer* scolded: "It seems as if Captain

[Tom] Carey was ignorant of the fact that the other fielders depend upon him to *call* one of them to take a fly when three or four are in position to capture it" (*Cleveland Plain Dealer*, August 13, 1879).

Since this made it necessary for the captain to play a central position, clubs began to fine-tune the system. The *Chicago Tribune* suggested in 1880, "The player running at full speed, with a chance of getting under the ball, should sing out as he runs, 'Let me have it!' and, whether he can get the ball or not, he should invariably have the right of way" (*Chicago Tribune*, May 19, 1880). Unfortunately, this advice wouldn't have been of much help if two players were running at full speed and called for the ball.

In 1888, Johnny Ward wrote, "The necessity of 'calling' for a fly hit applies with particular force to the centre fielder. As soon as he has seen that he can get to a hit and has decided to take it, he calls out loudly so that every one must hear, 'I'll take it,' and all other fielders near him respond, 'Go ahead'" (John Montgomery Ward, *Base-Ball: How to Become a Player*, 115).

4.3.2 Backing Up. Instances of one fielder backing up another date back to baseball's earliest days. In 1860, Henry Chadwick noted that the shortstop was expected to "back up the second and third bases when the ball is thrown in from the field" (*Beadle's Dime Base-Ball Player*, 23). His advice was heeded at least occasionally. For example, an 1864 account noted that the shortstop of the Excelsiors of Brooklyn "threw the ball over [second baseman Harry Brainard's] head: fortunately [right fielder George] Fletcher was backing up well, and securing the ball, rapidly returned it to Harry at second base in time to cut [Mutuals base runner Tom] Devyr off" (*Brooklyn Eagle*, August 18, 1864).

What is harder to determine is whether such isolated examples were designed or improvised, and when backing up became commonplace. As early as 1871, fielders were being counseled: "Every player should be active in 'backing up' in the in-field" (*New York Clipper*, March 4, 1871). Nonetheless such tactics were not routine in the 1870s, and this should not simply be attributed to a lack of industriousness.

Any time the ball was put in play, the basemen and catcher were expected to remain close to their respective bases and home plate. This left only the shortstop and pitcher available as convenient backups on plays in the infield.

Pitchers did occasionally fulfill this function, but it does not appear to have been widespread. Providence pitcher John Ward backed up the plate on a throw from the outfield in a game on May 30, 1879, but the technique was apparently considered innovative (Jim Charlton, ed., *The Baseball Chronology*, 38). One reason is that the pitcher's suitability as a backup was also limited by the blocked-ball rule (see **12.6**) and other rules that now seem quaint by which the ball needed to be returned to the pitcher in his box.

This left only the shortstop, as Henry Chadwick later noted: "In the old times the only infielder who ever thought of backing up a companion was the short-stop, and then he considered that his chief duty in this respect was to attend to the pitcher only. Base-players of the olden time, with some rare exceptions, never thought of leaving their positions to field a ball, or to assist in fielding it, which went to any position save their own" (*New York Clipper*, January 22, 1881).

In the 1880s the idea of backing up gained greater acceptance. Henry Chadwick, for example, commended the Chicago club at the end of the 1880 season because "the pitcher and catcher ran behind the first base to stop the ball in case of a wide throw" (*New York Clipper*, December 18, 1880). But the following examples suggest that execution of the theory sometimes lagged behind.

A *Sporting Life* correspondent observed in 1885, ". . . Every American Association club, with the possible exception of the Metropolitans [exhibits a] want of proper 'backing up' each other in the field. The Chicago League team gave some exhibitions in this line when here that reflect great credit upon the 'drill work' of their captain. When a ball, for example, is batted to left field, the centre fielder should run at full speed to a position on the line of the hit, back some distance of the left fielder, not with a view to catch the ball, but to stop it in case it passes the left fielder" (*Sporting Life*, June 3, 1885).

The blocked-ball rule was gradually superseded by ground rules, leading pitcher John Clarkson to note in 1888 that pitchers were free to act as backups: "In the event of a ball being thrown wide from the outfield or any other point, as the case may be, it is the pitcher's duty to be behind the player to whom the ball is thrown, backing him up." But, Clarkson added, "I make special mention of this because it is so seldom done, and I think it is more through carelessness than anything else" (*New York Sun*, May 6, 1888).

As noted earlier, Chicago catchers were backing up first base as early as 1880, but the practice may have been popularized by Charles Ganzel. Hughey Jennings stated in 1907, "I really believe that Herman Long and Bob Lowe when they were playing with that old Boston team used to throw wild to first purposely so that Ganzel could get the ball. The base runner would see the ball going over the first baseman's head and he'd start turning second or leaving first, forgetting the catcher. Charlie would be there with that wing and throw them out" (*Detroit News*, March 18, 1907).

Sportswriter Harold Burr reported that Philadelphia catcher Red Dooin revived this hustling play around the turn of the century (*Sporting News*, November 10, 1938). Dooin was a natural candidate to reintroduce the tactic, because he was a small, quick player at a time when the catcher's position was dominated by larger men. The much-larger Boss Schmidt was one of the catchers who followed Dooin's lead.

4.3.3   Decoys. It's especially difficult to pin down the first occurrence of an ad hoc play such as a decoy. This 1901 account at least gives some idea of the parameters: "[Cincinnati infielders Jake] Beckley, [Harry] Steinfeldt and [George] Magoon worked the old trick of getting a man on first to run on a fly ball to the outfield. [Tom] Daly [of Brooklyn] was on first and was playing the hit and run game with [batter Bill] Dahlen. Dahlen sent a fly to [outfielder Sam] Crawford. Daly did not see where the ball was hit, but Beckley, Steinfeldt and Magoon did everything in their power to make him turn back toward first. Daly, of course, would not follow their advice but continued on for third. In the meantime the fly had been caught and Crawford had passed it to Beckley, making a double play" (*Sporting News*, June 15, 1901). If the decoy was regarded as an "old trick" in 1901, it can be assumed to date well back into the nineteenth century.

Chicago second baseman Johnny Evers was particularly associated with the play. A 1905 account noted, "[Johnny] Evers' trick in the seventh was a clever one—and but for fate he would have trapped the cardinals [sic] into a double play. [Jack] Dunleavy was at first when [Jack] Warner poked out a short fly to center. Evers pretended the ball had skipped over second, running over and sliding as if trying to reach the ball. Dunleavy, seeing him, tore down to second and rounded towards third—then saw [Jimmy] Slagle tearing in to catch the fly, and he tried to get back to first. Slagle could not quite reach or it would have been an easy double" (*Chicago Tribune*, May 28, 1905). Evers frequently collaborated with Chicago shortstop Joe Tinker on the play and claimed to have fooled Sherwood Magee with it three times in the same season (John J. Evers and Hugh S. Fullerton, *Touching Second*, 205).

In 1912, Christy Mathewson described such decoys as being "as old as the one in which the second baseman hides the ball under his shirt so as to catch a man asleep off first base, but often the old ones are the more effective" (Christy Mathewson, *Pitching in a Pinch*, 136). Nonetheless he commented on their increasing frequency in recent years: "There is a sub-division of defensive coaching which might be called the illegitimate brand. It is giving 'phoney' advice to a base runner by the fielders of the other side that may lead him, in the excitement of the moment, to make a foolish play. This style has developed largely in the Big Leagues in the last three or four years" (Christy Mathewson, *Pitching in a Pinch*, 125).

This trend undoubtedly helped clubs recognize the value of hiring full-time coaches (see **7.2.1**), a development that came into vogue at the same time.

4.3.4   Reverse Decoys. The other main type of decoy, in which a baseman tries to convince a runner that no throw is on its way, also dates back to the nineteenth century. In 1892 the *Brooklyn Eagle* reported: "[Cleveland outfielder George] Davis threw the ball to [third baseman Patsy] Tebeau, who stood close to the base line, ready to touch [Brooklyn base runner Mike] Griffin as he was running for third, but Tebeau never moved as if the ball was coming to him, and Griffin, thinking himself safe, slacked up a little, and then it was that Tebeau got the ball and suddenly put it on the runner like a flash. It was a finely played point" (*Brooklyn Eagle*, June 5, 1892).

A similar play was made in 1899 by Brooklyn third baseman Doc Casey, who "hoodwinked [New York base runner Mike] Tiernan in the third inning. The little third baseman apparently paid no attention to Mike as he came up to third on [Parke] Wilson's hit, and the runner slowed up, believing that [outfielder Willie] Keeler was throwing to the plate to catch [Ed] Doheny. It was not until Casey received the ball that he turned in Tiernan's direction and Mike put a move on him when it was too late" (*Brooklyn Eagle*, June 16, 1899).

4.3.5 Cutoff and Relay Plays. The concept of a relay is an ancient one. Tim Murnane later explained, "In the early days [by which he apparently meant the 1850s] the game was played on large open fields, and the out-fielders had some long runs to get a ball hit by them. Sometimes they were obliged to go to the extreme end of the field. Men played but few games and their arms were not in condition to make long throws, and the basemen hugged their bases much closer than at the present time. The short-stop acted as a utility man and would go out in the field to take the ball from the out-fielders and send it to the home plate or to the in-field" (*Cincinnati Enquirer*, April 1, 1888).

As Murnane explained, the shortstop was responsible for all the relaying (and running) while the other basemen guarded their respective bases. By the 1860s the shortstop was beginning to be regarded more as an infielder than a rover, leaving no obvious candidate to relay throws from the outfield.

Henry Chadwick suggested in 1868 that the right fielder should sometimes fulfill this function: "If he sees a ball going over the centre fielder's head, he should at once run for the centre fielder's position, and be ready to help pass the ball in from the outer field, if necessary" (Henry Chadwick, *The American Game of Base Ball*, 23).

It seems reasonable to assume that the second baseman also inherited some responsibility for relays from right field. In many cases, however, the relay was simply scrapped, and the outfielder was expected to throw the ball into the diamond.

This trend was then furthered by two important changes in the playing conditions. By the end of the 1860s outfield fences (see 14.1.1) had become almost universal in professional play, and around 1870 the dead ball (see 9.1.5) came into favor. The combined effect of these two developments was to allow outfielders to play significantly closer to the infield.

Consequently the relay system fell into disuse in the 1870s. When a relay did take place, it was usually the result of spontaneous hustle, as is suggested by this 1878 game account: "Gardner had led off with a three-baser over [left fielder Jimmy] Hallinan's head. This hit would have given a home run had not [center fielder John] Remsen cleverly helped Hally field it in. It was not an unheard of point of play, but it pleased the people as showing the earnestness of the men" (*Chicago Tribune*, April 21, 1878).

By the late 1870s, Henry Chadwick was advocating that outfielders use the same teamwork practiced by infielders: "The idea that a left-fielder has only to attend to left-field balls and a right-fielder to those sent to right-field is an exploded rule of the old amateur days." He stressed the need for "good backing-up" among outfielders, noting that relays replaced or at least complemented the custom of "throwing home to the catcher from the outfield" (*New York Clipper*, December 27, 1879). But Chadwick was uncharacteristically vague in describing exactly how this was to be accomplished, and it does not appear that sophisticated cutoff and relay systems were yet in vogue.

It was not until the mid-1890s that such a systematic approach began to develop. According to *Babe Ruth's Own Book of Baseball*, John McGraw and Hughey Jennings invented the cutoff play "when they were playing with the old Baltimore Orioles, and it came near revolutionizing baseball. The Orioles worked it a hundred times in the course of a season, before the other clubs got wise" (Babe Ruth, *Babe Ruth's Own Book of Baseball*, 143). This account sounds a bit suspicious, and an 1895 article suggests that a different club of the same era may deserve credit: "The Boston outfielders are working together in a way different from the usual method. With men on the bases hits to the outfield are not fielded directly to the plate if a man is rounding third, but the ball is sharply thrown to one of the infielders, who is tipped off where to catch a runner. In this way long distance throws with crooked bounds are generally avoided" (*Atlanta Constitution*, May 3, 1895).

This certainly sounds like the rudiments of today's approach to cutoffs and relays. By 1904 it was becoming more common to use the pitcher as the cutoff man, as Connie Mack counseled pitchers: "Never fail to back up the catcher on all throws from the outfield to the plate. There are times, however, when it might be advisable to get in line in front of the catcher, to handle the ball, making the throw to second" (Connie Mack, "How to Play Ball," multi-part series, *Washington Post*, March 13, 1904).

A 1914 article indicated that Manager Buck Herzog of Cincinnati had recently changed the cutoff responsibility from the pitcher to first baseman Dick Hoblitzell: "Herzog knows that not one pitcher in ten knows whether to let the ball go on to the plate to try to catch the runner or catch the ball and shoot back to second to catch the batter who will attempt to take an extra base on the throw home. Therefore, he makes all of his pitchers go back of the catcher when a hit is made, and Hoblitzell comes to the middle of the diamond and handles all balls or decides to let them go" (*Washington Post*, July 12, 1914).

4.3.6 **Catchers Coaching Pitchers.** The value of catchers to early pitchers was recognized as being immense, because only a talented catcher allowed a pitcher to throw his best pitches with confidence. The catcher's primary role, however, was reactive, a function symbolized by the distance he stood behind the plate. That began to change once catchers began to assume responsibility for calling pitches. By the 1890s the position had gained prestige, as illustrated by comments like: "Of [Dick] Buckley it was said in the National League that his superior as a coaching catcher for young pitchers did not exist" (*Detroit Free Press*, December 30, 1896).

4.3.7 **Wheel Play.** Complex plays like the wheel play almost always develop by fits and starts rather than emerging full-blown. During the 1903 World Series, Pirates third baseman Tommy Leach threw to shortstop Honus Wagner covering third to foil a bunt (*Sporting Life*, October 17, 1903). Some observers considered the play new, but others said it was an element of the "sacrifice killer" play, described in the next entry.

4.3.8 **Sacrifice Killer.** The "sacrifice killer" was a play used to defense sacrifice bunts. As the following paragraphs show, there were two major variations of the play.

In 1900, Jimmy Callahan of Chicago told the *Chicago Chronicle*: "I was caught by the neatest trick in the world in one of the early Brooklyn games. This is the play: Man on first and second and nobody out. Now, everybody knows that it is good sense for the captain to tell the next man up to bunt into a sacrifice and advance the runners. So the Brooklyns all play in close for the bunt and the runners take good leads off their bases, seeing no chance for a throw from the pitcher to catch either of them. Suddenly [Bill] Dahlen, at short, wheels about and makes a dash for second, and the pitcher, turning at the same time, makes a bluff to throw to the base. Instead he turns and pitches one where it is certain to be a nice bunt for the batter. The batter, fulfilling orders, bunts. Either the pitcher or third baseman gets it and the runner at second, who has broken his spine trying to get back to the base to avoid the throw he thinks is coming to Dahlen, is an easy victim, for before he can get started back toward third he is out. . . . The only chance to avoid the play is to have a quick-witted batter up who will smash at the ball instead of bunting it" (*Chicago Chronicle*, reprinted in *Sporting Life*, December 8, 1900).

Around the same time, former Chicago third baseman Tommy Burns told a reporter, "Every now and then I see where some club is inventing new plays; for instance, the so-called 'sacrifice killer,' as used by the Brooklyns this year. Why, that play was used by the Chicagos fifteen years ago" (*Sporting Life*, November 17, 1900). It seems likely, though by no means certain, that he meant the same play described by Callahan.

In 1910, A. H. Spink quoted a recent article by first basemen Hal Chase that claimed: "Fred Tenney was the pioneer southpaw first sacker. He originated the sacrifice killing play. That is, on a bunt to him, he tried for the man that was to be advanced" (A. H. Spink, *The National Game*, 174). But Arthur Irwin maintained that the play had flaws that were soon exposed: "Back in the nineties Boston had [Billy] Nash for captain and third base, and the infield played for a bunt in the same way, [first baseman Fred] Tenney going in, [second baseman Bobby] Lowe going over to cover first, and [shortstop Herman] Long crossing to second base. Ordinarily the play worked well, and was a bunt killer. But for a heady bunch that could lay the ball down right it was soft. All that was necessary was to tap the ball where it would get by the third baseman—and, naturally, there was plenty of room for this, and both runner and batsman were safe. Boston didn't vary its play, and Baltimore took advantage of the knowledge of just how the infield would work. Boston didn't win a game from Baltimore that season" (*Sporting Life*, March 31, 1906).

Sportswriter J. Ed Grillo similarly believed that the play was far from foolproof. He observed in 1908, "One play which the New Yorks pulled off against the Nationals on Monday caused much surprise in the stands, and as it was Hal Chase who played a prominent part in it he was given a lot of credit for having performed a most miraculous feat, in that he threw a man out going from second to third on a bunt down the first base line. Chase really only took part in what is known as the 'sacrifice killer,' a play originated by the famous Baltimore Club of a few years ago. This is how it is done:

"With base runners on first base and second and none out, it is almost a certainty that the next man up will bunt. The shortstop allows the man on second to get a good lead, then suddenly runs for the bag, carrying the base runner back with him. As soon as the runner is headed back for second the pitcher lays the ball right over the plate, so it can easily be bunted. The first baseman runs in with the pitcher's motion, while the second baseman covers first. If the ball is picked up clean by the first baseman, he does not have to hurry to get his man at third coming from second, for he is going the other way when the ball is bunted. If the ball rolls to the right side of the pitcher, he makes the play at third, and if it happens to be fumbled by the first baseman, there is time enough to get the man at first base, which is being covered by the second baseman.

"This play is not tried with all batters up, but if it is a pitcher it is sure to go through, for they seldom know enough to switch the play, but usually carry out the orders as given to them by the manager. A wise player, when he sees the play being worked, does not bunt, but hits, and as he has every man on the infield out of position, he has but to keep the ball on the ground to get a hit; but it is not every player who thinks quick enough to switch the play" (*Sporting Life*, May 16, 1908).

Obviously there were a number of different interpretations of the origins of the "sacrifice killer," its effectiveness, and even what the play was. Nonetheless it seems likely that these preliminary efforts were the basis of the wheel play.

4.3.9   Bunt Defense. In 1892 the *New York Times* described an imaginative way of defending against the bunt: ". . . The science of 'bunting' has been so developed that it puzzles pitchers and the infield to meet it. Since the flat-sided bat has been admitted the most skillful pitcher cannot prevent a cool batsman from dribbling a grounder out toward third at so slow a pace that he can beat the ball to first.

"The fact that the entire team in the field knows just what the batter means to do seems to afford no assistance in the solution of the problem. Thus far in the presence of a good bunter the team in the field seems to be helpless. Few lovers of the game have ever before seen the expedient which the Yale boys tried in their recent game with Princeton in this city when [Yale catcher Walter] Carter left his place behind the bat, and, wearing his mask and pad, stood about thirty feet from the batsman, just inside the third base line. If the striker had bunted then, he would probably have been thrown out at first by Carter. The wily Princetonian, however, calmly made two strikes, whereupon the Yale catcher was forced to go behind the bat to catch the third. Then the Princeton man bunted and went safely to first" (*New York Times*, June 23, 1892).

At least one note suggests that the tactic may have been used the year before: "[St. Louis player-manager Charlie] Comiskey has another wrinkle this year. When a bunter is at the bat the catcher plays on foul ground toward third base, and the umpire is utilized to return balls the batsman lets go by" (*Williamsport Sunday Grit*, June 7, 1891).

Obviously this rather bizarre approach was only practicable when there were no runners on base. In 1901 the catcher's box was introduced, rendering this strategy impossible.

4.3.10   Influencing a Foul Ball. One of the more poignant moments in sports occurs when a supremely talented fielder charges a bunt too late and his only option is to watch helplessly and hope that it will roll foul. At least a few enterprising fielders have not been willing to remain passive spectators in such instances.

In a game on May 27, 1981, Seattle infielder Lenny Randle earned notoriety when umpire Larry McCoy ruled that Randle had blown a fair ball into foul territory. The umpire credited Kansas City's Amos Otis with a hit. Randle was indignant: "I didn't blow it. I used the power of suggestion. I yelled at it, 'Go foul, go foul.' How could they call it a hit? It was a foul ball" (*New York Times*, May 29, 1981).

Sixty years earlier, Eddie Cicotte tried a different method of exerting his will over a bunted ball. A sportswriter filed this account: "This is to notify A. D. B. Van Zant and all the rest of the goodly curling club clan that Eddie Cicotte, the White Sox pitcher, is stealing their stuff.

"In the eighth inning of Wednesday's game, [Detroit's] George Moriarty laid down a bunt which oozed along the foul line toward third base trying to make up its mind whether to roll foul or fair. Mr. Cicotte, knowing that he couldn't possibly make a play if the pill stayed in fair ground, assisted the wavering globule to make up its mind by scratching the dirt away from its path on the foul side and digging a little ditch that led it on to foul ground finally.

"In effect, Cicotte's action was exactly that of a curler in 'Sooping 'er up mon.' Just as the devotees of the indoor Scotch and sometimes Rye game sweep in front of a 'stane' to make it carry further, Eddie was aiding the progress of the ball to where he wanted it to travel. Alas for all his cunning, however, [umpire] 'Silk' O'Loughlin ruled that it didn't go. 'Silk' said that in doing his landscape work, Cicotte had accomplished the same object as though he touched the pill while in fair ground and knocked it outside the line. So it went as a base-hit for Moriarty" (*Detroit Free Press*, April 30, 1914).

Ed Wells reported that Joe Sewell of the Yankees once made handprints in the ground in front of a trickling ball in a game in Chicago. According to Wells, "The next day the American League made a rule and you could not do that anymore" (Eugene Murdock, *Baseball Between the Wars*, 74).

Joe Sewell gave this account of the play, which occurred while he was playing for the Yankees against the White Sox: "I knew I had no chance to throw [batter Lew] Fonseca out. [Pitcher Red] Ruffing came over to pick up the ball, but as he bent over I yelled, 'Let it roll!' And he did. I got out in front of that ball with my front spikes and scratched a trench across the foul line at a 45 degree angle. The ball hit that trench and rolled foul, and as soon as it did I grabbed it. Fonseca was already at first base, but old Bill Dinneen [sic], the umpire, yelled 'Foul ball!' Donie Bush was managing the White Sox then, and boy did they charge out at old Bill." Sewell added that Dineen told him the next day that League president Will Harridge had passed a temporary rule against such trench-building (Walter M. Langford, *Legends of Baseball*, 20).

(iv) Devising Alternate Methods of Retiring Players

Early fielders, playing without gloves or sunglasses, on uneven fields, and with stringent limitations on pitching, often found it hard to retire the other side at all. Single innings of twenty or thirty runs were not uncommon. Early reporters had a wonderfully apt word to describe the fielders on such a team: "demoralized." That is an understandable reaction to recognizing that none of the ways of retiring an opponent are easy to execute.

A few fielders, however, have turned that helpless feeling into something constructive by devising new ways to retire opposing batters and base runners. These were not, of course, actual additions to the four basic methods of recording an out. Rather they were new techniques that afforded new possibilities of recording outs, and thereby saved many a fielder from that sinking feeling of demoralization.

4.4.1   One-handed Catches. Early fielders did not wear gloves, so the two-handed catch was necessary for securing the ball and cushioning the impact. When outfielder Dan Patterson of the Mutuals of New York preserved the historic 1870 shutout of the White Stockings of Chicago with a one-handed catch, one game account raved that "such catches are rare as angels' visits" (*New York Tribune*, July 27, 1870).

As gloves were introduced and made bigger and better, the need for two hands became less apparent. Nonetheless the shift to one-handed catching was fitful, in large part because of the belief that one-handed catching was fundamentally unsound. There is an oft-told story that in 1882 first baseman Henry Luff of Cincinnati was fined for making a one-handed catch and quit the team in protest (William Curran, *Mitts*, 119). I have not been able to verify the details of this story, so it is possible that it is apocryphal or exaggerated. But there is probably at least a grain of truth in it, as there was a deep-seated and long-lasting hostility toward the one-handed catch.

At times it seemed that many believed it preferable for a fielder to miss a ball with two hands than to catch one with one hand. Chicago sportswriter William A. Phelon observed in 1906 that second baseman Johnny Evers of the local National League club "will be doing that one-handed grab act of his again this summer. Some of the scribes got the idea last summer that it was grand stand work and roasted Johnny. They were way off. Evers makes those one-handed plays because he can do the trick and get many a ball he could not reach with both hands" (*Sporting Life*, April 28, 1906).

Such logic gradually began to convince the skeptical that there were times when a one-handed catch was the only option available. This was most evident at first base, where the need to stretch to catch wide balls while remaining on the base made the need for one-handed catches apparent. As first basemen's gloves grew dramatically in size, one-handed catches made more and more sense.

The catcher, being the other fielder who was early equipped with an oversized glove, was the next battlefront. Many sources suggest that one-handed catching was introduced in the 1960s by Randy Hundley and popularized by Johnny Bench. As we shall see, Hundley and Bench did play an important role, but their contributions were not as dramatic a break with the past as is often imagined.

As is discussed at greater length under "Fielders' Gloves" (9.3.1) and "Catchers' Mitts" (9.3.2), early catchers used both hands to catch the ball. If they wore gloves at all, they sported a pair with very light padding to enable them to throw the ball. The advent of overhand pitching in the early 1880s forced them to rethink their technique, and the catcher's mitt had emerged by the late 1880s, allowing the catcher's nonthrowing hand to take more of the impact.

This led to a change in technique. Some sources suggest that backstop "Doc" Bushong pioneered the one-handed catch because he wanted to preserve his hand for dentistry. Bushong and other catchers of the early 1880s were undoubtedly allowing their nonthrowing hand to absorb more of the shock. An 1884 account explained that the catcher was trying to "do most of the stopping with his left hand, protected by a thickly padded glove. Such a glove cannot be worn upon the right hand as it renders accurate throwing impossible" (*Detroit Free Press*, May 2, 1884). Bushong's career ended just as mitts were developing, and the padded gloves worn before then could not firmly secure even a perfect pitch without help from the bare hand. As a result, the throwing hand was absorbing less of the impact in the first half of the 1880s, but catching continued to involve both hands.

Once catcher's mitts became larger and more efficiently designed, catchers gradually began to take greater advantage of the new possibilities. Carmen Hill claimed that catcher Earl Smith used a one-handed technique in the 1920s and, as a result, "He never had a bad finger on his right hand. His fingers were just as straight as they could be. Every other catcher I ever saw had banged up fingers" (Eugene Murdock, *Baseball Between the Wars*, 179).

Sportswriter H. G. Salsinger explained in 1935 that "the average catcher uses the bare hand simultaneously with the glove in receiving pitched balls and when he reaches for a wide pitch the hand does most of the work and, often, all of it." He noted, however, that catchers such as Mickey Cochrane and Ralph "Cy" Perkins were using a new technique that appeared to greatly diminish injuries to the bare hand.

Cochrane told Salsinger: ". . . Most catchers made the mistake of using the bare hand too soon and too much. They do not put enough dependence upon the glove and they do not know how to reverse with the glove and catch wild pitches. Also, they use the wrong kind of gloves."

Cochrane's novel approach was made possible by his use of "a glove that has a funnel-shaped indention [sic]. The padding at the top of the glove is about half as thick as the padding in gloves used by other catchers and there is no padding in the palm of the glove. The light top padding enables Cochrane to hook balls that he has to reach for. He takes more pitched balls with the glove hand than any other catcher. If the top of his glove were heavily padded this one-handed work would be impossible; the ball would glance off. Cochrane takes the pitched ball in the glove and then closes the bare hand over the ball" (*Sporting News*, January 3, 1935).

In his 1939 book, Cochrane credited Perkins with having taught him "to become in effect a one-handed catcher; to stop the pitched ball always with the gloved hand, holding your right hand with the finger tips folded against the heel of the hand and the thumb laid along the side of the hand. After a time it becomes natural not to open the unprotected hand until the ball is in the well padded glove. In that way Cy and I caught 2500 games for Mr. Mack without ever suffering a broken finger" (Mickey Cochrane, *Baseball: The Fans' Game*, 12).

Further tinkering with the design of the mitt enabled catchers to further reduce the use of their bare hands. Dan Gutman credited 1950s catcher Gus Niarhos with cutting an opening in his mitt so that he could squeeze the parts together and trap the ball (Dan Gutman, *Banana Bats and Ding-Dong Balls*, 180). Glove makers soon refined the idea and thereby changed the nature of catching.

Roger Angell noted that catchers almost universally referred to the result as the "one-handed glove." He explained: "Thanks to radical excisions of padding around the rim and thumb, it is much smaller than its lumpy, pillowlike progenitor, more resembling a quiche than a deep-dish Brown Betty. The glove comes with a prefab central pocket, but the crucial difference in feel is its amazing flexibility, attributable to a built-in central hinge, which follows the lateral line of one's palm. The glove is still stiffer and more unwieldy than a first baseman's mitt, to be sure, but if you catch a thrown ball in the pocket the glove will try to fold itself around the ball and hold it, thus simply extending the natural catching motion of a man's hand. Catching with the old mitt, by contrast, was more like trying to stop a pitch with a dictionary; it didn't hurt much, but you had to clap your right hand over the pill almost instantly in order to keep possession."

Angell characterized Randy Hundley as the one-handed glove's "first artisan" but contended that "Its first and perhaps still its greatest artist, its Michelangelo, was Johnny Bench" (Roger Angell, "In the Fire," reprinted in *Once More Around the Park*, 209). Bench benefited from further tinkering with the mitt, which included reducing the padding and redesigning the pocket so that "My glove squeezed the ball—you had to squeeze with the old mitt. You became another infielder in the sense that the glove just closed around the ball if it hit in there." Bench attributed his facility for catching balls backhanded entirely to the new design, explaining matter-of-factly: "You couldn't do that before" (quoted in David Falkner, *Nine Sides of the Diamond*, 302).

A similar series of design-based improvements have characterized the history of the fielder's glove. For many years the one-handed catch was stigmatized as a showy, unsound play. A 1930s list of baseball slang, for instance, defined a "Fancy Dan" as "a player who would rather make a one-handed catch than use two hands" (Bill Snypp, *Lima* [Ohio] *News*, April 27, 1937).

As Craig Wright has observed, this stigma reflected the reality that until the start of the 1960s gloves had to be small to be effective catching devices: "Fielding gloves really began to grow after the introduction of the Edge-U-Cated Heel in 1959. This new design eliminated the old open heel, which caused the glove to sit loosely on the hand. By providing a closing flex at the outer heel of the glove, it allowed the sides of the glove to more closely follow the contours and action of the hand and wrist. The hand could now reasonably control a much larger glove" (Craig R. Wright and Tom House, *The Diamond Appraised*, 259).

Longtime Rawlings glove designer Rollie Latina said the Edge-U-Cated Heel was probably the most important improvement to gloves in the twentieth century: "Before that all the gloves had a big, wide-open heel and there was never any actual snugging action of the glove on the hand. In other words it was more or less loose. The Edge-U-Cated Heel brought the sides of the glove into the contours of the hand and the wrist and the glove actually stayed on your hand better that way" (William Curran, *Mitts*, 83–84).

This innovation thus made the one-handed catch reliable in a way that it had never been before. 1930s star Charley Gehringer later observed, "I can't remember anybody catching one by jumping over the fence and it would stick in the big glove, 'cause it wouldn't. Maybe I dove for a ball once or twice, but you'd only hurt yourself probably and still wouldn't do more than knock it down. Now [the balls] stick and you can get up and throw them out if they're hit hard" (quoted in Jonathan Fraser Light, *The Cultural Encyclopedia of Baseball*, 258). In 1968, Joe DiMaggio noted that when he played, "you had to catch the ball in the pocket or you did not catch it" (*Chicago Tribune*, March 23, 1968).

Long after the one-handed catch became viable, coaches continued to preach that the two-handed catch was fundamentally correct. John Lowenstein complained in 1982, "They tell you always to catch a fly ball with two hands, but, if you think about it, you should almost always catch it one-handed off to the side so your arms don't block your own vision" (quoted by Tom Boswell, *Washington Post*, September 5, 1982; reprinted in Paul Dickson, ed., *Baseball's Greatest Quotations*, 257). No doubt the reluctance to accept the one-handed catch reflected the stigma that had long been attached to this style, but other factors may also have played a role.

First baseman Vic Power became one of the first fielders to make extensive use of the one-handed catch in the 1950s, because he thought it improved his "flexibility and range." He was almost universally criticized for his technique: ". . . Sportswriters wrote I was a showboat and opposing players and their fans cursed at me. Sometimes it even made my own fans nervous. I still get letters from people in Minnesota who remember how I caught the final pop-up of Jack Kralick's no-hitter: they say they almost had a heart attack because I used only one hand." Power was disturbed by all the uproar and asked his manager, Jimmy Dykes, if he should change. Dykes told him to stick with the technique as long as it worked; Power reported that he did so and never dropped a ball that way (quoted in Danny Peary, *Cult Baseball Players*, 368–369).

Detroit first baseman Norm Cash got a more tolerant reception when he began to use the "one-handed catch introduced by Vic Power" in 1961. His manager, Bob Scheffing, said: "I haven't said a word to Cash about it. And I won't either—until he misses one" (Warner Spoelstra, "Drydocking of Boros Helps Whet Tiger Flag Appetite," *Sporting News*, August 2, 1961). The fact that Cash was in the midst of an extraordinary batting season presumably contributed to his manager's indulgence, and followers are generally treated more leniently than trendsetters. But it's hard not to be troubled by the fact that Power, an African American, was perceived as a showboat while Cash, a white man, escaped a similar label.

4.4.2   Trapped-ball Plays. Researcher Eric Miklich reported that the infield fly rule was introduced by the Players' League in its lone season of 1890. The rule was adopted by the National League on February 26, 1894, and proved much more controversial. These late dates require some explanation, since clever fielders were trapping catchable balls in order to double up base runners as early as 1864.

The raging debate in baseball circles in the late 1850s and early 1860s was whether a ball caught on the first bounce should be an out (see **1.21**). Advocates of the "fly game" argued that a one-bounce catch took little skill. While they did not gain their point until December 14, 1864, they did get a concession that would change the way the game was played in the nineteenth century.

Until 1859 a caught fly ball was dead, so runners could return to their original bases without peril. A rule change that year allowed runners to be doubled up on a caught fly ball, thereby providing fielders with an incentive to catch such hits on the fly instead of one-hopping them. The rule must have proved popular, as it was retained even after the bound rule was eliminated. But the rule was less enjoyable for base runners, since it meant they could be placed in jeopardy by savvy fielders.

A game account in the *New York Clipper* in 1864 reported a "fine display of the fielding qualities of the Eurekas [of Newark], and a striking illustration of their peculiar strategy in playing the 'points' of the game." With runners on first and second, the batter hit an easy pop fly to pitcher Henry Burroughs. The writer explained that Burroughs "could easily have taken on the fly; had he done so, however, but one player could have been out, viz., the striker, while the others would have been on the third [sic] and second bases; for strategical reasons, therefore, he missed the catch, thereby allowing the striker to make his base, by which the others were forced off theirs, and the ball being passed rapidly to third and second and held well on each base, both the players forced off their bases were put out" (*New York Clipper*, June 25, 1864).

The account had no byline, but it seems to be in the distinctive style of Henry Chadwick, who usually expressed disdain for sneaky play. Considering that Burroughs was doing little more than exploiting a loophole in the rules, the language used in this account is strikingly commendatory. Instead of being condemned, the Eurekas were praised for the "fine display." The piece also twice made use of forms of the word "strategy," which had strong positive connotations in light of the ongoing Civil War.

A couple of possibilities present themselves. The first is that the play demonstrated two qualities that Chadwick regularly praised—heady play and knowledge of the rules. In addition, the requirement for base runners to attempt to advance was considered to be a characteristic that distinguished baseball from cricket. The *New York Herald*, for example, cited the fact that runners were forced to run in baseball to demonstrate its contention that "the English game is so low and tame, and the American so full of life" (*New York Herald*, October 16, 1859).

There is of course no way to be certain that Burroughs originated the so-called trapped-ball play. But the fact that his play warranted such a detailed description, and the use of the word "peculiar," suggest that this was at the very least one of the earliest instances. The only person for whom I have found a claim of inventing the trapped-ball play is Dickey Pearce, whom A. H. Spink cited as "the first player of his day to drop a fly ball in order to make a double play" (A. H. Spink, *The National Game*, 10). But Spink provided no specific basis for this claim.

In the years after the war, the play had plenty of imitators. Veteran sportswriter William Rankin recalled in 1908: "George Wright did that trick as early as 1870, and probably before that year. Certainly at that time. [Bob] Ferguson, [Ezra] Sutton, [Jack] Burdock and others were expert at that play shortly afterward" (*Sporting News*, December 24, 1908). Longtime National League president Nick Young cited Davy Force as another early master of the play (*Toledo Blade*, February 4, 1897).

It was George Wright with whom the play became especially closely associated. Tim Murnane credited Wright with introducing "what was called the trap ball" (*Boston Globe*, April 19, 1896). Nick Young described the play as the "pet trick" of Wright: "His equal trapping the ball was never known on the diamond in his or any other generation. George had something that I have never seen in a player, and that was a deft and delicate style in picking up a grounder. He was almost perfect in plowing into the ground and burrowing for a hot one that hugged the earth. And you must remember that the players were not shielded from cauliflower and pretzel fingers by large gloves in those days. George's skill in picking up grounders made him the past master of the trapped ball. Often I noticed that the latter day fielders could not rid themselves of the slow and clumsy habit of breaking into the orbit of the ball, catching it on the fly and deliberately dropping it whenever they were making a trap play. But George Wright was more accomplished. As the ball approached him he stepped back or forward, according to the distance. Planting himself for a pickup, he generally scooped it up on the first low bound, and turned like a flash for his double play" (quoted in *Toledo Blade*, February 4, 1897).

When executed by an alert and skillful fielder like George Wright, the play left base runners in an impossible situation. If they chose the Scylla of running, he could catch the ball and double them up. If they selected the Charybdis of holding their base, he would drop it and start a double play. In an 1872 game, the Empires of Detroit had runners on first and second with no outs when batter Harry Spence lifted an easy pop fly toward Wright. The other Red Stockings began to yell "drop it," so the Empire base runners began to run. Wright then caught the ball and started an easy triple play (Peter Morris, *Baseball Fever*, 290).

A much later account of this same game claimed that while the ball was in the air, Harry Wright yelled, "Drop it," and George replied, "No, I won't." The runners therefore held their bases, and George dropped the ball and started a triple play (*Saginaw Evening Express*, April 24, 1884). While it seems more likely that the contemporaneous accounts are accurate, either version illustrates the hopeless dilemma that the play could present to base runners.

It might be assumed that so lethal a play would become widely used, but that does not appear to be the case. One drawback was that the play relied on the umpire's indulgence. In a May 6, 1874, match against Philadelphia,

Ross Barnes of Boston tried the play on two successive pop flies. On the first attempt the umpire ruled that Barnes had held the ball too long and called only the batter out. Barnes executed the play more efficiently the next time, but the umpire pronounced it "too thin" and made the same ruling (Preston D. Orem, *Baseball [1845–1881] from the Newspaper Accounts*, 182).

Another complication was the risk of botching the play, which seems to have led many fielders to settle for one sure out. Indeed, after the infield fly rule was introduced, Nick Young contended that "The trap ball will never again be legalized" because it "would scarcely be fair in the up-to-date game, as there are so *few* players who have mastered it" (quoted in *Toledo Blade*, February 4, 1897, my emphasis).

The latter part of Young's claim seems very surprising, but he knew whereof he spoke. In 1883, as National League secretary, Young had tried to limit the play by instructing umpires to rule a catch if a fielder held the ball even momentarily and then deliberately dropped it. He drew sharp criticism for "restricting clever play in the field" from a writer in *Sporting Life* who added, ". . . Such an instruction as this is a mistake and a detriment, and will lead to mischievous results. A fielder who is clever enough to break the force of the ball and to recover it in time for a double play ought to be allowed to make the play, and to deprive him of that right is to diminish the fielding beauties of the game. . . . An umpire has all he can properly attend to when he undertakes to judge of facts; he should not be permitted, much less required, to rule on the question of intention" (*Sporting Life*, June 3, 1883).

In 1897, Young cited Fred Pfeffer of Chicago as the only infielder who was expert at making the play, though the article's unnamed author added another name: Bid McPhee of Cincinnati (*Toledo Blade*, February 4, 1897). The sportswriter E. S. Sheridan similarly contended in 1894 that only McPhee and Pfeffer were using the trapped-ball play (*Sporting Life*, April 28, 1894). After the infield fly rule was instituted, the *Chicago Tribune* reported: "This new rule effectually wipes out the play of trapping the ball for a double play, which was so successfully worked by McPhee and Pfeffer in particular" (*Chicago Tribune*, February 4, 1894). The sportswriter Ren Mulford later referred to the infield fly rule as "the old legislation passed to bottle up King Bid McPhee's famed trap ball play" (*Sporting Life*, October 1, 1904).

Later, the names of Boston's double-play combination, Herman Long and Bobby Lowe, were also added. In 1903 the *Chicago Tribune* observed: "It was to handicap [the Boston] team that the present rule against 'trapping' an infield fly with a runner on first was adopted" (*Chicago Tribune*, July 12, 1903). The following year the same paper specifically cited Long and Lowe (*Chicago Tribune*, June 26, 1904). The *Washington Post* echoed the claim: "Long and Lowe perfected the famous 'trapped ball' play until the National

League was compelled to legislate against it by making a batter out on an infield fly" (*Washington Post*, July 3, 1904).

So it seems clear that Chicago and Cincinnati were using the play in 1894, and Boston may have been doing so as well. Moreover the rise to prominence of the fielder's glove may have done more to hinder this tactic than to advance it. A scoop is easy to accomplish with today's fielders' gloves, but the gloves used by fielders in 1894 consisted primarily of padding. Since these gloves lacked pockets, it probably became harder to scoop a ball instead of easier. It is no coincidence that Bid McPhee, one of the masters of the trapped ball, was one of the few infielders still playing without a glove in 1894. (And perhaps it also accounts for why McPhee finally chose to wear one in 1896.)

This brings us back to the question we began with: why ban a play that had been around for thirty years, had initially been praised, and was not becoming more common? There are at least three reasonable possibilities.

The first is implied in Nick Young's comment that it "would scarcely be fair in the up-to-date game, as there are so few players who have mastered it." In a nutshell, the twelve-team league had two or three clubs that were able to use the tactic while the remaining clubs could not. It is pretty obvious which side would be likely to win a vote as to whether that tactic should remain legal. The majority might call this "preserving competitive balance" while the minority would be likely to describe it as jealousy or something worse.

The second reason is that the new approach made the umpire's onerous job less demanding. Nick Young explained that, "One of the objections to the trap play was the amount of kicking it caused between the players and umpires. The side that was made a victim of the trap play was naturally sore, and a kick generally followed the decision of the umpire" (*Toledo Blade*, February 4, 1897).

Third, the play had lost the novelty and aesthetic appeal that had once helped it gain support. As fielders used their gloves to catch and then deliberately release the ball, the perception of it as a "clever play" changed to "slow and clumsy."

Dramatic improvements in the quality of playing fields were also making the play appear tricky rather than clever. As John H. Gruber later explained, the trapped ball had long had "an element of danger connected with it"; if the ball were to "strike a pebble or take a 'funny' bound it was likely to shoot out of reach and result in both runners being safe." But as hillocks and other obstacles were removed from playing fields, the play began to look "so much like cold-blooded murder—the runners clearly having no chance." This in turn began to offend "the American idea of fair play" (John H. Gruber, "You're Out," *Sporting News*, February 17, 1916).

The Players' League's use of the infield fly rule seems to have attracted little comment, but when it was introduced to the National League four years later it proved tremendously unpopular. Many sportswriters assailed it, with Paul Chamberlin calling it a "libel on common sense" (*Sporting Life*, April 14, 1894). Fans were just as outraged, according to a *Cincinnati Commercial Gazette* reporter: "A ball crowd, nor any one else, for that matter, cannot see any justice in such rules. The sooner that splendid monument to ignorance is repealed, the better it will be for the game" (*Cincinnati Commercial Gazette*; reprinted in *Sporting Life*, April 21, 1894). At least one player was even more disdainful, as Arlie Latham sought to demonstrate "the asininity of the new rule" by folding his arms on a pop fly and making "no effort to get the ball, remarking, 'We don't have to catch that kind this year'" (*Sporting Life*, April 21, 1894; *Sporting Life*, April 14, 1894).

As a side note, the original infield fly rule stated: "The base runner is out if he hits a fly ball that can be handled by an infielder while first base is occupied with only one out" (*Sporting Life*, April 28, 1894). This clumsy wording left it ambiguous as to whether the rule applied with multiple runners on base, and also seemed to imply that it did not apply with none out. The wording was changed the following year to make clear that it applied with multiple runners on base, and in 1901 the rule finally made explicit that it also applied with none out.

Some have understandably concluded that the rule originally did not apply in those circumstances. The confusion was shared by umpires, with Ed Swartwood writing to Nick Young to request clarification. As far as I can determine, umpires were told to interpret the rule as applying with none out and with multiple runners on base, and the subsequent rewordings were clarifications rather than changes.

4.4.3 Catcher's Trapped Ball. Early catchers had an uncommon but highly lethal version of the trapped-ball play. The early rules specified that when the catcher did not catch or one-hop the final strike of a strikeout, the action proceeded as if the ball had been put in play. The *Brooklyn Eagle* pointed out in 1873 that, with the bases loaded, "it is a point in the game for the catcher to allow the ball, on a third strike, to be missed and not caught, in order that the base runners may be 'forced' to leave their bases" (*Brooklyn Eagle*, June 3, 1873). The catcher could then step on the plate and relay the ball around the bases for a double or triple play. While the play appeared clever at first, the novelty soon wore off since this play too "looked like cold-blooded murder, as it gave the fielder an unfair advantage over the runners." According to John H. Gruber, it was not until 1887 that runners were relieved of the obligation to run on a dropped final strike with less than two out (John H. Gruber, "You're Out," *Sporting News*, February 17, 1916).

This play was almost always used with the bases loaded, since only in that situation was at least one out easy. But at least one catcher was bold enough to use it in other situations, thereby giving up the certainty of one out for the possibility of two. Bill Craver made a specialty of deliberately dropping third strikes in hopes of starting such double plays (*National Chronicle*, May 29, 1869).

4.4.4 Outfield Trapped Ball. While the catcher's and infielder's versions of this play have not been legal since the nineteenth century, the outfielder's equivalent remains permissible to this day and has had an interesting history.

The *Washington Post* wrote in 1904: "[Herman] Long and [Bobby] Lowe [of Boston] perfected the famous 'trapped ball' play until the National League was compelled to legislate against it by making a batter out on an infield fly. Then these two conspired with [Tommy] McCarthy and [Hugh] Duffy, who were outfielders on that famous team, and they pulled off the 'trapped ball' in the outfield, something no other team has ever been able to work successfully" (*Washington Post*, July 3, 1904). While it seems surprising that the play should have emerged after the National League's 1894 adoption of the infield fly rule, that appears to be the case. Indeed, it followed almost immediately.

This account followed Boston's game at Baltimore on April 24: "In the third inning the home team had men on second and first, with one out, when [Willie] Keeler hit a line fly to McCarthy in left field. Mac dropped the ball intentionally, then lined it to [Boston third baseman Billy] Nash. The ball then went to Lowe, who touched his base, forcing the man who was still at first, and then touching the runner who had held second, completing a double play, the like of which was never accomplished before in a ball game" (*Boston Globe*, April 25, 1894).

McCarthy repeated the trick the following week against Philadelphia: "With no out [in the fourth inning], [Sam] Thompson hit a high fly to left field. Mac got under the ball. The base runners, knowing how quick he is, hung close to the bases. The ball was allowed to hit the palm of his hands with fingers raised, then bounded off several yards, but Mac was after it with a bound, and with an eye on the base runners, he jogged over to second, touched [base runner Charlie] Reilly with the ball, and then touched the base, completing a double play, as both men were forced. Umpire [Tim] Hurst, who had witnessed the same play made by McCarthy in Baltimore, promptly gave both men out" (*Boston Globe*, May 1, 1894). He turned another double play this way against Washington on May 25, perplexing the base runners so much that "it was some time before the visitors realized what had happened" (Timothy H. Murnane, *Boston Globe*, May 26, 1894).

Most journalists treated the play as a new innovation, but Baltimore sportswriter Albert Mott had a different perspective: "McCarthy rehabilitated an exceedingly ancient trick in Baltimore, which Tom Tucker announced to the stands as 'a new Boston thing, see?' It was so very ancient and had not been played in so long a time that the players had forgotten it, and it worked like a charm. Every amateur club in the country once used it— that is, when first and second are occupied, to muff a fly ball in the outfield, thus causing a force and making a double play" (*Sporting Life*, May 5, 1894).

McCarthy's success with the ploy encouraged imitators, but they usually were less proficient. Later in the season, a *Sporting Life* correspondent reported: "In the fifth inning of the New York-Cleveland game of August 30 [Cleveland outfielder Jimmy] McAleer attempted Tommy McCarthy's celebrated 'trapped ball' trick, but made a mess of it. Clark [Dad Clarke] was on second and [Mike] Tiernan on first, with one man out, when Davis sent a short fly to McAleer. The latter, instead of 'trapping' the ball, held it momentarily and then dropped it. He then threw to [second baseman Cupid] Childs, who touched Clark and the bag and made a claim of two out. [Umpire Tim] Hurst, however, declared Davis out, as McAleer had held the ball momentarily" (*Sporting Life*, September 8, 1894).

An effort the following year backfired more spectacularly: "[Boston right fielder Jimmy] Bannon tried the trapped ball trick in the fifth inning [on August 1], when if he had trapped the ball he could never have made a double play. He failed, and his error gave the Orioles five runs" (*Sporting Life*, August 3, 1895).

According to Hughey Jennings, another bungled attempt to imitate McCarthy led to a historic trade: "It was Tommy McCarthy, a famous outfielder with Boston, who developed the art of trapping a short fly with runners on first and second or with bases filled, and making a double play, instead of catching the ball off the ground and retiring only one man. It is the same play that Ty Cobb and other outfielders have used in modern base ball.

"George Van Haltern [sic], playing center field for Baltimore, tried to imitate McCarthy. Van Haltern tried the play with bases filled and none out. The batter hit the ball to short center and Van Haltern, after faking a catch, got down to take the ball on the short bound, but instead of hopping into his cupped hands the ball shot over his shoulder and before it could be recovered and relayed back to the infield it had become a home run, four men scoring.

"Van Haltern had not taken into consideration the condition of the ground. It was almost as hard as brick, due to a long drought. That attempt cost Van Haltern his job, for soon after Baltimore traded him to Pittsburgh for Joe Kelley, a grand swap for Baltimore as Kelley later proved" (Hugh Jennings, *Rounding Third*, Chapter 75).

Even McCarthy on at least one occasion "made a bad mess" of the play (*Boston Globe*, August 3, 1895). By 1903, Patsy Donovan remarked that "McCarthy's play of trapping the outfield flies isn't done nowadays" (*Washington Post*, August 9, 1903). As the *Chicago Tribune* aptly summarized that same year, "the play never became general in its use, because it required an artist like Duffy or McCarthy to do it and it was disastrous to a bungler" (*Chicago Tribune*, July 12, 1903).

The combination of the inherent risks and deeper play by outfielders made the play increasingly uncommon, though it did not become extinct. After Sandow Mertes pulled the play off and doubled up George Schlei in a 1906 exhibition game, John McGraw recollected: "In my career as a ball player I have seen the 'trapped ball' trick, as Mertes worked it on Sunday, performed perhaps a dozen times. The best man in the business on that trick—although he could not have worked it better than did Mertes in the game on Sunday—was Tommy McCarthy, left fielder of the Boston Nationals. He had the play down pat, and on more than one occasion saved his team by resorting to it. I recall one game in which McCarthy had the opportunity of using the play twice, and on both occasions he made a double play out of it, although working it differently. [Wilbert] Robinson, catcher of the old Baltimore team, was the victim on both occasions. The first occasion for performing the play came up in the early part of the game. Robbie was on second and some other player on first, when a little fly was hit to McCarthy in left. He came in on it, and just before it reached his hands he backed off a step, got the ball on a short bound, and tossed it to Herman Long at second, making the double play just as Mertes and [Bill] Dahlen did on Sunday, Robbie being a victim of the same character as Schlei. Later in the game Robbie was on second again, another runner on first, and only one out. Again the batter hit a short fly to left. 'You don't fool me this time,' yelled Robbie, as he started for third base. However, instead of trapping the ball, McCarthy caught it on the fly, threw to second, and again a double play was completed. Those of us who were on the bench almost rolled off with laughter over Robbie's break, but he was as sore as a man can get" (quoted in *Sporting Life*, April 7, 1906).

The researchers at Retrosheet found an instance in a July 3, 1935, game between Philadelphia and New York. The Giants had Mel Ott on first and Bill Terry on second with one out when Hank Lieber lifted a fly ball to shallow center field. Phillies center fielder Ethan Allen "intentionally dropped the ball, snatched it up and fired to [second baseman Lou] Chiozza, who stepped on second, forcing Ott and then shot the ball to [third baseman Johnny] Vergez, who tagged out Terry for a double play. Terry was in a hopeless situation for had he stayed on second Chiozza would have tagged him before stepping on the bag. Had he moved off the base while the ball was in the air Allen wouldn't have trapped it but would have caught it and doubled him anyway" (Richards Vidmer, *New York Herald Tribune*, July 7, 1935).

In 1938 sportswriter Harold Burr observed that the outfielder's trapped-ball play had come into use again that season, and noted that former Giants outfielder George Burns had been especially well known for the play (*Sporting News*, November 10, 1938).

4.4.5 Basket Catches. While now associated with Willie Mays, the basket catch had been the signature maneuver of Rabbit Maranville more than forty years earlier. A *Sporting Life* correspondent gave this description: "Shortstop Maranville, of the Braves, has his own copyrighted way of catching a fly ball. He never raises his hands, keeping them at his sides till the falling ball is level with his belt. Then he snaps his hands on the ball and clasps it to his belt with lightning speed, and, it is said, never misses one" (*Sporting Life*, August 30, 1913).

Hugh Jennings gave this account of its origins: "The first time that [Boston manager] George Stallings saw 'Rabbit' Maranville, he said that Maranville would never be able to make the major league grade if he did not change his style of catching fly balls. Maranville's style of catching was to cup his hands and press them against his chest, much in the manner used by most foot ball players in catching a punted ball. Stallings had never seen a similar style and decided it would not do in base ball, because there was no chance of recovering the ball if it bobbed from the hands. He told Maranville that he would have to change the style. Maranville replied that he had always used that style, had never fumbled fly balls, and if Stallings would permit him to use the system until it failed, he would gladly change, or try to. Nothing could be fairer, and Stallings consented. Maranville became one of the best shortstops in the game and he never changed his style" (Hugh Jennings, *Rounding First*, Chapter 75).

And in the years before gloves, Henry Chadwick reported that most players caught fly balls at breast level and that a player named Fred Calloway of the Eurekas of Newark "takes the ball with a spring-like movement of his hands about waist high" (Henry Chadwick, *The American Game of Base Ball*, 24).

4.4.6 Catchers Framing Pitches and Working Umpires. Once catchers began to play closer to the plate, they began to work on ways to influence umpires in the calling of balls and strikes. Umpire Billy McLean noted in 1884, ". . . Such catchers as [Sandy] Nava and Buck Ewing are in the habit of taking a ball from away out and quickly bringing it down in front of them as though it had come straight over the bag, and kicking when we call a ball on them. I tell you, ball players are up to all sorts of tricks, and nothing but the closest watch will keep us from being beaten by them" (quoted in *Boston Globe*, July 20, 1884).

The practice became even more prevalent once a 1901 rule change created the catcher's box and thereby required catchers to remain behind the plate throughout every at bat. Johnny Evers and Hugh Fullerton described Chicago catcher Johnny Kling in 1910 as "a past master of the art of working umpires on balls and strikes, which is one of the duties of a catcher that is not suspected by the spectators. The importance of 'getting the corners' is realized by all players, and the catcher who gets this advantage is invaluable to his club. Some umpires call strikes on both corners, some the outside, some the inside, and some force the pitcher to put the ball square over the plate. Many and varied are the schemes worked by catchers to 'get the corners.' The best tactics, however, are those employed by the catchers who seldom kick, and who win the friendship and confidence of the officials" (John J. Evers and Hugh S. Fullerton, *Touching Second*, 97).

4.4.7 Juggling Fly Balls. The early rules allowed that a runner could tag up and advance only after a fly ball settled in the hands of a fielder. A few outfielders daringly tried to take advantage of this wording by juggling fly balls, as this 1879 account shows: "[Buffalo's Dave] Eggler last week played a neat point on the Bostons. A base runner was on third base, when a high ball was hit to Eggler at centre field. In preparing to catch it he placed his hands in such a way that the ball would rebound from them in the air. The base-runner seeing the ball caught, as he supposed, ran for home. Eggler then took the ball on the fly as it came down, and, passing it to [Hardy] Richardson at third, put the base-runner out, the latter being obliged to return to the base on the fly-catch. [Wes] Fisler once played this point well while at centre field in a match at Brooklyn" (*New York Clipper*, May 17, 1879). Eggler repeated the same play a few weeks later, causing Providence to appeal the game.

At least a couple of other outfielders perfected the play. In an 1884 game Johnny Ward "was 'doubled-up,' being caught by the old 'juggling' act, which [Steve] Brady did cleverly" (*Sporting Life*, April 26, 1884). Baltimore sportswriter Albert Mott later recalled Jimmy Clinton pulling off the play several times for Baltimore, where he played in 1883 and 1884 (*Sporting Life*, May 5, 1894). Tommy McCarthy is sometimes credited with inventing this play, but his career began too late for that to be the case, and the attribution is likely the result of confusion with the outfield trapped ball (see **4.4.4**).

I have not been able to find a specific rule change that eliminated this practice, but the researcher Cliff Blau reports that it was removed some time between 1917 and 1922. Based on this lengthy delay, my inference is that after the adoption of gloves in the mid-1880s outfielders found such juggling too difficult.

4.4.8   Deliberate Passed Ball. Bill James once wrote that intentional walks make about as much sense as intentional passed balls. He was, of course, being facetious, but there have been at least a few instances of intentional passed balls.

In an 1870 exhibition game, the Atlantic Club of New Orleans had the bases loaded and no outs when catcher Bill Craver of the White Stockings of Chicago devised an imaginative ploy: "The back-stop stood sixty feet behind the plate, and its face was padded, and the ground in front covered with sawdust to prevent the bounding back of passed balls. Craver had shrewdly noticed the precise point at which every passed ball had stopped, and formed a plan to bag the man on third. He contrived to give Myerle [pitcher Levi Meyerle] a hint of his design, and as the striker stood at the bat, Craver being close behind, he gave the required sign to Myerle, who pitched a very low ball, giving it but a moderate rate of speed. Purposely Craver allowed the ball to pass between his legs and go rolling on toward the back-stop. The man on third saw the opening, and stepped into the trap. Quick as a flash, Craver wheeled and ran for the ball, while Myerle, well up to the dodge, ran forward to the home plate, and there received the ball from Craver in ample time." The inning ended without a run being scored (*Chicago Tribune*, May 19, 1870).

Hugh Jennings recounted another instance: "George Mullin told me about an unusual strategic move concocted by Charlie Schmidt, who used to be Detroit's first string catcher. In one game with a runner on third, two out and a dangerous man at bat, Schmidt walked down to the box and engaged Mullin in secret conference. He told Mullin: 'Now you heave the next ball over my head and put everything you got on it. This fellow on third will come dashing in. The ball will hit the stand so hard that it'll bound back and you come up and cover the plate. I'll toss the ball to you and we'll nail him.' The strangest part of it was that Mullin made the wild pitch, the runner tried to score, Schmidt recovered the ball and threw to Mullin who tagged the runner, just as Schmidt had planned it all" (Hugh Jennings, *Rounding Third*, Chapter 73).

Sportswriter Joe Jackson recalled in 1911: "At York, Pa., in the Tristate, they had a stand at one time that was almost on top of the plate. . . . The York catchers studied the angles for a little while and experimented with pitched balls. Then they were ready. With a runner on third they would signal for a wild pitch, and let it go to the stand. The runner would start home, the catcher would get the ball on the rebound, and the man would die at the plate. The trick was checked through adoption by the league of a permanent grounds rule for this park" (*Washington Post*, March 24, 1911).

4.4.9 Bounce Throws. Hall of Fame shortstop Pee Wee Reese remarked in the 1980s that there had only been one significant change in shortstop play in the fifty years since his major league debut (William Curran, *Mitts*, 148–149). That lone exception was the intentional bounce throw to first that was pioneered by Cincinnati shortstop Dave Concepcion.

As with so many firsts, the new technique was made possible by new conditions. In Concepcion's rookie season of 1970, artificial turf was installed at the Reds' home park of Riverfront Stadium on all areas except the mound and the cutoffs around the bases. This was more extensive than at any previous ballpark and it brought a new possibility to the shortstop position (Lonnie Wheeler and John Baskin, *The Cincinnati Game*, 51).

Concepcion found that on long throws, his first baseman had an easier time handling a ball that bounced off the turf than one that had to be scooped out of the dirt around the base. Moreover, the ball actually seemed to pick up speed when it skipped off the turf (David Falkner, *Nine Sides of the Diamond*, 153). This in turn enabled him to play deeper, especially against slow runners, and deliberately bounce throws.

Exactly when Concepcion began doing this is less clear. David Falkner indicated that it was not until after a 1980 elbow injury affected Concepcion's throwing ability (David Falkner, *Nine Sides of the Diamond*, 153). If so, other shortstops may have tried the approach earlier, since a 1976 article observed: "Chris Speier practices one-bounce pegs to first base from short left field so that he can play very deep shortstop on Astro Turf" (Dick Young, *Sporting News*, September 25, 1976).

Yet it was unquestionably Concepcion who ensured that the bounce throw was passed on. Ozzie Guillen recalled, "One day, we saw Davey Concepcion on TV throw the ball on the carpet—you know, one hop to the first baseman. We went out after that and every day [Luis] Aparicio's uncle worked with me on that . . . ever since, I've done that" (quoted in David Falkner, *Nine Sides of the Diamond*, 163).

4.4.10 Hidden-ball Trick. The hidden-ball trick has always evoked a wide range of responses. Some have sought to ban it and others have hoped that enough disdain would cause it to go away, while still others have taken a very different perspective by regarding it as the epitome of heady play.

The one thing that everyone agrees upon is that the play is very old. Depending on the source, the play was "the ancient hidden ball trick" (*Sporting News*, September 11, 1946); "born when the game was played in a cow pasture" (*Sporting Life*, February 3, 1894); "the old trick" (*Boston Journal*, reprinted in *Sporting Life*, May 20, 1905); "the trick of 1776 vintage" (*Indianapolis Star*, March 3, 1912); "such a hoary trick" (*Canton Repository*, April 27, 1888); "the hidden ball trick, so ancient that it is not used by pennant ball clubs" (Stanley T. Milliken, *Washington Post*, August 30, 1915); or "one of those old plays found in oil paintings" (Tim Murnane, *Boston Globe*, May 3, 1902).

No one tried to determine exactly how old it was until the researcher Bill Deane thought it might be fun to try to compile a list of occurrences. Deane has become the Gibbon of the hidden-ball trick, enlisting the help of a slew of baseball researchers to document well over two hundred instances of the play at the major league level. In the process, a picture has emerged of a play that, like Rasputin, has implausibly resisted all efforts to kill it.

It is safe to assume that the hidden-ball trick did not actually originate in a cow pasture or an oil painting. But, as befits the low regard in which the play has been held, there has been a noticeable shortage of claimants to patent rights. The only one I have unearthed appeared in *Sporting News* in 1888: "It was the late little Tommy Barlow who introduced the trick of hiding the ball under his arm after it was returned from the outfield when the hit had been made and then catch the base runner napping on a neat throw to the baseman, who would be on the lookout" (*Sporting News*, March 10, 1888). Note that even this assertion is made by a third party, who had waited until Barlow was dead and could not deny responsibility.

Tommy Barlow's playing days were in the late 1860s and early 1870s, and the play is first documented in those years. An 1873 article in the *Brooklyn Eagle* noted two recent examples. In one, Jack Burdock waited "quietly" until base runner Bob Addy stepped off second base, then applied the tag. The other saw Mutuals first baseman Joe Start take a more active role in instigating the action: "He argued with [Lip] Pike that he had been put out, whereupon Pike left his base for the purpose of explaining how he had overrun the base, and no sooner had Pike stepped from the sand bag than the wily Start touched him with the ball, thus putting him out, and it was so declared by the umpire" (*Brooklyn Eagle*, May 20, 1873). The *Eagle* commended Start for having "performed as clever a piece of base ball generalship as could be wished for." It even expressed compassion for his victim, noting, "It is not often Lip gets caught napping in this style" (*Brooklyn Eagle*, May 20, 1873).

Before long, however, familiarity with the play had begun to breed contempt. George Wright, after being caught by the play in an 1875 game, said in disgust that "he had been tried a hundred times before but that was the first time he had ever been caught" (*St. Louis Republican*, July 25, 1875). A *New York Clipper* reporter wrote later that year, "Tracy marred his fine play by a trick, in putting out Brasher, unworthy of a fair and manly player, by pretending to have thrown the ball to the pitcher while holding it under his arm. This is not legitimate ball-play" (*New York Clipper*, October 30, 1875). Another *New York Clipper* scribe commented three years later,

"We regretted to see Doescher [Herm Doscher] resort to one of [Jack] Burdock's old tricks of hiding the ball under his arm" (*New York Clipper*, November 2, 1878).

When Dan Brouthers hid the ball under his arm in an 1886 game and fooled base runner Ed Andrews, the *Boston Globe* referred to it as a "schoolboy play" (*Boston Globe*, June 26, 1886). While this may not sound particularly hostile, disapproval can be assumed in any wording that evokes childishness. The reception that greeted base runners who were victimized by the play was anything but subtle. When Brouthers caught Cleveland's Billy Taylor with the same ploy, "Taylor hung his head and walked home, nine Buffalos 'snickered,' and 700 Cleveland people said something which doesn't look well in print" (*Cleveland Voice*, reprinted in the *Chicago Tribune*, September 11, 1881).

Occasionally a new variant of the play would be cooked up, such as this one by Cincinnati in 1877: "[Catcher Nat] Hicks turned about carelessly, and, without calling time, purposely walked toward the Grand Stand. [Base runner Mike] Golden fell into the trap and started for home. [Pitcher Bobby] Mitchell, having the ball in his hand, easily ran in and caught him before he reached the home plate" (*Cincinnati Enquirer*, April 24, 1877). But far more often the play was executed in a much more rudimentary fashion.

As a result, the hidden-ball trick came increasingly to be viewed as a reflection of a base runner's recklessness rather than a fielder's cleverness. This perception was fostered by the advent of base coaches, since a successful play now required failure by two men. And the risk factor in the play was entirely one-sided. It was hard to give much credit to the defense for headiness when the nature of the play meant that they could tediously repeat the effort and would lose nothing when it failed.

As a result, opposition to the play steadily mounted. Harry Wright typically took the high road and "insisted that the trick was unprofessional and he would not allow his players to attempt it on opponents. Mr. Wright argued that the spectators were entitled to see how each man went out, and could not be expected to follow the ball when it was juggled by the players" (*Boston Journal*, reprinted in *Sporting Life*, May 20, 1905; describing Wright's days with Boston in the 1870s).

Others were less restrained, such as this writer in 1894: "It is noticed that [Brooklyn president] Charley Byrne sets his face against such stupid tricks on the field as hiding the ball under the arm to catch a man off his base. He is a whole heap right about such things. Fine points of play and new, snappy tricks are admired by most all spectators, but the loggy calf play of the ball under the arm was born when the game was played in a cow pasture and is the practice of a country lout and not of an up-to-date brainy ballplayer. Of all the stupid and disgust-breeding things among professional players, this ball-hiding custom is among the worst. The man who does it should be disciplined and the base runner who is caught by it should suffer more of a penalty than the usual disgust of spectators at his stupidity. Why, it is not playing ball. It is simply horse play."

Even those harsh words only scratched the surface of this writer's wrath. He went on to dismiss feints by basemen to draw runners off the base as a play performed by "all the children on the lots." He seemed unable to decide whether the bunt was more worthy of children or women, referring to it first as "infantile" and then as an "old woman's push-pin play." After condemning these examples of "exceedingly amateurish cow-pasture play," he concluded with a predictable paean to manliness: "Give us a rousing, bustling, athletic game and all those drawbacks will disappear and the sport will be far more popular even than it is at present" (*Sporting Life*, February 3, 1894).

While these comments may sound extreme, the underlying antipathy to the hidden-ball trick was a widely shared sentiment. Bill Deane discovered that Tim Murnane pulled it at least once during his playing days, in a September 20, 1875, exhibition game against Cincinnati (Bill Deane, "The Old Hidden Ball Trick: No Longer Banned in Boston," Mark Kanter, ed., *The Northern Game and Beyond*, 69).

Murnane had changed his tune by the time he became a sportswriter. In 1902 he wrote that the play was "not considered good sport in up-to-date ball" (*Boston Globe*, May 3, 1902). His opposition seems to have continued to deepen, because six years later he referred to it as a "trick as old as the game that should never be allowed to go in baseball. . . . Hiding the ball is an ancient trick, and long since barred from the game by custom. No Boston player has been allowed to attempt the trick since Harry Wright declared it was unsportsmanlike and an insult to the spectators" (*Boston Globe*, May 14, 1908).

Instead of prohibiting the hidden-ball trick, rule makers settled for discouraging it by passing a new rule in 1911 that the pitcher could not go "into his box" unless he has the ball "to render less easy of operation the hidden ball trick" (Joe S. Jackson, *Washington Post*, February 17, 1911). This did not entirely mollify the play's opponents. A note in *Sporting Life* in 1913 reported: "President Ban Johnson, of the American League, will issue an order forbidding the ancient 'hidden ball' trick, according to George Hildebrand, one of his umpires, hailing from the Pacific Coast. The latter says that President Johnson is opposed to it because of a tendency to delay the game" (*Sporting Life*, April 12, 1913). This rumor was widely disseminated, but nothing concrete ever came of it.

Two years later National League president John K. Tener tried a different approach: "Mr. Tener declares that the play is unsportsmanlike, and yet under the rules it is permissible. He says that he has told his umpires not only to watch the course of the ball from the time that it leaves the pitcher's hand, but if they suspect that an attempt is going to be made to work the hidden ball trick to look directly at the man who is holding the horsehide. In this way the runner or the coaches will be tipped off to what the opposition is trying to do, and the play may be prevented" (*Sporting Life*, May 20, 1915).

This effort seems to have been similarly short-lived. Even with the opposition of the presidents of both the National League and American League, the hidden-ball trick had again survived.

At the 1920 rules meeting at which the spitball was outlawed, Clark Griffith also proposed eliminating the hidden-ball trick. Griffith suggested doing so by rewriting the rule that the pitcher could not take a pitching position *on* the rubber without having the ball to instead read *on or near*. But this raised the insurmountable problem of how umpires would define "near."

In addition, the much-maligned hidden-ball trick now finally gained ideological support. The sportswriter John B. Sheridan contended that "The rule designed to curtail the hidden ball trick relieves the players of the responsibility of watching the ball, which is the first principle of baseball." He called it "another step in the direction of making players mere automatons moved by managers and by umpires" (*Sporting News*, February 19, 1920).

These failures seem to have chastened the opponents of the play, and calls to ban the hidden ball gradually subsided. The play's success rate gradually declined as professional base coaches became common, but some new twists were devised when gloves became large enough to conceal the baseball. Harold C. Burr observed in 1938, "Another old favorite brought forth from the mothballs is 'Frisco Frank Crosetti's hidden-ball trick. It is one of the most mortifying of tricks, yet one of the oldest, but Crosetti has smartly added an innovation. He conceals the ball inside the heel of his glove, so that he seems to be standing out there at shortstop innocently empty-handed" (*Sporting News*, November 10, 1938).

4.4.11 Catchers Blocking the Plate. The 1880s and 1890s saw more fielders obstructing base runners, taking advantage of the fact that a lone umpire worked most games (see **11.1.15**). A typical example of the rowdiness of the era occurred in a game between the Detroit Athletic Club and the New York Athletic Club on August 5, 1893, in Detroit. When Detroit catcher Frank Bowerman repeatedly attempted "the old 'block' act" by obstructing the plate, one New York runner responded by punching him in the eye (*Detroit Free Press*, August 6, 1893).

The obstruction seems to have generally been more of a nuisance than anything else. Tim Murnane complained in 1894, "The league rule makers would do the game a big favor by allowing the runner to get home without having to push the catcher out of the way" (*Boston Globe*, January 14, 1894).

Plate blocking became more sophisticated after the turn of the century. The sportswriter Ren Mulford, Jr., offered this account in 1902: "[Cincinnati base runner Harry Steinfeldt] beat Jack Farrell's relay at least a dozen feet, but the Texan found the way to home plate full of knees, legs and shoes. [St. Louis catcher John O'Neill] was squatted over the plate as if he owned it. Before Steinfeldt could bore through O'Neill got the ball, put it on him, [and umpire] Tom Brown called him out."

Mulford observed, "Under a strict interpretation of Section 6, of Rule 35, Steinfeldt might have been declared safe, but there isn't an umpire in the land who enforces that section if he can dodge it. The section in question says the base runner is entitled to his base, 'if he be prevented from making a base by the obstruction of an adversary, unless the latter be a fielder having the ball in his hand ready to meet the base runner.' In this case Steinfeldt beat the ball a full second, the fielder had his obstruction built and was compelled to wait for the ball to arrive to complete the play. Nice question to chew about" (*Sporting Life*, August 2, 1902).

This commentary is extremely revealing. Based upon Mulford's own description, there is no question that O'Neill's action was illegal. So clearly there was more at work here that caused Mulford to call this a "nice question to chew about."

My belief is that his ambiguous response resulted from a combination of several factors. The underlying one was that the size of the corps of umpires was increasing and a corresponding effort was being undertaken to crack down on obstruction. But with fires to put out all over the place, it was hard to know where to start.

As Mulford implied, the umpires realized that they would have a better chance of success if they did not appear too unreasonable in these efforts. So some form of compromise was advisable. That being the case, the drama inherent in the effort to score made plays at the plate the ideal place to turn a blind eye to obstruction.

What's more, blocking the plate took courage since base runners were already bowling over fielders (see 5.5.1). The resulting risk on both sides caused it to be viewed differently from efforts to trip and grab runners. *Sporting Life*, for example, noted: "Catcher [Fred] Abbott, of the Phillies, is a good plate blocker. He fears no man" (*Sporting Life*, April 15, 1905). Thus plate blocking began to emerge as a reputable practice even as other forms of obstruction were being weeded out.

Catchers gained a great advantage with the introduction of shin guards (see 9.4.6), which emboldened them to stand their ground against incoming base runners. Christy Mathewson seems to have had mixed feelings about the practice, writing, "Some catchers block off the plate so that a man has got to shoot his spikes at them to get through, and I'm not saying that it's bad catching, because that is the way to keep a man from scoring" (Christy Mathewson, *Pitching in a Pinch*, 267–268).

By 1914 plate blocking was becoming an art form: "There are no more expert backstops in the country, in the matter of stopping runners from sliding into the rubber than are Ed Ainsmith and John Henry, but the practice has developed in the last couple of years to such an extent that on close plays a catcher who does not plant himself in the lines is not considered as doing his duty" (*Sporting News*, March 5, 1914).

Clark Griffith explained that it was no easy matter to prevent this tactic: "There are two ways to stop blocking, one is to leave it to the judgment of the umpire whether the blocking is intentional and the other is to make the catchers shed their shin guards. . . . All blocking is done on close plays, and if you are going to force the umpire to watch blocking and at the same time judge whether the runner is out or safe, you will get a lot of bad umpiring. As for forcing the catcher to do away with his pads, you are taking an action that would be unfair to the catcher. A man who has to stand for fouls, flying bats, and such things as the catcher is now called upon to do, should be given all the protection possible. These are the reasons I would leave plays at the plate as they are" (quoted by Thomas Kirby of the *Washington Times*, reprinted in *Sporting News*, March 5, 1914).

As a result, plate blocking remained a part of baseball, despite occasional laments like this one by John Kieran in 1933: "A burly catcher, encased in protective armor, is a common sight blocking the road toward the plate for an incoming runner. But how many fans have seen an umpire pin the proper penalty on the catcher and declare the runner safe after he has been blocked off and tagged? It happens once in a long while, which isn't often enough" (John Kieran, "Collision Damage in Baseball," *New York Times*, May 1, 1933).

Bill James has suggested that plate blocking is a recent phenomenon, but the evidence he offers is largely recent and anecdotal (Bill James, *The New Bill James Historical Baseball Abstract*, 214–216). As the above examples demonstrate, this is simply not the case. James may be correct that blocking the plate is more extensive now than when he was a child, but if so, that is simply an example of the ebb and flow of historical patterns. Plate blocking is not new at all but is in fact the one surviving remnant of an era when obstruction was common.

4.4.12 Basemen Blocking a Base. As discussed in the preceding entry, there was a period when it was just as common for basemen to block their bases as for the catcher to block the plate. Base runners did not routinely slide until the 1880s, but once they began to do so, blocking soon came in its wake. Cap Anson said that Tommy Burns "excelled at the blocking game, which he carried on in a style that was particularly his own and which was calculated to make a base runner considerable trouble" (Adrian C. Anson, *A Ball Player's Career*, 129). Tim Murnane's account of a 1900 game noted that the winning run had scored on a passed ball in spite of the efforts of pitcher Bill Dineen: "Dineen took the throw from [catcher William] Clarke and blocked off his man, but [umpire Hank] O'Day could only see Pittsburg and the run was allowed to count" (*Boston Globe*, September 5, 1900).

Connie Mack recommended feet-first slides in 1904 because "A player is easily blocked off who slides with his head foremost" (Connie Mack, "How to Play Ball," multi-part series, *Washington Post*, April 17, 1904). Ty Cobb learned this the hard way in his first major league game. He had always slid headfirst on his way up through the minors, but when he tried this against New York: "Stepping on the bag to receive the ball from the catcher, [Kid Elberfeld] blocked my slide by coming down on my head with his knee. My forehead and face were shoved into the hard ground and the skin peeled off just above the eyebrows. The clever way in which he did this completely blocked me" (Ty Cobb, *Memoirs of Twenty Years in Baseball*, 42).

To prevent blocking, Cobb became a spikes-first slider, as did many other base runners of the period. He described this as "a case of beating the other fellow to the punch." To prevent fielders like Elberfeld from blocking his path to the base, "Instead of taking the long slide I would run close up to the base and then throw myself forward quickly—a sort of swoop. The force of a quick swoop or dart would swerve my body around more quickly. I would surprise the baseman and get out of his way before he knew it" (Ty Cobb, *Memoirs of Twenty Years in Baseball*, 43).

It appears that Elberfeld attempted to make an adjustment of his own. *Sporting Life* reported in 1908: "Elberfeld and Niles, of the Highlanders, wear shin guards to protect their legs from the base runners' spikes" (*Sporting Life*, May 2, 1908). Each player wore only a single shin guard, Elberfeld on the right leg, and Niles on his left. The effort was short-lived, however, and since then blocking bases has been used primarily against headfirst sliders.

4.4.13 Shortstop to Second Baseman to First Baseman (6-4-3) Double Play.

The *New York Clipper* recorded a 6-4-3 double play on August 17, 1861, and the play was still considered a novelty at that time. Within two years it was becoming common, as was the case with most of the other standard double-play combinations.

4.4.14 First Baseman to Shortstop to First Baseman (3-6-3) Double Play.

The 3-6-3 double play was first brought to prominence by longtime Boston first baseman Fred Tenney. Tenney is believed to have turned his first such double play on June 14, 1897, against Cincinnati. Tim Murnane reported the next day, "[Claude] Ritchey cracked a singing grounder at Fred Tenney. The ball was picked up clean and shot to [shortstop Herman] Long for a forceout, and then returned to Tenney at first for a double play" (*Boston Globe*, June 15, 1897). Tenney recalled later that after the play, "It seemed that you could have heard a pin drop for ten seconds, and then the crowd just let out a roar. It had seen something new" (quoted in Mark Sternman, "Frederick Tenney," Tom Simon, ed., *Deadball Stars of the National League*, 309). Boston second baseman Bobby Lowe discussed the play many years later and commented, "I believe Tenney was the originator, but I know any such observation will be subject to controversy" (*Sporting News*, July 16, 1942).

4.4.15   Triple Play. The earliest triple play I am aware of was turned by Jim Creighton of the Excelsiors of Brooklyn in an 1860 game in Baltimore (James H. Bready, *Baseball in Baltimore*, 7).

4.4.16   Bluff Tags. Henry Chadwick wrote in 1867, "Umpires, in judging of touching men on bases, have to decide according to the probabilities of the play, and not what in reality does take place, as they have no right to take the testimony of a player, even when, as in this case, the base player has the generosity to acknowledge that he did not touch him" (*The Ball Player's Chronicle*, July 25, 1867). While it undoubtedly wasn't Chadwick's intention, these instructions would seem to encourage fielders to apply phantom tags.

Bluff tags became prevalent in the 1880s as a natural response to increasingly sophisticated sliding tactics. Cub Stricker recalled, "I didn't put the ball on one out of four base stealers when I was playing second, but I almost always got the decision" (quoted in Gerard S. Petrone, *When Baseball Was Young*, 112).

Of course, the difficulty of being certain whether a tag was actually made could also work to the runner's advantage. The *Boston Globe* noted in 1886: "The *Newburyport Herald* says it is easy to steal bases on the Haverhill grounds if you know how. Simply make a long slide, and the effect will be to envelop the runner and baseman in such an impenetrable cloud of dust that no umpire can see either one for some seconds and naturally will be cautious about calling a man out" (*Boston Globe*, May 7, 1886).

4.4.17   Scoop Throws. The underhand toss on double plays may have been pioneered by Hall of Fame shortstop Rabbit Maranville. A 1914 article noted: "Maranville and [Braves second baseman Johnny] Evers are playing a lot of new stuff around second. The chief improvement is in Maranville's change of style of passing balls in force-outs and in starting double plays. He used to snap the ball at the second baseman, which is risky when the base-man is running at top speed toward him. Now he scoops it, getting a frac-tion of a second more speed and taking infinitely less risk of causing a muff" (*Washington Post*, July 12, 1914).

4.4.18 Glove Flips. Most fielders wore no gloves at all until the 1880s. When gloves finally came into vogue, they were so thin that it was absolutely necessary to use the throwing hand to secure the ball. It can therefore be safely assumed that the glove flip did not develop until much larger gloves came into use.

One might expect that a recent flashy fielder pioneered the glove flip, but that is not the case. Instead the earliest player whom I have been able to document using this technique was so fundamentally sound that he was nicknamed "The Mechanical Man." A 1932 *Sporting News* article described Detroit second baseman Charley Gehringer's approach when he fielded a ground ball up the middle with his momentum carrying him away from the bag. Instead of transferring the ball to his throwing hand, Gehringer had mastered the art of flipping the ball directly from his gloved hand to the shortstop covering second base (*Sporting News*, June 9, 1932).

4.4.19 Glove Throws. Orlando Hernandez fielded a comebacker in a 1999 game and found that the ball had become lodged so securely in his glove that he could not get it out. In desperation, he finally threw the glove to the first baseman to record the out. The play was understandably replayed on high-light shows, since most people had never seen anything like it before.

It turned out, however, that the same play had been made by Terry Mul-holland on September 3, 1986, as this account shows: "[Keith] Hernandez slammed the ball back to the mound, and it took one hard hop right into the rookie pitcher's glove. He turned toward first base and reached for the ball, but it was stuck in the webbing. Then he seemed to panic a little as he ran toward the base, yanking at the ball.

"Finally, he did the only sensible thing. He took the glove off his right hand and shoveled it—glove and ball—to [Bob] Brenly, the first baseman. The umpire, Ed Montague, after checking the glove to make sure the ball was still inside, waved his arm and called Hernandez out" (Joseph Durso, *New York Times*, September 4, 1986).

4.4.20 Extra Glove. In 1969 catcher Clay Dalrymple attempted to keep a glove in his pocket that would supplement his mitt. His intention was to switch to the glove if he anticipated a play at the plate, but he was told that he could not use the extra glove.

Chapter 5

BASERUNNING

BASERUNNING is the part of the game that young children most readily appreciate, and in many of the games that preceded baseball, the bat was little more than an excuse to begin a game of tag. A good example is a description, many years after the fact, by a man named Adam Ford of a game he played in Canada in 1838. Ford reported that the first "bye" was located only six yards from the home "bye" in order "to get runners on the base lines so as to have the fun of putting them out or enjoying the mistakes of the fielders when some fleet-footed fellow would dodge the ball and come in home" (*Sporting Life*, May 5, 1886).

A base runner's mad dash for a base remains one of the most thrilling plays for baseball fans. And yet the following entries show that even this simple act has been the subject of considerable forethought, scheming, innovation, and experimentation.

This section will be divided into six segments: (1) stolen bases, (2) slides, (3) pickoffs, pitchouts, and other countermoves by fielders, (4) plays like the squeeze bunt and the hit-and-run, where the batting is a pretext to set up running, (5) turf wars between base runners and fielders, and (6) novelty plays.

(i) Stolen Bases

5.1.1 **Stolen Bases.** It is often reported, even in usually reliable sources, that Ned Cuthbert stole the first base in 1865. That's a perfect indication of how much we still have to learn about early baseball. While there is some doubt about exactly how common stolen bases were in early baseball, there is no doubt that they were part of baseball well before 1865.

While base stealing is not specifically mentioned in the Knickerbocker rules, there is no reason to believe it wasn't legal. Tom Shieber discovered what seems to be the earliest explicit account of a stolen base, which appeared in 1856: "Mr. Valentine who succeeded Mr. Booth, made a good strike and reached the second base. He was followed by Mr. Abrams, a good and sure batter, and we felt certain that he would terminate the game in favor of the Union. Previous to his striking, however, Mr. Valentine run [sic] from the second to the third base, which he undoubtedly reached before being touched with the ball thrown to the guardian of that base; but the referee decided that he was out, and from that decision there was no appeal" (*New York Clipper*, August 7, 1856, based on an account in the *New York Sunday Mercury* of August 3, 1856; reprinted in Frederick Ivor-Campbell, "When Was the First? (Part 4)," *Nineteenth Century Notes* 95:3, 4 [Summer/ Fall 1995], 12). This may also be the first instance of an umpire being second-guessed and the first base runner to violate the precept about not making the last out at third base.

It remains unclear exactly how common base stealing was in the late 1850s and early 1860s. Paul Hunkele, a leading authority on the period, believes it was quite common. He cites Henry Chadwick's 1860 description of the catcher's responsibilities with a runner on first: "the moment the ball is delivered by the pitcher, and the player runs from the first to the second base, the Catcher should take the ball before bounding, and send it to the second base as swiftly as possible, in time to cut off the player before he can touch the base" (*Beadle's Dime Base-Ball Player*, 21).

Others are less sure, noting that while taking extra bases was common, it was not always by means of base stealing. Patient base runners realized that a passed ball would occur sooner or later, allowing them to advance without risk of being put out.

Indeed it was often alleged that batters would deliberately wait until a passed ball occurred before offering at a pitch. Henry Chadwick, for instance, later complained about "the habit the batsman had, under the old rules, of waiting at the bat until a passed or overthrown ball had enabled the base runner to leave the first base" (Henry Chadwick, *Haney's Base Ball Book of Reference for 1867*, 124).

The introduction of called strikes in 1858 was intended to address this tendency, but the rule was ineffectual because of umpires' reluctance to enforce it. Chadwick grumbled in 1860 about a "very tedious and annoying feature" of the way the game was being played. He asked rhetorically: "How often do we see the striker—the moment his predecessor has made his first base—stand still at the home base, and await the moment when the player on the first base can avail himself of the first failure of the pitcher and catcher to hold the ball, while tossing it backward and forward to each other." He noted that a batter was thus "frequently allowed to stop the progress and interest of the game, by his refusal to strike at good balls, under the plea that they do not suit him, when it is apparent to all that he simply wants to allow his partner to get to his second base" (*Beadle's Dime Base-Ball Player*, 16).

The situation began to change once the enforcement of the called strike rule improved. With batters no longer allowed to stand at the plate indefinitely, base runners could not simply wait for a passed ball, and stolen bases gradually became more common.

5.1.2 Leadoffs. The rules of baseball have never prevented a runner from leading off a base. It is sometimes suggested that leadoffs were not customary in early baseball, and such an assertion is difficult to disprove positively. But it is hard to reconcile with the fact that the leadoff's nemesis, the pickoff move (see **5.3.1**), was in vogue by 1860.

Pitchers' deliveries were severely constrained by the rules in most years before the 1880s, and this kept base runners close to the base. When windups (see **3.1.1**) became more elaborate, leadoffs developed in response. Tommy McCarthy suggested that Mike Kelly was one of the men responsible: "Kelly was a great base stealer for several reasons. In the first place, he always took plenty of room, more room than the average man of his time did. This counts a great deal in successful base-stealing" (quoted in A. H. Spink, *The National Game*, 103). Hugh Nicol also experimented with larger leads, explaining in 1888: "I play as far off of first as to make it nip and tuck which will get back first, me or the ball" (*Brooklyn Eagle*, March 11, 1888).

But the conventional wisdom continued to be that a large lead represented an unnecessary risk. Connie Mack wrote in 1904 that it was a mistake for a base runner to be far enough from the base to have to slide back on a pickoff attempt (Connie Mack, "How to Play Ball," multi-part series, *Washington Post*, April 10, 1904).

5.1.3 Delayed Double Steals. This is a play still in use by which, with runners on first and third, the offensive team tries to steal a run. The runner on first acts as though he is trying to steal, but his real intention is to draw a throw to second base that will allow the runner on third to score.

The venerable sportswriter William Rankin claimed in 1905 that the play had been around as long as he could remember, and it can be documented as early as 1873 (*Sporting News*, July 1, 1905). In a match that year between the Atlantics of Brooklyn and the Athletics of Philadelphia, Dickey Pearce was on first for the Atlantics and teammate Herman Dehlman on third: "Dick [Pearce] thought he would insure Dehlman's getting home, and so ran closely down to second. [Athletics catcher John] Clapp at once threw to [second baseman Wes] Fisler and Dehlman started for home. Dick stopped half way between first and second, and Fisler, hesitating between his desire to capture Pearce and to catch Dehlman at third, finally threw the ball to [third baseman Ezra] Sutton, who promptly forwarded it to Clapp, but too late to save the run, Pearce in the interim getting to second." But this was not the first occurrence, since the reporter observed that Pearce had "played the same point on the Philadelphians and it was a surprise to us to see the Athletics caught napping by the very same play" (*Brooklyn Eagle*, May 27, 1873).

By 1875 the play had become sufficiently common for Henry Chadwick to chide Ben Loughlin for not initiating it. In a game between the Confidence and Flyaway clubs of New York, "Quinn was on third and Loughlin at first, with two men out, when Spence came to the bat. Under these circumstances, with the Flyaways in the rear in the score, it was Loughlin's play to have drawn a throw from the catcher to second by an attempt to run down to second base, so as to have given a chance for Quinn to run home. By Loughlin doing this and getting caught between first and second, Quinn could have probably crossed home-plate before Loughlin was put out, in which case the run would have scored" (*New York Clipper*, October 6, 1875).

The play became still more commonplace in the next few years. Henry Chadwick wrote in his summary of the 1878 season that "sacrificing oneself between first and second base in order to get the runner at third home" had been one of "the points of baserunning generally played last year" (*New York Clipper*, January 18, 1879).

Naturally, when a play is common and successful, efforts arise to counteract it. The responses to the delayed double steal are discussed under "Short Throws" (5.3.13).

5.1.4 Two Bases on Balls. George F. Will reported that Detroit Tigers greats Ty Cobb and Sam Crawford used to run a play that operated on the same principle as the one described in the last entry. According to Will, the play was executed "when Cobb was on third and Crawford walked. Crawford would stroll toward first and then suddenly sprint around the base and tear toward second as Cobb was creeping down the line from third. If the startled team in the field threw to second, Cobb scored easily. Otherwise Crawford arrived at second with a two-base walk" (George F. Will, *Men at Work*, 74).

5.1.5 Steals of Home. In 1860, Henry Chadwick wrote of the pitcher, "when a player attempts to run in to the home base while he is pitching, he should follow the ball to the home base as soon as it leaves his hand, and be ready at the base to take it from the catcher" (*Beadle's Dime Base-Ball Player*, 22). Paul Hunkele reasons from this passage that if defenses were

planning strategies to combat steals of home, they must have been relatively common occurrences.

If so, the play seems to have almost entirely disappeared for many years.
Johnny Evers and Hugh Fullerton reported: "Ross Barnes, in a game between the Chicago and Rockford teams in 1870, stole home twice while the
pitcher was in the act of delivering the ball without finding imitators for
many years" (John J. Evers and Hugh S. Fullerton, *Touching Second*, 198).

Their belief that the play was highly unusual is supported by additional
evidence. In 1886, Ned Williamson of Chicago stole home and a Chicago
writer claimed that this was an unprecedented feat. But *Sporting News*
pointed out that Buck Ewing had pulled off a steal of home in 1885, while
the *New York World* noted that John Ward had done one in 1884, and the
Philadelphia Item recalled such a play by Jud Birchall in 1882. Obviously
though, a steal of home was still a very rare event in the 1880s (*Sporting
News*, August 2, 1886).

5.1.6 Triple Steals. The triple steal is perhaps the ultimate base running
feat. It is certainly the play on which the risks are divided most inequitably.
The runner on third is naturally the one upon whom a play will always be
made. The other runners, provided they are alert enough to follow the lead
runner's cue, can advance without peril.

Early in the 1908 season, with the Philadelphia Athletics hosting the
Washington Senators, the Athletics pulled off the play. In the second inning,
"There were two down, with [Harry] Davis on third, [Jack] Coombs on second, and [Rube] Oldring on first, and two strikes called on [Rube] Vickers.
Davis figured it out that [Senators pitcher Tom] Hughes would waste a ball,
and as it turned out he figured correctly. As soon as Hughes began to wind
up, Davis made a dash for the plate. He did not appear to be fifteen feet from
the plate when the ball left Hughes' hands, and he was over the plate when
the ball hit [catcher Jack] Warner's mitt" (*Washington Post*, April 28, 1908).

The *Post* described this triple steal as "something never before pulled off
in this city [Philadelphia]" and others went further by claiming that the play
had never before occurred. But Fred Clarke of the Pirates declared that he
had combined with Honus Wagner and Tommy Leach to pull the play
against both Louisville and Boston.

At least a couple of earlier instances have been uncovered. In the fourth
inning of a game on September 14, 1900, with Pink Hawley at bat and Virgil Garvin pitching, Jack Doyle, George Davis, and Mike Grady of New
York pulled off a triple steal against Chicago (*Sporting Life*, September 22,
1900). *Sporting Life* reported that Dick Padden, Joe Sugden, and Jesse Burkett of St. Louis pulled the play against the Athletics on September 26, 1904
(*Sporting Life*, October 8, 1904).

The inherent difficulty of stealing home and the need of having the bases loaded have combined to keep the play uncommon, though not unheard of. On April 30, 1914, Cleveland base runners Jack Graney (third), Ivy Olson (second), and Fred Carisch (first) pulled one off with two out and St. Louis' George Baumgardner pitching to Roy Wood. On July 25, 1930, the Athletics executed the play twice in a game against Cleveland.

5.1.7 Delayed Steals. A surprising number of players have been credited with inventing the delayed steal on the throw back from the catcher. Lee Allen tabbed Miller Huggins as the originator in 1903 (Lee Allen, *The Hot Stove League*, 97). In 1906, Kid Elberfeld helped popularize the play again, and some credited him with inventing the play. But the sportswriter H. G. Merrill wrote that Bill O'Hara had pulled off the same play a dozen times while playing for Wilkes-Barre in 1905 (*Sporting News*, December 22, 1906). Otto Jordan, another player of the era, also claimed to have invented the delayed steal (*Sporting News*, January 23, 1908).

Yet it was frequently used before any of these instances. Hugh S. Fullerton wrote in 1906: "Bill Lange used to pull off a trick that set catchers wild, and it was this trick that made him the champion baserunner of the league for two years. He had a habit of starting from first base at a terrific clip just as the pitcher pitched the ball, and then, instead of continuing, he would stop short and grin at the catcher, who was in position to throw. The moment the catcher started to throw the ball back to the pitcher or to shoot it to first Lange would make a dash for second, and eight out of ten times would land in safety. He always claimed that he could beat the relayed throw much easier than a straight throw from the catcher to second" (*Chicago Tribune*, April 15, 1906). While no year is specified, Lange retired after the 1899 season.

Johnny Evers and Hugh S. Fullerton accordingly categorized the delayed steal among plays that "have been 'discovered' about once a decade, and then neglected, if not forgotten, until some other genius brought them into action. . . . Frank Chance, in 1906, commenced to work the 'delayed steal' persistently and was proclaimed the discoverer of the play. Yet [nineteenth-century players Mike] Kelly, [Billy] Hamilton, [Bill] Lange, ['Tip'] O'Neill, [Charles] Comiskey, [Hugh] Duffy and many others used the play, and 'Sadie' Houck stole in that way with much success" (John J. Evers and Hugh S. Fullerton, *Touching Second*, 198, 203).

(ii) Slides

5.2.1 Slides. It is often reported that Eddie Cuthbert made the first slide. The origin of this story seems to be this passage in A. H. Spink's book: "The first attempt to steal a base by sliding head first for the bag was made on [the Capitoline Grounds in Brooklyn] during the summer of 1865. The honor belongs to Eddie Cuthbert, then a member of the Keystone Club of Philadelphia. It was during the progress of a game between the Keystones and the Atlantics of Brooklyn that Cuthbert surprised the spectators by trying to steal second base by diving headlong for the bag. His first attempt was successful, but on a second trial he was caught in the act and retired" (A. H. Spink, *The National Game*, 10).

The game in question occurred on July 29, 1865, but the *Brooklyn Eagle* had only a brief account and did not mention the play. It is quite possible that Cuthbert's slide was new to onlookers and conceivable that it incorporated elements not previously used by base runners. But he was definitely not the first ballplayer to hit the dirt as he approached the base.

An 1857 game account in the *New York Clipper* reported, "one of the Liberty's [sic], running to the first base and falling upon it with his hands, was decided in time" (*New York Clipper*, October 10, 1857). This description leaves the possibility that this player's slide was accidental or spontaneous.

Researcher David Arcidiacono discovered this account in James D'Wolf Lovett's 1908 book about early baseball in New England: "Mr. Chandler [Moses E. Chandler of the Tri-Mountains] also had the distinction of being the first ball player in New England who, when running the bases, made a 'dive' for one of them. This happened in 1859 in Portland, Maine, in a match between the Tri-Mountains and Portlands, and the feat fairly astonished the natives, who at first roared with laughter, *but Chandler scored the run*, and they then woke up to the fact that a large, new and valuable 'wrinkle' had been handed out to them" (James D'Wolf Lovett, *Old Boston Boys and the Games They Played*, 153). A similar description of Chandler's "original feature of diving at a base" appeared in a 1905 article that pinpointed the date as June 28, 1859 (*Boston Journal*, February 20, 1905).

Sliding does appear to have remained uncommon in the early days of baseball, and generally inadvertent. That is, a runner realized at the last moment that he would be unable to avoid overrunning the base and therefore chose instead to dive. Thus a premeditated slide in 1865 may have been regarded as a novelty.

Henry Chadwick reported in 1868, "Some base runners have a habit of sliding in to a base when they steal one." He was lukewarm about the practice, commenting that "sliding in is serviceable at times" but suggesting that a better approach was "getting around and back of the base player, and catching hold of the bag as he stoops to touch it" (Henry Chadwick, *The American Game of Base Ball*, 26).

In the 1860s runners could overrun bases only at their peril, and this rule was the primary impetus for sliding. In 1871 there was serious talk of allowing base runners to overrun bases and return at their leisure. Eventually it was decided to make this legal at first base. If overrunning had been allowed at all bases, it seems safe to assume that the uncommon practice of sliding would have pretty much died out, at least for many years.

As it was, it was not until the early 1880s that sliding became at all customary, and this did not happen until after there had been serious talk of banning the slide. The *St. Louis Post-Dispatch* noted later that when evasive slides had first emerged, "there was a long, loud and indignant kick that ended in smoke, and the boys kept sliding just the same" (*St. Louis Post-Dispatch*, July 31, 1886). The *New York Clipper* observed in 1881, "Sliding to bases is proposed to be put a stop to, as it results in too many accidents. [Arthur] Irwin broke his leg by it, and [Emil] Gross was disabled by sliding in. By requiring a player to touch a base on the run, the trouble would be stopped" (*New York Clipper*, September 3, 1881).

As this suggests, until the 1880s slides were defensive maneuvers rather than aggressive ones. The base runner's intent was generally to defend himself from going past the base and being tagged out. Since form follows function, his method was similarly defensive: to protect himself from injury as he fell. As a result, early base runners who hit the dirt were often not so much sliding as sitting down on the base.

That began to change in the early 1880s. Harry Wright said in an 1885 interview that John O'Rourke, who played for Wright in 1879 and 1880, was "the first man that I ever heard of sliding." Wright added, "Only once do I remember his being hurt," showing that fear of injury was one of the main objections to sliding (*St. Louis Post-Dispatch*, June 27, 1885).

Slides remained rare until a couple of years after this, when Mike Kelly demonstrated the lethal potential that the hook slide offered for evading tags. Copycats ensured that by the end of the decade slides had become commonplace and had undergone a transformation from defensive maneuvers to aggressive ones.

The *Cincinnati Enquirer* reported before the 1887 season, "It is the intention of the Cincinnati management to make a great effort to have one of the best baserunning teams in the profession this season. With this end in view, Manager [Gus] Schmelz has been drilling the men in the Gymnasium in this one specialty more than anything else. It has been his endeavor the past two weeks to train the players in the art of sliding both head and feet first. The first named style is the most effective, but any style that provides for the men going into bases near the ground is preferable to the don't-give-a-damn style of standing up and running into a baseman to be touched" (*Cincinnati Enquirer*, March 27, 1887).

There continued to be holdouts, and a reporter noted matter-of-factly in 1884, "Many [base runners] don't care to slide" (*New York Clipper*, October

18, 1884). Their reticence was understandable, as sliding on fields that were often strewn with pebbles could be a painful experience. Johnny Ward noted, "Sliding for bases is one of the most prolific causes of wounds and bruises. The hip generally suffers most in this exercise. Many a player, when he gets to his base, misses a patch of skin as big as the palm of his hand, but he doesn't say anything about it" (*San Francisco Examiner*, November 11, 1888). In addition to the pain, another consideration was that sliding created laundry bills that the players had to pay for themselves.

But the benefits of sliding were too obvious to ignore. Within a few years it was mostly veteran players who were resisting the change and even some of them were won over. An 1886 article reported that "Deacon White made his first slide since he began to play ball at Detroit Monday" (*Boston Globe*, June 26, 1886). Another old-timer gave in two years later: "Ezra Sutton, who began ball playing when this country was in its swaddling clothes, paralyzed the rest of the Boston team the other day by making a belly-buster slide. In his long career, it was the first time the old man ever soiled his clothes stealing a base" (*Cincinnati Enquirer*, April 22, 1888). The next season a scribe for the *Boston Globe* reported that veteran pitcher Jim "Pud" Galvin hated Pittsburgh's orange uniforms so much that he was threatening to slide for aesthetic reasons. The reporter quipped, "Just imagine James sliding into second base" (*Boston Globe*, April 16, 1889).

Arthur Irwin claimed later that Pete Browning had refused to slide when the two were teammates in 1890 because he "was afraid of twisting an ankle or springing a charley-horse" (*Washington Post*, July 26, 1899). But according to Johnny Evers and Hugh Fullerton, many base runners began to slide precisely because they feared getting a charley horse by stopping suddenly at bases (John J. Evers and Hugh S. Fullerton, *Touching Second*, 240–241).

By the 1890s the last holdouts had retired, and sliding had become virtually universal. Once again an exception helps to prove the rule. Jack Kavanagh noted that when a player named Hi Ladd reported to Pittsburgh in 1898, he informed manager Bill Watkins that he did not believe in sliding. Years later Ladd explained to a reporter: "I would see other players slide into bases and get badly hurt. I could hear their bones crack as they broke their legs. I didn't want it to happen to me." Watkins released him after one game ("Hi Ladd: The Man Who Would Not Slide," in Jack Kavanagh, *The Heights of Ridiculousness*, 145).

5.2.2   Headfirst Slides, Feet-first Slides, and Air Dives. The evidence as to whether headfirst or feet-first slides came first is confusing and often seems contradictory. One reason was that no form of slide was common before the 1880s, meaning that there was little reason to generalize about slides. As we shall see, it does not appear that either approach was ever used exclusively.

More important, nineteenth-century observers classified slides differently from the way we now do. Today we divide all slides into headfirst and feet-first varieties, but in the nineteenth century the slide on the side was often counted as a third type. In addition, many reporters appear to have differentiated a dive from a slide. This means that even contemporary accounts on the subject have to be read with great care.

For example, a *St. Louis Post-Dispatch* sportswriter explained in 1886 that there were three different slides: feet-first, the side slide, and the new headfirst dive. Diagrams illustrated each slide. The side slide was labeled the "old-fashioned method" and in it the player is on his side but with his feet foremost. In contrast, he made clear that the headfirst dive was new: ". . . The third slide and the most terrible of all is that adopted by the Philadelphia Club and practised by them this year. [Jim] Fogarty and [Ed] Andrews did the most of it in the early part of the season, but they must have noted the extreme danger attendant upon the act, for they have abandoned it of late. Right wisely did they encase their hands in the gloves mentioned before for better protection. This peculiar slide consists in the base-runner making an air dive for the bag head foremost and both arms stretched out to the full extent. In this daring act it is simply a matter of impossibility for a man to control himself and he risks broken arms or a cracked skull every time he makes the slide" (*St. Louis Post-Dispatch*, July 31, 1886).

The fact that only the headfirst slide was labeled new led me at first to assume that feet-first slides preceded headfirst ones. After considering all the evidence, however, I now believe that what was considered new about the Philadelphia players' approach was not the fact that their hands were foremost but that they were diving rather than sliding. Support is lent to this view by Harry Wright's mentioning in 1885 that several of the St. Louis Brown Stockings "have a way of sliding when 15 to 20 feet from a base that is awfully hard to cut off" (*St. Louis Post-Dispatch*, June 27, 1885).

This interpretation helps make sense of an account that otherwise reads like a fairy tale. William Stryker Gummere was born in 1850, attended Princeton in the late 1860s, and later became chief justice of the New Jersey Supreme Court. When he died in 1933, a *Sporting News* obituary described a slide he had made more than sixty years earlier while playing for Princeton in a game against the Athletics of Philadelphia. According to the account, when Athletics second baseman Al Reach went to tag Gummere:

"Gummere threw himself feet first at the bag—the original of the hook slide Ty Cobb was to use later—and buried his face in his right arm for protection.

"Reach turned to tag him and had to look for him.

"'What kind of damned fool trick is that?' he demanded.

"'That,' said Mr. Gummere with a dignity fitting to one destined to grace the Supreme Court, 'is a device to evade being put out when running bases.'

"Reach and his companions were quick to see the value of the play and congratulated the Princeton player and adopted the play for themselves" (*Sporting News*, February 2, 1933).

The authenticity of this story is debatable. The detailed account of such long-ago events is suspect, and it seems very likely that some of these were added or exaggerated after the fact. (Possible dates on which this game could have occurred include April 24, 1869, June 18, 1870, and June 28, 1870.) For one thing, the description does not sound like a hook slide. More important, there is no evidence that the Athletics adopted any kind of slide, so it would appear that this was just a way of claiming greater significance for Gummere's slide.

On the other hand, the questionable elements do not confirm that the account was entirely fabricated. It seems unlikely that the story was simply made up out of whole cloth. While a slide should not have been regarded as a novelty in 1869 or 1870, an air dive would have been. So the story of Gummere's slide seems to me to illustrate that base runners' slides in the 1860s or 1870s were customarily defensive in nature, and that what was new about his slide was the fact that he was trying to "evade being put out when running bases."

While Gummere's slide was described as being feet-first, other specific accounts are of headfirst slides. The slide described in the *New York Clipper* in 1857 is clearly of the headfirst variety, since the runner fell upon the base with his hands. Moses Chandler's 1859 "dive" would also appear to be headfirst. Cuthbert's 1865 slide was said to have been of the headfirst variety, and Harry Wright's account of John O'Rourke's slide makes clear that he too was a headfirst slider (*St. Louis Post-Dispatch*, June 27, 1885).

The fact that early slides seem to have been spontaneous rather than premeditated suggests they were often headfirst lunges. Another important factor is that the sharp spikes worn by many early players (see **9.5.4**) would have made sliding very dangerous. So it appears that headfirst slides were more common than feet-first slides in the 1860s and '70s, but as long as slides were defensive in nature, it was just regarded as a matter of personal preference.

That changed in the 1880s when base runners began sliding to evade tags and began aggressively launching themselves at bases. Fielders countered by trying to block them from the bases, and it suddenly mattered whether the runner led with his feet or head.

The account of the technique used by Ed Andrews and Jim Fogarty made clear that their air dives were headfirst. This undoubtedly made it easier for them to adjust and evade a tag, but it had a critical flaw. As discussed in the preceding chapter, fielders resorted to blocking headfirst sliders from the base (see **4.4.12**). Base runners realized that their spikes were their best response, and feet-first slides gradually gained favor.

Ed Williamson gave this account of the reprehensible origins of the foot-first slide in 1891: ". . . Ball players do not burn with a desire to have colored men on their team. It is, in fact, the deep seated objection that most of them have for an Afro-American professional player that gave rise to the 'feet first' slide. You may have noticed in a close play that the base-runner will launch himself into the air and take chances on landing on the bag. Some go head first, others with the feet in advance. Those who adopt the latter method are principally old-timers and served in the dark days prior to 1880. They learned the trick in the east. The Buffalos—I think it was the Buffalo team—had a negro for second base. He was a few lines blacker than a raven, but he was one of the best players in the old Eastern League. The haughty Caucasians of the association were willing to permit darkies to carry water to them or guard the bat bag, but it made them sore to have the name of one in the batting list. They made a cabal against this man and incidentally introduced a new feature into the game. The players of the opposing teams made it their special business in life to 'spike' this brunette Buffalo. They would tarry at second when they might have easily made third, just to toy with the sensitive shins of this second baseman. The poor man played in two games out of five perhaps; the rest of the time he was on crutches. To give the frequent spiking of the darkey an appearance of accident the 'feet first' slide was practiced. The negro got wooden armor for his legs and went into the field with the appearance of a man wearing nail kegs for stockings. The enthusiasm of opposition players would not let them take a bluff. They filed their spikes and the first man at second generally split the wooden half cylinders. The colored man seldom lasted beyond the fifth inning, as the base runners became more expert. The practice survived long after the second baseman made his last trip to the hospital. And that's how [Mike] Kelly learned to slide" (*Sporting Life*, October 24, 1891; reprinted in Jerry Malloy, ed., *Sol White's History of Colored Base Ball*, 140).

An Ohio paper made a similar point in 1890: "The Toledo men are dirty ball players. They slide feet first. It is contemptible work, and should be called down" (*Columbus* [Ohio] *Post*, April 19, 1890). While intimidation seems to have been one factor, it was not the only one. As is discussed in the next entry, Mike Kelly helped to popularize the foot-first slide by showing its potential to evade a tag.

Another factor was that in the early 1880s home plate was still made of marble or stone. In an 1880 game an African-American player named Howard from Utica, New York, was said not to slide with the customary "care." According to a game account, Howard "strikes every base head first.

This is not so dangerous on the bags, but it is a little risky when it comes to the home plate" (*New York Clipper*, March 6, 1880). This remained an issue until the middle of the decade, when the rubber home plate was introduced (see **14.3.2**).

As a result, feet-first slides gradually gained ascendance. Cap Anson later claimed that feet-first slides were more common than headfirst ones during the 1880s (Adrian C. Anson, *A Ball Player's Career*, 113–114). The *Chicago Tribune* reported in 1907 that the majority of major leaguers were sliding feet first (*Chicago Tribune*, March 31, 1907). Christy Mathewson noted in 1912, "The feet-first slide is now more in vogue in the Big Leagues than the old head-first coast, and I attribute this to two causes. One is that the show of the spikes is a sort of assurance the base runner is going to have room to come into the bag, and the second is that the great amount of armor which a catcher wears in these latter days makes some such formidable slide necessary when coming into the plate" (Christy Mathewson, *Pitching in a Pinch*, 267).

5.2.3 Hook Slides. Lee Allen wrote that the hook slide was first used by William Gummere of Princeton in a game in the 1860s (Lee Allen, *The Hot Stove League*, 97). But the description of Gummere's slide in the preceding entry suggests that this was not a hook slide at all.

Mike "King" Kelly is one of the names that come up in conjunction with firsts with implausible frequency, and few of the claims are solidly documented. While it is not clear when Kelly began to use the hook slide or whether he originated it, so many of his contemporaries gave him credit for the spectacular slide that it seems safe to assume that at least he was responsible for popularizing it in the early to the mid-1880s. Indeed the hook slide was sometimes referred to as the "Kelly slide," "Kelly spread," or "Chicago slide" before its current name was coined.

Sportswriter Hugh S. Fullerton explained, "Kelly invented the 'Chicago slide,' which was one of the greatest tricks ever pulled off. It was a combination slide, twist, and dodge. The runner went straight down the line at top speed and when nearing the base threw himself either inside or outside the line, doubled the left leg under him (if sliding inside, or the right, if sliding outside), slid on the doubled up leg and the hip, hooked the foot of the other leg around the base, and pivoted on it, stopping on the opposite side of the base. Every player of the old Chicago team practiced and perfected that slide and got away with hundreds of stolen bases when really they should have been touched out easily" (*Chicago Tribune*, May 20, 1906).

Mike Kelly's teammate, Tommy McCarthy, attested that "No man guarding a bag ever had more of Kelly to touch than his feet. He never came into a bag twice in the same way. He twisted and turned as he made his famous 'Kelly slide,' and seldom was he caught. He was a regular boxer with his feet when sliding into bases" (A. H. Spink, *The National Game*, 103).

Ted Sullivan added: "Many a time have I seen catcher or baseman waiting to touch [Mike Kelly], when with a lightning dart he would get under him by a curved slide and be declared safe by the umpire. I had better explain what a 'curved slide' means, as some people of to-day might think it belongs to the 'old rounder age.' A 'curved slide' is a play made by a runner coming into the home plate or other base, where he throws his body and feet one way and hands and head the other to deceive the man that has the ball as to the direction in which he is going to the plate or bag" (*Sporting News*, January 21, 1895).

Sullivan cited Johnny Ward, Ned Williamson, Jim Fogarty, Curt Welch, Sam Crane, Arlie Latham, Bill Gleason, and Ned Hanlon as other players who mastered the evasive slide in the 1880s. Another was Charlie Comiskey, who earned praise during the 1886 postseason series for "a wonderful slide to second in the seventh inning. A snakelike movement of his body twisted him out of the reach of [second baseman Fred] Pfeffer who had the ball but could not touch him" (*Chicago Tribune*, October 19, 1886).

The hook slide was particularly effective when a base stealer had a variety of slides in his arsenal, as this description of Kelly's technique attests: ". . . No man playing ball can match him in thinking on his feet. He can slide both head and feet first, but nine times out of ten will throw himself out of the reach of the baseman, and catch the base from the outside" (*Boston Globe*, June 8, 1889). Kelly's former teammate Hugh Nicol described his own technique in similar terms in 1888: ". . . Just the instant before making the dip, I look to see how the ball is coming. If it's coming high I take the belly buster in front of the baseman, for nine out of ten of them swing back with the ball, and I ain't there. That fools them. If it's coming low I go behind them and twist out with my right toe and left knee. If it's going to be a pretty close thing and the ground is good and dry, I've got all my legs and arms to kick up a big dust, so the umpire can't see how the thing is, and my story is as good as the second baseman's when the cloud clears away, don't you see?" (*Brooklyn Eagle*, March 11, 1888).

An offshoot of the hook slide was the scissors slide, which had the additional benefit that the runner's flailing legs could dislodge the ball from the fielder. Mickey Cochrane explained in 1939: "A few years ago in Boston Jojo White, a master of the scissors kick, gave a startling demonstration of kicking a ball around. He scored from first base on an attempt to steal second. Jojo was out by five feet at second base, but the infielder dropped his hand on a one-handed tag and White lashed out with his scissors slide and kicked the ball into left field." Cochrane added that White then repeated the play at third base and at home plate (Mickey Cochrane, *Baseball: The Fans' Game*, 41).

5.2.4 Stand-up Slides. The pop-up or stand-up slide seems to be one of those innovations that emerged several times before it caught on permanently. In 1887, with the slide still developing, the *New York Sun* observed, "The way that [Roger] Connor slides to bases, feet first, and rises upright as his feet strike the base, is stunning" (*New York Sun*, May 20, 1887). Another account that year maintained that Ed Williamson's "slide is different from that of any other ball player in America. He does not slide along the ground, but when within the proper distance of the base he is trying to make, the big shortstop leaps high in air, straightens out, and before the baseman can locate him he is standing up on the opposite side of the bag, wiping the dust from his uniform" (*San Francisco Examiner*, December 12, 1887).

A. H. Spink indicated that another star of the 1880s, Harry Stovey, used a similar technique: "Standing upward of six feet in his stockings, [Stovey] would slide to a base, feet first, and regain a standing position with less effort and greater speed than any other man who has ever played baseball. . . . Stovey always wore a pad on the left hip to protect the bones, and when some twenty feet from a base he would make a great forward feet-first plunge, plowing along on the side of his feet with his face turned toward the man making the throw intending to catch him. His hip would strike the ground about the time his feet reached the base bag, and, rebounding, he would come to a standing position fully prepared to continue his chase around the bases in case the throw was not right on the mark" (A. H. Spink, *The National Game*, 186).

But the pop-up slide appears to have been viewed still as a bit of a novelty in the early twentieth century. The *Washington Post* reported in 1904 that Billy Gilbert "slides more naturally than any other player on the team, with the possible exception of [Sandow] Mertes, in fact, it isn't a slide with Gilbert. He simply doubles up and then straightens out. When he straightens out he is on his feet" (*Washington Post*, September 25, 1904).

Christy Mathewson observed in 1912 that teammate Red Murray got to about eight feet from the base and then jumped "into the air, giving the fielder a vision of two sets of nicely honed spikes aimed for the base. As Murray hits the bag, he comes up on his feet and is in a position to start for the next station in case of any fumble or slip" (Christy Mathewson, *Pitching in a Pinch*, 265).

James Bready contended that this slide was reintroduced, with a new name, much later: "An example of Negro League style later adopted by the majors was the so-called scuttlefish slide: a runner goes into a base feet first and horizontal, but in the same motion bounces up, to end standing on the bag" (James Bready, *Baseball in Baltimore*, 182).

5.2.5 Sliding Drills. As noted under "Slides" (5.2.1), Gus Schmelz engaged his players in extensive sliding practice before the 1887 season. By the 1890s such drills were becoming more widespread. Walter C. Dohm noted in 1893, ". . . While the snow still lies deep on the ground, the collegian who hopes to get a place on the nine . . . practices base running by running at full speed, taking a dive that betrays a reckless disregard of life and limb, and slides along flat on his stomach on a narrow strip of oilcloth placed for that purpose on a thin gymnasium matting on the floor" (Walter C. Dohm, "College Baseball," *Los Angeles Times*, May 21, 1893).

By the early twentieth century the practice had made its way to the major leagues, as this 1913 account shows: "One feature [Cubs manager Johnny] Evers has insisted upon is a sliding pit. That consists of a pit of sand with a regular base attached to the ground in the middle. The athletes can take a good run and slide into the base with little danger of injury. Manager McGraw of the Giants has had this feature in his camp for a number of years and claims it has helped much in developing the great base running team he has" (*Chicago Tribune*, June 19, 1913).

Branch Rickey became widely associated with the sliding pit and he undoubtedly popularized it, but he obviously did not invent such drills.

(iii) Stop, Thief!: Pickoffs, Pitchouts, and Other Countermoves by the Defense

5.3.1 Pickoff Moves. The development of pickoff moves is nearly as old as pitching itself. The best indication of this is that as early as 1858 the rules specified that "whenever the pitcher draws back his hand, or moves with the apparent purpose or pretension to deliver the ball, he shall so deliver it." The addition of such a provision is a sure sign that pickoffs were already familiar sights.

In 1860 the *Brooklyn Eagle* recorded: "[Mattie] O'Brien played finely, both in pitching and watching the bases; in the latter respect he kept his opponents well on the bases when they reached them. He caught [Frank] Pidgeon napping at first base in capital style" (*Brooklyn Eagle*, October 30, 1860).

As the sophistication of pitchers' efforts increased, the *Detroit Advertiser and Tribune* reported after an 1866 match: "Never was better work done by the pitcher, catcher, and [first] baseman than by the Detroit nine." When an Excelsior base runner named McNally reached first base in the sixth inning, the teamwork of pitcher Henry Burroughs, catcher Frank Phelps, and first baseman John Clark "excited intense interest. McNally endeavored to 'steal,' but he was so closely watched that he dared not move his length from the base. The ball would pass with the rapidity of a cannon shot from the hands of Burroughs to Phelps, who stood close to the batsman and received it firmly in his hands, and if McNally was off the base the ball would fly to

Clark so quick that one would think it had actually bounded from Phelps' hands in that direction. Clark caught it with the same precision, and not merely caught it, but with the same motion brought it in contact with McNally. The latter soon learned not to leave his base further than his length, and as soon as he saw Burroughs or Phelps make the least motion towards the base, he would drop flat with his hands on it. This interesting scene was finally brought to a close by Burroughs getting the ball into Clark quicker than McNally could drop, and thus putting him out" (*Detroit Advertiser and Tribune*, July 3, 1866).

Henry Burroughs was a transplanted Easterner, and his technique for keeping runners close to the base attracted considerable notice. A Chicago paper was impressed by how he "springs from most perfect repose to lightning like pitching, which makes the bases look sharp" (*Chicago Times*, reprinted in the *Detroit Free Press*, June 30, 1866). Others were soon imitating him, such as Continental of Kalamazoo pitcher J. Ezra White, whose "pitching excited many comments, as it is different from anything we ever saw in that line. He stands squarely, facing the striker, both feet on a line parallel with the striker's position, and so that he can keep a watchful eye on first base, as many know to their sorrow. Many come to grief in attempting to steal bases, but White makes no preliminary movement in delivery before the ball leaves his hand, and the other players feared a throw from [catcher Jerome] Trowbridge" (*Detroit Advertiser and Tribune*, July 16, 1866).

Pitchers did not always earn such commendation for such attentiveness. Henry Chadwick grumbled in 1867, "The Rose Hill pitcher . . . has an objectionable habit of throwing to bases, which in this game delayed it nearly an hour. Not one time out of twenty does this style of play succeed, wild throwing generally giving men their bases ten times where one is caught napping; besides which, it ought never to be attempted unless by signal from the catcher" (*The Ball Player's Chronicle*, June 20, 1867).

Although these comments show that the pickoff move was established very early, a distinction must be noted. Since underhand pitching and one-step deliveries were mandated, pickoff moves did not have to simulate the windup, which meant that much of the interplay that now exists between pitchers and base runners did not exist. Most base runners began to take modest leads, and pickoff tosses accordingly became scarce in the 1870s. Henry Chadwick was only overstating the case a little when he wrote in 1881: "Throwing to first base to catch a runner napping was a frequent thing in the old days—now it is justly regarded as a play of only exceptional occurrence" (*New York Clipper*, January 22, 1881).

Then overhand pitching and windups came into vogue. Base runners had a brand-new opportunity and pitchers had a whole new problem. If a base runner broke when the pitcher began his windup, the catcher would have very little chance to throw him out. The only way to combat this was to evolve a windup that would keep the batter guessing as to whether the throw would go to first base or to the plate. Perhaps the most extreme approach was employed by Philadelphia's Con Murphy. Although Murphy was a right-hander, with a runner on first he stood facing the base runner until he suddenly pivoted and threw to the plate (*St. Louis Post-Dispatch*, September 24, 1884).

While the first truly deceptive pickoff move of the windup era is a subjective issue, there is a surprisingly firm consensus as to the man who deserves credit. The name that invariably is cited is left-hander Matt Kilroy. Ernest Lanigan wrote that "Matt was the best man in the country at picking men off base. It was suicide to take a lead of more than a foot off first" (Ernest Lanigan, *The Baseball Cyclopedia*, 86).

Sportswriter William Rankin noted that Kilroy "made the same step forward as though he was going to pitch, but would shoot the ball underhanded to first base, instead of 'putting it over the plate.' . . . A base runner had no more chance than has one when the baseman hides the ball. . . . Tim Keefe introduced the trick in the National League during the summer of 1886, I think it was, but being right-handed, he could not do it as cleverly as Kilroy did, but he got away with it for a while, and then there was such a grand howl over it that umpires were instructed to call it a balk. After Kilroy had 'turned his trick' at old Washington Park, I went to [Brooklyn owners Charles Byrne and Joseph Doyle] and showed them how it was done and told them that the base runner had no chance what ever, and they made a fight against it" (*Sporting News*, September 2, 1909).

Kilroy explained to Christy Mathewson how he developed his move: "I practised looking at the home plate stone and throwing at first base with a snap of the wrist and without moving my feet. It was stare steady at the batter, then the arm up to about my ear, and zip, with a twist of the wrist at first base, and you've got him!" (Christy Mathewson, *Pitching in a Pinch*, 224).

Sportswriter J. C. Kofoed claimed that Kilroy and Nick Altrock, another left-hander, were the first pitchers to develop deliveries so deceptive that base runners "had no idea whether the ball was going to home or to the plate" (*Sporting News*, December 8, 1921).

5.3.2 Ambidextrous Pickoffs. This tactic was surprisingly frequent in the days before it was common for pitchers to wear gloves. An 1867 account noted, "Schomp's pitching is worthy of notice, as he pitches with his right hand and throws with his left to second base without moving in his position" (*The Ball Player's Chronicle*, June 20, 1867). It was reported in 1886 that Icebox Chamberlain threw right-handed to home but left-handed to first base on pickoffs (*The Official Baseball Record*, September 20, 1886). Cliff Blau found an 1889 account that claimed that John Sowders had pitched left-handed while in the minors but made pickoff throws to first right-handed (*Sporting Life*, June 19, 1889).

David Nemec claimed that Tony Mullane sometimes carried this tactic still further, by hiding "his hands behind his back as he began his delivery, keeping a batter guessing until the last instant as to which arm would launch the ball" (David Nemec, *The Beer and Whisky League*, 130). In 1887 this tactic was eliminated by a new rule mandating that the pitcher "hold the ball, before the delivery, fairly in front of his body, and in sight of the Umpire."

5.3.3 Pickoffs at Second. The preceding entry included a description of an 1867 pitcher who used his nonthrowing hand to try to nab base runners at second base. Pickoffs were clearly established by that year, as Henry Chadwick observed a couple of weeks later: ". . . Not being aware of a sharp dodge which [Phonney] Martin plays to perfection, [base runner Crawford] was caught napping between second and third. The way of it was this: Martin would take his position facing the striker, as if to pitch, but without making any movement to deliver, would suddenly turn and face the second baseman, and nearly every time would catch the base runner off his base by the rapidity with which he would turn and throw the ball to second" (*The Ball Player's Chronicle*, July 4, 1867).

5.3.4 Seesaw Play. Once the shortstop began to share responsibilities for covering second base (see **4.2.6**), a runner at that bag was placed in a uniquely vulnerable position of being outnumbered by the enemy. His peril was increased by his status as the only base runner without a coach in the immediate vicinity to alert him to danger.

Harvard seems to have been the first club to begin systematically to exploit this weakness: "The Harvard base ball men have hatched up a trick which they claim will catch nearly every opponent who is lucky enough to steal second base. It is played between the pitcher, second baseman, and short stop, and its object is to confuse the player who may be stealing from second to third base. It is, as nearly as can be described, as follows: The player who has succeeded in reaching second base, on seeing that baseman step back to his usual position, about ten feet back of the base line, steals several feet down the path toward third. When he is about in front of the short stop that player makes a dash toward second base, which causes the runner to dart in that direction also, but the short stop's run is only a feint, and the runner, on seeing the short stop stop, also stops before reaching second, and the pitcher throws the ball to the second baseman, who is on base, and whom the runner has entirely forgotten, and the runner is out" (*New York Sun*, April 26, 1889).

As runners became more alert to this play, defensive players varied the method of attack. Dudley Dean of Harvard explained in 1892: "The see-saw play is sometimes well worked by short and second, the runner being caught by a sharp throw by the pitcher to one of the fielders mentioned when the runner's attention is diverted by the movements of the other" (syndicated article, *Atlanta Constitution*, June 5, 1892). Even when the seesaw play did not result in a pickoff, it could still benefit the defense by keeping a base runner closer to second base.

5.3.5 Pickoffs with Second Baseman Covering First. The seesaw play was effective because of the vulnerability of the outnumbered runner at second base. It was not long before defenses began to experiment with plays that would extend this principle to other bases.

Sporting Life's Pittsburgh correspondent reported in 1905: ". . . The Boston team worked a pretty fair trick here last season and one that looked to have some earmarks of newness at least. [Ed] Phelps was on first base. [Boston first baseman Fred] Tenney, after a few maneuvers to hold Phelps to the bag, pretended not to pay any attention to him and with the pitch started to 'run in' as if expecting the batsman to bunt the ball. Phelps, thus taken off his guard, began to assume a large lead for second base. Tenney again started to 'run in.' The next pitch was a wide one. Suddenly the catcher shot the ball to first base. [Fred] Raymer had run up to the bag without Phelps' knowledge. He caught the ball, blocked Phelps off the base and had him out by two yards" (*Sporting Life*, June 24, 1905).

5.3.6 Pickoffs with an Outfielder Covering Second. As if it weren't bad enough that runners on second base were double-teamed on pickoff plays, on a few rare occasions center fielders have also become involved.

On Decoration Day in 1887, New York's George Gore sneaked in on an unsuspecting runner at second base and Tim Keefe threw to Gore for the pickoff (*Cleveland Leader and Herald*, June 5, 1887). Johnny Evers and Hugh Fullerton reported that Chicago infielders Bill Dahlen and Bill Eagan would sometimes run a variation on the seesaw play in which center fielder Bill Lange would sneak in to apply the coup de grâce (John J. Evers and Hugh S. Fullerton, *Touching Second*, 216–217; Eagan had only a very short career with Chicago, so they may be mistaken about that part of their account).

Brooklyn center fielder Hi Myers provided a spectacular example in a game against the Cardinals on July 24, 1915. The game was tied in the ninth inning, but St. Louis had loaded the bases with only one out. Dodgers pitcher Sherrod Smith was engaged in a mound conference with several teammates when "Hi Myers ambled up from center as if to lend a hand to the discussion. He was within a few feet of second, and [Art] Butler, who held the bag, was paying no attention to him, nor were the coaches more wide awake, when Smith received the signal from Otto Miller to throw. Sherrod threw. He wheeled and let the ball go to second, leaving the rest up to Myers. It was a good heave. Myers grabbed the throw and tagged Butler, the while the other Cardinals were so astounded they never made a move." Smith retired the next batter and Brooklyn won the game in the tenth (*Brooklyn Eagle*, July 25, 1915).

Retrosheet uncovered another instance of this play in a game on September 13, 1949, with the Red Sox hosting the Tigers. Johnny Pesky was on second base with two out in the third inning when Detroit center fielder Hoot Evers sneaked in behind him to begin a 1-8-5 pickoff.

Center fielders also occasionally covered second base on bunt plays. Tris Speaker was renowned for playing a shallow center field and took advantage of this on at least one occasion to record a putout at second base. In a May 2, 1919, game, Detroit's Ira Flagstead had been advanced from first to second on a bunt. With the infielders in motion and nobody apparently covering second, Flagstead rounded the base. Speaker sneaked in behind him and took a snap throw to record the out (*Detroit Free Press*, May 3, 1919).

5.3.7   Fake to Third, Throw to First Pickoffs. This pickoff play is used with runners on first and third. It takes advantage of the fact that pitchers cannot fake a throw to first without being called for a balk, but can do so at other bases. Accordingly, the pitcher fakes a throw to third, then wheels and throws to first.

This tactic has only become common in recent years, and it is much maligned for the ostensible reason that it rarely appears to work. Tim McCarver, for example, wrote that it is successful "as often as the sun rises in the west" (Tim McCarver with Danny Peary, *Tim McCarver's Baseball for Brain Surgeons and Other Fans*, 300). McCarver did acknowledge that the Mets picked Cincinnati's Jon Nunnally off first with this play in 1997. It was also worked successfully on as savvy a base runner as Ichiro Suzuki in one of his first years in the American League.

In spite of these exceptions, there is no disputing the fact that the play rarely results in a pickoff. But those who criticize this play overlook its main purpose: to prevent the runner from breaking on the pitcher's first move. It not only accomplishes that goal but does so without the risk of a wild throw that usually accompanies a pickoff attempt.

Perhaps that lack of risk explains why this play is so frequently and roundly condemned by announcers and fans. Their displeasure is likely with the unfairness of the play, since the defense gains an advantage—albeit a small one—without any corresponding risk.

5.3.8   Pickoffs by Relay. In 1900, Arlie Latham attributed to Mike Kelly another play that used a base runner's aggressiveness against him. With Kelly catching and runners on second and third, "I've seen him whip the ball to third. That baseman would pay no attention to the runner at his bag, but relay the ball to second, and nine times out of ten the fellow at that base would be caught off his balance." Latham claimed that the play "rarely failed to land one man" (*Sporting Life*, December 15, 1900).

5.3.9   Pitching from the Stretch. Until the late 1880s, pitchers worked under restrictions that precluded elaborate windups. Once windups (see **3.1.1**) became legal, pitchers immediately began to use simpler deliveries when there were runners on base.

Pitcher Tim Keefe counseled in 1889, "When the bases are occupied by a base runner, the pitcher should shorten and quicken his delivery, so as to enable the catcher to dispose of the base runner in his attempt to steal a base, in case he should run" (*Sporting Times*, reprinted in the *Cleveland Plain Dealer*, May 19, 1889). A newspaper account that year observed: "[Bert] Cunningham, Baltimore's clever little pitcher, still does the 'wind-the-clock act' while delivering the ball when none of the bases are occupied" (*New York Sun*, April 30, 1889).

5.3.10   Slide Steps. The slide step became a standard part of the pitcher's repertoire in the 1960s in the wake of the revival of the stolen base. But there were forerunners of the slide step among the first wave of sophisticated pickoff moves that were developed in the late 1880s. In 1891 the *Williamsport Sunday Grit* gave this description of Pud Galvin's move to first: "Galvin is a short and rather fat old fellow, and the balk, or rather half-balk, by which he has caught many a good base-runner napping at first, consists of a jumping-jack movement which seems to be perpetual to the old fellow. The minute he steps in the box the movement commences. He always looks as if he were just ready to deliver the ball. He starts with a half-drop of his legs and forward movement of his body without removing one foot from the box. The runner takes a good lead off first. Then, with a smile that is childlike and bland, the veteran shoots the ball over to first and catches his man. Captains kick and claim that it is a balk, but Galvin gets right back at them and the best of the argument by claiming and proving that the movement is his natural one in the box" (*Williamsport Sunday Grit*, June 14, 1891). While this is less sophisticated than today's slide step, it does seem to include some of the key elements.

5.3.11   Pitchouts. In an 1874 game between the Mutuals of New York and the Atlantics of Brooklyn, Mutuals batsman Jack Burdock "in the seventh

was guilty of a very unfair piece of play in attempting to strike at a ball entirely out of his reach in order to keep [Atlantics catcher Jack] Farrow from
throwing out [base runner Candy] Nelson trying to steal. For this he should
have been declared out by umpire Allison but the umpire not being conver-
sant with the rules, he wasn't" (reprinted in Preston D. Orem, *Baseball
[1845–1881] from the Newspaper Accounts*, 185).

There is little in this account to suggest that the pitcher intentionally
threw the pitch out of the batter's reach. In one of life's little ironies, it thus
seems possible that the first attempt to foil a pitchout may have preceded the
development of the pitchout itself.

By the 1890s the pitchout had definitely begun to emerge. In 1894
catcher Heinie Peitz explained: "If I am reasonably sure that an attempt to
steal will be made on the next pitched ball, I signal for a high straight ball to
the right of the plate if the batter is right-handed, and to the left if he is a
south-paw, and if my throw is accurate and my pitcher has not allowed him
to get too much of a start, I'll nip my man every time" (*St. Louis Post-Dispatch*, September 23, 1894).

The popularity of this stratagem increased greatly after the turn of the
century. *Sporting Life*'s Chicago correspondent reported in 1902: "In the
New York games here it got so that after every runner got to first [catcher
Frank] Bowerman leaned far out on the next ball thrown, and called for a
wide one, so as to nip the expected steal" (*Sporting Life*, May 17, 1902).
When Cy Young coached at Mercer University in Georgia in 1903, he
taught the pitchout to the students, which was said to be new to the region
(Reed Browning, *Cy Young*, 125).

It took very little time before the strategy spread more widely. Deacon
Phillippe explained in 1904 that with the hit-and-run on, "the pitcher's play
is to deliver the ball so far from the plate that the batter cannot possibly hit
it and at the right height to enable the catcher to make a quick throw to second" (Deacon Phillippe, "Phillippe of Pittsburg Team Discusses Requirements of Successful Pitchers," *Syracuse Post Standard*, March 27, 1904).

Later that season the *Washington Post* observed, "Pitchers are so skillful
these days that when a batter reaches first base one or two balls may be
thrown wide to the succeeding batsmen at times when the twirler believes
the base runner is going to try to steal. Throwing the ball wide gives the
catcher the chance to receive the ball and throw it to second base without
being compelled to straighten out for the throw or side step the batter, who
usually attempts to block a throw through a little trickery" (*Washington Post*,
September 10, 1904).

Pitchouts became increasingly commonplace, as is shown by sportswriter
J. Ed Grillo's description in 1908: "A good catcher must, of course, be a good
receiver and thrower, but it is with men on bases that a catcher is required

to display judgment. He must know the game and realize when his opponents are going to do a certain thing and block their play. The hit and run game, for instance, can only be broken up by the catcher. He must know when the base runner is going to steal, and in order to prevent the batsman from helping the runner, he wastes the ball, which means to have the pitcher pitch it out of reach of the batsman, so that he cannot hit and at the same time gives the catcher a clear throw to second or third, as the case may be. A base runner, of course, tries to create the impression that he is going to steal when he isn't so that the catcher will waste the ball. By so doing he helps the batter, because he gets the pitcher in the hole. One frequently sees the catcher wasting two, and as many as three balls without seeing the runner leave first base, which indicates that the base runner has outguessed the catcher" (*Washington Post*, April 25, 1908).

5.3.12 Spontaneous Pitchouts. In 2000, *Sports Illustrated* reported on an innovative new version of the pitchout: "Padres catcher Carlos Hernandez has found a way to make up for righthander Stan Spencer's glacial move to the plate, against which the Marlins stole 10 bases on May 18. Hernandez told Spencer about a trick he learned while playing winter ball with former major league pitcher Urbano Lugo five years ago: When the catcher sees the runner take off, he jumps from behind the plate as if expecting a pitchout. Whereupon the pitcher throws a fastball, regardless of what was called. The tactic worked in Spencer's next start, against the Mets, when Hernandez gunned down Edgardo Alfonzo in the first inning. Alfonzo was the last Met to try to steal in that game" (*Sports Illustrated*, June 5, 2000).

5.3.13 Short Throws. The use of the short throw to defend against delayed double steals (see **5.1.3**) was already well known by 1874 when Henry Chadwick reported, "When a player is on the first base and one on the third, and the catcher holds the ball ready to throw to second, the short-stop should get nearly on the line of the pitcher and second baseman, and have an understanding with the catcher to have him throw the ball to short-stop instead of second base, for, seeing the ball leave the catcher's hands apparently for second base, the player on third will be apt to leave for home, in which case the short-stop will have the ball in hand ready to throw to the catcher on third base" (Henry Chadwick, *The American Base Ball Manual*, 28).

In 1879, Chadwick observed that a new wrinkle had been developed: "A point played last season with good effect at times was that of the catcher throwing to short-stop when a runner was on third, and another ran down from first to second to get the man on third home. This was not done in the old style of throwing to short-stop's position, but in throwing a little to the left of second base, the short-stop jumping forward and taking the ball and promptly returning it to the catcher in time. When the ball [sic] swiftly thrown and accurately returned, the play invariably yields an out; but it must be is [sic] understood by signal to be done effectively" (*New York Clipper*, December 20, 1879).

Another instance occurred in 1886 in an exhibition game between Boston's National League club and the Haverhills of the New England League. In the third inning the visiting Haverhills "were prevented from scoring by sharp fielding. In this inning McKeever got in a safe hit, stole second and went to third on [John] Irwin's single. With only one out the crowd fully expected a run, but [catcher Pat] Dealey and [second baseman Jack] Burdock rigged an amateur derrick on [James] McKeever, who was swung up on it like a lamb. Irwin made a break for second. Dealey threw the ball in the same direction. McKeever started home only to be met by the ball, which Burdock received just back of [pitcher Charlie] Parsons and returned to Dealey to McKeever's sorrow" (*Boston Globe*, June 10, 1886).

Although that account referred to the short throw rather condescendingly as an "amateur derrick," the play continued to develop in succeeding years and often proved effective. In 1904 the *Washington Post* noted: "Of the various problems that are presented in baseball, the proper time to steal a base and whether or not to try to prevent it is one of the most complicated. A puzzling feature of this important point of the game, and one that invariably causes comment among spectators is the ease with which a runner generally achieves a steal of second base with a team mate on third and none or one out. This play has resulted in the evolution of the 'short throw,' one of the best of baseball tactics, and a play that has been developed to a high state of efficiency by some catchers not identified with the clubs at present in the running in either the National or American League races. The idea of a runner stealing from first to second with a man on third is to draw a throw and allow the runner on third base to score during the resultant put-out or attempt to retire. Different managers hold various ideas about the wisdom of taking a certain put-out at the expense of a run. Some instruct their catchers in such cases to be guided by the score and to throw to second if their team is behind on the score board.

"The 'short throw,' however, while it allows the runner to reach second safely, usually results as intended—in catching the runner at third in an attempt to score on the play. It is not a throw to be relayed by the pitcher. Instead, the ball is jerked quickly to a point about ten feet short of second, to be met there by the shortstop, and as the man on third forms the conclusion that the ball was intended to go into play to catch the runner from first, he immediately starts for home, where quick return by the shortstop catches him off the plate. The advantage gained by shortening the throw is just what is required to get the ball back to the plate in time, and, unlike the relay from catcher to pitcher and to second, is quick and deceptive. Few pitchers are quick enough to take a throw and turn in time to get it to second to catch the runner from first. On the other hand, any shortstop can take a 'short throw,' provided he is looking for it, and the return to first or a throw to third involves no particular headwork. A third method of dealing with such a situation is the bluff by a catcher that he is going to throw to second, although the ball is not allowed to leave his hand in the swing around. At times this entices a runner to leave third base for the run home, but as a general thing he is not deceived and the base is stolen without effort" (*Washington Post*, September 18, 1904).

(iv) Plays

As discussed in the chapter on hitting, early batters had all the advantages and therefore had little reason to do anything other than swing from the heels. Only when pitchers began to gain the upper hand in the 1870s did batters begin to work on more innovative ways of getting on base. The origins of the bunt are discussed in the chapter on hitting, but by the 1880s the "baby hit" also had come of age and was spawning new plays, many of which turned back the clock to the pre-Knickerbocker games in which the bat was little more than a mechanism for commencing a lively chase.

5.4.1 Bluff Bunts. Once the bunt had become a major part of the offensive repertoire, players realized that a crafty fake bunt could sometimes accomplish the same end without sacrificing an out.

Johnny Evers and Hugh S. Fullerton explained in 1910, "The 'bluff bunt,' aimed to pull defensive infielders out of position, has resulted in a variety of plays, all based on the same principle. Possibly the cleverest variation is the 'bluff bunt' used as a substitute for the sacrifice hit to advance runners, especially from second to third base. . . . The batter was ordered to pretend to bunt, miss the ball purposely and shove his body over the plate so as to interfere slightly with the catcher's vision. The third baseman, expecting a bunt, comes forward rapidly, leaving the base unguarded. The runners, who have been signaled, start to run as the pitcher winds up, and the leading runner is expected to slide safe back of third base before the third baseman can get back to the base and catch the throw" (John J. Evers and Hugh S. Fullerton, *Touching Second*, 205–206).

The Detroit Tigers were masters of the play, as is shown by this 1914 account: "[Marty Kavanagh's] steal of third in the opening frame was a pretty play. [Ty] Cobb drew [Boston third baseman Larry] Gardner in with a bluff bunt and Marty beat him in a race to the bag after [catcher Bill] Carrigan had pegged to the baseman. This maneuver has been worked repeatedly since the start of the season and seldom fails to accomplish its purpose" (*Detroit Free Press*, May 17, 1914).

5.4.2   Push or Force Bunts. Johnny Evers and Hugh Fullerton explained in 1910, "The 'force bunt' was brought into prominence by little [Frank] Butler, of Columbus. . . . He pushed the ball slowly down the infield, striving to make it roll fast enough to pass the pitcher either to his right or his left, yet so slowly that the short stop or second baseman, playing deep, would have to take it while sprinting forward at top speed and make a perfect throw" (John J. Evers and Hugh S. Fullerton, *Touching Second*, 161–162).

5.4.3   Drag Bunts. F. C. Lane observed in 1925, "There is a method of diversified attack which has crept into batting which combines some of the peculiarities of the bunt and the hit. Players call it, 'dragging the ball.'" He quoted John Tobin: "Dragging the ball is simple on paper. Before the ball even gets to the plate, you start full speed for first. As the ball crosses the plate, you hook the bat around it and drag it past the pitcher. You hold the bat precisely as if you were going to hit the ball through the infielders. If you execute the play properly, you will have a grand lead to first base" (F. C. Lane, *Batting*, 85). Carson Bigbee added, "I use the drag play perhaps fifty times a year. It's a neat little play when properly executed" (F. C. Lane, *Batting*, 86).

5.4.4   Left-side Hit-and-run. Merwin Jacobson, who starred for the Baltimore Orioles' International League dynasty of the early 1920s, described a play that the club called the left-side hit-and-run: "[Fritz] Maisel, leading off, would get aboard; [Otis] Lawry would sacrifice; I was up next, the heavy hitter, and I'd bunt, toward third. Maisel, off with the pitch, would round third, never slowing. While the third baseman was running in after the ball and trying to throw me out, Maisel would score, most often standing" (quoted in James Bready, *Baseball in Baltimore*, 142).

5.4.5   Squeeze Play. The squeeze play was popularized and probably named by Clark Griffith's New York Highlanders in 1905.

   Early that season the *Chicago Tribune* referred to "the new 'squeeze' play" (*Chicago Tribune*, April 25, 1905). Nine days later the same newspaper described it as "Griffith's famed 'squeeze' play." The most popular version of the play's origins was that pitcher Jack Chesbro, after reaching third base in a 1904 game, broke for home because he mistakenly thought he had been given the steal sign. Batter Wee Willie Keeler alertly bunted, and Chesbro scored easily. Manager Clark Griffith saw promise in the play, practiced it during spring training in 1905, and began to use it.

Joe Yeager's obituary in 1937 credited him with inventing the squeeze play (*Sporting News*, July 15, 1937). The article offered no details, but Yeager was also on the Highlanders in 1905.

Other clubs soon began to imitate the play, though mostly in the American League. In 1907 the play was worked 108 times—87 times in the American League but only 21 times in the National League (*New York Sun*, March 3, 1918).

As soon as the squeeze play became popular, earlier claimants emerged. Algy McBride said: "I have been reading up a play where a man bunts with a fast runner on third base and the latter starts with the pitch. That isn't new. [Ned] Hanlon and his Baltimores when we faced them were always pulling off something that you wasn't [sic] looking for. This was one of their tricks. Of course they could not work it often, but when they had a rapid runner on third bag and a good bunter up, I tell you an infield had to be up and moving to get the ball home. Fact, the play wasn't good at home for the catcher often chased the bunt and there was no one to cover the plate" (quoted in *Sporting Life*, May 20, 1905).

Lee Allen credited Yale's George Case and Dutch Carter with using the play against Princeton in 1894 (Lee Allen, *The Hot Stove League*, 95). Others maintained that it dated back to Cap Anson, Mike Kelly, and the Chicago White Stockings (Lee Allen, *Cooperstown Corner*, 83).

An alternative view was that it was a play that had been tried previously and found wanting. Longtime player and manager Charley Morton contended, "I recall the squeeze play as early as 1883, but it was not worked extensively. Such plays then were considered 'freaks,' to be used only infrequently" (quoted in *Sporting News*, March 19, 1908).

The outspoken Joe Cantillon went further, contending that the play wasn't worth inventing in the first place. After proclaiming in 1914 that no new plays of merit had been invented in recent years, he added: "I will admit that the new school has brought the squeeze play into the game. I will also admit that it is the rottenest play in base ball when it fails. Furthermore it is an admission from the player who makes it on his own accord that he cannot hit and when the manager asks for it he shows that he has lost confidence in the hitting of the player asked to squeeze" (*Minneapolis Journal*, reprinted in *Sporting News*, May 28, 1914).

One candidate for the earliest squeeze play is one that occurred in 1877, when a game account recorded that Tim Murnane's "bunt near the home-plate allowed [Ezra] Sutton to score while [catcher Charley] Snyder was throwing the striker out" (*Louisville Courier-Journal*, July 13, 1877). But this raises the important and unanswerable issue of Murnane's intentions and the equally irresolvable philosophical question of whether something is really a first if it occurs by accident.

Clark Griffith answered the second query with a resounding no: "I don't doubt that base runners were scored years ago with the aid of bunts, but these plays were of a desultory and accidental nature. The highlanders were the first team to adopt the 'squeeze' as a regular play, as the first team to work it scientifically. The way we came to work the 'squeeze play' was this: We had several men on the team who, while they were good hitters, did not punch the ball any great distance, as a rule—men like Billy Keeler, 'Kid' Elberfeld and one or two others. Whenever we had a man on third and one of those chaps at the bat, we could not depend on them to drive out a long fly. Then the question arose: How could we best turn the batting ability of these men to account under such conditions? Every one of them could bunt, and so the idea of having them bunt at the same time that the man on third dashed for home occurred to us. And that's how the 'squeeze' play originated and was made a scientific adjunct to base ball" (*Sporting News*, March 25, 1909).

Griffith made a valid point, but he overstated his case in claiming that earlier squeeze plays had been "of a desultory and accidental nature." Doc Bushong of the St. Louis Brown Stockings wrote in 1887: "With a man on third, it is confessedly the play in base ball to bring him in. A man comes to the bat, and to make a successful 'bunt' he must bring the bat in front of the plate, the same as if he were batting, only not with the same force. If he bunts and it goes fair, the run is made" (letter to *National Base Ball Gazette*; reprinted in the *Cleveland Leader and Herald*, April 24, 1887). In addition, the next entry suggests that the double squeeze may have been in use as early as 1890.

It seems clear, then, that the squeeze play was far from unknown in the nineteenth century but was raised to a new level of prominence in 1905 by Clark Griffith and the New York Highlanders. The play then became enormously popular in the low-scoring environment of the next few seasons, but that level of frequency could not be sustained. John McGraw pronounced the play fundamentally unsound and used it rarely. Christy Mathewson explained: "McGraw objects to the squeeze play because he believes that a brainy pitcher ought to break up the play and prevent its success by pitching the ball so wide that the batsman is not able to bunt it" (quoted in A. H. Spink, *The National Game*, 281).

As defenses became more alert to the possibility, the play declined in effectiveness and frequency, leading one 1911 article to refer to the "practical abolishment of the squeeze play by managers" (*Mansfield* [Ohio] *News*, September 23, 1911). Of course the squeeze play did not entirely die but instead receded to a level of usage where it could again benefit from the element of surprise.

5.4.6 Double Squeeze Play. The double squeeze is an electrifying play that had a brief period of prominence but is largely forgotten today. With runners on second and third and less than two out, both runners break with the pitch. The batter then bunts, allowing the runner on third to score easily. When the infielder throws to first to retire the batter, the runner on second rounds third and continues home. Thus two runs score on a bunt.

There is at least one claim that the play originated as early as 1890. Sportswriter Stanley T. Milliken recorded in 1913, "As far back as the Brotherhood year, which was 1890, the Boston Players' League team used to use this scheme for acquiring runs. Arthur Irwin, scout of the Highlanders, has in his possession scrapbooks showing that Kelly's Killers frequently made two runs on a bunt to the infield" (Stanley T. Milliken, *Washington Post*, October 31, 1913).

Sportswriter Biddy Bishop wrote in 1911 that Pacific Coast League player Mike Lynch of Tacoma had invented the double squeeze in 1904. During an exhibition game, Lynch was on second when a squeeze was ordered. He broke with the pitch and scored, but captain Charley Graham dismissed the play as a fluke.

So Lynch "put the 'double squeeze' on record" in a game against Portland: "The opportunity came in the fourth inning. [George] McLaughlin was on third and Lynch on second as in the previous game. 'Happy' Hogan . . . was batting. The signal came on the third ball and McLaughlin took a long lead. As he did so Lynch was almost down to third. McLaughlin tore in and Lynch came on like a deer for third. Rounding the bag he dug his spikes into the dirt and beat it hard. . . . McLaughlin crossed the plate before the ball had hardly left the pitcher and Lynch was right at his heels, scoring standing up."

That still didn't convince Graham, who "declared he was taking a drink of water at the time and didn't see the play. 'Well, I'll show it to you again,' said Mike, and the very next day at Los Angeles he pulled off the same identical thing" (*Sporting News*, March 30, 1911).

The first known occurrence of the double squeeze in a major league game took place when the Cubs faced Brooklyn on July 15, 1905. With the bases loaded and one out in the fifth, "[Chicago base runner Jimmy] Slagle started for home and [Chicago batter Joe] Tinker bunted, going out on [Brooklyn catcher Bill] Bergen's throw to [Brooklyn first baseman Doc] Gessler, but before Gessler had returned the ball to the plate [Chicago base runner Billy] Maloney was over with the second run, making the record number of runs off the squeeze play" (*Chicago Tribune*, July 16, 1905; *New York Sun*, March 3, 1918).

A week later the play was copied by Detroit. Sportswriter Paul Bruske recounted: "The only time I ever saw the squeeze play worked for two runs at once occurred in the first game against Philadelphia Saturday [July 22]. With men on second and third, [Herman] Schaefer bunted. [Tom] Doran, on third, had started for the plate with the swing of [pitcher Eddie] Plank's arm and the Athletics' infield dashed to get the bunt. [First baseman] Harry Davis took it almost off the bat, but even then couldn't get Doran. Accordingly, he fired to [second baseman Danny] Murphy at first and retired Schaefer, never thinking of Dick Cooley, who had taken a big lead off second and never stopped, scoring with ease" (*Sporting Life*, July 29, 1905). That was likely also the first time Athletics manager Connie Mack saw the play, and it may have planted a seed in his mind.

The double squeeze continued to appear from time to time in the next few years but was generally regarded as a novelty. A 1907 article noted: "To add more interest to the uncertainty of the 'squeeze' play's birthplace 'Kid' Elberfeld and 'Hal' Chase have invented the 'double squeeze' and it is even more spectacular than its sensational predecessor. They tried the new play in a game with Boston at Highland Park and but for the fact that Elberfeld stumbled and fell on the base line both men would have scored on the out. Imagine what ball players twenty years ago would have said if such a play had been even suggested! For one runner to score on an infield out is hard enough, but for two to do so seems physically impossible. They are going to do it this summer, just the same" (*Sporting News*, May 4, 1907).

A 1909 account observed, "Down in the Virginia league some days ago the players of the Norfolk club made a double squeeze play, which is said to be the first one ever even tried. With men on second and third, both scored on the squeeze, the second base runner being a very fast man. The story giving an account of this freak thing says the infielders of the team that allowed this were the fastest in the Virginia League" (*Los Angeles Times*, July 4, 1909). The Giants pulled a double squeeze in a 1910 exhibition game against Jersey City (*New York Times*, April 12, 1910).

Sportswriter Abe Kemp must have been referring to some time around 1910 when he wrote in 1943: "Twice in one season, [Los Angeles] manager Frank Dillon successfully pulled off the double squeeze—unheard of today—in which runners score from second and third on a bunt. Each time the play was maneuvered, [Hughie] Smith was the batter" (*San Francisco Examiner*, January 17, 1943; Smith played for Los Angeles from 1909 to 1912).

In 1913 the play suddenly lost its novelty status. That was the year in which Harry Davis became a full-time coach for Connie Mack's Athletics; a later article credited him with refining and developing the play (*Sporting Life*, November 1922 [monthly]). The Athletics practiced the play extensively during spring training and unveiled it in an exhibition game in San Antonio (*Sporting Life*, March 22, 1913). Once the regular season began, they worked it successfully on no less than eight occasions. Three of those games—on May 22, June 5, and September 22—were against the same Detroit team that had used the play against the Mackmen eight years earlier. The Athletics also pulled off the play on August 2 and 26 versus St. Louis; on September 4 and 6 against Boston; and on September 1 versus Washington. Each time, shortstop Jack Barry was at the plate, and he beat out the bunt on three of those occasions (Stanley T. Milliken, *Washington Post*, October 31, 1913).

In the September 22 game the double squeeze brought home the winning runs in the game that clinched the pennant for the Athletics (*New York Times*, September 23, 1913). Philadelphia again tried "their famous double squeeze" in the eighth inning of the opening game of the World Series, but it failed and base runner Stuffy McInnis was picked off second (*New York Times*, October 8, 1913).

The Athletics continued to use the play in 1914 until it backfired spectacularly in a game against Washington on April 29. Jack Barry popped the bunt up and Chick Gandil caught it and started a triple play. Washington then rallied to win the game 6-4 (Stanley T. Milliken, *Washington Post*, April 30, 1914).

After this disaster, Connie Mack seems to have lost confidence in the double squeeze. According to an article tracked down by researcher Steve Steinberg, the play continued to be used in the major leagues at least a few times a year for the next few years, including at least six times in 1917 (*New York Sun*, March 3, 1918). When the home run era began a few years later, the play was almost entirely forgotten.

Retrosheet volunteer Greg Beston did find that Connie Mack brought the play out of mothballs in 1927. In the ninth inning of the nightcap of an August 16, 1927, doubleheader at Cleveland, Zack Wheat and Chick Galloway both scored on a sacrifice by Jack Quinn of the Athletics (David W. Smith, Retrosheet). But by 1933 sportswriter James M. Gould described the double squeeze as "a play which, in these modern days, never is seen and one which the writer saw completed only once" (*Sporting News*, January 19, 1933).

5.4.7   Hit-and-run. In the first series of the 1894 season, the Baltimore Orioles used the hit-and-run play repeatedly against the New York Giants. This brought a new level of prominence to the play and started a long debate about its origins.

Ted Sullivan later said of the hit-and-run, "The renowned Baltimore Club of '94, '95 and '96 was the team that perfected it and made it the dominant feature of their line of strategy" (*Sporting News*, January 21, 1905). Sportswriter and former player Sam Crane concurred, acknowledging that there were earlier accidental instances of the hit-and-run, but maintaining that it was "inaugurated as a run-making innovation and systematized to a science by the noted Baltimore Orioles in the early 1890s by the shrewdness of John McGraw and Willie Keeler" (Sam Crane, "Hit and Run Play an Oriole Discovery," *Sporting News*, February 10, 1916). But others cited earlier candidates.

Bill James noted that in 1893 John Ward of the New York Giants had credited the Boston club of the early '90s with popularizing the hit-and-run. Boston likely did play an important role in popularizing the play, but James was mistaken to conclude: "It is clear from [Ward's] comments that he had never seen this play before" (Bill James, *The New Bill James Historical Baseball Abstract*, 65).

In fact it can be said with certainty that the hit-and-run was in use before 1893, since the play was described in considerable detail in an 1891 *Sporting Life* article: "There is one point in baserunning which I believe wins many games if systematically carried out. That is the understanding that exists between the base-runner at first and the man at the bat; an understanding the man at bat has that the runner will start to steal on a certain ball pitched—the first, second, third, or whatever it may be. This being communicated to the batter by sign or previous agreement, it becomes his duty to strike at the ball if it be within bounds. Should it be wide the base-runner would probably reach second safely, anyhow.

"But if it be within reach it is the batter's plain duty to hit it or try to hit it. Why? Because the moment the base-runner starts he unsteadies or uncovers one field and sometimes both the second baseman's and short stop's territory. One and sometimes both are sure to start with him toward second base, and if the batter sends a grounder to the man's territory it is turned into a base hit by the tactics instead of a sure out or maybe a double play. This has happened a dozen times in Cleveland during the past season. It is much better to start the base-runner down and let the batsman strike at the ball than keep the runner hugging first and finally get put out in an easy double play" (*Sporting Life*, November 7, 1891).

David Ball discovered an 1890 article by Buck Ewing that makes it explicit that Ward was familiar with the play prior to 1893: "One piece of work that has been very successful with us in 1888 and 1889 was as follows: If [Mike] Tiernan, the batter who preceded me, got first he signaled me when he was ready to start for second, and I would strike at the ball, no matter where it went, endeavoring to put it between the bases toward right, for the second baseman, who was trying to catch Tiernan, would be out of the way. If I hit the ball the speedy Tiernan would surely reach third and Ward, the next batsman would bring in the score" (*Brooklyn Eagle*, November 24, 1890).

It seems just as clear that the play was being used at least occasionally before 1888, but that is where the situation becomes murky. Indeed, there is a baffling array of contradictory statements to sift through.

Longtime sportswriter William Rankin backed up Buck Ewing's claim by crediting Ewing, Johnny Ward, Mike Tiernan, and Danny Richardson of Jim Mutrie's Giants with being experts in the play in the late 1880s (*Sporting News*, July 1, 1905; *Sporting News*, March 3, 1910). Meanwhile columnist W. A. Calhoun wrote in 1900: "The 'hit and run' game of the champion Brooklyns is lauded as 'something new!' . . . Was not this very feature the main stay of the old St. Louis Browns and Detroits, both champion teams, and is not this very point a direct legacy to the Brooklyns from Detroit through Ned Hanlon?" (*Sporting Life*, December 15, 1900). Part of the problem is the difficulty of determining how regular a practice these clubs made of the play. Mickey Welch, for example, commented in 1901, "They played the hit and run game in the eighties; but . . . did not have as many players who could work it as now" (*New York Sun*, reprinted in *Sandusky Daily Star*, July 16, 1901).

Cap Anson's Chicago squad is the club mentioned most frequently. Cap Anson and Charlie Comiskey maintained that the White Stockings invented the hit-and-run in 1876 (*Sporting Life*, November 13, 1897). Ted Sullivan asserted: "The Chicago Club of the early '80's was the team which originated the hit-and-run we hear about so many times of late years" (*Sporting News*, January 21, 1905). A 1905 editorial in *Sporting Life* claimed that the hit-and-run "was in general use in the '80s, and the Providence and Philadelphia teams under Arthur Irwin, and the Chicagos under Anson had it down as fine as any teams in the '90s or the present time" (*Sporting Life*, July 8, 1905). On the other hand, longtime Chicago infielder Tommy Burns said in 1900, "The only thing absolutely new is the hit and run system, and that has only been perfected by a few teams" (*Sporting Life*, November 17, 1900).

The White Stockings of the early 1880s are one of those clubs that has been credited with a suspiciously large number of firsts, but in this case there are a couple of contemporaneous accounts that appear to offer confirmation. On October 7, 1882, in a postseason series against the American Association pennant winners from Cincinnati, Cap Anson's charges pulled a hit-and-run in the first inning. With George Gore running for second, Ned Williamson hit the ball into the hole vacated by second baseman Bid McPhee. The play led to two runs, which held up for a 2-0 Chicago win (Jerry Lansche, *Glory Fades Away*, 30). Researcher David Ball discovered an 1877 account that supports their claim: "Some chap stated the following conundrum, professing not to understand it: 'Why do batsmen strike a ball when a base-runner is half-way to second base on a clever steal?' The answer was found in Thursday's game, when [Cal] McVey started to second base, and [Cap] Anson hit the ball in the exact spot where [St. Louis second baseman Mike] McGeary had been standing before he ran to his base to catch McVey. It is really a clever batting trick to hit to right field when it lies all open" (*Chicago Tribune*, July 1, 1877).

When Tim Murnane heard of Anson and Comiskey's claim, he responded that Boston had invented the play in 1875. Murnane commented: "Other teams have tried it ever since, but usually give it up as a bad job, as it is not always possible to make this play a success" (*Sporting Life*, November 13, 1897). Jim O'Rourke claimed that Harry Wright was using the play in the 1870s.

There is no way to entirely reconcile such divergent claims from credible firsthand witnesses. Much of the confusion can be attributed to the fact that the play can be executed accidentally. For example, Lave Cross gave this account in 1905: "Pete Browning was the originator of the hit-and-run game. He was hard of hearing, and one day he couldn't hear the coacher after getting to first on a hit, and started for second on the first ball pitched. He ran like a wildcat and got to third on a single. Pete would not have gotten past second had he not misunderstood the signals, or if he could have heard the coacher. As it was, when he started off on his mad run he got to third safely, and would have been on the way home if he hadn't been held by the man coaching third. Hughey Jennings heard of it, and the system was introduced in Baltimore and worked with great success" (*Detroit Tribune*, March 16, 1905). Arlie Latham similarly recounted an incident during the glory days of the St. Louis Browns in which Tip O'Neill inadvertently executed a perfect hit-and-run but was bawled out by captain Charlie Comiskey because the club's system was that whenever a base runner took off, "the batsman was supposed to protect the steal by shoving his anatomy in front of his catcher" (*Washington Post*, March 19, 1899). Note that it is possible to read the two accounts of the White Stockings executing the hit-and-run as happenstance.

Moreover the play is not dissimilar to a play that was well known in 1877 when Henry Chadwick observed, "When a base-runner is on first base, not only is the first-baseman kept close to his position, but the second-baseman has to be near his, in readiness for a throw by the catcher. By this a wide, open space is generally left free for a successful hit" (*New York Clipper*, June 23, 1877).

As discussed under "Second Baseman Leaving the Bag" (4.2.5), the 1870s and 1880s saw the second baseman gradually position himself farther from the base. As he did, the hit-and-run saw a corresponding rise to prominence. Perhaps it is thus more accurate to view the hit-and-run as a play that slowly but surely developed in response, rather than one that was invented by anyone.

5.4.8 Steal and Slam.
John McGraw believed that plays like the hit-and-run and the squeeze were fundamentally unsound because an alert pitcher could detect the movement of the runner and pitch out. McGraw accordingly preferred a variant that he called the "steal and slam": "The man on

first would take a lead to actually steal the base. In that case, if the ball was a good one, the batter would slam at it. If the pitcher, expecting a hit and run, pitched out, the batter would simply let it go and take a chance on the runner stealing the base. The batter then would be in a better position than ever" (John McGraw, *My Thirty Years of Baseball*, 88).

(v) Turf Wars

5.5.1   Running into Fielders. In 1878 new rule 5.25 was introduced, which clarified that a fielder had to hold on to the ball after applying a tag. Henry Chadwick noted his concern that the amendment "offers a premium to collide with base players purposely to prevent their holding the ball" (*Brooklyn Eagle*, January 27, 1878). By the following season he was convinced that the rule was a mistake: "This vicious rule simply offers a premium to the runners to collide with the base player every time he can do so when the latter has the ball in hand ready to touch him." He incorrectly predicted that the rule would be repealed at the end of the season (*Brooklyn Eagle*, August 24, 1879).

Instead the rule remained, and contact between fielders and base runners did indeed become more common, spurred by a modest increase in the frequency of infield double plays over the next two seasons. The St. Louis Brown Stockings of the mid-1880s became particularly associated with the technique of bowling over the shortstop or second baseman to prevent a double play. In a game on May 14, 1886, Charles Comiskey caused a furor by running into Cincinnati second baseman Bid McPhee, but the umpire ruled the play legal. On June 16, 1887, St. Louis's Curt Welch ran over Baltimore second baseman Bill Greenwood to try to break up a double play and was arrested. Team owner Chris Von der Ahe had to bail his center fielder out of jail, and Welch was eventually fined $4.50.

Catchers also became targets for base runners, with Adrian "Cap" Anson being one of the leaders in this regard. An 1886 game account noted: "In Friday's game [against St. Louis] Anson was on third when [Tom] Burns knocked a fly to [John] Cahill at right field; the latter fielded it to catcher [George] Myers, who had Anson ten feet, and instead of stopping or sliding, Anson went up into the air and threw the full force of his 210 pounds against George Myers' 150 pounds. Myers was knocked almost senseless ten feet or more away from the home plate, but pluckily held on to the ball, thus retiring the side. Myers has not yet recovered from the severe shock. The storm of hisses which greeted Anson ought to admonish him that audiences do not consider brutal work of that kind ball playing" (*Sporting Life*, May 12, 1886).

With such tactics being associated with the champions of the respective major leagues, and with the umpires having limited recourse against offenders, they gradually became more common. Needless to say, Henry Chadwick continued to deplore this development, and most sportswriters followed his cue by raising an uproar whenever an especially violent incident occurred.

5.5.2 Low-bridging. Catchers had little recourse but to steel themselves for the impact of collisions with onrushing base runners. Middle infielders, however, soon found a way to get even with runners who attempted to "balk" them by going into second base standing up on potential double plays. *Sporting News* reported in 1890, "The so-called 'dirty ball' players who delight to prevent double plays by what they look upon as legitimate balking, have doubtless been taught a lesson by the accident that has overtaken [Joe] Mulvey of the Brotherhood. He attempted to balk [New York's] Arthur Whitney, but was hit in the face [with the ball] when not five feet off. He fell like a beef hit with a mallet. He will not try it again for some time" (*Sporting News*, June 28, 1890).

5.5.3 Nonviolent Ways of Breaking Up a Double Play. The early 1880s saw the conditions of playing fields improve and the introduction of fielder's gloves, both of which might have been expected to contribute to an increase in infield double plays. Instead, after increasing in 1880 and 1881, they returned to earlier levels.

The most logical explanation for this trend is to attribute it to a greater emphasis on base runners attempting to prevent double plays. As discussed in the two preceding entries, most of these endeavors were violent in nature, but gradually some less brutal tactics emerged.

In 1889, Mike Kelly unveiled a new method: ". . . When he is on first base and the ball is hit to second, and he sees that by running down the line he is likely to be the victim of a double play, he will turn back and run for first. This makes it hard for the second baseman to throw, and the chances are that he will hold the ball, and if he should let it go he is just as likely to hit Kelly as he is to get his man" (*Boston Globe*, June 8, 1889).

Honus Wagner described another approach in 1915: "My namesake, Heine Wagner, of the Boston Red Sox, told me a good one of how he endured the roasts for being a 'bonehead' on a really bright play. Heine was [a base runner] on second base and they had a hit-and-run play on. He started for third, but instantly saw a soft liner going square into the shortstop's hands. Unable to get back, Heine stopped and let the ball hit him.

"The crowd hooted and jeered and one Boston paper roasted Wagner and hailed him as 'the worst bit of ivory in the business.' They didn't realize that Heine's quick thinking had averted a double-play. In getting hit he prevented the catch from being made and a double play resulting from a toss to second" (syndicated column, *Detroit Free Press*, August 22, 1915).

Heine Wagner's tactic seems to have been a spontaneous onetime reaction to an unusual situation, but more than forty years later this ploy enjoyed a sudden renaissance. In a game at Boston on April 16, 1957, base runner George Kell of Baltimore intentionally allowed himself to be hit by a likely double-play ball. Following the game, Kell admitted not only that the tactic was deliberate but that it was one that the Orioles "have talked about and practiced all spring" under innovative manager Paul Richards.

Umpire Joe Paparella said that there was "nothing in the rules" that would permit him to rule the batter out on the play. He added, "I have always been surprised that more base runners don't do the same thing that Kell did. The base-runner can catch the ball, if he wants to be declared out. But once it touches him, the ball is dead. Jackie Robinson got away with the same trick several years ago for Brooklyn in a big game. It raised quite a controversy at the time, but nothing ever has been done by the rules makers to legislate against it. After all, who can assume the double play would have been made?" (*Baltimore Sun*, April 17, 1957).

The following week the Cincinnati Reds pulled this tactic on three successive days. In Milwaukee on April 20, Johnny Temple let a Gus Bell grounder glance off him. The next day Don Hoak was even less subtle, picking up a ground ball hit by Wally Post rather than risk a double play. One day later, this time in St. Louis, Post allowed himself to be hit by a ball off the bat of Ed Bailey (*Sporting News*, May 1, 1957).

The authorities had seen enough. On April 25 the American and National Leagues jointly announced that umpires would have the power to call a double play if a base runner allowed himself to be hit by a batted ball.

5.5.4 Another Dimension. David Falkner suggested that Joe Gordon, second baseman for the Yankees and Indians between 1938 and 1950, popularized the practice of middle infielders leaping in the air on double plays to avoid collisions (David Falkner, *Nine Sides of the Diamond*, 81–82).

(vi) Novelty Plays

5.6.1 Stealing First. Herman "Germany" Schaefer made a celebrated steal of first on September 4, 1908. The play has become a part of baseball lore, which is puzzling because the play was neither unique nor new.

In a game between Philadelphia and Detroit on August 13, 1902, Harry Davis stole second but did not draw a throw. He then stole first and then again attempted to steal second, this time drawing a throw that allowed the runner on third to score. Bob Davids discovered that Mickey Doolan of the Phillies pulled the play against the Braves on May 7, 1906 (*National Pastime*

[2001], 16). The tactic was also employed by Fred Tenney for Boston versus St. Louis on July 31, 1908, only five weeks before Schaefer's more celebrated stunt, but this was a lopsided game that featured considerable clowning. Researcher Norman Macht pointed out that Davis was the only one of these four to actually accomplish the aim of this play—to draw a throw from the catcher and enable the lead runner to score.

Hugh Jennings later claimed: "Although Herman Schaefer caused a new rule to be written into the base ball books by stealing first, he was not the originator of the idea. Dave Fultz used to do it while playing with the Athletics. He first tried it with [Harry] Davis on third and Fultz on first. Fultz stole second, but the catcher did not throw. Fultz ran back to first, hoping to draw a throw and give Davis a chance to score, but the catcher did not bite. He let Fultz run back and forth to his heart's content" (Hugh Jennings, *Rounding Third*, Chapter 72).

The practice was finally banned by a rule change in 1920.

5.6.2 Deliberately Not Advancing. A strategy occasionally used in the nineteenth century that will seem very strange to today's baseball fans was the tactic of intentionally turning down an opportunity to score.

J. P. Caillault, for example, found an account of an 1889 game in which Boston trailed New York by two runs in the ninth inning. With two out, Boston's Hardy Richardson "hit over the left-field fence for a home run, but preferred to remain at third base so as to make Catcher [Bill] Brown get close to the batter. The latter, however, did not bite at his bait. He paid no attention to Richardson, but retired the batsman after the occupant of third base had walked home" (*New York Times*, April 26, 1889; reprinted in J. P. Caillault, *A Tale of Four Cities*, 58).

The *Brooklyn Eagle*, however, placed a wildly different interpretation on the same events: "Richardson made a stupid play for Boston in the ninth inning. He hit the ball over the fence, and could easily have scored a run, but he stopped at third in order to keep the catcher close up behind the bat. This is one of those rutty notions that should be got rid of. It is stupid work to refuse a run when the chance is offered. It lost Boston the chance to tie the score" (*Brooklyn Eagle*, April 26, 1889).

Boston apparently worked this ploy more successfully in a game on May 19, 1893. Billy Nash of Boston hit a home run in the bottom of the ninth but elected to stay on third base to distract the Brooklyn pitcher (*Boston Globe*, May 20, 1893; the *Eagle*'s account, however, implied that Nash could not have advanced home). Boston rallied to tie the game but lost in extra innings.

David Nemec observed that this "was a well-respected tactical move that certain teams (Boston in particular) were not loath to try in the final inning of a tight game in the late 1800s." He explained that its usual intention was to allow the base runner to disrupt the pitcher. The strategy was no doubt influenced by the fact that one of the main functions of third-base coaches in this era was to annoy the opposing pitcher, as is discussed in the chapter on coaches.

5.6.3   Keep On Running. It seems hard to believe that a play like this was deemed legal as recently as 1926, but it's another reminder of how many of the entries in the baseball rulebook were written in response to an innovation. If nobody had ever thought to try something before, there might not be a rule that prohibited it. The Cubs and Dodgers were playing on June 17, 1926, and the Cubs loaded the bases in the sixth with one out. Joe Kelly hit a sharp ground ball to Dodger first baseman Babe Herman, who threw to shortstop Rabbit Maranville to force Johnny Cooney at second. Maranville returned the ball to first to try to complete the inning-ending double play, but his throw went astray—and then the fun began.

Brooklyn pitcher Jess Barnes retrieved the ball, saw a Cub runner headed for the plate and threw it to catcher Mickey O'Neil. The Chicago runner stopped short before reaching the plate and turned toward the dugout. O'Neil followed the runner into the Cub dugout and tagged him for the apparent third out. The problem was that the runner was none other than Cooney, who had kept running after being put out at second. Meanwhile Kelly had moved up to third.

After some thought, home plate umpire Bill Klem ruled that the inning had to continue. "There ought to be a law against such a thing, but there isn't," was the decision of the celebrated arbitrator. Chicago counted two more runs that inning, but Brooklyn eventually won the game. Columnist Thomas Holmes wrote, "Cooney's little 'joke' was unique. If it ever has been pulled in a ball game before it must have been pulled in China. Nobody ever saw or ever heard of anything quite like it" (*Brooklyn Eagle*, June 18, 1926).

5.6.4   Gag Rundowns. Johnny Evers and Hugh S. Fullerton noted that, when a pitcher was caught in a rundown, it was customary to keep running him back and forth in hopes of tiring him out (John J. Evers and Hugh S. Fullerton, *Touching Second*, 214–215). The play became prevalent enough that umpire John Gaffney suggested in 1898 that courtesy runners be allowed for pitchers (Gerard S. Petrone, *When Baseball Was Young*, 101).

The "old gag" was also tried on Cap Anson: "If they could get the Chicago man between bases they would run him up and down the lines until the big fellow dropped exhausted. On one occasion 'Buck' Ewing refused to touch Anson and called for a bat that he might warm him up" (*Grand Valley* [Moab, Utah] *Times*, September 1, 1899).

In 1903, Patsy Donovan lamented that fielders no longer tried to "catch the other side's pitcher and run him to death as they used to. Why, if the old boys could get a pitcher between second and third they'd keep him going for five minutes before they touched him, and he couldn't pitch for beans in the next innings" (*Washington Post*, August 9, 1903).

5.6.5   Not Running to First. Researcher Frank Vaccaro brought to my attention a novel ploy that Boston's Joe Hornung tried in a June 30, 1883, game against Providence. In the sixth inning, with no outs and runners on first and second: "Hornung hit to [Providence second baseman Jack] Farrell, and, instead of running and forcing [Ezra] Sutton and [Sam] Wise, he stood on the home plate. Wise started for second, and, not being a forced runner, he had to be touched by the ball before he could be declared out. While Farrell and [first baseman Joe] Start were engaged in doing this Sutton was speeding for the home plate and . . . scored the winning run" (*Sporting Life*, July 8, 1883). The *Boston Globe* confirmed this interpretation, explaining that Hornung was declared "out for not running on the hit" but that this removed the force (*Boston Globe*, July 1, 1883).

Chapter 6

MANAGERIAL
STRATEGIES

IN PRECEDING chapters I have tried to discuss strategies that could be implemented by a single player. In this chapter I describe changes made by managers. Of course there is a fine line between the two and plenty of overlap.

The task of drawing that line was made a little easier by the rule changes between 1889 and 1891 that legalized substitutions. These rules made many of today's most prominent strategies—pinch-hitting, relief pitching, platooning, etc.—possible for the first time. From that point on, managers became increasingly responsible for on-the-field decisions. By 1910, thanks to the savvy and forceful personalities of managers such as Ned Hanlon, Frank Selee, John McGraw, Connie Mack, Fred Clarke, and Clark Griffith, the prototype of today's manager was established and the related development of coaching staffs was beginning.

(i) Who's in Charge Here?

6.1.1 **Captains.** Captains were specified in the Knickerbockers' original rules, but their responsibilities appear to have been limited to choosing sides and determining who batted first. Moreover the position was not a permanent one but changed from match to match. Early clubs generally had few decisions to make, and those were settled democratically.

As the game increased in complexity, clubs began to centralize the decision-making process. In 1852 the Knickerbockers gave captains the authority to assign players to positions. Before the 1864 season the Star

Club of Brooklyn voted "to abolish the committee on nines, substituting the conferring of arbitrary power on the captains of the nines, whereby he can dismiss from the nine any unruly or rebellious player. This is a good rule, providing the captain is not one likely to play the tyrant" (*Brooklyn Eagle*, April 2, 1864). By 1865 the rules specified that clubs should have a captain, who assumed many of the functions now handled by managers.

The military connotations of the word "captain" bore special significance for a country that had just completed a long civil war. For example, the members of the Continental Club of Kalamazoo were praised in 1866 for giving "evidence of discipline and drill, the different players yielding implicit obedience to every suggestion of their captain" (*Niles* [Mich.] *Weekly Times*, May 24, 1866).

Baseball clubs were encouraged to adopt the military's hierarchical structure, with a Tecumseh, Michigan, newspaper noting that the local club "needs a smaller corps of Captains" and should "leave the command with Capt. Charles Augustus" (*Tecumseh Herald*, September 20, 1866). In 1887 a rule of the Zanesville, Ohio, club counseled: "Players must not criticize each other during play. The Captain will do that" (*Zanesville Times-Recorder*, May 2, 1887).

The responsibilities of the captain were reflected in a resolution adopted by the Excelsior Club of Chicago: "That a member be appointed Field Captain of this Club to serve during the current year, to have control of the several nines, select the same, and take general charge of the players on all occasions, except while the nine are engaged in a game" (*Chicago Tribune*, August 16, 1867). As discussed in the next entry, the captain was also responsible for directing base runners.

6.1.2 Managers. Harry Wright of the Red Stockings of Boston and Cincinnati deserves to be recognized as baseball's first manager, since he took charge of the strategy and finances of those clubs. Wright first assumed the dual role while with Cincinnati in 1868 and was acknowledged as the master of both jobs during the 1870s. Nonetheless, until the 1880s he had few counterparts (Henry Chadwick, *New York Clipper*, November 15, 1879).

The reason for this was simple. As Fred Stein noted, Harry Wright's duties with the Cincinnati club included "field manager, center fielder, relief pitcher, team trainer, tracker of team baseballs and field equipment, disciplinarian, schedule of games and travel arrangements, checker of game receipts, and bursar" (Fred Stein, "Managers and Coaches," *Total Baseball*, 2nd edition, 452). When he got to Boston, Wright relinquished the playing duties but continued in the other roles.

It was generally believed that no one else could hope to match Wright's versatility. As a result, Henry Chadwick called it a "blunder" to "give the club manager a double duty to perform, namely, the work of Captaining the nine in the field, as well as managing the business affairs of the team in general" (*New York Clipper*, November 17, 1877).

In 1882 the *Detroit Free Press* noted that future managing great Ned Hanlon, then still a player, "thinks it is a mistake to ask [George] Derby to both manage and captain the club. Derby would make a good manager, but a pitcher should be allowed to rest between innings, instead of being required to direct the running of bases" (*Detroit Free Press*, January 10, 1882). As this suggests, most clubs of this period delegated in-game strategy to the club's captain while letting a manager handle scheduling and finances. Meanwhile managers of the period were generally financial managers who had little or no playing experience.

The next few years would see this begin to change. Sportswriter William Perrin noted later that after the 1881 season the directors of the Providence club realized "the necessity of having a manager at the head of affairs who knew the game" rather than one who was "successful enough in business but innocent of baseball" (William Perrin, "Line Drives Then and Now," originally published in 1928 in an unknown source, reprinted in Jim Charlton, ed., *Road Trips*, 85). Other clubs began to follow suit. This did not, however, mean that a manager would simply make strategic decisions, as is discussed in the next entry.

The division of responsibilities was nicely summed up in a bylaw adopted by the Aetna Club of Detroit on November 27, 1874: "The captain shall have absolute control of the playing nine while on the field. . . . The manager shall have an absolute control over the financial affairs of the club" (*Aetna Base Ball Association Constitution and By-Laws*, 11).

As managers increasingly took control, the responsibilities of the captain were correspondingly reduced. Charley Snyder reported that in the early 1880s "a captain was often called upon to negotiate with the railroads for rates, look out for the baggage, and do all the business with the hotel people" (*Washington Post*, August 30, 1899). Once others were hired to handle these duties, the importance of the captain was further diminished. In 1899, Washington manager Arthur Irwin remarked, "The only use for a Captain on a ball team, when a manager is on the bench, is to answer all arguments in which any of his players are involved with the umpires" (quoted in the *Washington Post*, March 19, 1899).

Nevertheless it was many years before clubs saw fit to eliminate the role altogether. In 1917 a note remarked, "The Cleveland Americans went on the field yesterday without a captain. Lee Fohl, manager of the club, is to act in the dual capacity as captain and manager. 'The idea of a captain is a joke, in my way of thinking,' Fohl said in explaining why he would dispense with the figure-head" (*Warren Evening Times*, April 12, 1917).

6.1.3   Hustlers. The 1880s produced a new breed of managers who were often known as hustlers. These men were generally ex-players with a flair for salesmanship who could take on the role of finding and recruiting players while also scheduling matches and building up interest around town.

For example, the local papers in Grand Rapids, Michigan, criticized player-manager Henry Monroe Jones in 1883 for failing to schedule enough games against attractive opponents. This obviously wouldn't be expected of today's managers, but this was an essential function for clubs being run on razor-thin margins. As a result, the following year Jones was relieved of managing duties and replaced by "Hustling" Horace Phillips.

Horace Phillips was the epitome of a new breed of manager. He and kindred spirit Dan O'Leary were described as being "about as fine an article in the way of managers as there are in the profession. Either one of the above pair could go to Egypt, Honolulu or some other out of the way post and inside of a week organize a good base ball team and have the populace worked up to a high pitch of excitement over the game" (*Cincinnati Enquirer*, reprinted in the *Grand Rapids* [Mich.] *Daily Democrat*, August 14, 1883).

This could prove a mixed blessing, as the enthusiasm they drummed up was often short-lived. An 1886 article noted, "Mr. [Horace] Phillips is a 'hustler,' a faculty that Mr. [Harry] Wright does not lay claim to. 'Hustlers' seldom have the faculty of properly handling players after they get them" (*The Official Baseball Record*, May 14, 1886).

6.1.4   College of Coaches. Does one person have to be in charge? A hierarchical structure with one person overseeing everything entered baseball at the end of the Civil War and has been largely taken for granted ever since. But one notable effort to reexamine that premise occurred, appropriately enough, during the 1960s.

During the 1961 and 1962 seasons, innovative Chicago Cubs owner Philip K. Wrigley initiated a strange experiment in which the Cubs had no permanent manager. The club instead employed a group of coaches who rotated responsibilities every few weeks. Included in the rotation was the role of "head coach," as the manager was called.

It was an imaginative idea in theory but in practice was reportedly a disaster. The intention was to give the players the benefits of multiple coaches. Instead pitcher Don Elston later claimed that the opposite happened: ". . . Not one of them helped one of the others. My impression was that whoever was the manager—or the head coach—was pretty much on his own. All they did was wait until it was their turn" (quoted in Peter Golenbock, *Wrigleyville*, 371).

The Cubs remained near the bottom of the National League for the next two seasons, which was not unexpected. What was worse was that their young players didn't show much improvement. Elston recalled that players found the lack of continuity "very confusing." Ron Santo believed that the development of Lou Brock in particular was hindered by the College of Coaches (quoted in Peter Golenbock, *Wrigleyville*, 371, 375).

The experiment ended after two seasons when Bob Kennedy was appointed as permanent "head coach." The *Chicago Tribune* hailed the event with the headline, "CUBS COACHING STAFF STOPS REVOLVING" (*Chicago Tribune*, February 21, 1963).

6.1.5   Managers Are Hired to Be Fired. At least one nineteenth-century manager didn't accept the premise that managers are hired to be fired. Brothers George and Jacob Earl Wagner, who owned the Athletics in 1891, "called for the resignation of Manager William Sharsig. The latter refuses to step aside, declaring that he has a contract that holds good in law, and he proposes to stick. . . . As he proposes to stick, and the Wagners say he must go, there will be fun" (*Williamsport Sunday Grit*, May 10, 1891). Apparently the Wagners won the power struggle, as Sharsig was replaced soon thereafter.

6.1.6   Firing the Team. While it's a baseball commonplace that you can fire the manager but not the players, at least one minor league team tried the latter strategy. The event took place in 1902 in the Pennsylvania League. *Sporting Life* recorded: "The players of the Lebanon Club on Friday morning [May 23] revolted against Manager [M. F.] Hynes, with the result that all were fined seven days' pay and released. Manager Hynes went to Lancaster Friday after declaring he would return here on May 28 with an entirely new team" (*Sporting Life*, May 25, 1902). Instead the entire league disbanded.

6.1.7   Trading the Manager. Midway through the 1960 season, Cleveland and Detroit pulled the only trade of managers in major league history, with Joe Gordon and Jimmy Dykes changing jobs. The unique transaction cemented Cleveland general manager Frank Lane's reputation as "Trader Lane," but the swap apparently wasn't his idea. Lane later claimed that the deal was initiated by Detroit general manager Bill DeWitt, and Lane expressed his regret for agreeing to the trade. He explained, "There's a certain dignity to a manager and he shouldn't be subjected to a trade" (quoted in *Sporting News*, March 20, 1965).

6.1.8   Firing During Spring Training. The first manager to be fired during spring training was Phil Cavaretta in 1954. He has since been joined by Alvin Dark and Tim Johnson.

(ii) Substitutions

The manager's role became far more complex once substitutions became legal. A wide variety of previously impossible or impractical strategies, including pinch hitting, pinch running, and relief pitching, became viable. Managers became responsible for an increasing number of players and suddenly had the luxury of making in-game adjustments.

6.2.1 Insertion of Substitutes. As discussed under "Substitutions" (1.32), until the 1890s a player could not be replaced except under special circumstances. As a result, clubs tried to ensure that their nine contained several players capable of filling the key positions, especially the battery. By doing so they could move an injured player to the outfield and replace him with a healthy player. In 1873, Henry Chadwick referred to "the rule requiring two pitchers and two catchers in a nine" (*New York Clipper*, April 5, 1873). While this does not appear to have been an explicit rule, it only made sense to have players in the lineup who were able to fill in at these critical positions.

By the early 1870s top clubs generally had a tenth player on hand to play if needed. The *Chicago Tribune* aptly summed up his duties in 1870 when they described Clipper Flynn as "one of those thoroughly useful and sensible ball players who can afford to be the tenth, or general utility man, for the sake of the credit to be derived by doing everything well" (*Chicago Tribune*, June 1, 1870).

By the end of the decade, the role was a staple of professional clubs. Notes such as "The tenth man will be either [Doc] Bushong or [Joe] Roche" and "Mr. Michael Muldoon, the tenth man of the New Bedford club, arrived the first of the week" became commonplace (*Chicago Tribune*, December 15, 1878; *Boston Globe*, April 13, 1879).

Budgets remained very tight, however, and extra players were a luxury that clubs could ill afford. Many tried to justify the expense by assigning the substitute extra responsibilities. Ticket-taking duty was the most common task, but there were others. In 1876 a St. Louis club engaged a player named Al Turner as an umpire and extra man (*Detroit Free Press*, August 19, 1876). John J. Piggott was hired as a groundskeeper and occasional substitute (*Detroit Post and Tribune*, March 30, 1882; the *Detroit Free Press* of March 26, 1882, listed his duties as janitor and sub).

Clubs that engaged extra players were considered to be setting a bad example. When Chicago began rotating pitchers Larry Corcoran and Fred Goldsmith in 1880, it was said that "there is good ground for believing that certain of the league magnates wrote letters to the Chicago magnates, denouncing them for establishing a bad precedent in the matter of expense" (*Detroit Free Press*, March 31, 1895). In 1881 in-game substitutions were banned, except with the consent of the opposing captain.

Clubs continued to have a tenth man, but often he wasn't even in uniform. Before the 1884 season Washington manager "Holly" Hollingshead told a reporter, "the Washington nine will have one reserve man, who will be in trim and ready to play ball at a moment's notice. His name is 'Holly'" (*Washington Post*, March 16, 1884). But when a substitute was needed a few weeks later, the *Washington Post* chided: "[Bob] Barr was disabled in the fourth inning after just coming in to relieve [Ed] Trumbull. This necessitated quite a delay while Hammill [John Hamill] donned his uniform. It would be a good plan for Manager Hollingshead to have a substitute ready with uniform on, to take the place of any disabled player" (*Washington Post*, April 8, 1884).

The following year the *Boston Globe* observed: "The plan adopted by the St. Louis of having a tenth player on the grounds in uniform is a good one, and should be followed by all visiting clubs" (*Boston Globe*, August 7, 1885). A few clubs continued to balk at paying someone to do little or nothing, with Detroit manager Charlie Morton keeping in playing condition so that he could fill in if needed (*Detroit Free Press*, February 8, 1885). Most, however, gave in, and by mid-season it was reported that "Each league club seems to have one or more general utility men" (*Sporting Life*, July 22, 1885).

In 1889 a rule was adopted that allowed clubs to use one substitute. But his name had to be printed on the score sheet, and it appears that he could enter only at the start of an inning. The strategy immediately opened up new techniques: "Beginning the tenth inning [Cap] Anson relieved [Gus] Krock and put in [Frank] Dwyer, who was on the card as tenth man" (*Chicago Tribune*, April 30, 1889). It also opened managers up to second-guessing: "The tenth man rule should have been taken advantage of in the third inning, when it was seen that [Bob] Caruthers' pitching was being easily punished" (*Brooklyn Eagle*, April 26, 1889).

The next year the number of substitutions was increased to two. Their names still had to appear on the score sheet, but they could enter the game at any time (*Columbus* [Ohio] *Post*, November 13, 1889). Indeed minor league clubs were informed that they had to have two substitutes present for games. This prompted complaints that the extra expense was not feasible given the strict salary limits (*Columbus* [Ohio] *Press*, April 17, 1890).

The introduction of tactical substitutions created a new breed of player, and of course it was no honor to be relegated to the bench. The *Sporting News* noted: "'Bench warmer' is the most opprobrious epithet you can apply to a modern professional ball player" (*Sporting News*, December 24, 1892). Of course it was better than "unemployed."

6.2.2 Pitchers Being Required to Face One Batter. This requirement was first introduced in 1909 and has been the subject of considerable shenanigans, which have caused it to be modified several times.

In 1913 umpire Billy Evans explained the impetus for the rule's creation four years earlier, "Every umpire, player and fan can recall what a lot of jockeying a manager used to do when one of his pitchers suddenly showed signs of distress. In such cases, usually no pitcher would be warmed up. Naturally it would then become the purpose of the manager to consume enough time to allow his star twirler to get in proper shape to pitch. In response to a request for the name of a pitcher who would take the place of the man removed, the manager, after carefully looking over the available men on the bench, would inform the umpire that So and So would be the pitcher. The pitcher so announced would slowly remove his sweater, take a drink of water, a chew of tobacco, and then leisurely stroll out to the pitcher's box. In the meantime the twirler the manager really intended to use would be pitching his head off out by the club house in an effort to get in shape to stop the batting rally that had been going on at the expense of the pitcher just removed.

"The rules several years ago gave the new or substitute pitcher the right to throw five balls. The pitcher announced would take his time throwing the regulation number. Then the manager would hasten out to the box, and inform the umpire that he had decided not to use pitcher So and So, but would depend on pitcher Such and Such. Mr. Such and Such would then go through the same routine as did Mr. So and So, only to be recalled after throwing five balls, to allow the pitcher originally selected to take his place on the rubber. These two players by being so sacrificed enabled the real pitcher to get himself into shape to pitch, without possible injury to himself, or jeopardizing his club's chances by not being ready to give his best efforts.

"This practice was worked so much that it became a great nuisance to the spectators, delayed games 10 or 15 minutes, and was a custom generally obnoxious to the rooters who support the game. The rule makers realized the necessity of a change and incorporated a clause that practically did away with jockeying the pitchers for time. Now, when a twirler is substituted he must pitch until the batter has either been retired or reaches first. This condition made it foolhardy for a manager to substitute a man in whom he had no confidence. Incidentally it was the start of a system of constantly having a pitcher ready to step into the game.

"As a result of the change in the rules nearly every manager these days selects a couple of rescue pitchers at the start of the game. It is the duty of these players to keep limbered, and to start a real warming up at a signal, perhaps to desist when the pitcher in the box appears to have weathered the storm, but to be always at least half ready for a possible call that may be made upon their services" (*Sporting News*, January 9, 1913).

Illustrative of Evans's contention is John McGraw's use of Rube Mar-quard in 1908, the last year before the rule change. After he purchased Mar-quard for a record-breaking $11,000, McGraw twice ushered the rookie out to the mound during a game and had him warm up before he finally faced his first major league batter on September 25 (Larry Mansch, *Rube Mar-quard*, 43–44).

After the requirement of facing one batter was established, the desire to keep the game moving meant that relief pitchers were expected to be pre-pared to enter the game at all times. Their readiness was strictly enforced—sometimes more scrupulously than seemed fair. Billy Evans noted after the 1912 season that Clark Griffith had suggested allowing a new pitcher three minutes to warm up if the preceding pitcher had been ejected (*Sporting News*, November 28, 1912).

In a May 19, 1946, game between the Cubs and Braves, Cubs reliever Ray Prim came into the game but hurt his arm on his second pitch. The Cubs attempted to remove him but Boston manager Billy Southworth ob-jected, and the umpires ruled that Prim had to face at least one batter (Shirley Povich, *Sporting News*, June 5, 1946).

6.2.3   Interchanging Pitchers. In a National League game on August 13, 1880, right-hander Fred Corey and left-hander Lee Richmond swapped po-sitions between the pitching box and the outfield five times as Worcester beat Cleveland 3-1.

The strategy of shuttling pitchers in and out instead of replacing them reemerged in the early twentieth century after relief pitchers became com-mon. Washington sportswriter J. B. Abrams gave this description of a seventeen-inning tie game between the Washington Nationals and Chi-cago White Sox on May 13, 1909: "Though [Chicago pitcher] Doc White held the locals in the hollow of his hand and allowed but six hits and one pass in the full route, [Washington manager Joe] Cantillon kept his crowd abreast even to the finish by as clever a manipulation of his players as was ever seen. He outguessed [White Sox manager] Bill Sullivan, and deserved the victory, even though his pitchers were hit thirteen times and gave nine passes. Twenty White Sox were left on bases, which shows how the Na-tional pitchers rose to emergencies. [Walter] Johnson, [Bill] Burns, [Dolly] Gray and [Tom] Hughes were used in the box, the shifts from left to right-handers, and back, being made as occasion seemed to demand of Cantil-lon. He would pit against a batter of like ilk, and then, when another tight place arose, he would change to a starboard flinger. When he wanted to use Gray, he shunted Hughes to right field so that he could call Tom back to the box later, which he did. While Thomas was in right, though, there was many a prayer offered that no ball would be hit out that way. But for once, luck was with us, and the game was called with honors even" (*Sporting News*, May 20, 1909).

The account of the game in the *Washington Post* indicated that Cantillon's tactics were more effective because he was allowed to make unlimited switches. Although the rules specified that a pitcher had to face at least one batter, the wording of the rule began, "In the event of a pitcher being taken from the game . . ." Since Cantillon was not taking his pitcher from the game, the umpire decided that the rule did not apply. The *Post* noted: "This perhaps is not the spirit of the rule, but it certainly is the letter of it" (*Washington Post*, May 14, 1909).

Before the next season the wording was changed to read "In the event of the pitcher being taken from his position . . ." That modification seems to have eliminated the practice for many years, but it was brought back in the 1950s by innovative White Sox manager Paul Richards.

In a 1951 game Richards brought in left-handed pitcher Billy Pierce just to face Ted Williams and moved his pitcher, right-hander Harry Dorish, to third base. After Williams's at bat, the original pitcher returned to the mound (Red Smith, January 11, 1952, reprinted in *Red Smith on Baseball*; Joseph M. Overfield, "The Richards-Jethroe Caper: Fact or Fiction?," *Baseball Research Journal* 16 [1987], 33). Richards repeated the ploy in 1953—this time replacing Pierce with Dorish on the mound for two batters and having Pierce play first base—and on two occasions in 1954 (Joseph M. Overfield, "The Richards-Jethroe Caper: Fact or Fiction?," *Baseball Research Journal* 16 [1987], 33; David Nemec, *The Rules of Baseball*, 49–51).

The tactic has occasionally been used since then, though its usefulness was limited by the addition of a clause to rule 3.03 that a pitcher and position player could switch roles only once in an inning.

6.2.4 Double Switches. Researcher Frank Vaccaro has investigated double switches and has documented at least one occurrence in the 1906 season. In an August 2 game at Detroit, Highlanders manager Clark Griffith put himself in as a relief pitcher in the eighth inning and brought catcher Ira Thomas in at the same time. The previous catcher had batted eighth and the previous pitcher ninth, but Griffith reversed the order by putting himself in the eighth slot and Thomas ninth.

The tactic must have remained rare as it caused great confusion when Detroit manager Hughey Jennings used it in a 1913 game against Cleveland: "There was some confusion among the fans Thursday afternoon over the manner in which Jennings arranged his batting order after putting in substitutes.

"[Henri] Rondeau batted for [Ossie] Vitt and went in to catch in place of [Oscar] Stanage, thus keeping the second position in the swatting list throughout. [William] Louden, who replaced Stanage on the bases, was in turn replaced by Peplowske [Joseph Peploski] in the batting order, while Peplowske assumed [George] Moriarty's fielding position. [Les] Hennessey replaced [Jean] Dubuc, who batted for Moriarty, but went to second base instead of third.

"[Cleveland manager George] Stovall protested when Peplowske went to bat ahead of Hennessey in the ninth, claiming that 'Pep' was Moriarty's substitute. Jennings had explained to the umpire, however, that Hennessey was the man who had taken Moriarty's place and Peplowske was in for Stanage, and that he had changed their fielding positions after putting them in the game.

"A manager can make any shift in position he desires, but it is essential that a man remain in the same place in the batting order throughout the game, so Hughie was within his rights in arranging the two youngsters in the way he saw fit" (*Detroit Free Press*, June 27, 1913).

6.2.5 Pinch Hitters. The early history of the pinch hitter is confusing. The first issue is the term itself. What we have known since the 1930s as "clutch hitting" was by the early twentieth century called "pinch hitting." Substitute batters were almost always used in situations where a timely hit was needed—in a pinch—so they became known as pinch hitters.

The second issue is the history of the tactic, which is complicated by rules and customs that made it either illegal or impractical in early baseball. Substitutes were legal only under special circumstances in early baseball, and it was customary to have only nine players in uniform.

Thus there are only a few isolated incidents from the 1870s where an injured player was replaced by a substitute who essentially functioned as a pinch hitter. The first appears to have been Frank Prescott Norton, a star of the 1860s who made his only major league appearance on May 5, 1871, when Doug Allison was hurt. Jim Devlin pinch-hit for Philadelphia in a game played on October 2, 1873 (David Nemec, *Great Baseball Feats, Facts and Firsts*, 228–229). Researcher Al Kermisch found that Bobby Clack batted for Dave Pierson in a game on May 13, 1876 (*Baseball Research Journal* 19 [1990], 93).

Kermisch also compiled a list of several pinch hitters who were used during the 1880s (*Baseball Research Journal* 21 [1992], 112). The list, however, was a short one because a rule change in 1881 prohibited any substitutions except in case of an injury and agreed to by the opposing captain.

Substitutions were again legalized in 1889, but still on a very limited basis. Only one substitute could be used during a game, and his name had to appear on the scorecard before the game. Moreover he had to enter the game at the end of a complete inning, effectively making pinch hitting impossible.

The following year two replacements were allowed, but they still had to be designated on the scorecard. While the rules no longer explicitly prohibited pinch hitting, there appears to have been at least a tacit understanding that pinch hitting was not legal. The *Columbus Press* reported before the 1890 season that "a batsman cannot be superceeded [sic] by a player," which would seem to imply that pinch hitters could not be used (*Columbus* [Ohio] *Press*, March 16, 1890). In 1891 unlimited substitutions were finally allowed, but the strategy of pinch hitting remained extremely rare, with only seven documented attempts, all of them unsuccessful.

On July 25, 1891, Chicago led Cleveland 11-10 at the start of the ninth inning. Cleveland was the home team but was batting first and had two runners on and one out when the pitcher's turn came up: "Then from the brain of Patsy Tebeau sprang a brilliant idea. Ralph Johnson had been on the bench and Tebeau resolved to send him to the bat in place of [pitcher Lee] Viau, whose hitting ability has never yet threatened the world with a conflagration. The idea as far as Johnson was concerned was good enough, but Pat seemed to forget that by sending Johnson to bat he put Viau out of the game entirely." Cleveland scored four runs in its half to take a 14-11 lead. Unfortunately they "went out at last, and then Patsy Tebeau was confronted with a conundrum. He had no pitcher, and the best he could do was to send out [George] Davis, his center-fielder" (*Chicago Tribune*, July 26, 1891).

An account in *Sporting Life* three years later pinpointed this game as having "originated the trick of sending a heavy batter up to the plate in the final inning of a game to take the place of a pitcher. . . . Very few people in the stands understood the move, and neither did Anson. Uncle applied to the umpire for protection, but the rules say plainly enough that a captain of a team has the right to substitute one man for another at any time in the course of the game" (*Sporting Life*, October 6, 1894).

Unfortunately for the innovative Tebeau, Chicago scored four runs off Davis in its half to win the game. As this shows, pinch hitting remained a perilous strategy because of two practical considerations. First, clubs were very unlikely to have a healthy and dangerous hitter on their bench, since such a player would naturally be in the starting lineup. Second, even if one assumed that a hit would be delivered, the lack of capable relief pitchers meant that the benefits were unlikely to outweigh the harm done by removing the starting pitcher.

As a result, the use of pinch hitters increased only marginally in 1892, and there remained widespread confusion about the practice. Charles Reilly batted for pitcher Kid Carsey and singled in a game on April 28, 1892, but the *Chicago Tribune* left him out of their box score, explaining, "As he played no part in the game, he is given none in the score" (quoted in Paul Votano, *Stand and Deliver*, 17). Tom Daly hit a dramatic pinch-hit home run on May

14, 1892, to send Brooklyn's game against Boston to extra innings. But he hit not for pitcher Ed Stein but for the next batter, leadoff man Hub Collins, and then went to left field.

As pitching staffs and playing rosters expanded over the next decade, the strategy became more viable. John McGraw was a main proponent, though pinch hitting continued to be regarded with suspicion by many. Sportswriter W. A. Phelon reported that in a game on August 9, 1905, "One of New York's pet tricks went wrong. With the team a little behind, and the bases full of New Yorkers, [John] McGraw decided that the time was ripe for his favorite idea. He yanked [Leon] Ames, warmed up [Joe] McGinnity, and sent [Frank] Bowerman to bat. The trick fell down both ways. Bowerman forced a runner at the plate, and the Cubs knocked the stuffing out of McGinnity" (*Sporting Life*, August 26, 1905).

Pinch hitting thus was still problematic for managers. Even if a reliable relief pitcher were available, the likelihood that a bench player would come through with a key hit was not great. The wisdom of pinch hitting for the pitcher thus continued to appear dubious.

That began to change before the 1905 season when John McGraw purchased the well-traveled Sammy Strang. A major league regular from 1901 through 1903, Strang, like McGraw, was an infielder with an extraordinary ability to draw walks. His defense was shaky, however, and when he had an off year at the plate in 1904, he became available. McGraw realized that Strang could fill a role for his club and made him a utility infielder and pinch hitting specialist.

The *New York Telegram* observed in 1909: "One of the recent developments of base ball has been the 'pinch hitter.' Almost all of the teams in the National and American leagues carry some player these days who is supposed to be able to take his place at bat in an emergency and rap the ball out of the reach of the fielders, thereby restoring his club to good standing and keeping peace in the community. To some extent John J. McGraw of the New York Nationals is responsible for this innovation. He was quick to see the advantages which were likely to be gained when the rule was passed that one player could be substituted for another at any time, and after it was put into effect by the rules committee kept one or two men on his team for not much of any reason than that they could frequently walk to the plate and smash the ball safely to the field when needed. There was 'Sammy' Strang, for instance" (*New York Telegram*, reprinted in *Sporting News*, October 14, 1909).

Other clubs followed McGraw's example. Ham Hyatt was highly successful for the Pittsburgh Pirates. Dode Criss of the St. Louis Browns filled a dual function, as a pinch-hitting specialist who was also used as a relief pitcher. Harry "Moose" McCormick eventually succeeded Sammy Strang as McGraw's primary pinch hitter.

Not everyone welcomed this innovation. One sportswriter sniffed in 1913, "Manager McGraw, of New York, is credited with being the inventor of the pinch-hitter; at least he was the first manager to carry a hard-hitting player at great expense solely for the purpose of inserting him into games at critical stages for the chance of a timely safe hit. Inasmuch as all base ball managers are imitative all clubs now carry at least one pinch-hitter. For this may the Lord forgive McGraw, as there is no doubt that the system has added to the expense of the clubs, the length of the box scores, and the vexation of the scorers; while there is much doubt as to the practical value of the system" (*Sporting Life*, August 30, 1913).

In 1914 the *Detroit Free Press* observed, "It has become fashionable within recent years for a big league ball club to carry extra men who might be termed specialists. Washington has two comedy coaches, [Germany] Schaefer and [Nick] Altrock, the Athletics have their special coach, Harry Davis, and the Giants have their pinch hitter, Harry McCormick" (*Detroit Free Press*, September 30, 1914).

Even the players involved seem to have had reservations about taking specialization to such an extreme. Moose McCormick once said, "I wasn't a ball player, just a batter" (*Sporting News*, July 21, 1962). But it was not long before the pinch hitter began to be accepted as part of the game.

6.2.6 Courtesy Runners. Courtesy runners were an occasional feature of early baseball. When a batter was hurting but not incapacitated, one of his teammates—generally one who was already in the game—would act as a courtesy runner. The courtesy runner stood behind the batter and did his running, but the batter did not have to leave the game. For example, an 1867 article noted, "George [Wright] waited for a good length ball, and away he sent it 'over the hills and far away,' easily securing his second, or rather [Eb] Smith did for him, George being rather too lame for active running" (*The Ball Player's Chronicle*, July 25, 1867).

Like so many of the customs of the gentleman's era of baseball, this practice did not survive the transition to a more competitive environment. The intention of the rule was to make things easier for an ailing player, but clubs began using courtesy runners in order to have a swifter base runner or to get a running start. When the game's rule makers decided to take action, their efforts were not entirely effective.

In 1873 they decided that "When a substitute is presented to run a base for another player, the umpire must ask the captain of the field nine if he objects to him; if he does, the umpire must rule him out, as the captain of the fieldside can now select the substitute" (*New York Clipper*, April 5, 1873). Frequent violations of the rule caused Henry Chadwick to comment in 1875, "It has been customary to allow a substitute to run the bases for the pitcher, so as to save him from fatigue. This is unfair, and should be frowned down" (Henry Chadwick, *1875 DeWitt's Base Ball Umpire's Guide*, 83). After 1881 a courtesy runner could not be used at all unless the opposing captain or manager consented. It was not uncommon for this consent to be granted, and Tip O'Neill is said to have used a courtesy runner frequently in 1885.

When player substitutions were legalized in 1889, the use of pinch runners as we now know them became legal. But it did not become common to make a substitution in order to insert a faster base runner, and courtesy runners continued to be used. For example, the *Chicago Tribune* noted in 1905, "O'Neil [Jack O'Neill] took Ruelbach's [Ed Reulbach's] place on first in the ninth after he made the hit and scored the run for him, as he had a sore foot" (*Chicago Tribune*, May 28, 1905). A list of more than forty documented instances appears on the Retrosheet website, most of them between 1889 and 1949.

The courtesy runner was finally banned in 1950.

6.2.7   Pinch Runners. Pinch runners became legal at the same time that pinch hitters did, but early clubs used them sparingly. In particular, with constraints on budgets and rosters, it would not have been reasonable to make this a primary function of a player.

There were at least a couple of efforts to turn a track star into a well-rounded baseball player. Marty Hogan, an outfielder of the 1890s, once was reported to have tied the world record in the 100-yard dash with a 9.8 time (*Sporting Life*, July 20, 1895). A 1901 article noted: "B. J. Wefers, who is without doubt the greatest sprinter among all the athletes of the last decade, has been signed by the St. Louis National League baseball club as a substitute outfielder" (*Milwaukee Journal*, April 17, 1901). As fast as he was, "the trouble was that he had to get to first before he could give exhibitions of his speed, and the pitchers took care that he did not get there. Wefers could not hit a flock of barns, and he did not last long as a ball player" (*Washington Post*, January 7, 1908). Wefers never appeared in a major league game.

As with pinch hitters, John McGraw was the first manager to experiment with having a player who was primarily used as a pinch runner. In 1914, Sandy Piez filled this role for the Giants. Fifteen years later McGraw tried the concept again, using former pitcher Tony Kaufmann in this way for the 1929 Giants.

The idea was revived nearly forty years later by Charles O. Finley. As Rob Neyer and Eddie Epstein point out, while Herb Washington is better remembered, Allan Lewis was the first Oakland player to be used in that function (Rob Neyer and Eddie Epstein, *Baseball Dynasties*, 284–286). Lewis occasionally played the outfield or appeared at the plate, but in six seasons he took part in 156 regular season games and batted only 29 times. In his final season in 1973, he appeared in 35 games but only once played defense and never batted.

In 1974, Finley signed sprinter Herb Washington, who had never played professional baseball. He appeared in ninety-two games for Oakland that season as a pinch runner but never once batted or played the field. Washington stole twenty-nine bases but was caught stealing sixteen times. In that year's League Championship Series, Washington was caught stealing twice, and in the World Series he was picked off by Mike Marshall. (Coincidentally, Washington had once been a student in a course taught by Marshall at Michigan State University.)

Washington was released early the next season, but the experiment was not quite over. Oakland used Larry Lintz in the role of designated pinch runner in 1976 and 1977 before finally abandoning the scheme.

At the same time Finley was conducting these experiments, the Class A Midwest League adopted a designated-runner rule. In 1975 the Midwest League allowed managers to designate a player in this role on the lineup card. The designated runner could pinch-run no more than three times in the game, and the player he replaced did not have to leave the game. The rule was scrapped after one year (Glen Waggoner, Kathleen Moloney, and Hugh Howard, *Spitters, Beanballs, and the Incredible Shrinking Strike Zone*, 61).

6.2.8   Relief Pitching. Although substitutions were either impractical or illegal early on, relief pitching is almost as old as competitive baseball. Ineffective pitchers would simply switch positions with another player, and many early clubs specifically planned for this contingency. The 1868 Atlantics of Brooklyn, for example, penciled veteran pitcher Tom Pratt into the lineup in the outfield or infield "in matches where it is thought a change pitcher is necessary" (*Brooklyn Eagle*, August 15, 1868).

Henry Chadwick advocated the use of relief pitchers with a different pitching style from the regular pitcher. In one of his early books he counseled, ". . . A first-class team always has two pitchers in it, and it is in your management of these batteries that much of your success will lie. Put your swift pitcher to work first, and keep him in at least three innings, even if he be hit away from the start. . . . Supposing, however, that with good support in the field the swift pitching is being easily punished, and runs are being made too fast, if your pitcher is one who cannot drop his pace well without giving more chances at the bat, you should at once bring in your slow or medium-paced pitcher" (*Haney's Base Ball Book of Reference for 1867*, reprinted in *The Ball Player's Chronicle*, August 22, 1867). He regularly underlined the theme in game accounts, "In the previous innings Blakeslee had been put on to pitch in McNally's place, a change entirely useless, as the delivery of both was about the same, and unless a change of pitchers presents a different style of delivery, no benefit accrues from it" (*The Ball Player's Chronicle*, August 8, 1867).

In the 1870s and 1880s it was common practice to man one of the outfield positions with a "change pitcher" who could be moved to the pitcher's box if necessary. An account of an 1886 game observed: "Pitcher [Ed] Daily was stationed in [the left] garden . . . partly because Harry Wright thought an extra pitcher might come handy" (*Detroit Free Press*, May 19, 1886).

By the 1890s pitching staffs had expanded and substitutions were legal, which enabled relief pitchers to play a somewhat larger role. But the pitchers who were used in relief roles were starting pitchers between turns, and there continued to be resistance to the concept of pitchers not finishing what they started. As Al Pratt put it, "a man hired to pitch was expected to pitch" (quoted in *Sporting News*, March 23, 1895).

Before the 1902 season it was reported that White Sox manager Clark Griffith was "planning on using Virgil Garvin scientifically this season, letting the elongated twirler go his distance, and relieving him the moment that he begins to show his weakness, after the sixth inning" (*Mansfield* [Ohio] *News*, February 9, 1902). Traditionalists like Henry Chadwick were appalled by the notion of a starting pitcher who didn't finish what he started. Chadwick fumed, ". . . The argument used by the pitchers in 1901, that the most of them were 'overworked,' was little else than a 'bluff' on their part to avoid their due share of box work during the season. A pitcher occupies the box in a nine-innings games [sic] less than an hour on the average, and it is absurd to claim that an hour's work in the box during each day is either trying to his physique or to his powers of endurance" (*Spalding's Official Base Ball Guide*, *1902*, 86). Sound familiar?

The *Washington Post* observed in 1904, "As a general thing managers use their judgment as to when the proper time has arrived to replace a pitcher in a losing game, but some use a system of allowing a certain number of hits on a twirler in one or more innings in a game. Others figure that a pitcher is or is not in form by the number of batsmen he sends to first on balls. Many close observers are of the opinion that a pitcher should be allowed to remain in and 'take his medicine,' if the score is greatly against his team. Pitchers, as a rule, would prefer to remain in and try to turn defeat into victory. . . . The best-minded class of fans do not care to see a twirler replaced, especially if he is at all popular" (*Washington Post*, July 31, 1904).

Obviously no manager would assign an effective pitcher to regular relief duty as long as relievers were used only in lopsided games and the "best-minded class of fans" opposed their use.

6.2.9 **Relief Specialists.** As noted in the preceding entry, the relief pitchers who were used in the 1890s were simply starting pitchers on their day off—

there were no pitchers who worked exclusively in relief. The biggest reason was the mind-set that a relief pitcher should be used only if the situation was hopeless. As long as that was the case, it would make no use to pay even a struggling pitcher to fill that role, let alone an effective one.

One of the first to challenge that way of thinking was John McGraw, but not in the way that would later become standard. Sam Crane explained in 1903, "Manager McGraw has originated a new plan which he will put into operation when the championship season begins, and will be an entirely new departure in base ball. He intends to work his pitchers throughout the season as he has during the Southern trip, that is, he will use two pitchers in every game, one being in the points five innings and the other four. No manager but one who has originality and nerve would attempt any such innovation, but McGraw has both, and has made up his mind to adopt the plan. There are many things, too, in its favor. The pitchers can surely do more work and go in the box oftener than under the old plan, for a half game will hardly be more than pleasurable exercise for them. Then, again, most games are lost on one or two innings, and any ball player knows that any change of delivery during a game is more or less puzzling. McGraw says that the only thing to fear in adopting the plan is the 'roasting' he will get if the second pitcher should lose his game after the first pitcher had his opponents tied up. But he will take chances, just the same, and there is not a player among the Giants who does not favor the plan. It will be a radical and sensational plan" (*Sporting Life*, April 18, 1903).

Sporting Life editor Francis Richter commented disapprovingly: "McGraw's idea is by no means new, so far as the suggestion is concerned, although it has never yet been put into practice. No manager has yet had the nerve to try it out, and we have little doubt that McGraw will quietly weaken on it should he be bold enough to try it in championship games. It always was a poor scheme to swap horses crossing a stream, and it would be a still greater mistake to take out a pitcher who happened to be pitching winning ball just because he had completed five innings. The new pitcher would not be warmed up, and the change of style might be just what the batsmen were looking for" (*Sporting Life*, April 18, 1903).

As it turned out, Christy Mathewson pitched a complete game victory for the Giants on opening day, and Iron Man McGinnity followed with another the next day. McGraw essentially abandoned his scheme at that point, yet he does not appear to have entirely forgotten about it. For example, in a 5-2 loss to Chicago on May 23, 1907, he used the unheard of total of six pitchers.

In the ensuing years it became more common for teams to use an ace starter like the Cubs' Mordecai Brown to relieve at critical points in late games. An article in *Sporting News* after the 1912 season noted the success of pitchers like Walter Johnson, Vean Gregg, and Ed Walsh in relief roles and commented: "The pinch pitcher is becoming a factor in the big league races, and it may be only a short time until teams will have to carry great one and two-inning pitchers—men that hurl shut-out ball for a couple of rounds" (*Sporting News*, January 2, 1913).

Over the next two decades, pitchers like Doc Crandall of the Giants, Firpo Marberry of the Senators, and Wilcy Moore of the Yankees emerged as effective relief specialists. Yet the mind-set that it was wasteful to use a good pitcher in relief must have remained powerful, since none of these pitchers' managers could resist the urge to start them from time to time. As a result, the first effective pitcher to be used almost exclusively in relief was the Yankees' Johnny Murphy in the late 1930s and early 1940s.

Murphy explained that he was willing to accept this new role because he felt appreciated: "I don't know how I'd feel about it if I had to go to another club. On the Yankees they appreciate the necessity, the value of relief pitching. [Manager Joe] McCarthy repeatedly has told me that he rates me on a par with any of his starting hurlers. I am paid the starters' scale. I am happy" (quoted in John Thorn, *The Relief Pitcher*, 61–62).

6.2.10   Closers. John Thorn and John Holway characterized John Mc-Graw as "the first genius who suspected the value of the save, although again, even he only dimly grasped the importance of his discovery" (John Thorn and John Holway, *The Pitcher*, 108). McGraw, for example, used Claud Elliott ten times in 1905, and when saves were retroactively calculated in the 1960s it was discovered that Elliott had a then-record six saves in those ten appearances.

Nonetheless, with saves not becoming an official statistic until the 1960s, it was a long time before today's practice of reserving one pitcher for save situations emerged. This trend began in the late 1970s with Bruce Sutter of the Chicago Cubs being one of the first pitchers to be used primarily in save situations.

6.2.11   Designated Hitters. The American League's adoption of the designated hitter in 1973 was the culmination of a long and circuitous journey.

An 1891 article reported a conversation in which Ted Sullivan said that pitchers should not be allowed to hit, as they are a "lot of whippoorwill stickers." A. G. Spalding's brother J. Walter Spalding suggested that pitchers should just be skipped, leaving eight men in the batting order. Pittsburgh president William Chase Temple instead recommended "the substitution of another man to take the pitcher's place at the bat when it came his turn to go there." It was reported that the idea would be presented to the rules committee, but I found no indication that that had happened (*Sporting News*, December 19, 1891).

The idea continued to resurface from time to time, and in 1900 Tim Murnane voiced his support. Connie Mack brought the matter to the rules committee in 1906 (*Sporting Life*, February 3, 1906). John Heydler proposed the designated hitter at the annual National League meeting on December 11, 1928, and John McGraw thought it was a good idea. Ironically it was the American League that opposed the idea.

By the 1960s the idea had gained enough support for several minor leagues to express interest. The Pacific Coast League wanted to use the designated hitter in 1961 but was denied permission to do so by the Professional Baseball Rules Committee. During spring training in 1967, the Chicago White Sox experimented with allowing a designated pinch hitter to bat twice in a game.

The experimentation increased greatly in 1969, partly in reaction to the dominance of pitchers during the 1968 season. During spring training the major leagues experimented with a variety of ways of having a "designated pinch hitter." Researcher John Lewis drew my attention to an article about the different rules that appeared in the February 15, 1969, issue of the *Sporting News*. The designated pinch hitter, which was the equivalent of the current designated hitter, was used that year in four minor leagues: the American Association, the International League, the Eastern League, and the Arizona Instructional League. Meanwhile the Texas League used a wild-card pinch hitter who could bat for any player.

Researcher Kevin Saldana reported that Paul Flesner of the Dallas-Fort Worth Spurs became the first wild-card pinch hitter on April 11, 1969, going 2 for 4 with 4 RBIs. According to Lewis, the first true designated hitter in regular season professional baseball was either John Brandt of Oklahoma City, Larry Osborne of Omaha, or Charles Weatherspoon of Denver on April 18.

The American League finally approved the idea as a three-year experiment on December 10, 1972. On March 6, 1973, Larry Hisle became the first designated hitter to appear in an exhibition game and drove in seven runs. On April 6, Ron Blomberg of the Yankees became the first DH in a regular-season game. The AL made the rule permanent in December 1975.

According to sportswriter Red Smith, the National League almost adopted the designated hitter in 1980 (Red Smith, August 18, 1980, reprinted in *Red Smith on Baseball*). Nonetheless more than three decades after the American League first used the designated hitter this remains a major difference between two leagues that are otherwise virtually indistinguishable.

(iii) Lineups

Obviously, filling out a lineup card was a straightforward act in the days when clubs carried nine or at most ten players. But as roster sizes swelled during the 1880s, lineups increasingly assumed strategic implications.

6.3.1   Submitting Lineups. In early baseball there were some attempts to require clubs to submit their lineups before the start of the game, but they were not very successful. After the 1877 season the National League decided that a captain could send his players to bat in any order he wanted, though he had to continue that order in subsequent trips through the order (*Chicago Tribune*, December 9, 1877).

The *New York Clipper* reported at the start of the 1881 season: "A new rule adopted by the League requires the captain of each nine to furnish the exact batting order by nine o'clock on the morning of each game, and prohibits any change in the order so furnished, except in case of sickness or accident." One of the main reasons for the rule was reported to be that scorecard sales were dropping because the lineups were not reliable (*New York Clipper*, April 2, 1881).

The last clause of the rule made it difficult to enforce, as umpire Billy Evans explained in 1913: "Not so many years ago it was customary for the umpire to get the lineup some time prior to the start of the game. Often a manager would say either Jones or Smith would play left field that day, there being some doubt because Jones, who is the regular man, was said to be suffering with a bad ankle.

"The explanation listened swell, but in reality the manager was waiting to see who would pitch for the opposition before making his final selection. Jones, the regular player, happened to be weak when hitting against southpaws. Now the manager desired to use Jones if a right-hander was selected to pitch, but preferred Smith if a southpaw was selected. He saw two pitchers, one a right-hander and the other a left-hander, warming up for his rivals. That made him undecided. He hears the announcement that a right-hander will work for the opposition, whereupon he informs the umpire that Jones says his ankle is all right, and that he will play.

"Under the old ruling the fact that the manager had stated either of the two men might play did not affect the standing of the player not selected. He could enter the game later if the manager desired to use him.

"Under the ruling now in vogue the umpire accepts only one man for a position. If after the announcement of pitchers the manager desires to withdraw a certain player and substitute another, the player withdrawn is through for the rest of the afternoon, though the game has not really started. Now, if a manager desires to use strategy in finding out who is going to pitch, he must be prepared to sacrifice one of his players to accomplish his end" (*Sporting News*, January 9, 1913).

Enforcement of the revamped rule also seems to have grown lax. In 1923 a *Detroit Free Press* article observed: "Manager [Ty] Cobb's refusal to announce his pitchers prior to game time had Lee Fohl guessing. The Browns' pilot nominated both right and lefthand pitchers for his team's batting practice and then watched to see which of the Tiger gunners would participate in the clan's practice. Cobb continued the deception by instructing [right-handed pitcher Rip] Collins and [left-handed pitcher Ray] Francis to hit" (*Detroit Free Press*, April 19, 1923).

6.3.2 Batting Orders. Batting orders were fairly malleable in early baseball. A wide variety of theories were employed in devising them, and they tended to be general rather than specific. Henry Chadwick offered this advice in 1867: "In arranging your order of striking, see that strong hitters follow the poor batsmen, and that good base runners precede them. For instance, suppose that your best out-fielder, or your pitcher or catcher, is not as skilful at bat as the others, in placing him on the books as a striker put a good base runner's name down before him; by this means the chances for the first base being vacated by the time he is ready to make it, will be increased, as likewise those for two runs being obtained after he has made his base. Never put three poor hitters together, but support each, if possible, as above recommended" (*Haney's Base Ball Book of Reference for 1867*; reprinted in *The Ball Player's Chronicle*, August 15, 1867).

Even if a captain chose to follow this advice, it left him quite a bit of flexibility. With no dominant paradigm, it does not appear that captains of the period stayed awake at night worrying about their batting order, which is just as well. Sophisticated modern studies of batting orders show that the difference in runs created does not vary greatly from one lineup to another. Pete Palmer estimated that the worst possible lineup arrangement would score only twenty-five fewer runs per season than the best possible order (John Thorn and Pete Palmer, *The Hidden Game of Baseball*, 162–163).

By the 1880s the decision-making responsibilities were beginning to pass to managers, who were showing greater uniformity in devising their lineups. An 1884 piece explained, "The old plan of changing the order of batting every game is not now adopted by the best managed clubs. Experience has shown that better results follow where a regular order of striking is observed throughout the season. The first thing in settling upon the order of batting is to ascertain, by practical experience, which batsmen are best suited to follow each other. Thus a poor runner should be invariably followed by a good hitter, and a sharp runner should precede a poor or uncertain hitter. Then, too, when a regular order is observed, batsmen know what they have to do, alike in batting and base running. Thus, if the first striker makes his base and he knows that the batsman who follows him is not likely to bat him round the bases, he is prepared to take greater risks in base running than would be necessary if the succeeding batsman is a sure hitter. Then, too, the man at the bat is largely guided in his efforts in batting by what he knows of the runner's ability who preceded him to steal bases, etc. In fact a regular and sustained order of striking is the only way to promote team work in batting and base running, while the plan of changing the order, with a view of making it a species of reward, is a bad one in every way, it being neither an honor to be at the head of the list, nor any discredit to be the ninth man at the bat" (*Brooklyn Eagle*, August 10, 1884).

Some of the factors that the manager considered in arranging his lineup reflected the conditions of the day, such as the fact that base coaching was still done by players. Researcher David Ball discovered an 1889 account that explained that, as a result, Indianapolis manager Jack Glasscock spaced his three best base coaches in the lineup so that one of them would always be available to coach (*Sporting Life*, August 28, 1889).

By the 1890s managers were putting considerable emphasis on batting orders. *Sporting Life*'s Kansas City correspondent noted in 1892, "The question of the batting order of the team is worrying [Kansas City] Manager [Jimmy] Manning to some extent, as he is not acquainted with the hitting ability of his men" (*Sporting Life*, April 16, 1892). *Sporting Life* editor Francis Richter added in 1903, "A batting order is a serious matter. It can only be well made up on each player's ability in various departments, and once arranged should not be disturbed except when a man's failure to come up to form and expectation is complete and apparently irremediable" (*Sporting Life*, May 2, 1903).

6.3.3 Leadoff Batters. Today's model for a leadoff hitter developed very gradually. Henry Chadwick advised only: "Let your first striker always be the coolest hand of the nine" (*Haney's Base Ball Book of Reference for 1867*, reprinted in *The Ball Player's Chronicle*, August 15, 1867). An 1893 *Atlanta Constitution* article noted that Jimmy Stafford "always leads the batting order for the home team, because he is one of the hardest hitters on the team as well as the surest base getter and runner" (*Atlanta Constitution*, April 23, 1893). Researcher Tom Shieber directed my attention to an 1898 *Sporting Life* article that remarked: "It is customary to have a small, active fellow who can hit, run and steal bases, and also worry a pitcher into a preliminary base on balls, as a leader in the list" (*Sporting Life*, May 28, 1898). A 1906 article reported that Bill O'Neill "looks like a good lead off, being left handed, fast, and a good waiter" (*Chicago Tribune*, March 26, 1906).

6.3.4 Second-place Hitters. *Sporting Life's* Kansas City correspondent noted in 1892 that player-manager Jimmy Manning would lead off and "will be followed by [Arthur] Sunday, who is a left-handed hitter. This will give Manning a chance to steal second" (*Sporting Life*, April 16, 1892). The same 1898 *Sporting Life* article that noted the development of customs for leadoff batters added that clubs liked to place a "clever sacrifice hitter" in the second slot (*Sporting Life*, May 28, 1898).

6.3.5 Cleanup Hitters. Since home runs were rare occurrences between 1870 and 1920, the precept of batting a home run hitter fourth was naturally slow to develop. But the need for a good run producer in that slot was recognized from the early days in baseball history, and Cap Anson generally penciled his own name in there.

As power came to play a larger role in the game, the tendency to bat home run hitters fourth also developed. The 1898 article on batting-order customs gave this job description: "a massive slugger who can drive the ball out of the lot" (*Sporting Life*, May 28, 1898). Tim Murnane noted in 1904: "The heavy hitter of the team is located at the fourth place" (*Washington Post*, July 24, 1904).

The term we now use had come into vogue by 1908 when sportswriter Al Weinfeld wrote: "That he was the 'cleaner-up' of his team is shown by his being fourth on the batting order for Peoria all season" (*Sporting News*, December 24, 1908).

6.3.6 Spacing Left-handed and Right-handed Batters. Before the advent of relief pitching there would have been no logical reason to alternate left- and right-handed batters. Indeed, managers generally took the opposite approach.

Henry Chadwick noted at the end of the 1879 season that a significant development had been the "introduction of batting quartets of left-handed hard hitters" (*New York Clipper*, December 20, 1879). As is noted in the entry on "Platooning" (**6.3.9**), 1883 Grand Rapids player-manager Henry Monroe Jones moved all of the batters with the platoon advantage to the top of his lineup. Horace Phillips picked up this approach from Jones at Grand Rapids and then brought it along to Pittsburgh in 1888. A reporter explained: "The right and left-handed hitters will be dovetailed together. This is one of Horace Phillips' theories, and it is claimed that it will puzzle a great many pitchers" (*Detroit Free Press*, April 8, 1888).

Before the 1907 season it was reported that Boston manager Chick Stahl had made "a unique change in his batting order by alternating right and left-handed batters through the first seven men" (*Sporting Life*, March 30, 1907).

Sadly, Stahl had committed suicide two days before the press date of the issue. Since relief pitchers were still used sparingly, it seems likely that Stahl simply thought that an alternating sequence would keep pitchers off balance.

There were other isolated instances of this approach, but it didn't come to fruition until after the use of relief pitchers became common. (For example, the *Washington Post* of April 15, 1910, reported that Washington manager Jimmy McAleer had separated two left-handed batters against left-handed pitcher Eddie Plank.) Lee Allen credited John McGraw with being the first manager to deliberately space left-handed and right-handed batters in his lineup (Lee Allen, *The Hot Stove League*, 33). Allen did not specify a time frame, but it seems likely that McGraw did this in the late 1910s or 1920s in response to the increased use of relievers.

6.3.7　Shhh! If a batter steps to the plate when it is not his turn, the opposing manager is well advised to keep quiet about it. That enables him to let the result stand if the batter makes an out. But if the batter gets a hit, the manager can have him declared out for batting out of turn. Jim Bouton related in *Ball Four* how Seattle Pilots manager Joe Schultz filled out an incorrect lineup card for a game on May 28, 1969. Schultz's opposite number, Earl Weaver, noticed the error immediately but waited until Seattle had a rally going before pointing it out and nullifying the threat (Jim Bouton, *Ball Four*, 162–163).

6.3.8　Out of a Hat. Occasionally a manager attempts to change the luck of a slumping team by picking his lineup out of a hat. Billy Martin, for example, tried this approach while managing Detroit in 1972 (Red Smith, August 16, 1972, reprinted in *Red Smith on Baseball*). Don Zimmer also resorted to this method of shaking things up while managing the Red Sox. To his chagrin, "seven out of eight came out in the same place they'd batted in the day before. That's how bad I was going" (Roger Angell, *A Pitcher's Story*, 134).

6.3.9　Platooning. As with so many components of baseball, the emergence of platooning was impeded first by practical considerations and later by philosophical ones.

There were few left-handed pitchers in early baseball, and the curveball did not become a major force in most pitchers' arsenals until the late 1870s. Although Bobby Mitchell was briefly effective, the first left-handed pitcher to experience prolonged success was J Lee Richmond.

Richmond won thirty-two games as a rookie with Worcester in 1880, and "columns of room were given to discussion in the newspapers as to why the delivery of a left-hand pitcher should be harder to bat than that of a right-hand pitcher" (*Detroit Free Press*, March 31, 1895). In a game on June

26, 1880, three left-handed Chicago batters, Abner Dalrymple, George Gore, and Larry Corcoran, batted right-handed against Richmond.

Ned Hanlon, later a legendary manager but then an outfielder with Detroit, was another left-handed batter who was acutely aware of his disadvantage against Richmond. When Detroit and Worcester met for the first time in the 1881 season, it was reported, "for the reason that he had never been able to bat Richmond's left-handed curves, Hanlon was laid off by Manager Bancroft and Reilly was placed at center field" (*Detroit Free Press*, May 11, 1881). He returned the next day, and the *Free Press* chided: "The placing of Hanlon at center field yesterday proved the error of leaving him out of the nine on Tuesday . . . despite the belief that he cannot hit Richmond, [he] made one of the five base hits credited to Detroit" (*Detroit Free Press*, May 12, 1881). Nonetheless the next series between the clubs again brought word that "Hanlon did not play yesterday for the reason that he, being a left-handed batter, cannot hit Richmond" (*Detroit Free Press*, June 2, 1881).

The following season the *Free Press* reported with obvious pleasure that Ned Hanlon had gotten two hits against Richmond, though he "had solemnly affirmed a score of times that he cannot hit a left-handed pitcher" (*Detroit Free Press*, June 12, 1882). But Hanlon once again was on the bench when the Wolverines faced Richmond on September 12, 1882.

Henry Monroe Jones was player-manager of the Grand Rapids entry in the Northwestern League in 1883. Being a switch-hitter himself, Jones was very aware of the concept now known as the platoon advantage. The limited roster sizes and lack of in-game substitutions limited his flexibility, but he did what he could to give his team the edge. He had a couple of other switch-hitters on the club, and by using his extra players toward this end was able to get mostly right-handed batters in the lineup against lefties, and vice versa. He also moved batters with the platoon advantage to the top of his batting order.

By the mid-1880s left-handed pitchers were becoming more common, and an increasing number of clubs were doing what they could to fill their lineups with as many right-handed batters as possible when facing a southpaw. An article in *Sporting Life* in 1885 noted that Sam Wise was not playing shortstop for Boston due to a sore arm, explaining: "Another reason, and a very potent one, for not playing Sam on Thursday was because of his inability to bat [Dupee] Shaw, the latter being a left-handed pitcher and Sam a left-handed batter, consequently for the present [Tom] Poorman and Wise will alternate in right field" (*Sporting Life*, September 9, 1885).

The tactic spread further in 1886 when Detroit southpaw Charles "Lady" Baldwin had an outstanding season. When Harry Wright's Philadelphia charges faced Baldwin, "left field was not occupied by George Wood. Pitcher [Ed] Daily was stationed in that garden. This was partly because

Wood is averse to south-paws" (*Detroit Free Press*, May 19, 1886). Chicago's
Cap Anson took a similar approach: "Dalrymple and Gore being left-handed
batters, and not desiring to face Baldwin, [Jocko] Flynn and [Jimmy] Ryan
were substituted" (*Detroit Free Press*, May 7, 1886). Tom Nawrocki has argued that Anson was the first manager to use a platoon system (Tom
Nawrocki, "Captain Anson's Platoon," *National Pastime* 15 [1995], 34).

Bill James noted that outfielders Gid Gardner and Tom Brown of Indianapolis were platooned in 1887 (Bill James, *The New Bill James Historical
Baseball Abstract*, 117). Pittsburgh's Horace Phillips experimented with a like
arrangement in 1888: "[Abner] Dalrymple will lay off in all the games where
a left-handed pitcher twirls against the Pittsburg team this season, as he is
unable to hit a south paw's delivery" (*San Francisco Examiner*, April 2, 1888).

With so many managers already familiar with the technique, platooning
naturally increased in 1891 when unlimited substitutions were legalized.
Early in the season *Sporting Life* reported: "[Jack] Chapman, of Louisville,
was the first manager to take advantage of the new rule permitting the use
of an unlimited number of substitutions in a game, when he last Saturday
took out three left-handed batsmen who could not hit a left-handed pitcher
and substituted three right-handed hitters. This was also a new batting
wrinkle which is likely to find favor with many managers" (*Sporting Life*,
April 18, 1891).

Small roster sizes continued to limit this practice, as did the increasing
scarcity of left-handed infielders. But a number of clubs tried platoon
arrangements in the outfield. A *Sporting Life* correspondent reported in
1896, "When the Senators face a left-hander Captain [Bill] Joyce rearranges
the batting order and sends [Billy] Lush to the field in place of a left-hand
hitter" (*Sporting Life*, June 20, 1896).

A 1923 article offered this history of platooning: "Some left-handed hitters are easy picking for a classy southpaw hurler and it is for that reason that
a number of managers have devised what is known as the 'reversible outfield,' playing as many left-handers out there as possible when a regular
pitcher is in the box and switching to their string of right-handers when the
team is called to face a southpaw.

"The famous Buck Ewing, when he was manager of the Reds in the late
nineties, was the first manager to make this sort of shift. Buck was a fine
leader, a very close student of the game, and a man who played the percentage down to the finest point. On his team he had Dummy Hoy, a great
fielder and hardhitter [sic], especially against right-hand pitching. But Hoy
was not as strong against the southpaws, so when such men as Frank Killen,
Jesse Tannehill or Fred Klobedanz were working against the Reds, Buck
would retire Hoy for the day and send in a right-hand hitter" (*Cincinnati Enquirer*, March 4, 1923).

Platooning does not appear to have been common in the first decade of the twentieth century, though it certainly didn't disappear. Detroit manager Bill Armour began using such an arrangement with his catchers in 1906 (Bill James, *The New Bill James Historical Baseball Abstract*, 117). A 1907 article noted: "[Washington] Manager [Joe] Cantillon, when he was satisfied that [left-hander Rube] Kroh was going to pitch, decided that it would be too great a disadvantage to have five left-handed hitters in the game against a left-handed pitcher, and so decided to let [right-handed hitting Charlie] Jones take [left-handed hitting Clyde] Milan's place" (*Washington Post*, September 1, 1907).

George Stallings brought the tactic back to prominence with the Miracle Braves of 1914, and Tris Speaker made use of it in leading the Indians to the 1920 World Series title. The success of platoons on these World Series winners might have been expected to smooth the way for their acceptance, but instead it only increased the vehemence of detractors.

Sportswriter John B. Sheridan inveighed in 1924: "What is the effect of substituting right-handed hitters for left-handers when a left-handed pitcher is on the rubber? Spoon-feeding baseball players. Giving them setups. Making things soft for them. Coddling them. Softening them morally, by keeping them alternately on the bench and sending them in only to pick on crippled birds. Permitting them to become soft of muscle and weak of will, discontented loafers or semi-loafers. . . . Shifting players, in and out, utterly dislocates team work. Oh, yes, I know that George Stallings did win the world's championship in spite of having two sets of duplicate outfielders, but Stallings actually won in 1914 because he had three great pitchers going right, not because he shifted outfields to the opposing pitcher. . . . About the very worst thing that can happen to any young man in any business or profession is to have things 'made easy' for him. Hell's bells, the only way to make a young man worth a cent is to put him out there when things are hard for them" (*Sporting News*, August 7, 1924). Mickey Cochrane more succinctly called platooning "bunk" (Mickey Cochrane, *Baseball: The Fans' Game*, 174).

Platooning finally became established after World War II, thanks in large part to Casey Stengel, the Yankees manager. Even then, there remained many who were none too keen on the idea. In 1948, Red Smith wrote, ". . . Students interested in trends might find some profit in studying the current passion for 'percentages' among major-league managers. Unless the style changes, we've seen our last Joe DiMaggio or Stan Musial, because today's managers won't let a guy stay in long enough to become an all-around player. They consider it a mortal sin to let a left-handed batter swing against a left-handed pitcher, or a right-hander against a right-hander" (Red Smith, June 15, 1948, reprinted in *Red Smith on Baseball*).

6.3.10   Bait and Switch. An effective way to gain the upper hand on a club that uses platooning is for the opposing team to start one pitcher but soon switch.

Washington manager Bucky Harris started right-hander Curly Ogden in the seventh game of the 1924 World Series with the intention of having him only face one batter. After Ogden fanned leadoff hitter Fred Lindstrom on three pitches, "The crowd, in amazement, saw Ogden roll up his glove, stuff it into his hip pocket and start for the dugout. But [Bucky] Harris, impressed with the hurler's pitching against Lindstrom, sent the righthander back to the mound to pitch to Frankie Frisch" (*Sporting News*, March 14, 1962). Harris had outsmarted himself this time; Ogden walked Frisch, and Harris then made the switch. The Senators ultimately won the game and the Series in the twelfth inning.

San Diego manager Preston Gomez used the same ploy in a May 26, 1971, doubleheader against the Astros. Left-hander Al Santorini started the first game but pitched to only one batter before being relieved by a right-hander. Santorini was again the starter in the second game, and this time he remained in the game. The Padres were swept in the doubleheader.

6.3.11   Lineup Tricks. Managers do have an effective way to counteract an opposing manager who uses the bait-and-switch tactic described in the preceding entry. They can list pitchers whom they don't intend to use in their starting lineup, and this tactic has the additional benefit of allowing them to pinch-hit if a scoring opportunity arises. On September 11, 1958, Baltimore manager Paul Richards handed in a lineup card that included three pitchers. On June 29, 1961, Philadelphia pilot Gene Mauch listed four pitchers in his starting lineup in an attempt to outmaneuver Giants manager Alvin Dark.

6.3.12   Hitter to Be Designated Later. Researcher Wayne McElreavy noted that Baltimore manager Earl Weaver started making use of a similar idea as the result of the events of the first game of a doubleheader on September 8, 1980. The Orioles used a variety of designated hitters that year, with Lee May acting in that capacity in this particular game. May batted in the seventh slot, but Detroit pitcher Milt Wilcox was pulled from the game after facing only four batters. Although the Tigers brought in another right-hander, Weaver realized that he would have ended up wasting May if they had brought in a left-hander.

Accordingly, in twenty-one of the Orioles' remaining twenty-six games that season, Weaver listed a pitcher whom he did not intend to use as his designated hitter. When the player's turn came up, Weaver would insert a pinch hitter depending on which hand the pitcher threw with. Detroit manager Sparky Anderson also used this tactic on two occasions, both of them against Weaver's Orioles. The rule was changed over the offseason to require the starting designated hitter to bat at least once unless the opposing team had made a pitching change.

6.3.13   Rotations. It is sometimes said that early professional baseball clubs had only one pitcher. This is a misconception. In fact, as early as 1867, Henry Chadwick declared that "a first-class team always has two pitchers in it" (*Haney's Base Ball Book of Reference*, reprinted in *The Ball Player's Chronicle*, August 22, 1867).

These clubs generally had only one primary pitcher, but they always carried a "change pitcher" who would often pitch against the amateur and semi-pro clubs that made up a significant part of every club's schedule. Al Pratt later explained that in the early 1870s "there was a 'change pitcher,' who played the position when the regular man was sick, but a man hired to pitch was expected to pitch" (quoted in *Sporting News*, March 23, 1895).

As Pratt implied, good pitchers commanded top dollar, so clubs didn't spend comparable money on their "change pitcher." But sometimes they found they had two pitchers of roughly equal skill and tried to make use of both. George Zettlein and Tom Pratt appear to have been used in tandem by the Atlantics of Brooklyn in the late 1860s (William J. Ryczek, "George Zettlein," in Frederick Ivor-Campbell, Robert L. Tiemann, and Mark Rucker, eds., *Baseball's First Stars*, 182). The plans of the Forest Citys of Cleveland in 1872 were that "In some of the games [Rynie] Wolters will pitch, in others [Al] Pratt, according to circumstances" (*Cleveland Plain Dealer*, April 27, 1872). Tommy Bond and Arthur Cummings were hired by Hartford for the 1875 season and told they would both be "regular pitchers," though Cummings ended up getting the lion's share of the work (David Arcidiacono, *Grace, Grit and Growling*, 30).

It is often contended that Cap Anson used the first rotation in 1880 when he alternated Larry Corcoran and Fred Goldsmith. A December 19, 1891, *Sporting News* article may have originated this claim, and it was expanded by the *Detroit Free Press*: "Up to the innovation started by the Chicago club, when Corcoran and Goldsmith were hired by the Chicago team, and were pitched alternate days, one pitcher was supposed to do all the work. It created an immense amount of gossip among the baseball enthusiasts when the Chicago club adopted the new method, and the baseball cranks of those days, like the baseball cranks of the present, were disposed to be enraged at some of the other teams in the league because they did not engage another pitcher in order to be as well equipped as Chicago" (*Detroit Free Press*, March 31, 1895).

This, however, is a classic case of history being told from the perspective of the victors. Anson's alternate use of Corcoran and Goldsmith in 1880 is the first time that a National League club was very successful in dividing the pitching labors between more than one man, but it is inaccurate to call this a first.

In addition to the earlier examples already cited, Corcoran and Goldsmith had been used in the same manner for part of the preceding season when they were teammates for Springfield, Massachusetts. Goldsmith and Corcoran shared the pitching duties for Springfield until the club disbanded on September 6. While their starts did not follow a strict alternating pattern, neither man had a long skein as the primary starter.

Moreover, in pegging Anson's use of Corcoran and Goldsmith as a first, a slightly more complicated but far more interesting story has been overlooked. Here's what actually happened.

Before the 1880 season the National League club in Buffalo announced plans to balance the workloads of its two batteries: catcher Dude Esterbrook paired with pitcher Tom Poorman, and catcher Jack Rowe with pitcher Billy McGunnigle. The *New York Clipper* noted: "The two batteries will be brought to bear on the teams they are most successful against. Experience has shown that every pitcher in the arena finds one team with which he is invariably more successful than against any other, and the team he is able to pitch against with the most effect should, of course, be that one he selected to play against [sic]. Thus the two batteries will be regular, instead of one being regular and the other the change-battery" (*New York Clipper*, March 20, 1880).

A careful look at usage patterns reveals just how ludicrous it is to credit Anson with inventing the rotation. Buffalo started the 1880 campaign with two starts by McGunnigle, one by Poorman, two more by McGunnigle, and one more by Poorman. Chicago, in contrast, began the season with Larry Corcoran starting six straight games. In their seventh outing, Fred Goldsmith was finally given the nod and pitched a shutout.

At this point Chicago hosted Buffalo in a fateful three-game series. Goldsmith did the pitching for the home team in all three games and was outstanding. Buffalo tried both of their starters without success. Thereafter the 8-1 White Stockings and the 2-7 Buffalo squad exchanged tactics. Buffalo signed James "Pud" Galvin and made him their primary starter while Anson realized that he had two outstanding pitchers and began to balance their workloads.

For the next eight weeks, Goldsmith and Corcoran more or less alternated with spectacular results. The club ran off six more wins to push their winning streak to a National League record thirteen games. Chicago then dropped two games—one with each starter—before launching an incredible twenty-one-game winning streak (with one sixteen-inning tie), which has been surpassed only once in the major leagues in the years since.

The streak ended on July 10 when Fred Dunlap of Cleveland broke up a scoreless tie with the first "walkoff" home run in major league history (see **1.25**). Dunlap's blast not only finished the streak but also effectively ended Chicago's pitching rotation. Goldsmith contracted a fever shortly after the game and was sent home to recover. When he finally returned in September, Anson's use of his two ace starters was erratic. So Anson had taken an idea used by others, did so with the same two pitchers who had been used in similar fashion the preceding season, tried it reluctantly for eight weeks and gotten credit for inventing it because his borrowing corresponded with a twenty-one-game winning streak.

What Anson unquestionably did accomplish was to popularize the use of a pitching staff by showing that a rotation could be used successfully in the National League. The *Free Press* article was on much sounder ground when it contended that Chicago's success in 1880 "proved conclusively to many of the base ball managers that it was better to have an alternating pitcher for each series with a club, than to trust to one man to win all the games" (*Detroit Free Press*, March 31, 1895).

At season's end, Henry Chadwick commented that "the plan of having two regular batteries in working order and of working them in alternate games is a new one." He added that because of its success, "no club team of 1881 can be said to be fully organized unless it has two regular batteries, besides a reserve pitcher. A full team for a campaign, run as campaigns are now, must contain a dozen players, and of these there should be two pitchers, with two catchers to suit the pitchers and who are familiar with their peculiarities" (*New York Clipper*, November 20, 1880).

Until this time, roster sizes were generally limited to ten or at most eleven, so the notion of having to pay twelve salaries was met with resistance by owners. As the *Free Press* later quipped, ". . . There is good ground for believing that certain of the league magnates wrote letters to the Chicago management, denouncing them for establishing a bad precedent in the matter of expense" (*Detroit Free Press*, March 31, 1895).

These owners were no doubt pleased when Charley Radbourn brought back the one-man pitching staff in 1884, winning fifty-nine games and pitching Providence to the National League championship. A *Sporting Life* correspondent commented that Radbourn's "wonderful success has been achieved at the cost of the complete overthrow of the claim of pitchers being unable to stand the 'great fatigue' incident to continuous work in their positions. What Radbourne [sic] can stand hardier pitchers than he can stand more readily, and he has proved pretty conclusively the absurdity of the claim that consecutive work in the box is too trying an ordeal for pitchers to stand without their breaking down under the pressure" (*Sporting Life*, September 24, 1884).

But the advent of overhand pitching made it impossible for Radbourn to repeat his Herculean feat or for any other pitcher to approach it. The added strain of overhand pitching burned out many pitching arms and caused others to take unprecedented precautions. The slightly built Billy Mountjoy, for instance, signed a contract with Cincinnati with a clause "that he shall pitch but two games a week" (*Washington Post*, May 18, 1884).

Overhand pitching thus caused a rapid expansion in the size of pitching staffs, and within a few years most clubs were relying on at least three pitchers. The same 1895 *Free Press* article reported: "Nowadays no baseball team considers itself well equipped unless it carries a pitching force of four men." In 1904 the *Washington Post* observed that a few clubs got by with three pitchers, but most were using four (*Washington Post*, July 10, 1904).

Larger staffs did not necessarily mean pitching rotations, however. As pitching staffs expanded, managers faced large disparities in the quality of their starters. Thus they pursued all sorts of strategies to try to get more starts from their best pitchers, get those starts in the most critical games, and match specific pitchers against specific clubs. Today's idea of a pitching rotation, in which the starting pitchers go out in more or less unvarying order, would have been considered unimaginative and poor strategy.

Gradually, however, increasing credence was attached to the belief that pitchers did their best work when used in predictable sequence. A 1911 article noted that New York Highlanders manager Hal Chase was influenced by this way of thinking: "'Rotation' is the keynote of a new system of handling the pitching staff which has been adopted by the management of the New York Americans for the coming season. Six pitchers, [Russell] Ford, [Jack] Quinn, [Jim] Vaughn, [Ray] Fisher, [Ray] Caldwell and [Jack] Warhop, are relied on to carry the team throughout the summer, and they are to be worked in turn with clock-like regularity. Manager Chase believes that Ford's success last year was wholly due to the fact that he did not pitch out of his regular turn. . . . Ford knew exactly when he was expected to pitch and consequently nerved himself for the task. Chase maintains that if the other pitchers are worked in a similar manner they will prove vastly more effective and in this belief he is supported by many close students of the game. It is urged that a pitcher cannot be expected to do himself justice if he is suddenly called upon to enter the box at a time when he is hardly ready for a grueling test" (*Sporting News*, February 2, 1911).

Other managers seem to have experimented with this approach. Sportswriter James Crusinberry observed in 1916, "The [Cubs] pitchers who seem sure of places and who are likely to be worked in rotation the opening weeks are [Claude] Hendrix, [Jim] Vaughn, [George] McConnell, [Tom] Seaton and [Jimmy] Lavender" (*Boston Globe*, April 6, 1916). But a strict rotation remained uncommon for many years to come.

Johnny Vander Meer, for instance, described the rotation as if it were still a novelty in 1938 when he played for Cincinnati. Reds manager Bill McKechnie, he noted, "would put you on a system of starting every so many days, and we started regardless of who we were playing. He got you on that rotation, he got your system going, and he stayed with it" (Walter M. Langford, *Legends of Baseball*, 192).

6.3.14   Weekend Starters. After World War II, managers became increasingly prone to using strict rotations. Of course there continued to be exceptions when a manager wanted to give more work to one starter or have a pitcher face (or avoid) a particular pitcher or team.

One of the more novel exceptions was the once-a-week starter, which became a bit of a tradition for the White Sox. Ted Lyons became well known as Chicago's Sunday pitcher toward the end of his career. When Marty Marion managed the White Sox in 1955 and 1956, he revived the tradition: "I'd only pitch Billy Pierce on Sunday. Billy wasn't a very strong kid, and if you pitched him in rotation every fourth day he'd get murdered. But if you'd give him his rest he'd beat the opposition regularly" (Walter M. Langford, *Legends of Baseball*, 209).

6.3.15   No Starters. Are starters who get the lion's share of the work necessary at all? Several years ago Oakland manager Tony LaRussa tried a scheme in which several pitchers would be scheduled to work a few innings apiece in each game. This was not entirely new, however. As discussed in "Relief Specialists" (**6.2.9**), John McGraw had proposed a similar arrangement in 1903.

6.3.16   Personal Catchers. The idea of a personal catcher was revived in the 1970s with such pairings as Tim McCarver and Steve Carlton, and was considered by many to be new. It is more accurate, however, to see it as a throwback to a very common practice in early baseball.

Early catchers and pitchers were linked not only by their proximity on the field but also by a shared yoke of pain and suffering. Pitchers had the strain of backbreaking workloads, which were not entirely eased by the fact that overhand pitching was not yet legal. Catchers had an even more onerous job, with little or no equipment to protect them from foul tips. By the late 1870s, though clubs often carried only nine players, it was common to designate two of the outfielders as the "change catcher" and "change pitcher" and to use them to spell the regular battery members when needed. Within a few years many clubs were carrying ten or eleven players so that the change catcher and pitcher did not have to suit up every day.

As sharing the pitching load between two men became popular, many clubs chose to follow the same course with their catchers as well, creating two pairs of batterymates. In 1879 the *Chicago Tribune* noted, "Catchers and pitchers are beginning to make a point of practicing and hiring in teams. This is a good idea, and, if followed up, would produce much more effective catching and pitching" (*Chicago Tribune*, March 16, 1879). One of the more unique teams was the pairing of Frank Hengstebeck and Eugene Vadeboncoeur with the Port Hurons of 1882. When Vadeboncoeur was released, a nearby town's newspaper quipped, "now the Port Huron papers will have space for market reports, as well as base ball" (*Lapeer* [Mich.] *Democrat*, July 25, 1882).

The tactic of revolving batteries continued to be used throughout the 1880s. Catchers understandably thought the extra rest was a great idea, with Doc Bushong commenting, "The 'pairing' of pitchers and catchers so they can work steadily together, is always beneficial" (*New York Sun*, May 6, 1888). Henry Chadwick concurred, writing in 1890: "More than ever before was it plainly manifested last season that without team work together by the two battery players no pitcher, no matter what his individual ability in the position may be, can hope to be successful. 'How can I pitch to-day?' says the rattled star pitcher, 'when I have not got my regular catcher?' And that regular catcher is the player who knows every signal of his pitcher, and who is familiar with all his strategic points of play, and knows how to ably assist him in his work" (*Spalding's Official Base Ball Guide, 1890*, 45).

During the 1890s, however, such arrangements became increasingly rare. The strain of overhand deliveries was causing many clubs to use three or four pitchers. Meanwhile catcher's equipment was improving dramatically, and this enabled a team's best catcher to shoulder more of the load.

Personal catchers thus became rare again, though there were occasional exceptions. Russell Ford, for example, pitched almost exclusively to Ed Sweeney because of his knowledge of how to catch the emery ball (see **3.2.13**).

(iv) Intentional Walks

6.4.1 Intentional Walks. Bases on balls became part of baseball in the mid-1860s, and it did not take long before intentional walks were at least being considered. They were deterred, however, by doubts about the advisability of the strategy, since issuing a base on balls was inconsistent with the goal of preventing batters from reaching base. This is a very reasonable concern; indeed, while the intentional walk has now long been a regular feature of baseball, many analysts contend it is greatly overused.

The intentional base on balls thus was rare in the 1870s and 1880s, but it was used on occasion. Researcher Greg Rhodes found this newspaper account of a June 27, 1870, game between the Red Stockings of Cincinnati and the Olympics of Washington: "The pitcher of the Olympics did his best to let George Wright take his first every time on called balls, as he preferred that to George's style of hitting. George went to first twice on called balls, but on three or four other occasions he managed to strike the ball." Henry Chadwick wrote in 1873, "We have seen a pitcher purposely allow his adversary to take his base on called balls, simply because he knew him to be a skillful hitter, and chose rather to give him a base than let him make two or three by a good hit; and in doing this he purposely tempted the next striker to hit a ball to the shortstop, in order to capture the man on the first at second base" (*New York Clipper*, April 19, 1873).

Researcher David Arcidiacono discovered an account of what appears to have been an intentional walk that pitcher Bobby Mathews of the Mutuals issued to Hartford captain Lip Pike in an 1874 game (*Hartford Post*, September 2, 1874). A *Sporting Life* correspondent noted in 1884 that pitcher Will White had a hard time against left-handed hitters but "understands his weakness in this particular, and we have often seen him give the left-handed batsman a base rather than let him hit the ball when a safe strike would bring in a run" (*Sporting Life*, February 6, 1884). John Clarkson of Chicago twice intentionally walked St. Louis's Tip O'Neill in a postseason game in St. Louis on October 21, 1886. Chicago manager Cap Anson apparently tried to convince him not to issue the first free pass, but the equally headstrong Clarkson did so anyway (Jerry Lansche, *Glory Fades Away*, 84). Researcher Frank Vaccaro reports that a single "illegal" pitch could be used to send a batter to first base in the mid-1880s. He found that Philadelphia manager Harry Wright instructed his pitcher Charlie Buffinton to do that with Jim O'Rourke batting on August 19, 1887, only to have the next batter, Roger Connor, hit a grand slam.

Despite these examples, the intentional walk remained uncommon throughout the 1880s and was met with considerable resistance when it did occur. Clarkson's use of the tactic was denounced by the *St. Louis Globe-Democrat* as "contemptible" (*St. Louis Globe-Democrat*, October 22, 1886; quoted in Jon David Cash, *Before They Were Cardinals*, 129). Researcher Allan Margulies discovered an account of an 1887 minor league game in which Rochester's [Fred] Lewis, "probably the best batsman in the League," came to the plate with runners on second and third and two out. Syracuse pitcher Dug Crothers "whispered to [catcher Dick] Buckley and then sent in five balls wide of the plate, purposely giving Lewis his base," so as to instead face Doc Kennedy, who had "had little success in hitting him last season." Crothers retired Kennedy, but the reception was anything but warm: "The Rochester contingent in the crowd hissed, and dubbed the play a 'baby act,' and some Syracusans joined in the ungentlemanly demonstration." The *Sporting News* correspondent, however, defended this as a legitimate ploy: "Instead of censure, Crothers is deserving of the highest praise for the act. It proves that he is not a record player [one who thinks only of his own statistics]; but that he plays every point to win the game, and that is all he cares about" (*Sporting News*, May 21, 1887).

As will be discussed under "Playing for One Run" (**6.6.1**), offenses began to feature one-run strategies around 1890. It is thus not surprising that the intentional walk rose to prominence at the same time, since it enables the team in the field to mirror the batting team's strategy by going all out to prevent a single run while risking a big inning.

Patsy Tebeau, manager of the Cleveland Spiders in the 1890s, was one of the men most responsible for popularizing the intentional walk. A later article noted that Tebeau "was a believer in the intentional base on balls if a weak batter were to follow a strong batter whose turn it was at bat. . . . One might go further and say that Tebeau was a near pioneer in the giving of an intentional base on balls. The first few times that he tried it in Cleveland the bleachers jeered. It was a new move to them. It will be found that the bleachers usually are quick to jeer anything out of the ordinary in baseball. . . . The giving of intentional bases on balls went on for a while and then Cleveland discovered that Tebeau was winning games . . . by and by, those who had jeered the Cleveland man began to cheer" (*Sporting News*, December 2, 1920).

The once uncommon strategy had obviously become a familiar one by 1894 when pitcher Ted Breitenstein commented: "I seldom send a man to first on four bad balls purposely and resort to this move only when the game is at a critical stage and I have more confidence in my ability to dispose of the next man up" (*St. Louis Post-Dispatch*, August 12, 1894).

While the 1890s saw the intentional walk become prevalent, the strategy received a mixed reception. Some hailed it as heady strategy, but a majority opposed it. Much of the criticism focused on the scoring practice of considering a run to be unearned if a batter drew a walk and subsequently scored (see **17.5**). This prompted objections that "many pitchers save their records by deliberately giving bases on balls, knowing that earned runs cannot be secured, and thus they save their records" (*Sporting Life*, October 24, 1891).

Clark Griffith raised a very different concern: "The pitcher who is afraid of any batter ought to quit the business. If he doesn't it will not be long before he is proved a coward, and then he will have to quit. The crowd is not in sympathy with any pitcher who is not game enough to let any batter hit the ball, at the same time depending on his own ability" (*Boston Globe*, July 27, 1896).

Sportswriter Ren Mulford, Jr., gave an apt summation of the issue in 1900: "When the game has reached such a ticklish point that a hit will win it, is it good base ball to give a hard hitter his base on balls and take chances on the man who follows? Al Orth did it once in Cincinnati last May, and held the Reds at bay in the twelfth inning of a tie. Whenever the play succeeds the wise ones chuckle and say 'That was good head-work in sending Sluggers to his base.' On the other hand, if the fellow who is held cheaply cracks out a bingle the same W. M. [wise men] growl about the twirler who 'quit under fire.'" Mulford cited a number of examples of successes and failures of the strategy and concluded: "There will always be two warm sides to the argument, and winners from both ends. It is one of those 'nothing succeeds like success' sort of plays, as uncertain as the national game itself" (*Sporting Life*, September 22, 1900).

The early twentieth century saw regular discussion of banning the intentional walk. In 1913, American League president Ban Johnson said that he would like to ban the intentional walk since it was "one of the most, if not the most, unpopular plays in base ball" (*Sporting Life*, December 6, 1913). Hugh Jennings suggested that this could be accomplished by allowing the batter to step out of the batter's box but forcing the catcher to remain in the catcher's box (*Sporting News*, February 12, 1914). But the lack of consensus on a plan for eliminating the intentional base on balls seems to have killed the idea.

The dislike that Clark Griffith had felt for the intentional walk during his pitching career continued when he became an owner. On February 9, 1920, he presented a proposal to the major leagues' Joint Rule Committee that would allow base runners to advance one base on an intentional walk and two bases for the second offense. But the rule put the onus upon the umpire to determine the pitcher's intentions, and umpires Hank O'Day and Bill Klem successfully contended that this would lead to endless arguments about intentions (John B. Sheridan, *Sporting News*, February 19, 1920).

The issue was again raised at a special meeting of National League owners in 1924, where considerable support was expressed for a ban. Once more, however, no consensus could be reached on a practical scheme for doing away with the intentional walk (*Sporting News*, July 31, 1924).

After the 1933 season the Southern Association announced plans to institute a new rule intended to hinder the intentional walk. If there were two outs and runners on base, four consecutive balls would advance all base runners two bases (with the exception that a runner on second would advance only to third if there was a runner there). The rule change was greeted with excitement but also concern that the national rules committee would disallow the rule (*New York Times*, November 18, 1933). The new rule does not appear to have ever been implemented.

The idea resurfaced in 1937 when Sid Keener of the *St. Louis Star-Times* made an imaginative proposal. He suggested giving a batter who walked on four pitches the option of declining the free pass. If a second four-pitch walk resulted, the batter could choose between a walk to second or again declining the walk. If he declined again and another four-pitch walk ensued, the batter would walk all the way to third base (*Sporting News*, October 28, 1937).

Proposals for eliminating the intentional walk continue to emerge from time to time. But intentional walks—and the ensuing grumbles that they are unsporting—are now such traditions that it seems unlikely the status quo will ever be changed.

6.4.2   Intentional Walks with the Bases Loaded. Researcher Ev Parker cited two instances of this tactic being employed in the major leagues. The first occurred when Napoleon Lajoie came to the plate for the Athletics in the ninth inning of a game against the White Sox on May 23, 1901, with Chicago leading 11-7. Notwithstanding his dislike for this tactic (see the preceding entry), Clark Griffith deliberately walked Lajoie and then retired the next three batters to complete the victory.

The next bases-loaded intentional walk was ordered by Giants manager Mel Ott in the second game of a doubleheader at the Polo Grounds on July 23, 1944. The free pass was issued to Cubs slugger Bill Nicholson when he strode to the plate in the eighth inning with two out, the bases loaded, and the Cubs behind 10-7. The Giants hung on for a 12-10 victory (Ev Parker, "The Supreme Compliment," *National Pastime* 17 [1997], 138–139).

The year after Parker's article was published, Barry Bonds received a similar token of esteem in a May 28, 1998, game against the Diamondbacks. Arizona manager Buck Showalter ordered pitcher Gregg Olson to walk Bonds with two outs in the bottom of the ninth and a two-run lead. The next batter flied out to seal Arizona's 8-7 victory.

Of course there may have been additional instances in which a pitcher pitched around a dangerous hitter even with the bases loaded. Warren Spahn, for example, claimed that he once intentionally walked Stan Musial in that situation (Roger Kahn, *The Head Game*, 178).

6.4.3   Fake Intentional Walks. There is nothing particularly imaginative about the strategy of pretending to issue an intentional walk and then throwing a pitch across the plate. What is difficult is actually executing it, as the potential of a passed ball seems greater than the likelihood of catching the batter unaware. Nonetheless Oakland manager Dick Williams successfully employed this tactic against Johnny Bench of the Reds in a World Series game on October 18, 1972.

6.4.4   Lip Passes. There is always a risk of a wild pitch or a passed ball in the process of issuing an intentional walk. A couple of managers have devised imaginative ways to try to eliminate even that small risk.

During a July 9, 1924, game between Cincinnati and Philadelphia, Curt Walker came to the plate for the Reds with a runner on third base. On the instructions of Phillies manager Art Fletcher, pitcher Bill Hubbell threw to first baseman Walter Holke four times. According to the umpires' interpretation of a directive from league president John Heydler, each throw was ruled a ball, and Walker was sent to first base. Heydler closed the loophole by issuing a new directive, mandating that such acts be called balks (*Sporting News*, July 31, 1924).

Before the 1968 season, umpires were ordered to be more strict about calling a ball if a pitcher went to his mouth while on the rubber. Cubs manager Leo Durocher spent much of the exhibition season crusading against this directive. Finally, in a spring training game on March 23, Durocher instructed pitcher Jim Ellis to issue two intentional walks by licking his fingers, a tactic that was dubbed the "lip pass." This novel approach was not specifically banned, but a member of the rules committee suggested that Durocher would be fined $1,000 if another "lip pass" occurred. This effectively eliminated the lip pass, but Durocher did get some satisfaction, as umpires were instructed to be less vigilant about enforcing the rule.

6.4.5 Automatic Intentional Walks. After the 1955 season, American League president Will Harridge announced that the American League would experiment with automatic intentional walks during the following spring training. A manager wishing to intentionally walk an opposing batter could simply notify the umpire, who would wave the batter down to first base. If the trial proved successful, the rule would be retained for the regular season.

Harridge explained that such drastic measures were necessitated by significant increases in game times. It was "laughable," he said, to look back in his files and read about efforts to speed up the game in 1944, when an average game lasted less than two hours. Harridge noted that the average length of games in 1955 had been two hours and thirty-one minutes. Something had to be done, since "So many times nowadays you hear the comment, 'Oh, Mr. Smith used to be quite a fan but the games are getting far too draggy for him now'" (*Sporting News*, January 18, 1956).

Few, however, agreed that this seemingly minor adjustment was desirable. Sportswriter Dan Daniel observed, "The idea is not exactly new. It has been advocated for some twenty years and, in the past, ridiculed with vehemence by the league which is now going to give it a try" (*New York World-Herald*, quoted in *Sporting News*, February 15, 1956). Yankees general manager George Weiss said, "It is not a good idea because it goes against baseball tradition, tends toward mechanization, and takes away from the suspense of the game" (quoted in *Sporting News*, February 29, 1956). Umpire

Cal Hubbard cited the late Clark Griffith's comment that such a rule would "deprive the fans of four chances to boo" (*Sporting News*, March 7, 1956). Warren Giles similarly contended that fans needed the catharsis of booing (*Sporting News*, March 7, 1956).

Sporting News editorialized that the new rule "would remove from the game a small but colorful tradition." One might reasonably wonder how watching four wide ones could be characterized as colorful, so the piece explained: "There's a bit of drama in the picture of a Williams or a Berra or a Mantle standing helplessly in the batter's box, while the opposing manager tells him in actions which speak louder than words: 'You're too tough. In this situation, we can't take a chance on pitching to you.'" The editorial countered Harridge's argument by claiming: "Much of baseball's popularity depends on its allergy to change" (*Sporting News*, March 7, 1956).

Eventually the experiment died, not with a bang but a whimper. Earl Hilligan, chief of the American League's service bureau, explained, ". . . Not one manager experimented with the idea. Our managers were told the thing was strictly voluntary. They didn't have to use it. Evidently none of them wanted to use it" (quoted in *Sporting News*, April 25, 1956).

Similar plans were announced three years later by Texas League president Dick Butler, who explained that it was essential to speed up the game: "This is a different era, and we're competing with entertainment that moves faster and takes less time" (*Sporting News*, February 4, 1959). The automatic intentional walk, however, was immediately vetoed by Commissioner Ford Frick. Frick said the Texas League could experiment with the automatic intentional walk during spring training but would need permission to change the regular-season rules. He cited several reasons, including the importance of "the customer having his chance to boo" (*Sporting News*, February 4, 1959).

(v) Signs

6.5.1 Signs. Signs between ballplayers have been a feature of baseball since at least the 1860s.

Researcher Priscilla Astifan found an article in an 1860 Rochester newspaper describing the tactics of the visiting Excelsiors of New York: "The catcher was also proficient in his part, and won encomiums for the manner in which he would telegraph advantages to be gained, or the direction as to which one of the fielders should take a 'fly'" (*Rochester Evening Express*, July 9, 1860). Henry Chadwick added in 1867: "Always have an understanding with your two sets of fielders in regard to private signals, so as to be able to call them in closer, or place them out further, or nearer the foul-ball lines, as occasion may require, without giving notice to your adversaries" (*Haney's Base Ball Book of Reference for 1867*; reprinted in *The Ball Player's Chronicle*, August 22, 1867).

When the Red Stockings of Cincinnati toured California in 1869, the local paper was impressed by the trend-setting Ohio club's use of signs. One article noted that the Red Stockings "have perfected a system of telegraphic signals as easily recognized as if spoken words were used. . . . [They] have really two captains—the ostensible one is in the position of 'centre field' [Harry Wright], and directs the movements of the fielders, and the other is the catcher [Doug Allison], who indicates by signs to the pitcher and base-keepers the proper thing to do at the right moment" (*Daily Alta California*, September 26, 1869; quoted in Paul Dickson, *The Hidden Language of Baseball*, 31).

By the 1870s, Henry Chadwick was advocating a quite sophisticated system of signals. In 1873 he recommended that the catcher "always have a sign ready so as to signalize the pitcher where to send in the ball," while the pitcher "should never commence a match without having an understood arrangement with his catchers and outfielders in regard to their movements by signals" (*New York Clipper*, April 19, 1873). Chadwick elaborated the following year: "The pitcher and catcher should have a code of signals between them, and they should practice these signs until they can read them as easily as their letters. Thus, when a catcher sees an opportunity to catch a player napping off a base, a certain signal should be given by which the pitcher may understand that he is to throw to the base promptly. Again, if the pitcher is familiar with a certain habit of the batsman before him of hitting at a favourite ball, he should give the catcher a sign informing him that he is going to send in a slower or swifter ball or a higher or lower one than ordinarily is pitched" (Henry Chadwick, *Chadwick's Base Ball Manual*, 14–15).

Over the years, credit for originating signs between the catcher and pitcher has been claimed for many players of the late 1870s and early 1880s. These are obviously not firsts, in light of the examples already presented in this entry and in the earlier entry "Catchers Signaling to Pitchers" (**1.27**), especially the 1871 mention that it was common for the catcher to do "the 'headwork' in strategic play by directing—through private signals—the pitcher how to deliver particular balls" (*New York Clipper*, October 28, 1871).

Nonetheless the various claims are worth briefly reviewing to show how closely the emergence of the practice is tied to the parallel development of the curveball in the late 1870s (see **3.2.3**). Tim Murnane gave credit to Charles Snyder when with Louisville in 1877, while H. G. Merrill cited Little Joe Roche of the 1876 Crickets of Binghamton (*Sporting News*, July 16, 1908). A *Boston Globe* writer suggested that pitcher Jim Devlin had been the originator (quoted in *Sporting Life*, July 1, 1893).

In 1879 the *Boston Globe* noted, "It is said that [Silver] Flint, catcher of the Chicagos, by a system of sign-language, which no one has been able to fathom, wholly relieves [pitcher Terry] Larkin from the duty of watching either the first or second base. This is done by Flint, who, in the catcher's position, has a good view of all the bases. He signals Larkin to throw either to first or second, and by the same signal notifies [first baseman Cap] Anson, [second baseman Joe] Quest or [shortstop John] Peters to be on the lookout for the ball" (*Boston Globe*, May 18, 1879). A few days later the *Chicago Tribune* retorted, "There is nothing at all mysterious about the signal. It consists of Flint turning his cap around on his head. [Boston catcher Charles] Snyder's signal to [pitcher Tommy] Bond is made by putting his hands on his knees" (*Chicago Tribune*, May 25, 1879).

As signals between catcher and pitcher became routine, other types of signs also became more common. A Lansing, Michigan, newspaper complained in 1879 that the Lansing captain "had to resort to the questionable method of calling to [the outfielders], when a motion should have been sufficient" (*Lansing Journal*, July 24, 1879). An 1881 article counseled that outfielders "must be required to strictly obey the signals from the pitcher for all such changes of position. Time and again this past season we have seen a pitcher's strategy entirely nullified by the stupidity or obstinacy of some one or other of the outfielders to quickly obey the pitcher's signal to play deeper, or closer, or to get round more to the right or to the left, when he has been preparing to outwit a batsman by something besides the mere speed of his delivery" (*New York Clipper*, December 31, 1881).

Researcher David Ball found that signals were being used for base coaching by 1885: "The Baltimores have adopted a system for coaching baserunners a little out of the ordinary. Instead of yelling directions they give signs." But the *Cincinnati Enquirer* reported that spectators disliked this practice because they felt that yelling was a better way of showing spirit (*Cincinnati Enquirer*, May 3, 1885; reprinted in Frederick Ivor-Campbell, "When Was the First? [Part 4]," *Nineteenth Century Notes* 95:3, 4 [Summer/Fall 1995], 12).

It will be noted that most of the signs described in this entry were not given with much emphasis on secrecy. Umpire Tim Hurst claimed in 1894, "I know nearly all the battery signals now, and all signals made by the captain of a team, which is a great advantage for me in my work. . . . I have also to watch for switching of signals by a battery" (*St. Louis Post-Dispatch*, August 11, 1894). The *New York Press* noted in 1904: "For years the signals of professional baseball teams have been easily read by opponents. Their simplicity was readily fathomed, and lack of invention was displayed, which left the only chance of deception in reversing the system by a single sign. It was either a rubbing of the inside or the outside of a knee, the lacing of a glove or shoe, the dropping of a right or left hand to the thigh, the crook of a knee, or some similar expedient" (*New York Press*; reprinted in *Washington Post*, July 31, 1904).

As is discussed in the next entry, however, sign stealing was becoming prevalent by the 1880s, which in turn changed the way that signs were given.

6.5.2   Sign Stealing. Sportswriter Dan Daniel claimed that sign stealing was in use by 1876 (Paul Dickson, *The Hidden Language of Baseball*, 33). If so, it cannot have been extensive since signs themselves were still in their infancy.

By the 1880s the curveball (see **3.2.3**) had changed baseball, and one of the ripple effects was that the cat-and-mouse game between sign givers and sign stealers began in earnest. Initially not everyone thought it worth the bother to try to steal signs. An 1888 game saw Detroit captain Ned Hanlon figure out the signs being given by Pittsburgh's Fred Dunlap, but when he relayed the information to teammates Pete Conway and Charley Bennett, "they failed to grasp the idea" (*New York Sun*, April 29, 1888). Over the next few years, however, sign stealing would have an enormous impact.

George Smith claimed in 1891 that the key to his Brooklyn club winning two consecutive pennants was "our studying and learning the signs of the opposing pitchers. There wasn't a club in the League last year that we didn't know the signs of its pitchers. We always had a good deal of trouble with [Cincinnati catcher] Jim Keenan, for he generally made the signs to the pitchers, but we finally got on to him. Jim would crouch down close to the ground in giving the sign, and would use two fingers. The players in the base lines couldn't see him give it, but a man on the base could detect it. He would give the coacher a hand signal, who would in turn 'tip' the batter. . . . The Brooklyns would have beaten the New Yorks for the World's championship if [Buck] Ewing hadn't discovered that we were on to his signs'" (*Cincinnati Commercial-Gazette*, reprinted in *Sporting News*, April 25, 1891). That last claim is particularly intriguing because Brooklyn led the Series three games to one before New York swept the last five games.

Another article that same year reported that Oakland captain Norris O'Neill used sign stealing to nose San Francisco out by one game for the 1889 California League championship: "['Pop'] Swett was catching for San Francisco and when 'Pop' wiggled his right hand that meant that he wanted a straight ball. When he moved the left, a curve. O'Neill, who is an observing fellow, 'tumbled' to this sign manual late in the season, and then the Oakland men commenced to fatten up their batting average and make reputations as heavy hitters." The article explained that when a curve was signaled the coach would yell, "Take a good start" to the base runner, tipping the batter off to the pitch. When it was a fastball he would instead holler, "Cover a little ground" (*Williamsport Sunday Grit*, June 14, 1891).

As noted in the preceding entry, early signs were not terribly difficult to steal. That was changed when the emergence of the curveball meant that for the first time there were distinct types of pitches and by claims such as these that pennants could be won by sign stealing. Players naturally began to put an extra effort into encoding their signs. An 1889 account observed, "Arthur Irwin can find out the signs of opposing pitchers quicker than any other man in the League. [Ed] Morris of the Pittsburg team has been inventing signs all winter, and now claims that he will bother the Philadelphian's captain [Irwin] to call the turn" (*St. Louis Post-Dispatch*, April 1, 1889).

Signals now became increasingly complex and experimental. An 1896 article in *Sporting News* explained that catchers were signaling with nearly every part of their body—fingers, arms, mouth, hands, and feet—in hopes of ensuring their confidentiality (*Sporting News*, March 7, 1896). Gus Weyhing complained about the system used by Dallas manager Jack McCloskey during the 1897 season: "McCloskey operated his signals by a series of signs that involved more pantomime than a Mafia meeting. With a man on first Mac would give him the tip to steal by shifting the score card from his right to his left hand. If he scratched his left ear with his right mitt the base runner must anchor himself on the sack till further instructions, no matter if the runner had a 20-foot lead on the pitcher. If he jabbed the toe of his right shoe in the grass the runner on second base must steal third or make the bluff at it. If Mac took a chew of tobacco the batsman and the man on first were given notice that they were to work the hit-and-run scheme."

The obvious danger of an elaborate system was that the signs would be equally impenetrable to the players who were supposed to be receiving them. Weyhing noted that McCloskey confronted Dallas catcher Tub Welch after a game for missing a crucial sign. Welch responded in exasperation, "If you use your pipes so we can hear you and cut out de mitt stuff we can rap to exactly what you want. De reason I got twisted on dat hit-and-run gag is dat you put a chew of gum in your face instead of tobacco" (*St. Louis Post-Dispatch*, April 10, 1898).

Moreover even the most complex system could be breached. Connie Mack was especially renowned for his ability to decipher opponents' signs. Monte Cross noted that "Mack studies the moves of the other side closer than any manager I ever saw. At bat or in the field, he can tell exactly what his opponents are planning, and is often able to block them. Not many men try to figure out the signs of the other team, but an expert with good eyes by close attention can easily detect the hit-and-run, double steal and the many tricks of a crafty club. . . . Nearly all base ball signals are visible movements, such as spitting on the hands, hitching up the trousers, pulling at the cap, etc., and usually they are very simple, even those of the best teams" (quoted in *Sporting News*, April 16, 1908).

6.5.3   Shake Offs. As discussed in the entry "Catchers Signaling to Pitchers" (1.27), the first major response to sign stealing seems to have been the assignment to the catcher of pitch-calling responsibilities. Yet almost from the start, pitchers were exercising the veto power inherent in having the ball in their possession. John Ward wrote in 1888: "Until within a few years this sign was always given by the pitcher, but now it is almost the universal practice for the catcher to give it to the pitcher, and if the latter doesn't want to pitch the ball asked for he changes the sign by a shake of the head" (John Ward, *Base-Ball: How to Become a Player*, 53–54). Catcher Doc Bushong explained that "it has always been my practice to give the signs, and if satisfactory, the pitcher would deliver the ball as directed. If not, a shake of the head or a hesitation would lead to a change" (*New York Sun*, May 6, 1888). Pitcher Ted Breitenstein added, "The catcher calls for the kind of ball he thinks I should deliver, but if it is against my judgment, I reverse it by an agreed signal" (*St. Louis Post-Dispatch*, August 12, 1894).

6.5.4   Conferences to Go Over Signs. The earliest such conference that I have found occurred in 1886 and was not a popular success: "Then [James] McKeever held a long discussion with Pitcher [James] Harmon about signs. The crowd got impatient; one man yelled 'Get a telephone!' while the umpire ordered them to 'play ball'" (*Boston Globe*, May 13, 1886).

6.5.5   Signs from the Dugout. Bench managers were rare in early baseball, and signals originated from the field captain or a player in a critical position. An 1886 article noted, "Like Arthur Irwin, Captain [Tom] Burns of Newark, coaches by signals" (*Sporting Life*, May 19, 1886).

Even when bench managers became more common, there was still a widespread belief that signals should remain the responsibility of the players themselves. Catcher Tom Kinslow explained in 1899, "It's impossible for a manager to sit on the bench and direct the playing of his team by a secret service code, by dumb motion or pantomime. It doesn't require a razor-edge think-tank to study out and detect the most intricate of signals. In fact, the more complicated these pantomimics of signs are, the easier they are discovered. . . . The only signals required in the playing of a game are the battery signals, which are, of course, a positive necessity, and the signals for the hit-and-run play, which should be given by the batsman or the base-runner and not the manager on the bench" (quoted in *Sporting Life*, December 23, 1899).

Nonetheless signaling from the bench gradually became more common. Arthur Irwin's playing days essentially ended with the 1890 season, but he continued to direct the action from the bench. In 1895 his method gained another adherent: "Captain-manager [Buck] Ewing has adopted a code of signals by which he directs the movements of his men on the field. It is said that he does not have to get on the coaching lines and shout his commands to the players as [Charlie] Comiskey and [Arlie] Latham have in years gone by" (*Fort Wayne Sentinel*, May 3, 1895). By the early twentieth century it was becoming customary for the manager to signal from the bench.

6.5.6   Peeking. Batters trying to sneak a peek at the catcher's signal is another element that entered the game soon after signs themselves. An 1889 article observed: "[Bud] Fowler, the colored second baseman of the Greenvilles, is a tricky player. When at the bat he turns his head occasionally and catches the sign made by the catcher to the pitcher and lays his plans accordingly." But countermoves were also already being made. George Meakim, the opposing pitcher, "discovered the act yesterday and fooled him several times" (*Grand Rapids* [Mich.] *Daily Democrat*, June 16, 1889).

6.5.7   Combination Signs. As discussed under "Sign Stealing" (6.5.2), by the start of the second decade of the twentieth century sign stealing had reached epidemic proportions. Johnny Evers and Hugh Fullerton reported in 1910 that fielders were becoming increasingly paranoid in response: "The second baseman and short stop have from 20 to 24 signals to keep in mind, most of which are changed every day and sometimes three times during a game. In 1909, when the hint had gone through the American League that the New York team was stealing signals, the Chicago White Sox changed signals nine times in one game, no signal meaning the same thing in any two innings" (John J. Evers and Hugh S. Fullerton, *Touching Second*, 128–129).

According to sportswriter Stan Baumgartner, the solution was combination signs, introduced in 1905. At first catchers combined the pitch signal with a visual signal, such as touching the mask, the knee, or the back of the glove. Sign stealers soon caught on to this new wrinkle, but in 1915 Pat Moran finally gave the upper hand back to the sign givers.

When Moran was hired to manage the Phillies, "The first thing he did in the spring of 1915 was to line up his catchers on the top rail of a fence and teach them combination signs—using fingers exclusively—and giving as many as three or four signs, with only one of them to count. Thus base runners, signal tippers in the clubhouse and coaches were completely stymied. There was only one catch—some pitchers weren't quick enough on the trigger to use the combinations. These hurlers quickly passed out of the majors.

"Moran not only used combinations but he arranged a 'shift' sign by the pitcher so that he could 'rub off' the signal by the catcher and substitute one of his own by pushing his glove across his chest. The only hope left for opposing coaches was to pick what was being pitched by studying the pitcher. Moran made every attempt to thwart this by teaching his pitchers to throw everything with the same delivery" (Stan Baumgartner, "Signals," *Baseball Guide and Record Book* 1947, 133).

The Phillies were the surprise pennant winners in the National League that year. Just as important, their manager had finally ended the dominance of sign stealers.

6.5.8 Reading Pitchers. Connie Mack's 1911 Philadelphia A's were rumored to be great sign stealers, but several players on that team claimed that the team wasn't stealing signs at all but detecting pitchers who tipped their pitches.

Sportswriter Stan Baumgartner wrote later that Eddie Collins revealed this secret in a postseason article in *American Magazine*. Collins explained that every pitcher in the league had some telltale trait that gave away what he was going to throw. Many of Collins's teammates were angry with him for what they considered a betrayal. Catcher Ira Thomas said, "We felt he had sold us out" (Stan Baumgartner, "Signals," *Baseball Guide and Record Book* *1947*, 133).

According to Athletics pitcher Cy Morgan, the leader was Chief Bender, and he was so good at reading pitches that John McGraw sought to have him banned from the coaching box: "There are lots of little things almost unnoticeable about the motions different pitchers use in their delivery, and most of these motions have a meaning. We sit there in a row on the bench and study the pitcher, and if we detect any difference in his motion we watch to see what kind of a ball it means. Bender gets up on the coaching lines for a while, and if there is anything in it back he comes and tells us what kind of a ball that motion means. . . . Before I joined the Athletics they used to hit me. I did not know why. When I joined them Harry Davis came to me and told me. He said some other team might discover the little thing they had figured out, and then I changed my delivery so as to cut it out. The Athletics had not been able to hit me because they had my catcher's signs, but because they had my spitball figured out. That is all there is to any signal-tipping bureau, as they call it" (*Sporting Life*, April 6, 1912).

Collins's and Morgan's versions of events are confirmed by the Giants' Chief Meyers, who later recalled telling John McGraw during the 1911 World Series, "That coach on third base, Harry Davis, is calling our pitches. When he yells, 'It's all right,' it's a fast ball." McGraw suggested that Davis must have been stealing Meyers's signs, but the catcher responded that he had told the pitchers, "Pitch whatever you want to pitch. I'll catch you without signals" (Lawrence Ritter, *The Glory of Their Times*, 181). Obviously if no signs were being exchanged, the coach indeed must have been picking up clues from the pitchers' movements.

Clever sign stealers also became adept at deciphering signals from the actions of other players. According to sportswriter Stan Baumgartner, catchers were the favorite targets: "Big Frank (Pancho) Snyder, catcher of the New York Giants [in the early twenties], gave away every pitch by the way he held his glove after he got up from giving signals. If he held the glove up, it was a fast ball. If he held the glove pointed down, it was a curve. . . . Such a clever backstop as Roger Bresnahan gave a definite crook of the elbow of his right arm when he called for a fast ball, the batter could see the big muscle in his arm move up and down" (Stan Baumgartner, "Signals," *Baseball Guide and Record Book 1947*, 126–127).

The movements of infielders could also sometimes be giveaways. Baumgartner reported that even as savvy an infielder as Miller Huggins sometimes revealed a pitch by moving to the left or right after receiving a signal (Stan Baumgartner, "Signals," *Baseball Guide and Record Book 1947*, 127).

6.5.9 Cover Your Mouth. One innovation that has been introduced to baseball within the memory of most readers of this book is the custom of players covering their mouths with their gloves during mound conferences. It has long been the practice for infielders to do so when giving signals, as middle infielders often use an open or closed mouth—hidden by their glove—to signal which player will cover the base (George F. Will, *Men at Work*, 254–255).

But use of this tactic during mound conferences is a much more recent development, one that went from being unheard of to standard in a very short period of time. Tigers broadcaster Rod Allen said he first saw this while playing in Japan in the late 1980s. When he returned to the States in 1991 the practice had already caught on in the United States (Fox Sports broadcast, August 7, 2004).

One of the impetuses was Will Clark's grand slam off Greg Maddux in the 1989 National League Championship Series and Clark's subsequent claim that he had known what to expect from reading Maddux's lips during a mound conference. Maddux is dubious of this claim, as is Clark's teammate Bob Brenly, who noted that Clark never wanted to know what pitch was coming. But whether true or not, such a charge undoubtedly led many pitchers to cover their mouths (Cubs WGN broadcast, July 31, 2005).

Like so many strategies, lipreading can be used by either side. Mel Stottlemyre, Sr., claimed that he took advantage of Carl Yastrzemski's habit of talking to himself between pitches: "If I saw his lips saying 'Be quick, be quick,' I'd throw him a change-up. If he was saying 'Stay back, weight back,' I'd throw him a fastball" (quoted in George F. Will, *Men at Work*, 224).

(vi) Playing by "The Book"

Changes were made so frequently in the early days of baseball that the idea of an unvarying "book" of strategies would have made little sense. What's more, some of the now accepted dos and don'ts of managing would not have made sense given the frequent fluctuations in the era's rules and conditions. As a result, the network of tactics and principles known as "the book" developed in fits and starts.

6.6.1   Playing for One Run. The tactic of playing for one run has been a basic strategy for so many years that one might assume it could not be dated with much precision. The evidence suggests otherwise.

A *Sporting News* correspondent in 1897 quoted Baltimore manager Ned Hanlon as saying "we didn't play ball in 1889 as we play it now." The writer explained that before 1890 "the theory of playing at any and all times for a single run was practically unheard of. . . . The modern principle of baseball is to first make one run, if your opponents have none, and to continue always to try for one run as long as you are in the lead, or not more than a run or two behind. When your opponents have a lead of three or four science can be abandoned and chances taken on 'slugging.' . . . When a player in a team of the present era reaches first base the batsman succeeding him is instructed to go to the plate and advance his comrade, even at the expense of being retired himself. . . . In the old days once a man got to first base the next batter walked to the plate and promptly attempted to knock the cover off the ball" (*Sporting News*, October 30, 1897).

An 1891 *Sporting Life* article described how Columbus manager Gus Schmelz's "system of playing base ball for games rather than individual records is being adopted more or less by managers everywhere, as experience demonstrates that more games are won than lost by it, especially when the contestants are equally matched or the games are close. When the opposing team is several runs ahead, of course, it is necessary to try to bat it out and sacrificing will do very little good. But when one or two runs only are needed then Schmelz's system comes in play.

"The great object then is to get a man on first base and every scheme possible is used to accomplish that end. With a man on first base a hard hit is more likely not to go safe than to go safe, as the batting averages of the heaviest hitters in the profession will show, and a sharp infield hit is likely to result in a double play, while it is almost impossible with a hard-throwing outfield to make second base on a fly out. A slow hit, bunted, will certainly advance the man to second base, and the batter has a very good chance to beat the hit out himself.

"If the batter is thrown out there is no longer a danger of a double play, and the next man at bat should try to hit the ball hard, for the runner can easily score on a single or go to third on a fly out to the outfield. If the first bunter manages to beat out the ball, then there are two men on bases, with no one out, and in order to prevent a double or possibly a triple play, it is necessary again to bunt the ball or to push a fly into the outfield. In most cases the man would be held on first base in order to draw a throw out of the catcher in a subsequent attempt to steal second, and thus give the third man a chance to score.

"A bunted hit under these circumstances will about certainly score the man on third base, and a long fly out is even better. Of course, the programme is necessarily varied according to the abilities of the player or the weakness or strength of the opposing team. With a sore-arm catcher a double steal would be in order, and other tricks can be introduced as circumstances will permit. It will be seen that in order to carry out this system correctly the manager must have absolute control of his players and his discipline must be perfect" (*Sporting Life*, August 22, 1891).

Another article a few weeks later added, "The Schmelz system of playing ball has been made quite famous by the work of this team this year. With a nine of medium hitters Columbus has managed to play some very creditable games with the strongest teams in the Association, and has won a goodly number of them by clever team work. The men never play for records, and when a sacrifice hit is needed to advance a base-runner or bring him home it is forthcoming in most cases" (*Sporting Life*, September 5, 1891).

Gus Schmelz was a well-known manager of the 1880s and 1890s who is now almost forgotten. He does, however, deserve to be remembered for leaving baseball this important legacy.

6.6.2 Don't Put the Winning Run on Base.
Managers have always avoided this suicidal strategy except in exceptional circumstances. The surprising thing is that such a self-evident principle is considered to be part of the book at all.

6.6.3 Never Make the Third Out at Third Base.
This dictum makes sense today, but that would have been less the case in early baseball, since passed balls were then a much more common event. There was therefore more benefit to taking a risk to reach third than there is in today's game. For example, in the 1856 account of a steal mentioned in "Stolen Bases" (5.1.1), the runner made the third out of an inning trying to steal third.

Passed balls decreased steadily in the ensuing years, but attitudes were slower to change. As late as 1911 a sportswriter observed that "managers scheme with all their might and main to reach third, which doesn't do them any good after it's attained." He asked rhetorically, "Why is it that all sorts of schemes are worked to get a base runner round to third, but as soon as he reaches that corner all science is thrown to the winds and the issue is left to depend on simple, plain old slug it out?" (*Mansfield* [Ohio] *News*, September 23, 1911).

Nonetheless there were signs by this time that this mind-set was beginning to adapt to changing conditions. Christy Mathewson noted in 1912 that John McGraw "has favorite expressions, such as 'there are stages' and 'that was a two out play,' which mean certain chances are to be taken by a coacher at one point in a contest, while to attempt such a play under other circumstances would be nothing short of foolhardy" (Christy Mathewson, *Pitching in a Pinch*, 118–119).

This strongly suggests that the precept of not taking any chance of making the third out at third base had begun to emerge.

6.6.4 Don't Give Him Anything to Hit on 0-2. This basic principle was being cited even before it took three strikes to retire a batter. For example, in 1880, with the two-strike warning pitch (see **1.10**) still in the rulebook, the *New York Clipper* remarked, "The umpiring in Cincinnati, O., on the occasion when Will White pitched out [Cap] Anson on four balls delivered, must have been rather queer. No pitcher would deliver four fair balls in succession to such a batsman as Anson, especially when two men were on the bases" (*New York Clipper*, May 15, 1880).

6.6.5 Taking 3-0 and 3-1. A walk was not permanently made up of four balls until the late 1880s. Once it was, the idea of taking 3-0 and 3-1 pitches followed almost immediately, and appears to have been adhered to more rigidly than is the case today.

Ned Hanlon credited the Orioles of the mid-1890s with inventing the tactic of "hitting the ball with men on bases with three balls and no strikes on the batters." He cited this as an example of "tactics introduced by the Baltimores [that] were successful because they were unexpected" (*Washington Post*, August 14, 1904). This implies that most batters invariably took pitches in such situations.

Jack Doyle told a similar story, but with a twist. He claimed that pitchers like Clark Griffith took advantage of the fact that hitters wouldn't swing at a 3-0 or 3-1 pitch. So Griffith would deliberately throw three wide ones, and then toss two easy strikes, leaving the hitters with only one swing. Thus Doyle's perspective was that the Baltimore batters began swinging at 3-0 and 3-1 pitches out of "self-defense" (quoted in Ernest J. Lanigan's column, *Sporting News*, July 21, 1932).

Nineteenth-century player Jack Glasscock wrote an indignant letter to *Sporting News* in 1938 protesting the tendency of batters to swing at 3-1 pitches. He said that in his day they would have taken such pitches (*Sporting News*, October 20, 1938). Glasscock played in the majors from 1879 to 1895.

Just as noteworthy as how early this custom originated is the inflexibility with which it was followed. Cubs manager Bill Killefer reported in 1925, "It is best to ignore the established rules of baseball now and then. For example, in a game at Brooklyn I had [Charley] Hollocher hit with the count three and one. Most people would call this foolish." Even though Hollocher got a hit, Killefer reported that "the fans razzed me unmercifully. Some of them asked me if I didn't know anything about baseball" (quoted in F. C. Lane, *Batting*, 49).

(vii) Miscellaneous Managerial Strategies

6.7.1   Fifth Infielders. Today most managers bring an outfielder into the infield only when the situation is dire. The tactic is usually employed only when the winning run is on third base with less than two out, meaning that even a sacrifice fly would win the game.

George Sisler noted that the circumstances of its origin were different. While he called the play the "six-man infield" in this account, he was counting the pitcher as an infielder and was referring to what is now known as the five-man infield: "The six-man infield was originated and tried out at Vero Beach, Florida, in the spring of 1950 by Branch Rickey, then President of the Brooklyn Dodgers. . . . Here's the theory behind the six-man infield: When a poor-hitting pitcher comes up to the plate with a sacrifice in order, either with one down or no one out, it is wise to bring one of your outfielders from the outfield and place him at a definite place in the infield, making it defense with six rather than the normal five players. The idea, of course, is not to allow a weak-hitting pitcher to sacrifice the runner or runners to the next base or bases, but to put up such a defense that the pitcher will attempt to hit the ball, when he will probably strike out or hit into a double play" (George Sisler, *Sisler on Baseball*, 74).

Rickey's method of implementing the strategy was novel. Rather than keeping his intentions under wrap, Rickey announced plans to use the six-man infield at a banquet, and the scheme was widely publicized (*Sporting News*, February 1, 1950). Rickey contended that it would be very effective against a weak hitter.

The Dodgers tried this tactic during spring training and even used a variant in which two outfielders played the infield (*Sporting News*, April 9,

1952). They do not appear to have used it much if at all once the season began, but a couple of other managers did experiment with it. In the eighth inning of a game on September 30, 1950, Detroit pitcher Hal Newhouser came to the plate with a runner on second and no outs. Knowing that Newhouser would be asked to bunt, Cleveland manager Lou Boudreau "brought Bob Kennedy in from right field and put him midway between home and first on the grass. He put first baseman Luke Easter on third base and brought [third baseman Al] Rosen in close to have a six-man infield" (*Detroit Free Press*, October 1, 1950). All this planning went for naught when Indians pitcher Mike Garcia walked Newhouser on four pitches. Birdie Tebbetts of Cincinnati tried the same strategy against the Giants in a game on July 20, 1954, but infielder Rocky Bridges made an error.

6.7.2   Fourth Outfielders. An even more uncommon tactic has seen managers temporarily redeploy an infielder in the outfield. This move has been used almost exclusively against sluggers who are so feared that the opposition feels fortunate to hold them to a single. Cincinnati manager Birdie Tebbetts reportedly did this against Stan Musial in 1954, as did the Mets' Gil Hodges versus Willie McCovey in 1969 (Jonathan Fraser Light, *The Cultural Encyclopedia of Baseball*, 697).

Hodges then showed great courage by reprising the fourth outfielder at a critical moment in that year's World Series. Baltimore had won the opening game, and the second contest was tied until New York pushed across a run in the top of the ninth. In Baltimore's half, Mets starter Jerry Koosman got the first two men out, bringing Frank Robinson to the plate with a chance to tie the game with one swing of the bat.

Knowing that Robinson would be aiming for an extra-base hit, "Hodges made a rare strategic move. He shifted [Al] Weis from second base and made a fourth outfielder of him. Thus were the corners guarded as well as both power alleys in right center and left center" (Arthur Daley, *New York Times*, October 14, 1969). Robinson ended up walking, but the Mets hung on to win the game and swept the last three games of the Series.

Five years later another Mets manager revived this unusual defense under similar circumstances. New York was clinging to a 1-0 lead over Atlanta with two out in the ninth when Hank Aaron came up: "[Yogi] Berra called for an 'Aaron shift' in which Felix Millan was moved from second base to become a fourth outfielder. The strategy stemmed from the willingness by Berra to allow the home-run star to reach first if necessary but to cut down the chances of his getting to second and becoming a possible scorer" (Michael Stevens, *New York Times*, August 26, 1974). That script was followed precisely, as Aaron did indeed single—but the next batter whiffed to end the game.

6.7.3 Curfews. The *Springfield* [Mass.] *Republican* hinted in 1878: "attending a dance until 2 o'clock or later is not wise preparation for a game on the day following" (*Springfield Republican*; quoted in *New York Clipper*, May 18, 1878). That reality was undoubtedly understood by all early captains and managers, but acting upon it was another matter. After all, every employer would like to have their employees come to work well rested, but few would think seriously of trying to enforce such a rule.

Nonetheless clubs did begin to instigate curfews in the next few years. In 1879 the Albany club was reported to have a 10:30 curfew. In 1883, Fort Wayne manager Jack Remsen devised the first recorded method of enforcement: "Before eleven o'clock every night, players of the Fort Wayne Base Ball Club will be required to register in a book kept for that purpose at the Robinson House. Players retiring after that hour will be fined" (*Fort Wayne Daily News*, April 5, 1883).

6.7.4 Handwriting Analysis. In 1962, Charlie Metro was a member of the Chicago Cubs' "College of Coaches" (see **6.1.4**). Metro devised an original approach for gaining an advantage: "I had a handwriting expert analyze the signatures of all the National League managers to learn as much about my competition as quick as I could." The graphologist provided Metro with an analysis of each manager's character traits in hopes that Metro could use this information when making decisions. It doesn't seem to have helped much as the Cubs finished ninth, beating out only the expansion Mets. Metro also experimented with the still more novel tactic of using ventriloquism to disrupt opposing base runners, but couldn't master the skill (Tom Altherr, "Know Them by Their Autographs," *National Pastime* 18 [1998], 29–31).

6.7.5 Computers. The first manager to make extensive use of computers in his decision-making process was Oakland's Steve Boros in 1983 and '84. Boros never brought a computer into the dugout, but his reliance upon computer-generated data was publicized in such periodicals as *Newsweek*, *Sports Illustrated*, and even *Psychology Today*. When the A's struggled, their woes were blamed on the computers, and Boros lost his job (Alan Schwarz, *The Numbers Game*, 145–146).

Chapter 7

COACHING

BASEBALL coaches today have such a staid image that it will come as a surprise to many that the first coaches were so undignified that Christy Mathewson referred to them as the "old school of clowns" (Christy Mathewson, *Pitching in a Pinch*, 118).

The earliest coaching was just advice yelled from teammates on the bench and of course cannot be dated precisely. By 1872, however, the rules specified that a base runner's teammates had to remain at least fifteen feet away from him. Two years later the rules were amended to state that only the captain and one other player could approach that close. These players were known as coachers because, like stagecoach drivers, their job was to direct traffic. Only gradually did the name become shortened to coach.

When American ballplayers made a tour of England in 1874, the use of coaches was remarked upon as a characteristically American concept. One newspaper commented, "The employment of one of the side who are in to watch the movements of the field and advise the runner accordingly is a quaint device which savors of American acuteness" (quoted by William Rankin, *Sporting News*, February 25, 1909). This perception that coaching exemplified a peculiarly American approach to sporting activities was strengthened when the American Association was formed in 1882.

The upstart league was characterized by a brashness that contrasted dramatically with the more businesslike National League. One of the most conspicuous manifestations of this in-your-face attitude was the loud and annoying style of coaching. Many of the players who filled this role made little pretense of the fact that they went "in the line to disconcert the opposing players—generally the pitcher—not to 'coach' or assist the base-runner" (*Sporting News*, December 23, 1893).

Leather lungs were the primary requirement, as the *St. Louis Globe-Democrat* observed in 1888: "[Reddy] Mack, [George] Tebeau, and some of the local players' idea of coaching seems to be to stand on the line and yell as loud as they possibly can. It does not seem to matter what they say, just so they make a noise. A ball game at present more resembles a series of Indian war whoops than an exhibition of the national pastime" (*St. Louis Globe-Democrat*, reprinted in the *New York Sun*, May 9, 1888). But a voice that was both loud and annoying was even more effective, with an 1889 account noting, "Of all base ball coachers' voices that of Bug Holliday is the most excruciating" (*St. Louis Post-Dispatch*, April 26, 1889).

This style of coaching became increasingly associated with the St. Louis Brown Stockings. Arlie Latham had a particularly strong polarizing tendency, which was illustrated during the 1886 postseason series against Chicago. The *Chicago Tribune* felt that Latham's "insane whooping," "incessant howling," and "meaningless jumble of catch phrases" was "funny for about fifteen minutes. Then it grew tiresome, and before the fourth inning he was universally conceded to be the worst nuisance ever inflicted upon a Chicago audience" (*Chicago Tribune*, October 19, 1886). The *Chicago Inter-Ocean* chimed in with complaints about "the disgusting mouthings of the clown Latham." But the *St. Louis Post-Dispatch* praised Latham for "his excellent coaching" (both quoted in Jerry Lansche, *Glory Fades Away*, 79–80).

Some went so far as to attribute the club's success to its style of coaching: "It is a well-known fact that St. Louis won the pennant twice through this rowdyism on the field" (*Philadelphia Press*, reprinted in the *St. Louis Post-Dispatch*, July 7, 1887). Although this claim may seem farfetched, winners always attract imitators, and this approach to coaching soon spread.

When the Pittsburgh franchise moved from the American Association to the National League in 1887, it brought the upstart Association's coaching style with it. Its apostle was George Miller, who was known by such appropriate nicknames as "Foghorn" and "Calliope." As Miller made his way around the National League, he attracted considerable attention. On Pittsburgh's first trip to Detroit, he was described as being "a pronounced type of the American Association coacher, and nothing like his bray has ever before been heard at Recreation Park. It is startling to spectators seeing his squatty, Quilp-like form to suddenly hear his foghorn tones exhorting a Pittsburger to 'Getwaygetwaygetway'" (*Detroit Free Press*, May 10, 1887).

This state of affairs led to predictable efforts to abolish this style of coaching, or even coaching in general. The American Association held a special meeting on June 9, 1886, and decided, ". . . In order to prevent offensive coaching by captains, the lines being so changed as to keep the captain and his assistants at least 75 feet away from the catcher's lines and on a line 15 feet from and parallel with the four lines. A rule was adopted preventing the captain from addressing remarks to batsmen, except by the way of caution, or to the pitcher and catcher of the opposing team, and limiting coaching to base-runners under severe penalties" (*Chicago Tribune*, June 14, 1886).

The new rule was of some benefit, but the line between a comment directed at a teammate and an opponent was often a thin one. Moreover coaches were still free to make as much noise as possible, and some found imaginative new ways to cause a ruckus. At an 1894 game in Baltimore, the Orioles' Bill Clarke, "who was coaching from third base, walked out to the bleachers and raised his hands like a 'pop concert' leader, and a volume of sound filled the air, every man, woman and child yelling for all he or she was worth. This was done to rattle the pitcher" (*Boston Globe*, April 25, 1894).

This prompted renewed calls to ban coaching entirely after the 1895 season, but most thought that a prohibition would be going too far. The *New York Advertiser* argued: "To abolish loud coaching entirely would seriously hurt the game in some cities. . . . A game of ball isn't a game of lawn tennis, and one wants it to go through with a certain amount of dash and vigor. Lively coaching has often saved what would otherwise have been a most uninteresting contest. There is a robustness to base ball that will prevent it from becoming a parlor game, and coaching is part of its strength and life" (*New York Advertiser*, quoted in *Sporting Life*, November 2, 1895).

There continued to be occasional calls to abolish coaching. Predictably, Henry Chadwick wrote in 1904 that coaching has "degenerated into a dirty-ball method of annoying the pitcher" (*Sporting News*, December 17, 1904). But as signs and strategies increased in complexity, coaches gradually began to acquire prestige. By 1912, Christy Mathewson could look back and summarize: "the old school of clowns passed, coaching developed into a science, and the sentries stationed at first and third bases found themselves occupying important jobs" (Christy Mathewson, *Pitching in a Pinch*, 118).

Even so, there were few full-time coaches in the next decade, and the best-known one literally was a clown. Nick Altrock of the Senators, who was reportedly the only full-time nonplaying major league coach between 1914 and 1920, was best known for his shadow-boxing routines and other buffoonery (Fred Stein, "Managers and Coaches," *Total Baseball*, 2nd edition, 461). In 1914 the *Detroit Free Press* observed, "Washington has two comedy coaches, [part-time player Germany] Schaefer and Altrock" (*Detroit Free Press*, September 30, 1914).

Objections to coaches continued to surface from time to time, most notably in 1916 when former President William Howard Taft used the occasion of the National League's fortieth anniversary to denounce noisy coaching (*New York Times*, February 14, 1916). Not until the 1920s did coaching truly become established as a profession.

(i) Directing Traffic

7.1.1   Coaches' Boxes. As noted in the introduction to this chapter, restrictions were placed on coaches as early as 1872. During the 1886 season the coach's box was introduced to try to place some restraint on the mayhem that passed for coaching. Boston president Jim Hart blamed two St. Louis players: "[Charles] Comiskey and Bill Gleason used to plant themselves on each side of the visiting catcher and comment on his breeding, personal habits, skill as a receiver, or rather lack of it, until the unlucky backstop was unable to tell whether one or half a dozen balls were coming his way. . . . So for the sake of not unduly increasing the population of the insane asylums or encouraging justifiable homicide, the coach's box was invented" (quoted in Gustav Axelson, *COMMY*, 74).

7.1.2   Coaching Calls. As discussed in the introduction to this chapter, in early baseball it was not what a coach said but how loudly and gratingly he said it. This led to coaches developing a vivid but largely ad hoc vocabulary.

For example, in 1886, the *Chicago Tribune* reported, "In Tuesday's game at Kansas City, [Boston's] Joe Hornung cut quite a figure. In the sixth inning [teammate Billy] Nash was on first and Joe rushed down the coacher's line hollering 'Ubbo, Billy, Ubbo.' This was a new thing in coaching for a cowboy crowd, who imagined the mystic words were intended to hoodoo the home players. They were enlightened a moment after, when [Kansas City pitcher George] Weidman drawing back his arm to deliver the ball, Joe sang out to Nash: 'Now you, Ubbo' and Billy 'Ubbod' by sailing toward second bag. He made a fine slide, but the ball beat him there and [umpire Chick] Fulmer called him in [i.e., out]. The word was then caught up by the crowd and the small boy hollered himself hoarse crying 'Ubbo' at the Bostons. Hornung explained afterwards that the word was a tramp's term, which meant to move off" (*Chicago Tribune*, September 12, 1886; according to a version of these events in H. Allen Smith and Ira L. Smith, *Low and Inside*, 122, Hornung thought the term would be unfamiliar, but Weidman was familiar with it and he yelled 'Ubbo' to confuse Nash).

One of the most popular coaching cries was "That's the way," which Arlie Latham was using in 1886 (*Sporting Life*, June 9, 1886). Leather-lunged Detroit manager Hughey Jennings's famous cry of "ee-yah" was a simplified version of this call (*Sporting Life*, April 11, 1908). Sportswriter H. G. Salsinger traced its development: "In his early days of American League leadership he would jump about the coaching box at first or third and yell: 'That's the way.' Later he drew it out into a long 'That's the way-ah.' Then it became 'That's Swaya.' After a time he abbreviated it to 'Swaaa-ah.' And then 'Wee-ah.' But there came still another change. It was slight, but it converted the phrase into 'Eeyah' or 'Ee-yah'" (*Detroit News*, January 10, 1926; Peter Morris, "'Attaboy!' Originated from the Dynamic Managing Style of Hughie Jennings (Detroit Tigers) in 1907," *Comments on Etymology* 33, no. 1 [October 2003], 2–4).

Other early coachers pushed the limits of acceptable language. The *St. Louis Post-Dispatch* chided in 1889, "Such language as 'say, yer rotten, yer stinkin'" as [George] Tebeau yelled frequently at [Arlie] Latham yesterday is rather coarse to be used in the presence of ladies and should not be tolerated on the ball field" (*St. Louis Post-Dispatch*, April 27, 1889).

Once the rules specified that coachers could not directly address the opposing pitcher, they found clever ways around the restriction. Christy Mathewson noted that Clark Griffith used chants like "watch his foot" and "he's going to waste this one." While these calls were intended to intimidate the pitcher, they were not ostensibly directed toward him. Thus "if a complaint is made, Griffith declares that he was warning the batter that it was to be a pitchout, which is perfectly legitimate. The rules permit the coacher to talk to the batter and the base runners" (Christy Mathewson, *Pitching in a Pinch*, 132–133).

7.1.3 Amplified Coaching. Megaphones were brought to prominence by the U.S. Navy's effective use of them in 1898 during the Spanish-American War. With coaching putting a premium on leather lungs, it occurred to some unknown innovator that megaphones would be a natural. A 1902 article noted, "The megaphone ought to be barred from coaching. It was used on both sides in the great Harvard-Yale game, but there is really no place for it in base ball" (*Sporting Life*, June 28, 1902). That reasoning appears to have been persuasive, as megaphones quietly disappeared from the coaching lines.

7.1.4 First-base Coaches. Another way in which the game's authorities attempted to address the nuisance of noisy coaches was by limiting the number. An 1897 rule change restricted teams to one coach until they had multiple runners on base: "This change is recommended because it has been proven in the past that the presence of two coachers allow a 'cross fire' of talk between them foreign to the game and frequently of a character objectionable to spectators" (*Washington Post*, February 8, 1897). According to Benton Stark, in 1904 clubs were again permitted to use two coaches throughout their at bats (Benton Stark, *The Year They Called Off the World Series*, 102–103). The presence of another base coach made it much more difficult for catchers to shield their signs from being stolen and contributed to the introduction of the catcher's crouch (see **4.2.2**).

7.1.5 It's a Bird, It's a Plane . . . No, It's Only the Third-base Coach. When coaching was still in its "old school of clowns" era, a common ploy was to try to get the opposing fielders to mistake the base coach for a base runner or otherwise interfere. For example, base coach Mike Kelly of Chicago ran all the way out to the shortstop position to provide a distraction during an 1886 series against Detroit. At the end of the first full season of the coach's box, the *New York Times* observed that the new lines had succeeded at discouraging "the trick of personating runners from third base to the home plate" (*New York Times*, October 9, 1887). It doesn't seem to have entirely eliminated the practice. While coaching for Brooklyn in 1890, George Smith got carried away and ran home ahead of the base runner he was coaching. The catcher tagged Smith instead of the runner and, after a long argument, the umpire ruled the runner out (Robert L. Tiemann, "George J. Smith," in Frederick Ivor-Campbell, Robert L. Tiemann, and Mark Rucker, eds., *Baseball's First Stars*, 151). The tactic was explicitly prohibited by a 1904 rule change.

(ii) Coaching Staffs

7.2.1 Full-time Coaches. A few sources suggest that Bobby Mathews was the first paid coach, around 1888. I have found no contemporaneous documentation for that claim. Many other sources tab Arlie Latham with the New York Giants in 1909. That, however, can't be true because Latham had been employed as a full-time coach nine years earlier.

In July 1900, Latham was hired by the Cincinnati Reds as a coach. *Sporting Life's* correspondent enthused that "Cincinnati critics have it that Latham's coaching has greatly improved the Reds' base running" (*Sporting Life*, September 1, 1900). He later added: "Manager [Bob] Allen says he is delighted with the coaching of Latham. He says the base running of the team has improved fully 100% after the veteran got on the lines" (*Sporting Life*, September 29, 1900).

Sportswriter J. Ed Grillo painted a rather different picture. He noted that most of the players suspected that Latham had been hired by Cincinnati owner John T. Brush to spy on the newly formed Professional Ball Players' Protective Association. Others thought that Latham was "simply there to amuse the crowd with his coaching." In response to Brush's claim that Latham would teach some of the players the finer points of the game, Grillo wrote, "This might be construed as a direct slap at Manager Allen whose duty it was supposed was to give players such instructions" (*Sporting News*, August 4, 1900).

For whatever reason, it was an idea whose time had not yet come. During the first decade of the twentieth century, clubs made do with coaching from players, though the quality was often not high. A 1901 article, for instance, observed that Mike Donlin "likes to 'coach' but he has no conception of the meaning of the word. As he construes it, coaching consists entirely of saying mean and disagreeable things to the pitcher of the other team and showing off his own smartness. He does not aid the base runner at all, and the words of 'advice' that he shouts to the men on the bags are stereotyped and seldom timely" (*Sporting News*, March 16, 1901).

Between 1900 and 1910 the complexity of signals and managerial strategy increased greatly, and the need for full-time coaches became apparent. At least one minor league club had a full-time coach in 1908, with Perry Werden filling that role for Indianapolis (*Sporting Life*, May 1, 1909). In 1909, John McGraw hired Duke Farrell and Arlie Latham as full-time coaches for the Giants. Not everyone was impressed with Latham's work, and Fred Snodgrass later called him "probably the worst third-base coach that ever lived" (quoted in Lawrence Ritter, *The Glory of Their Times*, 94). Researcher Cliff Blau notes an additional problem: National League president Thomas Lynch ruled that coaches counted against a team's twenty-five-man limit (see **13.3.1**), though managers didn't (*New York Times*, May 10, 1910).

Nonetheless the benefits of Latham's coaching were sufficiently evident to journalist Ren Mulford, Jr., that he suggested in 1912 that Cincinnati follow New York's lead: "New York carries Arlie Latham, and the old boy is quite a card as a coacher and undoubtedly earns his salary. If there is any value at all in coaching surely 'Lath' delivers the goods. He was one of the game's best run-getters and he knows the way around the bases without a guide. Take it for granted that his coaching does get a percentage of runs across—runs that might not otherwise be made—then he is baggage well carried. Heiny Peitz was one of the prize coachers when he wore the red. His cheery voice was an inspiration to the players on base and as a matter of whispered fact there were qualities in that sarcastic little yelp of his that never helped the fellow on the firing line. . . . Cincinnati would have in Peitz a valuable all-season coach on the lines and one of the most valuable aids to good pitching in balldom" (*Sporting Life*, March 9, 1912).

In the next couple of years the benefits of skilled base coaching were attracting more general recognition. A 1913 article reported, "Pitcher Frank Allen cost Brooklyn a chance to tie a recent game with the Phillies in the ninth inning by bad coaching at third base, and yet managers—some of them—persist in sending pitchers to the coaching lines. In fact some managers seem to think that if a player is good for nothing else he is just the man to do the coaching. Such managers, however, never win pennants" (*Sporting News*, September 11, 1913). The growing perception that experienced coaching translated into victories paved the way for full-time coaches to become a permanent part of baseball.

As it grew increasingly common for the coaching lines to be manned by full-timers, the position assumed greater dignity. Nonetheless the men who manned it were veterans of the era when a prime goal was "to disconcert the opposing players," and some remnants of this approach persisted. Christy Mathewson observed in 1912: "There is a sub-division of defensive coaching which might be called the illegitimate brand. It is giving 'phoney' advice to a base runner by the fielders of the other side that may lead him, in the excitement of the moment, to make a foolish play. This style has developed largely in the Big Leagues in the last three or four years" (Christy Mathewson, *Pitching in a Pinch*, 125).

Nonetheless wartime austerity decreed only a few full-time paid coaches for the remainder of the decade. The profession of coaching made great strides toward respectability in the 1920s but was again threatened during the Great Depression. Many of the lower minor leagues reacted to the straitened economic climate by eliminating coaches. The International League announced plans to do so on May 5, 1933, but quickly reversed course. The major leagues appear never to have been forced to contemplate such measures (Jonathan Fraser Light, *The Cultural Encyclopedia of Baseball*, 204).

7.2.2   Bench Coaches. Leigh Montville credited Ted Williams with creating the position of the bench coach—a coach who, instead of being responsible for a specific department or group of players, aids the manager with strategy. When he was hired to manage the Washington Senators in 1969, Williams had no managing experience at any level. Accordingly, he offered the job to Johnny Pesky, who declined, and then hired Joe Camacho (Leigh Montville, *Ted Williams*, 273).

The 1980s saw the position become more common, though some questioned whether it was necessary. Columnist Gerry Fraley observed in 1999: "Twins manager Tom Kelly cannot understand the recent creation of 'bench coach.' Doesn't a bench coach do what a manager should be doing, Kelly has asked" (Gerry Fraley, *Baseball America*, December 27, 1999–January 9, 2000). But by then it had become almost standard for every major league club to employ a bench coach, and the position began to replace third-base coach as a stepping-stone to a managerial position.

Neither the function nor questions about its usefulness are entirely new. In 1877 the *Chicago Tribune* noted, "Joe Simmons is 'assistant manager' [of the Rochester club], whatever that may be" (*Chicago Tribune*, August 12, 1877). Christy Mathewson served as assistant manager of the Giants from 1919 to 1921 (Eddie Frierson, "Christy Mathewson," Tom Simon, ed., *Deadball Stars of the National League*, 36).

7.2.3 Pitching Coaches. The position of pitching coach took a long time to develop and did not become commonplace until the 1950s. Mel Harder is sometimes credited with being the first pitching coach, and he appears to have believed that to be the case: "During my active career they didn't have pitching coaches. At the end of the '47 season [Bill] Veeck gave me a job as pitching coach for the entire Cleveland organization. I went to the major league camp in spring training and when they broke camp I went to the minor league camp in Florida. I worked with their minor league teams for a while and then went back to the Indians and stayed there" (quoted in Walter M. Langford, *Legends of Baseball*, 72–73). But the evidence does not support Harder's claim.

A few signs indicate that pitching coaches were beginning to emerge before 1910, though the position was not yet a formal one. Pitching coaches were scarce before 1910, if they existed at all. If pitching legend Bobby Mathews did indeed become the first paid coach in 1888, it seems safe to assume that he was being paid for his ability to instruct pitchers. The great African-American pitcher Rube Foster is sometimes said to have worked as an informal pitching coach for John McGraw's New York Giants, though the evidence for this claim is not strong. Veteran catchers like Deacon McGuire often functioned as pitching coaches; during spring training in 1906 it was noted that "'Deacon' McGuire has charge of the pitchers of the Highlanders who are working at Hot Springs" (*Washington Post*, February 26, 1906).

By the teens there is much clearer evidence that the position had begun to emerge. Wilbert Robinson annually coached the Giants' pitchers during spring training from 1911 to 1913. One of Robinson's special projects was Rube Marquard, and the pitcher formerly dubbed the $11,000 lemon blossomed into a star. (Marquard lost his form when Robinson left the Giants in 1914 to manage the Dodgers, but bounced back when reunited with Robinson in Brooklyn.) At least once, McGraw called on Robinson during the season when he sensed that the team was "about to go to pieces" (Larry Mansch, *Rube Marquard*, 70–71, 82).

In the next few years pitching coaches began to become quite common, though like Robinson, many of these coaches concentrated on the pitchers during spring training and then assumed additional responsibilities once the season began. Others may have served only as instructors during spring training rather than being permanent members of the coaching staff.

It was reported in 1911 that Detroit owner Frank Navin offered Newark manager Joe Sugden "the job of teaching the Tiger pitchers and catchers this year and next season. The New York Highlanders have made Sugden a similar offer" (*Detroit News Tribune*, April 2, 1911). Jack Ryan was referred to in 1912 as "the Nationals' crack coach of young pitchers" (*Sporting Life*,

December 21, 1912). Pat Moran was said to have functioned as an informal pitching coach in the last few years of his playing career (Dan Levitt, "Patrick Joseph Moran," Tom Simon, ed., *Deadball Stars of the National League*, 207).

In 1915 the *Washington Post* mentioned "Charles 'Duke' Farrell's position as coach for the Yankee pitchers" (*Washington Post*, May 2, 1915). This was followed in 1920 by news that "The Joplin Club also has signed the veteran Jim Drohan to act as a coach of pitchers" (*Sporting News*, March 11, 1920). Two years later *Sporting News* referred to "Dan Howley, for the past four years coach of pitchers of the Detroit Tigers" (*Sporting News*, October 12, 1922). Grover Land was hired before the 1925 season "to coach the kid pitchers of the Reds" (*Zanesville Times Signal*, December 14, 1924). Hook Wiltse served as pitching coach for the Yankees in 1925 (Gabriel Schechter, "George LeRoy 'Hook' Wiltse," Tom Simon, ed., *Deadball Stars of the National League*, 54).

Since Mel Harder pitched in the major leagues from 1928 to 1947, it might be theorized from his claim to have been the first pitching coach that the position fell victim to depression-era and World War II cutbacks. But once again the evidence paints a very different picture. AP wire reports listed Ed Walsh as the White Sox' pitching coach in 1928, Chief Bender filling that role for the Giants in 1931 and being succeeded by Tom Clarke by 1933, and Johnny Gooch coaching the Pirates' pitchers in 1938 (*Reno Evening Gazette*, February 28, 1928; *Danville* [Va.] *Bee*, March 26, 1931; *Gettysburg Times*, July 27, 1933; *Wisconsin Rapids Tribune*, August 6, 1938). George Moriarty noted in 1928 that Allan Sothoron had recently been hired as pitching coach of the Braves (George Moriarty, syndicated column, *Lincoln* [Nebr.] *Evening State Journal*, June 26, 1928). Hank Gowdy was occupying that position five years later (Cleon Walfoort, "The Sport Dial," *Sheboygan* [Wisc.] *Press*, April 17, 1933). Charlie Berry was described as the pitching coach of the Athletics in 1937 (*Williamsport Gazette-Bulletin*, January 29, 1937). George Uhle claimed: "I was a coach with the Chicago Cubs in 1940. My job was to work with the pitchers" (Walter M. Langford, *Legends of Baseball*, 126). In 1941 the White Sox' and Senators' pitchers were coached by Muddy Ruel and Benny Bengough respectively (INS wire service: *Zanesville Signal*, October 14, 1941). Branch Rickey announced after the 1942 season that veteran pitcher Freddie Fitzsimmons would become an informal pitching coach for the Dodgers (*Coshocton* [Ohio] *Tribune*, December 11, 1942).

While pitching coaches do appear to have become less common during World War II, it is hard to understand how Mel Harder could have thought he was the first pitching coach.

7.2.4 Hitting Coaches. In 1912, Damon Runyon noted that Brooklyn owner Charles Ebbets was about to hire Willie Keeler "to coach the young Brooklyn players in the art of batting next Spring." While it was becoming common for clubs to bring a veteran player to training camp to tutor young players, Ebbets was reputedly "about the first to introduce a batting instructor" (*Sporting Life*, December 14, 1912).

Just as the earliest pitching coaches worked only during spring training, so too Keeler's duties apparently were limited to the preseason. It was not until the 1950s that the position emerged as full-time. Jonathan Fraser Light cited Harry Walker and Wally Moses as two of the first full-time hitting coaches (Jonathan Fraser Light, *The Cultural Encyclopedia of Baseball*, 84).

7.2.5 Strength and Conditioning Coaches. The Cincinnati Reds became the first club to have a full-time, season-long strength and conditioning coach in 1961 when they hired Otis Douglas, a former NFL player and head coach in the Canadian Football League (Greg Rhodes and John Snyder, *Redleg Journal*, 407). It seems to have paid off, as the Reds made it to the World Series that year and the players voted Douglas a full share (*Sporting News*, October 25, 1961).

As with pitching coaches and hitting coaches, however, a number of earlier clubs had engaged strength and conditioning coaches for spring training. Their programs were often quite rigorous, as this 1943 article shows: "Every club in baseball, large or small, has a trainer, but only the Philadelphia Phillies have a physical director. He is Harold Anson Bruce, internationally known track and field coach, who was appointed by owner Bill Cox to give the faltering Phils a taste of 'commando training' this spring and to keep them in condition after the season gets under way. Commando training is a catchword contributed to baseball terminology by Cox and what the Phillies' physical director really is giving them is an adaptation of the usual program of exercises given runners, jumpers, et al." (Judson Bailey, "Cox Gives Phillies Commando Drill," *Troy* [N.Y.] *Times Record*, March 24, 1943).

Many of these pioneers shared Douglas's football background. In 1948, Branch Rickey hired Brooklyn Dodgers football coach Carl Voyles to help condition his baseball team. In 1957, Gabe Paul brought in former Notre Dame football coach Terry Brennan to help the Reds get into shape during spring training (*Sporting News*, February 11, 1959).

7.2.6 Baserunning Coaches. The emergence of coaches whose primary responsibility is baserunning is mostly a recent development. But as discussed under "Full-time Coaches" (7.2.1), Arlie Latham was the first to have assumed that function. His main duty with the Reds in 1900 seems to have been baserunning and in 1909 he again served as third base and baserunning coach for the New York Giants.

(iii) Teaching Techniques

7.3.1 Charting Pitches. Longtime International League standout Eddie Onslow recalled that in the mid-1920s Rochester manager George Stallings had pitchers on the bench keep charts of "bases on balls, hits, and errors." Stallings apparently did this to demonstrate his contention that walks led to more runs than hits or errors. While this is not the same as the current practice of charting pitches, it may have helped to influence its development (Eugene Murdock, *Baseball Between the Wars*, 100).

Johnny Sain may have introduced the type of pitch-charting that is in vogue today (John Thorn and John Holway, *The Pitcher*, 174).

7.3.2 Pitch Limits. During the 1990s pitch counts and pitch limits went from being almost unheard of to becoming common and sometimes controversial. Pitch counts date back to the 1860s, but they were kept by the scorekeeper and no particular significance was attached to them.

According to Robin Roberts, Paul Richards was recording pitch counts when he managed Baltimore in the 1950s (Hal Bodley, "Teams Obsess Too Much Over Pitch Counts," *USA Today*, September 17, 2004, 4C). The idea of team-enforced pitch limits is a more recent one, but not as new as might be expected. As early as 1971, Roger Angell reported, "One team limits its youngsters to a maximum of a hundred pitches per game" (Roger Angell, *The Summer Game*, 267).

7.3.3 Batting Dummy. After abandoning Professor Hinton's pitching gun (see 14.4.11), the Princeton baseball club tried a new way of facilitating practice: "A 'dummy batter' was set up by the side of the home plate, and the Princeton twirlers took turns at pitching to it. The idea was to give the pitchers practice in accurate throwing without subjecting the batters to the dangers of being hit or having to dodge" (*North Adams* [Mass.] *Transcript*, June 13, 1898).

The concept made it to the major leagues in 1906 when Detroit manager Bill Armour placed a dummy in the batter's box during practice to help pitchers with their control. The players nicknamed the dummy "Hick" (*Sporting Life*, March 24, 1906).

7.3.4 Visual Aids for Coaching Hitting. Hitting coaches have long sought tools that enable them to *show* batters how they can improve instead of merely telling them.

Some hitters made use of visual aids even before coaches became involved in the process. George S. Davis observed in 1894, "I know a great many clever batsmen who practice daily before a looking glass just as actors and actresses do when they are rehearsing a part. By standing in front of a big glass, bat in hand, one can study his position and remedy any defects he may have" (George S. Davis, "How to Bat," syndicated column, *Warren* [Pa.] *Evening Democrat*, May 26, 1894).

Detroit manager Hughey Jennings appears to have been the first to use technology to improve this process. Jennings started in 1908 by showing his hitters a photograph of Honus Wagner to exemplify an ideal stance. During spring training in 1910 he took photographs of Joe Casey's ungainly stance, causing the rookie to exclaim that it "must be awful to look that way at the plate" (*Detroit News*, March 7, 1910). Jennings then hired a photographer to snap his players so he could discuss their stances with them (H. G. Salsinger, *Detroit News*, April 25, 1910).

Some hitters turned to photographs on their own, as described in a 1921 article: "When [George] Burns was enjoying his greatest batting season in 1918, he was photographed, in action, by a Cleveland camera man. This spring, he felt that something was wrong with his position at the plate and accordingly hunted up the film shooter to get one of his 1918 photos, figuring that would show up any differences in his stance or way of holding his bat" (*Sporting News*, May 19, 1921).

Photographs did not entirely drive out older methods of hitting instruction, as shown by this 1942 account: "[Ted] Williams has stood before a mirror by the hour and practiced his swing. And that is the pet method of old Hugh Duffy for improving the hitting of batting pupils in his care. . . . In his time old Hughey has seen many a great batter come and go. He has helped to make some of them great with his 'looking glass' method of batting instruction" (Dwight Freeburg, "Batter Number One," *Baseball Magazine*, January 1942).

By the 1940s film was being used by innovative football coaches like Paul Brown. Baseball, however, was slow to follow the lead of football. Joe Morgan said that Ted Kluszewski was the first to make extensive use of videotape while coaching the Reds in 1975 (ESPN broadcast, June 25, 2000). Tony Gwynn helped to popularize videotape instruction in the 1980s and 1990s by making extensive use of it to refine his own technique and study opposing pitchers.

Chapter 8

UMPIRES

"The umpire is the sole judge of play, and is entitled to the respect of the spectators, and any person hissing or hooting at, or offering any insult or indignity to him, must be promptly ejected from the grounds."—(1876 National League Constitution)

THE ROLE of the umpire is to ensure that things are even. But the word "umpire" itself is derived from an Old French word that literally means uneven. That is somehow appropriate, as it has always been the role of the umpire to be alone and friendless. While still true today, imagine how much more evident it was in the early days of baseball, when a lone umpire had to keep track of all of the action on the field.

The evolution of the umpire's general role is discussed in Chapter 1 (see **1.12** and **1.13**). In this chapter, the origins of more specific elements will be examined.

(i) Growth of the Profession

8.1.1 Professionals. In the earliest days of baseball, being chosen to umpire was an honor, and there was no thought of paying for these services. As competitiveness changed the nature of the game, it became increasingly difficult to find qualified men who were willing to volunteer. When an umpire was verbally abused following an 1868 game, a reporter asked rhetorically, "Who, after this exhibition, wishes to act as umpire? . . . If this continues we will loose [sic] all our good umpires" (*Brooklyn Eagle*, August 15, 1868).

The idea of professional umpires was resisted, with Henry Chadwick warning in 1871, "The fraternity should bear in mind the important fact that the moment they legalize the system of paying umpires impartial umpiring will become a thing of the past" (*New York Clipper*, November 25, 1871). Nonetheless it became increasingly clear that the abuse being heaped upon umpires and the low quality of many volunteers left little alternative. In 1874 the rules acknowledged that clubs could pay umpires—as long as both clubs paid him equal amounts!

Thus if one defines the first professional umpire as the first man to earn money from umpiring, there is no way to be sure who holds the distinction. But the first man to make umpiring a profession appears to have been Billy McLean, who was sent on the road by the National League in 1878 and received five dollars per game plus all his expenses. It is apt that McLean was a former boxer, for umpiring was a very tough profession at the time (Larry R. Gerlach, "William H. McLean," in Frederick Ivor-Campbell, Robert L. Tiemann, and Mark Rucker, eds., *Baseball's First Stars*, 110).

8.1.2 Assignments. The dawn of the professional umpire was accompanied by another development that umpires were less grateful for, but which was just as crucial for maintaining the integrity of the game. This was the transition from the umpire being chosen by one or both of the teams to his being designated by an ostensibly neutral officer of the league.

Until well into the 1870s, games were umpired by locals who were hired by the home team, which led to frequent howls from the visitors. Everyone agreed that this system was less than ideal, but it was not easy to devise a better one without breaking the razor-thin budgets. The result was that arguments about who would umpire were frequent in the ensuing years. In the mid-1870s the rules called for the visitors to submit five names, the home team to winnow the list to two, and the visitors to try to hire one (*St. Louis Globe-Democrat*, April 4, 1875). The complexity of this process led to numerous snags, and more than a few games were never played at all because the issue could not be resolved.

Perhaps the ultimate such instance came during the 1884 best-of-three postseason series between New York and Providence. Providence clinched the series by winning the first two games and didn't want to play the third game, so New York manager Jim Mutrie offered to let Providence choose the umpire. Providence then selected New York's star pitcher Tim Keefe to umpire, and were able easily to beat New York's change pitcher (Jerry Lansche, *Glory Fades Away*, 42–43).

In 1879, the National League introduced the prototype of an umpiring staff (James M. Kahn, *The Umpire Story*, 30). The fact that these men had ongoing roles gave the league some much-needed control over quality. But, with the exception of Billy McLean, these umpires did not generally travel, which still left their objectivity open to question.

On July 2, 1882, the American Association held an emergency meeting and replaced the use of locals with the first staff of umpires who traveled to games (David Nemec, *The Beer and Whisky League*, 34). This proved satisfactory enough that at season's end the rules were amended to reflect the fact that umpires were now salaried employees.

Sporting Life gave this summary of the issue in 1885, though it was mistaken about the year in which the change took place: "There was a time when mediocre ability, if supplemented by known fairness on the part of the umpire was acceptable, but that day has gone by, for in these days of great skill and close championship contests the umpiring must be on a par with the other features of the exhibition.

"To make this attainable, all professional associations now have a corps of professional umpires, selected for their abilities and paid by the association, and hence with no incentive for unfairness.

"Up to 1883 [sic] it was customary to appoint a corps of umpires at large in the League, and the different clubs agreed upon which of them should umpire their games, but as there was no steady employment it was hard to get good men to serve. This plan, however, developed some good men, notably [John] Kelly and [Charles] Daniels, neither of whom has a superior in the profession today.

"The American Association depended upon the selection of umpires in each city, but this was soon found to have its objections. The rivalry became so intense that local umpires were compelled to succumb to partisan influence, and it seemed almost impossible for a club to get a square deal in a strange city. This finally culminated in a big squabble in St. Louis in the latter part of June, 1883 [sic], during which the Louisville Club left the field. The result of the trouble was the meeting of the American Association in Cincinnati July 2, 1883 [sic], at which meeting a regular corps of Association umpires were chosen at a fixed salary and expenses. Since that time all the associations have a regular corps of umpires, and the best umpiring ever done in the history of the game was done last year" (*Sporting Life*, June 3, 1885).

The benefits of such a staff became evident to the major leagues, but the perennially cash-strapped minor leagues continued to wrestle with the question. When the Southern League began in 1885, it was reported that "games are umpired by local umpires, who, the game being new, are inexperienced and not well posted on the rules, and also lean to their home club. This has threatened serious trouble and Secretary Deadrick proposes to take the bull by the horns and appoint a regular staff, as all the other associations have. He has the legal power to do this and should not hesitate to use it, as good umpiring is essential to the proper conduct and enjoyment of the game. He should appoint a staff of competent men at once" (*Sporting Life*, April 29, 1885).

8.1.3 You've Got a Friend. By the 1880s the need for more than one umpire was very clear. Base runners were increasingly taking advantage of the umpire's helplessness by cutting bases (see **11.1.5**). The advent of evasive slides (see **5.2.3**) made the inadequacy of long-distance umpiring all the more obvious.

The desirability of at least one additional umpire didn't mean that owners were anxious to assume the added expense. As a result, A. G. Spalding's brother Walter proposed an idea that reprised the much earlier system of two umpires and a referee (see **1.13**). In Walter Spalding's scheme, the two umpires would be members of the respective teams while the referee was a neutral party who would only have "a voice when a decision is questioned" (*Chicago Tribune*, October 19, 1886). It was also hoped that this would cut down on arguments: "unless the in umpire's decision is questioned by the out umpire it shall stand . . . on balls, strikes, and base decisions the only man entitled to appeal is the opposing umpire. On a question of rules the captain may appeal. In no case has a player other than the captain a right to protest or appeal to the referee" (*Chicago Tribune*, October 20, 1886).

The idea had the obvious advantage of increasing the number of officials without adding any expense. As a result, it was decided to experiment with it in the 1886 "World's Series" between Chicago and St. Louis, "and upon the result may depend the introduction of some such scheme into the league next year." But one critical change was made for the purposes of the test— all three arbiters were experienced major league umpires. This meant that the most vulnerable part of Walter Spalding's idea would not be tested: "With three experienced men, it should work well; whether it would be satisfactory were the umpires members of the contesting clubs, instead of outsiders, is a question" (*Chicago Tribune*, October 19, 1886).

The concept was first tried in an October 19 game in Chicago, with John Kelly serving as referee and Joe Quest and John McQuaid as umpires. Things ran smoothly for most of the game, but the one exception revealed a critical flaw. On a close play, McQuaid's ruling was questioned by the players but not by Quest. Nonetheless Kelly overruled the call, which naturally led to subsequent appeals of all close plays: "Yesterday the players seemed to think that any one of them had a right to appeal to the referee, and there was much needless waste of time" (*Chicago Tribune*, October 20, 1886).

This made it clear that Walter Spalding's system would fail for the same reason that a nearly identical one had had to be abandoned three decades earlier (see **1.13**). The same three men officiated again in the fifth game of the series with no major problems, but the scheme does not appear to have ever been used with club members serving as umpires (*Chicago Tribune*, October 23, 1886).

The following year John Gaffney and John Kelly, both nicknamed "Honest John," teamed to umpire the fifteen-game 1887 World's Series. The innovation was considered a complete success and led to sporadic attempts to introduce an extra official in the years that followed, even in semipro games. Immediately after the 1887 World's Series, it was announced in San Francisco that "The double umpire system will be worked for the remainder of the season at Central Park" (*San Francisco Examiner*, December 19, 1887). In an 1891 game in Henderson, Minnesota, two umpires rotated between the plate and field, but the resulting inconsistency caused the scheme to be termed "a rank failure" (Tom Melchior, *Belle Plaine Baseball, 1884–1960*, 42).

The Players' League of 1890 became the first league to mandate a second umpire, but the circuit lasted only the one season. The American Association occasionally experimented with a second umpire between 1888 and its demise following the 1891 season. The National League similarly used a base umpire from time to time between 1888 and 1897 (John Schwartz, "From One Ump to Two," *Baseball Research Journal* 30 [2001], 85–86).

While almost everyone recognized that a second umpire would benefit the game, there continued to be concerns about the expense. One reporter observed in 1897, "The cost of the experiment, $12,000, will scarcely warrant the engagement of another crew, and on this point the Little Five and the Big Seven heartily concur, as they do on every question where the wallet comes directly into play" (*Washington Post*, February 17, 1897).

The National League finally mandated the second umpire in the 1898 season. The change necessitated a new nomenclature that did not last long: "When two umpires are assured one shall be known as the 'referee umpire' and the other as the 'assistant umpire'" (*Washington Post*, February 23, 1898). The two-umpire system didn't last much longer, as the National League again shelved it after two seasons.

Researcher John Schwartz has meticulously examined early-twentieth-century umpiring assignments. He reported that the National League used only 1.13 umpires per game in 1901, and the American League 1.21. The rate increased gradually, and by 1908 the figures were 1.39 in the senior circuit and 1.51 in the junior circuit, meaning that more often than not a major league umpire was still unaccompanied (John Schwartz, "From One Ump to Two," *Baseball Research Journal* 30 [2001], 85–86).

Researcher David W. Anderson analyzed 1908 assignments carefully and found, not surprisingly, that two umpires were generally assigned to games between contenders and to ones where a sizable crowd was expected (David W. Anderson, *More Than Merkle*, 102–103). What's more surprising is that some veteran umpires, including Tom Connolly and Hank O'Day, expressed a preference for working without a partner (David W. Anderson, *More Than Merkle*, 88–89).

Other umpires, however, including Bill Klem, were vocal supporters of the two-umpire system. Their viewpoint carried the day, as the number of umpires per game rose dramatically to 1.72 (National League) and 1.91 (American League) in 1909 and 1.99 and 1.83 in 1910. It was not until 1911 that the second umpire was required by the rulebook. According to Schwartz, the last major league umpire to work a game entirely by himself was Cy Pfirman, who did so in the second game of a doubleheader in Philadelphia on July 11, 1923, after his partner Ernie Quigley was injured in the opener (John Schwartz, "From One Ump to Two," *Baseball Research Journal* 30 [2001], 85–86).

8.1.4 Three-man Crews. Like the second umpire, the three-man umpiring crew was introduced to regular-season major league baseball in fits and starts. The American League began the 1917 season with nine umpires, so it used an extra umpire on a regular basis until August. In the next few years the league president would occasionally assign a third arbiter to a big game (*Chicago Tribune*, August 9, 1920). The American League returned to nine umpires in 1921, and two years later it went to ten and the National League to nine. By the mid-1920s the major leagues began to hire ten umpires, which meant that three-man crews could be used in half the games if all the umpires were healthy (*New York Times*, April 13, 1925; research by John Schwartz). The number had increased to eleven or twelve umpires in the late 1920s. In 1932 both leagues went back to ten umpires to save money, but the three-man crew was restored at season's end (*Washington Post*, April 12, 1932; *New York Times*, November 5, 1932). John Schwartz reports that the number fluctuated for several years, and it was not until 1944 that both leagues permanently employed enough umpires to ensure three-man crews at each game. As far as he can tell, the last major league game with only two umpires on the field occurred in St. Louis on August 19, 1951—a game better remembered for the pinch-hitting appearance of midget Eddie Gaedel (see **2.3.3**). A few innings later, first-base umpire Art Passarella was injured, and the game was completed with two arbiters.

8.1.5 Four-man Crews. The now-customary practice of using four umpires likewise has a very sporadic history.

The first major league game that appears to have made use of four umpires occurred by accident during the Players' League's sole campaign of 1890. For a July 14 game with Brooklyn hosting Pittsburgh, "There was no room for any kicking, as owing to an error in calculation Secretary [Frank] Brunell had assigned four umpires to the Brooklyn game instead of sending two to New York and two here. It was the first championship contest ever decided with the aid of an umpire at each bag and one behind the catcher. The game began with Mr. [Bob] Ferguson judging balls and strikes, Mr. [Lon] Knight at first base, Mr. [Charles] Jones at second and Mr. [Bill]

Holbert at third. They moved round at the conclusion of every inning, each taking his turn at each base" (*Brooklyn Eagle*, July 15, 1890).

The 1909 World Series saw four-umpire crews become a custom for the World Series. The plan was to alternate two two-men crews: Jim Johnstone of the National League and "Silk" O'Loughlin of the American League rotating with Bill Klem of the National League and Billy Evans of the junior circuit. But the erection of temporary seating for the overflow crowds made life very difficult for the arbiters.

Evans and Klem officiated the second game on October 9 and were forced to determine whether a ball that bounced into the stands had landed in the permanent seats (making it a home run) or the temporary seats (making it a double). After a long huddle, they eventually ruled it a double but admitted afterward that the decision was little more than a guess, and were fortunate that it did not affect the outcome (James M. Kahn, *The Umpire Story*, 121–125).

The series resumed two days later with Johnstone and O'Loughlin scheduled to umpire. Before the game a conference about the ground rules took place with the result that Klem was asked to stand down one of the outfield lines in an "advisory capacity" (*Los Angeles Times*, October 12, 1909).

Before the next game the decision was made to make use of all four umpires for the remainder of the series. All four men took the field for game five on October 12, causing Ring Lardner to chronicle: "Klem was behind the bat and Evans on the bases. Silk O'Loughlin was out in left field to help decide whether balls were fair or foul and Johnstone was in right on the same job. Another reason for using the two extra ones was to avoid disputes over balls hit into the stands. There didn't happen to be any over which any discussion could arise, so Silk and Johnstone almost froze to death standing still" (R. W. Lardner, *Chicago Tribune*, October 13, 1909).

Despite the hardship, frozen umpires seemed preferable to having the outcome of the World Series potentially decided by a guess from hundreds of feet away on where a ball had landed after leaving the playing field. Thereafter four umpires became a World Series tradition.

A similar reason led to four umpires next being used in a regular-season major league game in Cincinnati on August 3, 1919. With a crowd of some 33,000 necessitating seating in the outfield, National League president John Heydler assigned four umpires to the game. Bill Klem was behind the plate and Bob Emslie covered the bases, with Pete Harrison and Barry McCormick stationed on the foul lines to make rulings on balls hit into the overflow crowd.

It was another three decades before today's system of umpires at each base came into use. According to John Schwartz, the National League went to thirteen umpires in 1945, which meant that—barring injuries—a four-man crew would work in one game out of four. The number rose steadily until 1953 when both leagues engaged sixteen men, and since then four-man crews have been standard except when unusual circumstances arise.

8.1.6   Five-man Crews. Ed Sudol explained to Larry Gerlach how he became part of the first five-man crew. National League umpire Dusty Boggess suffered a heart attack in late June 1957, and Sudol was called up to replace him. When Boggess returned in late August, the league was pleased with Sudol's work and let him remain in the major leagues as a fifth umpire. Sudol recalled, "For the rest of the season I alternated working the foul lines" (Larry R. Gerlach, *The Men in Blue*, 222).

David W. Smith of Retrosheet used the Retrosheet database to corroborate Sudol's account. He found seventeen games in September 1957 where five umpires were used, all of them involving Sudol. Smith also found that Bill Jackowski was used as a fifth umpire for two games in 1959 and John Kibler for three games in 1964. In 1961 the National League made extensive use of five-umpire crews to break in the new umpires who would be necessary in 1962 due to expansion.

8.1.7   Six-man Crews. Beginning in 1939, six umpires were on hand for all World Series games in case of an injury to any of the four who actually officiated the game (James M. Kahn, *The Umpire Story*, 233). The practice of using all six umpires in the World Series began with the 1947 Fall Classic. The decision to use two extra arbiters was made by Commissioner Happy Chandler shortly before the start of the series. Chandler reasoned that since two "active alternates" were always on hand in case of illness or injury to one of the regular umpires, they might as well be put to use. So the two umpires were assigned to "sit in the park at first and third base to determine if balls are fair or foul, to decide if outfielders trap or actually catch fly balls on shoestring catches, and rule whether or not fans interfere with balls close to the railing" (AP: *Washington Post*, September 30, 1947).

8.1.8   Rotations. It took some time after it became customary for multiple umpires to work major league games before a rotation became conventional. Bill Klem, most notably, continued to monopolize home-plate assignments for many years.

Sportswriter Herbert Simons noted in 1942 that a rotation had become the norm. He explained: "The stationing of umpires on bases and at the plate is up to the men themselves. It is a tradition, however, that the veteran in point of service opens the season behind the plate, the next oldest umpire at first and the junior member at third. They then rotate clockwise with each game for the rest of the season. . . . Sometimes an umpire may seem more proficient calling 'em on the bases than he is behind the plate, but he rarely is assigned to specialize, barring injury" (Herbert Simons, "Life of an Ump," *Baseball Magazine*, April 1942; reprinted in Sidney Offit, ed., *The Best of Baseball*, 156–162).

8.1.9   Chief of Umpires. When the legendary Harry Wright was fired as Philadelphia manager after the 1893 season, it caused a public outcry. As a result, the position of chief of umpires was created for him. Some claim this was an honorary position, but that was not the case. While National League president Nick Young continued to be in charge of appointing umpires, Wright took his duties seriously in 1894, visiting ballparks to observe umpires, asking Young for rule clarifications, and lobbying for greater respect for umpires (*Sporting Life*, April 14, 1894).

During the 1895 season, Wright's deteriorating health interfered with his duties. He died on October 3, and the position was not again filled until John B. Day was appointed in 1897. Longtime umpire Tommy Connolly was appointed as the first supervisor of American League umpires on June 17, 1931.

8.1.10   Umpire School. The earliest umpire school may have been one operated by Nick Young in Washington in the late nineteenth century (Richard Puff, "Nicholas Emanuel Young," in Frederick Ivor-Campbell, Robert L. Tiemann, and Mark Rucker, eds., *Baseball's First Stars*, 181). It seems unlikely that the instruction was extensive; most umpires continued to learn on the job. In 1899, Cleveland and St. Louis owner M. Stanley Robison advocated "the establishment of a school for umpires." Robison argued that better officiating was necessary for the sport to continue to advance and that the National League should sponsor the school. His fellow owners apparently did not agree (*Grand Valley* [Utah] *Times*, August 11, 1899). It was not until the 1930s that umpire schools with systematic instruction began to appear, with George Barr operating one of the first prominent ones.

8.1.11   Unions. In 1963 National League umpires secretly formed a union. According to Tom Gorman, Augie Donatelli was the driving force behind the movement. The umpires hired negotiator Jack Reynolds to represent them, and he won improvements in salaries, benefits, and working conditions (Tom Gorman as told to Jerome Holtzman, *Three and Two!*, 38).

American League umpires had initially declined to join the union, but after five years they changed their minds. An Association of Major League Umpires was formed on September 30, 1968, but it was met with greater resistance. One of the union's first demands was the reinstatement of Al

Salerno and Bill Valentine, two American League umpires who had been fired two weeks earlier. The umpires alleged that the pair was fired for their role in helping to start the union.

The umpires' union has attracted less attention than the players' union, but it has had its share of showdowns with the owners. The umpires staged a one-day walkout on October 3, 1970, and there have been several subsequent ones, one of which forced the 1979 season to begin with replacement umpires. A disastrous union tactic in 1999 saw the mass resignation of fifty-seven of the sixty-six major league umpires. Union head Richie Phillips intended to evade a no-strike clause in their contract, but his ploy backfired when major league baseball accepted many of the resignations. Twenty-two umpires lost their jobs, though most of them have since been rehired. A new union now represents the umpires.

(ii) Kill the Ump!

8.2.1 Verbal Abuse. It is hard to imagine any professional more prone to being second-guessed than the baseball umpire. In the early 1950s the wife of Supreme Court Chief Justice Fred Vinson reported that one of her husband's favorite forms of recreation was watching baseball on television and "hollering at the umpire whenever he thinks a poor decision is made" (James M. Kahn, *The Umpire Story*, 4).

Of course the umpires could not hear Vinson's catcalls, but that consideration has not deterred fans since the earliest days of baseball from heaping verbal abuse on umpires. As early as 1861, Henry Chadwick was chiding, "Clubs should remember that the umpire in a match confers a favor by accepting the office, and tries his best to act fairly in every instance; and common courtesy should lead them to act respectfully towards him, no matter how he may err in his decisions. This grumbling at adverse decisions is unworthy of true ball players" (*New York Clipper*, October 19, 1861).

It was not long before spectators were following the players' lead. By 1867 a Boston crowd was being taken to task by Chadwick for having "hissed nearly every decision of the Umpire" and an audience in Chicago for "hissing the umpire" (*The Ball Player's Chronicle*, June 6, 1867; *Detroit Post*, October 8, 1867). Chadwick reiterated this theme at every opportunity, but it soon became clear that he was fighting a losing battle. This did not deter him in the least, and the topic would be a recurrent theme of his writing for the next forty years.

8.2.2 Cotton. The *Brooklyn Eagle* reported in 1896 that one umpire had found a unique way to shield himself from verbal abuse: "The latest story is that [umpire William] Betts puts cotton in his ears and does not hear the players' abusive language" (*Brooklyn Eagle*, July 18, 1896).

8.2.3   Physical Abuse. It would be nice to report that early umpires were subject only to verbal abuse. Direct physical assaults on umpires were rare, though not unheard of, but a far more common menace was objects being thrown from the stands. As noted in an earlier entry (see **1.12**), umpires of the 1860s were customarily offered the largest glass of beer. Before the end of the century, the glasses of beer were instead being thrown at them.

Nor did the defenseless umpires have any recourse, as was shown by a National League game on August 4, 1897. When a fan threw a beer glass at umpire Tim Hurst, Hurst threw it back but hit a different spectator and was arrested for assault and battery.

The autobiography of Harry "Steamboat" Johnson, a prominent minor league umpire from 1909 to 1935, regularly refers to spectators throwing pop bottles at umpires (Harry "Steamboat" Johnson, *Standing the Gaff*, 62, 68–70, 112, etc.). In spite of the obvious dangers, baseball clubs moved very slowly to address the issue.

The 1907 season saw umpire Billy Evans and Cubs player-manager Frank Chance both seriously injured by flying bottles. The possibility of a ban on bottles was raised at the league meetings before the 1908 season, but no action was taken. *Sporting Life* editor Francis Richter felt this was a reasonable course since fans ought to be able to quench their thirst (*Sporting Life*, February 15, 1908; quoted in David W. Anderson, *More Than Merkle*, 18). Others felt that the owners were putting concession revenues ahead of safety, with sportswriter I. E. Sanborn observing, "Whenever the good of the game conflicts too seriously with the pockets of the club owners, no reform ever has been made until something happens to unite the public in demanding reform" (*Chicago Tribune*, March 1, 1908; quoted in David W. Anderson, *More Than Merkle*, 18).

As a result, this easily preventable hazard continued to menace umpires. Umpire Red Ormsby, who had fought in World War I and escaped unscathed, almost had his career ended by a pop bottle that gave him a severe concussion and caused him to miss nine weeks of action (*Sporting News*, May 12, 1932). Not until the late 1920s and early 1930s did owners agree to prohibit pop bottles from stadiums (Joe Williams, *New York World Telegram*, July 24, 1930, reprinted in *The Joe Williams Baseball Reader*).

(iii) The Umpire Strikes Back: Discipline

Umpires have never had much recourse against fan abuse unless they chose to emulate umpire William Betts and stick cotton in their ears. But over the years they have been given a number of ways of responding to impertinent players and managers.

8.3.1 Fines. In early baseball the umpire enforced discipline by assessing fines for misbehavior. As noted in Chapter 1, this practice dates back to the Knickerbockers. The most common fine was for swearing, and the score-keeper would record the fine—and sometimes the offending word—in the club's scorebook. Because club membership was highly valued, there was no difficulty in collecting these fines. The 1860 bylaws of the Excelsior Base Ball Club of Brooklyn, for instance, prescribed, "All fines incurred for violation of Sections 9, 10 and 11 must be paid to the umpire, before leaving the field."

This worked only as long as the umpire and players were members of the same club and collection of the fines was ensured by the value attached to membership. Once the gentlemanly era of baseball began to wane, fines disappeared, and they were not again practical until the dawn of professional leagues with their centralized power.

It is usually reported that professional umpires did not issue fines until 1879, but this is not technically correct. In fact National League umpires could assess fines in 1878, but they also had the authority later to cancel them. The result was that, "out of all fines imposed, only one was enforced during the year 1878" (*New York Clipper*, December 14, 1878). Even that lone fine was never collected by the league (*New York Clipper*, March 8, 1879).

Consequently the National League created a rule after the 1878 season "to remedy the evil of forgiveness" by making it impossible to revoke a fine (*New York Clipper*, December 14, 1878). Collecting fines still remained problematic, as is demonstrated by an 1889 rule adopted by the Michigan State League: "If [the umpire] fines a player during the game, the contest stops until the fine is paid. If the assessment is not settled within fifteen minutes, the game is awarded to the other club. This . . . may seem severe, but was thought necessary, as of the twenty fines imposed in the league this season, the only one which has been paid was the $5 Keyes assessed [Edward] Phalen for calling him a fool in a recent Grand Rapids game" (*Grand Rapids* [Mich.] *Daily Democrat*, July 3, 1889).

In the early 1890s the National League attempted to deal with player misconduct by allowing umpires to issue heavy fines. Unfortunately the fines seem to have done more to create ill will between players and umpires than anything else. Sportswriter H. G. Merrill asked in 1897, "Can anyone state where anything is gained by the fining system? The umpire in the heat of passion, exasperated as well, imposes a fine—large or small. The player loses a portion of his salary and in his sober moments ruminates over his indiscretion. He realizes he was wrong in abusing the umpire, but there rankles in his breast the thought that the umpire took away his money. . . . The player views the umpire as a highwayman and subsequently this same player and umpire are likely to have another tilt" (*Sporting News*, October 9, 1897).

Fines were further undermined by the fact that owners often paid them on the player's behalf. As one unidentified former umpire asked rhetorically, "Of what benefit are the rules when the players are tacitly encouraged to their erasion and infraction by the clubs paying the fines of players imposed by the umpire to enforce discipline?" (*Cincinnati Times-Star*, May 21, 1892).

Former American Association umpire John Dyler added that "all the fines in the world—unless the players themselves are compelled to pay them—will never stop the rowdies." He suggested that umpires needed the power "to fine them good and hard and not only put them out of the game, but stop them from playing for a time, and you'll soon put an end to the fighters and toughs" (*Sporting News*, October 30, 1897).

The 1890s saw the legalization of substitutions and increasing roster sizes, which made it possible for umpires to eject players instead of fining them. This had some advantages, but ejection by itself came to be perceived as too lenient a punishment, so rules were enacted in the early twentieth century that made fines mandatory for ejected players. This still had the disadvantage of creating resentment between players and umpires.

The change to the current practice of assessing fines from the league offices was a gradual one, but one of the prime movers was Tom Lynch, a former umpire who in 1910 became president of the National League. Lynch was determined to reduce the amount of umpire-baiting and concluded that "if I could touch the players' pockets I could stop this foolishness. So I notified each of the club owners that hereafter when a player was benched for using profane or indecent language on the field he would be suspended indefinitely. Lo, and behold, I haven't had a complaint from an umpire since!" (*Washington Post*, July 24, 1910). American League president Ban Johnson joined Lynch in imposing more severe penalties, and this course relieved umpires of some of the pressure.

8.3.2 Ejections. In 1867, Henry Chadwick noted that an "umpire has the power to order the dismissal of any player from a nine in a match" if he learned that that player had bet on the outcome (Henry Chadwick, *Haney's Book of Base Ball Reference for 1867*, 58). Other than this, before 1889, the rulebook gave the umpire no authority to remove a player, though it appears there were a few ad hoc ejections. For example, Gerard S. Petrone reported that John Gaffney once ejected Cap Anson from an 1884 game (Gerard S. Petrone, *When Baseball Was Young*, 131).

In 1889, with player substitutions legal, a rule was added that stated: "After a player has been once fined for abusing the umpire, that official shall retire said player from game, and substitute one of the men in uniform" (*Washington Post*, April 7, 1889). The rule did not prove effective, though there were different opinions as to whose fault that was.

Henry Chadwick blamed the umpires, writing in 1890: "Umpires did not enforce the rule last year, of removing an offending player from the field for repeatedly disputing an Umpire's decision, as they should have done" (*Spalding's Official Base Ball Guide, 1890*, 180). The umpires, however, saw the matter in a different light. An unidentified former umpire replied in 1892, "When writers like Chadwick inform umpires that an umpire can only remove a player upon the repetition of his offense, of what use is that rule?" (*Cincinnati Times-Star*, May 21, 1892).

In 1896 the National League made a renewed effort to crack down on troublemakers by emphasizing that umpires were expected to eject unruly players. This reflected a growing perception, mentioned in the preceding entry, that umpires who doled out fines created long-term animosity. Soon fines became the prerogative of the league presidents and ejections became the umpire's primary method of disciplining unruly players and managers.

In 1933, Heinie Manush became the first player to be ejected from the World Series. Commissioner Kenesaw Mountain Landis announced that in the future only he would have the authority to eject players from the World Series. While no such rule was specifically enacted, it appears that umpires adhered to this precept for the remainder of Landis's tenure.

8.3.3 Limiting Arguments. When umpires were given new and more effective disciplinary tools in the 1890s, with them came a renewed effort to restrict the arguing over calls. For example, the *Brooklyn Eagle* reported in 1892: "Hereafter no player—captain or subordinate—will be allowed to dispute any decision marked by a simple error of judgment, such as that involved in the question as to a base runner being touched or not, or on called balls or strikes. Only in cases where an illegal interpretation of a special rule is involved will any appeal from the umpire's decision be allowed" (*Brooklyn Eagle*, March 3, 1892).

Needless to say, adherence to such guidelines was not universal. But disputes came to be more and more governed by some basic conventions. It became accepted that a team's manager would take the lead in arguments and that umpires had the authority to cut short discussions of judgment calls. Matters were further eased as playing managers gave way to bench managers, since this enabled umpires to eject managers without costing a team the services of a star player.

Once this principle was in place, it led to other forms of détente between umpires and managers, such as the understanding that a manager would be automatically ejected if he came on the field to argue balls and strikes. I have not been able to determine the precise origins of this restriction, but it occurred some time after World War II (Larry R. Gerlach, *The Men in Blue*, 106).

Nonetheless, among the major professional sports baseball remains the most tolerant of stoppages of action to dispute an official's decision.

8.3.4 Clearing the Bench. In another effort to limit disputes, in 1910 the major leagues gave umpires the authority to clear the bench. *Sporting News* found the new measure effective: "The new rule adopted this year empowering umpires to 'clear the bench' has emphasized the need of regulating the retirement of players. Until this season offending players have been sent to the clubhouse singly, except in a few instances and comparatively few players in any one game" (*Sporting News*, July 28, 1910). Apparently when the bench was cleared, those players could still enter the game; they simply could not sit on the bench when not playing.

(iv) Making the Call

8.4.1 Making Up Rules. Like judges, umpires are not supposed to make up rules, just enforce the existing ones. But there have been occasions, especially in the early days of baseball, when they had little choice.

Not only were there major omissions in the scope of the rules, but there was also often ambiguity in the points that were covered. An amusing commentary in 1884 claimed: "Disputes over points of play have been unusually frequent this season, for the reason that many of the rules are ambiguous, improperly worded and capable of widely different constructions. In fact the playing rules are anything but models of pure or ordinary good English. An attempt has been made to clothe them in a sort of legal phrase. Evidently the author has taken a wild delight in seizing as many 'thereafters,' 'suches,' 'saids,' 'provides' and the like as he could lay his hand upon, impressing them into the service of the League to the entire neglect of the usual parts of speech, many of which, in these astounding paragraphs, wander up and down like [Dickens character] Mr. Pickwick trying to find his room in the dark and quite as disconsolate. It wouldn't be a bad idea for a joint committee to revise the entire code" (*Sporting Life*, July 30, 1884).

In 1867 a poorly thought-out rule specified that a batter had to be alongside the plate when he hit the ball, but specified no penalty. Accordingly, the accepted practice became for the umpire to call "no play" if the batter moved forward. In one game, umpire Phonney Martin decided to consider such balls "foul," an imaginative ruling that meant the batter could not profit by breaking the rules, but that he could be put out if his hit was caught. (Not coincidentally, Martin was one of the best pitchers of the day.) This led to one batter being called out on a "foul ball" caught by the center fielder. Henry Chadwick lambasted Martin: "This usurpation of the powers of the National Association by an umpire is something new in the history of the game" (*The Ball Player's Chronicle*, August 29, 1867).

For other instances of umpires becoming legislators, see the entries on "Brushback Pitching" (3.3.2) and the "Kimono Ball" (3.2.17).

8.4.2 Positioning. In early baseball the sole umpire stood behind the plate and well off to the side, a placement that was necessary for his protection since the catcher stood well behind the plate (see 4.2.1). This meant that his vision of the field was less than ideal, a problem that was exacerbated in the 1880s when base runners developed evasive slides (see 5.2.3).

The difficulty of umpiring from behind the plate was further emphasized by having to enforce restrictions on the pitcher's delivery. It was this requirement that may have first prompted an umpire to experiment with a different positioning. An account of an 1885 game noted that Kansas City pitcher Billy O'Brien "persisted in leaving his box with each pitch, until finally the umpire stationed himself back of the pitcher and closely watched his delivery during three or four pitches" (*Milwaukee Daily Journal*, May 26, 1885).

The first umpire to make a regular practice of standing behind the pitcher was John Gaffney in 1888. He introduced the system during the pre-season and drew a puzzled response: "Gaffney inaugurated a new style of umpiring here to-day. When the bases were clear he stood behind the catcher, but as soon as a man reached a base he went behind the pitcher. This is practically the double umpire system. It caused no end of comment among the spectators, who could not understand why he kept changing" (*Detroit Free Press*, April 5, 1888).

Gaffney found it effective and continued to use it in the regular season. At least one colleague, Billy McLean, also experimented with standing behind the pitcher and commented favorably (*Detroit Free Press*, June 15, 1888). The *Chicago Tribune* reported the following year that "[George] Barnum goes behind the pitcher as soon as two strikes or three balls have been called, and remains there while men are on base" (*Chicago Tribune*, April 30, 1889). The fact that the positioning of McLean and Barnum drew attention, however, suggests that umpires who stood there remained a distinct minority. Eventually the issue was rendered moot by the two-umpire system (see 8.1.3).

8.4.3 Home Umpire. Accusations that an umpire favored the home side, and the obligatory denials, are a familiar part of baseball. It would thus seem safe to assume that major league umpires have always strived for complete neutrality. This isn't quite the case.

National League president Nick Young specifically instructed umpire John Kelly in 1888 to give the benefit of the doubt to the home team. He explained: "To carry out this idea it is not necessary to be 'a home umpire,' but where an honest doubt exists the home club should not be the sufferer" (*Detroit Free Press*, July 1, 1888).

8.4.4   Appeals on Checked Swings. The automatic appeal on the checked swing is a fairly recent innovation, and several of the umpires interviewed in Larry Gerlach's *The Men in Blue* had strong opinions about it. Shag Crawford maintained, "It's the plate umpire's call, and he should make it." Ed Sudol concurred that the plate umpire had a better view of the play, and also felt that the appeal put the base umpire on the spot. Lee Ballanfant similarly felt that it was passing the buck. On the other hand, Bill Kinnamon liked the checked-swing appeal because it "takes some of the heat away from the home-plate umpire" (Larry R. Gerlach, *The Men in Blue*, 45, 207, 231–232, 245). None of these umpires specified exactly when this custom originated, so I hope a reader will be able to fill in this gap.

8.4.5   Tie to the Runner. This principle is often mentioned when a bang-bang play occurs at first base. Knowledgeable baseball fans sometimes retort that this precept does not appear in the rulebook. In fact the issue is more complex and the history more convoluted.

In 1860, Henry Chadwick counseled umpires, "When toe [sic] point, on which judgment is required, is a doubtful one, the rule is to give the decision in favor of the ball" (*Beadle's Dime Base-Ball Player*, 29). This would certainly appear to mean that a tie went to the defense, which was confirmed by an 1865 game account that observed, "the rule of 'favoring the ball' was followed" (*Detroit Advertiser and Tribune*, October 19, 1865).

But Chadwick removed this advice from the 1864 edition of *Beadle's* and in 1867 suggested just the opposite by noting that "the umpire—who gave excellent decisions as a general thing, erred in giving men out on the base when the ball was held simultaneously with the player's putting his foot on the base. Now the rule in each case requires that if the ball be not held before the player reaches the bases, the latter is not out" (*The Ball Player's Chronicle*, August 1, 1867). No reason was given for the apparent about-face, but it would seem likely that it reflected the fact that outs were becoming more routine.

This rule of thumb continued to be affirmed by Chadwick for many years and was reiterated by other sources. In 1886 a reader wrote to the *Chicago Tribune* to inquire: "When the umpire has a very close decision to make—as, for instance, where both base-runner and ball reach the base at the same time—is the preference given the runner or the club in the field?" He was told that "the base-runner is given the benefit under the rules" (*Chicago Tribune*, September 12, 1886). And in 1888 the *St. Louis Post-Dispatch* reported that the umpires' instructions included this guideline: "The umpire must call the man running to first base safe, if he gets to the base at the same time the ball is held on the base" (*St. Louis Post-Dispatch*, April 9, 1888).

It is easy to imagine that a fielder who protested on such a play and was told that it was a tie would not find this answer very satisfying. As a result, the precept that "a tie goes to the runner" was gradually de-emphasized in umpire instruction. Early-twentieth-century umpire "Silk" O'Loughlin became famous for saying, "There are no close plays. A man is always out or safe" (quoted in Christy Mathewson, *Pitching in a Pinch*, 168). Since then, umpires have been taught to call bang-bang plays one way or the other and "sell" their conviction.

(v) Communicating

8.5.1 Calling "Play Ball." The early rules required the umpire to call "Play" to commence the proceedings. The word "ball" must have been added before long, as an 1867 account noted, "'Play ball' was the cry of the umpire" (*The Ball Player's Chronicle*, August 8, 1867).

In 1915 the *Detroit Free Press* noted, "According to the rules, the umpire is supposed to call 'play' after every foul that is not caught. If you don't believe it read rule 36 in any guide or rule book. That the umpire doesn't call this after [every] foul is due to habit. That formality has been neglected so long that it has come to be understood that play shall be suspended until the runner gets back. Legitimately, the umpire is required to call 'play' at the start of a game or an inning before the pitcher delivers the ball, but only a few of them do it nowadays. Perhaps this disregard of a minor formality is responsible for growth of the misapprehension that the batsman must get out of position after a foul to keep the ball out of play" (*Detroit Free Press*, September 26, 1915).

The *Sporting News* had reported in 1911 that an appeal had been launched on the grounds that the umpire had neglected to call "play" after every foul. The appeal was understandably dismissed (*Sporting News*, June 29, 1911).

8.5.2 Ball and Strike Signals. It is often written that umpires began to use hand signals for the benefit of William "Dummy" Hoy, a deaf outfielder. This attribution is appealing for a number of reasons. Hoy overcame both his physical handicap and a diminutive stature to become a star major league outfielder from 1888 to 1902. He collected more than two thousand hits and nearly six hundred stolen bases while playing primarily for second-division teams. While it would make a wonderful story for umpires' signals to be Hoy's legacy to baseball, the evidence for this contention is weak.

Bill Deane's research has found that Hoy was indeed informed of the count by means of hand signals. These cues came not from the umpire, however, but from his own third-base coach. Deane cited an article from Hoy's rookie season of 1888 that said of Hoy, "When he bats a man stands in the Captain's box near third base and signals to him decisions of the umpire on balls and strikes by raising his fingers" (*Washington Evening Star*, April 7, 1888). Another article similarly observed: "Hoy is the only deaf and dumb [sic] player in the League. When he is at bat a man must be stationed at third base to sign with his fingers the number of balls and strikes that are called on him" (*St. Louis Post-Dispatch*, March 24, 1888; Hoy was not actually dumb).

In 1900 a Cincinnati fan named Warren Lynch suggested: "If every time an umpire called a ball he would raise his right hand and every time he pronounced a strike he would lift up his left hand there would be no trouble to follow the game." Hoy pronounced this a "splendid" idea and commented, "The act of lifting up the right hand by a coacher while I am at bat to denote that the umpire has called a strike on me and the raising of the left hand to denote that a ball has been called has come to be well understood by all the League players. The reason the right hand was originally chosen to denote a strike was because 'the pitcher was all right' when he got the ball over the plate and because 'he got left' when he sent the ball wide of the plate. I have often been told by frequenters of the game that they take considerable delight in watching the coacher signal balls and strikes to me, as by these signals they can know to a certainty what the umpire with a not too overstrong voice is saying." The *Sporting News* endorsed this idea in an editorial, but there is no evidence that it was tried at that time (*Sporting News*, January 27, 1900).

Hoy reported the following season that he also received other types of signals in a similar fashion: ". . . My team mates tell me whether a ball or strike is called by using the left fingers for balls and the right fingers for strikes. In base running the signals of the hit and run game and other stratagems are mostly silent, and the same as for the other players. By a further system of sign [sic] my team mates keep me posted on how many are out and what is going on around me. . . . So it may be seen the handicaps of a deaf ball player are minimized" (*Grand Valley* [Moab, Utah] *Times*, July 12, 1901).

Thus there is clear evidence that during his career Hoy received signals about balls and strikes from his teammates rather than from the umpire. The only eyewitness source that linked Hoy to umpire signals is his statement more than fifty years later that "the coacher at third kept me posted by lifting his right hand for strikes and his left for balls. This gave later day umpires an idea and they now raise their right . . . to emphasize an indisputable strike" (*The Silent Worker*, April 1952).

Even here, Hoy suggested only that his deafness had an influence on umpires' hand signals, not that there was a direct connection. Such a claim is conceivable, and it can never be positively refuted. And yet a review of the evidence reveals that umpire signals had occasionally been used before Hoy's career but did not become common until afterward.

In early baseball the ideal umpire was a leather-lunged man whose decisions could be heard all over the field and throughout the stands. This was not merely for the benefit of the audience. An umpire's lung capacity could have a direct impact on the outcome of the game, since base runners could be put out if they did not return promptly to their bases after a foul ball had been called.

The idea of replacing this hollering with signals was raised on several occasions. For example, an 1870 letter writer proposed: "If the umpire would hold a small flag or some other signal in his hand and elevate it above his head when a ball is struck 'foul'; every player in the field could see it, and it would do away with mistakes as regards 'fouls.' The signal might also be used to advantage in calling 'in' players who are 'out' on bases, & c.; but, of course, this could not relieve the umpire from giving his signals orally" (*Chicago Tribune*, June 18, 1870).

Bill Deane noted that Harry Wright wrote in 1870: "There is one thing I would like to see the umpire do at [a] big game, and that is, raise his hand when a man is out. You know what noise there is always when a fine play is made on the bases, and it being impossible to hear the umpire, it is always some little time before the player knows whether he is given out or not. It would very often save a great deal of bother and confusion" (letter to the *New York Sunday Mercury*, March 27, 1870).

At least a few umpires put this idea into practice during the 1880s, though they were prompted to do so by unusual circumstances. Al Kermisch discovered that umpire Robert I. McNichol was hit in the throat with a foul ball in the seventh inning of an American Association game between St. Louis and Columbus on August 11, 1883. Temporarily unable to speak, he used hand signals for the remainder of the game to register his decisions (Al Kermisch, "Umpire Used Hand Signals in 1883," *Baseball Research Journal* 21 [1992], 111).

Several other members of the school where Hoy learned to play baseball, the Ohio School for the Deaf in Columbus (see **20.3.5**), also relied upon signals. When the school team went on a tour in 1879, one account noted that "only one player speaks, he acting as captain, giving them signs for strikes, called balls, etc." (*New York Clipper*, July 19, 1879).

In 1886 another alumnus, former major leaguer Ed Dundon, umpired a minor league game and communicated his decisions by means of signals: "Dundon, the deaf and dumb pitcher of the Acid Iron Earths, umpired a game at Mobile between the Acids and Mobiles, on October 20. . . . He used the fingers of his right hand to indicate strikes, the fingers of the left to call balls, a shake of the head decided a man 'not out,' and a wave of the hand meant out'" (*Sporting News*, November 6, 1886).

Paul Hines, who starred in the major leagues from 1872 to 1891, suffered from a serious loss of hearing by the end of his career. One contemporary claimed many years later that sympathetic umpires such as John Gaffney, Phil Powers, Sandy McDermott, and Tom Lynch held up "their fingers to indicate balls or strikes to [Hines]" (Guy Smith, *Sporting News*, July 25, 1935; quoted in Tony Salin, *Baseball's Forgotten Heroes*, 86).

By the end of the 1880s crowds had grown larger and more dispersed, which meant that more spectators "in case of unusual noise cannot hear the umpire's decision" (*New York Sun*, May 27, 1888). A reader named John J. Rooney wrote to the *New York Sun* in 1889 to complain that the umpire's decisions could not be heard by much of the audience. He suggested hiring a "man or boy with a pleasant-sounding gong" to convey the umpire's rulings to the spectators (*New York Sun*, April 14, 1889). A second reader, James Sullivan of New Haven, Connecticut, suggested that, instead of using a gong, the umpire should "telegraph his decisions." His idea was, "For every strike the umpire shall raise one hand straight over his head; for a ball he shall make no significant motion. Whenever a man is out he shall raise both hands over his head, and if a man is safe, whether at the bat or running bases, he need make no significant motion" (*New York Sun*, April 16, 1889).

Rooney replied that "the umpire has enough to do in watching the game. . . . His attention must be centred on the play, and any distraction or unnecessary increase of duties weakens and burdens him. The umpire would be compelled to shout, throw up his hands and work the hand register at the same time." He contended that the umpire would resemble a "jack-in-the box" and further argued that hand signals were not sufficiently "emphatic." By contrast, he claimed, "A bell demands attention, speaks unmistakably, and at once stamps the decision with authority" (*New York Sun*, April 18, 1889).

The powers-that-be turned a deaf ear to the complaints of fans like Rooney and Sullivan for more than a decade. The press also remained largely unsympathetic to this viewpoint, with one correspondent writing in 1896, "Last season some of the umpires had a habit of indicating their reasons for giving judgment on balls and strikes by a gesture of the hand, indicating too high, too low, too wide, etc. It is not a good plan. When one gives reasons there are thousands to differ as to the facts. . . . An umpire serves best when he confines his work to giving judgment on plays and going no farther until the decision is protested by the captain of the team. . . . Even the old 'what's-the-matter-of that' from the pitcher had best be replied to, if at all, by the quiet rejoinder that 'it is a ball'" (*Sporting Life*, March 7, 1896).

By the turn of the century, growing crowd sizes were making the need for a new means of communicating the umpire's decisions too obvious to ignore. Sportswriter W. A. Phelon wrote in 1901: "Noiseless umpiring is to be attempted at the South Side park Monday afternoon. Impossible as this may seem at first hearing, it is to be attempted, and there are even bets that it will be a go. George W. Hancock, famed in Chicago as the man who invented indoor base ball, will be responsible for the success or failure of the scheme. The umpire is to wear a red sleeve on the right arm and a white one on the left. For a strike he will raise the right arm, for a ball the left; for an out he will hoist the right arm, for a ball [sic] the other. People at the far end of the park, unable to hear even that human buffalo, [Jack] Sheridan, can see the colors, and there seems a good chance for the trick to make a hit" (*Sporting Life*, September 14, 1901).

Coincidentally, "Dummy" Hoy was on that Chicago team, though it is clear from the account that the experiment had nothing to do with him. But I could find no indication that the scheme was actually tested. The White Stockings' last home Monday appearance came with a doubleheader on September 9, and the *Tribune*'s account of the game gave no mention of such an experiment. Game accounts over the next couple of weeks made no other mention of the scheme.

It was not until a few years after Hoy's retirement that the idea of umpires using signals began to gather momentum. Researcher Dan Krueckeberg reported that umpire Cy Rigler introduced the practice in a Central League game in 1905: "One feature of Rigler's work yesterday that was appreciated was his indicating balls by the fingers of his left hand and strikes with the fingers of the right hand so everyone in the park could tell what he had called" (*Evansville Courier*, May 1, 1905). Krueckeberg added that "When Rigler entered the National League a year later, he found that his raised-arm call had preceded him and was in wide use" (Dan Krueckeberg, "Take-Charge Cy," *National Pastime* 1 [Spring 1985], 7–11). This latter assertion is not documented, and the evidence I have found clearly suggests that it was not until 1907 that pressure from fans and reporters led to the change.

New York Highlanders manager Clark Griffith proposed that umpires gesture with their right hand on any called strike (*Chicago Tribune*, February 24, 1907). Umpires continued to resist the idea, and before the season umpire Tom Connolly "presented a strong argument against the proposed rule to have umpires wave their arms to designate balls and strikes" (*Washington Post*, March 1, 1907).

They seemed to have agreed to experiment with signals during spring training, and the *Chicago Tribune* offered this report of the results: "'The *Tribune's*' agitation for a system of umpire's gestures to indicate decisions seems to be as far reaching as popular. Chief Zimmer has been using signs for balls and strikes and delighting New Orleans patrons. Today Collins, who officiated here [Memphis], adopted the same system and used it successfully, with the result the crowd forgave him for not calling everything the local twirler pitched a 'strike.' To date Hank O'Day appears to be the only opponent of the idea" (*Chicago Tribune*, March 24, 1907; Collins must have been a local umpire as he did not umpire in either major league that season).

The possibility of receiving more sympathetic treatment from the fans must have been alluring to umpires, and by opening day even O'Day had overcome his reservations. Researcher Greg Rhodes noted that an account of the season opener in Cincinnati reported: "Hank O'Day used the arm signals yesterday and they were satisfactory. He raises his left hand for a ball. In case he raises neither hand, it is a strike" (*Cincinnati Commercial-Tribune*, April 12, 1907).

When the opening-day umpire in Chicago didn't follow O'Day's lead, he was lambasted by the *Tribune*: "There is nothing but this habit of looking at baseball matters through the umpire's eyes to explain the failure of the big league presidents to answer the public's demands by instructing their umpires to adopt a simple code of signals to indicate doubtful decisions on pitched balls, the same as on base decisions. The umpires objected to being overworked by the necessity of moving an arm to indicate a 'strike.' Consequently the public must continue to guess, until electric score boards are installed and perfected, and then miss some of the play while studying the score board" (*Chicago Tribune*, April 14, 1907). The following day the *Tribune* reported approvingly that umpire Bill Carpenter had been a big hit with the fans by raising his right hand to indicate a strike.

Obviously umpires still had some work to do to synchronize their signals, but once this had been accomplished umpire signals became a permanent and essential part of baseball. The *1909 Spalding Guide* observed: "Two or three years ago Base Ball critics in the East and West began to agitate the question of signaling by the umpires to announce their decisions. At first the judges of play did not want to signal. They thought it detracted from their dignity to go through a dumb show resembling the waving of the arms of a semaphore. . . . It was finally experimented with and has been one of the very best moves in Base Ball as a medium of rendering decisions intelligible, and now there is not an umpire but uses his arms to signal. If he did not, two-thirds of the spectators . . . would be wholly at sea as to what is transpiring on the field, except as they might guess successfully. Even the older umpires, who were more loath to give their consent to the new system on the field, are now frank enough to admit that it has been of invaluable assistance to them in making their decisions understood when the size of the crowd is such that it is impossible to make the human voice carry distinctly to all parts of the field."

8.5.3   Embellished Signals. Bill Klem is sometimes credited with pioneering umpire signals. While I have found no evidence to support that contention, it does appear that Klem was among the first to give added emphasis to his signals. His work inspired sportswriter Sid Mercer to file this whimsical report in 1909: "Some of the fans thought that Mr. Klem was picking posies for a while. When the first good one came over he would describe a semi-circle with his right arm somewhat after the manner of a romantic young man blowing a kiss to a fair young maiden. His manner seemed to say: 'There, now, you saucy thing. I'll take you from over there and place you over there, and you've got to be good.' To denote a second strike, Mr. Klem used a sign that is universally recognized as a silent order for two beers. It is also used sometimes by goats butting into the press box" (*New York Globe*; reprinted in *Sporting News*, May 27, 1909).

8.5.4   Safe and Out Signals. Somewhat surprisingly, umpires appear to have been signaling out and safe before it became customary to have signs for balls and strikes. In 1907, when the *Chicago Tribune* was agitating for umpires to have signs for balls and strikes, the newspaper noted, "There is no rule compelling an umpire to motion 'safe' or 'out' on the bases, but nearly all of them do by force of habit on plays which are not at all close" (*Chicago Tribune*, February 24, 1907).

8.5.5   Wired for Sound. Cy Rigler became the first umpire to be wired for sound in a game at the Polo Grounds on August 25, 1929 (see **14.5.13**).

(vi) The Tools of the Trade

8.6.1   Blue. Umpires were wearing blue as early as 1884, when the American Association required its arbiters to wear suits of "blue yacht-cloth" and a black cap (*New York Clipper*, April 12, 1884). Blue had become customary by the early twentieth century and remained so for most of the century (Beth Martin, "Hey, Blue!," *National Pastime* 18 [1998], 36–46).

8.6.2   Masks. Early umpires stood a safe distance from home plate and therefore did not need protective equipment. As catchers moved closer to the action, so did umpires, and they began to adopt similar forms of protection.

Larry Gerlach credited Dick Higham, who was banished from the National League in 1882 (see **11.1.3**), with being the first umpire to wear a mask. Ironically Higham was a former catcher who had not used a mask during his playing days (Larry Gerlach, "Richard Higham," in Frederick Ivor-Campbell, Robert L. Tiemann, and Mark Rucker, eds., *Baseball's First Stars*, 77).

It was not long before masks were accepted as a necessity. An 1884 game account in the *Washington Post* noted, "The umpire, Mr. [Arthur] Allison, was struck a terrible blow in the head in the fourth inning, but pluckily continued in his position. He should have followed [Sam] Trott's example on Thursday, and worn a catcher's mask" (*Washington Post*, April 12, 1884).

8.6.3   Chest Protectors. Once umpire's masks were accepted, it was only a matter of time before chest protectors were added. The originator appears to have been John Gaffney, who at the start of the 1888 season was reported to be wearing "an ingenious breast and stomach protector. It is made of pasteboard in sections, joined together with elastic, and made to fit tight around. When Gaffney buttons up his cardigan jacket no one would know that he is provided with a protector. He said he was hit so often in the chest and over his heart that he had to take some means to save his life. The contrivance is Gaff's own make" (*New York Sun*, April 22, 1888).

By the end of the 1891 season, most umpires were following Gaffney's lead by donning cork chest protectors. In the meantime, Gaffney had become convinced that he was catching colds because of the device and was planning to switch to a "wire body protector" (*Sporting Life*, October 17 and 24, 1891).

At least one minor league umpire was so concerned about his safety that he outfitted himself like a medieval knight. An 1889 account noted that "McDermott, one of the Western Association umpires, is bound not to be killed by a pitched ball this season. He has made a helmet and cuirass of stout bull's hide, steel bound and brass riveted, which shields his head and body. The suit is ingeniously constructed to yield with the movements of the wearer, while light but strong steel ribs offer stout resistance from assaults from without. The helmet is lined with a combination of steel bars and springs and cotton wool in such a way that not even the most powerful blow from an irate batsman would be felt on the wearer's head. In fact, the only vulnerable spot in the helmet is the hole necessarily left for the umpire's mouth, and even this is in a measure protected by a wire netting. For his legs he has devised a covering somewhat resembling cricketers' leg pads, but much thicker and stronger, constructed of heavy bull's hide" (*Brooklyn Eagle*, April 1, 1889).

A 1913 article credited Bill Klem with having invented the aluminum rib protector, which was worn inside the coat (*Sporting News*, January 30, 1913).

For much of the twentieth century, National League umpires followed Klem's lead and wore inside protectors while American League umpires wore outside protectors. In the 1930s and '40s, minor league umpires discovered that their choice of chest protector style was a factor in which major league was more likely to offer them a promotion (Beth Martin, "Hey, Blue!," *National Pastime* 18 [1998], 36–46). American League umpires finally began to switch in the 1970s.

8.6.4   Headgear. An 1886 article suggested, "Base ball umpires should call at the C. J. Chapin Arms Company's store and see their new sunshade hat for $1. It does away with the nuisance of holding an umbrella in the hand and annoying the catcher. They are lighter than an ordinary hat and much cooler on account having [sic] a space between the head and the inside of the hat, allowing a free circulation of air" (*Sporting News*, June 21, 1886).

8.6.5   Shin Pads. When I was growing up in Canada, an old joke asked: "What was the number one song in Canada when 'Wake Up Little Susie' was number one in the United States?" The answer was, "I don't know, but six months later it was 'Wake Up Little Susie.'" Similarly, the equipment of nineteenth-century umpires generally remained in lockstep but well behind catcher's equipment.

By the twentieth century the gap had pretty much been eliminated and, reflecting their closer proximity to the action, umpires sometimes led the way. Bob Emslie reportedly showed up for a 1900 game wearing cricket pads (Gerard S. Petrone, *When Baseball Was Young*, 143). A 1905 article noted, "Umpire Tom Connolly is wearing shin pads" (*Sporting Life*, June 17, 1905).

At the same time some umpires were going the other direction. Jack Sheridan became known for refusing protective equipment and instead shielding himself by crouching behind the catcher (*Detroit News-Tribune*, September 18, 1904; James M. Kahn, *The Umpire Story*, 41).

8.6.6   Foot Protectors. Toe pads were introduced by Umpire Jim Johnstone in 1912 (*Sporting Life*, June 15, 1912).

8.6.7   Indicators. Not long after the advent of balls and strikes, umpires began using devices to keep track of balls and strikes. Henry Chadwick noted in 1874: "In counting balls unfairly delivered, the umpire should be furnished by the club with a counting tally, consisting of pieces of wood moving on a wire, like a billiard tally. It should be made small, so as to occupy but three or four inches in length" (*New York Clipper*, April 11, 1874).

In 1875, Peck & Snyder's was selling an "Umpire's Assistant" for one dollar. The device was made of black walnut, with "each Ball or Strike . . .

registered by turning the thumb-screw," and was endorsed by Chadwick (advertisement in Henry Chadwick, *DeWitt's Base Ball Umpire Guide*). Before long the devices were improved so that they could keep other running tallies as well: "The scoring dial is the latest thing out in the form of a method for keeping the score of runs at a match. It is manufactured by Casseno, May & Shepard, of Glen Allen, Va. It is the handiest thing out for umpires to count balls and strikes" (*Brooklyn Eagle*, August 4, 1885).

8.6.8   Whisk Brooms. Umpires used large brooms to clean home plate until a game on May 14, 1904, when Cubs outfielder Jack McCarthy stepped on one and sprained his ankle. The injury led National League president Harry Pulliam to mandate the use of whisk brooms, and the American League followed suit.

8.6.9   Glasses. Eyeglasses are, of course, not standard equipment for an umpire, but a few brave arbiters have donned spectacles. The first to do so may have been Billy McLean, who was also the first major league umpire to be paid to travel: "Some fun is being poked at Umpire McLean for using glasses. Now, why shouldn't McLean wear glasses? Will White has used glasses ever since he has been on the ballfield; and he continues to see a good deal of base ball and know it, too" (*Sporting Life*, July 16, 1884). McLean may have been spared from ridicule due to having formerly been a prizefighter. McLean's eyesight continued to deteriorate and eventually forced him to quit the profession (*Williamsport Sunday Grit*, July 19, 1891).

As the vision of umpires became the subject of derision, there arose an increasing unwillingness to acknowledge that the eyesight of the men in blue was imperfect. Minor league umpire Bob O'Regan wore glasses throughout a career that began in 1939, but he never made it to the majors and his eyewear may have been responsible (Gary Waddingham, "Irish Bob O'Regan: A Bespectacled Ump in the Bush Leagues," *Minor League History Journal* 1:1, 33–36).

It was not until 1956 that another major league umpire donned glasses. Frank Umont did so in a game between Detroit and Kansas City on April 24, 1956. Umont was a former NFL tackle, which no doubt limited the abuse he took.

Ed Rommel told sportswriter Paul Menton that he had beaten Umont to the punch, wearing glasses in an April 18 game between the Yankees and Washington. No one noticed Rommel's glasses because he was umpiring on the bases. Rommel indicated that he intended to wear the glasses only when he was a base umpire during a night game (*Lima* [Ohio] *News*, April 27, 1956; attributed to Paul Menton, *Baltimore Sun*, April 26, 1956, though I checked that issue and could not find the article).

The initial reception accorded Umont and Rommel was generally favorable. Columnist Arthur Daley reasoned, "Arbiters in spectacles are operating on firmer ground. Their eyesight has been tested by experts and the specs give 20-20 vision" (Arthur Daley, "Eyes Like Eagles," *New York Times*, May 13, 1956). Organized baseball did not prove to be as receptive. Bespectacled umpires who apply for umpire schools are now told that they may attend the school but will not be considered for positions in professional baseball (Gary Waddingham, "Irish Bob O'Regan: A Bespectacled Ump in the Bush Leagues," *Minor League History Journal* 1:1, 35).

8.6.10 Lena Blackburne's Mud. When Lena Blackburne, a longtime major league infielder, coach, and manager, was growing up in Clifton Heights, Pennsylvania, he often waded in the Pennsauken Creek, a branch of the Delaware River. He discovered that "the outgoing tides purified the mud at the bottom of the creek, leaving it inky black and sticky. I was a kid pitcher in those days and I often used the mud on a new ball—when we were lucky enough to get one" (quoted in *Sporting News*, March 16, 1968).

After Blackburne reached the majors, he heard umpire Harry Geisel complaining about how difficult it was to get the slickness off of new baseballs. That fall Blackburne dug up a supply from his old location and experimented with it. He discovered a secret ingredient that prevented the mud from staining the balls (*Sporting News*, March 16, 1968). Next spring he presented Geisel with a can of the mud. Geisel found it very effective, and word soon spread.

According to *The Baseball Chronology*, umpires in both leagues began rubbing down balls with Blackburne's clay on June 13, 1921 (Jim Charlton, ed., *The Baseball Chronology*). But Blackburne himself gave the year as 1939, and that date is more consistent with other factors, especially the fact that Geisel did not beginning umpiring in the major leagues until 1925 (Joseph F. Lowry, "Baseball's Magic-Mud Man," *Family Weekly*, September 5, 1965).

At first Blackburne looked at the mud as an amusing way to make a few extra bucks. But as time went by it grew into a lucrative business, and the exact source of the mud and the added ingredient became closely guarded secrets. In 1965 he drove a reporter to Pennsauken Creek but explained, "This isn't the exact spot where I get my goo. Nobody ever will know where that is. But this is close enough. Where I get my mud, two streams come together. That means the mud is filtered twice and is very fine" (Joseph F. Lowry, "Baseball's Magic-Mud Man," *Family Weekly*, September 5, 1965). Blackburne died in 1968, but his family is still supplying mud to the major leagues. As of the mid-1990s they charged $75 for a can of mud; no doubt it has gone up since then (Dan Gutman, *Banana Bats and Ding-Dong Balls*, 161–162).

Chapter 9

EQUIPMENT

(i) Baseballs

An 1884 article gave a fascinating description of the "rude, homemade balls" that were used before 1850. These balls "were made of rubber and were so lively that when dropped to the ground from a height of six or seven feet they would rebound ten or twelve inches. A blow with a bat would not drive them so far as one of the balls now in use can be driven with the same force, but when they struck the ground they were generally much more difficult to stop on account of their bounding propensities. Fifty years ago there were no professional ball players and the demand for manufactured base balls of any description was very small. Many of the balls then in use—in fact nearly all of them—were home made. An old rubber overshoe would be cut into strips a half inch wide and the strips wound together in a ball shape. Over this a covering of woolen yarn would be wound and a rude leather or cloth cover sewn over the yarn. Sometimes the strips of rubber were put in a vessel of hot water and boiled until they became gummy, when they would adhere together and form a solid mass of rubber. This, after being wound with yarn and covered with leather by the local shoemaker, was a fairly good ball and one that would stand considerable batting without bursting. In the lake regions and other sections of the country where sturgeon were plentiful, base balls were commonly made of the eyes of that fish. The eye of a large sturgeon contains a ball nearly as large as a walnut. It is composed of a flexible substance and will rebound if thrown against a hard base. These eyeballs were bound with yarn and afterward covered with leather or cloth. They made a lively ball, but were more like the dead ball of the present than any ball in use at that time" (*Brooklyn Eagle*, February 3, 1884).

9.1.1 **Manufactured Balls.** A. J. Reach, one of the first professional players and later a sporting goods magnate, wrote in 1909: "As to the first base balls, my recollection of them dates from about 1855 or '56. The most popular ball in those days was the Ross ball: Harvey Ross, the maker, was a member of the Atlantic Base Ball Club, of Brooklyn, and a sail-maker by trade; his home was on Park Avenue, where he made the balls. John Van Horn was a member of the Union Club, of Morissania [sic], New York; he had a little boot and shoe store on Second Avenue, New York City. These two makers turned out the best base balls for some years, and they were used in nearly all of the match games that were played up to the early '70s" (*Sporting Life*, March 13, 1909).

Henry Chadwick indicated that even with only two ball makers, the demand in the 1850s was so limited that Ross and Van Horn were able to meet "it very readily without entrenching upon the time required for their ordinary avocations." The limited demand also meant that there was no need to mechanize, and "Van Horn used to cut up old rubber shoes into strips from which he wound a ball of about from two to two and a half ounces of rubber, and then covering this with yarn and the yarn with a sheepskin cover" (*Spalding's Official Base Ball Guide, 1890*, 35).

By the end of the decade baseball had begun to catch on in earnest, and this changed baseball manufacturing. As an 1867 article observed, "Five or six years ago clubs procured the balls they played with from two or three makers, and one bat maker could supply almost the whole demand. Now there is a regular bat and ball manufactory in each city . . . turning bats out by the thousand, and balls by the hundred, where they were previously sold by the dozen and singly" (*The Ball Player's Chronicle*, June 27, 1867). In 1870 a single baseball manufacturer turned out 162,000 new balls. Even this vast quantity did not suffice for the demand, which was estimated at half a million balls per year ("Bats, Balls and Mallets," *New York Times*, May 30, 1871).

This brought many new manufacturers into the business, including "a man named Rice, who commenced business in a small room in a frame building on Nassau street, New York. He continued in the business until about 1870, and became quite an expert base ball maker, although he was never able to make more than a living out of the business. About 1870 he sold out to S. W. Brock, a Brooklyn man who was then doing a small novelty business in the same locality. The new owner soon became convinced that the manufacturing of base balls was likely to become a large and lucrative business. He disposed of his novelty business and invested his entire capital—only about two hundred thousand dollars—in base ball material. From that time the demand for base balls began to increase and the success of the business was assured. It soon became necessary to have more room, and in order to obtain it the business was removed to a large building on Dey street, where it still remains" (*Brooklyn Eagle*, February 3, 1884).

Dan Gutman described several earlier patents of machinery designed for manufacturing baseballs. Since none of these were marketed commercially, it is impossible to say how feasible they were (Dan Gutman, *Banana Bats and Ding-Dong Balls*, 151). Ben Shibe of the A. J. Reach Company is generally credited with inventing the machinery that made it possible to mass-produce standard baseballs. The Reach Company was mass-producing cheap baseballs by 1883, though official balls still had to be hand-sewn.

By 1884 there were major baseball-making factories in Brooklyn, New York City, and Massachusetts, and the manufacturing process was becoming increasingly elaborate: "Over twenty different grades and varieties of base balls are made, and the prices obtained by the manufacturers vary from twenty-eight cents per dozen up to ten dollars per dozen, according to the grade. Those sold at the latter prices are the finest base balls made. Each one of these balls is carefully packed in a paper box by itself and sells at retail at one and a half dollars. The balls being made for next season's use are generally being wound on a small base of rubber, which gives them more elasticity and life than is possessed by the dead balls which have been in use for some time past. The dead balls are said to be going out of favor, because of their liability to burst when struck a hard blow with the bat.

"The first steps to be taken in making base balls is to cut the covers and wind the yarn. The covers are made of sheepskins and are cut into the proper shape by means of a large steel punch. The sheepskins are spread out on large wooden blocks. The operator, with the steel punch in his left hand and a wooden mallet in his right, cuts the covers by placing the sharp edges of the punch on the sheepskin and striking the punch a smart blow with the mallet.

"The covers, when cut, are almost exact imitations of the sole of a shoe. After being cut they are sent into the sewing room, where they are sewn together by girls, one end being left open so that the ball can be placed inside. The balls are wound by men. Each man has a reel in front of him on which a skein of yarn is placed. He also has a block of wood, which stands perpendicularly upon the floor. In the upper end of this block there is a polished indentation somewhat resembling a teacup, though not so deep. When the operator has wound off yarn enough to make a ball as large as a black walnut he stops winding, places the ball in the cup-like form on the block of wood and with a small club which he has close at hand, strikes it several hard blows. He then winds on more yarn and repeats the blows. In this way he proceeds until the ball is large enough to receive the cover. The blows are given for the purpose of hardening the ball. After the covers are put on the balls are rolled, under considerable pressure, in a polished groove. After being rolled they are perfect and present a very smooth and pretty appearance, all the roughness of the seams being completely removed by this operation. They are now thrown into barrels and removed to the packing room, where they are packed into boxes for the trade.

"Base ball makers are paid for their work by the piece. The sewing is all done by girls, and they make as much money as the men. All average from ten dollars to fifteen dollars per week the year round" (*Brooklyn Eagle*, February 3, 1884).

9.1.2 **Dimensions.** As early as 1854, there were broad guidelines for the size of baseballs. The 1857 rules specified that the baseball weigh between 6 and 6.25 ounces, with a circumference of not less than 10 and not more than 10.25 inches. Rules amendments in 1859, 1861, 1868, 1871, and 1872 reduced the size of the ball. By 1872 the weight was between 5 and 5.25 ounces, with the circumference between 9 and 9.25 inches. Those dimensions have not changed since. Roger Kahn pointed out that these dimensions are very close to the ones that had been established for a cricket ball long before baseball had formal rules (Roger Kahn, *The Head Game*, 34–35).

9.1.3 **Covers.** Creating a crude semblance of the innards of a baseball has never been that difficult, but making a cover that fit snugly over it has been another matter. A man named Charles Haswell recalled many years later that around 1816 boys wound yarn over a variety of objects to form the core of the baseball but then "some feminine member of his family covered it with patches from a soiled glove" (Charles Haswell, *Reminiscences of an Octogenarian, 1816 to 1860* (New York, 1896), 77; quoted in Thomas L. Altherr, "A Place Leavel Enough to Play Ball," 245).

Daniel Adams, one of the leading members of the Knickerbockers, originally made the club's baseballs, and he found the covers the most difficult part. He later recalled: "I went all over New York to find someone who would undertake this work, but no one could be induced to try it for love or money. Finally I found a Scotch soldier who was able to show me a good way to cover the balls with horsehide, such as was used for whip lashes." Adams continued to make the covers himself until "some time after 1850," when "a shoemaker was found who was willing to make them for us. This was the beginning of base ball manufacturing" (*Sporting News*, February 29, 1896).

An early Boston ballplayer explained that the baseball of the era was "covered with alum-dressed horse hide, that being the strongest leather known, being very elastic when water soaked, in which way it was used. The body of the horse being smoother, rounder and harder than that of other animals it follows that the skin would be more even throughout. The alum makes the leather white and may add some strength. . . . Sometimes balls would not last through a game and balls were made with two covers, but the Boston manufacturing broke down that business. When leather was not to be had, a cheap and easy way to cover a ball was with twine in a lock stitch, called quilting" (*Boston Journal*, March 6, 1905).

John Gruber offered this history of baseball covers: "Leather coverings were used from the very start. Before 1880, any kind of leather was allowed, sheepskin being mostly preferred, because it was the universal belief that it lasted longer. But in 1880 the rule was changed to read that the ball 'must be composed of woolen yarn and two horse-hide covers, inside and outside, with yarn between said covers.' From that year dates the familiar expression of 'hitting the horse-hide.' However, the 'horse-hide covers, inside and outside,' were in use a couple of seasons only, 1880 and 1881. In 1882, the simple words 'covered with leather' were reinserted. In 1887 'leather,' like 'yarn and rubber,' was scratched off the books altogether" (*Sporting News*, November 11, 1915).

This last change was part of a decision to simplify the rulebook by merely specifying that the official league ball be used (*Sporting News*, November 11, 1915). Horsehide became the standard cover and remained so until December 2, 1974, when major league baseball announced that cowhide would also be permitted. This followed a similar change of baseball gloves from horsehide to cowhide that took place around 1940 (Dan Gutman, *Banana Bats and Ding-Dong Balls*, 206).

9.1.4   Cover Design. Some sort of stitching was almost always used to secure early baseball covers, but there was no uniformity in the pattern. There are a number of candidates to have originated the figure-eight design still used today, but not much firsthand evidence.

A leather goods worker named Ellis Drake claimed many years later to have developed several designs but found that the corners and joins gave out. After a lot of trial and error, he hit upon the figure-eight design but never patented it (*Boston Globe*, March 28, 1909). Researcher Bob Schaefer, however, noted that Drake makes some implausible claims that weaken his credibility.

A report by the Natick, Massachusetts, Historical Society claimed that a Natick resident named Colonel William Cutler designed the figure-eight cover. Cutler is said to have hit upon the design in the kitchen of his home about 1858 and sold it to early baseball manufacturer William Harwood.

A couple of sources claim the current design was invented by C. H. Jackson in 1860 and subsequently patented (Lee Allen, *Cooperstown Corner*, 84; "Designing a Baseball Cover," by Richard B. Thompson, of the Department of Mathematics, University of Arizona). But Bob Schaefer was unable to locate such a patent in the records of the U.S. Patent Office.

Finally, an 1888 article noted vaguely: "The cover consists of two pieces, each cut in the shape of the figure '8.' By bending one section one way and the other in an opposite direction a complete cover is obtained. That was the discovery of a college boy. For years the balls were covered with four pieces of leather, but the genius of the college chap has proved of great benefit to the manufacturers" (*San Francisco Examiner*, January 8, 1888).

9.1.5 Insides. John Gruber noted in 1915 that "India rubber and yarn were from the very first the chief substances of which the ball was made" (*Sporting News*, November 11, 1915). An early ballplayer later recollected the process of scrounging up the innards: ". . . It was not difficult to procure an old rubber shoe for the foundation of a ball. Many a dear old grandma or auntie of today will remember having stockings and mittens being begged of them, which were knit at home by hand, to be unraveled for ball stock" (*Boston Journal*, March 6, 1905).

With availability playing a crucial role, only the weight and the two basic components were initially specified. This meant enormous variations in the liveliness of the balls, and the ideal mixture of rubber and yarn rapidly became a subject of considerable controversy.

The early balls created for the Knickerbockers by Daniel Adams were soft and didn't travel far (*Sporting News*, February 29, 1896). This didn't suit their aims of making the game manlier while also eliminating "soaking" (see **1.22**), so the ball was tinkered with to make it livelier.

Henry Chadwick later reported that, "in the days when the Knickerbocker and Gotham Clubs were the crack organizations of the metropolis," which would be the mid-1850s, "the leading ball maker of New York only used *an ounce and a half* of rubber in the composition of the balls he manufactured" (*New York Clipper*, April 16, 1870).

With no standard, the 1860s saw clubs choosing baseballs with significantly more rubber. This produced a great deal of scoring but became tedious to many observers, and a backlash ensued. Harry Wright's Red Stockings popularized a dead ball, and Henry Chadwick began to crusade for less rubber.

John Gruber explained in 1915: ". . . In the first year of the Professional Association, 1871, the quantity of rubber was limited to one ounce, 'no more, no less,' the rule makers declaring that 'this makes the ball lively enough for the purposes of good batting.' But it seems the manufacturers used strips of rubber which made the ball rather too lively and so the next year, 1872, it was decreed that 'the rubber used shall be vulcanized and in mold form.'"

This was the last time the specifications for the amount of rubber changed, but it was hardly the end of the issue: "In 1883, the American

Association eliminated the yarn and rubber qualifications and ordained that the ball must be manufactured from the patent plastic composition under the specification and proposition made by A. J. Reach. The National league, however, adhered to the yarn and vulcanized rubber.

"But, in 1887, when the joint rules committee came into life, the words 'yarn' and 'rubber' disappeared from the rules forever. It was simply stated that the Spalding league ball or the Reach American Association (later the American League) ball 'must be used in all games played under these rules.' Therefore, during the past 29 seasons, from 1887 to date, the manufacturers apparently used any kind of material just so they remained within the limits of weight and measurement. Lately one of the manufacturers sprung a surprise by announcing a 'cork' center for every ball" (*Sporting News*, November 11, 1915).

The type of yarn to be used was not specified by the early rules, but in 1874 it was decreed that it had to be woolen. This requirement was never changed, but in 1877 there was a brief and unsatisfactory experiment with cotton yarn. Shortly before the season the National League had informed official ball maker Louis Mahn that his product was too soft. So Mahn attempted to remedy the situation by replacing the woolen yarn with cotton yarn.

The resulting balls were anything but too soft; in fact, they were so hard that fielders feared for their safety. The *Chicago Tribune* explained that with the woolen yarn, "after a few innings' use the outside of the ball becomes 'mellowed,' so that it can be handled without pain. The ball with the cotton outside cannot by any possible amount of use be softened at all."

Complaints about the new ball flooded in. Harry Wright and Louisville owner Walter Haldeman registered their objections in a vociferous yet tactful form. Cincinnati owner Si Keck "also expressed a most decided opinion in the same direction, but it was so marked up by dashes as to be necessarily omitted" (*Chicago Tribune*, May 17, 1877). The old baseball was swiftly brought back.

9.1.6 Cork-center Balls. Cricket was using cork-center balls as early as 1863. Baseball, however, stuck primarily with India rubber and yarn, though there were occasional exceptions. Henry Chadwick observed in 1869, ". . . Some base balls are made—illegally—with a small ball of cork in the centre, covered with nearly *three ounces of hard* rubber, and this with about two ounces of yarn and leather. The result is a ball which will rebound on hard ground from 20 to 30 feet, and one which a fielder finds it very difficult to hold" (*National Chronicle*, July 17, 1869).

After the 1880 season Harry Wright staged an exhibition game using a square bat and a ball composed of a "small globe of cork wound round with string, rubber and yarn." Neither innovation was deemed a success. Players complained that the cork-center ball did not "sound natural when hit with the bat and that the infielders had trouble fielding it" (Preston D. Orem, *Baseball [1845–1881] from the Newspaper Accounts*, 335–336). This suggests that the cork center upset the always delicate balance between offense and defense, and it would not be until gloves were being universally worn that the game would prove to be ready for cork-center baseballs.

By the 1890s the fielder's glove was well established, and in the early twentieth century, as noted in the preceding entry, "one of the manufacturers sprung a surprise." Around 1900, A. G. Spalding & Brothers began experimenting with a cork-center ball.

They met with initial problems because the wool yarn tended to expand after the stitching was in place. But by 1909 this problem had been addressed, and the cork-center ball was tested during the latter part of the season (according to an advertisement in *Sporting News*, March 2, 1911). (Curiously, pitcher George Winter later claimed that when the cork-center baseball was introduced, it became lopsided after being hit a couple of times. Since Winter last pitched in the American League in 1908, this suggests that the cork-center ball may have been experimented with still earlier) (Don Basenfelder, unpublished manuscript in *Sporting News* morgue, cited in Bill James and Rob Neyer, *The Neyer/James Guide to Pitchers*, 430). It must have passed the tests in 1909, as it was unveiled in 1910 by the A. J. Reach Company, which had come under Spalding's control (David Pietrusza, Lloyd Johnson, and Bob Carroll, ed., *Total Baseball Catalog*, 55).

It is frequently claimed that the cork-center ball was secretly introduced during the 1910 season, but nothing could be farther from the truth. The *Los Angeles Times* noted in May, "Manufacturers of the American League official baseball have announced that this year's ball has a cork instead of a rubber center. The cork was dipped in rubber and the rest of the process was the same as usual. The makers say the cork center has resulted in a much livelier baseball" (*Los Angeles Times*, May 8, 1910).

Popular Mechanics explained, "The cork makes possible a more rigid structure and more uniform resiliency. It is said to outlast the rubber center balls many times over, because it will not soften or break in spots under the most severe usage" (*Popular Mechanics*, reprinted in *Washington Post*, July 31, 1910). The manufacturers did their best to herald the new ball, contending "that of 280 clubs over the country using the cork-center ball, not one has been returned from losing its shape" (*Sporting News*, July 28, 1910). The ball was used in that year's World Series, where both managers expressed satisfaction with it.

At the annual meeting in February 1911, the major leagues signed a twenty-year contract to use the cork-center ball. Again, far from being secretive about the fact, the manufacturers took an ad in *Sporting News* to publicize this milestone for their new ball (*Sporting News*, March 2, 1911).

Once the cork-center ball came into general use, it became clear that the "lively ball has brought a lot of hitting" (*Sporting Life*, May 27, 1911). This led to some controversy, and Garry Herrmann of the National Commission threatened to return to the old ball (*Washington Post*, May 25, 1911).

A. J. Reach's son George "deemed it necessary to give official and emphatic denial to the reports and to add that no change whatever would be made in the ball, as the cork-centre had been designed to make a perfect and durable ball and not solely with an eye to increasing the batting, though that was a satisfactory and popular incident. The dean of the National league umpire staff, Hank O'Day, who usually sizes up a situation shrewdly and correctly, struck the nail on the head when he said last Wednesday: 'Modify the ball to make it deader eh? What do they want? Before the cry was against pitchers' battles; now there is too much hitting'" (*Sporting Life*, May 27, 1911). St. Louis Browns president Robert L. Hedges similarly thought it much ado about nothing: "The fans have been crying for more hitting. They have it now" (*Sporting Life*, June 3, 1911). The controversy quickly simmered down.

Harry Davis showed a more sophisticated understanding of the properties of the new ball when he contended: "The new ball is no livelier than the old one. It retains its resiliency longer than the old ball and that's all there is to it. The rubber-centre began to lose its shape and liveliness after it had been in play a couple of innings, while the cork-centre sphere will stay right much longer" (*Sporting Life*, March 30, 1912).

9.1.7 Cushioned Cork Centers. The baseball's interior was again modified in 1925 with the introduction of the cushioned cork center. Its manufacturers, the A. J. Reach Company, explained the differences: "The old cork center consisted of a live cork core inside a center of pure para rubber. The center of the Reach cushioned cork center ball is made of a lathe-turned perfect sphere of live cork, surrounded by black semi-vulcanized rubber, which is vulcanized by another cover of red rubber" (*Port Arthur* [Tex.] *News*, October 25, 1925).

As with the introduction of the original cork-center ball, there has been confusion about the year of this innovation, with William Curran placing it in 1926 and the *Total Baseball Catalog* listing the year as 1931 (William Curran, *Big Sticks*, 79–80; David Pietrusza, Lloyd Johnson, and Bob Carroll, ed., *Total Baseball Catalog*, 56). Once again, however, not only was there no secrecy but in fact a press release was issued. The Reach press release following the 1925 season declared: "The new cork center ball, the Reach official American league cushioned cork center ball, patented March 1, 1925, is far

superior to its predecessor of fifteen years ago. Use in this year's world's series and other games proved that, while it has better balance, and greater
wearing and enduring qualities than the former ball, it is neither less lively
nor more lively in play" (*Port Arthur* [Tex.] *News*, October 25, 1925).

9.1.8   Rabbit Balls. What is more American than a . . . conspiracy theory?
It's pretty much a given that if there's even a small increase in home runs, or
even just a slow news day, there will be talk about a rabbit ball. Sometimes
there is at least some basis for speculation, but often it seems to have been
entirely fueled by paranoia.

Such rumors date back to the nineteenth century, with the *Cleveland
Leader and Herald* writing in 1886: "The Western Association clubs suspect
that Al Reach is quietly supplying a livelier ball in order to give the public
what they want—heavy batting" (*Cleveland Leader and Herald*, May 16, 1886).

The term "rabbit ball" had come into use by 1907 when sportswriter Joe
S. Jackson wrote, ". . . The Cleveland camp followers, when Macon won on
Wednesday, went to the old family chest and brushed the moth powder off
the 'rabbit' ball story that was sprung a dozen times during the championship series a year ago" (*Detroit Free Press*, March 31, 1907).

This seems to have begun with the introduction of the cork-center ball.
Dan Gutman reported that the new ball was secretly introduced during the
1910 World Series (Dan Gutman, *Banana Bats and Ding-Dong Balls*, 152). In
fact, as noted earlier, (see **9.1.6**), the manufacturers had been advertising
their new ball in the sporting press throughout the 1910 season.

The issue was reprised a decade later, and it is often reported today that
a livelier ball was introduced to the major leagues in 1920 (William Curran,
Big Sticks, 84). But William Curran has argued convincingly that no such
event transpired (William Curran, *Big Sticks*, 65–85). He noted that the 1922
Reach Guide contained a full-page ad stating, "There has been no change in
the construction of the CORK CENTER BALL since we introduced it in 1910"
(William Curran, *Big Sticks*, 78).

In 1925 the major leagues hired Harold A. Fales, a professor of chemistry at Columbia University, to study the new cushioned-cork-center baseball. Fales tested balls manufactured in 1914, 1923, and 1925 and concluded
that the elasticity was "practically the same" (*New York Times*, July 16, 1925).
He did acknowledge differences in the cover that might affect the ball's
flight. Yet even the *New York Times* reported his findings that there was *no*
proof of the existence of a rabbit ball under the headline, "Magnates Approve The 'Rabbit Ball.'"

While denials by manufacturers and other authority figures only fuel
such conspiracy theories, Curran noted that a more telling sign is the lack of
complaints from pitchers. He cited pitcher Vean Gregg's 1925 assertion that

the baseball was no livelier than it had been before the war (William Curran, *Big Sticks*, 81). Curran argued that the increased power of the 1920s can be attributed to more frequent replacement of used balls, banning of trick pitches, and fuller swings by batters.

Nonetheless, the die was cast. The press had figured out that the public gobbled up conspiracy stories about changes inside the baseball and was happy to oblige. When the cushioned-cork-center baseball was introduced in 1925, the para rubber inside might as well have been short for paranoia. While others were suggesting that a rabbit ball had been unleashed, Arthur Mann wrote that the manufacturer had been part of a conspiracy to deaden the ball (Arthur Mann, "The Dead Ball and the New Game," *Baseball Magazine*, August 1926; quoted in William Curran, *Big Sticks*, 80).

In 1929, *Scientific American* compared a 1924 baseball with a 1929 ball and found no difference. It attributed the increase in offense entirely to the greater frequency with which old balls were replaced. Louis S. Treadwell explained that "when a ball is struck a few times it softens up. Its original structural aspect is changed and it becomes slower" (*Scientific American*, quoted in *New York Times*, August 28, 1929). But such sober accounts never had the impact of wild claims about rabbit balls.

Rabbit balls have remained a perpetual topic of speculation among baseball fans ever since. Perhaps the most novel theory to date was described by George F. Will: "In 1987 a sudden increase in home runs produced the 'Happy Haitian' explanation: Baseballs were then manufactured in Haiti and the theory was that the fall of the Duvalier regime so inspirited Haitians that they worked with more pep, pulling the stitching tighter, thereby flattening the seams—and flattening curveballs. The smoother balls had less wind resistance to give them movement when pitched, or to slow their subsequent flight over outfielders" (George F. Will, *Bunts*, 245).

9.1.9 Colorful Baseballs. The baseball has been white throughout most of baseball history, but experiments with other hues have been conducted from time to time.

Early players couldn't be choosers and used whatever color of ball was available. Gradually white became the predominant color. Then, in 1870, Peck & Snyder introduced a "Dead Red Ball," which was dark red in color. The intention, according to an advertisement placed by the company that year, was "getting rid of the objectionable dazzling whiteness of the ball which bothers fielders and batsmen on a Sunny Day" (quoted in Dan Gutman, *Banana Bats and Ding-Dong Balls*, 162).

The Dead Red remained popular for several years. Henry Chadwick liked the ball and recommended "a clause requiring the cover to be of some dark color. The cricketers have found red to be the best color, and this has been the color of cricket balls for fifty years past. White, in the air, is daz-zling to the eyes; and when the ball becomes soiled, it is difficult to find it in the grass. There is in fact, nothing to commend the white color, while there is everything in favor of the dark" (*New York Clipper*, December 4, 1875).

The red balls gradually lost favor, though A. G. Spalding & Company continued to sell them into the 1880s. Legendary football coach Amos Alonzo Stagg noted their passing in 1892: "Only a few years ago every boy dreamed of 'red dead' balls, and was discontented until he could have one. Both the 'red' and the 'dead' have since passed away" (Amos Alonzo Stagg, "Ball for the Boys," *Atlanta Constitution*, May 29, 1892).

It was not until 1928 that a colored ball was again seriously considered. A yellow ball was experimented with in the second game of a doubleheader on August 28, 1928, between Milwaukee and Louisville of the American As-sociation. An AP report of the game noted: "The new balls are said to have greater visibility than white ones, particularly with a bleacher background of white shirts. They are not easily discolored and therefore should give longer service. Further experiments will be made and if successful the ball will be officially adopted for 1929" (AP–*New York Times*, August 29, 1928).

Nothing came of that effort, but the idea was revived a decade later. Columnist Irving T. Marsh explained, "In an experiment to eliminate the menace of the 'bean' ball, Columbia and Fordham will play their game next week with a spectrum yellow baseball which, in the opinion of its sponsor, can be more quickly and easily seen than the white ball used now. The orig-inator of the colored ball is Frederic H. Rahr, New York color scientist. He believes that not only will it eliminate 'bean' balls but that better hitting will result, since the sphere can be seen more easily. The yellow ball was given a preliminary test in practice at Columbia a few weeks ago and after that Andy Coakley, coach, suggested that it have a trial in a regular game. He advanced the idea to Jack Coffey, Fordham coach, and Coffey agreed. So it will be tried at Baker Field next Wednesday [April 27th] and the re-sults of the experiment will be watched with interest" (*New York Herald Tri-bune*, April 21, 1938).

The newspaper gave this account of the actual game: "This was 'the game of the yellow ball,' with the chief interest presumably the debut of the colored missile in actual competition." But the yellow ball was overshad-owed by a tight, exciting game, capped by a game-winning triple by future NFL star Sid Luckman. "About the yellow ball, both coaches were agreed that the fancy spheroid had not had exactly a fair test. 'One game isn't enough,' said Andy Coakley, of the Lions, 'but I'm inclined to like it'" (*New York Herald Tribune*, April 28, 1938).

On August 2, 1938, Brooklyn general manager Larry MacPhail intro-duced yellow baseballs to the major leagues during the first game of a doubleheader against St. Louis. According to Dan Gutman, the balls had the curious side effect of turning the pitchers' fingers yellow (Dan Gutman, *Banana Bats and Ding-Dong Balls*, 163). The Dodgers used them again in games on July 23 and September 17, 1939, and the Cardinals tried them in a game on July 31, 1939.

In 1965, when it was discovered that outfielders could not gauge fly balls at the newly opened Astrodome, the team experimented with yellow, orange, red, and cerise baseballs. Charles Finley's Oakland A's used gold-colored baseballs in a game on April 13, 1970, and attracted considerable publicity. But there was nothing new about the idea.

9.1.10 Clunk Balls. Wartime restrictions threatened the quality of baseballs used in 1943. The horsehide, which had previously been imported from Belgium and France, was replaced with horsehide first from Bolivia and then from the United States. Then cork became scarce and was replaced with balata, a hardened form of gum. When the balata ball was introduced at the start of the 1943 season, it was so dead that it was dubbed the "clunk" ball. Major league baseball and suppliers A. G. Spalding and Brothers claimed that the problem was with the rubber cement: "The cement used in the 'clunk' ball was made from a poor grade of reclaimed rubber" (AP: *Milwaukee Journal*, May 5, 1943).

An improved version was introduced on May 8: "The new and lively Balata ball made its appearance Saturday. . . . The speedier ball has replaced the dead or 'clunk' ball with which the majors opened the season. The manufacturer discovered that the original ball had hardened when an inferior rubber cement seeped into the wool and dried. The mistake was corrected in the new ball" (AP: *Milwaukee Journal*, May 9, 1943).

(ii) Bats

9.2.1 Types of Wood. Henry Chadwick reported in 1860, "The description of wood most in use is ash, but maple, white and pitch pine, and also hickory bats are in common use, weight for the size governing the selection. For a bat of medium weight, ash is preferable, as its fiber is tough and elastic. The English willow has recently been used, and is favorably regarded by many. This latter wood is very light and close in fiber, and answers the purpose better than any other wood for a light bat" (*1860 Beadle's Dime Base-Ball Player*, 19).

Batters evidently agreed, as George Wright recalled in a 1915 interview that many types of wood were used in early bats, "but the favorite wood was willow, hence the expression, 'Use the willow'" (*New York Sun*, November

14, 1915). Isaac G. Kimball remembered many years later that during the earliest days of baseball in Fort Wayne the "bats were made of elm at a Fort Wayne spoke factory," but later poplar and basswood were used (E. L. McDonald, "The National Game of Base Ball Was Born in Fort Wayne," *St. Louis Republic*, reprinted in *Fort Wayne Journal Gazette*, January 26, 1902). Chadwick remarked in 1868 that, "Frank Wright, of Auburn, has got up a fine sycamore bat" (Henry Chadwick, *The American Game of Baseball*, 50). Spruce, cherry, and chestnut were also used on occasion, with availability often being the determining factor (*Colorado Daily Chieftain* [Pueblo], August 18, 1876; A. G. Spalding & Co. advertisement, *New York Clipper*, May 26, 1877; Clarence Deming, "Old Days in Baseball," *Outing*, June 1902, 359).

As baseball grew in popularity, batters were able to become choosier and take more factors into account, as an 1870 article described: "White ash bats are now generally used, weighing from 24 to 48 ounces, and from 34 to 40 inches in length. Michigan furnishes much of the material. Basswood and willow are also used to some extent, and Balm of Gilead wood bats, polished, are very highly recommended; though their cost is [35 cents] more than the ash bats." Basswood and willow were the cheapest varieties (*Chicago Post*, reprinted in *Detroit Advertiser and Tribune*, August 1, 1870). An 1896 article claimed, "Twenty years ago about half the bats were poplar but the style has now changed" (*Sporting News*, March 7, 1896).

After 1870 white ash emerged as the predominant wood for professional bats, with Henry Chadwick recommending "a well-balanced light bat, made of tough and elastic ash" (*New York Clipper*, April 12, 1873). Ash became even more commonplace when soft woods were banned in 1893. A machinist for a leading bat manufacturer said in 1901, "In selecting the bats for the best sticks I am careful to use nothing but second growth white ash. It is the only wood that stands the test and can be made light and still preserve a correct size" (*Grand Rapids* [Mich.] *Evening Press*, April 20, 1901).

Ash was the overwhelming preference of major leaguers for most of the twentieth century but apparently never became their exclusive choice. In recent years a new challenger has emerged. Harmon Killebrew may have been the first to experiment with a maple bat, but he eventually abandoned it (Dan Gutman, *It Ain't Cheatin' If You Don't Get Caught*, 78). In the 1990s a Canadian named Sam Holman revived the idea, and his maple "Sam Bat" has become a favorite of many major leaguers, including Barry Bonds.

9.2.2 Dimensions. Early batters "selected the wood and whittled their own bats . . . there are stories told of enthusiasts who faced the pitcher with bats five feet long and nearly as thick as wagon tongues. It was a happy-go-lucky crowd, those pioneers of the national game, and quite as much in earnest as were their fathers who cleared the forests to erect homes, and spoiled many a good bat in doing so" (John H. Gruber, *Sporting News*, November 11, 1915).

In 1857 the rules specified that a bat could not exceed two and a half inches in diameter. The diameter was changed to two and three-quarters inches in 1895 and has never changed since. In 1868 bats were limited to forty inches in length; the next year this was modified to forty-two inches. This rule remains on the book, but it is pretty much moot, as no major leaguer is known ever to have used a bat that long. George Wright explained in 1888 why the rule had been thought necessary in the first place: "It is queer what an effect experience, change in playing rules, and especially the science of curving the ball, have had upon [baseball bats]. Formerly long bats were all the rage, and players, both professional and amateur, held up logs of wood, some of them three and a half feet in length, and fanned the air in a way that would seem perfectly ridiculous for the average player today. . . . The reason for the substitution of the short for the long bat is its lighter weight and the sharp, quick blow one can give with it" (quoted in *Boston Herald*, reprinted in *Cincinnati Enquirer*, April 29, 1888). As we shall see in the next entry, the same issue has been a recurrent theme in the weight of baseball bats.

9.2.3 Weights. There have never been any restrictions placed on the weight of a baseball bat, but there have been a number of changes over the years in the preferences of batters.

As noted in the entry on "Types of Wood" (**9.2.1**), in 1870 bats ranged from twenty-four to forty-eight ounces in weight. There was no obvious correlation between bat weights and hitting style, so the choice appears to have been simply a matter of personal preference. Henry Chadwick reported that hollow bats were also experimented with but "have been proven failures" (*New York Clipper*, April 12, 1873).

By the early twentieth century most batters were swinging significantly heavier bats than the ones favored today. A 1912 article reported that Charlie Hickman's thirty-four-ounce bat was one of the lightest in the majors (*Washington Post*, September 5, 1912). The heaviest bats in that period were often used by singles hitters like Bill Sweeney and Chief Meyers, who took short, compact swings and tried to drive the ball between the infielders and outfielders.

Babe Ruth's success led to a reexamination of bat weight. Since Ruth was a pitcher, not much was expected of him at the plate (Ty Cobb, quoted in F. C. Lane, *Batting*, 71). That factor, combined with his willful personality, enabled Ruth to disregard the conventional wisdom about hitting. The extraordinary results he produced naturally attracted many copycats, and they mimicked what they perceived to be the three keys to Ruth's success: his free swing, his full follow-through, and his heavy bat.

The first two have remained the hallmarks of power hitters ever since. The heavy bat was also obligatory for the generation of power hitters who succeeded Ruth. It was many years before sluggers began to realize that the bat speed that could be generated with a light bat more than offset the extra weight of a heavier bat. So Ruth's example, so influential to the home run era in many ways, probably proved a detriment in this regard.

At least a couple of Ruth's contemporaries had figured this out. In 1925, Rogers Hornsby observed, "It doesn't follow, however, that a heavy bat is necessary [for a slugger]. Some sluggers use heavy bats. Chief Meyers did and so does Babe Ruth. Most batters will find that an extra heavy bat cuts down the speed of their swing more than enough to offset what the extra weight of the bat can accomplish. I prefer a rather light bat. . . . There are two things which drive a baseball hard; the weight of the bat and the speed with which it moves. The two are direct opposites. No matter how much strength a batter has, he cannot handle a heavy bat with as much speed as he would a light bat . . . in general the chop hitter would best use a heavy bat and the slugger a light one" (quoted in F. C. Lane, *Batting*, 67). And Harry Heilmann added, "I discount weight in a bat almost entirely. In fact, I use a light bat and I think Babe Ruth, with all his success as a slugger, would be a greater hitter if he discarded that wagon tongue of his" (quoted in F. C. Lane, *Batting*, 67).

9.2.4 Shapes. There was no requirement that early baseball bats be rounded, yet John Gruber reported that "bats were invariably round and not flat like those used in cricket" (John H. Gruber, "The Ball and the Bat," *Sporting News*, November 11, 1915). This reflects the fact that early hitters generally took lusty swings and tried to hit the ball as far as they could without regard to placement. In 1857 the rules incorporated what was already customary by specifying that bats be round.

By 1870 the dead ball was leading to new approaches to hitting. In a game on May 3, 1875, several Hartford players used a bat that had been whittled down on one side so as to be nearly flat. The Philadelphia captain eventually protested, and the bat was removed from play.

In 1880 the body governing amateur baseball legalized square bats. Henry Chadwick reported: "The new bat, in its widest part, viz., from corner to corner at its end, is not wider than the round bat. Its four sides only extend to the handle. It is just as if a round bat had been planed off on four sides. This bat will admit of harder wood for its size than the round bat; that is, two bats of the same size and material, one being made round and the other four-sided, the latter would necessarily be lightest by several ounces. The idea of changing the form from the round to the four-sided is to enable the batsman to 'place' the ball better than is possible with a round bat" (quoted in John H. Gruber, "The Ball and the Bat," *Sporting News*, November 11, 1915; Gruber did not specifically credit Chadwick, but the piece is in his distinctive style and nearly identical portions appeared in a Chadwick article in the *New York Clipper* on January 10, 1880).

There seems to have been little enthusiasm for the square bats. Even Chadwick had to report after an exhibition game at which the new bats were to be tested: "Unluckily, the Park groundkeeper had only provided three of the new four-sided bats and as these were all broken before two-thirds of the game were finished, the contest did not present a fair opportunity for testing the merits of the new sticks" (*New York Clipper*, April 5, 1879).

Following the 1880 season, Harry Wright staged an experimental game that featured cork-center balls and flat bats. Neither innovation was considered a success, with the flat bats being particularly unpopular. Not only did they reduce hitting, they also stung the batters' hands. The bats were abandoned partway through the game (Preston D. Orem, *Baseball [1845–1881] from the Newspaper Accounts*, 335–336). According to John Gruber, the square bat was not popular among amateurs and was soon dropped (John H. Gruber, "The Ball and the Bat," *Sporting News*, November 11, 1915).

Nevertheless after the 1884 season the National League legalized flat bats. While these bats were described as flat, actually they were only flattened. A diagram of the new bat in *Sporting Life* showed that only about one-sixth of it had been shaved off (*Sporting Life*, February 25, 1885).

Several reasons for legalizing the flat bat were offered, yet none of them mentioned what would end up being the main function of the flat bat. Harry Wright expressed optimism that, with this new style of bat, "'placing the ball' will be made easier" (*Sporting Life*, December 3, 1884). Researcher Tom Shieber discovered a *New York Times* article that suggested that the aim instead was to "do away with so many foul tips and high fly balls, and in a measure improve batting" (*New York Times*, November 21, 1884). Another article described the rule change as an acknowledgment of the reality that "players have frequently used such bats for a long time without detection" (*Sporting Life*, February 25, 1885).

A few batters experimented with it in 1885, with the *Detroit Post* noting that "Scheffer" of St. Louis—presumably George Shafer—was using a flat bat (*Detroit Post*, May 18, 1885). It was only in 1886, however, that the flat bats seemed to become commonplace, and it was for a purpose no one seems to have anticipated. The bunt (see **2.2.1**) made a dramatic comeback in 1886 after a decade of disuse, and the new flat bats played a major role. An 1892 article observed, "Since the flat-sided bat has been admitted the most skillful pitcher cannot prevent a cool batsman from dribbling a grounder out toward third at so slow a pace that he can beat the ball to first. The fact that the entire team in the field knows just what the batter means to do seems to afford no assistance in the solution of the problem" (*New York Times*, June 23, 1892).

This feeling that the flat bats had made bunting too effective led to widespread calls for banning the bunt. Instead flat bats were permanently banned in 1893.

9.2.5   Soft Bats. John Gruber observed that "Scientific batting, especially bunting, was the general craze in the eighties" and led to the use of a "soft" or "sacrifice" bat. He explained, "The bat was made of wood so soft that it was hardly possible for the batter to drive the ball beyond the diamond. The ball became dead after coming in contact with the mush-like bat and dropped to the ground" (John H. Gruber, "The Ball and the Bat," *Sporting News*, November 11, 1915). Connie Mack later remarked: "Remember the bunting bats they had for one season? Soft wood and flattened at the business end" (*Sporting Life*, December 14, 1912). When the rule banning flat bats was adopted in 1893, it was also specified that bats had to be made of hard wood, effectively eliminating the soft bat.

9.2.6   Mass-produced Bats. The *New York Times* reported in 1871 that demand for bats was so great that one firm kept two mills running year round just to turn out baseball bats ("Bats, Balls and Mallets," *New York Times*, May 30, 1871). By 1879 it was becoming evident that "large bat manufacturers have deprived the carpenter, the turner and other hewers of wood of a considerable share of profitable business done on a small scale" (*New York Clipper*, April 26, 1879). That November, A. G. Spalding & Company began mass-producing cheap bats at a factory in Hastings, Michigan. Before the factory burned down in December 1887, it was reported to be producing more than a million bats a year (*Sporting News*, April 2, 1887). By 1909 it was reported that "a kiln-dried bat wouldn't be given honorable mention by the poorest swatter on the Kokomo team. The timber that is to be made into a first-class bat must be seasoned out doors at least four years, and seven is better. Then it is ready to be put into a lathe and turned into a $1.50 club" ("The Great National Game in Dollars and Cents," *Washington Post*, May 9, 1909).

9.2.7   Models. Lee Allen reported that in 1878 Providence batters began to select their own model of bats (*Sporting News*, April 20, 1968). By 1896 it was reported that "Some of the crack players will not condescend to use a stock bat, but go to the factory and have bats of the size and weight they desire made for them" (*Sporting News*, March 7, 1896).

The introduction of individual models was the culmination of a trend that had begun to emerge in the 1860s. John Gruber pointed out that, in early baseball, hitters chose any bat they fancied, whether it belonged to a teammate or even an opponent. Batters gradually became more proprietary about their weapons, and disputes ensued. As a result, a rule was passed in 1872 that "The striker shall be privileged to use his own private bat exclusively, and no other player of the contesting nines shall have any claim to the use of such bat, except by the consent of its owner" (John H. Gruber, *Sporting News*, January 27, 1916).

9.2.8 Trademarks. An A. G. Spalding & Brothers ad in 1888 declared that "Spalding's Trade-Marked bats were first introduced in 1877" (advertisement, *Spalding's Official Base Ball Guide, 1888*). The company claimed the trademark "was stamped on each bat to insure its genuineness" (advertisement, *Spalding's Official Base Ball Guide, 1883*). Not everyone accepted that explanation, and slugger Ed Delahanty is said to have told batmaker John "Bud" Hillerich, "You didn't need to put an ad on that bat. If the bat makes good, I'll tell everybody where I bought it—don't you think I'm square enough to give you credit if it's coming to you?" (W. A. Phelon, *Sporting News*, December 19, 1912).

Youngsters today are told not to hit the ball on the trademark, but it is important to note that the opposite advice was given in the nineteenth and early twentieth centuries. An 1885 article reported, "McVey says he hit that first ball on the handle of his bat yesterday. Where would it have gone if he had hit it where it says 'A. J. Reach'?" (*Atlanta Constitution*, May 14, 1885). One of the bats pictured in the 1888 *Spalding's Guide* has the words "Strike This Way Up Grain" on the same side as the trademark. George S. Davis noted in 1894 that "Smacking the ball on the trade mark" had become synonymous with making solid contact (George S. Davis, "How to Bat," syndicated column, *Warren* [Pa.] *Evening Democrat*, May 26, 1894). Cap Anson inscribed copies of his autobiography with the words, "Always hit the ball on the trade-mark" (*Sporting Life*, November 29, 1902).

The difference appears to be mostly one of nomenclature. At some point the trademark seems to have been rotated slightly, so that the batter could easily see it while batting. Thus while the bat's sweet spot continued to line up with the trademark, it became desirable not to hit the ball right on the trademark.

Yogi Berra liked to meet the ball with the trademark, so Hillerich & Bradsby shifted the trademark on his model to accommodate him (Dan Gutman, *Banana Bats and Ding-Dong Balls*, 34).

9.2.9 Louisville Sluggers. The usual story of the first Louisville Slugger goes something like this: Early in the 1884 season, Louisville's star outfielder Pete Browning broke his favorite bat. A local apprentice woodworker named John "Bud" Hillerich offered to make him a new bat at his father's job-turning shop. Browning was pleased with the result and experienced immediate success. Orders from other players soon followed, and a new business was born.

If this story sounds too good to be true, there's a good reason for that. Researcher Bob Bailey discovered that as late as 1914 Hillerich was saying he had made a bat for himself in 1884 and had given it to pitcher Gus Weyhing (Bruce Dudley, "Every Knock Is a Boost for the Louisville Slugger Bat," *Louisville Herald Magazine*, September 27, 1914). Weyhing began using it, and other local players soon inquired about it and then began requesting their own. The bats became known as Hillerich Bats, then as Falls City Sluggers. They assumed their current name around 1894.

Bailey found that the now familiar story did not begin to emerge until the late 1930s. In 1937, Arlie Latham claimed he triggered the chain of events when he broke his bat while playing in Louisville and happened into the Hillerich shop. Two years later a similar version appeared in *The Sporting Goods Dealer*, a trade publication, but this time Browning had replaced Latham as the central figure.

The author of the article was Sam Severance, head of marketing for Hillerich & Bradsby. Severance didn't even pretend that the story was true; he merely related it as a "legend around the Hillerich & Bradsby factory." It must have struck a chord, however, because it was reprinted in the *Famous Slugger Yearbook* for the next decade and supplemented with new and increasingly melodramatic details. By 1949, Hillerich was "tugging at Browning's sleeve" to offer him the bat.

Such stories, all too often, become accepted as baseball "history" (Bob Bailey, "Hunting for the First Louisville Slugger," *Baseball Research Journal* 30 [2001], 96–98).

9.2.10 Burning Bats. Many nineteenth-century hitters applied their own treatments to bats after receiving them from the factory. St. Louis Browns secretary George Munson explained in 1894, "The Browns were burning bats when I left the park an hour ago. It was a comical sight to see them in variegated uniforms crowding around a miniature camp fire. 'Burning' a bat properly is considered quite an accomplishment. The 'stick' is first immersed in a preparation of boiled linseed oil and shellac. It is then held over the flames until it has become perfectly dry. Great care is required to prevent the bat's being scorched during the toasting process. When perfectly dry it is rubbed for an hour or more with a piece of flannel" (*St. Louis Post-Dispatch*, June 28, 1894).

Bat manufacturers soon began to offer this feature. A 1901 article offered this explanation, "There is a superstition widely current among professionals to the effect that a scorched bat is less prone to meet the ball on the top or bottom, but sends out straight line hits. When so ordered a bat is 'burned' by the application of a piece of hard wood to the bat's surface as it turns in the lathe. The result is seen in the series of brown rings which are so common on the bats of the big league players" (*Grand Rapids* [Mich.] *Evening Press*, April 20, 1901).

9.2.11   Tapers. Most early baseball bats had a similar diameter from the handle to the barrel. While they generally had a taper, the taper was so gradual that the difference between the two ends was minimal. This design reflected, among other things, the reality that bats were expensive; broken bats needed to be avoided if at all possible.

The idea of a more dramatic taper was around as early as 1880, when it was reported that "George Wright is manufacturing bats of regulation length, which, instead of gradually tapering from butt to handle, have long, small, round handles with the full swell at the centre of the bat" (*New York Clipper*, May 1, 1880). The results are unknown, but it seems likely that they broke too frequently to be practical.

By the early twentieth century, handles were becoming slimmer. Dan Gutman noted that "Rogers Hornsby is usually cited as the first player to use a truly tapered bat" (Dan Gutman, *Banana Bats and Ding-Dong Balls*, 9). This appears to be another example of a great player being credited with a first, not because he introduced it but because he was great. Hornsby did not reach the major leagues until 1915, while a 1910 article indicated that the bat used in the 1870s "was more slender than the one used today, the tapering being more gradual" (*Chicago Tribune*, July 10, 1910). Two years later the *Washington Post* noted that Charlie Hickman used a bat that "loses weight in the handle, which is remarkably slender." The piece described another player's bat as "chopped off about where most bats are beginning to taper." While the most popular model was reported to be the Harry Davis bat, which had no taper, it is clear from this article that a significant number of major leaguers were using tapered bats before Rogers Hornsby (*Washington Post*, September 5, 1912).

Bill James suggested that Ernie Banks may have started the trend to ultra-thin handles in the 1950s (Bill James, *The New Bill James Historical Baseball Abstract*, 320). Banks, however, gave this version: "When I first came up I used a 35-ounce bat. Late in the season when I got a little tired I switched to a lighter bat after talking to Ralph Kiner. Now I use a 31-ounce all the time" (quoted in AP wire story, *Lima* [Ohio] *News*, July 11, 1956). Whoever was responsible, this was not merely a design innovation but a sign that baseball's growing prosperity was making it possible—even necessary—to trade a lot of broken bats for an improvement in performance.

It seems likely that the increased prominence of narrow handles led pitchers to place a greater emphasis on pitches that moved in on batters.

9.2.12 Bottle Bats. The most novel offspring of the experimentation with tapers was Heinie Groh's bottle bat. Groh explained that in 1913 John McGraw suggested he try a larger-barreled bat. But the five-foot-seven, 160-pound Groh's hands proved too small to grip a large handle. So he went to Spalding headquarters and, in the basement, "we whittled down the handle of a standard bat, and then we built up the barrel, and when we were finished it looked like a crazy sort of milk bottle or a round paddle—real wide at one end and then suddenly tapering real quick to a thin handle" (Lawrence Ritter, *The Glory of Their Times*, 302).

The finished product weighed forty-six ounces, and Groh found that if he held it anywhere near the knob, pitches would knock the bat right out of his hands. By choking up and chopping at the ball, however, Groh became very proficient at driving the ball over the infielders' heads. Occasionally he would also "slide one hand down to the end of the handle and swing more like a slugger" (quoted in F. C. Lane, *Batting*, 30).

As Groh became a star player, it is curious that the bottle bat attracted few imitators. Groh was also puzzled, telling F. C. Lane: "I am convinced that many other chop hitters would find this peculiar bat much better for them than the ordinary club" (quoted in F. C. Lane, *Batting*, 30).

9.2.13 Extra Knob. Quite a few hitters around the turn of the century batted with their hands apart, most notably Ty Cobb and Honus Wagner (see 2.1.5). The sporting goods firm of Wright & Ditson responded by marketing a bat with two knobs, which was known as "The Double Ring Handle" (Dan Gutman, *Banana Bats and Ding-Dong Balls*, 15).

9.2.14 Cupped Ends. Bats with an indentation scooped out of the end were made legal by the major leagues in 1975, and Lou Brock helped popularize them. The idea, however, was not new. The Hanna Manufacturing Company of Athens, Georgia, began making bats with cupped ends around 1936 (Dan Gutman, *Banana Bats and Ding-Dong Balls*, 26; Dan Gutman, *It Ain't Cheatin' If You Don't Get Caught*, 127). Researcher John Schwartz discovered that pitcher Elden Auker used such a bat in an American League game on July 19, 1942. Auker came to the plate with a bat "with a depression in the business end." Plate umpire Ed Rommel scrutinized it and allowed its use (*Washington Post*, July 20, 1942).

9.2.15 Laminated Bats. Laminated bats, which were molded from several pieces of wood, became popular in the early 1950s. Their history had eerie parallels with the later development of aluminum bats. Their use was approved by the American Association of College Baseball Coaches because of their durability (*Syracuse Herald Journal*, April 18, 1954). The laminated bats came to be used extensively by college teams as well as "smaller budgeted school, sand-lot, semi-pro and little league clubs." Professional baseball, however, resisted the innovation on the grounds that the bats were too lively and gave too much advantage to batters (Ed Lukas, *St. Joseph* [Mich.] *Herald Press*, March 30, 1954).

9.2.16   Aluminum Bats. In the late 1960s a Pennsylvanian named Anthony Merola, who had been manufacturing aluminum pool cues, turned his attention to baseball and designed an aluminum bat. A bat manufacturer named Worth, Inc., contracted to mass-produce them. The turning point for aluminum bats came in 1971 when Little League baseball adopted them to eliminate the cost of broken bats. High school and colleges began using them in batting practice at about the same time for the same reason. They were approved for play by schools over the next couple of years, and by 1975 sales of aluminum bats topped those of wood bats (Dan Gutman, *Banana Bats and Ding-Dong Balls*, 36; "Aluminum Bats Stand the Test of Time," *Baseball America*, September 1–14, 2003). Professional leagues have been reluctant to adopt them because of fears that the speed of the ball off an aluminum bat poses a hazard to pitchers. In recent years, modifications have been made to aluminum bats and tests conducted to address such concerns.

9.2.17   Pine Tar. George Brett will always be associated with pine tar, because of his July 24, 1983, home run that was disallowed by the game umpires, who in turn were overruled by American League president Lee MacPhail. The issue, however, is of much longer standing. As early as 1886 the rules specified that bat handles could be made of twine or "a granulated substance applied, not to exceed 18 inches from the end." A 1948 article indicated: "Baseball rules prohibit any foreign substance or markings on a bat higher than 18 inches" (*Washington Post*, July 6, 1948).

On July 19, 1975, Thurman Munson of the New York Yankees singled home a run in a game against the Minnesota Twins. The Twins pointed out that Munson's bat "had pine tar rather far up the handle." Umpire Art Frantz declared Munson out and took the run off the board in what turned out to be a one-run loss. Frantz stuck with his ruling even though manager "Bill Virdon and a group of Yankees followed Frantz around shouting." *New York Times* sportswriter Paul L. Montgomery explained to readers that according to Rule 1.10B, "if there is a foreign substance on a bat within 18 inches of the fat end, the bat is illegal and anyone who uses it at the plate is automatically out" (Paul L. Montgomery, "Yanks Take Suspended Game, Then Lose 2-1," *New York Times*, July 20, 1975).

Just over a month later, new Yankees manager Billy Martin protested that the Angels were using bats with pine tar too far up the handle. Umpire George Maloney denied his protest, saying that he couldn't tell whether the substance was dirt or pine tar. Martin later complained, "The rule says that if a batter gets a hit with an illegal bat, he's automatically out" (*New York Times*, August 23, 1975).

(iii) Gloves

9.3.1 Fielders' Gloves. Gloves are one of a handful of inventions that can be reasonably argued to have had the single most comprehensive effect on every element of the game of baseball. Nonetheless there has been no rush to claim credit for introducing them to the game.

The reason for this is simple: fear of ridicule for violating the ideal of manliness. While many early players must have considered wearing gloves, they were deterred by the possibility of being stigmatized. Those who did wear gloves, rather than advertising the fact, often wore flesh-colored gloves to avoid criticism (A. G. Spalding, *America's National Game*, 476).

Cricket players had been wearing India rubber gloves since the 1830s. They were introduced when bowlers began to throw from shoulder level and were initially "found an impediment and laughed at by older players" (Henry Chadwick, *New York Clipper*, March 20, 1880). Gloves eventually gained acceptance in cricket, but it took much longer in baseball.

A 1905 reminiscence described a game played in Boston on May 31, 1858, with a baseball that had a bullet at its center: "Heavy gloves had to be used with such a ball, for bare hands could not hold it and it would twist more fingers and do more injury than the ball of the national game. Gloves had not been seen in play before, neither were gloves used in the national game in old amateur times" (*Boston Journal*, February 22, 1905).

The first baseball player to wear gloves regularly may have been a catcher named Ben Delavergne, around 1860. In 1886, *Sporting News* wrote that "Delavarge [sic], the catcher of the old Knickerbockers, an amateur club of Albany, used gloves when playing behind the bat in the sixties" (*Sporting News*, June 28, 1886). The *Detroit Free Press* of May 17, 1887, also credited Delavergne.

An 1867 *Detroit Free Press* account of a major tournament being held in Detroit provided an important revelation: "We have noticed in all the matches played thus far that the use of gloves by the players was to some degree a customary practice, which, we think, cannot be too highly condemned, and are of the opinion, that the Custers [of Ionia] would have shown a better score, if there had been less buckskin on their hands" (*Detroit Free Press*, August 15, 1867).

While the *Free Press* seems to imply that players all over the field were wearing gloves, there is little evidence of players other than the catcher and first baseman wearing gloves before the mid-1880s. As had been the case in cricket, there was a close correspondence between the use of gloves and pitchers' release points. As the release points moved higher in the 1870s, the use of gloves gradually caught on among catchers and first basemen. Then when all restrictions were dropped in the 1880s, they quickly became standard at all positions.

As a result, in the early 1870s there are an increasing number of references to catchers and first basemen wearing gloves. Doug Allison, catcher of the Red Stockings of Cincinnati, played in a game on June 28, 1870, with very sore hands. Researcher Darryl Brock alerted me to the note in the *Cincinnati Commercial* the next day that "Allison caught . . . in a pair of buckskin mittens, to protect his hands" (*Cincinnati Commercial*, June 29, 1870). The following year the *New York Sunday Mercury* replied to a letter writer: "Of course a player may wear gloves if he likes. A half glove covering the palm of the hand and first joints of the fingers is excellent in saving the hand of the catcher and first baseman" (*New York Sunday Mercury*, June 25, 1871; quoted in Jim Charlton, ed., *The Baseball Chronology*).

The stage was set for gloves that not only cushioned the hand but helped make the catch. An 1887 article gave this description: "Al Pratt and Jim White faked up the first pair of catcher's gloves ever worn, and Jim was the first man to wear them. Jim was much younger than he is now, but his hands were sore. He and Pratt dropped into a store on Broadway, New York, and purchased an old-fashioned pair of buckskin gloves. They cut the fingers off the gloves, split them and inserted lacing, until they had a pair of catcher's gloves quite to their liking. If they had had any idea to what extent base ball playing was going to grow, they could have made a ten-strike by getting out a patent on them" (*Pittsburgh Dispatch*; quoted in *Detroit Free Press*, April 28, 1887).

That article did not provide a precise date, but White himself placed these events in 1872, when he was playing for the Forest Citys of Cleveland: "as early as '72, I bought myself a large buckskin glove, put my own padding in it, and stood up behind the batter at the start of an inning as well as when men were on base" (David McCarthy; *Aurora* [Ill.] *Beacon-News*, May 7, 1939). Al Pratt attested that during the 1872 season Deacon White bought a pair of heavy driving gloves and wore one on his left hand (quoted in *Sporting News*, March 23, 1895). While White's glove primarily protected his hand, it paved the way for the revolution that followed, in which the glove actually began to do the catching.

A. G. Spalding claimed that the first player he saw wearing a fielder's glove was Charles Waitt, in 1875. As a result, Waitt is often mistakenly credited with having pioneered the baseball glove. But Spalding's claim is noteworthy because Deacon White was his catcher from 1873 to 1876. It therefore seems reasonable to assume that White had abandoned the glove by the end of the 1872 season and that few others followed his lead.

Another statement by Spalding has attracted far less attention but is probably more important because it suggests that he played a major role in fielder's gloves gaining acceptance. When Spalding switched permanently to first base in 1877, not only did he don a glove but also deliberately chose a black one to make his decision conspicuous. The glove was met with "sympathy" rather than "hilarity," showing that attitudes toward gloves had changed (A. G. Spalding, *America's National Game*, 476). Probably it is no coincidence that Spalding was starting his sporting goods empire at this time.

9.3.2 Catchers' Mitts. The catcher's mitt originated in the 1880s, but the particulars are more difficult to disentangle. The biggest complication is that catchers of the 1870s and 1880s were faced with an enormous number of changes in their role. Handling speedier pitching while often standing closer to the plate, catchers were forced to improvise rapidly. As a result, the transition from gloves to mitts was a chaotic one, with the same idea sometimes emerging from independent sources.

As noted in the preceding entry, several players had experimented with gloves in the 1860s, but these gloves offered only minimal cushioning. By the mid-1870s, liberalized delivery rules were leading to much faster pitching and in turn to greater protection for catchers. These comments in the 1876 *DeWitt's Base Ball Guide* also make clear that catchers wore these gloves on both hands: "The catcher will find it advantageous when facing swift pitching to wear tough leather gloves, with the fingers cut off near the joint, as they will prevent him having his hands split and puffed up. If he has the fingers of the glove on he can not retain his hold on the ball so well" (*DeWitt's Base Ball Guide*, 1876, 19).

An 1890 article in the *New York Sun* described how the catcher's mitt gradually began to develop from these early efforts. According to the article, the initial events took place in 1875, but it is more likely that the year was actually 1877. Billy McGunnigle was the catcher for the Fall River Club, and his hands had become very sore. Before a game against Harvard, he went to a glove store and bought a pair of bricklayer's gloves made of thick, hard leather. During preliminary practice he found that he could not throw properly with the gloves on, so he cut off the fingers. It was still awkward to throw the ball with these gloves on, but not impossible. Harvard catcher Jim Tyng borrowed them in the third inning and found them useful. He later bought a pair and increased the protection they afforded by lining them with lead (*New York Sun*, April 27, 1890).

Within the next few years, sporting goods manufacturers began to make gloves specifically designed for catchers, but their efforts were rendered difficult by a fundamental issue: it was necessary to use two hands in order to catch the ball, which meant that equal protection was needed on both hands. One firm placed an advertisement in 1882 that read: "Our new design, open back, catchers' gloves, made out of very thick buckskin, and padded is the best protection for catchers' hands of anything yet devised. They do not interfere with throwing and no catcher or player subject to sore hands, should be without a pair of these gloves" (quoted in John H. Gruber, "The Gloves," *Sporting News*, December 2, 1915).

Catchers would have been delighted if a glove that could adequately protect the hand without hindering the throwing motion really existed. But the reality was that no glove could do both at once. Chief Zimmer recalled many years later that when he debuted in the majors in 1884, "a mitt similar to the present-day outfielder's glove was in vogue. A hand glove with the fingers cut off was used on the other hand" (Hal Lebovitz, "Zimmer, Oldest Catcher, Leafs Memory Book," *Sporting News*, January 12, 1949).

And things would get worse before they got better. During the next couple of years, pitchers began to throw overhand with hop, step, and jump motions, and the strain on catchers' hands became unbearable. Gigantic pitchers like Boston's Jim Whitney threw with such "frightful power" that "he used up both Mike Hines and Mertie Hackett, his backstops," in a single season (*Washington Post*, February 11, 1906). Boston was far from unique, with Henry Chadwick later recalling that "the wear and tear upon catchers" became so great that "clubs had to engage a corps of reserve catchers, in order to go through a season's campaign with any degree of success" (*Spalding's Official Base Ball Guide, 1895*, 71).

The beleaguered catchers were willing to try almost anything, with Deacon McGuire of Toledo reportedly having placed a steak in his glove in 1884 to catch the heavy ball thrown by pitcher Hank O'Day (Norman L. Macht, "Henry Francis O'Day," in Frederick Ivor-Campbell, Robert L. Tiemann, and Mark Rucker, eds., *Baseball's First Stars*, 123). Chief Zimmer also claimed to have used beefsteak in his glove (Hal Lebovitz, "Zimmer, Oldest Catcher, Leafs Memory Book," *Sporting News*, January 12, 1949). Others, such as Doc Bushong, padded their gloves with sponges (*San Francisco Examiner*, December 12, 1887). These methods undoubtedly eased the pain inflicted on these catchers' hands, but it made it harder to snag the ball.

As discussed under "Windups" (3.1.1), the situation was so dire by 1886 that it forced two important adjustments. The first was the familiar effort of rule makers to place restrictions on pitchers' deliveries. The more startling development was that some pitchers concluded that too much "pace is useless" and began to put more emphasis on deception than on raw speed.

During these years, however, a new solution emerged as catchers learned to modify their receiving techniques. By 1884 it was recognized that a catcher could "do most of the stopping with his left hand, protected by a thickly padded glove. Such a glove cannot be worn upon the right hand as it renders accurate throwing impossible" (*Detroit Free Press*, May 2, 1884). As more and more catchers discarded the traditional two-handed catching method for one in which the nonthrowing hand would "bear the brunt of the shock," the search for a way to wear a heavier glove on that hand and a light one on the throwing hand began (*New York Sun*, April 27, 1890). As a result, almost every backstop began to experiment with modifications that would make a padded glove easier to catch with. The sense of urgency helps explain why there are so many nearly simultaneous claimants to having invented the mitt.

It would simplify matters if some of these claims were earlier than others. Indeed, Charley Snyder said he switched from a finger glove to a mitt in 1885, and Connie Mack recalled the big mitt originating in 1885 or 1886 (*Cleveland Press*, reprinted in *Sporting News*, December 26, 1907; Connie Mack, "Memories of When the Game Was Young," *Sporting Life* [monthly], June 1924). Unfortunately both Snyder and Mack gave their accounts many years after the fact, and it seems likely they were mistaken about the exact year. All of the other claims date to 1887 or 1888.

Ted Kennedy's name is cited by several sources. Owney Patton said that the first catcher's mitt was made by Kennedy and worn by Bill Traffley with Des Moines in 1888 (*San Francisco Examiner*, March 28, 1909). Joe Cantillon stated: "All catchers after the '80's had good large catcher's mitts and the first good one was made by Ted Kennedy of Des Moines" (*Minneapolis Journal*, reprinted in *Sporting News*, May 28, 1914; the year cited by Cantillon appears to read 1883 but is difficult to read. Traffley and Kennedy played for Des Moines in 1888).

Jack McCloskey gave this version: "I claim to be the inventor of the original catcher's glove. In 1888, I was catching Red Ehret for the El Paso Club, and used at that time a padded finger glove, called the Sawyer glove, which came from Milwaukee. I improved on that glove, putting a circle of wire around it and filling it with padding. In addition I put a piece of leather on the pocket of the glove.

"In 1887 I met Ted Kennedy, the old pitcher and former glove manufacturer, of St. Louis. I explained the glove to him and he modified it in some respects, which made an improvement, and the glove was afterwards improved by others until the present glove was produced. I think all the credit should go to Kennedy, although the original idea was mine. Of course, many have claimed this honor, but I think that Ted Kennedy and myself were the originators" (*Sporting News*, December 30, 1926).

Another name frequently cited is Joe Gunson. Catcher Sam Trott recalled: "It was Joe Gunson, the catcher of many years ago, who invented the
mitt. He made the first one himself and caught with it at Kansas City"
(*Sporting Life*, March 26, 1910). Gunson said he first wore one in a Decoration Day doubleheader in 1888 to protect an injured finger. In Gunson's
words, fifty years later, "I took the glove I was then wearing—a glove which
was something like the kid gloves they wear today—stitched all of the fingers together and made a mitt. Then I fixed up a padding and put it all
around the finger ends, sewed a wire in it to help keep its shape, padded the
center of the glove with sheepskin and wool and covered the entire mitt with
buckskin. The next afternoon I kept my promise to [manager Jimmy] Manning and caught both games" (Charley Scully, "'Father of the Catching
Glove' Admits Split Finger Fifty Years Ago, with Twin Bill Ahead, Was
'Mother,'" *Sporting News*, February 23, 1939).

At another point Gunson told a somewhat different version in which he
made a few innovations before the doubleheader but then did additional
work on the glove afterward: "I stitched together the fingers of my left hand
glove, thus practically making a mitt; and then I caught both games. It
worked so well that I got to work, took an old paint-pot wire handle, the old
flannel belts from our castoff jackets, rolled the cloth around the ends of the
finger, and padded the thumb. Then I put sheepskins with the wool on it in
the palm and covered it with buckskin, thus completing the mitt" (quoted in
Dan Gutman, *Banana Bats and Ding-Dong Balls*, 178).

According to Gunson, the mitt became popular around the league, and
he realized that he should patent it. He and Manning decided to produce the
mitt jointly, but their plans were delayed when Manning went on a world
tour after the 1888 season. By the time Manning returned, Gunson had received a letter from a man in Des Moines—presumably Kennedy—who had
designed and patented a mitt identical to Gunson's.

Gunson gave this summary: "I wasn't really interested in making a fortune
out of my idea, but I do want the credit for designing and making the original glove. I have in my possession documentary evidence which proves that
my glove was made long before any of the gloves designed and patented by
others who claimed to have been the original creators of the mitt" (Charley
Scully, "'Father of the Catching Glove' Admits Split Finger Fifty Years Ago,
with Twin Bill Ahead, Was 'Mother,'" *Sporting News*, February 23, 1939).

This is a strong statement and cannot be entirely reconciled with the
other accounts. Gunson did indeed lose the opportunity to profit from his
innovation when a patent was awarded on August 8, 1889, to E. Harry
Decker, a catcher of the era who was a habitual thief, forger, and counter-
feiter. But whether Gunson's efforts preceded those of McCloskey and
Kennedy is much harder to determine.

The use of catcher's mitts had become widespread by the end of the 1888 season, and their impact on the game was immediate. An 1899 article in the *Cincinnati Enquirer* observed that "in the latter part of 1888 came the big glove into use, and from that day began the decline in base running" (*Cincinnati Enquirer*, January 2, 1899).

Buck Ewing appears to have introduced the catcher's mitt to the National League in 1888 and played an important role in popularizing it. An 1890 article explained: "It is just two years since Buck Ewing created a sensation by wearing an immense glove on his left hand while taking Tim Keefe's hot shot behind the bat at the old Polo grounds. His first appearance with the glove, which looked for all the world like a big boxing glove crushed out flat by a road roller, caused a shout of laughter from the assemblage, but when the game was over Buck declared that his hand was not swollen a particle, and that thereafter nothing could tempt him to relinquish his new guard to his big left hand. All through that season Buck wore the glove, and soon it was recognized as indispensable in the paraphernalia of the big back stop" (*New York Sun*, April 27, 1890).

In addition to its advantages in functionality, Ewing's glove was also visually memorable: "Buck continued to add stuffing to the glove and covering it with patches of new leather. The growth of the glove was closely watched by the fans, who marveled at its expansion. Any rip in it was instantly mended by Buck himself with any kind of leather, so that it sure was one of the most conspicuous things on the ball field, with its patches of all sorts of hide. It really became one of the attractions of the game, and scores of fans, influenced by newspaper comments, went to the game merely to get a look at Buck's glove. Naturally, manufacturers took the hint and began making the big glove" (John H. Gruber, "The Gloves," *Sporting News*, December 2, 1915).

In the next two years, mitts were refined and improved, as is shown by an 1890 article that reported: "One of the best gloves on the market to-day is that called a 'perfect pillow.' It is made of the choicest Plymouth buckskin. A continuous roll or cushion, tightly packed with curled hair, is firmly stitched around the palm, forming a deep hollow, and the thumb of the glove is a sufficient bulwark to make it impossible for a foul tip, fly, or hand-thrown ball to put the human thumb out of joint.

"The 'flexible glove' is made of the choicest buckskin, and is thoroughly padded with chinchilla. The padding extends from the wrist to the finger tips, but there is a break at the roots of the fingers forming a sort of hinge by which the fingers are practically separate from the hand. The right glove is of a lighter grade of buckskin, well padded or not, as the purchaser desires, and fingerless" (*New York Sun*, April 27, 1890). By 1890 the annual *Spalding's Guide* was offering a wide selection of mitts for the catcher's left hand and throwing gloves for the right hand.

As noted earlier, a decline in base stealing was attributed to the new mitts, and this was not the only significant change they helped effect. The Knickerbockers' initial rules had specified that a caught foul tip was an out, and the rule had stood ever since, because catching a foul tip with bare hands or kid gloves was a feat that required great skill. That perception changed almost immediately after the introduction of the catcher's mitt. According to John Gruber, "an element of pure luck or ill luck, depending on the viewpoint, guided the whole proceeding," and fans accordingly "growled and grumbled at the injustice of the rule" (John H. Gruber, "Out for Interference," *Sporting News*, February 24, 1916). As a result of this new perspective and the prevalence of fake foul tips (see **11.1.11**), the rule was changed in 1889 and a caught foul tip became simply a strike.

9.3.3 Snaring Nets. 1920s star Frank Frisch wrote in his 1962 autobiography, "We used to have leather pancakes for gloves. We had to make stops with our hands. Now they have snaring nets they call baseball gloves. The first baseman's glove is like a basketball hoop with a net on it" (Frank Frisch and J. Roy Stockton, *Frank Frisch: The Fordham Flash*; quoted in Dan Daniel, "Fordham Flash Casts Vote for Old-Timers," *Sporting News*, August 4, 1962, 5). Umpire Tim Hurst similarly told the *St. Louis Post-Dispatch*, "It makes me indignant to see a nice, clean grounder smothered by a big glove. Why, it has come to such a pass that the infielder who wears a big glove depends entirely upon his pillow to stop a ball with. None of them ducks do any clean fielding" (*St. Louis Post-Dispatch*, July 3, 1894). The catch, however, is that Hurst was speaking in 1894. Clearly the history of the glove's evolution from cushion to "snaring net" is a complex and often emotionally charged one.

Until some time in the 1880s, almost all reliable sources agree, most catchers and first basemen were wearing no more than simple finger gloves, and most other fielders were bare-handed. As John Gruber noted, "Before 1880 few fielders even thought of wearing hand-shoes, because nobody could see any advantage in them. On the contrary, there was a prevailing idea that they would prove a handicap, a hindrance to stopping the ball" (John H. Gruber, "The Gloves," *Sporting News*, December 2, 1915). During the next decade, fielders adopted gloves and catchers switched from gloves to mitts. There are different versions of when and how these innovations were introduced and a still wider range of opinion as to whether these changes were improvements or signs of collective madness.

John K. Tener took the latter view, recalling many years later that "in my day they would no more think of wearing a glove than they would of wearing skirts" (*Sporting News*, April 10, 1942). His recollection was that catchers and first basemen wore pads but kept their fingers free, and other fielders remained bare-handed until gloves caught on around 1889. George P. Scannell wrote similarly in 1905 that in the 1870s and 1880s gloves were used mostly by catchers and first basemen. Scannell claimed that it was not until 1889 that Arthur Whitney popularized the use of gloves by other players. He indicated that the practice "jumped into permanent favor" in 1890 (*Sporting Life*, April 1, 1905).

The more common version of events has the padded glove being popularized by Arthur Irwin, who began wearing one after an injury to his hand sidelined him from early July 1885 until August 12. Irwin gave this account: "I started the infielders wearing gloves . . . I reached for a hot one from the bat. Gloves were not known for us in those days. I stopped the ball right, but broke my finger. I had to play later, but my finger was terribly sore. I decided to wear a glove and made one. When I trotted out on the field I was the object of all sorts of joshing, but it proved a success. I studied the thing out and improved on it. I found even after my finger was better that it helped me. Other players grew curious and I made for them too [sic]. The Spalding and Reach people sent in orders for them too. For four years I made all the gloves they sold. When they started making them I quit" (*Sporting News*, December 9, 1905). A. H. Spink added that Irwin broke the third and fourth fingers of his left hand and "consulted a glover, bought a buckskin glove many sizes too large for his injured hand, padded it, and sewed the injured fingers together to make way for the bandages" (A. H. Spink, *The National Game*, 228).

An amateur player named C. Wickliffe Throckmorton later recollected, "In the Eighties, when I came north from New Orleans, I thought it was 'sissie' to wear a fielder's glove, but I soon got over that" (letter to the *New York Times*, July 6, 1940). Most other players showed a similar adaptability, though a few holdouts remained.

By the mid-1890s fielding gloves were becoming common. Moreover they were no longer being used merely to cushion the hands but were rapidly increasing in size and were beginning to make the catch for the fielder. The trend climaxed in 1894 when Lave Cross wore a catcher's mitt to play third base. Henry Chadwick denounced this as "making a travesty of skilful infield play" (*Spalding's Official Base Ball Guide, 1895*, 121). Tim Hurst quite accurately predicted, "Why, it will be so after awhile that a player will provide himself with a fan-like contrivance which he will open when he sees a hard grounder coming toward him" (quoted in *St. Louis Post-Dispatch*, July 3, 1894).

This unwelcome development understandably led to a backlash. After the 1894 season several prominent players came out in favor of allowing only catchers and first basemen to wear gloves. The National League enacted a restriction that players at all other positions could not wear gloves that exceeded ten ounces or fourteen inches in circumference. The *St. Louis*

Post-Dispatch was pleased that "players can no longer take refuge behind 'pillows,' but are allowed only plain kid or buckskin gloves" (*St. Louis Post-Dispatch*, March 3, 1895). Others felt this was still not enough, and there continued to be complaints that "One way to bring baseball back to the good old days would be to bar the big mitts from all but the catchers and the first basemen. Outfielders would then have to play the ball properly and not catch flies in a big pillow" (*Boston Globe*, July 5, 1899).

9.3.4 Pitchers Wearing Gloves. Pitchers were the last players to don gloves. A 1906 article claimed that the first pitcher to wear a glove was Nig Cuppy (*Sporting News*, November 17, 1906). Cy Young repeated the assertion three years later, adding that "Many base ball critics of the old school rushed into print declaring that the pitcher could not grasp the ball properly because the glove would interfere" (*Cleveland Leader*, quoted in *Sporting Life*, May 15, 1909).

Cuppy reached the majors in 1892 when pitchers wearing gloves were undoubtedly still a novelty, since the *St. Louis Post-Dispatch* thought it noteworthy in 1894 that "[Mike] Sullivan and Cuppy of the Clevelands use a glove on the left hand while pitching so as to handle hot grounders with safety" (*St. Louis Post-Dispatch*, September 4, 1894).

But Cuppy wasn't the first. The *New York Sun* remarked in 1888, "[Cannonball] Crane generally has a catcher's glove on his left hand when he pitches" (*New York Sun*, April 14, 1888). And later that year the *St. Louis Post-Dispatch* observed, "[Kid] Gleason, the Philadelphia pitcher, wears a glove on his left hand while pitching" (*St. Louis Post-Dispatch*, September 10, 1888).

9.3.5 Last Gloveless Player. The last player to take the field in a major league game without a glove was almost certainly a pitcher. Dan Gutman cited Gus Weyhing in 1901. But the following year *Sporting Life* reported, "Pitcher [Joe] Yeager's split hand is due to the fact that he refuses to wear a fielding glove" (*Sporting Life*, August 9, 1902).

The last prominent nonpitchers to reject gloves were Bid McPhee and Jerry Denny. Denny's career ended in 1894, and Bill James described him as the "last position player who did not wear a glove" (Bill James, *The New Bill James Historical Baseball Abstract*, 68). This, however, can't be true since, as James himself noted, Bid McPhee didn't start wearing a glove until 1896 (Bill James, *The New Bill James Historical Baseball Abstract*, 503). Perhaps James meant that Denny was the last player to retire without ever wearing a glove. But this too is incorrect since Pat Flaherty succeeded Denny as Louisville's third baseman and also played without a glove (*St. Louis Post-Dispatch*, July 30, 1894).

Apparently there were gloveless players in the minor leagues well into the twentieth century. A 1909 article estimated that only two-thirds "of the small leaguers" wore gloves ("The Great National Game in Dollars and Cents," *Washington Post*, May 9, 1909).

9.3.6   Pockets. The pocket in gloves developed gradually as a result of numerous modifications. As early as 1898 the *Boston Globe* suggested that outfielder Billy Hamilton "should wear a larger mit and one with a pocket in it. Billy is fast, but has a poor grip after a sharp run" (*Boston Globe*, October 1, 1898). Pockets of this era, however, were still relatively negligible in size and effectiveness. Pitcher Bill Doak made the big breakthrough in 1919 when he devised the idea of a glove with a pocket between the thumb and index finger that could be adjusted by manipulating the leather laces. Doak sold the idea to Rawlings Sporting Goods, and it became the basis of today's fielder's glove. But, as discussed under "One-handed Catches" (4.4.1), it was still many years before the glove was able to secure the ball reliably without help from the bare hand.

9.3.7   Flexible Heels. As described in the entry on "One-handed Catches" (4.4.1), the introduction of the flexible heel in 1959 further eased the fielder's task and brought gloves closer to the snaring nets that Frank Frisch derided.

9.3.8   Slot for Index Finger. William Curran gives this account of the origin of the small slot for the index finger in the back of gloves: "Sometime in the 1950s, Yankees catcher Yogi Berra injured the index finger on his left hand. To spare the tender digit some of the pounding it would take inside the catcher's mitt, Yogi slipped it outside and continued to catch. The finger felt so good out there in the air and sunshine that Yogi did not bother to put it back into the mitt after it had healed. Other American League catchers, sensing that the perennial MVP winner had discovered some arcane method for eliminating passed balls, quickly pulled their fingers from the mitt in imitation." Naturally this created a demand, and it eventually also became standard for fielders' gloves to be made with a special slot for the index finger (William Curran, *Mitts*, 82–83).

9.3.9   Breaking In. The technique of breaking in a glove must be almost as old as gloves themselves, as the *Milwaukee Journal* reported in 1901: "Jimmie Burke is mourning the loss of his fielding glove. Someone stole it while at the Springs, and Jimmie sort of suspects that it left with the Chicago team. 'I would not care so much,' said Jimmie, 'only I had just got it broke in'" (*Milwaukee Journal*, April 15, 1901).

9.3.10   Six-fingered Gloves. The six-fingered glove was invented by glove-maker Harry Latina for Ken Boyer. Its best-known user was Ozzie Smith (Vince Staten, *Why Is the Foul Pole Fair?*, 99).

9.3.11   Oversized Catchers' Mitts. Frustrated by his catchers' inability to control Hoyt Wilhelm's knuckleball, on May 27, 1960, Baltimore manager Paul Richards introduced an enormous catcher's mitt. Such mitts were banned after the 1964 season by a rule restricting catchers' mitts to no more than thirty-eight inches in circumference and a maximum distance from top to bottom of fifteen and a half inches.

9.3.12   Gloves Being Left on the Field. Until the 1954 season it was common practice for fielders to leave their gloves on the field while their team batted. The outcome of one pennant race was affected by this custom. On September 28, 1905, the Athletics beat the White Sox 3-2, with Topsy Hartsel scoring the winning run after Harry Davis's line drive deflected off Hartsel's own glove. The Athletics ended up beating Chicago for the pennant by two games (Robert L. Tiemann, "Hartsel Scores on Hit Off Hartsel's Glove," *Baseball Research Journal* 17 [1988], 33).

Researcher Frank Vaccaro noted that the impetus for banning the practice may have been provided by a game between the White Sox and Senators on July 12, 1952. The hometown Senators were behind 1-0 in the fifth when Chicago shortstop Sam Dente tripped over the glove of opposing number Pete Runnells on what would have been the third out. Washington then rallied for two runs and hung on for a 2-1 victory.

In spite of the apparent need to end this practice, researcher Wayne McElreavy reports that news of the ban in November 1953 was not received warmly. American League president Will Harridge threatened to ignore the rule after seven of the league's eight clubs voiced opposition. Casey Stengel complained: "There is no sensible reason for the rule which forces the players to carry their gloves off the field after each half inning. . . . We are trying every which way to speed up games. Now we have a rule which makes for delays. I don't get it. I would like to see the rule repealed" (Dan Daniel, "A. L. Balks Over Rule on Bringing Gloves Off Field," *Sporting News*, March 24, 1954).

The Eastern League notified its clubs not to observe the rule. Other minor leagues discussed following suit, with one even threatening to fine players if they carried their gloves off the field (*Sporting News*, March 24, April 14, 1954). But Commissioner Ford Frick and National Association President George Trautman stood by the new rule, and eventually the uproar died.

(iv) Protective Equipment

The introduction of almost every piece of protective equipment in the nineteenth century was met with resistance. The first and foremost objection was that the new piece of equipment conflicted with the ideal of manliness. A secondary consideration, but a far from trivial one, was the reality that players had to pay for their own garb.

Once a piece of equipment passed these tests, however, the "tipping point" occurred, and generally in little time its usage became universal. Obviously this was first and foremost the result of the natural instinct for self-preservation. It also reflected the enormous incentive that clubs and players had to avoid serious injuries. A club was unlikely to have an adequate replacement available, while the injured player himself was even worse off, as his contract could be terminated with ten days' notice.

9.4.1 Rubber Mouthpieces. The first form of protective equipment was the rubber mouth plate. The *Williamsport Sunday Grit* later explained that before masks were invented the catcher used "to hold in his teeth a large piece of solid rubber for the purpose of protecting them" (*Williamsport Sunday Grit*, June 7, 1891).

Rubbers seem to have encountered less resistance than any other form of equipment, which makes their introduction difficult to date. It does seem safe to assume that they were in use by 1870, since a rubber mouthpiece belonging to catcher Doug Allison of the Red Stockings of Cincinnati was auctioned off in 1916 (Jonathan Fraser Light, *The Cultural Encyclopedia of Baseball*, 142).

The rubber appears to have become quite common by the middle of the decade. An 1883 account reported, "Before [1877] the catcher's rubber had been the only safeguard adopted by the catchers, but this did not come into general use, and protected the teeth and mouth only" (*Grand Rapids* [Mich.] *Morning Democrat*, September 4, 1883). A Michigan newspaper informed its readers in 1875: "Couch keeps a piece of rubber in his mouth to protect his lips from foul tips" (*Jackson Citizen*, August 16, 1875). The *Atlanta Constitution* later wrote of an 1877 game: "[Frank] Foster caught the game in magnificent style. He had no mask, only a rubber mouth plate" (*Atlanta Constitution*, February 12, 1893). Scott Hastings of Chicago also used a rubber mouthpiece in 1877 (*Chicago Tribune*, July 26, 1877).

The advent of the mask quickly made the rubber obsolete, and the game's first piece of protective equipment passed out of baseball with no more fanfare than had been caused by its introduction.

9.4.2   Catchers' Masks. The first catcher's mask was designed by Harvard baseball captain Fred Thayer in the mid-1870s. But the identity of the first catcher to don a mask was the subject of lively controversy in the nineteenth century and may never be definitively resolved. What is puzzling is that the two main claimants both attended Harvard, and only a year apart.

Howard K. Thatcher, a Maine physician, staked his claim in 1896. He explained that the development of the curve led to the protective device: "I used to wear a rubber band over my mouth, but I decided that this was not enough protection for me. When we played our first game in the Spring of 1876, I put on a mask which I had made from heavy wire. The edges were wound with leather, and I had a strap on the chin and another at the forehead. My chum, Fred Thayer, helped me to make it, and I confess it was a queer-looking thing. It was ridiculed the first time I wore the mask, partly because it was a new thing, and partly because the people considered that a catcher did not need any protection for his face. I threw the mask away" (reprinted in A. H. Spink, *The National Game*, 384; cited as appearing in the *New York Sun* on June 30, 1896, but I could not locate the original for this or the subsequent quotations).

James A. Tyng, Thatcher's successor as Harvard's catcher, responded angrily and termed Thatcher a "prevaricator." He gave this version: "The first public appearance of the mask was in the Spring of 1877, not 1876, as he places it. I was at the time a member of the Harvard nine, and Thayer, who was then captain of the nine, wanted me to fill the position of catcher. To this my family were opposed, on account of the danger, and I suggested to him the idea of having a mask made that would protect my face. He followed my suggestion and a wiremaker in Boston made me a mask, which, although heavy and clumsy, compared to the one now in use, answered the purpose for which it was intended, and this mask was worn by me in the three remaining years that I played and caught on the nine" (reprinted in A. H. Spink, *The National Game*, 385; cited as originating in the *New York Sun*).

Two eyewitnesses give equally contradictory accounts. Warren R. Briggs, a contemporary and acquaintance of both men, favored Thatcher's claim. He wrote to the *Sun* that in the early summer of 1875 he was catching for an amateur nine in Boston when he heard rumors "of a face protector or mask that Fred Thayer, captain and third baseman of the Harvard nine, was getting up, and which Thatcher, who was catching for Harvard at that time was to use. Naturally I was interested in the new-fangled protector and went to Thayer's room some time during the Summer or Fall of '75, saw a working model of the device, and, if I remember rightly, made some suggestions concerning it. Soon after this, either in the Fall of 1875 or in the Spring of 1876, I procured one of these masks, of whom I cannot remember, but I think through Thayer, and used it a little during the early games of 1876. I left Boston on the 5th of July, 1876, and came to this city, where I have resided ever since. I brought with me at that time the mask to which I have referred, and have it in my possession today, a relic of the past and, I believe, one of the first things of its kind ever used. Later I saw Tyng using the same thing, but as I left Boston a year before the date he mentions, and as I saw a model of the device some months before in Thayer's room, I do not think there can be any doubt about the accuracy of my statements" (reprinted in A. H. Spink, *The National Game*, 384; cited as originating in the *New York Sun*).

A. G. Spalding addressed the topic in 1911, claiming, "That Dr. Thatcher was *not*, and that James Tyng *was*, the first catcher to wear the mask in a regular game it is quite possible to demonstrate by competent witnesses" (A. G. Spalding, *America's National Game*, 478). As with so many of Spalding's claims, however, his rhetoric outpaced the facts. He offered two pieces of support for his claim. One of these is a letter from George Wright, who indicated that Tyng was the first man whom he saw wearing a mask. Obviously this does not mean that Thatcher did not wear one earlier.

The more substantive piece of evidence is a 1911 letter from Fred Thayer himself. Thayer indicated that Thatcher was the Harvard catcher in 1876 but left school at the year's end. Thayer thought Tyng would be the best man to play the position, but Tyng proved "timid." Accordingly, Thayer designed a mask based upon the fencing mask, and he said that Tyng first wore it against the Live Oaks of Lynn in April 1877 (the entire letter is reprinted in A. G. Spalding, *America's National Game*, 478–479).

There is no way to reconcile such contradictory accounts, making it impossible to be certain whether Thatcher or Tyng first wore the catcher's mask. Nonetheless it seems easier to imagine that Thayer had forgotten and that Tyng had never known about Thatcher's brief experiment with the mask than it is that both Thatcher and Briggs made up or fantasized their accounts.

What is beyond question is that Tyng's use of the mask caused it to become popular, and this happened surprisingly quickly. Reports about the mask were circulating by the end of January, when Henry Chadwick remarked: "The baseball players used to laugh at the idea of cricketers wearing batting pads and gloves, until they faced swift bowling themselves; then they thought better of the idea. Recently defensive articles have been introduced in baseball, Mr. Thayer of the Harvard College Club having invented a steel mask for protecting the face of the catcher of the nine. It is constructed of upright bars about an inch apart, and stands out from the face 3 or 4 inches, being fastened at the top of bottom. It has proved a valuable protection to the face, and is in daily use at the gymnasium" (*New York Clipper*, January 27, 1877). Word spread rapidly, and by March accounts were springing up in far-flung places of the catcher from Harvard who had "invented a brass wire mask for the face" (*Woodstock* [Ont.] *Review*, March 9, 1877).

Reactions were mixed. The *Providence Dispatch* sneered at Tyng's mask: "The near future may bring about many other improvements in the equipments of a base ball player, and we shall probably soon behold the spectacle of a player sculling around the bases with stove funnels on his legs, and boiler irons across his stomach" (*Providence Dispatch*, reprinted in *Boston Globe*, May 19, 1877). Another newspaper added, "There is a great deal of beastly humbug in contrivances to protect men from things which do not happen. There is about as much sense in putting a lightning rod on a catcher as there is a mask" (quoted in Dan Gutman, *Banana Bats and Ding-Dong Balls*, 186).

Henry Chadwick took the opposite position: "Thayer's invention to protect the catcher from dangerous hits in the face when playing close up behind the bat attracted considerable attention. In fact the wire mask is something all catchers who face swift pitching should have. It is light, simple and a sure protection, not in the way in any respect" (*Brooklyn Eagle*, May 19, 1877).

He reiterated this theme in succeeding months, with increasing conviction (*Brooklyn Eagle*, June 15 and August 13, 1877). When these calls were not heeded, he remarked, "The amateur catchers have wisely adopted this valuable invention, and why the professional catchers do not use it, is a puzzle." He suggested that the solution was that professional catchers "have not, as a class, the moral courage to face the music of the fire of chaff and raillery from the crowd, which the wearing of the mask frequently elicits. Plucky enough to face the dangerous fire of balls from the swift pitcher, they tremble before the remarks of the small boys of the crowd of spectators, and prefer to run the risk of broken cheek bones, dislocated jaws, a smashed nose or blackened eyes, than stand the chaff of the fools in the assemblage" (*Brooklyn Eagle*, August 16, 1877).

The poor catcher of 1877 was in the unenviable position of being accused of not being "plucky or manly" if he wore a mask, but equally likely to be insulted if he shunned the protective device (*New York Clipper*, August 25, 1877). Given those alternatives, it is not surprising that the professionals soon donned masks to avoid adding injury to the inevitable insults.

The first professional to wear the mask may have been Pete Hotaling, the catcher for the Syracuse Stars who was still recovering from the effects of being struck in the eye with a foul tip. He acquired his mask by a circuitous route, as sportswriter P. S. Ryder later explained: "Pete Hotaling was the first player to don a mask. A graduate of Harvard invented the mask and sent it to Homer Ostrander. Homer showed me the new article and I gave it to Hotaling. Peter donned it and afterwards brought it with him to Chicago.

He loaned it one day to Cal McVey, the Chicago backstop. When President [William] Hulbert saw the mask he gave orders to McVey to take it off and never wear it again. 'Don't you ever let me see you with that trap on in a game,' was Hulbert's order to McVey" (*Sporting News*, October 30, 1897).

Hotaling began wearing the mask in July 1877. When he wore it during a game in Chicago, bemused reports indicated that it "had never before been seen on the Chicago grounds. The crowd variously named it 'the rat-trap' and 'the bird-cage'" (*Chicago Tribune*, July 20, 1877). On August 8, 1877, Mike Dorgan became the first National League catcher to wear one. Like Hotaling, Dorgan was recovering from an injury and does not appear to have continued wearing the mask.

Scott Hastings was yet another catcher who experimented with the mask after being hit in the face with a foul, but he was uncomfortable with it: "The use of the wire mask he finds bothers his playing, and it has been discarded for the teeth rubber" (*Chicago Tribune*, July 26, 1877). This was not the only complaint about the new device. The *New York Clipper* reported: "This 'mask' is composed of brass wires, and fastened around the head by a strap. It works fairly well, but needs a powerful thrower to use it, as it is apt to jar the head, thereby upsetting the aim of the thrower" (*New York Clipper*, April 14, 1877). In addition, several catchers discovered that a hard foul ball could drive the wires into their face and cut them.

Nonetheless most catchers found these drawbacks preferable to the alternative, and interest in the new invention continued to spread. Soon after designing the mask, Fred Thayer "visited the club room of the Boston nine, then at 39 Eliot street, and spoke to Harry and George Wright and others of the players present about the new invention. Most of them laughed at the idea of a man going around with a cage on his head. Harry, however, always ready and curious enough to look at anything new in base ball, asked Thayer to bring in the affair. The young man accordingly did so, and stood at one end of the room with it on, allowing the players to throw balls at it, which he easily butted off" (*Grand Rapids* [Mich.] *Morning Democrat*, September 4, 1883).

Thayer received a patent for the mask in 1878 and he arranged to have George Wright's sporting goods firm of Wright & Ditson manufacture it. By the early 1880s the mask had become a standard piece of the catcher's gear and Thayer was using his law degree to defend his patent. Among his successful lawsuits was one against A. G. Spalding and Brothers in 1886 for patent infringement.

Even after the mask became commonplace in the East, it continued to encounter resistance when it made its first appearance in new areas. For example, when Rooney Sweeney introduced the mask to California while playing for Oakland in 1883, he "was 'booed' until he took it off in disgust. Later the fans began to see the benefits of the wire covering and it gradually became popular" (*San Francisco Chronicle*, reprinted in *Sporting News*, December 30, 1909).

9.4.3   Billy Goats. In 1976, Dodgers catcher Steve Yeager was standing in the on-deck circle when his teammate's bat shattered and splinters lodged in Yeager's neck. When he returned to action, he introduced the "billy goat" neck guard, which hangs down from the mask to protect the catcher's throat. It soon became popular with major league catchers.

This was not an entirely new concept. Researcher Reed Howard alerted me to an 1887 description of National League umpire Herman Doscher wearing a mask that had "a protection attachment for the throat" (*Sporting Life*, August 31, 1887). In the 1888 *Spalding's Official Base Ball Guide*, A. G. Spalding & Brothers advertised a newly patented neck-protecting mask with a "peculiar shaped extension at the bottom which affords the same protection to the neck as the mask does to the face." The ad claimed that the neck protector "does not interfere in the slightest degree with the free movement of the head." But the fact that it did not catch on in the major leagues until nearly a century later suggests that the catchers who tried it may have felt otherwise.

9.4.4   Hockey-style Masks. Catchers' masks have of course changed considerably in the years since Thayer modeled one on the fencer's mask. The alterations, however, have primarily been evolutionary in nature.

Arguably the most radical change to the mask came in 1996 when Blue Jays catcher Charlie O'Brien donned a hockey-style mask. After attending a Toronto Maple Leafs hockey game, O'Brien became convinced that a goalie's mask would be more effective for catchers. He helped design a prototype based upon the goalie's mask, but which was designed to offer greater vision and protection. He first wore the hockey-style mask in a major league game on September 13, 1996. The new design caught on quickly, and its greater protection allowed catchers to shed the "billy goat" neck guards.

9.4.5   Chest Protectors. Sportswriter William Rankin wrote in 1910, "During the summer of 1876 Denny Clare, now a Brooklyn politician and known as one of the cleverest domino players in the country, wore a padded vest, from which, I believe, the chest protector had its origin" (*Sporting News*, February 3, 1910).

The description suggests that Clare probably wore his vest under his uniform, but by the early 1880s catchers were wearing chest protectors over their jerseys. The first seems to have been Charley Bennett of the National

League Detroit Wolverines, in 1883. Interestingly, Lee Allen reported in 1968 finding an article crediting Bennett with pioneering the chest protector.

The article in question was probably one by Maclean Kennedy that appeared in 1914. In it, Bennett explained that his wife was concerned about his health and with his help created a "crude but very substantial shield . . . by sewing strips of cork of a good thickness in between heavy bedticking material." When Bennett tried it out, it proved so effective that he allowed pitches to hit him square in the chest and did not experience "the slightest jar" (Maclean Kennedy, "Charley Bennett, Former Detroit Catcher, Inventor of Chest Pad," *Detroit Free Press*, August 2, 1914; *Leslie's Illustrated Weekly* printed a similar article on October 15, 1914, which is quoted in Vince Staten, *Why Is the Foul Pole Fair?*, 263).

Allen wisely cautioned that "the exact year was not given, so it is impossible to say that Bennett's contribution was a 'first,' a very dangerous word to employ in writing baseball history" (*Sporting News*, April 6, 1968; reprinted in Lee Allen, *Cooperstown Corner*). Fortunately the increased availability of microfilm now makes it possible to date Bennett's contribution with greater precision, and he does appear to have been first. At the start of the 1883 season, the *Detroit Free Press* commented: "A heavy cork pad protects Bennett's chest from foul tips this season" (*Detroit Free Press*, May 1, 1883). A couple of weeks later another Michigan newspaper remarked on the "heavy cork chest-protectors" being worn by catchers (*Lapeer Democrat*, May 16, 1883). Catcher Phil Baker was also reported to have used a chest protector in 1883 (*Cincinnati Enquirer*, June 8, 1884).

Use of the devices became far more widespread during the following season. The 1884 *Reach Guide* had an ad for Gray's Patent Body Protector. The chest protectors attracted comment for their unusual appearance: "[Ed] McKenna, the catcher of the Nationals, wore in yesterday's game the first body-protector ever used in a championship game in this city. It is made of rubber cloth and inflated with air. He looked like a knight of old equipped in armor for a battle when he donned his mask and other trappings" (*Cincinnati Enquirer*, May 29, 1884). The *Columbus Dispatch* wrote that Rudolph Kemmler "looks like a back-stop when he wears the body protector," which may be how the catcher came to be referred to as the backstop (*Columbus* [Ohio] *Dispatch*, May 21, 1884).

While these descriptions suggest bemusement, there seems to have been little of the resistance that usually met new kinds of protective equipment. By June, *Sporting Life* reported that many catchers were now using chest protectors (*Sporting Life*, June 10, 1884). The following month a correspondent commented, "The chest protector is coming into general use. It is as necessary as the mask" (*Sporting Life*, July 23, 1884).

As with the catcher's mask, the *Brooklyn Eagle* offered a staunch defense of the chest protector: "the catcher who refuses to wear such a protector from severe injuries simply because 'it looks so queer,' or because a lot of fools in the crowd laugh at him, is no better than the idiots who quiz him" (*Brooklyn Eagle*, June 1, 1884). The support was echoed by *Sporting Life*: "The usefulness of the Rubber Body Protector was fully illustrated in a recent game in Hartford. . . . The usefulness of the Body Protectors have [sic] become an established fact, and the sooner all catchers adopt them the sooner we shall see more confidence displayed in them" (*Sporting Life*, July 30, 1884).

By the end of the 1884 season it was catchers who *didn't* wear the new gear who were being mocked. One game account reported that rookie New York catcher Henry Oxley must have arrived from the "Green Mountains" because he wore neither a mask nor a chest protector. Oxley saw "the catcher of the other club strapping on a chest protector, so he asked him what he was doing that for." He then put it on, but wore it without blowing it up until another player took pity on him and explained that it had to be inflated to offer protection (*St. Louis Post-Dispatch*, August 23, 1884).

It wasn't long before other possible uses were noticed. A want ad in *Sporting Life* after the season that read: "Wanted, a base ball catcher's body protector till April 1, '85 for polo playing. If any damage is done will fully repay" (*Sporting Life*, February 4, 1885). This was no small consideration in the days when players paid for their own equipment.

Curiously, an 1890 article gave this account: "The catcher's breast-protector, or the 'sheepskin,' as it is often contemptuously referred to, is neither neat nor gaudy, but, like a trick mule in a kicking match, it gets there just the same. This most useful piece of the base-ball paraphernalia had a hard time getting a foothold. The catchers were slow in adopting it, and the spectators at first guyed as baby-play. [Jack] Clements, the great catcher of the Philadelphia League team, was the first to wear a catcher's protector in a game before a Cincinnati crowd. He was then back-stopping Jersey Bakely with the Keystone Unions, at Philadelphia, in 1884. Considerable fun was made of the protector, and the writer distinctly remembers that it was made the subject of adverse newspaper comment by one of the best base-ball authorities in America. Now it is different" (*Sporting News*, November 1, 1890).

This description sounds credible, yet contemporary articles give little indication of such ridicule. Perhaps the truth lies somewhere in between. It should also be noted that this article's claim that Jack Clements was the first to wear a chest protector in Cincinnati is contradicted by the *Cincinnati Enquirer* of May 29, 1884, which gave the distinction to Ed McKenna.

In any event, by 1890 the chest protector had become established. In succeeding years the inflatable rubber vests gave way to leather and canvas protectors filled first with cotton felt, then with kapok, and eventually with foam.

9.4.6   Shin Guards. New York Giants catcher Roger Bresnahan is generally credited with introducing them to baseball in 1907. As with so many claimed firsts, a closer look reveals a somewhat different picture, though Bresnahan unquestionably played a major role.

Shin pads were used by cricket batsmen long before they were used in baseball. They entered cricket in the 1830s as a direct result of the introduction of over-the-top bowling deliveries. They were more necessary in that sport because of the batsman's need to protect the wicket, whereas "in base ball there is no need of leg guards or pads for the batsmen, as they can jump aside and avoid balls likely to hit them" (*Brooklyn Eagle*, August 16, 1877). By 1893 shin pads were being worn by hockey players and soon became common in that sport (Michael McKinley, *Putting a Roof on Winter*, 33). At least some football players were also using shin guards in the nineteenth century (Robert W. Peterson, *Pigskin*, 19).

Their use in nineteenth-century baseball, however, was sporadic. Tim Murnane claimed that in 1871 the King Philip club of East Abington, Massachusetts, had a young pitcher "named 'Ferd' Thompson, who wore high-legged boots with his trousers tucked inside, and I believe was the first man to wear any protection on his shins" (*Boston Globe*, January 17, 1915). It is said that nineteenth-century black pioneers Frank Grant and Bud Fowler wore primitive shin guards because they were spiked so often by vindictive white players. (See Ned Williamson's comments under "Feet-first Slides" [5.2.2] for details.) A 1930s newspaper article stated that Morgan Murphy briefly wore shin guards in the early 1890s. He was catching for Cincinnati at the time and "was spiked, but he was needed so badly that a light temporary shin guard was arranged to wear under the stocking of his left leg" (Harry A. Williams, *Los Angeles Times*, February 28, 1932).

Harry Steinfeldt, who went on to fame as the fourth member of the Chicago Cubs' Tinker-to-Evers-to-Chance infield, definitely experimented with shin guards in 1897: "Steinfeldt, a Detroit infielder, wears a pair of shin guards during play. They are an excellent protection against spikes and do not impede his running to any extent" (*Cleveland Plain Dealer*, August 6, 1897). As the last comment indicates, a major problem with such devices was that most versions of them were a severe impediment for running. John B. Foster recalled many years later that the catcher on his amateur team in the 1880s wore rubber boots with cotton batten in them, but found that he could barely move (*Sporting News*, January 31, 1935).

By the early twentieth century new types of shin guards were earning trials. According to researcher Dan Hotaling, early-twentieth-century catcher Mike Kahoe told his family he had been the first player to wear shin guards. Kahoe's obituary in *Sporting News* stated: "Roger Bresnahan's claim that he was the first catcher in the majors to wear shinguards was always disputed by

Kahoe. It was asserted that Kahoe, while with the Cubs in 1902, donned the protection when struck on the leg by a pitched ball. A British cricket player and sporting goods salesman suggested the catcher try on a pair of shin-guards used in cricket, which he did. However, he did not use them regularly until later. Bresnahan is credited with having introduced the shinguards to the majors in 1907" (Frederick Ivor-Campbell, "When Was the First? [Continued]," *Nineteenth Century Notes* 95:1, [Winter 1995], 1; *Sporting News*, May 25, 1949). There does not appear to have been any contemporary documentation of Kahoe's contention. Instead, when shin guards began to catch on in 1907, Kahoe was quoted at length on the new equipment and made no mention that he had ever worn them before (*Washington Post*, June 17, 1907).

But there is clear evidence that shin guards were being used in the major leagues by 1904. Sports columnist A. R. Cratty wrote in that year that Boston catcher Tom Needham "earned fame over the circuit for getting his man at the rubber. He stood right there and defied spikes. As a result, the youth was laid up a number of times. The Reds gave it to him once in their tour. The sore had to be scraped day after day for two weeks. Then Needham was forced to go to Philadelphia, where a metal shin guard was made for him. George Wright, the veteran, made the protection and declared that this was the first time he had produced anything of that kind for a base ball player" (*Sporting Life*, October 15, 1904).

There seem to have been several other similar experiments in the next couple of years. The *Chicago Tribune* reported in 1905, "[Billy] Sullivan is considering adopting shin guards as a protection from the eels [spit balls]. He got two nasty blows on the shin, the second one making him dance merrily for a time" (*Chicago Tribune*, May 1, 1905). Nig Clarke later claimed that "in 1905, while with Cleveland, he took to wearing the brand of shin guards which are used in football. However, these did not seem to cover enough territory, and late that season he switched to the cricket shin guards, which provide protection for the knees as well as the front of the lower leg." Clarke showed sportswriter Harry A. Williams a photo to support his contention (*Los Angeles Times*, May 10, 1915).

Lee Allen noted that Red Dooin also claimed to have preceded Bresnahan by a couple of years: "I had a special type made, substituting papier-mâché for rattan to make them lighter. One day Bresnahan crashed into me at the plate and somehow came in contact with my legs. 'What have you got on under your stockings?' he asked. I told him they were shinguards." Dooin kept these shin guards on while batting (Lee Allen, *The Hot Stove League*, 96).

It is obvious that Roger Bresnahan did not invent shin guards, nor was he the first to wear them in a major league game. In fairness, it must be noted that he never claimed to have invented this form of protective equipment. What Bresnahan did do was play a crucial role in popularizing them.

He did this by taking the revolutionary step of wearing shin guards over his pants in the Giants' opening day game on April 11, 1907. The *New York Times* described the reaction: "Bresnahan created somewhat of a sensation when he appeared behind the bat for the start of play, by donning cricket leg guards. . . . The white shields were rather picturesque, in spite of their clumsiness, and the spectators rather fancied the innovation. They howled with delight when a foul tip in the fourth inning rapped the protectors sharply" (*New York Times*, April 12, 1907).

The reception around the league was mixed. Pittsburgh owner Barney Dreyfuss tried to have them banned but won little support for this view. The general feeling seems to have been that the day had passed when manliness could be deemed more important than safety. One reporter commented that there was now "no chance for any such interference with a player's right to wear what protection he pleases, provided it is not injurious to other players" (*Washington Post*, May 16, 1907).

Giants manager John McGraw had to overcome his initial misgivings, as Bresnahan explained: "McGraw thought they would interfere with my running, and looked askance at them at the beginning of the year, but he has changed his mind. . . . Last year my legs were bruised from the knees down, and part of the time it was all that I could do to walk after a game. That interfered with my running a great deal more than the shin guards possibly can interfere" (*Washington Post*, May 12, 1907).

The reaction of rival catchers was aptly summarized by Cubs receiver Johnny Kling, who said he would follow Bresnahan's lead "as soon as I can muster up nerve enough." He explained, "The roasting the rooters gave Bresnahan during the New York series here has taken away my nerve and I cannot muster up courage enough to wear them at home. I guess I will try them away from home first and then it won't be too bad" (*Washington Post*, June 17, 1907).

As shin guards became common, descriptions of them usually included references to Bresnahan. William J. Hennessey, writing about the Connecticut League in 1909, observed, "Shinguards, a-la-Bresnahan, is [sic] the vogue this season. Last year Beaumont was the only backstop to don the leg armor and the idea was looked upon as a novelty, but the value of them is becoming more apparent each season" (*Sporting News*, April 29, 1909).

As acceptance of the use of shin guards by catchers grew, a number of variants were attempted. Cleveland catcher Nig Clarke, for instance, wore thin pads that "do not interfere with his running, so he does not have to discard them when he is not behind the bat" (*Washington Post*, August 9, 1907). Detroit's Charley Schmidt donned "an elaborate suit of armor on his left leg . . . concealed under his uniform. Its sole purpose is to protect him from the spikes of runners whom he is blocking off, and it does him no good in case of wild pitches or foul tips. Some of the third basemen follow the Schmidt system to greater or less extent" (*Detroit Free Press*, April 30, 1910).

As this last comment suggests, other fielders were also experimenting with shin guards. At the outset of the 1908 season it was reported that "shin guards are to be worn by [second baseman Harry] Niles and [shortstop Kid] Elberfeld, according to the latest edict of the Yankee commander. The kind selected are not as bulky as those worn by Roger Bresnahan" (*Sporting Life*, April 4, 1908). For greater mobility, each player wore only one shin guard: "Elberfeld and Niles, of the Highlanders, wear shin guards to protect their legs from the base runners' spikes. Elberfeld wears his on the right leg and Niles has his on the left" (*Sporting Life*, May 2, 1908). Unfortunately Elberfeld was injured later that week when a runner slid into his unprotected left leg, and the experiment was discontinued.

A few pitchers even joined the trend. In 1910 a Houston pitcher named Merrill "trotted out to the slab wearing one guard on his right leg. It was one of the short guards, such as were made popular by Nig Clarke, with no loose extensions to come above and to protect the knee cap" (*Detroit Free Press*, April 30, 1910). Tim Murnane reported in 1915 that several pitchers were sporting shin guards (*Boston Globe*, January 17, 1915).

9.4.7   Knee Caps. Knee caps began to appear at about the same time as shin guards and appear to have been a direct borrowing from football. A 1906 note observed: "Catcher [Howard] Wakefield, of Cleveland, has purchased a pair of foot ball knee caps and will wear them this coming season. He claims they will protect his knees when catching" (*Sporting Life*, March 24, 1906).

9.4.8   Knee Savers. The Knee Saver is the name of the foam pads that today's catchers strap on behind their shin guards. The device was introduced by AliMed in 1997 to support the knees and reduce strain while crouching.

9.4.9   Batting Helmets. Many years after the fact, a man named C. Wickliffe Throckmorton claimed that in the late 1880s "a player from the New York A. C. was hit in the head by a pitched ball. Shortly afterward he appeared on the field wearing a helmet. He was laughed at and gave up the idea" (letter to the *New York Times*, August 28, 1937). This would be one of the earliest instances of what would become an extraordinarily fierce resistance to head protectors.

In the same season that Roger Bresnahan introduced shin guards, he was hit in the head with a pitch in a game on June 18, 1907. While hospitalized he decided to use a primitive helmet known as the Head Protector, invented in 1905 by Frank Mogridge and marketed by the A. J. Reach Company (Dan

Gutman, _Banana Bats and Ding-Dong Balls_, 211). Sportswriter J. Ed Grillo commented, "If Bresnahan continues his policy of protecting himself against injury with all sorts of devices, it will require a small express wagon to drag his pharphernalia [sic] to and from the grounds before and after each game" (_Washington Post_, July 11, 1907).

Bresnahan's experiment was short-lived as were several others in succeeding years. _Sporting Life_ noted the following year, "Freddie Parent, of the White Sox, has discarded his head protector" (_Sporting Life_, April 25, 1908). Frank Chance donned protective headgear in 1913, but it was little more than a sponge wrapped in a bandage (Gerard S. Petrone, _When Baseball Was Young_, 84). In 1914 the _Toronto Globe_ reported, "Pitcher Joe Bosk of Utica wears a headgear with a pad on one side as a protection while he is batting. Bosk was a victim of a bean-ball in 1911, and he doesn't want to run any chances of having the same thing happen again" (_Toronto Globe_, April 27, 1914). A 1917 article noted, "Manager Pat Moran, of the Phillies, has adopted the new cork-cushioned caps for his ball players, believing them a fine thing to minimize injuries from bean balls. If they prove satisfactory it is likely other clubs will take the idea" (_Sporting Life_, April 7, 1917).

The fatal beaning of Cleveland's Ray Chapman in 1920 brought calls for protective headgear. During spring training the following season, the Indians experimented with leather helmets similar to the ones then being used by football players. But the players found them uncomfortable, and the effort was abandoned.

At some point Negro Leaguer Willie Wells wore a modified construction worker's hard hat following a beaning. John Holway reported that this happened in 1925 (John Holway, "Willie Wells: A Devil of a Shortstop," _Baseball Research Journal_ 17 [1988], 52). Other sources, however, list the date as July 4, 1940, or as sometime in 1942. Researcher Larry Lester appears to have pinpointed the events as actually occurring in 1937 and cites an August 26, 1937, account in the _New York Age_. Lester reports that Wells was expected to miss the rest of the season after being beaned by Ray Brown, but instead he made an amazing recovery and soon returned to the field with the hard hat.

The subject gained additional attention from the near-fatal beaning that same year of Mickey Cochrane of the Detroit Tigers. Clark Griffith tried to convince his Washington players to wear helmets but "the players, after taking a look at the lop-sided caps, vowed they wouldn't wear the dizzy-looking things. They'd rather get hit in the heads, they said" (Shirley Povich, _Washington Post_, August 1, 1937). Modifications to the helmet did nothing to lessen their opposition: "Most players argue against the helmets that have been suggested for them. They say such headgear would be too heavy or cumbersome, might make it more difficult for them to see or would not really protect all the vital spots. The real reason is that baseball resists a change and the old Oriole tradition that a player should show no fear, just as he should try to conceal an injury, still holds on" (Hugh Bradley, *New York Evening Post*, reprinted in *Sporting News*, May 2, 1938).

Several serious beanings in 1940, especially one suffered by Brooklyn's Joe Medwick, brought renewed attention to the issue. An advertisement for a batting helmet with earflaps appeared in *Sporting News* on July 14, 1940. Larry MacPhail began to look into the issue and he insisted that all players in the Brooklyn organization wear some kind of head protection in 1941, though he gave them a choice about what type of headgear they wore.

Ford Frick had designed a full-fledged helmet, but the Dodgers' players found it uncomfortable. Instead they chose a design created by two Johns Hopkins surgeons, Dr. George E. Bennett and Dr. Walter Dandy. Their creation, which became known as the "Brooklyn safety cap," was described as follows: "Zippered pockets are cut in each side of a regulation baseball cap. Into one of these pockets on the side he faces the pitcher, the batter will slip a plastic plate which is about a quarter of an inch thick and little more than an ounce in weight. The plate, about the width and length of a man's hand, covers the vulnerable area from the temple to about an inch behind the ear" (*Chicago Tribune*, March 9, 1941).

The Washington Senators also required players to wear protective head-gear, and the press hailed the clubs for breaking "a stubborn Big League stand against this sensible protection" (Bob Considine, *Washington Post*, May 15, 1941). By this time several minor leagues were starting to mandate that players wear helmets as well. Nonetheless major leaguers continued to resist such headgear, and they again fell into disuse.

Branch Rickey brought helmets back with the Pirates in 1952, and required his players to wear them in 1953. The plastic caps, made by Rickey's own company, elicited the usual backlash from fans and players. Joe Garagiola recalled, "It was awful. You see, we wore them all the time, not just at bat. And in the bullpen, the kids would be bouncing marbles off our helmets all day long. The fans called us coalminers, and the things were really heavy to wear" (quoted in Mike Sowell, *The Pitch That Killed*, 289). Meanwhile "rival players thought those helmets were really funny and made such knee-slapping remarks as: 'Where's the polo match?'" (Bob Addie, *Washington Post*, May 5, 1960).

This time the batting helmets finally gained acceptance, though the Pirates soon began wearing them only while batting. By 1958 both major leagues required players to wear either helmets or plastic liners inside their caps. As Fred Hatfield later recalled, "Some of us used to kid guys in helmets by saying they looked ready to play football. If you played before the rule came in, you didn't have to wear one. I never wore one. I had to have something, so all the time I had this little plastic liner inside my baseball cap, on the sides of my head" (quoted in Danny Peary, *We Played the Game*, 278).

Hatfield and his peers gradually gave way to a generation of players who had grown up wearing helmets and had no such qualms. By 1971 all batters were required to wear one.

9.4.10   Earflaps. Helmets with earflaps began in Little League and, as with regular helmets, encountered considerable resistance when first worn by adults. Sportswriter Bob Addie reported in 1960, "The 'earmuff' or Little League helmet made its major league debut last night when Jim Lemon became the first major leaguer to wear the new type protective helmet" (*Washington Post*, May 3, 1960). The sight of a major leaguer wearing a Little Leaguer's equipment provoked "much merriment" (Bob Addie, *Washington Post*, May 5, 1960). Other players bolstered their opposition to the innovation by contending that "the new helmet doesn't give complete vision" (Bob Addie, *Washington Post*, May 3, 1960). But the new helmets steadily gained popularity and in 1974 were made mandatory in the major leagues.

9.4.11   Batters' Shin Guards and Shields. A. G. Spalding's sporting goods firm was offering shoe plates and pitcher's toe plates in the 1880s, but the intention was to protect the shoe rather than the wearer (Dan Gutman, *Banana Bats and Ding-Dong Balls*, 224–225). As noted in the entry on shin guards (see **9.4.6**), turn-of-the-century catchers Red Dooin and Nig Clarke wore light shin guards that they did not have to take off between innings. The custom of batters trying to protect themselves from fouling balls off their shins is of much later vintage.

The first batter regularly to wear a shin guard to protect himself against foul balls appears to have been Vic Wertz, who reportedly began wearing "a fiber shin guard when batting" in 1952 (Louis Effrat, *New York Times*, September 30, 1954). Wertz is best remembered for hitting the ball in the first game of the 1954 World Series on which Willie Mays made a spectacular running catch. What is forgotten is that Wertz's shin guard also played a key role in the game, and that afterward he was more frustrated about that than by Mays's catch.

Wertz led off the sixth with a single, one of his four hits in the game. An outfielder's throw behind him got away and Wertz could have advanced to third except for his shin guard: "When he returned to first and kicked the bag, he inadvertently opened the clasp of the guard. This flapping fiber, which weighs approximately a pound, hampered his running and he elected to remain at second" (Louis Effrat, *New York Times*, September 30, 1954). He was stranded there, setting the stage for the Giants to win in extra innings on Dusty Rhodes's home run. After the game Wertz complained, "I've worn that thing all season and I have my first trouble with it in the World Series" (AP: *Los Angeles Times*, September 30, 1954).

These protective devices played a more positive role in the following year's World Series when the Yankees' Joe Collins hit two home runs in the opening game while wearing a shin guard (Red Smith, September 29, 1955, reprinted in *Red Smith on Baseball*). Collins had begun wearing a "leather and sponge-rubber covered metal guard" after fouling a ball off his ankle in June that led to phlebitis. Sportswriter Joseph M. Sheehan explained, "Self-inflicted foul injuries are not uncommon in baseball. But, except to a few unfortunate players, like Collins and Cleveland's Vic Wertz, they happen only once in a blue moon. Wertz . . . has worn a guard on his right leg for several years. Collins joined Vic in this practice a couple of weeks ago. If Joe has anything to say about it, the guard will be standard equipment for him from now on" (Joseph M. Sheehan, *New York Times*, September 10, 1955).

Since shin guards could pose an obstacle while running, by the 1960s some batters were opting for guards that protected only the feet. *Sporting News* reported in 1965 that Al Kaline was wearing a specially designed shoe with a toe guard on his left foot to protect him against foul balls (*Sporting News*, March 13, 1965).

9.4.12 Sliding Pads. Henry Fabian claimed many years later that he had introduced the sliding pad while playing for New Orleans in 1883. His sister had made it for him, which caused his teammates to tease him that he had simply borrowed her bustle (*Sporting News*, February 15, 1934).

In 1886, Sam Morton took out a patent on a sliding pad that protected the side and hip. The *St. Louis Post-Dispatch* observed, "Those players of the Browns who have sliding proclivities will have the danger of an injury averted the coming season by the use of the Morton patent sliding pad" (*St. Louis Post-Dispatch*, March 13, 1886). The device encouraged hook slides like the one being popularized by Mike Kelly: "Mike Kelly has given Sam Morton's sliding-pad his hearty indorsement. This little invention is to enable runners to steal bases without injury to their cuticle" (*Sporting News*, March 17, 1886).

In 1899, Fred Clarke introduced a "new style of sliding pads. The new pads are adjustable affairs, and are separate from the pants. The old style, which were sewed to the pants, were not suitable because they became stiff and hard from usage and washing" (*Sporting Life*, April 21, 1899). He continued to modify it and finally patented it in 1912 (Dan Gutman, *Banana Bats and Ding-Dong Balls*, 230).

Despite improvements, many felt that sliding pads were more of a liability than an asset. Old-time ballplayer Dasher Troy explained in 1915, "A player does not have to slide often, but if he wears pads he has to carry them around all through the game. They interfere with free motion and are a hindrance to him in every way. With practice he can do without pads quite as well and with little risk" (John [Dasher] Troy, "Reminiscences of an Old-Timer," *Baseball Magazine*, June 1915, 94).

9.4.13   Sliding Gloves. At about the same time, a few base runners began wearing gloves while running the bases. When Ed Andrews and Jim Fogarty of Philadelphia reached base during the 1886 season, they would don "a huge pair of buckskin gloves" to protect them during their headlong "air dives" that became known as the "Philadelphia patent" slide (*St. Louis Post-Dispatch*, May 31, 1886).

9.4.14   Jockstraps. Jockstraps were being advertised by the sporting goods stores by the 1880s (Dan Gutman, *Banana Bats and Ding-Dong Balls*, 227). The identity of the first baseball player to wear one is unknown, and perhaps that's just as well.

(v) Miscellaneous Equipment

9.5.1   Bat Bags. Bat bags have long been a part of baseball. While it is probably impossible to date their entry into the game with much precision, it seems reasonable to assume that they originated as soon as clubs had to carry more than a handful of bats. Bob Leadley, for instance, later recalled that when the Cass Club of Detroit traveled in the 1870s, "We carried our uniforms in a large trunk and bats in a large bat-bag" (*Detroit Free Press*, February 10, 1889).

9.5.2   Doughnuts. Elston Howard was responsible for pioneering the use of the weighted doughnut on bats, which was originally known as "Elston Howard's On-Deck Bat Weight." Howard's widow says the device was invented by a New Jersey construction worker named Frank Hamilton, who showed up at Howard's door around 1967 looking for someone inside baseball to help him market them. Howard became an enthusiastic proponent of the doughnut, explaining, "Instead of swinging two or three assorted bats like warclubs, you swing your own bat with the added weight. It slips right off when you go up to the plate and then your own bat feels as light as a toothpick" (Arlene Howard with Ralph Wimbish, *Elston and Me*, 153–154).

9.5.3   Batting Gloves. In 1901 sportswriter John B. Foster described Hugh Jennings's proclivity for being hit by pitches. Foster observed, "Hughey Jennings had lots of fun flirting that big glove of his into the ball, and many and many a time he was made a present to first when he was no more entitled to it than the Kohinoor [a very valuable diamond]" (*Sporting Life*, April 6, 1901). This certainly seems to indicate that Jennings wore some form of glove while batting, but I have found no other confirmation of this.

Batting gloves can next be documented to have appeared on a major league baseball diamond in 1932, when *Sporting News*' Brooklyn correspondent informed readers that local players "Johnny Frederick and Lefty O'Doul have introduced something new in the way of shock absorbers for their hands when at bat. When Frederick is about to take his turn at the plate, he bandages his left thumb with the same sort of material that is used to stuff shoulder pads worn by football players. O'Doul wears an ordinary street glove when he's facing the pitcher. Injuries led the two Brooklyn players to introduce the new-fangled devices and they contend their methods are better than the ordinary sponge usually held onto the handle of the bat with strips of adhesive tape. Frederick . . . injured his thumb late in the season of 1930 . . . and as the injury seems a permanent one, Johnny probably will employ the shock absorber all the time. O'Doul, however, will discard the glove as soon as his right wrist, injured when struck by a pitched ball in the training campaign, entirely mends" (*Sporting News*, May 12, 1932).

That year Frederick hit six pinch-hit home runs, doubling the previous best and establishing a major league record that still stands. Nonetheless batting gloves disappeared from baseball for many years. Bobby Thomson was given one by a golf pro in 1949, and they were occasionally used in batting practice and spring training during the 1950s (Jonathan Fraser Light, *The Cultural Encyclopedia of Baseball*, 85). Ken Harrelson is credited with reintroducing them in the 1960s and Rusty Staub with helping popularize them.

9.5.4   Spikes. Spiked shoes go all the way back to the Knickerbockers, who in turn borrowed them from cricket. Researcher John Husman reported that the Knickerbocker records show they were using metal spikes with canvas shoes in 1849. In 1859 the *New York Herald* explained, "In both games [baseball and cricket] the players wear a peculiar kind of buckskin shoes with a long spike in the sole, to prevent them from slipping" (*New York Herald*, October 16, 1859). The following year Henry Chadwick counseled: "The bases should be made of the best heavy canvas, and of double thickness, as there will be much jumping on them with spiked shoes" (*1860 Beadle's Dime Base-Ball Player*, 18). The *Brooklyn Eagle* added in 1865, "Every ball player should wear shoes with good spikes, that he can break up at short notice, and stop short, without slipping down" (*Brooklyn Eagle*, June 19, 1865).

A more difficult question to answer is how sharp these spikes were. It is safe to say they varied widely, since those who could afford baseball shoes wore ones of "homespun pattern, with spikes made by the village blacksmith and set in the soles of ordinary shoes by the local cobbler" (Clarence Deming, "Old Days in Baseball," *Outing*, June 1902, 358). Several photographs on the website of the Vintage Base Ball Association (http://www.vbba.org) confirm that quite a few base runners of this era wore footgear that would have been very dangerous to any fielders who got in their path.

At first this wasn't a great concern since sliding was rare in early baseball and was usually headfirst (see **5.2.2**). Yet even without sliding, a sharp spike poses a considerable risk. An 1867 match in Rockford, Illinois, saw two players be "frightfully lacerated by being spiked," which prompted a reporter to suggest that ballplayers "discard the use of spikes" (*Chicago Tribune*, July 6, 1867). Henry Chadwick advised the following year that baseball shoes "should be made with stout soles, having four short spikes instead of three long ones; the injuries from large spikes being very severe at times when running the bases" (Henry Chadwick, *The American Game of Base Ball*, 23).

When sliding became commonplace in the 1880s, the dangers of spikes became increasingly evident. At first, fielders bore the brunt of the damage, but soon they began to retaliate; Jimmy McAleer later recalled that Jack Glasscock positioned himself so that "if you slid into the base it was right into his spikes, blocking off the bag like a barb-wire fence" (quoted in the *Los Angeles Times*, February 7, 1904).

The result was that spikes were banned for a couple of years (Harold Seymour, *Baseball: The Early Years*, 187). The prohibition proved ineffective as the club most associated with sliding, the St. Louis Brown Stockings, began to "wear gigantic shoe plates made of fine steel, and sharp enough to whittle a stick of wood. So it's the same as if they had the biggest kind of spike" (*Philadelphia Herald*; quoted in the *Cleveland Leader and Herald*, May 3, 1886).

Moreover they were greatly missed since, as Topsy Hartsel explained in 1904, "the spikes now used by all players seem to be the only thing now devised which will keep a man from slipping and falling as he runs down the base line." Hartsel reported that no other footwear suited the peculiar needs of baseball: "Various trials of rubber soles and leather cleats, like those of football players, have been made, but nothing except the spikes proved satisfactory" (*Washington Post*, September 11, 1904).

In consequence, spikes were brought back, apparently with an informal understanding that forbade the razor-sharp spikes used by track stars and golfers. Nonetheless it took some time for a consensus on the ethics of sliding with spiked shoes. Base runners such as Ty Cobb felt that flashing the spikes was "a case of beating the other fellow to the punch" since otherwise they were liable to be blocked by an infielder (Ty Cobb, *Memoirs of Twenty Years in Baseball*, 43).

According to the 1928 *Babe Ruth's Own Book of Baseball*, deliberate spiking had gone from being common in the 1890s to being virtually unheard of by the 1920s (Babe Ruth, *Babe Ruth's Own Book of Baseball*, 235–239).

9.5.5 Sunglasses. Looking into a blinding sun was one of the greatest torments faced by early ballplayers. They would have been very grateful to be able to leap forward in time and purchase a pair of sunglasses.

By the 1880s players were experimenting with smoked or tinted glasses. A number of sources report that Paul Hines wore sunglasses as early as 1882 (for example, David Pietrusza, "Famous Firsts," *Total Baseball* VI, 2507). In 1886 the *Boston Globe* noted, "[Tom] Poorman wears blue goggles to keep the sun out of his eyes" (*Boston Globe*, June 9, 1886). Three years later St. Louis owner Chris Von der Ahe remarked, ". . . The grounds there [Kansas City] are the worst I ever saw. They are laid out so that the sun shines in all the players' eyes. Why the right fielder has to wear smoked glasses. That is a fact. [Tommy] McCarthy had to buy himself a pair with which to play" (*St. Louis Post-Dispatch*, May 7, 1889).

Von der Ahe's remark makes clear that such devices were still uncommon at the end of the 1880s, but the next few years saw them begin to catch on. A clear indication of this occurred when Cleveland outfielder Jesse Burkett was criticized for not wearing a pair in a game on August 12, 1893 (*Washington Post*, August 13, 1893). Nonetheless the inconvenience of taking them on and off and the glare created by the metal dissuaded some outfielders from wearing them. In the early twentieth century some opted for eye black (see 26.1.3) instead. Thus the innovation described in the next entry was a godsend for outfielders.

9.5.6 Snap-down Sunglasses. *Sporting Life* reported in 1912, "Manager Fred Clarke, of the Pittsburgh club, has received a model of his latest improved 'sun-cap' for outfielders. This idea is an improvement over the cap worn by the boss last season, in that it permits of the wearer snapping the glasses into place with a flick of the finger, and at the same time doing away with the glare of metal which formerly was found obnoxious. The glasses are now fastened in an aluminum sheath, which is fitted above the peak. There is a small lever which releases the spring and this allows the glasses to drop down into position before the wearer's eyes. Fred showed the idea to several of the St. Louis outfielders and all were loud in their praise for it" (*Sporting Life*, April 6, 1912).

Clarke filed a patent for the device in 1915 and received it the following year (Dan Gutman, *Banana Bats and Ding-Dong Balls*, 216).

9.5.7 Rosin Bags. Of all the items in the baseball firmament, the innocuous rosin bag would seem one of the least likely to prompt a heated debate.

And yet the rosin bag was at the center of one of baseball's most singular controversies.

Rosin (also spelled resin) is a natural substance derived from sap that retains some of its stickiness even in powdered form. Its value in helping the pitcher grip the ball was recognized as early as 1893, when an article noted: "About a half dozen times last year the ball got pretty greased in the outfield, and it was pretty hard to hit. In using a greased ball our pitchers always had a lot of powdered rosin in their pockets, and it wasn't very hard to keep control of the ball" (*Sporting News*, January 21, 1893).

But it seems to have been several years before rosin became a more regular feature of baseball. Christy Mathewson claimed in 1912 that this came about in an unusual way: "An old and favorite trick used to be to soap the soil around the pitcher's box, so that when a man was searching for some place to dry his perspiring hands and grabbed up this soaped earth, it made his palm slippery and he was unable to control the ball.

"Of course, the home talent knew where the good ground lay and used it or else carried some unadulterated earth in their trousers' pockets, as a sort of private stock. But our old friend [pitcher Arthur "Bugs"] Raymond hit on a scheme to spoil this idea and make the trick useless. Arthur always perspired profusely when he pitched, and several managers, perceiving this, had made it a habit to soap the dirt liberally whenever it was his turn to work. While he was pitching for St. Louis, he went into the box against the Pirates one day in Pittsburg. His hands were naturally slippery, and several times he had complained that he could not dry them in the dirt, especially in Pittsburg soil.

"As Raymond worked in the game in question, he was noticed, particularly by the Pittsburg batters and spectators, to get better as he went along. Frequently his hands slipped into his back pocket, and then his control was wonderful. Sometimes he would reach down and apparently pick up a handful of earth, but it did no damage. After the game, he walked over to Fred Clarke, and reached into his back pocket. His face broke into a grin.

"'Ever see any of that stuff, Fred?' he asked innocently, showing the Pittsburg manager a handful of a dark brown substance. 'That's rosin. It's great—lots better than soaped ground. Wish you'd keep a supply out there in the box for me when I'm going to work instead of that slippery stuff you've got out there now. Will you, as a favor to me?'

"Thereafter, all the pitchers got to carrying rosin or pumice stone in their pockets, for the story quickly went round the circuit, and it is useless to soap the soil in the box any more" (Christy Mathewson, *Pitching in a Pinch*, 294–295).

Umpire Billy Evans observed in 1914: "The use of rosin carried in the hip pocket has been for many years a practice resorted to by many pitchers.

By placing rosin on the hands, a pitcher is enabled to get a much better grip on the ball, and in the use of the curve, is able to produce a much better break. This practice has also been much discussed, but nothing has been done relative to its abolition" (Billy Evans, syndicated column, *Atlanta Constitution*, November 8, 1914).

After the 1919 season a wide variety of "foreign substances" were banned in an effort to eliminate trick pitching and rosin was construed as falling under this heading. John McGraw complained that "the rule which prevents the pitchers from using resin on their fingers in order to remove the gloss from the cover of the ball is largely responsible for the fact that they are not getting much stuff on it" (*Lima* [Ohio] *News*, June 17, 1920). Pitcher Slim Sallee was ejected from a 1920 game for using rosin and suspended for ten games (Paul Sallee and Eric Sallee, "Harry Franklin 'Slim' Sallee," Tom Simon, ed., *Deadball Stars of the National League*, 347).

As a rule, however, the prohibition appears to have proved unenforceable. Since rosin left no discernable mark on the ball and pitchers needed only a few grains to dry their fingers, the rule was easy to get around. As columnist Westbrook Pegler explained, some pitchers "would sprinkle the powder on their handkerchiefs, which they kept in their hip pockets, and between throws they would finger the handkerchief, ostensibly to wipe off the perspiration. Or if a pitcher was not addicted to any such refined apparatus as the hankie he would dab his fingers in a bag of resin on the bench. Every well equipped bench had its resin bag, concealed in the trainer's satchel, and one good dab was sufficient to last almost for a full inning" (*Chicago Tribune*, February 14, 1926).

Another ruse that pitchers employed was "using resin as batsmen. It was not against the rules for a pitcher or any other player to rub a little resin on his hands to keep his bat from slipping. And as there are no wash basins on the average playing field, of course, the pitchers have not been able to get the proscribed stuff off before they went back to the pitcher's box. Some pitchers are alleged to have developed an idea that they had to bat every inning, judging from the frequency with which they prepared to grapple with the slippery willow" (John B. Foster, *Detroit News*, February 4, 1926).

As a result, the use of rosin seems to have continued unabated. This caused very little consternation until the notion of legalizing the substance was raised. Most people in baseball seem to have assumed that pitchers derived little or no benefit from rosin and given it even less thought. And yet there must have been a little spark of suspicion that was ready to ignite into a firestorm of controversy.

At a 1925 mid-season meeting to discuss the explosion of offense, National League owners concluded that the ball was not livelier. They decided, however, to toss pitchers a bone by authorizing league president John Heydler "to confer with Ban Johnson, President of the American League, as to the advisability of the umpire bringing a bag of resin to each game and placing it behind the pitcher's box for the pitcher's use in drying his perspiring hands and enabling him to get a better grip on the ball, which now is being done in the Southern Association" (*New York Times*, July 16, 1925).

The joint rules committee followed up that winter by passing a rule instructing umpires to prepare a rosin bag that pitchers "may" request to use. The choice of the word "may" would prove fateful. In February, American League owners voted not to approve the rule, citing the possibility that it would lead to the return of freak deliveries. They contended that the word "may" gave them the choice of whether to adopt the new rule (*Los Angeles Times*, February 10, 1926). Commissioner Kenesaw Mountain Landis told reporters that the option belonged to the pitcher rather than the league, but he made no immediate formal response.

Members of the press were as usual eager for any whiff of controversy to enliven the clichés of spring training. They were therefore delighted by the opportunity to portray the rosin bag as "another test of strength" between Landis and his longtime nemesis, Ban Johnson (Frank Young, "Landis Wants Uniform Code," *Washington Post*, April 11, 1926). Westbrook Pegler fanned the flames of controversy with a very fanciful analogy: "The law was being flouted, so the major leagues, unable to abolish the evil practice, got around the trouble by abolishing the law that made it an evil practice. . . . The same idea might be helpful elsewhere. If homicide were legalized there would be no murder" (*Chicago Tribune*, February 14, 1926).

Reporters also tried to draw pitchers into the maelstrom, but most did not seem terribly excited. When a *Chicago Tribune* reporter polled the Cubs' pitchers, youngsters like Fred Blake and Tony Kaufmann expressed interest, but the great Grover Cleveland Alexander begged to differ. Alexander explained, "Why, a lot of fellows have been fooling around with the stuff under cover for three or four years, and it hasn't helped many of them. I don't like it because I can't handle it. I tried it some years ago, but my hand became so sticky that I was helpless" (Irving Vaughan, "Alex's Off Resin Ball, He Says as Cubs Roll West," *Chicago Tribune*, February 12, 1926).

Another veteran pitcher, Jimmy Ring, was even more emphatic: "All this talk about the resin bag bringing back trick pitching is simply hysterical talk. . . . By the time the resin is sifted through a silk bag, as provided by the rules, it will be of no aid to trick pitching" (quoted in *New York Times*, February 20, 1926).

By this time seven minor leagues had joined the American League's insurrection, forcing Commissioner Landis to issue a carefully worded edict. He observed that "Allowing the pitcher to dry his hands by the use of powdered resin, as specifically limited by the hereinafter rule, does not affect the prohibition against the resin ball, any more than allowing him to dry his hands with dirt (which is universally permitted, despite the absence of any rule allowing it) affects the prohibition against the mud ball, or dirt ball" (letter to John H. Farrell, president of the minor leagues, *Los Angeles Times*, April 2, 1926). He accordingly ordered all leagues, including the American League, to ensure that its umpires had a rosin bag on hand for any pitcher who requested one.

This still left the American League with a loophole, and Ban Johnson was quick to take it. He announced that the junior circuit would comply with the letter of Landis's order by requiring umpires to prepare rosin bags for each game. At the same time he instructed managers not to allow their pitchers to request to use one!

And so the regular season began with the issue still unresolved. By this time the whole escapade had begun to resemble nothing so much as the story of the Emperor's New Clothes. As obvious as it seemed that there was nothing to be seen, there was still the lurking suspicion that someone else might really be seeing something. In the intensely competitive world of sports, the smallest suspicion that an advantage is being gained can easily develop into rampant paranoia.

The atmosphere that resulted is nicely captured in this bizarre account: "[Cubs pitcher] Bob Osborn was guilty of a terrible crime when he started to pitch in the fifth. He picked up the resin bag and dusted it on the ball. Umpire [Charlie] Moran called time and threw the pill out of play. The rule says you must put the resin on the hand and then on the ball. The effect is the same" (*Chicago Tribune*, April 29, 1926).

The 1926 season proceeded with neither side flinching. National League pitchers used the resin bag when needed, though there were no obvious signs that it helped much. American League umpires prepared resin bags for every game, and the league's pitchers obediently refrained from using them, with apparently only one minor breach. On a rainy August day, Yankee pitcher Dutch Reuther asked the home-plate umpire for resin while batting so that he could get a better grip on his bat (James R. Harrison, "40,000 See Yankees Divide Homecoming," *New York Times*, August 15, 1926).

That year's World Series brought renewed attention to the year-long standoff between Landis and Johnson. It was one thing for all teams in the league to comply with Johnson's instructions, but quite another for the American League champion Yankees to concede any potential advantage to their National League opponents, the Cardinals. At least one New York pitcher did succumb to temptation, and it was the same moundsman who had earlier experimented with resin.

The *Chicago Tribune* recounted in mock horror after the third game: "Dutch Reuther was detected in a horrible blunder in the first inning. He picked up the resin bag and dusted his fingers, though it is restricted for use only by National League pitchers. President B. B. Johnson of the American League was looking the other way" (*Chicago Tribune*, October 5, 1926). The *New York Times* reported that Reuther also used the rosin bag in the second inning. But the controversy that had made for such lively press during spring training seemed tepid in the midst of a dramatic World Series, and the issue soon died.

The following spring a *New York Times* reporter tried to revive the controversy when rookie Yankee pitcher George Pipgras used the rosin bag during an exhibition game against the Boston Braves. The reporter observed mischievously that Pipgras "had better look out or the Goblins will get him. This constitutes a high crime and misdemeanor in the American League. There is no rule against it, but the managers have requested the pitchers to refrain, and sometimes a request is as good as an order" (*New York Times*, March 20, 1927).

But it was no longer possible to generate much interest in "the resin bag, which was supposed to work such miracles but which in reality is nothing more than a joke" (Irving Vaughan, *Chicago Tribune*, May 16, 1927). Paradoxically, as it became generally accepted that the resin bag was of relatively little help, this only strengthened the American League's resolve since a competitive advantage was not at stake. Johnson was succeeded as American League president by E. S. Barnard, but both sides remained firmly entrenched in their positions. American League umpires continued to prepare rosin bags for each and every game, American League pitchers continued to refrain from asking for them, and the press and public paid no attention.

That was how matters still stood in 1931 when Barnard and Johnson died, their passings separated by a single day. Newly elected league president Will Harridge announced that the rosin bag would be allowed in the American League, but the resolution of the once contentious issue barely warranted mention in the sports pages (*Chicago Tribune*, May 28, 1931). Three days later American League pitchers were finally at liberty to use the resin bag in a game in the nation's capital. In a fittingly anticlimactic resolution, neither pitcher used it until the fourth inning (*Washington Post*, May 31, 1931).

Chapter 10

UNIFORMS

JERRY SEINFELD has observed that, as a result of free agency, longtime fans of a club are rooting for little more than laundry. The quip is apt, but it must be noted that baseball uniforms have always held a deep significance for fans. As early as 1869, Henry Chadwick recognized that "one of the last things a club should find occasion to do is to change the colors or form of its uniform" (*National Chronicle*, March 20, 1869). By the 1880s it was already recognized that the color of a club's "hosiery . . . has, in some sense, become its trade-mark" (*Detroit Free Press*, December 11, 1881). This tradition is maintained by such current nicknames as the Red Sox and White Sox.

The earliest baseball uniforms borrowed touches from military attire and from firefighter's uniforms (most notably the bib, which was intended to protect the shirt from cinders and other debris). These highly respected associations helped convey a sense that the game was worthy of adult attention. Clubs that took pride in their uniforms have always been viewed as commanding respect while derision has been accorded those who neglected their garments.

Those wishing to visualize the development of the uniform are directed to this fine website, created by Tom Shieber of the Baseball Hall of Fame: http://baseballhalloffame.org/exhibits/online_exhibits/dressed_to_the_nines/

10.1 Uniformity. Uniforms of a team were not required to be identical "in color and style" until 1899. Uniformity had been the custom long before then, though, but occasionally a player did not conform. The most notable example came in the wake of the Great Chicago Fire of 1871, which destroyed the ballpark and possessions of that city's entry in the National Association. The club mustered on in pursuit of the pennant, wearing a piebald mix of uniforms borrowed from other clubs: "[Ed] Pinkham wore a Mutual shirt, Mutual pants and red stockings. Bannock [Michael Brannock], a player picked up for this eastern trip, wore a complete Mutual uniform, except the belt which was an Eckford. [Tom] Foley was attired in a complete Eckford suit. [George] Zettlein, 'he of the big feet,' wore a huge shirt with a mammoth 'A' on the bosom. [Ed] Duffy appeared as a Fly Awayer. Some wore black hats, a few regular ball hats, others were bare-headed" (Preston D. Orem, *Baseball [1845–1881] from the Newspaper Accounts*, 140).

10.2   Caps. The first uniform adopted by the Knickerbockers in 1849 included straw hats to shield the players' eyes from the sun. It wasn't long before the need for headwear that stayed on the head while running became apparent. Around 1851 the Knickerbockers and other early clubs adopted baseball caps, which were already being used in cricket.

10.3   Cap Backward. The sporting of a backward baseball cap (by players other than the catcher) is a recent fashion trend that is sometimes viewed as disrespectful to baseball traditions. Not surprisingly, however, it is not unprecedented. Bryan Di Salvatore observed that 1880s outfielder George Gore would sometimes "play the clown by turning his cap brim backward" (Bryan Di Salvatore, *A Clever Base-Ballist*, 207).

10.4   Knickerbockers. While the Knickerbocker club of New York was responsible for many firsts, knickerbockers (or knickers) weren't one of them. Early uniforms generally consisted of "white duck trousers, full length, a white flannel shirt, and a white flannel jockey cap" (*Williamsport Sunday Grit*, June 7, 1891). To prevent tripping over the long pants, early "ball tossers either strapped their trousers around their shoes, as Uncle Sam does in pictures, or wore them clamped about their ankles like the bicycle riders with trouser guards" (*St. Louis Post-Dispatch*, April 4, 1898).

By the late 1860s baseball was borrowing the use of shorter pants from cricket. The first baseball player to adopt this fashion statement may have been Charley Walker of the Actives of New York, whose 1881 obituary described him as "one of the first to adopt the now prevalent custom of wearing knee-pants and stockings as part of the uniform" (*New York Clipper*, June 11, 1881). The article does not specify when Walker first wore knickerbockers, but the heyday of Walker and his club came between 1864 and 1866.

Although Walker probably preceded them, the Red Stockings of Cincinnati were the first entire club known to have worn knickerbockers and undoubtedly were responsible for popularizing them. They were wearing them as early as 1867 when *The Ball Player's Chronicle* described "the Cincinnatians in white flannel suits, with knee breeches and red stockings, a la Young America Cricket Club" (*The Ball Player's Chronicle*, July 25, 1867). Before the club's historic 1869 season, this fashion statement was already associated with the Red Stockings (Henry Chadwick, *National Chronicle*, March 20, 1869).

Harry Wright is often credited with bringing knickerbockers to the Red Stockings, which would seem a logical assumption because of his cricket background. But researcher Mark Alvarez suggested that George Ellard, who brought Wright to Cincinnati, may have been responsible (Mark Alvarez, "William Henry Wright," in Frederick Ivor-Campbell, Robert L. Tiemann, and Mark Rucker, eds., *Baseball's First Stars*, 177). This contention was supported by Ellard's son, who reported that his father arranged for a tailor named Bertha Bertram to make the Red Stockings' uniforms from 1867 to 1870. While knickerbockers were not specified, the younger Ellard wrote that the style introduced by Mrs. Bertram "has been changed but very little up to the present day" (Harry Ellard, *Base Ball in Cincinnati*, 54).

The Red Stockings' fashion statement was widely copied. A group of Chicago residents who were unwilling to concede baseball supremacy to Cincinnati formed the White Stockings in 1870. Partway through that same season the Mutuals of New York adopted "corduroy knee-breeches" (*New York World*, June 7, 1870). With the country's top clubs wearing knickerbockers, it was not long before they were a standard part of the baseball uniform.

They also became part of the identity of baseball. The shorter pants made long stockings essential and led to nicknames like Red Stockings and White Stockings. No fewer than three current major league teams—the Boston Red Sox, Cincinnati Reds, and Chicago White Sox—are direct descendants of those clubs.

10.5 Uniform Colors. Early baseball clubs had one uniform; it would have seemed extravagant to have another for changing. If they had a spare uniform, it was generally for other purposes. The *Fort Wayne Daily News* reported in 1883, "The Fort Wayne nine will have two suits, one to play ball in and the other to wear when they call on their girls" (*Fort Wayne Daily News*, April 3, 1883).

Moreover most clubs used white as the base color and were distinguished only by the color of such accessories as their stockings, belts, and armbands. This made it difficult for spectators, umpires and fellow players to distinguish the players at the best of times. If two clubs happened to use similar secondary colors, it became virtually impossible to tell the fielders from the base runners.

As noted in the next entry, at least one club appears to have experimented with separate road and home uniforms in the early 1870s, but this was an expense that most clubs were unwilling to assume. Consequently, before the idea of separate home and road uniforms was permanently adopted, efforts to make it easier to distinguish the players were regularly made every three or four years and were just as regularly greeted with ridicule.

In 1872 the Lord Baltimores donned yellow silk shirts and black pantaloons. The enterprising club hoped to remind observers of the state bird of Maryland, the oriole, but instead they were dubbed the Canaries.

The White Stockings of Chicago decided in 1876 that it would help matters if every player wore a different-colored cap. Initial reports on the experiment were favorable, but when some mocking comments were made, the scheme was quickly abandoned (*Chicago Tribune*, April 21 and 23, 1876; Neil W. Macdonald, *The League That Lasted*, 90–91; Susie McCarthy in Bill James, *The New Bill James Historical Baseball Abstract*, 23).

A similar scheme was tried before the 1879 season. The *Chicago Tribune* reported that the White Stockings would be wearing a "queer uniform" that "will consist of a white shirt and white knee-breeches as in former years, but each player will have different colored cap, belt, necktie, and stripe around stocking at calf of leg" (*Chicago Tribune*, March 16, 1879). The *Boston Globe* noted the convenience of this scheme for spectators, who would "be able to follow a man wherever he may go around the field, either in base running or change of position. The colors will be placed opposite the player's name on the score sheets furnished at the gate" (*Boston Globe*, March 21, 1879).

Another National League club announced intentions to follow suit. The Worcesters made plans for each player to wear "a band of his color an inch wide on his cap" with the name of the color being "printed against the player's name on the scorecard" (*Boston Globe*, April 8, 1879). Not everyone greeted the new scheme enthusiastically, with the *Syracuse Courier* dubbing the White Stockings "the Chicago Rainbows" (quoted in the *Chicago Tribune*, March 30, 1879).

The experiment proved short-lived, but in 1882 the National League made a more ambitious effort along the same lines. It is often reported that only the Detroit Wolverines implemented the innovation, but the following accounts leave no doubt that it was a league-wide endeavor. The *Detroit Free Press* offered this preview: "The new system uniforms by position. All the catchers in the league will be dressed precisely alike with the exception of their hose, which will be of their club color, and so of all the pitchers, first basemen, and so on through the list. The report fixes the color of each article of dress for each player. The shirts, belts, and caps for the various positions are to be as follows: Catcher, scarlet; pitcher, light blue; first base, scarlet and white; second base, orange and black; third base, blue and white; short-stop, maroon; right field, gray; center field, red and black; left field, white; first substitute, green; second substitute, brown. The trousers and neck-ties of all players are to be white, and the shoes leather. In the matter of the colors of stockings, the committee, as far as possible, allowed each club to retain the hosiery which has, in some sense, become its trade-mark. The stockings to be worn by the members of the different nines are as follows: Boston, red; Chicago, white; Detroit, old gold; Troy, green; Buffalo, gray; Cleveland, navy blue; Providence, light blue; Worcester, brown.

"This will give a rainbow hue to the diamond and make the spectators wish they were color blind. Picture [Detroit catcher Charley] Bennett in leather gaiters, golden stockings, white trousers and red belt, red shirt and white tie, a red cap crowning the whole! With the addition of mutton-chop whiskers, he could easily be mistaken for a Canada milkman, while [first baseman Martin] Powell will look as if his uniform was made of the pieces that were left over after Bennett's and [outfielder George] Wood's had been constructed. The umpires seem to have been entirely overlooked. Serpentine pantaloons, in imitation of a barber's pole, harlequin jacket and a circus clown's wool hat, would give them a neat and not particularly gaudy suit, and afford a kaleidoscopic effect as they skipped up to first base along with a batsman. A log cabin bed quilt, worn as a toga, would highten [sic] the effect and add dignity to the office. A revived interest in the national game may reasonably be expected all over the country" (*Detroit Free Press*, December 11, 1881).

The *Free Press*'s sarcasm proved justified. Spectators ridiculed the uniforms, which became known as "monkey suits" or "clown suits." If the batting team's first baseman reached first, the pitcher could not tell the two men apart and was liable to throw to the wrong one on a pickoff attempt (William Perrin, "Line Drives Then and Now," originally published in 1928 in an unknown source, reprinted in Jim Charlton, ed., *Road Trips*, 85–86).

Early in the season the *Boston Post* remarked, "Every time a league team appears on the ball field in uniform, the absurd legislation of the League relative to the colors and style of the uniform is universally commented upon and condemned. None feel more sensitive over the situation than the players themselves. The sentiment will be overwhelmingly in favor of the repeal of the rule at the next meeting of the League" (reprinted in *Cleveland Leader*, May 4, 1882). The league held an emergency meeting and revoked the colorful uniforms.

At least one American Association club, the Cincinnatis, also adopted this scheme in 1882. David Nemec claimed that the National League was following the lead of the American Association (David Nemec, *The Beer and Whisky League*, 37). But since the National League had adopted the new uniforms by December 1881, when the Association was still in the planning stages, this seems unlikely.

10.6 Road Uniforms. After the unsuccessful experiments described in the preceding entry, an older idea was revived. The St. Louis club of the Union

Association of 1884 unveiled a dark blue traveling suit. A writer for the *St. Louis Post-Dispatch* noted that another newspaper was describing this as a first, but he claimed that Troy had unsuccessfully tried the same idea in 1871 (*St. Louis Post-Dispatch*, February 21, 1884).

Baseball was still not quite ready to embrace the added expense of separate road and home uniforms. But the game's growing prosperity and the continued need to distinguish players made the idea's eventual acceptance inevitable. A fan wrote to the *Cleveland Leader and Herald* in 1887 suggesting that clubs should wear blue on the road and white at home (*Cleveland Leader and Herald*, May 29, 1887).

Researcher David Ball discovered evidence suggesting that one of the reasons for white becoming customary for the home team was a practical consideration. In 1889, John Morrill became captain and manager of the Washington team and expressed a preference for "having two uniforms entirely distinct, and yet not so different in color and style as to prevent the team being known by its regular uniform. In all probability the two uniforms will be two shades of gray, with blue stockings for both. The darker uniform will be best adapted for traveling purposes and the lighter for use at home, where laundries are more convenient" (*Washington Star*, April 13, 1889).

Over the next couple of years it gradually became customary for the home side to wear white and the visitors colored uniforms (George L. Moreland, *Balldom*, 20). This practice was finally mandated by the rulebook in 1904 and thereafter was strictly enforced. In the opening game of the 1907 World Series, the host Chicago Cubs wore spiffy new gray uniforms with slight pinstripes. But National Commission chairman Garry Herrmann was disturbed by "the fact that it was difficult to distinguish the players of the two teams, and an order was issued that the Cubs must wear their white uniforms to-morrow, while the Tigers will have to wear theirs in Detroit" (*Washington Post*, October 9, 1907). The Cubs reverted to "their soiled and worn white home uniforms" for their remaining home games (AP: *New York Times*, October 10, 1907). Sportswriter Joe S. Jackson noted in 1911 that the Giants and Phillies had had to get permission to sport a black pinstripe on their home uniforms (Joe S. Jackson, *Washington Post*, February 17, 1911).

10.7 Shorts. Short skirts were a feature of the All-American Girls' Professional Base Ball League, which lasted from 1943 to 1954. The intention, however, was to emphasize the players' femininity, and the strawberries that resulted when they slid made it clear that the uniforms were designed with fashion rather than function in mind.

The Hollywood Stars of the Pacific Coast League had a very different motivation for taking the field on April 1, 1950, wearing "T-type rayon shirts and white pin-striped flannel shorts with hose rolled below the knee."

Manager Fred Haney denied that the experiment was an April Fool's Day gag or a sign that the club was "going Hollywood." He said his club would wear the shorts on warm days and even nights and predicted they would become "standard equipment."

Haney explained that he came up with the idea after reading an article about how record-breaking performances in other sports were being attributed to improvements in equipment. He began to think about the baseball uniform and concluded that it was not built for speed. Haney elaborated: "It stands to reason that players should be faster wearing them—and that half step going down to first alone wins or loses many a game. These outfits weigh only a third as much as the old monkey suits and when both are soaked in perspiration the difference is greater yet. And if a couple of pounds makes so much difference in a horse race, think what shedding them should do in baseball." He also felt the shorts would provide a "greater freedom of motion in fielding and throwing."

Haney was aware of concerns about sliding, but he was convinced this would not prove a problem. He explained that he and Stars second baseman Gene Handley had "spent over an hour trying slides in them and we never got a scratch. The boys still wear sliding pads under their shorts and the roll of the sox protects their knees. There may be a little reluctance at first to hit the dirt, but I think they'll soon get over that" (Al Wolf, "Hollywood Stars Blossom Out in Shorts (for Speed)," *Los Angeles Times*, April 2, 1950).

Several other clubs in warm-weather climates experimented with shorts. Branch Rickey liked Haney's idea and ordered a similar set for the Dodgers' farm club in Fort Worth. Pueblo of the Western League announced on May 29, 1950, that they would also wear shorts that summer. Abilene of the West Texas–New Mexico League tried shorts for two games later that season but went back to regular uniforms due to mosquitoes. The other clubs that had tried them also abandoned them before long.

It was another quarter of a century before maverick owner Bill Veeck reintroduced shorts to professional baseball in 1976. Veeck's White Sox became the first major league team to experiment with shorts when they donned Bermuda shorts for a game against the Royals on August 8, 1976. Veeck explained, "We had to wait until this late in the summer to wear them because we had to get the right pads under the socks to protect the knees." The team stole five bases in the game and manager Paul Richards reported "no skinned knees" (*Chicago Tribune*, August 9, 1976).

10.8   Short Sleeves. As with pants, early uniform shirts were quite formal and gradually became more casual. Many shirts of the 1860s featured bibs and neckties, a fashion statement borrowed from the fire companies with which they were often closely connected. They gradually became more casual in the

1870s, and the first club to wear short-sleeve shirts may have been a Harvard club (Susie McCarthy in Bill James, *The New Bill James Historical Baseball Abstract*, 23). Researcher Tom Shieber reports that the Chicago Cubs were the first club to wear sleeveless uniforms in 1940.

10.9   Fabrics. Henry Chadwick declared in 1869, "Flannel is, of course, the only suitable article for pants and shirt" (*National Chronicle*, March 20, 1869). Most early clubs followed this guideline, but not all. Harry Ellard, for example, reported that the Louisville Base Ball Club of 1865 sported blue jeans (Harry Ellard, *Base Ball in Cincinnati*, 54).

According to Marc Okkonen, until well into the twentieth century baseball uniforms remained either 100 percent wool flannel or a blend of wool and cotton. Okkonen observed that the "weight of these wool and cotton flannels was gradually reduced in half by the 1940s but the problems of durability and shrinkage had not improved much. The advent of synthetic fibers in the post-WWII era (NYLON, DACRON, ORLON) paved the way for improved blends." The 1960s saw a blend of Orlon and wool gain popularity. Double knits were introduced in 1970, and their superiority in comfort and durability soon made them standard (Marc Okkonen, *Baseball Uniforms of the Twentieth Century*, 1).

10.10   Team Names and Logos on Uniform Fronts. In the 1860s it was uncommon for clubs to spend money to place lettering on their uniforms. Those that did generally economized by placing only a single letter (see, for example, Mark Rucker, *Base Ball Cartes*, and the special pictorial issue of the *National Pastime*, issue 3, 1984). Clubs instead often wore monogrammed belts or armbands (see *The Barry Halper Collection of Baseball Memorabilia: The Early Years*, 88, 95).

By the 1870s names on uniforms were becoming more common. Susie McCarthy noted that by 1876 a couple of clubs—the Maple Leafs of Guelph, Ontario, and an amateur Massachusetts club called the Skull and Bones—had logos on their shirts instead of the team name (Susie McCarthy in Bill James, *The New Bill James Historical Baseball Abstract*, 23). The Maple Leafs earned widespread praise for their natty appearance: "The breast is ornamented with a maple leaf of fine green silk, which shows the natural 'ribbing' of the leaf, and is artistically done" (*St. Louis Globe-Democrat*, May 6, 1877). It does not appear that the Skull and Bones Club attracted similar compliments.

Researcher Tom Shieber discovered that the Buffalo entry in the Federal League in 1914 was the first major league club to spell out its name in script lettering rather than block lettering. The Cardinals experimented with script lettering in 1918 and 1919 but soon abandoned it. Marc Okkonen reported that the Detroit Tigers brought the feature back in 1930 and popularized it (Marc Okkonen, *Baseball Uniforms of the Twentieth Century*, 4).

10.11   Sanitary Hose. The generally accepted story is that when Nap Lajoie was spiked badly while playing for Cleveland in 1905, the dye in his stockings contributed to a case of blood poisoning. As a result, players began to wear white sanitary hose under their colored socks to guard against infection (Dan Gutman, *Banana Bats and Ding-Dong Balls*, 224). A 1912 article observed: "These days up-to-date basemen not only wear an asbestos or leather pad around each foot and ankle, but have white stockings under their colored ones, if their uniforms call for colored stockings. White stockings prevent blood poisoning if a man is spiked" (*Indianapolis Star*, March 3, 1912). I'll leave it to readers to decide whether the use of asbestos as a protective device represented progress.

Marc Okkonen pointed out that another practical consideration undoubtedly was a major factor: white socks would have been much easier to wash every day, especially while a team was on the road.

10.12   Jackets. The idea of wearing some form of jacket over the uniform goes back to at least 1869, when Henry Chadwick noted, "It is advisable to have a flannel jacket to wear in case of a sudden change of weather, or to throw over the shoulders when in a perspiration and resting after play" (*National Chronicle*, March 20, 1869).

The earliest jackets were designed for appearance rather than functionality, however, as the *Chicago Tribune* explained: "The White Stockings players are hereby served with notice that the audience have seen and admired their new white coats, and generally approve them. They are no part of a player's field uniform, however, and look wonderfully out of place buttoned around a player as he goes to bat or takes his position in the field" (*Chicago Tribune*, May 11, 1877). The *Indianapolis Journal* was similarly critical of the local team when they wore their jackets during an exhibition game on a cold day (quoted by the *Louisville Courier-Journal*, May 13, 1877). Henry Lucas's St. Louis entry in the Union Association was even reported to have jackets made of the "finest silk" (*Sporting Life*, April 30, 1884).

Marc Okkonen reported that by the turn of the century the standard garb was a double-breasted coat "with large pearl buttons and 2-tone trimmings on the sleeve ends, pocket flaps and collar" (Marc Okkonen, *Baseball Uniforms of the Twentieth Century*, 8). In 1906 the New York Giants began wearing a new garment over their uniforms as they made their way to the ballpark and back. It was described as a cross between a bathrobe and an ulster (*Sporting Life*, April 21, 1906).

About the same time clubs started to wear team sweaters over their uniforms on cold days, and the concept of warm-up jackets that were more
suited to the exigencies of baseball soon followed. The *Detroit Free Press*
reported in 1909: "One innovation, made at the suggestion of Ed Killian,
is the ordering of jackets, in addition to the sweaters, to fit over the latter,
for the pitchers" (*Detroit Free Press*, March 2, 1909). A 1913 article noted,
"Ollie Chapman, a Cincinnati ball player, has invented a protective sleeve
for pitchers and catchers to prevent their arms from cooling off between
innings" (*Sporting News*, January 30, 1913). Chapman intended to apply for
a patent on the protective sleeve. By the 1920s the windbreaker style of
jacket had begun to appear (Marc Okkonen, *Baseball Uniforms of the Twentieth Century*, 8).

10.13 Numbers on Uniforms. The idea of adding a unique distinguishing
element to the uniform of each player was around as early as 1879. In that
year the Worcesters announced plans for each player to wear "a band of his
color an inch wide on his cap." The idea seems to have been as much to
stimulate sales of scorecards as to help fans, as the name of the corresponding color was "printed against the player's name on the scorecard" (*Boston
Globe*, April 8, 1879).

Over the next half-century the idea of having numbers on players' uniforms was regularly proposed but was met with surprisingly stout resistance.
Cincinnati apparently discussed the idea in 1883, and it was proposed again
in 1894. Players, however, appear to have believed that the numbers would
make them look like prisoners, and the plans were shelved.

Researcher Tom Shieber discovered that in 1907 innovative minor
league manager Alfred Lawson ordered numbers for his Reading club.
Whether the numbers were actually worn is unknown (*Sporting Life*, April
27, 1907). Shieber also reports that the Cuban Stars, one of the greatest
African-American clubs of the era, wore numbers on their sleeves in 1909.

Hockey teams began wearing numbers on their jerseys in 1912, and this
renewed talk of bringing the feature to major league baseball (Michael
McKinley, *Putting a Roof on Winter*, 85). The Cleveland Indians wore numbers on their sleeves in a game on June 26, 1916. They were soon done away
with, partly because the numbers proved too small to read.

The St. Louis Cardinals announced before the 1923 season that their
players would wear six-inch high numbers on both sleeves that corresponded to their place in the batting order. Manager Branch Rickey explained, "I think we owe it to the patrons. . . . The fans do not know all the
players. Even I, a manager in the same league, when away from home, must
often call an usher aside and ask him who this or that player is. And, if I do

not know the players, how is any ordinary person to figure it out" (*St. Louis Post-Dispatch*, March 6, 1923). The plans were delayed, but the Cardinals wore small numbers on their sleeves on April 15, 1924. The experiment ended after the 1925 season.

On January 22, 1929, the Yankees announced that their players would wear numbers on the backs of both their home and road uniforms. The numbers corresponded to their spot in the batting order, which is why Babe Ruth wore number 3 and Lou Gehrig number 4. The Cleveland Indians joined them in part by adding numbers to their home uniforms. The Yankees' opening day game was rained out, giving the Indians' players the distinction of being the first major leaguers to play a regular season game with numbers on their backs. The Indians won the historic April 6 game in eleven innings over the visiting Tigers.

This time the innovation finally caught on in the American League. The National League actually banned uniform numbers for several years afterward, but by 1933 all teams in the major leagues were wearing numbers.

10.14   Player Names on Uniforms. White Sox owner Bill Veeck pioneered the use of players' names on road uniforms in 1960 during spring training. As with numbers, the new addition was met with resistance. Sportswriter Bob Addie noted that it was a scheme that would "delight fans and disturb concessionaires" (*Washington Post*, March 3, 1960). The vendors who sold programs were not the only ones to express hostility. When the uniforms were unveiled, opposing players dubbed them the "silent scoreboard" uniforms. Addie reported a few weeks later that the names had "been cause for much hilarity among the brothers in arms. A ballplayer beats a joke to death. There are the same old cracks with few variations. The White Sox must be getting a trifle nauseated at the constant ribbing" (*Washington Post*, March 31, 1960).

The kidding must have grown old very quickly. A few weeks later the innovation was reported to have "met with such favor that it will be continued throughout the regular season." White Sox manager Al Lopez commented, "What difference does it make? After a while you don't even think about it. I can remember when I first came up in the late twenties, the players weren't even wearing numbers" (*New York Times*, April 10, 1960).

10.15   Pinstripes. The Yankees first wore their signature pinstripes in 1912 but were far from the originators of this fashion trend. Researcher Tom Shieber discovered that three major league clubs experimented with pinstripes in 1888—Washington and Detroit of the National League and Brooklyn of the American Association. Marc Okkonen reported that around 1907 pinstriping returned in the form of "a fine, narrowly spaced line on the road grays that was barely visible from a distance. The Chicago Cubs were probably the first to use this pattern, but the Boston Nationals went a step further with a discernable green pin stripe on their 1907 road suits. The Brooklyn club was yet more daring with a fine blue 'cross-hatch' pattern on their '07 road grays" (Marc Okkonen, *Baseball Uniforms of the Twentieth Century*, 1).

Within a few years the pinstripes became much more conspicuous. Before the 1911 season *Sporting News* reported that Giants manager John McGraw "has a new idea, a white uniform with black perpendicular stripes" (*Sporting News*, February 16, 1911). Over the next two seasons the Phillies and several other clubs adopted visible pinstriping on their home uniforms. By the time the Yankees permanently joined the trend in 1915, about half of all major league teams sported distinct pinstripes on their home uniforms (Marc Okkonen, *Baseball Uniforms of the Twentieth Century*, 1).

10.16   Patches. Clarence Deming reported that in the early days of baseball it was "the habit of the better class of clubs [to exchange], just before each match, silk badges imprinted with the club name. The players wore these accumulated trophies pinned upon the breast, sometimes with startling color effects; and the baseball man was proud, indeed, who could pin on the outside of his deep strata of badges a ribbon from the mighty Atlantics, Mutuals, or Eckfords, attesting his worth for meeting giants, if not mastering them" (Clarence Deming, "Old Days in Baseball," *Outing*, June 1902, 359).

Marc Okkonen believes that the Chicago White Sox ushered in the custom of sporting shoulder patches in 1907. While the wording on the small patch cannot be read clearly, it seems likely that it proclaimed the club's status as world champions. American flags and other patriotic emblems became a familiar sight during World War I, and commemorative patches have made regular appearances on baseball uniforms ever since (Marc Okkonen, *Baseball Uniforms of the Twentieth Century*, 5).

10.17   Armbands. It was not uncommon for early baseball clubs to wear some form of mourning when appropriate. When Tommy Miller died in 1876, each of his St. Louis teammates wore "a badge of mourning" for thirty days (*New York Clipper*, June 10, 1876). An 1884 account noted: "The Fort Waynes will wear white and black rosettes in memory of their late captain, John McDonough" (*Sporting Life*, August 13, 1884). There were many other instances; Tom Shieber has compiled a list on the Hall of Fame website.

10.18   Retired Numbers. Lou Gehrig, in 1939, was the first player to have his uniform number retired. Retired uniform numbers remained uncommon until the 1960s.

10.19   Rally Cap. A "rally cap" can be seen when all the players on one team's bench wear their caps in an unusual fashion, such as inside out, in hopes of stimulating a comeback. *The New Dickson Baseball Dictionary* indicated that rally caps were introduced by the Texas Rangers in 1977 (Paul Dickson, *The New Dickson Baseball Dictionary*). It seems more likely that it was actually the University of Texas.

The world champion 1986 Mets seem to have ensured the popularity of the rally cap on the major league level. Howard Johnson claimed to have introduced this innovation to the club but noted that he had borrowed it from collegians: "All the colleges have them. One day [after a loss] . . . I was sitting on the bench thinking: 'Why not us?'" (Joseph Durso, "Mets Wear Their Own Style," *New York Times*, July 14, 1986).

Chapter 11

SKULLDUGGERY

"In the scrub games tricks were often resorted to for advantage. . . . These antics prevented the exercise for which the game was instituted and had no good effect."—*Boston Journal*, March 6, 1905

"A winning team is made up of men who will 'turn tricks' when they have a chance—men who study points, and work every advantage to win. All is fair in love and war, and the same may be said of baseball."—Charles Comiskey, quoted in *Chicago Tribune*, April 28, 1889

MANY ENTRIES in this book concern players who sought to bend, reinvent, or subvert the game's rules, practices, or customs to their own advantage. Some went further, perhaps crossing the imaginary line between stretching and flouting the rules. To outsiders that line often seems to be drawn in an incomprehensible manner, yet ballplayers have little trouble understanding it. Consider, for example, the comments of Christy Mathewson and Ty Cobb, two all-time greats with very different reputations for ethics.

Mathewson explained, "Even though the Athletics are charged with stealing the signs whether they did or not, it is no smirch on the character of the club, for they stole honestly—which sounds like a paradox." He then modified Charles Comiskey's dictum slightly by adding: ". . . All is fair in love, war, and baseball except stealing signs dishonestly, which listens like another paradox" (Christy Mathewson, *Pitching in a Pinch*, 143–144).

Ty Cobb had virtually the same viewpoint: "In the minds of the public there seems to be an impression that sign stealing is illegal—at any rate, unsportsmanlike." He explained that sign stealing "is not so regarded by ballplayers" as long as it was done on the field. But as soon as mechanical devices were introduced, Cobb described the practice as "reprehensible" (Ty Cobb, *Memoirs of Twenty Years in Baseball*, 83).

(i) Garden Variety Trickery

11.1.1 Fixed Games. The Mutual club of New York were beaten 23-11 by the Eckford club of Brooklyn on September 28, 1865. The uncharacteristically poor play of Mutual catcher William Wansley attracted considerable attention. After he committed his sixth passed ball, he was moved to the outfield.

After the game a committee of players accused Wansley, and he acknowledged that he had received $100 from a gambler named Kane McLoughlin to throw the game. He had split the money with two teammates, Edward Duffy and Tom Devyr, in order to ensure the success of the plot. The three players were barred from baseball, but all were eventually reinstated (Dean A. Sullivan, ed., *Early Innings*, 49–53).

The extent of game fixing in early baseball is difficult to establish, as suspicions and accusations were far more common than actual proof. The best-of-three or best-of-five format was particularly vulnerable to manipulation and led to direct charges of "hippodroming." In 1871 a Chicago sportswriter wrote in disgust: "According to previous arrangement, the Chicago base ball club was yesterday beaten again—the Olympics of Washington making 13 to their 8. The horse-racing program was as follows: These two clubs were to play each other for 'the best three in five games.' The Olympics had beaten once and the Chicagos twice, and if the latter had made yesterday's game they would have won the best three out of five, and the two clubs could have played together no more this season. So to secure the gate money of another game it was agreed that yesterday's contest should result in a tie [in the series], and thus another game would be necessary" (*Chicago Evening Mail*, July 1, 1871; reprinted in *Baseball in Old Chicago*, 25).

When the National League was formed in 1876, it went to great lengths to depict its product as clean baseball. How much this was reality and how much propaganda is debatable. The 1877 National League pennant race was tainted by a game-fixing scandal while the 1876 race was affected by the "Double-ball Racket" (see **11.1.12**). What is beyond dispute is that professional baseball was greatly damaged in the late 1860s and early 1870s by the public perception that games were often not on the level. The message that the National League had ended such practices, whether true or not, was enormously important to the future of the game.

11.1.2 Double Fix. Baseball's troubles with gambling reached a nadir in a game between Chicago and Philadelphia on October 14, 1875, when "It was openly charged on the field that it was a 'hippodroming' affair or 'double-cross,' players on both sides endeavoring to 'throw' the game" (*New York Clipper*, October 23, 1875).

11.1.3   Umpire Implicated in a Fix. National League umpire Dick Higham was accused of involvement in fixing games in 1882 and was fired. Higham's behavior was suspicious, but his descendant Harold Higham and Larry Gerlach have researched his case extensively and shown that his guilt is not entirely clear (Larry R. Gerlach and Harold V. Higham, "Dick Higham," *National Pastime* 20 [2000], 20–32). Higham is the only major league umpire to be fired for game fixing.

In the years before Higham there were sporadic attempts to bribe umpires, and accusations of crooked umpires were made from time to time. There is, of course, no way to prove or disprove such allegations now. But it seems safe to assume that the majority were simply sour grapes.

Since the Higham case there have been no serious accusations of umpire corruption. That is, of course, first and foremost a tribute to the integrity of the men in blue. In fairness, however, it should be noted that the presence of four umpires would make it very difficult for gamblers to be confident that a single umpire could decide the outcome of a game.

11.1.4   Doing It with Mirrors. A manager who wins games without much apparent talent is said to be "doing it with mirrors." The metaphor corresponds to an actual practice that was occasionally attempted in early baseball. In 1886 a rumor was "afloat that they have a new scheme in Kansas City to disable batters. A small boy perches on a roof outside the grounds, and with a piece of looking-glass reflects the sun's rays into the batter's eyes" (*Boston Globe*, May 18, 1886). A 1905 article reported: "A Toledo bleacherite used a mirror to blind the Columbus players when at bat. Manager Clymer was backed up by the other occupants of the bleachers in having the disreputable and dirty practice abated" (*Sporting Life*, June 10, 1905). Bill Veeck reported that in 1935 the Cubs sold "Smile-with-Stan-Hack" mirrors and added that it was "rather strange how often the makeup of female bleacherites seemed to need attention when the opposition was hitting" (Bill Veeck with Ed Linn, *Veeck—As in Wreck*, 160).

11.1.5   Skip Play. The skip play, by which a runner took advantage of the single umpire to cut inside of a base, was associated with Mike Kelly in the 1880s (*Detroit Free Press*, May 10, 1886; *Boston Globe*, June 8, 1889). Kelly biographer Marty Appel has demonstrated that Kelly had a reputation for using this tactic, but he was far from alone (Marty Appel, *Slide, Kelly, Slide,*

48–49). It was a fairly regular practice in the 1870s and almost certainly originated not long after the rules specified that runners had to touch each base.

11.1.6 Electronic Sign Stealing. Throughout the 1900 season the Philadelphia Phillies were very successful at home. Two men who turned out to have a great deal to do with this were a seldom-used reserve player named Pearce "Petey" Chiles, who usually coached third base, and an even more infrequently used catcher named Morgan Murphy. There was widespread suspicion that the two were stealing signs. Indeed, when Murphy had signed his contract, the *Boston Herald* remarked, "Hereafter it will be the proper thing for a club to carry with it a sign discoverer" (*Boston Herald*, reprinted in *Brooklyn Eagle*, February 4, 1900).

But it was not until Cincinnati visited Philadelphia for a game on September 17, 1900, that the secret was revealed. The *Philadelphia Inquirer* described the bizarre scene that interrupted the game: "There was a scene not down on the striking order at Philadelphia Park yesterday. In the third inning of the first game Tommy Corcoran, the captain of the Cincinnati team, walked over to the coachers' box at third base and began to scratch gravel in a way that made Petey Chiles look like a blacksmith. But there was an apparent purpose in Tommy's scratching. In fact, his actions caused consternation on the bench which is held down by the genial Shettsline, for, while Corcoran was in the midst of his energetic endeavors, Groundkeeper [Joe] Schroeder, accompanied by a sergeant of police, swooped down upon the Cincinnati generalissimo, but not before he had lifted a board, disclosing a nicely prepared hole, in which was snugly fitted an electric apparatus.

"Of course, there was considerable commotion among the players and the spectators, the latter of whom had no idea what was coming off. Arlie Latham was among the first to get a peep in the little vault.

"'Ha! Ha!' he said. 'What's this? An infernal machine to disrupt the noble National League, or is it a dastardly attempt on the life of my distinguished friend, Col. John I. Rogers?' . . .

"Cleverly concealed in the cache was a little telegraphic instrument, by which Morgan Murphy, chief of the signal service, tipped off to the coacher the kind of ball that the pitcher was about to deliver. The coacher in turn tipped off the batsman and there you are.

"Before he arrived in this city, Manager Bob Allen, of the Cincinnati Club, was told that the Phillies were using some sort of electric signals on the pitchers. Allen started an investigation, with the disclosure stated above.

"This may be honest base ball, but the general public has nothing but contempt for people who play with marked cards" (*Philadelphia Inquirer*, September 18, 1900).

Arlie Latham later explained that he concluded there must be something buried under the third-base coaching box because Chiles was standing with one foot in a puddle (Christy Mathewson, *Pitching in a Pinch*, 145–148— though there are many errors in this account). The fact that Chiles's leg often seemed to twitch while he was coaching likely also contributed to the discovery (Joe Dittmar, "A Shocking Discovery," *Baseball Research Journal* 20 [1991], 52).

The buzzer scheme sent—ahem—shockwaves through the baseball world. Two days later Petey Chiles got a bit of revenge on the Reds. He spent the game coaching from first base while standing in the position and regularly twitching. The Reds came out again and began digging furiously but found only a piece of wood that Chiles had buried there (Joe Dittmar, "A Shocking Discovery," *Baseball Research Journal* 20 [1991], 53).

Ten days later the Reds uncovered a more conventional sign-stealing ring in Pittsburgh. It transpired that Pittsburgh and Philadelphia had been aware of each other's systems but had agreed not to reveal the other club's secret (Joe Dittmar, "A Shocking Discovery," *Baseball Research Journal* 20 [1991], 53).

Christy Mathewson contended that Philadelphia gained an important residual benefit from their buzzer. He claimed that the Philly batters had convinced pitchers that they could hit high fastballs during the 1900 season, and as a result got a steady diet of curves in the years that followed (Christy Mathewson, *Pitching in a Pinch*, 48).

The Phillies' buzzer scheme was many years ahead of its time. Nothing as sophisticated is known to have been used again, though clubs have of course used binoculars and the like. George Will noted that in recent years clubs have used satellite dishes and telecasts to learn their opponents' signals (George F. Will, *Men at Work*, 53–54).

11.1.7   Jewelry. According to Patsy Donovan, 1880s pitching star John Clarkson wore "a big belt buckle in such fashion that it flashed light into the batters' eyes" (*Washington Post*, August 9, 1903). The issue of batters being distracted by pitchers' apparel has resurfaced in a number of different guises over the years, as reflected in a series of rules changes to eliminate items that might distract batters.

In 1931 the major leagues banned pitchers from having glass buttons or polished metal on their uniforms. Eight years later it was mandated that the pitcher's glove could be only one color. In 1950 pitchers' gloves were further restricted from being either white or gray. The pitcher was also prohibited from having ragged sleeves or attaching items of different colors to his uniform.

Nonetheless it is safe to assume that rule makers in 1950 could not have anticipated the manifestations of this issue that have occurred in recent seasons. Arthur Rhodes, for example, was ordered to remove an earring that was said to be distracting hitters. Trever Miller was told that he would have to wear long sleeves to obscure the tattoos that cover his arms.

11.1.8 Jumping Jacks. In a game on August 9, 1950, Boston Braves batter Bob Elliott asked the second-base umpire to move out of his line of vision. This gave Giants second baseman Eddie Stanky an idea, and he deliberately moved to exactly where the umpire had been standing and moved around to distract Elliott (*New York Times*, August 14, 1950).

His tactic attracted little attention, so Stanky refined it. When the Giants played the Phillies two days later, Stanky "drove Andy Seminick, Philadelphia's catcher, all but crazy with his annoying habit of planting himself behind second and waving his arms to distract a batter as the pitcher delivers" (Joseph M. Sheehan, *New York Times*, August 12, 1950).

The umpires could find no rule to prevent it, so after the game they attempted to contact National League president Ford Frick for a ruling. Unable to track him down by the opening of the next day's game, they asked Giants manager Leo Durocher not to repeat the tactic until Frick could render a decision. Durocher agreed, but during the game Seminick precipitated a brawl with a hard slide into third base. Durocher then told Stanky to do what he pleased, so he did his jumping jacks again and the umpires ejected him (Joseph M. Sheehan, *New York Times*, August 13, 1950).

A heated debate ensued. Phillies manager Eddie Sawyer called it "unsportsmanlike and strictly bush league stuff." Durocher, however, maintained: "Smart ball players have been pulling stuff like that for all the twenty-five years I've been in baseball and it's perfectly legal as far as I'm concerned. . . . After all, this is not Chinese checkers we're playing" (Joseph M. Sheehan, *New York Times*, August 13, 1950).

Additional arguments were advanced on both sides. Some wondered how Stanky's tactic was any different from a base runner who jockeys off a base to disconcert the pitcher. But others felt that distracted batters would be unable to avoid pitched balls and noted that Seminick had been hit by a pitch while Stanky was distracting him (*Washington Post*, August 14, 1950).

Ford Frick ended the debate by instructing umpires to eject fielders for "antics on the field designed or intended to annoy or disturb the opposing batsman" (*Chicago Tribune*, August 14, 1950).

11.1.9 Corked Bats. The art of corking bats is an ancient one. In 1888, George Wright claimed that around 1860 "a hollow ash bat, loaded with a movable ball of lignum vitae, was used as an experiment by some players. A hole was bored some distance into the larger end of the bat, the lignum vitae ball inserted, and the hole stopped up. This ball played freely back and forth in the hollow, and whenever the batsman brought forward the bat for the stroke the ball rolled toward the end away from the handle and the ball sent in by the pitcher struck the bat at a point opposite the lignum vitae ball. There was little advantage gained by this, however, as the rolling and snapping of the ball inside of the bat often sounded like the 'tick' of a foul ball, and occasioned considerable trouble."

Later in the same article, Wright added, "A laughable thing happened in connection with another 'crank' bat once while I was testing it. . . . Some person had taken a bat, bored a hole in the larger end for about six inches, inserted several small rubber balls about two inches in diameter and plugged up the end with cork, so as to give the bat no additional weight. The idea was to have a springy bat that would not crack.

"I was striking, and neither the pitcher nor catcher knew any thing at the time about the 'crank' bat. A ball was pitched and I struck at it, but unfortunately the stopper in the end of the bat came out, and three or four of the rubber balls flew out in all directions. . . . I was put out on a 'foul,' one 'liner,' one 'pop fly,' and two 'sky-scrapers' all at once. This was certainly discouraging for a batsman, and I need hardly say that this unfortunate episode brought its career to a timely close" (*Boston Herald*, reprinted in *Cincinnati Enquirer*, April 29, 1888).

An 1883 article recalled: "In 1865 and 1866 a perfect frenzy of ball-playing swept over the United States. . . . The game as played then had a breezy range and flavor. The ball, charged to its full with rubber, bounded among the fielders with the ricochet of a cannon ball. One country nine, famous for its prowess in hitting, had its bats made of huge square pickets 'whittled' down at one end. Another team bore vast round beams of bass-wood as large as a man's thigh, bored out and charged with cork to make them light" (*New York Evening Post*, reprinted in the *Detroit Free Press*, May 23, 1883).

John Gruber noted that by the 1870s bats were subject to "desecration by having holes bored into them, in which metal, particularly lead, was poured." As a result, the National League approved a rule change in 1876 that added the word "wholly" to the requirement that bats be made of wood (John H. Gruber, *Sporting News*, November 11, 1915).

The new wording did not of course eliminate the practice of tampering with bats. A game between the Blue Sox of Owosso and the Brown Stockings of Flint prompted charges of doctored balls and "corked bats" (*Owosso* [Mich.] *Press*, August 8, 1877). A St. Louis man named Charles Held even patented a corked bat in 1903 (Dan Gutman, *Banana Bats and Ding-Dong Balls*, 24–25).

Dan Gutman noted that it is safe to assume there was very little bat-corking from the 1920s to the 1950s. This wasn't the result of a change in ethics but rather a change in batting philosophy (Dan Gutman, *It Ain't Cheatin' If You Don't Get Caught*, 77). As discussed under "Weights" (**9.2.3**), Babe Ruth's success with massive bats led to these becoming the weapons of choice among sluggers. Since cork makes a bat lighter, the hitters who did doctor their bats during this era did so by adding heavier substances such as nails (Dan Gutman, *It Ain't Cheatin' If You Don't Get Caught*, 72–73). When batters began to realize that bat speed generates more force than bat weight, corking again made sense.

11.1.10   Ejection Scoffing. It is common knowledge that ejected managers continue to make decisions from the tunnel or the clubhouse. A few have attempted to be more blatant.

Browns manager George Stovall was indefinitely suspended by American League president Ban Johnson following a run-in with umpire Charley Ferguson on May 4, 1913. But the *Washington Post* observed, "Although George Stovall is supposed to be an exile from baseball, he sits near the St. Louis bench and directs his team through a hole. Looks like a case of making a farce of Ban Johnson's sentence" (*Washington Post*, May 12, 1913).

Venice manager Hap Hogan was ejected from a Pacific Coast League game the following season. When he tried sitting in the stands in his uniform and signaling to his players, the umpire again tossed him out. Hogan responded by putting a Panama hat and frock coat over his uniform and continuing to pass instruction along to his players (*Los Angeles Times*, April 18, 1914).

On June 29, 1989, Boise manager Mal Fichman was ejected from a game but returned to the field disguised as team mascot Humphrey the Hawk. He received a one-game suspension.

In a June 9, 1999 game, Mets manager Bobby Valentine was ejected but "reappeared on the bench in a disguise: black Mets t-shirt, baseball-type cap, sunglasses and a fake moustache" (Murray Chass, "Mets Woes Are Hard to Conceal," *New York Times*, June 11, 1999). Valentine initially denied that it was him but eventually owned up and was suspended for two games. He maintained that his action was not that singular: "I've heard of managers coming back as part of the ground crew, or sitting in a front-row seat and giving signs. Or sitting in the bleachers with binoculars, or standing behind a photographer or a TV cameraman" (Dave Anderson, "Manager Issued a Foolish Challenge," *New York Times*, June 12, 1999).

11.1.11   Fake Foul Tips. As described under "Foul Ground" (**1.20**), most of the bat-and-ball games that preceded the Knickerbockers did not include the concept of foul territory. This meant that, as noted under "Bunts" (2.2.1), it was considered good play in some versions for the batter to deliberately tip the ball over the catcher's head. It therefore seemed only fair to credit a catcher with an out if he thwarted this tactic, and this continued to be the rule under the Knickerbockers' rules. That remained the case until enterprising catchers began to find ways to exploit this rule.

Tim Murnane reported that Bill Craver, who was banned from baseball after the 1877 season, "had a way of snapping his fingers, claiming the ball tipped the bat, and often making outs in this way" (*Boston Globe*, January 17, 1915). *Sporting News* noted in 1886, "Ball players in Pittsburg are talking about the smart young catcher of an amateur club, who was remarkable for catching many batsmen out on foul tips, even when the bat didn't seem to strike within three or four inches of the ball. An investigation revealed that the catcher had a gum band attached to his glove, and when he desired to foul out a man he would raise the band with one finger, and when the ball passed under the bat release it. The band would snap against the glove and all within hearing would hear a supposed foul tip" (*Sporting News*, June 21, 1886).

Connie Mack was particularly associated with this tactic, and he later explained how it was eliminated: "Probably a little trick which I introduced and worked repeatedly under the old 'foul tip' rule was responsible for the change in this rule. When the batter was declared out on a 'foul tip' caught directly off the bat, and after the introduction of the big mitt for catchers in 1885 or 1886, as a batter would swing at a ball and miss it cleanly I would frequently clip the tip of my big mitt with the finger tips of my right hand, making a sound exactly as though the batter had tipped the ball with his bat and, as I caught the ball, the umpire invariably called the batter out on a caught 'foul tip.' In fact, in the majority of cases the batter himself was fooled and actually thought he was legitimately retired. Subsequently the rule was changed so that a foul ball had to go at least ten feet in the air or be caught ten feet away from the plate for the batter to be declared out, so this trick was no longer possible" (Connie Mack, "Memories of When the Game Was Young," *Sporting Life* [monthly], June 1924).

An article in the *Williamsport Sunday Grit* in 1891 observed, "Several seasons ago, when foul tips were out, it used to be an easy play for catchers to snap their fingers, making a noise resembling a foul tip and securing a putout whenever necessary. Mike de Panger [De Pangher] used to work this dodge in a more artistic fashion than any other catcher" (*Williamsport Sunday Grit*, June 7, 1891). Charles "Pop" Snyder was also said to have been a master of snapping his finger to simulate a tip (R. M. Larner, "Old-Time Baseball in the White Lot," *Washington Post*, June 26, 1904).

The issue was resolved after the 1888 season with the rule change noted by Mack. The tactics of catchers such as Craver and Mack were an important reason for the rule change, but another major factor was the introduction of catchers' mitts (see **9.3.2**). Thereafter a caught foul tip counted only as a strike rather than an out.

11.1.12   Double-ball Rackets. The fact that only one ball was used in early baseball left considerable room for shenanigans. The St. Louis club of 1876 was later accused of using the "double-ball racket." Whenever St. Louis went to bat a lively ball was used, but when their opponents were at bat a dead one would be substituted. The ploy was said to have been used in a three-game series against Hartford from July 11 to 15 (*Sporting News*, March 10, 1888). Hartford entered the series in a tight race with Chicago for the pennant, but after three straight shutout losses the race was essentially over.

An 1878 game account reported: ". . . Early in Tuesday's game the ball all of a sudden became soft and mushy. No one could account for it, but the general impression was strong among the players that a soft ball had been run in between innings by the visitors. To prevent the repetition of the 'same old game,' the Umpire took possession of the ball just so soon as an inning was finished and held it till the pitcher was in his position ready to deliver it" (*Cincinnati Enquirer*, May 31, 1878).

Researcher A. D. Suehsdorf found an article describing an exhibition game between the Baltimore Unions and the Athletics of Portsmouth, Virginia. In the sixth inning it was discovered that the visiting Baltimore club was substituting a livelier ball for their at bats, and spectators mobbed the field in protest (*Wilmington Every Evening*, August 14, 1884; reprinted in the *National Pastime* 21 [2001], 8).

Alert clubs began to take precautions against such tricks. An unspecified player explained in 1893, ". . . Whenever a new ball was thrown out last season and we were in the field it was tossed to the pitcher, who put his private mark on the same, so the visitors could not change the ball. With our pitchers it was the custom to put two marks with a long finger nail on the ball across one of the seams which would remain there as long as the ball was in play" (*Sporting News*, January 21, 1893).

But new variants continued to emerge, as Arthur Irwin noted. In 1899, Irwin singled out Minneapolis manager John S. Barnes for waiting until his team was ahead and bringing out "a stack of springy balls on tap in his ice chest. The refrigerator warped the rubber in the sphere and when it met the bat, it sputtered feebly into the hands of an infielder like the last dying kick of a Fourth of July skyrocket." Irwin reported that another team's captain "dropped half a dozen balls into a flour sack and pounded them with an ax" (quoted in Gerard S. Petrone, *When Baseball Was Young*, 118).

According to Irwin, New Orleans manager Charlie Frank took such shenanigans to a new level in the early twentieth century. Frank brought to each game a valise that contained "four rows of baseballs. The first row consisted of new, good baseballs; the second row, new punk balls. Those in the third row were balls that had an abnormal amount of rubber in them. The fourth row also held dirty balls, but they were as dead as Caesar. And accordingly, as Charlie's team was in the lead or behind, he would throw out those balls.

"The scheme Charlie worked was this. He'd break the seal of the box, of course, take out the balls, tie a piece of cord around them, and hang them up in a dry refrigerator for a few days. At the end of that time, you could slam them on the ground with all your might but they wouldn't bounce half an inch. The fourth row of balls he had in his valise were of the same sort."

Thus prepared, Frank was able to supply whatever type of baseball would be most advantageous to his team. Irwin added: "Of course, it is customary for the umpire to examine the cover of the new balls to see that the seal is not broken. But Frank had a way of getting around that too. Instead of handing the ball to the umpire, he'd take it out of his valise and slam it on the ground. The box would burst open, the ball would roll out, and the ump, suspecting nothing, would hand it to the pitcher" (quoted in Gerard S. Petrone, *When Baseball Was Young*, 119).

As a result, by the early twentieth century, umpires were taking responsibility for the supply of balls before the game started, which made it virtually impossible for the home team to change to dead balls after grabbing the lead. Even this did not entirely eliminate such chicanery. Dan Gutman reported that in the 1960s light-hitting clubs were still freezing balls before games to handicap the opposing team's sluggers (Dan Gutman, *It Ain't Cheatin' If You Don't Get Caught*, 83–84).

11.1.13 Hidden-potato Tricks. Minor league catcher Dave Bresnahan of Williamsport pulled the hidden-potato trick on August 31, 1987. He threw a peeled potato wildly to third base and then tagged the runner out when he trotted home. The umpire ruled the runner safe and fined Bresnahan, who was released by the Indians the next day. While the play received enormous publicity, there was nothing new about it.

In 1889 a member of the Staten Island Athletic Club pulled a similar play in a game against Yale. The umpire ruled the runner safe, and the player was asked to resign from the club (H. Allen Smith and Ira L. Smith, *Low and Inside*, 116).

Legendary umpire Bill Klem observed in 1908: "An old gag they used to spring was that of pelting some object high over a base-runner's head and then nailing him with the ball in play. Of course that sort of thing was not covered in the rules. But the trick was never tolerated. Umpires invariably sent the man back. Some half dozen narrowly escaped lynching, however, on the stand" (quoted in *Sporting Life*, May 16, 1908).

A player named Marshall Mauldin recalled a Lafayette teammate attempting the play in a 1934 Evangeline League game. With runners on second and third, the catcher "threw wild into left field and the man on third and the man from second came legging it home. Imagine their embarrassment when our catcher stood right in front of the plate and tagged each one out with the ball. While the boys, out yonder, were chasing an iced potato, whitewashed. He brought it along from home for an emergency. The umpire, of course, was standing behind the pitcher with men on the bases and a big beef went up, naturally. Our catcher claimed he just happened to see the potato lying there and was throwing it off the ballfield, but I guess the umpire didn't believe him 'cause he just put the men back on base" (quoted in Dennis Snelling, *A Glimpse of Fame*, 169).

Harold Seymour cited a couple of additional instances of the hidden-potato play being used in nonprofessional games (Harold Seymour, *Baseball: The People's Game*, 127, 588). So Bresnahan's tactic was not new but the reemergence of a seemingly forgotten ploy from an earlier era.

11.1.14   Chalk Erasing. It is a curious paradox that the pitcher's area was being delineated by permanent markings in the 1880s (see **14.3.8**) while batters continue to be confined by chalked lines. As early as 1906 umpire Hank O'Day suggested that white rubber strips be used to mark the batter's box so that batters could not obliterate the lines. But batters continue to stand between chalk lines that they can and do erase.

11.1.15   Obstruction. In spite of rules to the contrary, many clubs of the 1880s and 1890s took advantage of the single umpire to obstruct base runners. The ploy is usually associated with the Baltimore Orioles of the 1890s, but they were not the first to use it.

An 1888 note explained: "The St. Louis Browns are playing as tricky ball as ever, and have added this new wrinkle: Whenever an opposing base-runner is on third, as soon as the ball is hit the entire infield, except the man to whom the ball is batted, will start for home, ostensibly to back up the catcher, but really to block the runner, as each one after the other will cross the base path in front of him and thus retard his progress. They do not injure him, but simply block him adroitly" (*Toledo Blade*, May 26, 1888).

Once it became common to have more than one umpire (see **8.1.3**), fielders were much more unlikely to obstruct a base runner without being detected. But as discussed under "Catchers Blocking the Plate" (**4.4.11**), an unwritten exception seems to have been made for the catcher.

11.1.16 Who's on Second (and Third)? Fred Clarke tried a novel tactic in 1897: "In Sunday's game at Chicago Captain Clarke of the colonels quietly detached the second base from its moorings, ran down to third and, when caught, showed the base to [umpire Hank] O'Day and claimed that he had stolen it and was safe as long as his hands were on the bag. It was a new point in baseball and the crowd laughed weirdly through the misty rain. O'Day called him out, and the joke was on little Freddie. Clarke was sorry a moment later, when [Hans] Wagner hit sharply into center—a hit that would have tied the score" (*Nebraska* [Lincoln] *State Journal*, August 4, 1897).

(ii) Gardening Variety Trickery

The phrase a "level playing field" is now largely used as a metaphor, but that wasn't always the case. In early baseball, clubs often derived obvious advantages from a groundskeeper who could tailor the ballpark to their strengths. Christy Mathewson noted, "For a long time it was considered fair to arrange the home field to the best advantage of the team which owned it, for otherwise what was the use in being home?" (Christy Mathewson, *Pitching in a Pinch*, 291).

Nowadays major league baseball goes to considerable lengths to ensure that ground conditions are standard at all major league parks. Groundskeepers at grass parks still find ways to help the home club, but they do so in comparatively subtle ways. George F. Will explained that a good groundskeeper can greatly increase the chance of a bunt staying fair or rolling foul: "A determined groundskeeper for a bunting team should be able to build an inward slope on the foul lines, a decline of as much as two inches in the two feet from the foul line to the infield grass. Such a slope radically improves the odds on a bunt staying fair" (George F. Will, *Men at Work*, 267). Similarly, groundskeepers can still aid the home club by keeping the grass longer or shorter and the ground harder or softer, depending on the makeup of their club. But these methods are a far cry from the much more brazen tactics of earlier years.

11.2.1 Unplayable Grounds. The *St. Louis Post-Dispatch* reported in 1884 that Cleveland had had several injuries at once during the previous season. So when a slight rain fell, manager Frank Bancroft attached a hose to a hydrant and flooded the grounds. Providence manager Harry Wright had to agree to a postponement (*St. Louis Post-Dispatch*, August 25, 1884).

11.2.2 Slow Base Paths. In an 1886 series in Philadelphia, the home club had pebbles put on the base paths to deter St. Louis's base stealers. The

Browns brought out brooms and swept them away. Charley Comiskey claimed there was fully a foot of sand around the bases to impede them (*Sporting News*, June 7 and 14, 1886).

This tactic and similar ones have remained part of the arsenal of groundskeepers ever since. The most notable instance occurred in 1962 when San Francisco Giants groundskeeper Matty Schwab, Jr., flooded the infield to slow down Maury Wills. The resulting mess was known as "Lake Candlestick." The Giants rewarded Schwab by voting him a full World Series share.

11.2.3   Mound Building. Until 1950 the rules specified that pitchers' mounds could be no more than fifteen inches high, but did not require a standard height. The early history of the mound is discussed in a later entry (see **14.3.9**).

Altering the height of the mound gradually developed into an art form. Researcher Steve Steinberg alerted me to this explanation by Arthur Daley: ". . . Home teams build them high or low in order to take advantage of whatever special deliveries their star hurlers possess. As a means of utilizing to the full the blinding side-arm speed of Walter Johnson, Washington leveled off the 'mound' so completely that it almost was a depression instead of an elevation. Usually it was so scuffed that finding the rubber was not easy. Hence Senator pitchers acquired the understandable habit—shame on them!—of edging up a few inches before each pitch" (Arthur Daley, *Inside Baseball*, 61).

Bill Veeck described the mound as one of the prime concerns of the man whom he referred to as "the Michelangelo of grounds keepers," Emil Bossard. Veeck explained, "Our mound at Cleveland always changed according to the pitcher of the day. Bob Feller always liked to pitch from a mountaintop so that he could come down with that great leverage of his and stuff the ball down the batter's throat. Ed Lopat of the Yankees liked a wide, flat mound. When Lopat was pitching against Feller, we'd make it so high that if he had fallen off he'd have broken a leg. An artist like Bossard takes both pitchers into consideration and keeps sculpting and shaping the mound daily to give the greatest possible advantage to the home team" (Bill Veeck with Ed Linn, *Veeck—As in Wreck*, 161).

Until 1950 there was nothing illegal about such tactics. In that year a standard mound height of fifteen inches was finally written into the rulebook. Groundskeepers continued to tailor the slopes to the preference of the home pitchers, but the growing prominence of relievers limited the effectiveness of these shenanigans. Yankees reliever Ryne Duren explained, "Bob Turley wanted the mound at Yankee Stadium to be flat and since he was the top gun of the staff in 1958, the groundskeepers kept in that way. I preferred it to be sloped. . . . One day, I threw my first pitch and my foot hit the ground and I thought my knee was going to hit me in the chin" (quoted in Danny Peary, *We Played the Game*, 420).

In 1969, after the most dominant season for pitchers in recent history, the mound was lowered to its current height of ten inches. Major league baseball now regularly measures mounds to ensure compliance.

11.2.4   Dimensions. On April 25, 1981, Seattle manager Maury Wills had the grounds crew enlarge the batter's box because Oakland had been complaining that Seattle player Tom Paciorek was stepping out of the box. Wills was suspended for two games.

11.2.5   Soaping the Soil. Another trick of early groundskeepers was adding soap to the soil around the pitching area. Christy Mathewson explained the purpose: when an opposing pitcher "was searching for some place to dry his perspiring hands and grabbed up this soaped earth, it made his palm slippery and he was unable to control the ball" (Christy Mathewson, *Pitching in a Pinch*, 294).

Groundskeepers who used this technique, such as Tom Murphy, tipped off the home pitchers as to where they could find reliable soil (Burt Solomon, *Where They Ain't*, 71). The entry on rosin bags (see **9.5.7**) explains how pitchers eventually discovered an effective remedy to soaping the soil.

Chapter 12

TIMEOUTS

Reader: "Why does a batter get out of the box when a foul ball is knocked and there is a man on base?" Answer: "For the same reason that a hen crosses a dusty road. There is no known reason for either."—(*Washington Post*, October 11, 1908)

IF A nineteenth-century ballplayer could view baseball as it is played in the early twenty-first century, he would undoubtedly be amazed at how the game has grown and shocked at how it has changed. Of all the changes, perhaps none would surprise him more than the frequency with which the action halts. In nineteenth-century baseball something was always happening and players and fans were always kept on their toes, as the examples in this chapter will show.

This was not merely a feature of the game—for many it was baseball's distinguishing characteristic. When American baseball players toured England in 1874, a London sporting paper remarked, "In the cricket field there is at times a wearisome monotony that is entirely unknown to baseball. To watch it played is most interesting, as the attention is concentrated but for a short time and not allowed to succumb to undue pressure of prolonged suspense . . . it is a fast game, full of change and excitement and not in the least wearisome" (*London Field*, quoted in Adrian C. Anson, *A Ball Player's Career*, 73–74). Another British reporter marveled, "In base ball, action is continuous and rapid" (*Saturday Review*, August 15, 1874; reprinted in *Sporting News*, February 25, 1909).

Such statements would certainly not be made about baseball today. Fans accustomed to nine-inning games that often last well over three hours will be startled to learn of sportswriter Charles Peverelly's 1866 pronouncement that "An American assemblage cannot be kept in one locality for the period of two or three hours, without being offered something above the ordinary run of excitement and attraction. They are too mercurial and impulsive a race not to get too drowsy and dissatisfied with anything which permits their natural ardor to droop even for a brief space of time" (Charles Peverelly, *The Book of American Pastimes*, 338).

The change in the pace of the game reflects a more dramatic revolution in the way Americans view time. There is a simple explanation for why baseball is the only major team sport played without a clock: baseball came of age as a professional sport in the 1860s and 1870s while sports like football and basketball did not reach a similar stage until three or four decades later. In the interim, Americans' attitudes toward time had been fundamentally changed by the 1883 introduction of standard time at the behest of the railroads.

Historian Michael O'Malley portrayed this event as a fundamental break: "Once individuals experienced time as a relationship between God and nature. Henceforth, under the railroad standards, men and women would measure themselves in relation to a publicly defined time based on synchronized clocks" (Michael O'Malley, *Keeping Watch*, 145). The result was that the final decades of the nineteenth century saw "a constant process of negotiation and redefinition of time's role and meaning in daily life" (Michael O'Malley, *Keeping Watch*, 148).

This chapter assesses the impact of this society-wide redefinition of time on the game of baseball—how the pace of action on the diamond went from rapid and continuous to leisurely and disjointed, and how other aspects of baseball were affected by that change.

12.1 Calling Time. While they may not be happy about it, today's fans are accustomed to "time" being called on countless occasions in the course of a game. Although players can only request that an umpire call a timeout, these requests are routinely granted unless action is under way. But it wasn't always this way.

The game's early rules specified only that the action began when the umpire called "Play" and continued until he called "Time." The expectation was that a timeout would be called only when absolutely necessary, such as when the ball was lost. Lest there be any doubt, the National League advised in 1877 that "The umpire shall suspend play only for a valid reason, and is not empowered to do so for trivial causes at the request of any player" (Section 7, Rule 2).

That season a batter named John Remsen asked for time in the middle of an at bat. When the umpire granted the request, he was lambasted by the *Chicago Tribune*: "It can hardly be said to come within this rule to stop play to throw the other side off their balance, or to give time to a rattled player to collect his thoughts. It is doubtful whether any excuse can be found for

Remsen's conduct in standing astride of the plate so as to stop the game until he got ready to have it go on again" (*Chicago Tribune*, May 20, 1877).

As a result, at season's end umpires were instructed to be much stingier about granting stoppages. The *Brooklyn Eagle* explained that the umpire "can now only call 'time' when a player has been actually injured or taken ill. Before, the rule was that a player could call time to dispute the umpire's decision even" (*Brooklyn Eagle*, January 27, 1878). The *Chicago Tribune*'s baseball reporter expressed satisfaction that the power to call time, which had "always been vested in, and generally abused by, an umpire, is now restricted to cases 'of illness or injury to himself or a player'" (*Chicago Tribune*, December 9, 1877).

Umpires can be presumed to have been considerably less happy about receiving this instruction. Already filling a most unenviable position, they must have been reluctant to be vigilant about enforcing this dictate. How does one tell a batter that he doesn't have something in his eye?

The result was that the game started down a slippery slope. While the rule makers did their utmost to keep the ball continuously in play, more and more exceptions became necessary. A new rule in 1887, for instance, specifically gave the umpire the right to call time "in case of annoyance from spectators."

Rain also had to be added to the list of reasons for stopping the action, though every effort was again made to keep such interruptions as rare as possible. Henry Chadwick counseled umpires not to "suspend play on account of rain, unless it rains so heavily that spectators are obliged to seek shelter from 'the severity of the storm.' An ordinary drizzle or gentle shower does not produce this effect as a rule" (*Spalding's Official Base Ball Guide, 1890*, 179).

Another issue was blocked balls (see **12.6**)—balls that were touched by spectators. Everything possible was done to keep the ball live under such circumstances, but this only encouraged onlookers to try to help one side by interfering. The rule makers reluctantly had to add a provision that stopped play if a spectator ran off with the ball or deliberately knocked it out of reach.

With each additional new reason for stopping the action, umpires became more lenient toward discretionary requests for timeouts. In turn, such requests gradually became more common and the resultant timeouts more lengthy. Sometimes this was simply stalling, but there were also practical considerations.

Substitutions became legal in the 1890s (see **1.32** and **6.2.1**), which slowed the place of the game. So could the increasing amount of equipment, as was suggested by the reporter who complained in 1898 that "the spectacle of a batsman selecting a bat, fumbling over a pile of sticks like an old lady gathering huckleberries, breeds a tired feeling among spectators" (quoted in Gerard S. Petrone, *When Baseball Was Young*, 63).

As coaching and sign stealing (see **6.5.2**) became important parts of the game, signals increased in complexity. The time that was necessary to send and receive them created additional delays that gradually became routine. Pitchers eventually began to step off to receive signs and thereby put the ball out of play, a practice described as early as 1913 (*Washington Post*, July 13, 1913).

In addition, it had been customary for nineteenth-century baseball games to be played with a single ball. At one time a rule on the books required the game to be stopped for five minutes so that everyone could search for a lost ball. Even after this quaint rule was abandoned, a new ball was generally put in play only when the original one was lost. Only in the early twentieth century did it become customary to replace balls that had become worn or damaged (see **1.26**).

This meant yet another reason for "time" being called on a regular basis, and then an additional pause in the action while the pitcher rubbed the new ball until it met his satisfaction. After the hullabaloo over the emery ball (see **3.2.13**), there were still more interruptions in the form of requests from batters for the umpire to inspect the ball. And when these requests were granted, the entire ritual started anew.

By the early twentieth century the game had assumed a more leisurely pace, and a new generation of players found the rules on timeouts archaic and perplexing. This was aptly described in a 1915 article: "For a good many years you probably have wondered why a batsman always steps out of his box and carefully remains out of it while baserunners return to their bases after a foul ball has been batted. If the batsman forgets to do so he is almost sure to be ordered by the manager or coacher to get out of the box in such cases. This applies, of course, to fouls that are not caught . . . ignorance of the playing rules is usually responsible for this practice.

"Ninety-nine out of every 100 average players will tell you if you ask them, that if a batsman stands in his box after hitting a foul ball, the pitcher can deliver the sphere as soon as he gets it again. But if the batsman gets out of his box, that stops play until the runner gets back. They will tell you that if the batsman remained in his position and the pitcher delivers the ball before the runner touches his base after a foul, the runner will have to go back anyway, before he can advance on a base hit. This isn't true.

"It doesn't make a bit of difference whether or not the batsman gets out of his box after a foul. It doesn't make a bit of difference whether the pitcher waits for the runner to go back before delivering the ball, and if the batsman should whale a pitched ball over the fence while a base runner was on the way back to his base after a foul hit. It would not make a bit of difference either.

"The reason is that the ball is automatically put out of play when a foul is made and not caught. It is just the same as if the umpire called 'time' for an injury or change of players. Nothing can happen legally until the ball is put in play again by the umpire. According to the rules, the umpire is supposed to call 'play' after every foul that is not caught. If you don't believe it read rule 36 in any guide or rule book.

"That the umpire doesn't call this after [every] foul is due to habit. That formality has been neglected so long that it has come to be understood that play shall be suspended until the runner gets back. Legitimately, the umpire is required to call 'play' at the start of a game or an inning before the pitcher delivers the ball, but only a few of them do it nowadays. Perhaps this disregard of a minor formality is responsible for growth of the misapprehension that the batsmen must get out of position after a foul to keep the ball out of play" (*Detroit Free Press*, September 26, 1915).

What's more, as is discussed under "Quick Pitches" (see **12.9**), the unfairness of allowing pitchers to hold the ball without pitching while giving batters no recourse was becoming increasingly apparent. The cumulative effect of these factors was for umpires to gradually become still more lenient about granting requests for time—but not without a fight.

When Ernie Stewart began umpiring in the American League in the early 1940s, supervisor Tom Connolly counseled umpires to "Keep the ball in play" and "not to call time unless there was an injury or something of that nature." Stewart even boasted about denying players' requests for timeout (Larry R. Gerlach, *The Men in Blue*, 122–123). Bill James confirmed that before World War II, umpires "were very much in the habit of enforcing a certain degree of attention to time." Ones who were lax about this "were subject to criticism from the press, and were sometimes fined by the league, simply for failing to 'move the games along'" (Bill James, *The New Bill James Historical Baseball Abstract*, 320).

The fight seems to have gone out of umpires for a very simple reason: night games (see **14.1.3**). James perceptively observed, "Baseball's poetic and lyrical celebrants are fond of pointing out that baseball is the only major team sport without a clock. What these people don't understand is that, until about 1945, baseball *did* have a clock. It was called the sun" (Bill James, *The New Bill James Historical Baseball Abstract*, 319–320). When most stadiums suddenly acquired lights, there was no longer a sense of urgency about moving games along. The effect was dramatic.

By the time Larry Gerlach interviewed Ernie Stewart in the 1970s, Stewart complained, "One thing I detest about the umpire today is that they call time too often. They'll call time twenty times in a ball game" (Larry R. Gerlach, *The Men in Blue*, 122–123). Nowadays twenty stoppages in a game would be a remarkably small number, and too much has changed for it to be likely that this trend will ever be reversed.

But it is worth noting that frequent timeouts not only slow the pace of the game but have also reduced its spontaneity. Early ball games frequently featured players stealing bases while a fielder was busy arguing with the umpire or otherwise distracted. Quick pitches (see **12.9**) have become essentially obsolete. Hidden-ball tricks (see **4.4.10**), often madcap affairs in early baseball, have been rendered more difficult to execute. Other plays that defied categorization are described in the next few entries.

While the increased length of ball games has spawned many complaints, there has been less attention to the specific issue of timeouts. Yet it is important to recognize that the shift from a game in which time was rarely out and in which the action was virtually continuous to one in which timeouts are frequent has removed one of the features that initially distinguished baseball. This has occurred as the result of a series of accommodations to new conditions rather than as a conscious decision.

It is striking to compare baseball to the other major sports in this regard. While baseball has moved steadily toward discontinuous action, the opposite trend has occurred in other sports. In early basketball, for example, every basket was followed by a tip-off at center court. In hockey's early days, play stopped every time the puck went behind the goal line (Michael McKinley, *Putting a Roof on Winter*, 29). In football, the offensive side's option to begin play at any point is increasingly utilized by no-huddle and two-minute attacks.

12.2 Pay Attention! The rules that were devised to ensure nonstop action led to many plays that seem absolutely bizarre to current sensibilities. In many instances the rule makers recognized that their intentions were being subverted and modified the rule in question. Yet each of these examples stays true to the basic principle that players—as well as spectators and umpires—had to be constantly paying attention at early baseball games because action was likely to break out when least expected.

A perfect example is an 1888 account of a game between the Mutuals of New York and the Eurekas of Newark in 1862. In the bottom of the tenth inning, Ed Brown of the Mutuals reached first with two out, took second on a passed ball, and stole third on a close play. He then loudly offered to fight any of the Eureka players. As soon as they had gathered around him, he ran home with the winning run (*Sporting News*, March 10, 1888; the Mutuals did indeed beat the Eurekas 14-13 in ten innings in a game on August 21, 1862).

Another instance was described in 1905: "At the Lowell-Harvard game on the Common May 15, 1867, a new rule was nicely demonstrated; the pitcher must be at his plate after 'called balls' before he could play, but the pitcher had followed the ball too near the striker and Mr. [George A.] Flagg, who was on third base, made a dash home and got there before the pitcher could resume play" (*Boston Journal*, March 6, 1905).

Part of the appeal of such plays was the risk on both sides. A perfect example is a rule that specified that a runner could not advance after a foul ball until the pitcher had possessed the ball. A few heady clubs realized that this presented a golden opportunity for the defense, as is shown by this 1861 account of a match between the Enterprise of Brooklyn and the Gotham of New York: "Ibbotson [of the Enterprise] was the fourth striker, and began with a high foul ball over the catcher's head. Cohen the catcher returned the ball to McKeever the pitcher, who purposely allowed it to slip through his hands towards right field, seeing which, [Enterprise base runner] Smith forgetting that it was a returned foul ball, and that he could not make his base until the ball had been settled in the hands of the pitcher, ran for his third base, when McKeever immediately picked up the ball and stood on second base, thus putting out Smith, it not being requisite to touch the player in such cases" (*New York Clipper*, August 31, 1861).

12.3   Hat Catches. As the preceding entry showed, the emphasis on keeping the action going sometimes led to imaginative efforts to take advantage of loopholes in the rules. Another instance was based upon Section 22 of the 1857 rules, which stated, "If any adversary stops the ball with his hat or cap, or takes it from the hands of a party not engaged in the game, no player can be put out unless the ball shall first have been settled in the hands of the pitcher."

This rule was obviously intended to penalize a player who used his cap, but the Red Stockings of Boston recognized that there was another possibility. They found an opportunity to test their interpretation in a game on September 14, 1872. A. G. Spalding was pitching. The opposing team had loaded the bases with no one out when an easy pop-up was hit to Boston shortstop George Wright. Wright removed his cap and "deftly captured the ball therein. He then quickly passed it to me, standing in the pitcher's box. Under the rule, the ball was now in play. I threw it home, from whence it was passed to third, second and first, and judgment demanded of the umpire on the play." After deliberation, the umpire decided that, the rules notwithstanding, the play would not count at all (A. G. Spalding, *America's National Game*, 165–166).

A new, clearer rule was enacted in 1873 and modified in 1874. The revised wording awarded base runners a base if a fielder used his cap.

12.4   Broom Makers' Trots. Another example of the difficulty of designing rules to ensure a lively pace was an 1877 rule which specified that a base runner had to run back to his base after a foul ball or he would be called out. On May 5, 1882, Cap Anson was ruled out for *walking* back to his base, which naturally caused a storm of protest (Jim Charlton, ed., *The Baseball Chronology*, 47). Most "runners evaded the law generally by adopting the 'broom maker's trot,' a mere leisurely jog" (John H. Gruber, "The Baserunner—Part Two," *Sporting News*, March 9, 1916).

12.5 The Litmus Test. Tim Murnane offered this description of a play that took place in a game on June 27, 1911: "[Stuffy] McInnis of the Athletics went to the plate as the first man up in the eighth. [Ed] Karger, pitching for Boston, had hurried to the box and Nonnemacher [catcher Les Nunamaker] was back of the plate, without his mask on. Karger found the players still walking on and off the field and tossed the ball to the catcher. McInnis reached out and tapped the ball to center, the Athletic players yelled 'Run!' and away went McInnis around the bases for a 'home run,' as no Boston player went after the ball.

"When the ball was hit, [Philadelphia outfielder Bris] Lord was crossing the field to the visitors' bench, and even [Philadelphia second baseman Eddie] Collins, who had stopped to talk to [Boston's Tris] Speaker, was still on the infield. Umpire [Rip] Egan allowed the run. The Boston spectators, the best posted fans in the world, lost their respect for Connie Mack's boys then and there" (*Sporting News*, July 6, 1911).

This play is as good a litmus test of two mutually incompatible outlooks as can be imagined. To the sensibility that dominated nineteenth-century baseball, McInnis's tactic is a heady one that exemplifies the goal of keeping the action as continuous as possible and of ensuring that players remain alert at all times. But to a new generation that accepted frequent interruptions in the action as the price to pay for a game that rewarded planning and preparation, this was nothing but a cheap trick. The fact that this play occurred in 1911 is appropriate because, as will be clear throughout this chapter, the second decade of the twentieth century saw baseball make many steps away from continuous to disjointed action.

12.6 Blocked Balls. A major obstacle to keeping the action nonstop was the fact that spectators often stood very near the field of play. At an 1860 game the field was so closely surrounded by onlookers that "players on the second base are frequently at a loss to know whether the third base is occupied or not" (*Philadelphia Morning Philadelphian*, August 27, 1860; quoted in George B. Kirsch, *The Creation of American Team Sports*, 192). Occasionally spectators were actually in fair territory.

In response, the blocked-ball rule was instituted to keep the action going when the ball was touched by a spectator. Since it was generally the fielding team that benefited if the ball was stopped by a spectator, the rule required the fielders to return the ball to the pitcher in his box before they could retire a base runner. Thus the blocked-ball rule essentially gave the runner a risk-free opportunity to take extra bases.

Play was supposed to be stopped if a spectator actually ran off with the ball or deliberately knocked it out of reach. But since the intention was to keep the action going, play generally continued if at all possible. For example, in an 1882 game, "the ball went into the crowd and became a block ball. Connolley went to field it, and as a small boy tossed it to him, [Joe] Weiss of the Cass struck it with his bat, allowing [Tommy] Shaughnessy to reach third base before the ball could be sent to center. This was not exactly right, but as there is no rule covering such work, it was passed by" (*Grand Rapids* [Mich.] *Democrat*, August 18, 1882).

The blocked-ball rule created some scenarios for which there are no contemporary equivalents. This 1894 account is a prime example: "[Second baseman] Joe Quinn was the only one of the Browns equal to an emergency which arose in the second game at Sportsman's Park Sunday afternoon. [Ollie] Smith, the Louisville left fielder, hit down to short stop. [Shortstop William] Ely made a great stop, but his quick throw went ten feet over Connor's head. One of the spectators, who was inside the ground, picked up the ball. This made it a blocked ball, and it had to be held by the pitcher while standing in his position before it was in play. [Pitcher "Pink"] Hawley had run over to back up [first baseman Roger] Connor. The Louisville players yelled 'Blocked ball' to Smith, who was sprinting around the bases, while Hawley started for the box on the run."

It was obvious that Hawley could not get back to his position in time, and the quick-thinking Quinn realized that only a decoy could save the day. He "ran to the pitcher's box and called to Connor to throw the ball. When Joe caught it, he made a bluff of throwing it to cut off Smith, who was ready to turn third base." If Smith had recognized that it was Quinn rather than Hawley in the box, he could have run home with impunity. But he didn't, and hustled back to third base. By the time Smith realized that he had been deceived, "it was too late for him to make another effort to score, as Hawley had reached the box and the ball was in play" (*St. Louis Post-Dispatch*, July 31, 1894).

This account also suggests one of the reasons why teams were reluctant to use pitchers to back up throws from the outfield (see **4.3.2**).

The blocked-ball rule was still on the books in 1916 and, as far as I can tell, for many years after that (*Washington Post*, July 30, 1916). But long before it was eliminated the rule had been rendered obsolete by several developments. The first was that the building of permanent stadiums made fan interference a rare occurrence. When overflow crowds did occur, it became increasingly common to institute special ground rules and, as the *Chicago Tribune* explained in 1909, "when ground rules are made that disposes of the blocked ball rule" (*Chicago Tribune*, July 11, 1909). Finally, as we have seen throughout this chapter, changing times meant that there was no longer an expectation of nonstop action.

12.7   Throw Me the Ball. During an 1889 game, while Chicago's Cap Anson was arguing with the umpire, "[Chicago pitcher Ad] Gumbert, who held the ball, turned around and faced [Pittsburgh base runner Al] Maul. The latter invited him to 'throw it here,' and he accommodatingly made the throw. Maul let the ball pass him and bolted for home, which he reached before [Chicago outfielder Jimmy] Ryan could field the ball and get it to the plate. Anson did not realize what was going on until the run was scored. Then he began to inquire how the ball got to centerfield. Gumbert answered: 'I thought the umpire had called time, and threw the ball to Maul when he asked me to.' The spectators became hysterical over the performance" (*Chicago Tribune*, April 26, 1889).

The same trick was used in at least three other professional games that season, prompting Henry Chadwick to scold: "It is bad enough in players to stoop to such contemptible tricks, but a line should be drawn when managers take a hand in any such work" (*Spalding's Official Base Ball Guide, 1890*, 132–133).

In 1896, while coaching at third base, Pittsburgh's Denny Lyons fooled future Ivy League professor and university president Ted Lewis with what was even then described as "one of the moldiest chestnuts known to baseball." Lyons "called to Lewis to let him see the ball, and the youngster, never dreaming of a trick, tossed it toward Denny. Of course the latter stepped aside, and then broke for the plate, which he reached in safety, while [base runner Connie] Mack went to second. It was the old, old trick, and [umpire William] Betts refused to send Lyons back to third" (*Boston Globe*, July 15, 1896).

In 1908 umpire Bill Klem referred to this tactic as if it were a part of the past: ". . . The coacher used to tell the pitcher the ball was ripped or something like that, asking him to throw it to him that he might examine it. Then the coacher would side-step the throw and let the base-runner advance. According to the rules, this ruse is permissible to this day. But what umpire would stand for it, even if a big league pitcher were foolish enough to be hoodwinked?" (quoted in *Sporting Life*, May 16, 1908).

Klem was wrong, however. In a 1915 syndicated column by Honus Wagner, Al Mamaux described falling for this trick in one of his first appearances in the major leagues: "It was in Chicago, and I obligingly tossed a ball to Roger Bresnahan, of the Cubs, and darned near lost the ball game then and there.

"There were two men out and Chicago players on first and second bases. Roger was coaching at third base. He was talking to me—not trying to kid me or get me up in the air, but chatting in a friendly sort of way. Finally, there was some sort of an argument at the plate. The ball had been returned to me by our catcher, and I was standing near the pitching mound trying to steady myself and looking at the ball.

"'Say, Al, toss that ball here so I can take a look at it,' Bresnahan yelled to me.

"I didn't give the thing a second thought. I just tossed it to him, and darned if he didn't step to one side and yell to the runners to 'Come on.' They came, all right. Each advanced a base, and they would have gone farther if [Pittsburgh infielder] Jimmy Viox hadn't run like an Indian and retrieved that ball in a hurry.

"Well, maybe our gang didn't ride me. I heard nothing else for a month or more. But it cured me. I wouldn't toss a baseball to an opposing coacher now if the umpire told me to do it. I'd hand the onion to the ump and let him do what he wanted with it" (*Detroit Free Press*, July 25, 1915).

Mamaux debuted in 1913, but he pitched only one game that season and was not charged with an error. So most likely this took place in 1914.

Wagner's column describing Mamaux's blunder appeared in late July 1915. Whether the article inspired him or it was just a coincidence, St. Louis manager Miller Huggins revived the moldy chestnut two weeks later. On August 7, 1915, while coaching at third, Huggins took advantage of Brooklyn pitcher Ed Appleton: "In the seventh inning of the Saturday game, with the score a tie and three Cardinals on bases, Miller Huggins was coaching at third base. Youngster Appleton was pitching and was more or less befuddled by the situation he was facing. Huggins, an alert student of things psychological, suddenly called to Appleton to throw him the ball; he wished to see if it had John K's [National League president John K. Tener's] signature on it, perhaps. The innocent boob on the pitching box accommodatingly tossed the ball to Huggins; the Cardinals' manager sidestepped, the ball went to the grandstand and the runner on third scampered home with the run that was enough to win" (*Sporting Life*, August 12, 1915).

The reception to the play was lukewarm. *Sporting Life* wrote: "It was a smart trick, at least a sharp one, and it is not the intention to criticize Huggins for his part, since such tricks are permitted, but we do protest that such a thing makes a farce of the game, stirs ill feeling and bring [sic] down ridicule upon the hapless wight who is made the victim." Noting President Tener's efforts to eliminate the hidden-ball trick, the article suggested that it was only right to "place the 'Throw me the ball' trick in the same category as the hidden ball trick. If there is no room for one in the game there certainly can be no room for the other" (*Sporting Life*, August 12, 1915).

It does not appear that a specific rule was passed to forbid this tactic, but it seems to have died out at this point, yet another casualty to baseball action becoming discontinuous.

12.8   Team Stalling. Early ballparks did not have lights, which meant that a club with a small lead could stall in order to preserve a victory. This practice had already begun to emerge before the Civil War, causing Henry Chadwick to write in 1860, "There has been one or two instances where this contemptible conduct has been resorted to" (*Beadle's Dime Base-Ball Player*, 30). Stalling became much more prevalent after competitiveness began to transform the game. In a typical example, an 1866 article noted: "the Resolutes began to play a 'waiting' game, by which they succeeded in prolonging the contest till it began to grow dark and the Umpire called the game" (*Brooklyn Eagle*, September 3, 1866).

This tactic was rendered obsolete by rule changes that designated five innings as an official game and introduced the concept of suspended games. But even today clubs occasionally stall if rain is on the way and they think they may be able to avert defeat by preventing the game from becoming official. Such tactics also date back to the nineteenth century. An 1880 article, for instance, noted that, "[Cap] Anson's sharp practice in getting the Umpire to call 'Time' twice on account of a slight fall of rain let the Chicagos out of what promised to be a defeat at the hands of the Cincinnatis on May 8, and finally prevented the playing of five full innings" (*New York Clipper*, May 22, 1880).

12.9 Quick Pitches. The changing perception of the quick pitch is one of the best indicators of the shift in the pace of baseball. In the twentieth century the quick pitch came to be viewed as a dubious tactic and in time was effectively eliminated. There was no such stigma attached to it in the nineteenth century. Once called strikes were introduced, the batter was expected to be ready at all times for the pitcher to deliver the ball.

This precept couldn't be strictly enforced in the 1860s because batters were allowed to be very specific about the pitches they requested. But when the strike zone became larger in the 1870s, pitchers were able to exploit inattentive batters with quick pitches. Henry Chadwick counseled in 1873: "From the moment the batsman takes his stand at the bat, to the time he strikes a fair ball, he should stand in proper form for hitting at every ball, or he will be sure to be caught napping by a skillful pitcher" (*New York Clipper*, April 12, 1873). As this suggests, pitchers and catchers who combined on a quick pitch were not viewed as behaving unethically but as forcing the batter to remain alert.

By the mid-1870s quick pitches had become a big part of the confrontation between pitchers and hitters. Henry Chadwick gave this description of a September 8, 1876, game between the White Stockings of Chicago and the Mutuals of New York: "[A. G.] Spalding's rapid style of sending in ball after ball as quickly as returned to him, together with his frequent change of pace, bothered the Mutuals strikers exceedingly. After striking at a ball, they would take things leisurely, instead of always being ready to strike, and the result was a fair ball would come to them before they were prepared to hit it, and a strike would necessarily be called" (*New York Clipper*, November 4, 1876).

The following season another newspaper account commended St. Louis pitcher Fred "Tricky" Nichols for "having improved greatly since last season, and the rapidity with which the ball was transferred backwards and forwards between [catcher John] Clapp and himself proved very puzzling to several of the Louisville batsmen" (*Louisville Courier-Journal*, May 30, 1877). At the season's end Henry Chadwick reported: "A feature of the season's catching was the general introduction among the best catchers of the leading nines of the rule of a prompt return of the ball to the pitcher . . . [which] enables the pitcher to take advantage of a batsman's being off his guard" (*New York Clipper*, December 1, 1877).

Hitters gradually learned to keep their guard up. The frequency of successful quick pitches declined, but the tactic remained part of every savvy pitcher's repertoire. Some pitchers devised new variations on the old theme. In 1878 pitcher Gid Gardner of the Clinton Club combined with catcher Barney Gilligan on an effective ruse. Gilligan "would turn around as if to walk toward the fence, the batter would wait for him to get in position. Gardner would shoot the ball over the plate. Gilly would turn around and meet it and 'one strike' would send a shiver down the spinal cord of the batsman" (Frank H. Pope, *Boston Globe*, March 24, 1889). In 1884, *Sporting Life* reported another new wrinkle: "[Charlie] Sweeney, of the Providence Club, catches the batsman napping thuswise: The catcher trundles the ball slowly to him; he picks it up, and before he has fairly straightened himself in his position the ball is driven over the plate for a strike" (*Sporting Life*, May 28, 1884).

Some pitchers turned the screws still further by deliberately keeping the batter waiting for the pitch. When complemented by the threat of the quick pitch, such stalling was a very effective way of keeping batters off balance. In considering these descriptions, bear in mind that the impression of never-ending delay is largely a result of the contrast to the usual rapid-fire pace of the game.

One of the earliest masters of the art of purposeful stalling was A. G. Spalding. The *New York Star* offered this description of Spalding's pitching style: "On receiving the ball, he raises it in both hands until it is on a level with his left eye. Striking an attitude, he gazes at it two or three minutes in a contemplative way, and then turns it around once or twice to be sure that it is not an orange or a cocoanut. . . . Assured that he has the genuine article, he then winks once at the first baseman, twice at the second baseman, and three times at the third baseman, and after a scowl at the short stop and a glance at the home-plate, finally delivers the ball with the precision and rapidity of a cannon shot" (*New York Star*, reprinted in *Chicago Tribune*, June 2, 1870).

Another reporter nominated 1890s star pitcher George Cuppy as "the 'slowest ever' and then some," but explained that "There was method in his intolerable loitering. While the hungry spectators were looking at their watches and swearing, the impatient batter was sweating from nervousness and that was what Cuppy wanted" (*Sporting News*, September 22, 1906).

An 1885 piece nicely described the effects of "the tedious slowness of some pitchers in handling the ball. When a pitcher, after getting it into his hands, invariably goes through a large variety of twistings and turnings, changes his position, rubs his arm and his spine and feels if all the bones are in proper position for a great (?) effort before delivering the ball, and repeats the same manoeuvers each time, the spectators get restless and lose interest. The query is often heard 'Is ——— going to pitch to-day?' And if answered in the affirmative, 'Well, I guess I won't go, he's too slow. Life is too brief and the benches too hard'" (*Sporting Life*, August 19, 1885).

The *San Francisco Examiner* reported that George Nicol "is the most energetic young man, perhaps, in his line of business that ever worked here. It is estimated that he walked 10 miles yesterday between the pitcher's box and home. Every time he pitches a ball he walks up so that the catcher can hand it to him. This delays the game somewhat and gives the spectators a tired feeling, but it affords Nicol exercise" (*San Francisco Examiner*, April 15, 1893). St. Louis pitcher Silver King was said to take "as much time to deliver each ball as [deliberative] Senator [William M.] Evarts does to write a sentence" (*Cincinnati Times-Star*, May 4, 1892).

Lee Richmond, before delivering a pitch, went "through the boa-constrictor performance of sliming the ball, spitting on his hands, rubbing them on the ball, and then rubbing off the ball." Once this was completed, he began "a painful working of the shoulders, as though something was biting them between the blades. After this is kept up for some time, and the batter's arms are reasonably supposed to be limp from holding up the bat, the pitcher apparently says to himself, says he, 'Well, I guess I'll send one in'" (*The Capital*, reprinted in *New York Clipper*, March 20, 1880). Batters naturally squirmed during such routines, but they could not afford to relax or a quick pitch might suddenly whistle past them.

By the early twentieth century the legitimacy of such tactics began to be questioned, since all the risk was on one side. In 1910 sportswriter J. Ed Grillo criticized Eddie Plank for causing "a lot of delay by his antics on the rubber. His great scheme is to pretend that he does not see the catcher's sign, thus making the batsman wait until he is nervous" (*Washington Post*, April 15, 1910).

Batters who were put in this situation understandably began to ask for time, and umpires became increasingly lenient about granting such requests.

In 1917 sportswriter I. E. Sanborn denounced umpires for having "allowed the batsman to stop plays by stepping out of the batsman's box while the pitcher was ready to deliver the ball, or even after he had started his windup. You have seen it. With a pitcher stalling for time on the slab, the batsman often gets nervous, steps out of his box, and feigns to have something in his eye or to need more dirt on his hands. In such case the umpires have let him get away with it, calling time illegally in many cases" (*Sporting Life*, June 2, 1917).

While Sanborn was indisputably correct in his interpretation of the rules, he ignored a more basic point. Allowing the pitcher to stall indefinitely but providing the batter with no recourse did not satisfy most people's idea of fair play, with the result that umpires became increasingly sympathetic to requests for timeouts.

Toward that end, American League umpires were instructed around 1913 not to recognize the quick pitch (Eugene Murdock, *Baseball Between the Wars*, 21). The quick pitch remained legal in the National League and, according to Fred Snodgrass, who played in the National League from 1908 to 1916, it was a constant threat for batters. Snodgrass recalled: "You didn't dare step into the batter's box without being ready, because somebody with a quick delivery would have that ball by you before you knew what happened. That was part of the game. The instant you stepped into that batter's box you had to be ready. If you were looking at your feet or something, the way they do today to get just the right position and all, well by that time the ball would already be in the catcher's mitt" (Lawrence S. Ritter, *The Glory of Their Times*, 99–100).

This meant that the World Series became the main battleground for the issue. After the 1913 Series a *Sporting News* reader inquired: "In fourth game of World's Series, [Philadelphia's Rube] Oldring stepped out of batter's box to smear his hands with dirt and took an unreasonably long time to do it. [New York pitcher Rube] Marquard shot one over and Giants claimed a strike, which [umpire "Rip"] Egan refused to allow; was Egan correct; where does Oldring get his authority to suspend play at will?" The paper responded, "It is up to the umpire to keep the game going without unreasonable delays; evidently Egan did not think Oldring was unnecessarily delaying the game; it's all up to his judgment" (*Sporting News*, October 30, 1913).

In the ensuing years the increasing latitude with which umpires granted time to batters gradually rendered the quick pitch obsolete. Its swan song may have occurred in the final game of the 1928 World Series. With the score tied in the seventh inning, Cardinals pitcher Willie Sherdel apparently struck Babe Ruth out on a quick pitch. But Commissioner Landis had ruled before the Series that quick pitches would not be allowed. Granted another swing, Ruth homered and the Yankees went on to complete the four-game sweep (Marshall Smelser, *The Life That Ruth Built*, 384).

While the demise of the quick pitch was largely unlamented, its passing removed another of the elements that had once made baseball a game associated with spontaneity.

12.10   Human Rain Delays. In the 1970s and '80s, Mike Hargrove became known as the "Human Rain Delay" for his painstaking preparations while batting. Deliberate batsmen such as Hargrove and Nomar Garciaparra often take the brunt of the frustration that many fans feel over the slow pace of today's game. But they were far from the first to attract such criticisms.

As noted in the preceding entry, in the early days of baseball batters could not afford to stall lest they fall victim to a quick pitch. Moreover they weren't even supposed to take their time coming to the plate, with an 1880 article declaring: "It should be the duty of each Captain and his assistant to see that every player who is next at bat has his bat in hand, and that he runs to the plate and gets ready for striking. A good way to secure this would be to fine a few of the laggards who keep the spectators waiting for their laziness" (*Chicago Tribune*, May 7, 1880). This precept was reinforced by an 1882 rule that counseled the next two batters to be waiting for their turn with bats in hand.

When umpires began to grant discretionary timeouts, stalling by batters began to be part of the game. The *Youngstown Vindicator* reported in 1898: "[Thayer] Torreyson at the bat is a study. He takes a crouching position, lunges fiercely at the first high one pitched; if he misses connection, down goes the bat, he expectorates in both hands, grabs up two hands full of earth, drops it, rubs his hands on his new uniform, snatches up the stick and resumes his crouching posture" (*Youngstown Vindicator*, April 26, 1898).

Hugh S. Fullerton enumerated several other slowpokes: "Did you ever watch Frank Chance come to bat? He steps up, grasps his bat, taps the plate, holds his bat in his right hand, while he pulls up his belt with his left, places his bat between his legs, pulls his cap on tighter, pulls up his trousers, grabs the bat again, taps the plate, and is ready. He goes through these same motions every time he faces a pitcher, and it is a cinch he wouldn't hit .200 if forced to leave them out.

"Kip Selbach was another who had a pantomime he had to perform before hitting. He adjusts belt, cap, trousers, then raps his left foot with the bat, holds up his right foot and raps that, knocking all the dirt out of his spikes, and then, after another pull at his cap, is ready for business. He is a nervous hitter, and pitchers like Clark Griffith used to take advantage of his nervousness and keep him fretting by delaying the pitch until he couldn't hit much of anything. Dad Clarke vowed that Selbach couldn't take the ball in his hands and make a hit if the pitcher was slow, and it is notorious that Selbach never could hit those slow ball pitchers—especially the infamous Nig Cuppy.

"Another pantomimist was Pete Browning, who went through all sorts of antics before settling down to hit. He rearranged most of his clothing before he stepped up" (*Chicago Tribune*, April 29, 1906).

Hughey Jennings recalled that "every time ['Socks' Seybold] went to the plate he felt obliged to go through a whole rigmarole of stunts which would take him a full minute or more to perform" (quoted in F. C. Lane, *Batting*, 208). Walter McCreedie was described as going "through the tactics in preparing to bat that made Al. Selbach famous. He knocks the dirt off the soles of his shoes, gives his trousers a hitch, pulls down the peak of his cap, gives his trousers another hitch, and pulls down the back of his cap. Then he is ready for action" (*Sporting Life*, May 2, 1903).

It might be assumed that the difference between these early "pantomimists" and the more recent vintage is that today's batters are allowed to go through these rituals *between every pitch*. But Sy Sutcliffe was described in 1885 as "very anxious to hit the ball, and looks as though he can hardly wait to have it pitched to him. He gives his shoulders a rock, hitches up his pants nervously, spits on his hands, rocks again, taps the plate hurriedly and shifts about restlessly until he strikes. Then, if he misses, he hurriedly taps the plate again and goes over the previous performance" (*Sporting Life*, September 23, 1885).

12.11   Commercial Breaks. When baseball games first began to be televised, the assumption was that any commercials would be worked around the action, rather than the other way around. In 1965 columnist Bucky Summers observed of an ABC telecast: "There was a commercial at the end of each half inning, but this was expected. Much to the credit of baseball was the fact that the game was not held up in order to complete the speel before play was resumed. . . . This in itself was refreshing after suffering through football season when the paying customers are forced to wait until the commercial is over before anything happens" (Bucky Summers, "Still Baseball on TV," *Frederick* [Md.] *Post*, April 20, 1965). It would not be long before baseball would go the way of football.

Bibliography

BOOKS

1864 American Boy's Book of Sports and Games (New York, 1864; reprint New York, 2000)

Melvin L. Adelman, *A Sporting Time: New York City and the Rise of Modern Athletics, 1820–70* (Urbana, Ill., 1986)

Aetna Base Ball Association Constitution and By-Laws (unpublished logbook; Burton Collection, Detroit Public Library)

Lee Allen, *Cooperstown Corner: Columns from the Sporting News, 1962–1969* (Cleveland, 1990)

Lee Allen, *The Hot Stove League* (New York, 1955; reprint Kingston, N.Y., 2000)

David W. Anderson, *More Than Merkle* (Lincoln, Nebr., 2000)

Will Anderson, *Was Baseball Really Invented in Maine?* (Portland, Me., 1992)

Roger Angell, *Once More Around the Park: A Baseball Reader* (New York, 1991; reprint Chicago, 2001)

Roger Angell, *A Pitcher's Story: Innings with David Cone* (New York, 2001)

Roger Angell, *The Summer Game* (New York, 1972)

Adrian C. "Cap" Anson, *A Ball Player's Career* (Chicago, 1900; reprint Mattituck, N.Y., n.d.)

Marty Appel, *Slide, Kelly, Slide: The Wild Life and Times of Mike "King" Kelly, Baseball's First Superstar* (Lanham, Md., 1999)

Marty Appel, *Yesterday's Heroes* (New York, 1988)

David Arcidiacono, *Grace, Grit and Growling* (East Hampton, Conn., 2003)

Jean Hastings Ardell, *Breaking into Baseball: Women and the National Pastime* (Carbondale, Ill., 2005)

Gustav Axelson, *Commy: The Life Story of Charles A. Comiskey* (Chicago, 1919)

Walter Bagehot, *The English Constitution* (London, 1867)

Red Barber, *The Broadcasters* (New York, 1970)

The Barry Halper Collection of Baseball Memorabilia (New York, 1999)

Gai Ingham Berlage, *Women in Baseball: The Forgotten History* (Westport, Conn., 1994)

Charles W. Bevis, *Sunday Baseball: The Major Leagues' Struggle to Play Baseball on the Lord's Day, 1876–1934* (Jefferson, N.C., 2003)

David Block, *Baseball Before We Knew It* (Lincoln, Nebr., 2005)

Don Bollman, *Run for the Roses: A Fifty Year Memoir* (Mecosta, Mich., 1975)

Bill Borst, *Baseball Through a Knothole: A St. Louis History* (St. Louis, 1980)

Talmage Boston, *1939, Baseball's Pivotal Year: From the Golden Age to the Modern Era* (Fort Worth, Tex., 1994)

Jim Bouton, edited by Leonard Shecter, *Ball Four: My Life and Hard Times Throwing the Knuckleball in the Big Leagues* (New York, 1970)

Larry G. Bowman, *Before the World Series: Pride, Profits and Baseball's First Championships* (De Kalb, Ill., 2003)

James H. Bready, *Baseball in Baltimore* (Baltimore, 1998)

Eric Bronson, ed., *Baseball and Philosophy: Thinking Outside the Batter's Box* (Chicago, 2004)

Jim Brosnan, *The Long Season* (New York, 1960; reprint Chicago, 2002)

Warren Brown, *The Chicago Cubs* (New York, 1946; reprint Carbondale, Ill., 2001)

Lois Browne, *Girls of Summer: The Real Story of the All-American Girls Professional Baseball League* (Toronto, 1992)

Reed Browning, *Baseball's Greatest Season, 1924* (Amherst, Mass., 2003)

Reed Browning, *Cy Young: A Baseball Life* (Amherst, Mass., 2000)

Robert F. Burk, *Much More Than a Game: Players, Owners and American Baseball Since 1921* (Chapel Hill, N.C., 2001)

Robert F. Burk, *Never Just a Game: Players, Owners and American Baseball to 1920* (Chapel Hill, N.C., 1994)

J. P. Caillault, *A Tale of Four Cities* (Jefferson, N.C., 2003)

Bob Carroll, *Baseball Between the Lies* (New York, 1993)

Robin Carver, *The Boy's and Girl's Book of Sports* (Boston, 1834)

Jon David Cash, *Before They Were Cardinals: Major League Baseball in Nineteenth-Century St. Louis* (Columbia, Mo., 2002)

Jerrold Casway, *Ed Delahanty in the Emerald Age of Baseball* (Notre Dame, Ind., 2004)

David Cataneo, *Tony C.: The Triumph and Tragedy of Tony Conigliaro* (Nashville, 1997)

Henry Chadwick, *Chadwick's Base Ball Manual* (London, 1874)

Henry Chadwick, *The American Game of Base Ball* (aka *The Game of Base Ball. How to Learn It, How to Play It, and How to Teach It. With Sketches of Noted Players*) (1868; reprint Columbia, S.C., 1983)

Henry Chadwick, *Beadle's Dime Base-Ball Player* (1860) (reprint: Morgantown, Pa., 1996) (later editions are occasionally cited, but this guide changed little from year to year)

Henry Chadwick, *DeWitt's Base Ball Umpire's Guide* (various years)

Henry Chadwick, *Haney's Base Ball Book of Reference for 1867* (aka *The Base Ball Player's Book of Reference*) (New York, 1867)

James Charlton, ed., *The Baseball Chronology: The Complete History of Significant Events in the Game of Baseball* (New York, 1991)

James Charlton, ed., *Road Trips* (Cleveland, 2004)

Seymour R. Church, *Base Ball: The History, Statistics and Romance of the American National Game from Its Inception to the Present Time* (San Francisco, 1902; reprint Princeton, N.J., 1974)

Dick Clark and Larry Lester, eds., *The Negro Leagues Book* (Cleveland, 1994)

Jerry E. Clark, *Anson to Zuber: Iowa Boys in the Major Leagues* (Omaha, 1992)

Ty Cobb, *Bustin' 'Em and Other Big League Stories* (New York, 1914; reprint William R. Cobb, ed., Marietta, Ga., 2003)

Ty Cobb, *Memoirs of Twenty Years in Baseball* (1925; reprint William R. Cobb, ed., Marietta, Ga., 2002)

Mickey Cochrane, *Baseball: The Fans' Game* (New York, 1939; reprint Cleveland, 1992)

William Curran, *Big Sticks: The Phenomenal Decade of Ruth, Gehrig, Cobb, and Hornsby* (New York, 1990)

William Curran, *Mitts: A Celebration of the Art of Fielding* (New York, 1985)

Arthur Daley, *Inside Baseball: A Half Century of the National Pastime* (New York, 1950)

Bill Deane, *Award Voting* (Kansas City, 1988)

Jordan Deutsch, Richard M. Cohen, Roland T. Johnson, and David S. Neft, eds., *The Scrapbook History of Baseball* (Indianapolis, 1975)

Donald Dewey and Nicholas Acocella, *The Ball Clubs: Every Franchise, Past and Present, Officially Recognized by Major League Baseball* (New York, 1996)

Paul Dickson, ed., *Baseball's Greatest Quotations* (New York, 1991)

Paul Dickson, *The Hidden Language of Baseball: How Signs and Sign-Stealing Have Influenced the Course of Our National Pastime* (New York, 2003)

Paul Dickson, ed., *The New Dickson Baseball Dictionary* (New York, 1999)

Paul Dickson, *The Worth Book of Softball: A Celebration of America's True National Pastime* (New York, 1994)

James M. DiClerico and Barry J. Pavelec, *The Jersey Game: The History of Modern Baseball from Its Birth to the Big Leagues in the Garden State* (New Brunswick, N.J., 1991)

Bryan Di Salvatore, *A Clever Base-Ballist: The Life and Times of John Montgomery Ward* (New York, 1999)

Phil Dixon and Patrick J. Hannigan, *The Negro Baseball Leagues: A Photographic History* (Mattituck, N.Y., 1992)

Dick Dobbins and Jon Twichell, *Nuggets on the Diamond* (San Francisco, 1994)

Bert Dunne, *Play Ball!* (Garden City, N.Y., 1947)

Bob Edwards, *Fridays with Red: A Radio Friendship* (New York, 1993)

James E. Elfers, *The Tour to End All Tours* (Lincoln, Nebr., 2003)

Harry Ellard, *Base Ball in Cincinnati: A History* (1907; reprint Jefferson, N.C., 2004)

John J. Evers and Hugh S. Fullerton, *Touching Second: The Science of Baseball* (Chicago, 1910; reprint Mattituck, N.Y., n.d.)

David Falkner, *Nine Sides of the Diamond: Baseball's Great Glove Men on the Fine Art of Defense* (New York, 1990)

Federal Writers' Project, *Baseball in Old Chicago* (Chicago, 1939)

G. H. Fleming, *The Unforgettable Season* (New York, 1981)

Stephen Fox, *Big Leagues: Professional Baseball, Football, and Basketball in National Memory* (New York, 1994)

Joel S. Franks, *Whose Baseball? The National Pastime and Cultural Diversity in California, 1859–1941* (Lanham, Md., 2001)

Ford Frick, *Games, Asterisks and People: Memoirs of a Lucky Fan* (New York, 1973)

Cappy Gagnon, *Notre Dame Baseball Greats: From Anson to Yaz* (Charleston, S.C., 2004)

Larry R. Gerlach, *The Men in Blue: Conversations with Umpires* (New York, 1980)

Michael Gershman, *Diamonds: The Evolution of the Ballpark* (Boston, 1993)

A. Bartlett Giamatti, *Take Time for Paradise: Americans and Their Games* (New York, 1989)

Malcolm Gladwell, *The Tipping Point: How Little Things Can Make a Big Difference* (Boston, 2000)

George Gmelch and J. J. Weiner, *In the Ballpark: The Working Lives of Baseball People* (Washington, D.C., 1998)

Warren Goldstein, *Playing for Keeps: A History of Early Baseball* (Ithaca, N.Y., 1989)

Peter Golenbock, *Wrigleyville: A Magical History Tour of the Chicago Cubs* (New York, 1999)

Roberto Gonzalez Echevarria, *The Pride of Havana: A History of Cuban Baseball* (New York, 1999)

Tom Gorman, as told to Jerome Holtzman, *Three and Two!* (New York, 1979)

Guy W. Green, *Fun and Frolic with an Indian Ball Team* (1907; reprint Mattituck, N.Y., 1992)

Robert Gregory, *Diz: The History of Dizzy Dean and Baseball During the Great Depression* (New York, 1992)

Stephen Guschov, *The Red Stockings of Cincinnati: Base Ball's First All-Professional Team and Its Historic 1869 and 1870 Seasons* (Jefferson, N.C., 1998)

Dan Gutman, *Banana Bats and Ding-Dong Balls: A Century of Unique Baseball Inventions* (New York, 1995)

Dan Gutman, *It Ain't Cheatin' If You Don't Get Caught: Scuffing, Corking, Spitting, Gunking, Razzing, and Other Fundamentals of Our National Pastime* (New York, 1990)

Allen Guttmann, *Sports Spectators* (New York, 1986)

David Halberstam, *October 1964* (New York, 1995)

John Helyar, *Lords of the Realm* (New York, 1994)

Robert W. Henderson, *Ball, Bat, and Bishop: The Origin of Ball Games* (New York, 1947; reprint Urbana, Ill., 2001)

J. Thomas Hetrick, *Chris Von der Ahe and the St. Louis Browns* (Lanham, Md., 1999)

Laura Hillenbrand, *Seabiscuit* (New York, 2001)

Frank W. Hoffmann and William G. Bailey, *Sports and Recreation Fads* (Binghamton, N.Y., 1991)

Jerome Holtzman, *No Cheering in the Press Box*, revised edition (New York, 1995)

Arlene Howard, with Ralph Wimbish, *Elston and Me: The Story of the First Black Yankee* (Columbia, Mo., 2001)

Colin Howell, *Northern Sandlots* (Toronto, 1995)

Frederick Ivor-Campbell, Robert L. Tiemann, and Mark Rucker, eds., *Baseball's First Stars* (Cleveland, 1996)

Bill James, *The 1990 Bill James Baseball Book* (New York, 1990)

Bill James, *The Bill James Baseball Abstract* (various years)

Bill James, *The Bill James Guide to Baseball Managers: From 1870 to Today* (New York, 1997)

Bill James, *The New Bill James Historical Baseball Abstract* (New York, 2001)

Bill James, *The Politics of Glory: How Baseball's Hall of Fame Really Works* (New York, 1994)

Bill James and Rob Neyer, *The Neyer/James Guide to Pitchers* (New York, 2004)

Hugh Jennings, *Rounding First* (n.p., 1925)

Harry "Steamboat" Johnson, *Standing the Gaff* (Nashville, Tenn., 1935; reprint Lincoln, Nebr., 1994)

Lloyd Johnson, *Baseball's Book of Firsts* (Philadelphia, 1999)

Lloyd Johnson and Miles Wolff, eds., *The Encyclopedia of Minor League Baseball*, 2nd edition (Durham, N.C., 1997)

James M. Kahn, *The Umpire Story* (New York, 1953)

Roger Kahn, *The Head Game: Baseball Seen from the Pitcher's Mound* (New York, 2000)

Roger Kahn, *Memories of Summer* (New York, 1997)

Roger Kahn, *A Season in the Sun* (New York, 1977)

Mark Kanter, ed., *The Northern Game and Beyond: Baseball in New England and Eastern Canada* (Cleveland, 2002)

Lawrence S. Katz, *Baseball in 1939: The Watershed Season of the National Pastime* (Jefferson, N.C., 1995)

Jack Kavanagh, *The Heights of Ridiculousness: The Feats of Baseball's Merrymakers* (South Bend, Ind., 1998)

Jack Kavanagh and Norman Macht, *Uncle Robbie* (Cleveland, 1999)

Kevin Kerrane, *Dollar Sign on the Muscle: The World of Baseball Scouting* (New York, 1984)

George B. Kirsch, *The Creation of American Team Sports: Baseball and Cricket, 1838–72* (Urbana, Ill., 1991)

Charles P. Korr, *The End of Baseball as We Knew It: The Players Union, 1960–81* (Urbana, Ill., 2002)

Bowie Kuhn, *Hardball: The Education of a Baseball Commissioner* (New York, 1988)

Bruce Kuklick, *To Every Thing a Season: Shibe Park and Urban Philadelphia, 1909–1976* (Princeton, N.J., 1991)

Robin Tolmach Lakoff, *The Language War* (Berkeley, Calif., 2000)

F. C. Lane, *Batting* (1925; reprint Cleveland, 2001)

Walter M. Langford, *Legends of Baseball* (South Bend, Ind., 1987)

Ernest J. Lanigan, *The Baseball Cyclopedia* (New York, 1922; reprint St. Louis, 1988)

Jerry Lansche, *Glory Fades Away: The Nineteenth-Century World Series Rediscovered* (Dallas, 1991)

Irving A. Leitner, *Baseball: Diamond in the Rough* (New York, 1972)

Peter Levine, *A. G. Spalding and the Rise of Baseball: The Promise of American Sport* (New York, 1985)

Frederick G. Lieb, *The St. Louis Cardinals: The Story of a Great Baseball Club* (New York, 1944; reprint Carbondale, Ill., 2001)

Jonathan Fraser Light, *The Cultural Encyclopedia of Baseball* (Jefferson, N.C., 1997)

Michael E. Lomax, *Black Baseball Entrepreneurs, 1860–1901: Operating by Any Means Necessary* (Syracuse, 2003)

Lee Lowenfish, *The Imperfect Diamond: A History of Baseball's Labor Wars*, revised edition (New York, 1991)

Philip J. Lowry, *Green Cathedrals: The Ultimate Celebration of All 271 Major League and Negro League Ballparks Past and Present* (Reading, Mass., 1992)

Neil W. Macdonald, *The League That Lasted: 1876 and the Founding of the National League of Professional Base Ball Clubs* (Jefferson, N.C., 2004)

Connie Mack, *My Sixty-Six Years in the Big Leagues* (Philadelphia, 1950)

Jerry Malloy, ed., *Sol White's History of Colored Base Ball, with Other Documents on the Early Black Game, 1886–1936* (original version 1907; reprint Lincoln, Nebr., 1995)

Larry D. Mansch, *Rube Marquard: The Life and Times of a Baseball Hall of Famer* (Jefferson, N.C., 1998)

William Marshall, *Baseball's Pivotal Era, 1945–1951* (Lexington, Ky., 1999)

Christy Mathewson, *Pitching in a Pinch* (New York, 1912; reprint Mattituck, N.Y., n.d.)

Ronald A. Mayer, *Perfect!* (Jefferson, N.C., 1991)

Bill Mazer, with Stan and Shirley Fischler, *Bill Mazer's Amazin' Baseball Book* (New York, 1990)

Kevin M. McCarthy, *Baseball in Florida* (Sarasota, 1996)

Tim McCarver with Danny Peary, *Tim McCarver's Baseball for Brain Surgeons and Other Fans* (New York, 1998)

John J. McGraw, *My Thirty Years in Baseball* (New York, 1923; reprint Lincoln, Nebr., 1995)

Michael McKinley, *Putting a Roof on Winter: Hockey's Rise from Sport to Spectacle* (Vancouver, 2000)

William B. Mead, *Even the Browns* (Chicago, 1978)

Tom Melchior, *Belle Plaine Baseball, 1884–1960* (Belle Plaine, Minn., 2004)

Tom Melville, *Early Baseball and the Rise of the National League* (Jefferson, N.C., 2001)

Frank G. Menke, *The Encyclopedia of Sports* (New York, 1955)

Dick Miller and Mark Stang, eds., *Baseball in the Buckeye State* (Cleveland, 2004)

Stephen G. Miller, *Arete: Greek Sports from Ancient Sources* (Berkeley, Calif., 1991)

Leigh Montville, *Ted Williams: The Biography of an American Hero* (New York, 2004)

George L. Moreland, *Balldom* (Youngstown, Ohio, 1914; reprint St. Louis, 1989)

Peter Morris, *Baseball Fever: Early Baseball in Michigan* (Ann Arbor, Mich., 2003)

W. Scott Munn, *The Only Eaton Rapids on Earth* (Eaton Rapids, Mich., 1952)

Eugene Murdock, *Baseball Between the Wars: Memories of the Game by the Men Who Played It* (Westport, Conn., 1992)

Eric Nadel and Craig R. Wright, *The Man Who Stole First Base: Tales from Baseball's Past* (Dallas, 1989)

David Nemec, *The Beer and Whisky League* (New York, 1994)

David Nemec, *Great Baseball Facts, Feats and Firsts*, revised edition (New York, 1999)

David Nemec, *The Great Encyclopedia of 19th Century Major League Baseball* (New York, 1997)

David Nemec, *The Rules of Baseball* (New York, 1994)

Rob Neyer and Eddie Epstein, *Baseball Dynasties: The Greatest Teams of All Time* (New York, 2000)

Robert Obojski, *Baseball Memorabilia* (New York, 1992)

Robert Obojski, *Bush League: A History of Minor League Baseball* (New York, 1975)

Sidney Offit, ed., *The Best of Baseball* (New York, 1956)

Marc Okkonen, *Baseball Uniforms of the Twentieth Century: The Official Major League Guide* (New York, 1991)

Marc Okkonen, *Minor League Baseball Towns of Michigan* (Grand Rapids, Mich., 1997)

Marc Okkonen, *The Ty Cobb Scrapbook* (New York, 2001)

Michael O'Malley, *Keeping Watch: A History of American Time* (New York, 1991)

Preston D. Orem, *Baseball (1845–1881) from the Newspaper Accounts* (Altadena, Calif., 1961)

Danny Peary, ed., *Cult Baseball Players* (New York, 1990)

Danny Peary, *We Played the Game: 65 Players Remember Baseball's Greatest Era, 1947–1964* (New York, 1994)

Harold Peterson, *The Man Who Invented Baseball* (New York, 1969)

Robert W. Peterson, *Only the Ball Was White: A History of Legendary Black Players and All-Black Professional Teams* (New York, 1970)

Robert W. Peterson, *Pigskin: The Early Years of Pro Football* (New York, 1997)

Gerard S. Petrone, *When Baseball Was Young* (San Diego, 1994)

Charles Peverelly, *The Book of American Pastimes* (New York, 1866)

David Pietrusza, *Judge and Jury: The Life and Times of Judge Kenesaw Mountain Landis* (South Bend, Ind., 1998)

David Pietrusza, *Lights On! The Wild Century-Long Saga of Night Baseball* (Lanham, Md., 1997)

David Pietrusza, *Minor Miracles: The Legend and Lure of Minor League Baseball* (South Bend, Ind., 1995)

David Pietrusza, Lloyd Johnson, and Bob Carroll, eds., *Total Baseball Catalog: Great Baseball Stuff and How to Buy It* (New York, 1998)

Joseph V. Poilucci, *Baseball in Dutchess County: When It Was a Game* (Danbury, Conn., 2000)

Murray Polner, *Branch Rickey* (New York, 1982)

R. E. Prescott, *Historical Tales of the Huron Shore Region* (Alcona County, Mich., 1934)

Richard A. Puff, ed., *Troy's Baseball Heritage* (Troy, N.Y., 1992)

Martin Quigley, *The Crooked Pitch: The Curveball in American Baseball History* (Chapel Hill, N.C., 1988)

Reach's Official Base Ball Guide, various years

Greg Rhodes and John Erardi, *The First Boys of Summer* (Cincinnati, 1994)

Greg Rhodes and John Snyder, *Redleg Journal* (Cincinnati, 2000)

Francis C. Richter, *Richter's History and Records of Base Ball* (Philadelphia, 1914; reprint Jefferson, N.C., 2005)

Branch Rickey, *Branch Rickey's Little Blue Book* (New York, 1995)

Lawrence S. Ritter, *The Glory of Their Times* (New York, 1966; reprint New York, 1984)

Mark Rucker, *Base Ball Cartes: The First Baseball Cards* (Saratoga Springs, N.Y., 1988)

Mark Rucker and Peter C. Bjarkman, *Smoke: The Romance and Lore of Cuban Baseball* (Kingston, N.Y., 1999)

Babe Ruth, *Babe Ruth's Own Book of Baseball* (New York, 1928)

William J. Ryczek, *Blackguards and Red Stockings: A History of Baseball's National Association, 1871–1875* (Jefferson, N.C., 1992)

William J. Ryczek, *When Johnny Came Sliding Home: The Post–Civil War Baseball Boom, 1865–1870* (Jefferson, N.C., 1998)

Tony Salin, *Baseball's Forgotten Heroes: One Man's Search for the Game's Most Interesting Overlooked Players* (Indianapolis, 1999)

Alan Schwarz, *The Numbers Game: Baseball's Lifelong Fascination with Statistics* (New York, 2004)

Michael Seidel, *Ted Williams: A Baseball Life* (Lincoln, Nebr., 2000)

Harold Seymour, *Baseball: The Early Years* (New York, 1960)

Harold Seymour, *Baseball: The Golden Age* (New York, 1971)

Harold Seymour, *Baseball: The People's Game* (New York, 1990)

Bruce Shlain, *Oddballs: Baseball's Greatest Pranksters, Flakes, Hot Dogs and Hotheads* (New York, 1989)

Tom Simon, ed., *Deadball Stars of the National League* (Washington: 2004)

Tom Simon, ed., *Green Mountain Boys of Summer: Vermonters in the Major Leagues 1882–1993* (Shelburne, Vt., 2000)

George Sisler, *Sisler on Baseball: A Manual for Players and Coaches* (New York, 1954)

Marshall Smelser, *The Life That Ruth Built: A Biography* (New York, 1975 reprint: Lincoln, Nebr., 1993)

Curt Smith, *Voices of the Game*, revised edition (New York, 1992)

H. Allen Smith and Ira L. Smith, *Low and Inside: A Book of Baseball Anecdotes, Oddities, and Curiosities* (Garden City, N.Y., 1949; reprint Halcottsville, N.Y., 2000)

Red Smith, *Red Smith on Baseball* (Chicago, 2000)

Robert Smith, *Baseball* (New York, 1947)

Dennis Snelling, *A Glimpse of Fame: Brilliant but Fleeting Major League Careers* (Jefferson, N.C., 1993)

Burt Solomon, *Where They Ain't* (New York, 1999)

Mike Sowell, *July 2, 1903: The Mysterious Death of Hall-of-Famer Big Ed Delahanty* (New York, 1992)

Mike Sowell, *The Pitch That Killed* (New York, 1989; reprint Chicago, 2003)

Albert Goodwill Spalding, *America's National Game: Historic Facts Concerning the Beginning, Evolution, Development, and Popularity of Base Ball, with Personal Reminiscences of Its Vicissitudes, Its Victories, and Its Votaries* (New York, 1911; reprint Lincoln, Nebr., 1992)

Spalding's Official Base Ball Guide, various years

Alfred H. Spink, *The National Game* (St. Louis, 1910; reprint Carbondale, Ill., 2000)

Sporting News *Baseball: A Doubleheader Collection of Facts, Feats and Firsts* (New York, 1992)

Benton Stark, *The Year They Called Off the World Series: A True Story* (Garden City Park, N.Y., 1991)

Paul Starr, *The Creation of the Media* (New York, 2004)

Vince Staten, *Why Is the Foul Pole Fair? (Or, Answers to Baseball Questions Your Dad Hoped You'd Never Ask)* (New York, 2003)

Dean Sullivan, ed., *Early Innings: A Documentary History of Baseball, 1825–1908* (Lincoln, Nebr., 1995)

Dean Sullivan, ed., *Late Innings: A Documentary History of Baseball, 1945–1972* (Lincoln, Nebr., 2002)

Dean Sullivan, ed., *Middle Innings: A Documentary History of Baseball, 1900–1948* (Lincoln, Nebr., 1998)

Jim L. Sumner, *Separating the Men from the Boys: The First Half-Century of the Carolina League* (Winston-Salem, N.C., 1994)

James L. Terry, *Long Before the Dodgers: Baseball in Brooklyn, 1855–1884* (Jefferson, N.C., 2002)

John Thorn, ed., *The Armchair Book of Baseball* (New York, 1985)

John Thorn and Pete Palmer, with David Reuther, *The Hidden Game of Baseball* (Garden City, N.Y., 1984)

John Thorn, ed., *The National Pastime* (New York, 1988)

John Thorn and John Holway, *The Pitcher* (New York, 1987)

John Thorn, *The Relief Pitcher* (New York, 1979)

John Thorn and Pete Palmer, et al., *Total Baseball*, various editions

Robert L. Tiemann and Mark Rucker, eds., *Nineteenth Century Stars* (Kansas City, 1989)

Cliff Trumpold, *Now Pitching: Bill Zuber from Amana* (Middle Amana, Iowa, 1992)

Brian Turner and John S. Bowman, *Baseball in Northampton, 1823–1953* (Northampton, Mass., 2002)

Jules Tygiel, *Baseball's Great Experiment* (New York, 1983)

Jules Tygiel, *Past Time: Baseball as History* (New York, 2000)

Bill Veeck, with Ed Linn, *The Hustler's Handbook* (New York, 1965; reprint Durham, N.C., 1996)

Bill Veeck, with Ed Linn, *Veeck—As in Wreck* (New York, 1962)

David Quentin Voigt, *American Baseball, Volume I: From the Gentleman's Sport to the Commissioner's System* (Norman, Okla., 1966)

David Quentin Voigt, *American Baseball, Volume II: From the Commissioners to Continental Expansion* (Norman, Okla., 1970)

David Quentin Voigt, *American Baseball, Volume III: From Postwar Expansion to the Electronic Age* (University Park, Pa., 1983)

David Quentin Voigt, *The League That Failed* (Lanham, Md., 1998)

Paul Votano, *Stand and Deliver: A History of Pinch-Hitting* (Jefferson, N.C., 2003)

Glen Waggoner, Kathleen Moloney, and Hugh Howard, *Spitters, Beanballs, and the Incredible Shrinking Strike Zone: The Stories Behind the Rules of Baseball*, revised edition (Chicago, 2000)

John Montgomery Ward, *Base-Ball: How to Become a Player* (Philadelphia, 1888; reprint Cleveland, 1993)

Don Warfield, *The Roaring Redhead* (South Bend, Ind., 1987)

Ty Waterman and Mel Springer, *The Year the Red Sox Won the Series: A Chronicle of the 1918 Championship Season* (Boston, 1999)

Lonnie Wheeler and John Baskin, *The Cincinnati Game* (Wilmington, Ohio, 1988)

G. Edward White, *Creating the National Pastime: Baseball Transforms Itself, 1903–1953* (Princeton, N.J., 1996)

George F. Will, *Bunts* (New York, 1999)

George F. Will, *Men at Work* (New York, 1990)

Pete Williams, ed., *The Joe Williams Baseball Reader* (Chapel Hill, N.C., 1989)

Ted Williams, with John Underwood, *My Turn at Bat: The Story of My Life* (New York, 1969)

Craig R. Wright and Tom House, *The Diamond Appraised* (New York, 1990)

Marshall D. Wright, *The American Association: Year-by-Year Statistics for the Baseball Minor League, 1902–1952* (Jefferson, N.C., 1997)

Marshall D. Wright, *The National Association of Base Ball Players, 1857–1870* (Jefferson, N.C., 2000)

David W. Zang, *Fleet Walker's Divided Heart: The Life of Baseball's First Black Major Leaguer* (Lincoln, Nebr., 1995)

Joel Zoss and John Bowman, *Diamonds in the Rough: The Untold History of Baseball* (New York, 1989)

NEWSPAPERS AND MAGAZINES

This study relies upon an enormous number of articles and notes from newspapers, magazines, and journals, many of them untitled and having no bylines. In many cases the entire note has already been quoted, which would mean that a researcher would gain little by going back to the original. Rather than trying to list every single article, I have included some of the most valuable ones and those with scopes that go well beyond documenting a particular event or game, since these are the ones a researcher is most likely to benefit by consulting. The list of articles is followed by a list of all the periodicals I utilized.

Dr. Daniel L. Adams (early Knickerbocker), interview, *Sporting News*, February 29, 1896, 3

Melvin L. Adelman, "The First Baseball Game, the First Newspaper References to Baseball, and the New York Club: A Note on the Early History of Baseball," *Journal of Sport History* 7, No. 3 (Winter 1980), 132–135

William P. Akin, "Bare Hands and Kid Gloves: The Best Fielders, 1880–1899," *Baseball Research Journal* 10 (1981), 60–65

Thomas L. Altherr, "A Place Leavel Enough to Play Ball," reprinted in David Block, *Baseball Before We Knew It* (Lincoln, Nebr., 2005), 229–251

Thomas L. Altherr, "Know Them by Their Autographs," *National Pastime* 18 (1998), 29–31

Priscilla Astifan, "Baseball in the Nineteenth Century," *Rochester History* LII, No. 3 (Summer 1990); "Baseball in the Nineteenth Century, Part Two," *Rochester History* LXII, No. 2 (Spring 2000); "Baseball in the Nineteenth Century, Part Three: The Dawn of Acknowledged Professionalism and Its Impact on Rochester Baseball," *Rochester History* LXIII, No. 1 (Winter 2001); "Rochester's Last Two Seasons of Amateur Baseball: Baseball in the Nineteenth Century, Part Four," *Rochester History* LXIII, No. 2 (Spring 2001); "Baseball in the Nineteenth Century, Part Five: 1877–Rochester's First Year of Professional Baseball," *Rochester History* LXIV, No. 4 (Fall 2002)

Bob Bailey, "Hunting for the First Louisville Slugger," *Baseball Research Journal* 30 (2001), 96–98

Stan Baumgartner, "Signals," *Baseball Guide and Record Book 1947* (St. Louis, 1947), 124–135

Jay Bennett and Aryn Martin, "The Numbers Game: What Fans Should Know About the Stats They Love," in Eric Bronson, ed., *Baseball and Philosophy: Thinking Outside the Batter's Box*, 233–245

Mike Berardino, "Economic Climate Could Snuff Out Waiver Blocking," *Baseball America*, September 1–14, 2003

Gai Ingham Berlage, "Women Umpires as Mirrors of Gender Roles," *National Pastime* 14 (1994), 34–38

Charles W. Bevis, "Family Baseball Teams," *Baseball Research Journal* 26 (1997), 8–12

Charles W. Bevis, "Holiday Doubleheaders," *Baseball Research Journal* 33 (2004), 60–63

Charles W. Bevis, "A Home Run by Any Measure," *Baseball Research Journal* 21 (1992), 64–70

Dennis Bingham and Thomas R. Heitz, "Rules and Scoring," *Total Baseball*, 4th edition, 2426–2481

Peter Bjarkman, "Cuban Blacks in the Majors Before Jackie Robinson," *National Pastime* 12 (1992), 58–63

Hal Bodley, "Teams Obsess Too Much Over Pitch Counts," *USA Today*, September 17, 2004, 4C

Larry G. Bowman, "The Monarchs and Night Baseball," *National Pastime* 16 (1996), 80–84

Randall Brown, "How Baseball Began," *National Pastime* 24 (2004), 51–54

Bozeman Bulger, "Pitching, Past and Present: The Evolution of the Twirler's Art," *Baseball Magazine*, February 1912, 71–73

Pete Cava, "Baseball in the Olympics," *National Pastime* 12 (1992), 2–8

O. P. Caylor, "The Theory and Introduction of Curve Pitching," *Outing*, August 1891, 402–405

Henry Chadwick, "The Art of Pitching," *Outing*, May 1889, 119–121

Irwin Chusid, "The Short, Happy Life of the Newark Peppers," *Baseball Research Journal* 20 (1991), 44–45

Eddie Cicotte, "The Secrets of Successful Pitching," *Baseball Magazine*, July 1918, 267–268, 299

Robert Cole, "Ball, Bat and Ad," *Baseball Research Journal* 8 (1979), 77–79

T. Z. Cowles, multi-part series on early Chicago sports history, *Chicago Tribune*, May 26, June 2, June 16, and June 30, 1918

"Cummings Tells Story of Early Days of Curve Ball," *Sporting News*, December 29, 1921, 7

"Curved Balls," *Sporting News*, February 20, 1897, 2

Dan Daniel, "Batters Going Batty from Butterflies," *Sporting News*, June 12, 1946, 3

George S. Davis, "How to Bat," syndicated column, *Warren* (Pa.) *Evening Democrat*, May 26, 1894, 2

Bill Deane, "The Old Hidden Ball Trick: No Longer Banned in Boston," in Mark Kanter, ed., *The Northern Game and Beyond: Baseball in New England and Eastern Canada* (Cleveland, 2002), 69–72

Clarence Deming, "Old Days in Baseball," *Outing*, June 1902, 357–360

Joe Dittmar, "A Shocking Discovery," *Baseball Research Journal* 20 (1991), 52–53, 65

Walter C. Dohm, "College Baseball," *Los Angeles Times*, May 21, 1893, 10

Joseph Durso, "Slider Is the Pitch That Put Falling Batting Averages on the Skids," *New York Times*, September 22, 1968, 198

Stefan Fatsis, "Mystery of Baseball: Was William White Game's First Black?," *Wall Street Journal*, January 30, 2004, 1

"The First Detroit Base Ball Club Formed in the *Free Press* Office Twenty-Seven Years Ago," *Detroit Free Press*, April 4, 1884

Val J. Flanagan, "Rain-Check Evolved to Check Flood of Fence-Climbers, Says Originator, Now 83," *Sporting News*, April 8, 1943, 2

Russell Ford (as told to Don E. Basenfelder), "Russell Ford Tells Inside Story of the 'Emery' Ball After Guarding His Secret for Quarter of a Century," *Sporting News*, April 25, 1935, 5

John B. Foster, "Buckeye Boys," *Sporting News*, December 28, 1895, 3

John B. Foster, "The Evolution of Pitching" (part 1), *Sporting News*, November 26, 1931, 5; "The Evolution of Pitching" (part 2), *Sporting News*, December 10, 1931, 6; "The Evolution of Pitching" (part 3), *Sporting News*, December 24, 1931, 6; "The Evolution of Pitching" (part 4), *Sporting News*, January 7, 1932, 6

Duane Frazier, "Wellington Celebrates the Evening It Lit Up High School Football," *Wichita Eagle*, September 10, 2004, 1D, 6D

Larry R. Gerlach, "Death on the Diamond: The Cal Drummond Story," *National Pastime* 24 (2004), 14–16

Larry R. Gerlach and Harold V. Higham, "Dick Higham," *National Pastime* 20 (2000), 20–32

"The Great National Game in Dollars and Cents," *Washington Post*, May 9, 1909

Barbara Gregorich, "Jackie and the Juniors vs. Margaret and the Bloomers," *National Pastime* 13 (1993), 8–10

William Ridgely Griffith, *The Early History of Amateur Base Ball in the State of Maryland*; reprinted in *Maryland Historical Magazine* 87, No. 2 (Summer 1992), 201–208

John H. Gruber, multi-part series on baseball rules and customs under a variety of headings, weekly series in *Sporting News*, November 4, 1915–April 6, 1916

Bob Hoie, "The Farm System," *Total Baseball,* 2nd edition, 644–647

John Holway, "Willie Wells: A Devil of a Shortstop," *Baseball Research Journal* 17 (1988), 50–53

"How to Hit a Ball," *New York Sun,* reprinted in *Birmingham* (Ala.) *Evening News,* October 2, 1888

"Dan Irish," "System Is Bad: Ball Players Not Properly Trained," *Sporting News,* February 19, 1898, 2

Frederick Ivor-Campbell, "Extraordinary 1884," *National Pastime* 13 (1993), 16–23

Frederick Ivor-Campbell, "Postseason Play," *Total Baseball* IV, 281–282

Frederick Ivor-Campbell, "When Was the First? (Continued)," *Nineteenth Century Notes* 95:1 (Winter 1995), 1–2

Frederick Ivor-Campbell, "When Was the First? (Part 4)," *Nineteenth Century Notes* 95:3, 4 (Summer/Fall 1995), 10–12

Frederick Ivor-Campbell, "When Was the First Match Game Played by the Knickerbocker Rules?" *Nineteenth Century Notes* 93:4 (Fall 1993), 1–2

Bill James, "A History of the Beanball," *The Bill James Baseball Abstract 1985,* 131–140

Willis E. Johnson, "The Player's Life in the Major Leagues," *Sporting Life,* March 4, 1916

Gene Karst, "Ready for the New Asterisk War?," *Baseball Research Journal* 26 (1997), 66–67

Seamus Kearney, "Bill Thompson, Pioneer," *National Pastime* 16 (1996), 67–68

Maclean Kennedy, "Charley Bennett, Former Detroit Catcher, Inventor of Chest Pad," *Detroit Free Press,* August 2, 1914

Al Kermisch, "Umpire Used Hand Signals in 1883," *Baseball Research Journal* 21 (1992), 111

Gene Kessler, "Deacon White, Oldest Living Player, at 92 Recalls Highlights of Historic Career That Started in 1868," *Sporting News,* June 22, 1939, 19

Bill Kirwin, "The Mysterious Case of Dick Brookins," *National Pastime* 19 (1999), 38–43

J. C. Kofoed, "Early History of Curve Pitching," *Baseball Magazine,* August 1915, 55–57

Leonard Koppett, "The Ex-National Sport Looks to Its Image," *New York Times,* December 20, 1964, SM18

Dan Krueckeberg, "Take-Charge Cy," *National Pastime* 4, No. 1 (Spring 1985), 7–11

F. C. Lane, "The Emery Ball Strangest of Freak Deliveries," *Baseball Magazine,* July 1915, 58–72

R. M. Larner, "Old-Time Baseball in the White Lot," *Washington Post,* June 26, 1904, S4

R. M. Larner, "Beginning of Professional Baseball in Washington," *Washington Post,* July 3, 1904, S3

Hal Lebovitz, "Zimmer, Oldest Catcher, Leafs Memory Book," *Sporting News,* January 12, 1949, 11

Larry Lester, "Only the Stars Come Out at Night!: J. L. Wilkinson and His Lighting Machine," Lloyd Johnson, Steve Garlick and Jeff Magalif, eds., *Unions to Royals: The Story of Professional Baseball in Kansas City* (Cleveland, 1996), 8–10

Frederick G. Lieb, "A Man Who Has Made Millions from By-Products of Sport," *Sportlife,* December 1925, 94

Joseph F. Lowry, "Baseball's Magic-Mud Man," *Family Weekly,* September 5, 1965

Connie Mack, "How to Play Ball," multi-part series, *Washington Post*, March 13, March 20, March 27, April 3, April 10, April 17, 1904

Connie Mack, "Memories of When the Game Was Young," *Sporting Life* (monthly), June 1924

Jerry Malloy, "Out at Home," in John Thorn, ed., *The National Pastime* (New York, 1988), 209–244

David Mandell, "Reuben Berman's Foul Ball," *National Pastime* 25 (2005), 106–107

Larry Marthey, "Park Tampering Is Old Custom," *Detroit News*, April 7, 1959, T-15

Beth Martin, "Hey, Blue!," *National Pastime* 18 (1998), 36–46

Andy McCue, "The King of Coolie Hats," *National Pastime* 19 (1999), 24–27

David McDonald, "The Senators' Diamond Dynasty," *Ottawa Citizen*, March 25, 2003

E. L. McDonald, "The National Game of Base Ball Was Born in Fort Wayne," *St. Louis Republican*, reprinted in *Fort Wayne Journal Gazette*, January 26, 1902

P. A. Meaney, "Who Invented the Spit Ball," *Baseball Magazine*, May 1913, 59–60

Leigh Montville, "Field of Screams," *Sports Illustrated*, May 22, 2000

Peter Morris, "'Attaboy!' Originated from the Dynamic Managing Style of Hughie Jennings (Detroit Tigers) in 1907," *Comments on Etymology* 33, No. 1 (October 2003), 2–4

Peter Morris, "Baseball Term 'Bunt' Was Originally Called 'Baby Hit'; Popular 19c. Lullaby 'Bye, Baby Bunting' May Have Produced 'Baby Bunting Hit,' Shortened to 'Bunt,'" *Comments on Etymology* 34, No. 1 (October 2004), 2–4

Edgar Munzel, "Daily Workouts Put Shaw in Pink for Comeback Pitch," *Sporting News*, November 16, 1960, 9

"Jim Nasium" [Edgar Wolfe], "'Ted' Sullivan, Baseball Pioneer," *Sporting Life* (monthly), January 1923

Tom Nawrocki, "Captain Anson's Platoon," *National Pastime* 15 (1995), 34–37

Amy Ellis Nutt, "Swinging for the Fences," in Lissa Smith, ed., *Nike Is a Goddess: The History of Women in Sports* (New York, 1998)

Robert A. Nylen, "Frontier Baseball," *Nevada*, Volume 50, Number 2 (March/April 1990), 27–29, 56

James O'Rourke, "Forty Two Years of Base Ball: Wonderful Life Story of Jim O'Rourke" (multi-part series), *Kalamazoo Evening Telegraph*, February 24, 25, 26, March 1, 2, 3, 1910

Steve Orr, "MSU Police Get Radar Gun," *State News*, October 10, 1974

Joseph M. Overfield, "The Richards-Jethroe Caper: Fact or Fiction?," *Baseball Research Journal* 16 (1987), 33–35

Joseph M. Overfield, "You Could Look It Up," *National Pastime* 10 (1990), 69–71

Ev Parker, "The Supreme Compliment," *National Pastime* 17 (1997), 138–139

Ted Patterson, "Jack Graney, The First Player-Broadcaster," *Baseball Research Journal* 2 (1973), 80–86, reprinted in *Baseball Historical Review* 1981, 52–57

William Perrin, "Line Drives Then and Now," originally published in 1928 in an unknown source, reprinted in James Charlton, ed., *Road Trips* (Cleveland, 2004), 81–91

William A. Phelon, "Shall We Have a Third Big League?," *Baseball Magazine*, March 1912, 10–12, 92

Deacon Phillippe, "Phillippe of Pittsburg Team Discusses Requirements of Successful Pitchers," *Syracuse Post Standard*, March 27, 1904, 10

David Pietrusza, "The Cahill Brothers' Night Baseball Experiments," *Baseball Research Journal* 23 (1994), 62–66

David Pietrusza, "The Continental League of 1921," *National Pastime* 13 (1993), 76–78

David Pietrusza, "Famous Firsts," *Total Baseball* VI, 2507

Bill Plott, "The Southern League of Colored Base Ballists," *Baseball Research Journal* 3 (1974), 91–95, reprinted in *Baseball Historical Review* 1981, 75–78

Barry Popik and Gerald Cohen, "Material on the Origin of the Spitball Pitch," *Comments on Etymology* 32:8 (May 2003), 21–28

Robert Pruter, "Youth Baseball in Chicago, 1868–1890: Not Always Sandlot Ball," *Journal of Sport History*, Spring 1999, 6

Chris Rainey, "A Cincy Legend: A Narrative of Bumpus Jones' Baseball Career," in Dick Miller and Mark Stang, eds., *Baseball in the Buckeye State* (Cleveland, 2004), 3–7

Bob Rives, "Good Night," *National Pastime* 18 (1998), 21–24

Emil H. Rothe, "History of the Chicago City Series," *Baseball Research Journal* 8 (1979), 15–24

Robert H. Schaefer, "The Lost Art of Fair-Foul Hitting" *National Pastime* 20 (2000), 3–9

John Schwartz, "From One Ump to Two," *Baseball Research Journal* 30 (2001), 85–86

Alan Schwarz, "Real-time Broadcasts Lead to Copyright Questions," *Baseball America*, September 15–28, 2003

Charley Scully, "'Father of the Catching Glove' Admits Split Finger Fifty Years Ago, with Twin Bill Ahead, Was 'Mother,'" *Sporting News*, February 23, 1939, 9

Peter Segroie, "Reuben's Ruling Helps You 'Have a Ball,'" *Baseball Research Journal* 20 (1991), 85

Tom Shieber, "The Earliest Baseball Photography," *National Pastime* 17 (1997), 101–104

Tom Shieber, "The Evolution of the Baseball Diamond," originally printed in the *Baseball Research Journal* 23 (1994), 3–13; reprinted in an expanded version in *Total Baseball* IV, 113–124

Herbert Simons, "Life of an Ump," *Baseball Magazine*, April 1942; reprinted in Sidney Offit, ed., *The Best of Baseball*, 156–162

Duane Smith, "Dickey Pearce: Baseball's First Great Shortstop," *National Pastime* 10 (1990), 38–42

Deron Snyder, "A Stat Worth Saving," *USA Today Baseball Weekly*, July 21–27, 1999

Fred Stein, "Managers and Coaches," *Total Baseball*, 2nd edition, 452–463

Bucky Summers, "Still Baseball on TV," *Frederick* (Md.) *Post*, April 20, 1965, 9

Scott S. Taylor, "Pure Passion for the Game: Albany Amateur Baseball Box Scores from 1864," *Manuscripts* LIV, No. 1 (Winter 2002), 5–13

Dick Thompson, "Matty and His Fadeaway," *National Pastime* 17 (1997), 93–96

George A. Thompson, Jr., "New York Baseball, 1823," *National Pastime* 21 (2001), 6–8

Ken Tillman, "The Portable Batting Cage," *Baseball Research Journal* 28 (1999), 23–26

E. H. Tobias, sixteen-part history of baseball in St. Louis up to 1876, *Sporting News*, November 2, 1895–February 15, 1896

M. E. Travaglini, "Olympic Baseball 1936: Was Es Das?," *National Pastime* (Winter 1985), 46–55

"Tri-Mountain," three-part series on early baseball in Boston, *Boston Journal*, February 20 and 22, March 6, 1905

John (Dasher) Troy, "Reminiscences of an Old-Timer," *Baseball Magazine*, June 1915, 93–94

Gary Waddingham, "Irish Bob O'Regan: A Bespectacled Ump in the Bush Leagues," *Minor League History Journal* 1:1, 33–36

William J. Weiss, "The First Negro in Twentieth Century O.B.," *Baseball Research Journal* 8 (1979), 31–35

H. H. Westlake, "The First Box Score Ever Published," *Baseball Magazine*, March 1925; reprinted in Sidney Offit, ed., *The Best of Baseball*, 156–162

William Wheaton (early Knickerbocker), interview, *San Francisco Examiner*, November 27, 1887

Tim Wiles, "The Joy of Foul Balls," *National Pastime* 25 (2005), 102–105

Bob Wolf, "Controversy Like Screaming at Danforth 40 Years Ago," *Sporting News*, May 1, 1957, 15

James Leon Wood, Sr. (as told to Frank G. Menke), "Baseball in By-Gone Days," syndicated series, *Indiana* (Pa.) *Evening Gazette*, August 14, 1916; *Marion* (Ohio) *Star*, August 15, 1916; *Indiana* (Pa.) *Evening Gazette*, August 17, 1916

ADDITIONAL PERIODICALS CONSULTED

Adrian (Mich.) *Press, Adrian Times and Expositor, American Chronicle of Sports and Pastimes, Atlanta Constitution, Atlanta Journal, Aurora* (Ill.) *Beacon-News, The Ball Player's Chronicle, Baltimore Sun, Baseball America, Baseball Magazine, Baseball Research Journal, Bay City* (Mich.) *Journal, Boston Globe, Brooklyn Eagle, Canton* (Ohio) *Repository, Chicago Inter-Ocean, Chicago Tribune, Christian Science Monitor, Cincinnati Enquirer, Cincinnati News-Journal, Cincinnati Times-Star, Cleveland Herald, Cleveland Leader, Cleveland Leader and Herald, Cleveland Plain Dealer, Colorado Daily Chieftain* (Pueblo), *Columbus* (Ohio) *Dispatch, Columbus* (Ohio) *Post, Columbus* (Ohio) *Press, Columbus* (Ohio) *Sunday Morning News, Comments on Etymology, Coshocton* (Ohio) *Tribune, Danville* (Va.) *Bee, Dayton Journal, Decatur Review, Delphos* (Ohio) *Herald, Detroit Advertiser and Tribune, Detroit Evening News, Detroit Free Press, Detroit News, Detroit Post, Detroit Post and Tribune, Detroit Tribune, Elyria* (Ohio) *Chronicle Telegram, Family Weekly, Fort Wayne Gazette, Fort Wayne Journal Gazette, Fort Wayne News, Fort Wayne News and Sentinel, Fort Wayne Sentinel, Frederick* (Md.) *News, Frederick* (Md.) *Post, Fremont* (Mich.) *Indicator, Gettysburg Times, Grand Rapids* (Mich.) *Democrat, Grand Rapids* (Mich.) *Evening Press, Grand Rapids* (Mich.) *Herald, Grand Rapids* (Mich.) *Leader, Grand Rapids* (Mich.) *Times, Grand Rapids* (Wisc.) *Tribune, Grand Traverse* (Mich.) *Herald, Grand Valley* (Moab, Utah) *Times, Harper's Weekly, Hawaiian Gazette, Holland* (Mich.) *Evening Sentinel, Indiana* (Pa.) *Gazette, Indianapolis Sentinel and News, Indianapolis Star, Ionia* (Mich.) *Sentinel, Jackson* (Mich.) *Citizen, Jonesville* (Mich.) *Independent, Kalamazoo Gazette, Kalamazoo Telegraph, Lansing* (Mich.) *Journal, Lapeer* (Mich.) *Democrat, Lima* (Ohio) *News, Lincoln* (Nebr.) *Evening Journal, Lincoln* (Nebr.) *Evening State Journal, London* (Ont.) *Free Press, Los Angeles Times, Louisville Courier-Journal, M.A.C.* [Michigan Agricultural College] *Record, Manistee* (Mich.) *Advocate, Mansfield* (Ohio) *News, Manufacturer and Builder, Marion* (Ohio) *Star, Marshall* (Mich.) *Statesman, Michigan Argus* (Ann Arbor), *Milwaukee Journal, Minor League History Journal, Muskegon News and Reporter, Mutes Chronicle* (Ohio School for the Deaf, Columbus), *National Chronicle, National Pastime, Nevada* (Reno) *State Journal, Newark Advocate, New England Base Ballist, New York Clipper, New York Herald, New York Herald Tribune, New York Sun, New York Times, New York Tribune,*

New York World, Niles (Mich.) *Republican, Niles* (Mich.) *Times, Nineteenth Century Notes, North Adams* (Mass.) *Transcript, The Official Baseball Record, Ohio State Journal* (Columbus), *Oshkosh Northwestern, Ottawa Citizen, Ottumwa* (Iowa) *Courier, Outside the Lines, Owosso* (Mich.) *Press, Paw Paw* (Mich.) *True Northerner, Perry* (Iowa) *Chief, Perry* (Iowa) *Pilot, Philadelphia Inquirer, Portage Lake* (Houghton, Mich.) *Mining Gazette, Port Arthur* (Tex.) *News, Port Huron Times, Reno Evening Gazette, Rochester History, Rocky Mountain* (Denver) *News, Saginaw Courier, Salisbury* (Md.) *Times, Sandusky* (Ohio) *Star, Sandusky* (Ohio) *Star-Journal, San Francisco Examiner, Sheboygan* (Wisc.) *Press, South Haven Sentinel, Spirit of the Times, Sporting Life, Sporting News, Sportlife, Sports Illustrated, St. Joseph* (Mich.) *Herald Press, St. Louis Globe-Democrat, St. Louis Post-Dispatch, St. Louis Republican, State News* (Michigan State University), *Steubenville Herald Star, Stevens Point* (Wisc.) *Journal, Syracuse Herald, Syracuse Herald Journal, Syracuse Post Standard, Tecumseh* (Mich.) *Herald, Titusville* (Pa.) *Morning Herald, Toledo Blade, Toronto Globe, Trenton Times, Troy* (N.Y.) *Times Record, USA Today, USA Today Baseball Weekly, USA Today Sports Weekly, Virgin Island News, Warren Evening Times, Washington Evening Star, Washington Post, Wellsboro Agitator, Wichita Eagle, Williamsport Gazette-Bulletin, Williamsport Sunday Grit, Winnipeg Times, Wisconsin Northwestern, Wisconsin Rapids Tribune, Woodstock* (Ont.) *Review, Woodstock* (Ont.) *Sentinel Review, Youngstown Vindicator, Zanesville Signal, Zanesville Times-Recorder, Zanesville Times Signal*

SPECIAL COLLECTIONS AND ARCHIVAL SOURCES

Allen County (Indiana) Public Library; Chadwick Scrapbooks; Bentley Library, University of Michigan; Burton Collection, Detroit Public Library; Cincinnati Reds Collection, Cincinnati Historical Society; Michigan Pioneer and Historical Collections; Michigan State University Library; Library of Michigan; Ohio Historical Society; William Rankin Scrapbooks; Peter Tamony Collection, University of Missouri; University of Michigan Library; Wazoo Records, East Lansing

ON-LINE RESOURCES

While on-line resources are always prone to disappearing, a few websites seem well enough established and were valuable enough in my research that it would be inexcusable not to mention them. The Baseball Index (http://www.baseballindex.org), compiled by the Bibliographic Committee of SABR, is an invaluable tool for tracking down sources. The wonderful Retrosheet website (http://www.retrosheet.org) has also been a constant aid in my research. The websites of the Vintage Base Ball Association (http://www.vbba.org) and the National Baseball Hall of Fame (http://www.baseballhalloffame.org) also have considerable relevant material. The early card mentioned in entry 15.4.3 can be viewed at the website of Frank Ceresi and Associates (http://www.fcassociates.com/ntearlybb.htm).

I have also benefited greatly from the free on-line archives of the *Brooklyn Eagle* (http://www.brooklynpubliclibrary.org/eagle/index.htm), the newspapers of Utah (http://www.lib.utah.edu/digital/unews), Missouri (http://newspapers.umsystem.edu) and Colorado (http://www.cdpheritage.org/newspapers/index.html), and the diverse offerings of the Amateur Athletic Foundation of Los Angeles (http://www.aafla.org). My work has also been made easier by the subscription-based archives of ProQuest (available to SABR members at http://www.sabr.org), newspaperarchive.com and Cold North Wind (http://www.paperofrecord.com).

Index

A NOTE ON THE AUTHOR

Peter Morris was born in Birmingham, England, and studied English at the University of Toronto and Michigan State University. His first book, *Baseball Fever: Early Baseball in Michigan*, received the coveted Seymour Medal from the Society for American Baseball Research as the best book on baseball history published in 2003. A former world Scrabble® champion, Mr. Morris is now a researcher for the Michigan Public Health Institute and lives in Haslett, Michigan.